Crime Prevention and Security Management

Series Editor
Martin Gill, Perpetuity Research, Tunbridge Wells, UK

It is widely recognized that we live in an increasingly unsafe society, but the study of security and crime prevention has lagged behind in its importance on the political agenda and has not matched the level of public concern. This exciting new series aims to address these issues looking at topics such as crime control, policing, security, theft, workplace violence and crime, fear of crime, civil disorder, white collar crime and anti-social behaviour. International in perspective, providing critically and theoretically-informed work, and edited by a leading scholar in the field, this series will advance new understandings of crime prevention and security management.

Ligia Maura Costa

Brazil's Biggest Corruption Scandal

Testimonies From Operation Car Wash

palgrave
macmillan

Ligia Maura Costa
FGVethics
Fundação Getulio Vargas Escola de
Administração de Empresas
de São Paulo - FGV EAESP
São Paulo, Brazil

ISSN 2946-3513 ISSN 2946-3521 (electronic)
Crime Prevention and Security Management
ISBN 978-3-031-99077-9 ISBN 978-3-031-99078-6 (eBook)
https://doi.org/10.1007/978-3-031-99078-6

The original submitted manuscript has been translated into English. The translation was done using artificial intelligence. A subsequent revision was performed by the author(s) to further refine the work and to ensure that the translation is appropriate concerning content and scientific correctness. It may, however, read stylistically different from a conventional translation.

This Palgrave Macmillan imprint is published by the registered company Springer Nature Switzerland AG
The registered company address is: Gewerbestrasse 11, 6330 Cham, Switzerland

(Org.)
Alberto Zacharias Toron
Alexandre Knopfholz
Antonio Carlos De Almeida Castro (Kakay)
Antônio Sérgio Altieri De Moraes Pitombo
Carlos Fernando Dos Santos Lima
Deltan Dallagnol
Eliana Calmon
Hermes Magnus
João Pedro Gebran Neto
Jorge Pontes
Marcelo Zenkner
Marco Aurélio Mello
Maria Cristina Pinotti
Michel Temer
Modesto Carvalhosa
Orlando Martello Júnior
Pierpaolo Bottini

Rafael Vela Barba
Roberto Livianu
Rodrigo Chemim
Sergio Fernando Moro
Stefan Lenz

For my mother, Clotilde

Foreword

Corruption is often perceived as an isolated deviation from legal and ethical norms. However, as this volume on Operation Car Wash (*Operação Lava Jato*) compellingly illustrates, corruption can become deeply systemic, entrenched within the very institutions designed to uphold integrity. The Brazilian case has become emblematic not merely for the vast sums of money laundered or the number of high-ranking individuals implicated, but for the way it unveiled an entire architecture of dishonesty and impunity: a sprawling network of collusion between political elites, corporate executives, and public officials (Anselmo & Pontes, 2022; Lagunes & Švejnar, 2020). This book offers the world an invaluable and enjoyable look "under the hood", the perspectives and views of those who played a key role, and the impressive integrity fighters in their own words.

Sadly, Operation Car Wash is neither unique in its scope nor unprecedented in its implications, prompting the academic and policy communities to continue our critical and comparative work and learn valuable lessons. Similar cases—each shaped by local histories, legal cultures, and political economies—have exposed straightforward criminality as well as the limitations of formal legality and the inadequacy of narrow definitions of corruption. Examples that can be cited include the Operation Clean Hands in Italy (Burnett & Mantovani, 1998; De Cesare, 1999; Manzi, 2023) or the 1MDB scandal in Malaysia (Rethel, 2021; Wright & Hope, 2018). The 2023 Tempi train crash in Greece, where 57 people lost their lives in a head-on collision, revealed not only technical or operational failures but also a deeper pattern of bad governance in a context of regulatory evasion, political recklessness, outdated infrastructure, and administrative negligence (Georgoulas et al., in press). The tragedy underscored the human cost of both numerous crimes and "lawful but awful" practices: actions that may comply with the letter of the law but violate its spirit, eroding institutional trust and endangering lives (Passas, 2005; Passas & Goodwin, 2004).

This book offers a rich, empirically grounded analysis that affirms insights I have been able to draw from my own work: that corruption is not merely a legal infraction, but often a systemic condition maintained through criminogenic asymmetries, that is imbalances in legal, economic, political, and cultural systems across jurisdictions (Passas, 1999, 2000). As exemplified by Odebrecht and other multinational actors in the *Lava Jato* case, corruption flourishes in networked interfaces between legal and illegal actors, in spaces where regulatory arbitrage and institutional weaknesses allow powerful actors to exploit gaps in enforcement, evade accountability, and obscure culpability through legal complexity (Costa, 2021, Passas, 2003).

Such criminogenic factors are not confined to Latin America. The 1MDB scandal in Malaysia, involving billions embezzled from a state development fund, implicated domestic elites and global financial institutions in the United States, Switzerland, and Singapore (Wright & Hope, 2018). In South Africa, the "State Capture" inquiry revealed how the Gupta family, alongside former President Jacob Zuma, repurposed state institutions for private enrichment, facilitated by weak governance and permissive global finance (Madonsela, 2016).

Rather than being marginal, corruption in these instances is integral to governance. The underlying factor connecting these diverse situations is the breakdown of a shared normative framework, a condition I have characterised as global anomie (Passas, 2000). In environments of inequality and institutional fragility, boundaries between legitimate and illegitimate conduct blur. Self-enrichment is normalised as entitlement; bribery as a cost of doing business; and compliance regimes as instruments of obfuscation rather than accountability.

Operation Car Wash demonstrates both the possibilities and limitations of criminal justice in addressing entrenched corruption. On the one hand, it disrupted powerful networks, prosecuted and convicted influential actors, and renewed civic discourse. On the other, it illustrated how legal tools like plea bargains, when deployed without sufficient oversight, can be politicised or weaponised. The subsequent backlash, including judicial reversals and allegations of prosecutorial overreach, reflected the precarious balance between procedural and substantive justice.

Similar patterns are observable elsewhere. Italy's *Mani Pulite* in the 1990s revealed systemic corruption but failed to institutionalise long-term reforms (Della Porta & Vannucci, 1999). In Greece, public tragedies such as the Tempi crash, the 2007 wildfires, and the 2009 fiscal crisis have revealed the costs of clientelism, opacity, and institutional decay (Georgoulas et al., in press; Sotiropoulos, 2014).

To understand and address these systemic failures, we must consider conduct along the corruption continuum, including lawful but awful actions. Practices like regulatory capture, institutionalised lobbying for harmful policies, use of shell companies, and predatory procurement may not violate penal statutes, but they produce outcomes functionally indistinguishable from illegal corruption: measurable harm to the public, erosion of trust, and institutional corrosion (Amit et al., 2017; Lessig, 2013; Passas, 2005).

Accordingly, anti-corruption strategies must be preventive, multi-level, and systemic. This includes designing institutions that control discretion, enhance transparency, close regulatory gaps that facilitate arbitrage, and produce accountability. It also requires confronting the complicity of enablers: banks, law firms, lobbyists, and consultancies that operate within the bounds of legality while facilitating impunity (Passas, 2020; Vogl, 2021; Wedel, 2016).

Corruption is transnational. The harms it produces—and the mechanisms it exploits—are global. The proceeds of bribery are laundered in financial centres; contracts are masked by opaque corporate structures;

and reputation is rehabilitated through public relations and legal firms with plausible deniability. The global financial system, far from neutral, functions as an enabling infrastructure of misconduct (Christensen, 2011; Passas, 2003).

This book contributes meaningfully to the scholarly and policy dialogue on governance and integrity. It provides empirical grounding, theoretical insight, and comparative breadth. It exemplifies the systemic and global nature of corruption and affirms the urgency of integrated, long-term, and justice-centred responses. Most importantly, it sends messages of grounded hope: that people of integrity can make a difference, speak truth to power, and achieve accountability in very high places. It is also a reminder that the battle continues and requires constant effort and concerted actions from legal, civil society, corporate, and international actors. So, the story of *Operation Car Wash* serves as both inspiration and cautionary tale. It reminds us that the protracted war against corruption demands vigilance, innovation, and unwavering commitment to the rule of law.

This book is a vital contribution to this fight. By amplifying the voices of those who led *Operation* Car *Wash*, it ensures that their efforts and the lessons they learned will not be forgotten.

Niko Passas
School of Criminology,
and Criminal Justice
Northeastern University
Boston, USA

References

Amit, E., Koralnik, J., Posten, C., & Lessig, L. (2017). Institutional corruption revisited: exploring open questions within the institutional corruption literature. *Southern California Interdisciplinary Law Journal*, *26*, 22.

Anselmo, M., & Pontes, J. (2022). Operation car wash: Brazil's institutionalized crime, and the inside story *of the biggest corruption scandal in history*. Bloomsbury Academic.

Burnett, S. H., & Mantovani, L. (1998). *The Italian guillotine: Operation clean hands and the overthrow of Italy's First Republic*. Rowman & Littlefield Publishers.

Christensen, J. (2011). The looting continues: Tax havens and corruption. *Critical Perspectives on International Business, 7*(2), 177–196.

Costa, J. (2021). *Revealing the networks behind corruption and money laundering schemes: An analysis of the Toledo–Odebrecht case using social network analysis and network ethnography*. Working Paper 36: Basel Institute on Governance Working Papers, 1–35.

De Cesare, C. (1999). Borrelli, corruzione e giustizia: "Mani pulite" (1992–1998) nelle parole del procuratore Francesco Saverio Borrelli (1. ed.). Milano: Kaos Edizioni.

Della Porta, D., & Vannucci, A. (2012). *Corrupt exchanges: Actors, resources, and mechanisms of political corruption.* Aldine de Gruyter.

Georgoulas, S., N. Passas, C. Kouroutzas, D. Paraskevopoulos (in press). *State-corporate crimes and risk in mass transportations: The tempi train crash case.* Antigoni.

Lagunes, P., & Švejnar, J. (Eds.). (2020). *Corruption and the Lava Jato scandal in Latin America*. Routledge.

Lessig, L. (2013). "Institutional corruption" defined. *The Journal of Law, Medicine & Ethics, 41*(3), 553–555.

Madonsela, T. (2016). *State of capture: Report no. 6 of 2016/17*. Office of the Public Protector, South Africa.

Manzi, L. (2023). *Among equals: the causes of effective corruption prosecution in Italy*. Lexington Books.

Passas, N. (1999). Globalization, criminogenic asymmetries and economic crime. *European Journal of Law Reform, 1*(4), 399–423.

Passas, N. (2000). Global anomie, dysnomie, and economic crime: A criminological perspective. *European Journal of Law Reform, 1*(4), 517–543.

Passas, N. (2003). Cross-border Crime and the Interface between Legal and Illegal Actors. *Security Journal, 16*(1), 19–37.

Passas, N. (2005). Lawful but awful: Legal corporate crimes. *The Journal of Socio-Economics, 34*(6), 771–786.

Passas, N. (2020). Anti-corruption beyond illusions: The pressing need to make a difference. In B. Makowicz (Ed.), *Yearbook of global ethics, compliance and integrity* (pp. 329–339). Peter Lang.

Passas, N., & Goodwin, N. (Eds.). (2004). *It's legal, but it ain't right: harmful social consequences of legal industries*. University of Michigan Press.
Rethel, L. (2021). *The political economy of financial development in Malaysia: From the Asian crisis to 1MDB*. Routledge.
Sotiropoulos, D. A. (2014). Southern European governments and public bureaucracies in the context of economic crisis. *European Journal of Social Security, 16*(2), 225–245.
Vogl, F. (2021). *The enablers: How the West supports kleptocrats, facilitates money-laundering and corruption, and endangers our democracy*. Rowman & Littlefield.
Wedel, J. R. (2016). *Unaccountable: how elite power brokers corrupt our finances, freedom, and security*. Pegasus Books.
Wright, T., & Hope, B. (2018). *Billion dollar whale: the man who fooled Wall Street, Hollywood, and the world*. Hachette Books.

Competing Interests The author has no competing interests to declare that are relevant to the content of this manuscript.

Introduction

Brazil's Biggest Corruption Scandal: Testimonies from Operation "Car Wash"

The book, titled Brazil's Biggest Corruption Scandal: Testimonies from Operation "Car Wash", compiles oral testimonies from individuals directly involved in Operation Car Wash ("Lava Jato"), Brazil's most prominent anti-corruption initiative. Launched on 17 March 2014 and officially concluded on 1 February 2021—although investigations and legal proceedings have continued beyond that period—Operation Car Wash represents a pivotal chapter in Brazil's efforts to combat corruption. This book seeks to document the historical trajectory of corruption in the country, with particular emphasis on the operation's focus on Petrobras, Brazil's largest state-controlled oil and gas company. It also explores the far-reaching impact the investigation had on Brazil's leading engineering and construction firms, many of which were central to the illicit schemes uncovered.

Car Wash stands as the most extensive corruption investigation in Brazil's history, revealing a sophisticated network dedicated to the misappropriation of public funds involving politicians, business leaders, and high-ranking officials from both the public and private sectors. The investigation uncovered a range of criminal activities linked to Petrobras and major Brazilian engineering and construction companies, resulting in the arrest of numerous prominent figures from the political and corporate spheres, and promoting significant changes in the country's anti-corruption framework.

This book stands as a historical record of Operation Car Wash, assembling first-hand accounts through oral testimonies of individuals directly or indirectly involved in the investigation. The *narratives*—provided by prosecutors, judges, lawyers, and anti-corruption specialists, many of whom are key figures in Brazilian civil society—offer a range of perspectives and insights into this pivotal period. Interviewees were selected based on their expertise, their engagement in anti-corruption initiatives, and their willingness to share their experiences and contribute to the construction of Brazil's institutional memory. Although many individuals were invited to participate, some were ultimately unable to do so due to scheduling constraints or personal circumstances.

In the chapters that follow, readers will encounter the voices of key figures who played central roles in the Car Wash Operation, offering nuanced reflections on the challenges faced by prosecutors, criminal defence lawyers, judges, and civil society activists. These testimonies provide an insider's perspective on the complex legal mechanisms underpinning the investigative process, including negotiations and plea agreements, which collectively shaped the course of Operation Car Wash. Taken together, these accounts contribute to a deeper historical understanding of one of the most significant anti-corruption efforts in Brazil's democratic trajectory.

The interviews—conducted with key actors in the investigation and recorded via the Zoom platform in both audio and video formats—adopt a documentary-style approach, capturing the breadth and complexity of Operation Car Wash. This book seeks to preserve the historical memory of the investigation, ensuring that its essential elements are not lost to time. A total of twenty-two individuals, each of whom played a pivotal role, were interviewed, offering distinct yet intersecting perspectives on the operation. Their testimonies are presented across four thematic sections, each shedding light on different dimensions of this landmark anti-corruption effort.

Chapter 1. The Car Wash Investigation and theProsecutor's Office
This chapter examines the initial phase of Operation Car Wash, focusing on the Federal Public Prosecutor's Office and its central role in launching and advancing the investigation. Through first-hand accounts, it sheds light on the institutional dynamics, prosecutorial strategies, and legal innovations that marked the early development of the case. The testimonies included here illustrate the internal deliberations, inter-agency coordination, and the complex legal environment in which prosecutors operated, offering a unique perspective on the foundations of one of the most consequential anti-corruption operations in Brazil's history.

Chapter 2. The Car Wash Investigation and the Criminal Lawyers
This chapter presents the perspectives of lawyers who represented individuals and corporations implicated in the investigations and legal proceedings of Operation Car Wash. Their testimonies offer critical insights into the legal strategies employed by the defence, the procedural and constitutional challenges raised, and the broader implications for due process and the rights of the accused. These accounts illuminate the adversarial dimension of the operation and contribute to a more comprehensive understanding of its legal and institutional complexities.

Chapter 3. The Car Wash Investigation and the Judiciary
This chapter gathers reflections from members of the judiciary, including judges from first- and second-instance courts, as well as from Brazil's higher courts—the Superior Court of Justice and the Federal Supreme Court. Many of these judges have authored landmark rulings that shaped the legal trajectory of anti-corruption enforcement in Brazil. Their testimonies reveal the judicial reasoning behind key decisions, the institutional pressures faced, and the evolving jurisprudence that emerged during the course of Operation Car Wash.

Chapter 4. The Car Wash and the Civil Society
The fourth and final part of the book presents the testimonies of prominent figures from Brazilian civil society—experts and advocates

dedicated to combating corruption—whose perspectives offer a crucial complement to the institutional narratives of Operation Car Wash. Their reflections illuminate the role of non-state actors in demanding transparency, shaping public debate, and sustaining pressure for reform. As the concluding section, these accounts are essential for a comprehensive understanding of the investigation's legacy and its implications for democratic accountability and the future of anti-corruption efforts in Brazil.

The interviews are arranged alphabetically within each of the four chapters described above. They were conducted with key individuals selected from the main institutional and societal fronts involved in Operation Car Wash. This chapter-based structure reflects a commitment to editorial neutrality, allowing each voice to be presented on its own terms. By engaging directly with a range of diverse—and at times conflicting—perspectives, readers are invited to form a comprehensive and critically informed understanding of one of the most significant anti-corruption investigations in Brazil's contemporary history.

The book poses critical questions to its interviewees regarding the broader societal, institutional, and legal implications of Operation Car Wash. What transformations did the investigation bring about in Brazil's political and legal culture? What were its principal achievements, limitations, and unintended consequences? In what ways did it expose structural vulnerabilities in the country's anti-corruption framework? And, perhaps most importantly, what enduring lessons can be drawn to inform the prevention of future large-scale corruption?

Presented in a format that balances academic rigour with narrative accessibility, the book offers a rare, behind-the-scenes view of one of the most far-reaching anti-corruption investigations in Brazil's democratic history. The testimonies—rich in detail and drawn from the lived experience of central figures—contribute to an empirically grounded and multidimensional account of Car Wash, making this work a valuable resource for scholars, practitioners, and policymakers in the fields of law, governance, and public integrity.

As a documentary and analytical record, this book does not seek to deliver a definitive judgement on Operation Car Wash. Rather, it presents a curated set of testimonies that allow readers to engage directly with the diverse and often conflicting perspectives of those who played central roles in the investigation. By doing so, it encourages a reflective and critical reading—one that recognises the complexities of the operation and its long-term consequences for Brazilian democracy and the rule of law. From a legal standpoint, the narratives gathered here offer a rare look into how institutions developed and applied new instruments—such as plea bargains, leniency agreements, and international legal cooperation—in the face of unprecedented corruption schemes. From a political science perspective, the testimonies illuminate the tensions between anti-corruption enforcement and democratic stability, the role of judicial institutions in political transformation, and the fragility of institutional legitimacy under public pressure.

Although the interviewees represent different branches of government, sectors of society, and ideological positions, a common thread runs through their accounts: the recognition of Car Wash as a turning point. Much like Italy's Mani Pulite, the operation revealed both the depth of systemic corruption and the capacity of state and societal actors to confront it. In bringing these voices together, this book contributes to Brazil's institutional memory and offers an invitation to the reader: to consider what Operation Car Wash was, what it became, and what it continues to mean in Brazil's ongoing struggle against corruption and in the pursuit of a culture of public integrity.

Contents

1

Car Wash and the Prosecutor's Office

Introduction to Chapter 1

In the opening Chapter of this book, titled "The Car Wash and the Prosecutor's Office", readers are introduced to the landscape of corruption investigations and the subsequent legal proceedings initiated by the Federal Public Prosecutor's Office in response to the evidence uncovered. This chapter marks the beginning of the narrative surrounding Operation Car Wash, offering insights into the testimonies of prominent Brazilian prosecutors who were key members of the Car Wash Task Force and who played critical roles in this complex investigation.

Among the prosecutors featured, Carlos Fernando dos Santos Lima, Deltan Dallagnol, and Orlando Martello Júnior stand out as central figures in the Car Wash Task Force. Carlos Fernando dos Santos Lima, renowned for his dedication and expertise, played a pivotal role in the investigation, becoming widely recognised as a key figure in the legal landscape for his commitment to uncovering corruption and advocating for justice.

Deltan Dallagnol gained widespread recognition for his leadership and instrumental role within the Car Wash Task Force. As a prosecutor, he has been at the forefront of efforts to combat corruption, contributing

L. M. Costa, *Brazil's Biggest Corruption Scandal*, Crime Prevention and Security Management, https://doi.org/10.1007/978-3-031-99078-6_1

to the success of high-profile cases and demonstrating an unwavering commitment to upholding the rule of law.

Orlando Martello Júnior, another prominent member of the Car Wash Task Force, made significant contributions to Brazil's fight against corruption, particularly through international cooperation with other countries entangled in the Car Wash Operation's web of corruption. His legal expertise and dedication to justice positioned him as a key figure within the prosecutorial team.

Together, these individuals exemplify a steadfast commitment to the principles of justice and the relentless pursuit of accountability in the face of corruption. Their roles within the Car Wash Task Force have left a lasting impact on Brazil's legal landscape, as well as on the international stage.

Additionally, Peruvian prosecutor Rafael Vela Barba, tasked with overseeing local investigations into corruption uncovered by Operation Car Wash across Latin America—particularly in Peru—adds a crucial international dimension to the discussion. In Peru, the operation was designated "Odebrecht", named after the Brazilian engineering and construction company at the centre of the scandal, which had ramifications across Latin America and Africa. Vela Barba's extensive experience and commitment to justice play a central role in Peru's efforts to combat corruption and promote transparency within its legal system. His leadership in Peru's Odebrecht Operation underscores the importance of cross-border collaboration in addressing corruption that transcends national boundaries.

Readers are also introduced to the significant contributions of Swiss prosecutor Stefan Lenz, who oversaw international cooperation in freezing assets held in Switzerland. Renowned for his expertise in navigating complex financial investigations, Lenz's work highlights the critical role of cross-border collaboration in combating transnational crimes, particularly money laundering and corruption. His active participation in the Car Wash Operation underscores the global dimension of the investigation and the essential cooperation between nations in addressing the financial ramifications of this extensive corruption network. This opening chapter offers a detailed understanding of the strategies, challenges, and behind-the-scenes dynamics faced by the Car Wash Task

Force at the outset of the investigations. It marks the beginning of a compelling exploration into the complexities of the legal battle against corruption in a country plagued by endemic issues—an operation whose impact resonated far beyond Brazil's national borders.

Testimony of Carlos Fernando dos Santos Lima

Abstract

This section presents the testimony of Carlos Fernando dos Santos Lima, a former Regional Prosecutor of the Republic and key member of the Car Wash Task Force in Curitiba (2014–2018). Lima recounts his career trajectory and the connections between Car Wash and earlier investigations, particularly Banestado, which played a crucial role in shaping Brazil's modern anti-corruption efforts. He provides insights into financial crime mechanisms, plea bargains ("colaboração premiada"), leniency agreements, and the significance of international cooperation in corruption cases.

His testimony highlights the legal and political challenges surrounding Car Wash, including judicial decisions, institutional resistance, and the evolving legal framework. He also discusses the task force's investigative techniques and how they contributed to exposing systemic corruption in Brazil. Lima reflects on the impact of Car Wash, addressing both its successes and limitations. He examines the role of the media, public perception, and political reactions in shaping the operation's trajectory.

His testimony offers a critical perspective on the complexities of combating corruption and the lasting influence of Operation Car Wash on Brazil's legal and political landscape. By analysing operational strategies and legal instruments, this section provides valuable lessons on governance, compliance, and the rule of law—contributing to the broader global discourse on anti-corruption efforts.

Could you elaborate on your academic background and personal trajectory to help contextualise your standpoint?

I come from the state of Paraná and a family with a long-standing, uninterrupted tradition of service in the Public Prosecutor's Office, spanning more than seventy-five years. Two of my brothers also pursued careers as public prosecutors—one now retired and the other still in active service. Of the six siblings in our family, five followed our father's path into the legal profession. I mention this because, from an early age, I was deeply immersed in the institutional culture of the Public Prosecutor's Office. It has really been part of my path from the start. At the age of fourteen, my mother secured a position at Banco do Brasil—she could no longer tolerate having me at home, quite understandably. At fifteen, I passed the internal exam and assumed the role of clerk, a position I would hold for several years. In the end, I stayed at the bank for twelve years. The experience proved invaluable, shaping my character through the steady reinforcement of routine and discipline. At that time, Banco do Brasil functioned almost like a training ground, particularly for those preparing for a career in public service.

While studying law in Curitiba, I often walked past pass the Federal Prosecutor's Office and thought to myself, "One day, I will be a federal prosecutor." That aspiration ultimately materialised. I began my professional journey as a state prosecutor in Paraná, a role I held for four years before qualifying through the federal examination. Upon passing, I was appointed to Foz do Iguaçu, where I was responsible for establishing the local Federal Prosecutor's Office from the ground up. As one might anticipate in a tri-border region, the jurisdiction posed considerable challenges, including pervasive drug trafficking, smuggling, and contraband-related offences. Around 1995–1996, investigations were initiated into financial offences associated with the so-called CC5 accounts—banking instruments frequently used to facilitate international fund transfers.[1] While not all such transactions were inherently unlawful, many exhibited signs of irregularity or illicit financial activity, warranting thorough scrutiny. That investigation marked the outset of a sustained and complex engagement with financial crime enforcement. Following my return to Curitiba, I served two consecutive terms as Regional Prosecutor for Citizens' Rights and assumed the role of Criminal Coordinator. Although the CC5 investigation had commenced in 1996, it remained ongoing into 2003, by which time the proceedings faced the imminent threat of statutory limitation. In response, a specialised prosecutorial unit—the Banestado[2] Task Force—was formally constituted to consolidate efforts and prevent the potential collapse of the case. I was invited to join the task force at a time when the investigation had reached a particularly sensitive and high-stakes phase, marked by increasing institutional and political tension. There were two teams involved—one based in Curitiba and the other in Foz do Iguaçu—and they were in conflict, each either asserting jurisdiction or seeking to avoid it altogether. I had a good relationship with both sides, so, despite my background in civil matters, I was asked to step in as a kind of mediator. That is how I became part of the task force.

Could you elaborate on Operation Banestado and its relevance, particularly in terms of how it may have shaped or foreshadowed the investigative approaches and institutional dynamics later seen in Operation Car Wash?

Operation CC5—or Banestado, as it came to be known—stemmed from investigations into the use of CC5 accounts to send illicit funds abroad. So, what was going on at the time?

Well, during the Fernando Henrique[3] government there was an effort to artificially maintain parity between the US dollar and the Brazilian real. Under the pretext of allowing Paraguayan merchants to bring Brazilian currency—which had been spent in Paraguay—back to Foz do Iguaçu to be deposited into CC5 accounts, the government effectively enabled these accounts to function as foreign accounts. The idea was that the money could then be converted into another currency and sent abroad. In practice, this created enormous pressure on the parallel exchange rate. In my assessment, the government appeared to be utilising the CC5 mechanism as a form of institutionalised safety valve—an unofficial channel to relieve pressure on the parallel foreign exchange market. This, in my view, reflects a tacit strategy to accommodate systemic imbalances outside the formal regulatory framework.

These accounts ended up being used in various ways to move money from across Brazil. Funds were deposited into fake or "dummy" accounts, which in turn deposited money into Brazilian banks under the guise of transfers originating in Paraguay. That was the central element of what was uncovered. However, at that time—around 2004—there were dozens of ongoing inquiries, many of which consisted of little more than photocopied documents. There was a marked absence of oversight and institutional coordination, which significantly hindered our ability to conduct the investigations in a systematic and effective manner. One of the major challenges in Foz do Iguaçu was the constant turnover of personnel: prosecutors typically did not remain in their posts for more than a year. The same situation applied to agents of the Federal Police and the Federal Revenue Service. As a result, the investigations made very limited progress at that stage. In 2004, once the seriousness of the situation had become clear, the prosecutors in Foz do Iguaçu, with the judge's authorisation, decided to transfer all case records to Curitiba. The transfer gave rise to a significant institutional challenge—after all, few would welcome the sudden arrival of a large volume of cases nearing the statute of limitations. A large meeting was convened, including congresspersons, prosecutors from Brasília, and it was ultimately decided to formally request the creation of a task force. At that time, the concept of a task force did not yet exist within the Public Prosecutor's Office—it was an entirely new model. A task force represents a modern approach to conducting investigations: a dedicated team established specifically to address a single complex case or issue. I therefore sought out Marcela[4] and Nazareno,[5] and together met with Dr Geraldo Brindeiro, who was at the time serving as the Attorney General and the highest authority within Brazil's Federal Public Prosecutor's Office.[6] He expressed full support for the proposal, and authorisation was granted to proceed. The task force brought together prosecutors from Foz do Iguaçu, Curitiba, and various other regions across the country. By 2003, the inquiries initially opened in Foz do Iguaçu had already been resolved.

Would you consider Operation Banestado to have marked the emergence of the first structured investigative task force in Brazil?
I would not go so far as to claim definitively that it was the very first, as there may have been other groups formed earlier. However, in terms of its characteristics—the formal adoption of the term "task force," its internal structure, and the clarity of its mandate—it was, in effect, the first of its kind. Or at the very least, it was the first significant initiative to operate in that manner.

What institutional or investigative framework, if any, inspired the structure and approach of the Banestado task force?
The Banestado task force—also referred to as the CC5 task force, with the terms used interchangeably—represented a highly pioneering model. Its success stemmed, in large part, from the decision to extend efforts beyond domestic inquiries, actively tracing funds that had been illicitly transferred abroad. At that time, Banestado (the Bank of the State of Paraná) had already been privatised and acquired by Itaú. Banestado maintained a branch in New York, and Itaú soon identified that this branch had been used for money laundering purposes. When funds passed through Paraguay, access to information was severely limited. The situation changed, however, when Itaú—demonstrating a positive example of compliance and cooperation in anti-money laundering efforts—voluntarily stepped forward. A proposal was made to engage an American lawyer to file a civil action that would enable the bank to release the necessary information to the Brazilian authorities. That is precisely what occurred.

One of the key figures in this operation was the well-known black-market currency dealers Alberto Youssef.[7] He had an account at Banestado's New York branch, and from there, funds were transferred to other accounts that were essentially "contaminated" by their connection to him. With the support of US authorities—particularly the New York District Attorney's Office and the US Attorney's Office in Newark—access was successfully obtained to records from dozens of financial institutions, leading to the uncovering of thousands of offshore accounts. A significant number of these accounts were held by Brazilian nationals who had received funds laundered through complex transnational schemes.

As a result, the Brazilian tax authorities issued assessments totalling approximately 8 billion reais. On the criminal side, however, the same level of success was not achieved. Charges were brought, primarily against Paraguayan brokers and financial institutions, but ultimately, criminal accountability remained limited. That outcome reflects a broader pattern in Brazil. Personally, I filed charges against Banestado itself—which was the largest case—and secured a conviction. But by the time enforcement was possible, only two bank executives remained, both elderly and under house arrest. So, while the criminal consequences were limited, at least there were those tax assessments. Whether the funds made their way back into the public coffers, I could not say. Still, 8 billion reais was a significant amount—at least it was at the time.

By 2003, I had been promoted to Regional Prosecutor in São Paulo, a role I undertook while simultaneously managing the complex Banestado investigations. Despite the significant progress already achieved, I became aware of a gap in my own legal training. To address this, I decided to pursue an LL.M. in the United States, enrolling at Cornell Law School, where I studied from 2008 to 2009. I was not alone in seeking further education abroad—several of my colleagues in the Public Prosecutor's Office followed a similar path. Deltan Dallagnol,[8] for example, studied at Harvard and later succeeded me in leading the Banestado case.

Thus, Operation Banestado was not only the precursor to the investigative practices later refined in Operation Car Wash—it also served as a training ground, a nucleus of prosecutorial expertise. Four of the prosecutors who worked on Banestado would later play key roles in Car Wash.

Which members of the Federal Prosecutor's Office were involved in both Operation Banestado and Operation Car Wash, and how did the institutional and procedural lessons drawn from Banestado influence the strategic and legal approaches later adopted in Car Wash?

Myself, Deltan, Orlando Martello,[9] and Januário Paludo.[10] In addition to our team, there was also a core team from the Federal Police who had worked on the Banestado case and later became part of Car

Wash. Márcio Anselmo,[11] for instance, who initiated the first Car Wash investigations—around 2013—was then a clerk at the Federal Police. Erika Marena[12] and Luciano Flores,[13] both Federal Police delegates in Car Wash, had also been involved in Banestado. We also had Roberto Leonel,[14] who later served at the Council for Financial Activities Control. He was part of the Federal Revenue's intelligence team and had worked with me for over twenty years on various cases. He participated in both Banestado and Car Wash. Then there is Judge Sergio Moro,[15] who worked on both cases. Although not close friends, there was mutual respect and familiarity. A shared sense of public duty significantly facilitated collaboration during Operation Car Wash.

After I returned from Cornell, I was invited to serve as Deputy Secretary for International Legal Cooperation—an invitation that arose from the work I had done in the Banestado and Car Wash operations. I owe that opportunity to Vladimir Aras,[16] who had also worked on Banestado and later served as Secretary-General during the Janot administration.[17] At Vladimir's request, I helped restructure and organise the new secretariat, even though international legal cooperation had never truly been my area of expertise. Around that time, Deltan was putting together a new task force. Vladimir proposed my name, and since Deltan and I had previously worked together, he readily agreed. They invited me to join, and although I was already quite senior within the Public Prosecutor's Office, I still had a strong desire to contribute and make a difference.

I had been working at the regional level for a long time and, as many in our career path know, it can feel like a kind of professional limbo. Justice Joaquim Barbosa, for instance—who himself served as a regional prosecutor before joining the Supreme Court—used to say that regional prosecutors often experience a form of "ostracism." The most meaningful activity tends to occur at the trial level or in the higher courts, while the regional tier is generally less dynamic. I did feel somewhat underutilised in that role. So, when I was invited to join Operation Car Wash, I accepted without hesitation.

Upon returning from Suriname, I joined the task force, and the investigation commenced without delay. At the outset, our attention was directed towards four "doleiros", black-market currency dealers.[18] At first, I even questioned why I had been brought into the case—it did not seem particularly significant. But one of those doleiros was Alberto Youssef, who had given a Land Rover to a former Petrobras director. That is not the kind of gift one offers to someone of little importance. That seemingly minor detail turned out to be the spark that ignited Operation Car Wash.

Those initial investigations into the black-market currency dealers eventually became part of our routine casework, but the Land Rover case developed into the centrepiece of Operation Car Wash. It was a clear indicator of money laundering. The investigative methodology employed was grounded in the strategies developed during the Banestado case—refined and enhanced by the knowledge and experience acquired in the intervening years.

When you joined the Car Wash task force, did you anticipate that the operation would uncover such vast amounts of illicit funds involving one of Brazil's largest corporations, its top executives, and high-ranking political figures?

The prevailing impression—one that I believe resonated with many Brazilians—was a pervasive sense that something was fundamentally wrong. While corruption was plainly visible, its true scale and systemic entrenchment were not fully understood. What ultimately emerged from our investigations was a sobering realisation: corruption was not an occasional deviation, but rather a structural component of the political and economic fabric of the country. Operation Car Wash essentially revealed how political financing in Brazil operated: it was built on illicit money. The opportunity to generate illicit funds emerges anywhere public power is used to negotiate with private interests—for instance, in the drafting of legislation, provisional measures, and public procurement. Corruption was uncovered in connection with legislative processes, large construction firms, major infrastructure projects, and even seemingly routine activities such as the supply of materials to the public administration.

Of course, many critics argue that Operation Car Wash did not go far enough—that it did not reach certain areas or people. In my assessment, a significant portion of the truth remains hidden. The truth is that the system was simply not prepared to handle the magnitude of what was being revealed. That became clear in the way institutional powers and investigative tools were systematically stripped away from the task force. Its capacity to act was deliberately suffocated. Whether one agrees with that or not is beside the point—the fact is, there was a concerted effort to shut it down. And that effort succeeded.

In the early days, no one could have foreseen the scale the operation would eventually attain. Yet, the investigative groundwork laid, and the methodologies employed enabled its exponential expansion. Foremost among these was the strategic use of collaborative mechanisms—particularly plea bargain agreements—which proved instrumental in unveiling the systemic nature of the crimes under investigation. These were mechanisms that Vladimir Aras and I introduced as early as 2003 during Operation Banestado. In fact, the first plea bargain agreement was made by Alberto Youssef.

Later, in 2015 and 2016, leniency agreements—already provided for under the Clean Company Act[19]—were also employed. Until then, these instruments had not been effectively applied by the Public Prosecutor's Office. They were incorporated into the strategy, adapted accordingly, and made operational within the Federal Prosecutor's Office. These tools became key drivers of the Car Wash investigations. I used to say, even during the Banestado case, when speaking with early collaborators: "Your head for ten others—equal to or greater than yours." The aim was always to pursue the leadership of criminal organisations. The principle was to "collaborate upwards," never downwards—not necessarily within the same case, but across all proceedings in which the individual had been involved. A person who took part in a bribe or money laundering operation in Banestado might also have been involved in Petrobras, Eletronuclear, or elsewhere. Within this logic, the expansion of the investigation became inevitable. Alongside this, there were three essential pillars to our work. First, collaboration mechanisms. Second, legal and procedural tools. And third, communication. A strong effort was made to uphold transparency and open communication—not only through the Public Prosecutor's Office presenting its account of events (a practice now under serious threat due to ongoing attempts to silence the institution), but also through public access to electronic legal proceedings. This access enabled both journalists and the wider public to follow developments in real time. The approach was guided by a shared understanding—within both the judiciary and the Prosecutor's Office—that secrecy serves only the interests of the investigation. There is no "right to secrecy" for the defendant when measures such as search, and seizure or arrest are executed. Once those measures are implemented, public awareness of the facts becomes essential. In retrospect, it is evident to me that both the rapid expansion of the investigation and the backlash it provoked were not only foreseeable but, perhaps, inevitable.

The decision by the Federal Supreme Court to dismantle Operation Car Wash had significant repercussions for anti-corruption efforts in Brazil. In your view, what were the principal gains and setbacks brought about by this ruling in terms of the broader institutional fight against corruption?

Admittedly, I may not be entirely impartial in this assessment. The entire development of Operation Car Wash was anchored in the principle of probative connection. The investigation originated in the state of Paraná, initially focusing on black-market currency dealers, but also involving early suspicions of overpricing in construction works at Repar—the Presidente Getulio Vargas Refinery, also located in Paraná. From that starting point, we were able to establish evidentiary links to major Petrobras projects across the country.

There is no public interest in fragmenting these investigations, because when you do that, you lose sight of the bigger picture. The corruption at Repar is not fundamentally different from what happened at Abreu and Lima, or at the refinery in Rio, or even in the World Cup construction projects. It is all part of the same phenomenon. Drawing on the concept of probative connection—and supported by information obtained through plea bargains—the investigation was able to advance and expands.

This exponential growth brought both advantages and challenges. Naturally, each new operation led to the discovery of further documents, which in turn encouraged new collaborators to come forward. These collaborators and materials revealed a range of new facts. From that pool, three or four of the most relevant and promising leads would typically be identified for further investigation, serving as the basis for new operations. However, this cycle repeated itself continuously—with each new phase producing more documents, more collaborators—ultimately resulting in a significant backlog.

At a certain stage, the evidentiary links began to lose strength—and I fully recognise that this enters the realm of interpretation. One might plausibly trace the investigative thread from the initial corruption schemes to later projects, such as the Metropolitan Arch in Rio or the Olympic developments. However, over time, that thread began to fray. It would be equally reasonable to argue that the causal connection had dissipated—or, conversely, that it remained intact. In my view, some of these investigative offshoots were entirely valid and legally sound; much depends on one's interpretive approach. The truth is that Operation Car Wash did not possess the institutional capacity to cover the entire country. While many prosecutors demonstrate profound dedication to investigative work, there are moments when they may not fully appreciate the structural and operational limits inherent to their role. At the height of its activity, the Car Wash task force comprised thirteen prosecutors—an expansion from the original team of just seven.

One of the first major setbacks for the task force occurred when the material related to Eletronuclear[20] was transferred to Rio de Janeiro. A separate task force was established there, which conducted a full investigation and ultimately led to the downfall of the Sérgio Cabral administration.[21] The Eletronuclear case eventually developed into a separate investigation based in Rio de Janeiro, with clear links to the Sérgio Cabral administration. That case became an independent operation within the Rio de Janeiro jurisdiction. In fact, the first arrest of Sérgio Cabral was carried out jointly by teams from Curitiba and Rio. It was based on a dual warrant—one issued in Curitiba and the other in Rio—executed simultaneously. From that point onward, the Rio task force gained momentum. Even today, operations stemming from that investigation are still ongoing. It became what one might describe as a "second Car Wash", and it was successful demonstrating that some spin-offs can indeed be effective. However, not all of them were. São Paulo, for example, never truly gained traction. The challenges there likely had more to do with the specific nature of the investigations and with the functioning of the São Paulo courts and judiciary. I cannot say with certainty why it failed to advance—they made efforts, but the initiative was consistently met with resistance, both from the judiciary and from political circles.

Much of the outcome ultimately depended on a degree of luck—having the right judges in the right positions. In Curitiba, the circumstances were favourable. Judge Sergio Moro was presiding at first instance, Gebran[22] as the rapporteur at the appeals court, Felix Fischer[23] at the Superior Court of Justice, and, at the Federal Supreme Court, initially Justice Teori Zavascki,[24] followed by Fachin.[25] That alignment was a stroke of real luck. In Rio, by contrast, they were not as fortunate. Their cases ended up with Justice Gilmar Mendes[26] at the Supreme Court, which made everything far more difficult.

Spin-offs are undoubtedly useful and serve an important function. However, not all decisions taken in the fragmentation of the investigations were viewed favourably. Take, for example, the decision to refer certain cases to the electoral courts—a move that altered the established understanding of jurisdiction and institutional independence. Electoral matters remained with the electoral courts, while non-electoral cases were left in a sort of procedural limbo, with no clear obligation to remain connected. That jurisdictional shift was grounded in a precedent we had believed to be long superseded. Politically, however, it was convenient. Electoral justice in Brazil operates as a "borrowed" system—it is composed of judges and prosecutors who serve temporarily and often hold other positions concurrently. It is not structurally equipped to handle complex criminal investigations.

For this reason, the notion of an "electoral spin-off" was consistently opposed. That position was made clear at the time, and I continue to regard it as a mistake. In hindsight, some spin-offs were entirely justified and led to robust legal outcomes—such as the case in Rio. Others, in my view, were not; they appeared to be motivated more by political pressure than by sound legal reasoning. Perhaps Operation Car Wash had grown too powerful, and certain judges and justices felt compelled to reassert institutional control. The decision to fragment the investigations may well have been a way of curbing what they perceived as an excessive concentration of prosecutorial authority.

What role have plea bargains played in advancing the fight against corruption in Brazil? In your view, how have recent legislative developments impacted the effectiveness and integrity of this legal instrument?

As previously mentioned, it was our team that developed the foundational model for plea bargains in Brazil—an assertion I make with confidence, as it reflects the historical record. While cooperation agreements existed prior to Alberto Youssef's 2003 arrangement, the specific framework that became standard—contractual in form, structured through explicit clauses, negotiated penalties, and subject to judicial oversight—was established during the Banestado operation. That investigation alone involved seventeen plea agreements, all of which were validated by the Judiciary, not only for their evidentiary outcomes but also for their legal soundness, including affirmation by the Federal Supreme Court.

Even before the enactment of the 2013 Clean Company Act, which formally introduced the concept of plea bargaining into Brazilian legislation, the Supreme Federal Court had already made use of such agreements in at least two cases—if memory serves me correctly.[27] The Supreme Court itself relied on testimony provided by cooperating witnesses. If one examines the indictment in the Mensalão case,[28] for instance, one finds repeated references to a particular black-market currency dealers who, notably, was not indicted. He is referred to exclusively as a witness—a procedural choice that appears incongruent with the factual elements detailed in the indictment. To the best of my understanding, this was due to a cooperation agreement he had entered into, which had been negotiated Antonio Fernando,[29] then serving as Prosecutor General of the Republic. To my knowledge, however, this agreement was never formally ratified by the Federal Supreme Court. Nevertheless, it was operative, and it predated the 2013 Clean Company Act, which would later codify such mechanisms. In this sense, the use of plea bargain agreements as a prosecutorial tool emerged from our practice, preceding formal legislative recognition. Given my prior experience with complex, high-profile cases, I was consistently very cautious in my approach to plea bargain agreements. In fact, I developed a detailed internal protocol to guide their handling. Until quite recently, I was still providing training to Federal Prosecutors on what I consider the most critical and intricate phase of the process: the pre-agreement stage. This is the phase in which the possibility of collaboration is first raised, negotiations are initiated, terms and conditions are outlined, and the clauses begin to take shape—all before the agreement is formally executed. In my view, the legal framework tends to oversimplify the process, as though the act of signing the agreement was the decisive step. But that is not the case; the most challenging and delicate work takes place long before the signature.

Following the pre-agreement stage comes the management phase, which I often describe as a kind of marriage of convenience. This is precisely why it is so important to structure the pre-agreement carefully and to address the principal points of contention early in the process. Our approach was always characterised by caution and rigour, as a poorly drafted agreement could pose a serious risk to the integrity of the investigation. To mitigate this, a series of safeguards was implemented. A prosecutor would never engage directly with a cooperating witness without the presence of their defence counsel. Moreover, the prosecutor was never alone; each interaction was accompanied by at least one other prosecutor. Every negotiation and decision had to be expressly recorded in a formal clause. Institutional memory is fragile—people change, recollections fade—and without clearly drafted provisions, interpretation becomes highly problematic. Even with meticulous documentation, disagreements may still arise. For that reason, additional layers of precaution were introduced to ensure both legal soundness and procedural transparency.

In both the Banestado and Car Wash operations, no effort was made to actively seek out potential collaborators. The consistent practice was to wait for defence counsel to initiate contact with a proposal. This approach served to protect the integrity of the process and avoid any potential misinterpretation of conduct. One fundamental principle was always upheld: any agreement must be capable of public justification. In other words, the rationale for granting a particular benefit must be evident. Plea bargain agreements often provoke mixed reactions, and clarity in their rationale is essential to maintaining public confidence. On the one hand, the public demands access to the facts—they want the truth to come to light. On the other, they expect accountability and punishment. It is often difficult for people to accept that collaboration entails compromise: the collaborator receives a benefit in exchange for the information they provide. That benefit is only justifiable if the information proves to be of demonstrable value.

What matters, therefore, is the quality of the information—not just in terms of its content, but in its potential to generate meaningful, long-term investigations. That was always the guiding principle. A plea bargain agreement is not a right; it is a matter of mutual interest. Either party is free to withdraw. For us, as prosecutors, an agreement only made sense if it promised exponential progress in the investigations—results that could stand on their own. That is precisely why Palocci's[30] proposal was declined on two occasions: the Public Prosecutor's Office simply did not consider it viable.

I often say that a collaborator goes through several distinct phases. I tend to explain this to fellow prosecutors—with a touch of humour, of course. The first is the denial phase: "Doctor, I did not do it." To which I reply, "Then you should speak to the judge—acquittals are up to the judiciary, not the Public Prosecutor." Next comes the euphemism phase: "It was not a cartel, it was more of a gentlemen's agreement"; "It was not a bribe, it was a commission." Everything is rebranded in softer, more palatable terms. They need to move through these stages until, eventually, a moment comes when you find yourself thinking: "All right, now they're telling me something I believe to be true." I am not suggesting it is the whole truth—it rarely is—but there comes a point when you sense that they are genuinely trying to disclose the bulk of what they know.

Then comes another phase—which I sometimes jokingly refer to as the "Marcelo Odebrecht phase"[31]—in which the collaborator, feeling abandoned or disillusioned, becomes so frustrated that they begin to uncover and submit additional material even after the agreement has been formally concluded.

There is an entire psychological dimension to the process. Well-constructed plea bargain agreements take time.

I won't deny that, on occasion, we expedited the process—Barusco's[32] case, for example, was concluded in a single day: he arrived in the morning and left at dawn with the agreement signed. But that was the exception, not the rule. The standard approach involves careful deliberation, proceeding methodically through each phase and negotiating every clause with precision—especially given that these agreements must ultimately be explained and justified to both the public and the press.

We had a protocol in place, and it was followed diligently in Operation Car Wash, in Curitiba. Unfortunately, I have been quite critical of certain other cases—particularly of the agreements led by Marcelo,[33] who was an advisor to Prosecutor General Janot. The plea bargain deals negotiated by the Office of the Federal Prosecutor General did not adhere to the same protocols. There was too much eagerness, too much voluntarism. I always tell prosecutors: "*When you are feeling too eager, that is precisely the moment to pause and take a broader view.*" At times, a piece of evidence can strike an emotional chord—and that is when caution is most necessary. Every prosecutor wants a strong outcome in a high-profile case. So when something dramatic is presented—such as the recordings by Sérgio Machado,[34] involving Sarney,[35] Renan,[36] and Jucá,[37] if I recall correctly—it can be almost hypnotic.

The same happened in the case of Cerveró.[38] That agreement was signed without prior knowledge on my part or that of the task force. The response was one of outrage, and it was firmly communicated to the Office of the Prosecutor General that involvement was essential in any agreements concerning defendants linked to cases under the responsibility of the team. But in that instance, the agreement was imposed from above—entirely top-down. Once again, it was an environmental recording that triggered the decision to proceed.

I experienced this dynamic first-hand in the JBS case[39]—once again, it began with a covert recording. These secret audio recordings often attract significant media attention, but they do not always yield substantive investigative value. It is essential to distinguish between material that can genuinely support a sustainable line of inquiry and that which merely serves to generate headlines.

That was the level of caution consistently observed. The office in Rio de Janeiro, in particular, demonstrated a strong commitment to this deliberate and methodical approach. This is precisely what is emphasised at the training school of the Public Prosecutor's Office: that effective plea bargain agreements require meticulous attention to detail. A well-constructed agreement is one that triggers a series of robust and credible investigations. The more investigations it leads to, the stronger the collaborator's negotiating position becomes.

The key question is always: is this in the interest of the Public Prosecutor's Office? If the answer is yes, then it must be because the facts disclosed are highly relevant, capable of generating multiple investigations, and because these crimes were previously unknown. That is what places the collaborator in a strong position.

It is often described as a reversal of conventional logic: "the dirtier, the better." Admittedly, it is an unfair rationale, but the process is not about moral judgement—it is about pragmatism. The more information the collaborator possesses—and the deeper their involvement in the scheme—the more valuable their contribution becomes. Ideally, they will also provide documentary evidence, though not all do. And it is important to be clear: no one who has not committed a crime enters into a plea bargain agreement. Their participation in the wrongdoing is a fundamental prerequisite.

This brings us to leniency agreements, which are applicable to legal entities rather than individuals. Our work with leniency began in 2015, following the introduction of the Clean Company Act. This legislation incorporated the concept of leniency, drawing heavily on the model established under the Administrative Council for Economic Defence Law,[40] which had long governed competition-related leniency. The issue, however, is that the Clean Company Act essentially replicated the Administrative Council for Economic Defence legal framework without fully accounting for the fact that corruption presents a fundamentally different challenge from anti-competitive conduct—particularly in a context like Brazil, where a significant portion of companies are family-owned and closely held.

Under the Administrative Council for Economic Defence framework, parties that self-report anti-competitive conduct may be granted immunity from related sanctions. By contrast, the Clean Company Act offers no protection from criminal liability, which represents a significant disincentive. Consider the implications: if I am running a family-owned business, what incentive do I have to come forward and implicate executives who may be close relatives and who, in many cases, hold actual control over the company? In this sense, the leniency mechanism under the Clean Company Act was not structurally designed to function effectively—at least not within the context of Brazil's corporate landscape, where family ownership is prevalent. The incentive structure proved insufficient, as it was largely confined to the reduction of administrative sanctions. This limitation was soon recognised. Yet, as with plea bargaining, it became evident that the Public Prosecutor's Office possessed sufficient legal latitude to develop a robust and operational framework for negotiating leniency agreements, even in the absence of detailed legislative regulation. I was able to persuade the other members of the task force, and the proposal was jointly presented to the 5th Chamber of the Public Prosecutor's Office in Brasília.[41] Agreement was reached, and a model of leniency was then developed in collaboration with the task force. The underlying premise was that the Public Prosecutor's Office needed to proactively engage with companies and convey the message: "There is a new product on the market. It is called leniency."

The first corporate leniency agreement was then successfully secured. I gave an interview—if I recall correctly, it was with *Valor Econômico*—in which I remarked, somewhat provocatively: "I have created a prisoner's dilemma," which, of course, lies at the heart of the leniency framework.[42] In other words: the first one in gets the benefit, and the others will face the full force of the law for everything that is been revealed. It is a form of strategic engineering. You break the loyalty between companies, between companies and their corrupt partners, between companies and their executives. It starts a kind of internal race—no one really wants to run, but everyone's watching their neighbour, wondering, "Will I be the one left behind?" That is the logic: to create mistrust and disrupt the internal solidarity of a criminal network. You break the *omertà*, that code of silence. That was the spirit behind my interview with *Valor Econômico.* I said that the Prosecutor's Office would start signing leniency deals with companies. The first one in gets the benefits, and the rest will be held accountable. And it worked. That idea—that a race had started—caught on. To make it feel real, I added a detail: "We already have a company interested." That took it from being a theoretical race to a real one. The gun had fired. People were already running.

Sure enough, a week later, a company stepped forward. And funnily enough, it was the ideal company to start with in the Petrobras case. It was small enough not to spark huge public outrage—it was not Odebrecht, Camargo, or Andrade—but it was still big enough to matter. It had always been part of the cartel's inner circle, so it had a wealth of information. At the same time, it did not come with a huge reputational cost. Every agreement comes with a reputational cost for the Public Prosecutor's Office. There is always a big debate about whether it is even appropriate to make a deal with a particular company. But then one company came forward, we signed the first leniency agreement, and soon after that, there was a wave—an avalanche, really—of other companies wanting to do the same. The same rule applied in the Administrative Council for Economic Defence's leniency model was adopted: the first company to come forward would receive the benefits, while those that followed would incur significantly higher costs. This principle formed the foundation of the leniency framework established in Brazil.

Why did it succeed? Because the Prosecutor's Office occupied a unique institutional position, capable of engaging with both the enforcement and negotiation dimensions of the process. It was this convergence—this "marriage of perspectives"—that created the institutional synergy essential to rendering the leniency agreements viable from the outset.

At that time, the implementation of this model in Brazil was still in its early stages, even as the sanctions imposed on companies were rapidly increasing. I recall that the penalty imposed on Camargo Corrêa reached approximately 700 million reais. At the time, it was difficult to persuade legal counsel that this figure was accurate. Then came Andrade Gutierrez—with a penalty of 1 billion—and subsequently Odebrecht, which exceeded 2 billion. This brings us to an important point: these values are not fixed. There is no absolute number, as the full extent of the harm is often uncertain. As a result, determining penalties becomes a matter of arbitration—dependent on the methodology used to calculate the losses. But as the process unfolded, the scale of the sanctions escalated. Once a company was no longer the first to come forward, the cost of leniency increased significantly. That is the underlying logic of the system: "the first to cooperate drinks the clean water." The entire structure of incentives is built around that principle.

With these two tools—the individuals who agree to collaborate, and the documentation provided by the companies—we created what I sometimes call an investigative monster. A machine with immense power and efficiency, capable of dismantling criminal organisations.

Now, companies do not always know what their own executives or business partners are going to say—many won't speak unless there is a benefit for them. At the same time, the individuals who are willing to talk often do not have access to the hard evidence—the e-mails, the accounting records, the phone logs. That kind of material tends to be in the company's systems. So, when you bring both together—the personal testimony and the documents—they complement each other, and the investigation gains real strength.

As Operation Car Wash proved increasingly effective, there came a point when many of those involved began to realise it might be in their best interest to make a deal. In Curitiba, it was not us—the task force—chasing after companies and collaborators. It was the other way around. The initiative came from the companies themselves. It was simply made clear that there was readiness and capacity to engage in negotiations. These agreements serve a very specific and complex purpose. Take Odebrecht, for instance: that agreement involved three countries and dozens of jurisdictions. The facts extended across Latin America and beyond. A deal was reached across three jurisdictions, with a single value agreed upon and allocated among them. The negotiation lasted nine months and proved to be one of the most complex agreements ever handled. At the same time, it provided invaluable experience. The process yielded a much deeper understanding—not only of corporate decision-making and internal dynamics, but also of how to conduct cross-border negotiations effectively. And that is why these negotiation processes are so key to understanding the success of the Car Wash Operation and, more broadly, Brazil's fight against corruption.

To what extent did international cooperation—through mutual legal assistance, international conventions, and treaties—contribute to the success of Operation Car Wash?

Much of the progress achieved over the years in establishing robust legislative frameworks has been driven by soft power—particularly pressure exerted by the international community. Key developments, such as anti-money laundering legislation and the Clean Company Act, were largely influenced by external forces, particularly from the United States. Since 9/11, international legal cooperation—along with the exchange of information and best practices—has assumed increasing importance. These developments are part of the broader process of globalisation, which I view, overall, as a positive and necessary force.

Globalisation has undoubtedly made it easier for assets and financial values to move across borders. At the same time, however, it has played a key role in closing the very loopholes that once enabled illicit flows to go undetected. The objective of anti-money laundering initiatives is not to eliminate such practices entirely—that would be unrealistic—but to raise their cost. The more complex, risky, and expensive the process becomes, the greater the deterrent effect. Within this framework, international legal cooperation is indispensable—particularly the timely and effective exchange of intelligence.

There has been significant ideological resistance, with some arguing that "the task force should not be engaging with the FBI." But let me be clear: during the Banestado case, I personally visited the FBI. Meetings were also held with the US Attorney's Office in Newark, the Department of Homeland Security, and the New York District Attorney's Office. Why? Because in cross-border investigations, the cooperation of foreign authorities is not merely beneficial—it is indispensable. The exchange of information is a cornerstone of effective transnational enforcement. Much of that information is, of course, requested through formal channels. However, over time, as institutional relationships develop, you begin to understand which requests are likely to be met—because contact has already been established, and dialogue has taken place. It is not a matter of obtaining early access to the data, but of knowing which avenues are viable and how best to navigate them. This type of expertise—grounded in communication and the development of mutual trust—plays a central role in enabling effective international cooperation. We first developed that skillset through our cooperation with the United States during the Banestado case. Later, in the context of Operation Car Wash, our most significant partnership was with Switzerland. This collaboration proved so effective that it led the Swiss judiciary to revise its own approach to money laundering. In terms of both impact and efficiency, the cooperation between Brazil and Switzerland was historic. The relationship was marked by openness and candour—they visited Brazil on several occasions, and we reciprocated. It was a matter of sitting around the same table, engaging in constructive dialogue, and jointly addressing complex challenges. I recall travelling to the United States to observe how their experts managed the accounting aspects of cooperation agreements, simply to learn from their experience. Exchanges of this nature are indispensable for building institutional capacity and fostering mutual trust.

There remains a considerable degree of ideological resistance on this subject—remarks such as "You should not work with the Americans; they are imperialists, they are Yankees" are not uncommon. Frankly, I do not consider this type of argument productive. The reality is that Brazilian authorities operate strictly within the bounds of the law when providing assistance to foreign investigations, and, in turn, we request their cooperation through the appropriate legal channels. That is how international legal collaboration functions.

The exchange of information—alongside logistical and technical support—has evolved in a remarkably positive manner. We have received strong backing from public prosecutors in other jurisdictions. A notable example is Peru: following the disclosure of the Odebrecht agreement, Peruvian authorities initiated their own investigations, ultimately opening a major chapter of Operation Car Wash within their own jurisdiction—one that implicated several former presidents. This illustrates both the effectiveness and the necessity of international cooperation. Transnational corruption cannot be addressed in isolation.

A significant part of our decision to conclude an agreement with Odebrecht stemmed from observing how swiftly investigations were advancing abroad. We came to realise just how much we could contribute to the efforts of other countries—because to be frank, the Brazilian model of corruption had been exported. Our construction companies were replicating the same practices in other jurisdictions. We therefore felt a moral obligation to cooperate with foreign judicial authorities and to support their investigations. It was no longer solely about Brazil.

International legal cooperation is essential. It operates within strict legal frameworks and depends heavily on intelligence work, but it is both effective and indispensable. In several instances, Monaco provided valuable support, and Switzerland, once again, played a decisive role. In the Odebrecht case, for example, we received critical documents from the Swiss authorities just three days before the deadline for bringing charges—and that changed everything. It is one thing to build a case on circumstantial evidence suggesting a link between certain funds and Odebrecht; it is quite another to hold in your hands an official Swiss document confirming that a particular Odebrecht executive, responsible for a specific offshore account, was indeed the account holder. That type of evidence is powerful—not only from a legal standpoint, but also in terms of reinforcing public confidence and institutional legitimacy. Ultimately, it was communication, international cooperation, negotiated agreements, and coordinated teamwork that lay at the core of Operation Car Wash's success.

While the Mensalão scandal was still under adjudication, γOperation Car Wash was already underway. Even at present, it is likely that other corrupt practices continue to occur. In retrospect, what might have been done differently? And which measures could have contributed to more enduring and positive outcomes for Operation Car Wash?

I always find this kind of reflection quite difficult. During the task force years, I had a friend who kept a notebook solely to record things I said—he wrote everything down. The truth is, Operation Car Wash could very easily have been far less successful. Just yesterday, for example, we witnessed an injunction issued by a Supreme Court justice in response to what is clearly a political backlash—what I see as the persecution of prosecutors. Now, someone might ask: "Did Operation Car Wash make mistakes?" Perhaps. But I tend to think of it in terms of that scene from the film *City of God*,[43] you know? The boy has photographs of Zé Pequeno's murder—he has got undeniable proof. And he says something like, "This photo could win me a prize, I will be recognised, but I will also be persecuted for the rest of my life. If I hand over the other photos, I will get a job." And so, he chooses the photos that get him a job. That is somewhat how I feel. Perhaps we failed to recognise that there comes a moment when you need to stop pulling the rope—to loosen your grip and allow others to take the lead. This is often misunderstood. I have seen members of the Public Prosecutor's Office—including Deltan—face the threat of losing their careers, which, let's be honest, is the one true asset most prosecutors possess: a career that provides stability and supports their families.

I used to say to Deltan—one of my many well-worn phrases—that an operation is like an aeroplane: it needs a flight plan, a clear direction, and a true north. It takes time to build momentum and reach the point of lift-off. And that take-off phase is the most precarious. Had Justice Teori Zavascki's first injunction gone the other way, it is entirely possible that Operation Car Wash would never have taken off at all. That is how fragile it was in the early days. Once airborne, things appear stable. You reach cruising altitude, the speed is steady, and everything seems to be going according to plan. But the destination is always the ground. One way or another, the aircraft must land—because if it does not, it will eventually crash. Those are the only two options. It is not a satellite—it cannot remain in orbit indefinitely. Perhaps the real challenge of Operation Car Wash was knowing when to land, when to hand things over. I am not entirely sure how that should have been done. It is a highly theoretical question: at what point should a step back have been taken to allow the operation to expand more organically across the country? Such an approach might have alleviated some of the pressure experienced in Curitiba.

The second point—though I would not necessarily call it a mistake—was something the system struggled to accept: our communication with the public, particularly in relation to the *Ten Measures Against Corruption*. At that moment, Operation Car Wash began to take on a more proactive, public-facing role. The second point—though I would not necessarily call it a mistake—was something the system struggled to accept: our communication with the public, particularly in relation to the *Ten Measures Against Corruption*. At that moment, Operation Car Wash began to take on a more proactive, public-facing role.[44]

Anyone with a degree of common sense recognises that the criminal justice system alone cannot transform societal reality. We are confronted with deeply rooted problems regarding the effectiveness of our criminal procedures. I often say it is like a one-legged creature: so much emphasis is placed on the "guarantee leg"—the rights of the accused—while the other leg, which should ensure the enforcement of criminal sentences following conviction, is largely neglected. And in Brazil, that second leg is virtually non-existent.

What is truly needed is a system that operates with greater efficiency and timeliness—one capable of delivering clear outcomes, whether acquittals or convictions, and ensuring that such outcomes are enforced. This is not necessarily a call for harsher penalties, but for resolution. It is disheartening to witness cases lost in endless appeals or overturned on procedural grounds. Judgements should be rendered on the merits of the case. Yet that, regrettably, is not the prevailing reality in Brazil. The *Ten Measures Against Corruption*, as conceived by Deltan Dallagnol, sought to address this institutional gap. However, I have always maintained that a fundamental element remained unaddressed. The problem of corruption in Brazil is not solely a matter of the state's inability to sanction wrongdoing; it is also—and perhaps more profoundly—about the sheer volume of financial resources demanded by the political system. That, in my view, is the more structural and enduring challenge.

The real debate should centre on the proportional electoral system used to elect deputies and councillors—a system that is extraordinarily costly. It also concerns the excessive number of political parties, as well as the lack of transparency and internal democracy within those parties. A significant portion of political financing ends up concentrated in the hands of party leaders—those who exercise control over the machinery. There has even been the emergence of informal—or de facto—'parties', such as the one associated with Eduardo Cunha,[45] which was, in essence, constructed through corrupt practices.

Operation Car Wash marked the beginning of efforts to address issues that, for many, had long been regarded as purely political in nature. In my view, however, this did not represent an overreach of our institutional role or a breach of constitutional boundaries. Rather, it was an expression of citizenship—an exercise of our civic and professional responsibility to participate in discussions that any citizen is entitled to have, particularly those concerning the future of the country. That said, this position deeply unsettled the political establishment. Once you begin to question practices long regarded as "normal," discomfort inevitably follows. There is a widespread belief—one we often encountered in conversations with collaborators—that this is simply how politics functions. Many of them genuinely believed there was no other way for the system to operate. So, when we began to identify these practices for what they were—criminal—there was a strong reaction: "You are criminalising politics!" But this was not a rhetorical accusation. The issue lies in the fact that many continue to draw a sharp distinction between politics and criminality, even in cases where the two are demonstrably intertwined.

All this likely contributed to the system's backlash. I am not suggesting that we were responsible for what followed—none of us ever supported Bolsonaro.[46] However, I do believe that the movement created conditions that gave rise to a populist wave. Someone recognised the opportunity to capitalise on anti-corruption sentiment and presented himself as an "anti-system" figure—when the truth was quite the opposite.

Within the operation—particularly among members of the Public Prosecutor's Office and the Federal Police—there was no alignment with or sympathy for Bolsonaro. I would go so far as to say that the prosecutors, almost unanimously, did not support him. It is often said that his election represented the peak of Operation Car Wash, but in my view, it marked the beginning of its decline. Why? Because from that moment onward—especially following Sergio Moro's entry into politics and subsequent departure—the political establishment identified an opportunity. They used that perceived association to launch a counteroffensive, particularly after media support began to diminish. Suddenly, we found ourselves in the eye of the storm. Public enthusiasm began to wane amid the constant stream of new revelations. The media withdrew. And the political system, sensing an opening, responded with a concerted pushback. It was at that point that Operation Car Wash—especially in Curitiba—began to lose momentum and confront significant challenges.

In the final two years, we spent more time managing the fallout from Operation Car Wash than conducting substantive investigations. In retrospect, I wonder whether we missed the right moment to begin the descent—to start bringing the plane down, or at least to prepare for landing. Perhaps we aimed for too much change, too quickly—an ambition that is inherently difficult to realise within the constraints of a democratic institutional framework. As a result, Car Wash has found itself fighting for its own survival. Many prosecutors are now simply trying to preserve their careers.

I used to say this often to younger prosecutors—particularly during lectures for new inductees into the Public Prosecutor's Office: the system is inherently unfair. At some point, it will turn against you. And when that happens, your only defence is the strength and integrity of the institution you serve. I experienced this personally during the Banestado case. Regrettably, I am no longer certain that full reliance can be placed on the institution. The current situation is markedly precarious. What is unfolding today bears a striking resemblance to the fate of Operation Clean Hands in Italy. People frequently ask me about this comparison, and my answer is always the same: the reaction of a cornered political system follows a predictable pattern—and it is, in many respects, inevitable.

There are, in truth, few effective safeguards against this dynamic, because political influence has permeated nearly every institution. It extends to appointments to the higher courts and to oversight bodies within both the Public Prosecutor's Office and the judiciary. It also exerts considerable influence over the media, where many public officials act as sources. And once an individual becomes a source, they often enjoy a degree of protection from journalistic scrutiny. The result is a complex web of influence and insulation. If you take aim at large-scale corruption—if your objective is to dismantle entrenched political corruption—you will inevitably encounter serious resistance. There is no avoiding that. That said, over the long term, I remain hopeful that progress can be made towards a cleaner and more transparent system. At present, however, the challenges faced are immense.

Would you like to offer any final reflections or concluding remarks to round off this discussion?

From a historical perspective, I believe I have already addressed the most important points. Naturally, there are always additional details—some more anecdotal in nature—but they are not especially significant in the broader context. Stepping back and viewing the events from a wider angle, I would say that this provides a fair summary of what truly matters.

Carlos Fernando dos Santos Silva was born in Apucarana, Paraná, Brazil, and is a lawyer and compliance consultant. He previously served as Regional Prosecutor of the Republic in São Paulo and was a key member of the Car Wash Task Force in Curitiba from 2014 to 2018, in addition to his involvement in the task force for Operation *Banestado*. From 1991 to 1995, he held the position of Public Prosecutor in Paraná. He is now a retired prosecutor from the Federal Public Prosecutor's Office. His testimony was recorded on 18 August 2021 via the Zoom virtual platform and lasted 1 hour and 22 minutes. The transcript was subsequently reviewed by the interviewee on 1 April 2022.

Testimony of Deltan Dallagnol

Abstract

In this testimony, Deltan Dallagnol reflects on his personal and professional trajectory leading to his central role in Operation Car Wash. He recounts his early academic formation at the Federal University of Paraná, his motivation to join the Public Prosecutor's Office grounded in a sense of civic duty and Christian ethics, and the early disillusionment with systemic impunity in high-profile corruption cases such as Banestado. These frustrations led him to pursue further studies at Harvard, where he encountered more efficient judicial models. Upon returning to Brazil, he was invited to join the emerging Car Wash task force. Drawing on prior experience in task forces, particularly Banestado, he helped build an innovative investigative model grounded in strategic collaboration between institutions, the use of plea bargains, and phased operations.

Dallagnol offers a detailed institutional history of the task force's formation, the rationale behind its design, and the significance of its structure in enabling the largest anti-corruption operation in Brazil's history. He reflects on the unprecedented scale of the investigation, its reliance on plea bargaining, and the legal safeguards employed to protect its legitimacy. He also addresses the political and institutional backlash that followed, linking the operation's temporary success to broader systemic resistance and legal setbacks—including changes to pre-trial detention rules, weakened anti-corruption laws, and the persistence of privileged jurisdiction. Finally, he presents a civic and ethical argument for sustained engagement in anti-corruption efforts, framing the fight as a generational endeavour rooted in democratic resilience and public accountability.

For contextual purposes, could you reflect on your educational background and the personal journey that shaped your professional path?

I graduated in Law from the Federal University of Paraná. In my final year, I decided to pursue a career in the Public Ministry, as I felt a strong calling for public service. That decision really took shape when I read the law governing the Public Ministry—it struck me as a law about the many ways one can love their neighbour and serve others. With my Christian worldview, I identified deeply with that mission. I saw it to serve a greater purpose.

Upon completing university studies in 2002, I began preparing for public service examinations and went on to pass several, including the competitive exam for the Federal Prosecutor's Office. I officially entered the Federal Prosecutor's Office at the start of 2003. From the outset, I was driven by a desire to serve justice and make a meaningful impact—particularly in the fight against corruption among the powerful. I grew up witnessing major corruption scandals, such as the Anões do Orçamento[47] scandal in the 1990s, go unpunished. These events left a lasting impression on my generation. I believed that through dedication and rigour in my work, it would be possible to achieve concrete results—securing convictions and recovering misappropriated public funds. But reality proved quite different.[48] In 2004, I worked on my first major corruption case, which involved phantom employees and embezzlement within the Legislative Assembly of Paraná. Today, more than seventeen years later, no one has been held accountable, and not a single real has been recovered. Then came the Banestado case,[49] in 2005, a task force was established, through which charges were brought against more than 680 individuals for serious financial crimes. Yet again, more than sixteen years on, accountability has remained elusive, with very few facing any real consequences.

My next major case was Operation Curaçāo,[50] and once again, the results were minimal. In 2006, I led another major corruption case in which convictions were secured against two individuals for corruption and corporate fraud, including the use of offshore schemes. Prosecution was brought against both businessmen and tax auditors—the businessmen were each sentenced to more than forty years in prison. Yet, in retrospect, what became of those three major cases? One was overturned, and the other two expired without ever reaching a final resolution.

My professional trajectory has been shaped by a sense of persistent frustration—marked by repeated efforts to hold powerful white-collar offenders accountable, often with limited tangible results. This sense of institutional inertia led me, in 2012, to take a temporary leave in order to pursue further studies at Harvard. That experience significantly broadened my perspective. I became more familiar with the American legal system which, while firmly grounded in the protection of fundamental rights, appeared to operate with greater efficiency in producing concrete outcomes. I returned to Brazil in 2013 with a renewed outlook and new ideas. Around that same time, my first child was born—a moment of personal transformation that coincided with a particularly intense and formative period in both my private and professional life.

Then, in early 2014, I was invited to what would become known as Operation Car Wash. I hesitated at first. My previous experiences had shown that anti-corruption work, while vital, often produced limited results. Yet I also believed deeply in the importance of the task—it was work that needed to be done. I could not simply walk away. I felt a responsibility to persist. Perhaps fatherhood influenced that decision as well; becoming a parent shifts one's perspective, prompting reflection on the kind of future we hope to help shape for the next generation. And so, despite knowing it would entail long hours and a demanding workload, I accepted the challenge.

At that stage, Operation Car Wash had not yet reached the political sphere. During the first phase, a search and seizure operation was conducted, resulting in the collection of over 80,000 documents—a staggering volume of material. The evidence was highly complex and related primarily to money laundering carried out by black-market currency dealers. Given my prior experience with such cases—particularly Banestado, the CC5 task force,[51] and Operation Curação—several colleagues invited me to join the investigation. And that was how my involvement in Operation Car Wash began.

How effective do you consider the task force model to be in addressing complex corruption cases, and is it the most appropriate approach within the Brazilian context?
My first experience with a task force dates back to 2004, when the Banestado task force—also known as the CC5 task force—was established in the state of Paraná. At the time, I had just relocated from Campinas to Curitiba to begin my work with the Federal Public Prosecutor's Office. Although I was not initially a member of the task force, I began to follow its work closely and with great interest. In 2005, I was officially invited to join the task force, and I decided to accept. I was genuinely intrigued by the model—it was yielding tangible results, which was encouraging. The CC5 task force was responsible for drafting what is widely regarded as the first written plea bargain agreement in Brazil's history. At the time, no specific legal framework existed to govern such agreements, but the team identified practical ways to proceed, drawing extensively on the American model. Many of the clauses adopted closely mirrored those found in plea agreements used in the United States.

In many ways, that task force functioned as an incubator—not only for what would later become Operation Car Wash, but also for the very practice and legal culture of plea bargaining[52] in Brazil. It was only years later, in 2013, that the Law on Criminal Organisations formally recognised and regulated written plea agreements. When I joined the CC5 task force, the work was coordinated by Januário Paludo[53], a highly respected prosecutor with vast experience. Orlando Martello Júnior[54] was also part of the team at the time. As it turned out, many of those involved in the CC5 task force would later find themselves working together once more on Operation Car Wash. Carlos Fernando[55] was also involved in CC5. It was a very collaborative environment—there was constant exchange of ideas, strategies, and information, both among us prosecutors and with other key institutions, like the Federal Revenue Service and the Federal Police.

It was during this time that I first met Roberto Leonel,[56] an auditor from the Federal Revenue, who would later become a key figure in Car Wash. He was the one who really taught me how to handle large-scale investigations. I also first crossed paths with, Érica Marena,[57] a Federal Police officer who would later lead much of the Federal Police's work in Car Wash.

That is why I view the CC5 task force as the true forerunner—or even incubator—of Operation Car Wash. The experience I gained during those one, two, or three years within the task force was likely equivalent to what I might have acquired over fifteen or twenty years in a more traditional prosecutorial setting. The pace, the collaboration, the intensity—it was a period of extraordinary learning and sustained effort. Everyone was deeply committed to a common objective, working overtime on a daily basis, constantly exchanging insights and refining strategies. It was an intellectually demanding environment, but also a profoundly stimulating one—and it produced results. Only later did I come to realise that similar task force models existed in other countries as well. In fact, some of the colleagues from those early days later authored a manual on task forces, drawing on both our domestic experience and international best practices.

What were the circumstances that led to your appointment as coordinator of the Car Wash task force?

In 2014, I was invited to take the lead on Operation Car Wash. At the time, I knew I would need someone to work alongside me from the outset—largely for a rather circumstantial reason: I had an international surfing trip already planned. It was a long-anticipated journey to the Mentawai Islands in Indonesia, a true paradise for surfers. Cancelling or rescheduling was not a realistic option. The trip had been meticulously planned over an extended period, was financially significant, and involved a group of friends who had each organised their schedules to make it possible. For any dedicated surfer, the opportunity to surf in the Mentawai Islands is almost a rite of passage—it represents the fulfilment of a long-held dream. As it happened, the trip coincided exactly with the launch of the first phase of Operation Car Wash. It was immediately clear to me that I could not lead the investigation single-handedly. To move forward in a structured and effective manner, it would be essential to assemble a team of trusted colleagues to share the responsibility from the outset.

It is important to recall that, at that stage, the investigation was focused exclusively on money laundering operations. Petrobras was not yet part of the picture, and the full extent of political corruption had not come to light. Even so, the case was already large in scale and complex in structure, with significant potential implications. This context was presented to the Prosecutor General[58] and proposed the formation of a dedicated task force. He endorsed the creation of the task force. At the time, he was working closely with Prosecutor Vladimir Aras,[59] who had previously been involved in the CC5 task force. That proved to be a decisive factor—Vladimir's direct experience with the task force model, and his understanding of its effectiveness, lent credibility and institutional weight to our proposal.

His experience helped the Prosecutor General understand that the model offered more than administrative structure—it was a strategic framework capable of delivering results—it was a practical, results-driven approach. At that stage, as previously noted, the investigation was still confined to money laundering. Yet establishing the task force early on made a significant difference as the investigation expanded and evolved.

To what extent is it common for the Prosecutor General to authorise the establishment of a task force in complex investigations?

Authorising a task force is not a straightforward decision for the Prosecutor General. Once one is created, it is almost certain that, by the following day, prosecutors from across the country will begin requesting similar arrangements for their own high-profile cases. Task forces are intended for truly exceptional circumstances; they are not the standard institutional response. From the Prosecutor General's perspective, such authorisation carries significant costs—not only in terms of financial resources, but also in political capital. Approving one task force often means having to deny similar requests from others facing equally complex investigations, which can generate internal pressure and criticism. The reality is that there are simply not enough personnel or resources to support the creation of multiple task forces simultaneously. Therefore, when one is approved, it signals that the case is of extraordinary scope, complexity, or national relevance.

Could you describe how the task force for Operation Car Wash was formed and organised in its initial stages?

It was agreed with the Prosecutor General that, as the lead prosecutor on the case, I would be responsible for assembling the team. The first person I contacted was regional prosecutor Orlando Martello Júnior. I made it clear from the outset that I would only accept the position if he agreed to join me; I was not prepared to undertake such a responsibility alone. He accepted immediately. From there, I began reaching out to colleagues with whom we had previously worked and who had demonstrated both technical competence and an unwavering commitment to public service. Among those invited were Carlos Fernando dos Santos Lima and Januário Paludo, both of whom had prior experience in task forces and were widely respected within the institution. I also invited Andrey Borges de Mendonça,[60] another highly regarded colleague, and Diogo Castor de Mattos,[61] a prosecutor who had previously completed an internship under my supervision and had consistently demonstrated a strong commitment to addressing organised crime and complex financial offences. In this way, the initial composition of the Car Wash task force was defined—a group built on professional trust, shared experience, and a collective sense of purpose.

Over time, more than twenty colleagues from the Federal Prosecutor's Office joined the Car Wash task force. They came from different backgrounds, brought different perspectives, and had varied world views—but they were all united by the same purpose: to serve society with excellence in criminal cases and to deliver real, concrete results.

Which structural and operational features of the task force do you believe were most instrumental in allowing Operation Car Wash to become the largest anti-corruption operation globally?

What made the difference was a shared commitment to innovation—a willingness to think beyond conventional approaches, to adopt new techniques, tools, and strategies, always within the bounds of the law. As with the Banestado task force, Operation Car Wash fostered an environment that promoted close institutional collaboration. It strengthened ties with the Federal Police—who had established their own task force—as well as with the Federal Revenue Service and other public agencies, including the Office of the Comptroller General. The operation effectively became a kind of incubator for best practices and a new investigative model. Plea bargaining was once again employed, but this time with the addition of a crucial new dimension: a strategic communication plan. This proved essential, given that the individuals now being confronted possessed far greater political and economic power than those involved in earlier cases.

One of the defining features of this new investigative model was the decision to structure the operation in sequential phases, each unfolding as multiple lines of inquiry progressed. This approach kept the public engaged—almost as if they were following a television series. Behind the scenes, we were working continuously, often into the early hours of the morning, to advance several investigations simultaneously. People grew accustomed to that rhythm, eagerly awaiting each new development, as if watching a real-life version of *House of Cards* or *Game of Thrones*—not in the sense of fictional political drama, but in the sense of relentless action, complex narratives, and high-stakes consequences. Each phase involved judicially authorised measures that regularly made headlines, uncovering large-scale corruption involving millions—or even billions—of reais, and implicating major political and corporate figures. For the first time in Brazilian legal history, we extended the use of cooperation agreements to legal entities as well as individuals—an important milestone in the country's fight against corruption.

When you assumed coordination of the task force, did you anticipate that Operation Car Wash would reach the scale it eventually did? In retrospect, what most surprised you—the magnitude of the corruption uncovered, the profile of those implicated, the longevity of the investigation, or something else entirely?

The greatest surprise—and something I genuinely did not anticipate—was that we were able to carry out the investigation without it being shut down by the higher courts. That, more than anything else, was the most unexpected development. Historically, major anti-corruption operations in Brazil have often been curtailed or obstructed at higher judicial levels. In that context, the fact that Operation Car Wash was allowed to advance as far as it did marked a significant and unforeseen departure from precedent operations like Boi Barrica[62] (literally "Barrel Ox"), Sancastle (Castelo de Areia in Portuguese),[63] Flood (literally "Dilúvio" in Portuguese),[64] and Satiagraha[65]—each of which collapsed once they began to implicate powerful individuals—often for a range of procedural or technical reasons. That was the pattern. That pattern was deeply entrenched. In Brazil, it is extraordinarily difficult to carry out major investigations involving influential figures—unless the subject is drug trafficking. Cases related to trafficking invariably proceed; they are almost never obstructed or annulled by higher courts. But when it comes to corruption involving politically or economically powerful actors—no matter how grave or well-documented the misconduct—the historical tendency has been for such investigations to stall. There are empirical studies that confirm precisely this dynamic. So, without question, the greatest surprise for me was that we managed to overcome that barrier. The fact that Operation Car Wash was not blocked or annulled by the higher courts was entirely unprecedented. And for me, that changed everything.

In your view, why was Operation Car Wash not blocked or annulled by the higher courts, as had occurred with previous anti-corruption operations such as Boi Barrica, Castelo de Areia, Dilúvio, *and* Satiagraha? What factors do you believe made the difference?
In my view, the plea bargain agreement with Paulo Roberto Costa was the turning point that gave Operation Car Wash its structural solidity and momentum.[66] That agreement was virtually impossible to annul or obstruct—not only due to the scale of the crimes and the facts it brought to light, but above all because Paulo Roberto Costa was, at the time, returning a substantial sum of money. If I recall correctly, it amounted to approximately twenty-three million dollars. The combination of concrete evidence and significant asset recovery gave the agreement a level of legitimacy that made it very difficult to challenge.[67] To put that into perspective, the amounts in question ranged from fifty to sixty—perhaps

even seventy or eighty million reais. The most significant safeguard—the real form of institutional insurance for Operation Car Wash—was this multimillion-dollar plea bargain with Paulo Roberto Costa. From that point forward, any attempt to annul the investigation would have entailed returning an extraordinary sum to the defendant—something close to eighty million reais. For a plea agreement, this was unprecedented in Brazil. No previous case had ever resulted in such a substantial recovery of assets at such an early stage. The sheer magnitude of the restitution created a kind of structural protection: annulling the operation would have meant reversing the recovery of public funds, a politically and legally untenable outcome. That, in my view, was the operation's strongest shield.

Of course, getting to that point was not without considerable difficulty. There were moments when we genuinely feared that the entire operation might collapse. One such instance was when Justice Teori Zavascki[68] ordered the suspension of Car Wash, based on concerns that the investigation might involve individuals with privileged jurisdiction.[69] That decision introduced a high degree of uncertainty and raised the very real possibility that the case would be removed from our hands altogether. He suspended the investigations and ordered the release of all suspects who were in custody. In response, former federal judge Sergio Moro[70] acted with considerable skill, submitting a formal document within the case record that raised several critical questions. For instance: would the Justice also intend to release individuals arrested for money laundering and drug trafficking involving more than one hundred kilograms of narcotics[71]? And would he likewise authorise the release of suspects apprehended while attempting to flee the country with cash concealed in their underwear[72]?

Following that submission, Justice Teori Zavascki upheld the release of Paulo Roberto Costa but reversed his decision with regard to the other defendants, ordering that they remain in custody. This was a rather unusual outcome; logically, if the original decision was to be reconsidered, one would have expected either all the defendants to be released or all to remain detained. However, the Justice maintained Costa's release—likely because that decision had already been taken—while reinstating the detention of the others. At that stage, Paulo Roberto Costa arguably should have remained in custody as well, but the prior ruling stood. What proved crucial was that the remaining suspects were not released. Had they been the investigation would likely have faced a prolonged suspension. It could have taken more than a year for the Justice to issue a final ruling on whether the case involved individuals with privileged jurisdiction, potentially paralysing the inquiry during that time.

By keeping some of the defendants in custody, however, Justice Zavascki was compelled to act with greater urgency, and within approximately a month, Operation Car Wash was allowed to resume. Had no individuals remained in pre-trial detention, the process would likely have stalled, potentially resulting in a suspension lasting up to a year—during which time we would have had little operational capacity. For approximately a month, the investigation remained in a holding pattern: internal work continued, available material was analysed, but meaningful progress could not be made. During this interim period, new intelligence emerged concerning Paulo Roberto Costa, revealing the existence of an offshore account containing over twenty million dollars. This discovery provided the legal basis for a renewed request for his pre-trial detention, which enabled us to reassert control over the case once the files were returned from the Federal Supreme Court.

The use of pre-trial detention in Operation Car Wash has generated significant public and academic discussion. What do you consider to be its most positive contributions—and its most problematic consequences—in the context of anti-corruption enforcement?
Operation Car Wash faced considerable criticism, particularly regarding the allegedly excessive use of pre-trial detention. However, I believe much of that criticism was overly general and failed to engage with the substance of the legal decisions involved. The more relevant question is: in which specific case was the use of pre-trial detention excessive? A serious debate cannot proceed without reference to concrete examples. And when those cases are examined individually, what one finds is that the detentions were based on robust evidence of criminal activity and clear indications that the individuals in question posed a risk to the investigation or to public order. The legal grounds for

those measures were well established, supported by detailed and well-reasoned judicial decisions—often ten, fifteen, sometimes twenty pages in length—meticulously analysing the facts and the available evidence.

Consider, for example, the very outset of Operation Car Wash on 17 March 2014. At that point, the objective was simply to collect evidence in the possession of Paulo Roberto Costa. No decision had been taken to place him in preventive custody. However, while the Federal Police were executing search and seizure warrants, he took active steps to obstruct the investigation—with the assistance of family members. As police officers retrieved the keys to his office from his residence and prepared to return to complete the search, Costa contacted relatives and instructed them to go to his office and remove several boxes and envelopes—possibly containing money, documents, or other forms of evidence. This conduct was captured on the building's surveillance camera system. This act of obstruction, which in itself constituted a separate criminal offence, led to a renewed application for his pre-trial detention.

Nor was this an isolated incident. Similar conduct by other individuals also led to requests for pre-trial detention. However, such measures were applied with considerable restraint and were generally reserved for central figures—those most directly and persistently involved in criminal activity. Pre-trial detention was only requested when the legal criteria were unequivocally met. This included not only robust evidence of criminal conduct and the identity of the perpetrator—the basic threshold for any such measure—but also the presence of risk factors such as threats to public or economic order, risk of flight, or interference with the judicial process. In practical terms, individuals were detained preventively only when there were clear indications of flight risk, potential obstruction of the investigation, or involvement in dozens—or even hundreds—of criminal acts. These were often ongoing criminal enterprises requiring immediate disruption.

The guiding principle throughout Operation Car Wash was that pre-trial detention, while undoubtedly severe, is at times necessary. When applied with precision and in accordance with legal standards, it served as an essential tool for protecting the integrity of the investigation and upholding the public interest.

To what extent did Operation Car Wash succeed in breaking the long-standing link between corruption and impunity among Brazil's political and economic elites—a dynamic that had largely prevailed until 2014?

Operation Car Wash undoubtedly disrupted the entrenched relationship between corruption and impunity—at least temporarily. In essence, what the operation achieved was the exposure of a deeply rooted system in which powerful individuals forged alliances to accumulate even greater power and wealth. It brought to light a culture of systemic looting, orchestrated from the highest levels of political and economic influence. By confronting impunity directly, Car Wash placed at risk not only the power but also the wealth and personal freedom of many influential actors. Unsurprisingly, this provoked a significant backlash.

In the years that followed, a series of setbacks unfolded—many of them deliberate—aimed at weakening the operation, diluting anti-corruption legislation, and ultimately paving the way for the resurgence of the very same corruption schemes it had exposed. Objectively, I would say that the operation succeeded in suspending the functioning of large-scale corruption networks for a time. And this was not merely our perception: numerous politicians, business leaders, and journalists privately acknowledged that a shift had indeed occurred.

Now, seven years later, with significant setbacks in anti-corruption efforts and little meaningful progress in addressing the structural roots of the problem, it is entirely possible—if not likely—that the old schemes are gradually re-emerging. It is essential to emphasise that this was never about corruption confined to a single administration or political party. What was uncovered were systemic practices embedded in the political culture for decades. Take, for example, Pedro Corrêa,[73] a veteran politician from the Progressive Party, who, in his plea bargain, stated unequivocally that the practice of appointing political allies to public office for the purpose of extracting bribes had been in place for decades.

The mechanism typically functions as follows: corrupt political parties and politicians appoint loyalists to head public agencies—whether at the federal, state, or municipal level. Once installed, these individuals manipulate procurement processes, delay regulatory approvals, or obstruct administrative procedures in exchange for bribes from companies or businesspeople seeking favourable treatment. The illicit proceeds generated from these transactions tend to flow in two primary directions. First, into the personal accounts of those involved, enabling illicit enrichment; and second, into the financing of expensive electoral campaigns. This is where the deeper structural problem lies. The use of bribe money to fund campaigns perpetuates a vicious cycle: corrupt politicians secure re-election, consolidate their power, and repeat the scheme—bringing in additional allies, expanding the network, and extracting even greater sums. It becomes a self-reinforcing system of finance political corruption.

This dynamic reflects a form of adverse selection. Whereas in nature it is typically the strongest who survive and thrive, in this system it is often the most corrupt who prevail—precisely because they have access to substantial financial resources through illicit means. Empirical studies have demonstrated a strong correlation between campaign expenditure and electoral success: the more money a candidate channels into their campaign—frequently from bribes—the greater their chances of winning. Once in office, they possess both the incentive and the mechanisms to perpetuate the scheme. That, in essence, is what Operation Car Wash laid bare: a deeply entrenched structure that long predates the investigation and has shown itself to be remarkably durable.

Unless there is a fundamental shift in how Brazil addresses impunity—through the swift removal of corrupt individuals from public office and comprehensive reform of a permissive electoral system—the cycle is likely to persist for decades to come.

In your view, how central was plea bargaining to the progress of Operation Car Wash, and what impact did it have on the outcomes of the investigation?

Plea bargain agreements were central to Operation Car Wash. They were the driving force—the heartbeat—of the entire investigation. Without them, it simply would not have reached the scale that it did. Why is that? Well, corruption is notoriously difficult to uncover and prove. But once you have someone who is directly involved and willing to talk, everything changes.

Investigating a single count of corruption is already a complex task. But when a suspect agrees to a plea bargain, the scope of the investigation expands dramatically. Instead of providing information solely about the offence under investigation, the individual may disclose details about crimes B, C, D, E, F—an entire alphabet of illicit conduct. Each new revelation introduces additional actors, some of whom may also choose to cooperate. This cumulative dynamic creates a cascading effect, allowing the investigation to expand exponentially. And that is precisely what occurred in Operation Car Wash.

It all began with what appeared to be a relatively narrow investigation: a money laundering case involving former Petrobras director Paulo Roberto Costa. At that stage, the inquiry was not even focused on corruption. However, once Costa agreed to cooperate, the scope of the investigation expanded dramatically. His testimony revealed not only irregularities in a single Petrobras contract, but systemic corruption across multiple contracts within his division. It soon became clear that the scheme extended beyond his area of responsibility to other divisions of Petrobras, other companies, and other contracts entirely. And it was not limited to Petrobras. As Costa himself put it, "this is not just a Petrobras thing—it is a political party-based scheme." If the root of the scheme is party based, then of course it is going to extend far beyond one state-run company. And that is precisely what began to be uncovered. Costa provided that first big wave of evidence, and then Alberto Youssef confirmed much of it and added new layers—bringing in links to other agencies altogether.

Then came the engineering and construction company executives. Once they began cooperating, the scope of the investigation widened even further. Their statements made clear: "*This is not just about Petrobras, or even federal agencies—there is corruption at the state and municipal levels as well.*" A single major company alone implicated individuals linked to twenty-six political parties, totalling more than four hundred politicians. This reinforced what had already become evident: the scheme was systemic. It was not an isolated episode, nor was it confined to a single government, party, or institution. It was deeply embedded in the political and economic structure of the country.

To answer your question directly: plea bargaining was the mechanism that enabled the investigation to expand across so many layers of the system. It was the engine room of Operation Car Wash—the strategic tool that exposed the breadth of corruption in Brazil and allowed prosecutors to follow the evidence wherever it led.

Were any individuals prosecuted or convicted in Operation Car Wash solely on the basis of plea bargain testimony, without independent corroborating evidence?

No, absolutely not. That is not how plea bargains work.[74] No one has ever been accused or convicted solely on the word of a collaborator in Operation Car Wash.[75] The collaborator's testimony is not used to convict—it is used to investigate. It is a tool to help uncover corruption schemes and point investigators in the right direction, so they can find solid, independent evidence. Let me give you an example. A collaborator might say, "There is an offshore account being used by a politician to receive bribes." That gives us a lead. We then follow that lead, go abroad, find the account, and obtain official records showing the bribe payments. The plea bargain agreement serves as a starting point, not an endpoint. It is the trigger for proper investigative work—not the sole basis for judicial decision-making.

Plea bargains were employed extensively during Operation Car Wash in a manner that had no real precedent in earlier investigations. Why was this the case? Because Car Wash introduced a crucial element that had long been absent: the genuine prospect that justice would be done. Consider the rationale—why would an individual under investigation agree to a reduced sentence, admit guilt, return illicit funds, and potentially implicate themselves and others—often at considerable personal risk—unless they were convinced that the alternative was worse? This kind of cooperation only becomes viable when individuals believe they are likely to face serious legal consequences if they do not cooperate.

The effectiveness of plea bargaining is directly tied to the credibility of the justice system. When enforcement mechanisms function properly—such as the imposition of custodial sentences following second-instance convictions[76]—it closes off the traditional escape routes, including procedural delays and the expiration of statutory limitations. According to some studies, in Brazil, 97 out of every 100 proven corruption cases have historically failed to result in a conviction. In such a context, without the credible threat of punishment, there would be little incentive for anyone to enter into a plea bargain agreement. After all, without a credible threat of punishment, why would anyone agree to a plea deal in the first place?

This is where a fundamental principle of negotiation becomes relevant: BATNA—Best Alternative to a Negotiated Agreement.[77] Individuals only choose to cooperate when doing so is preferable to the alternative. In the context of Operation Car Wash, that alternative—real and immediate prison time—became, for the first time in many years, a credible prospect. This is precisely what made plea bargaining such an effective tool. It was not about producing scapegoats; rather, it created conditions under which individuals were willing to come forward because, for once, the justice system was demonstrating its capacity to function effectively.

Why did this dynamic—where cooperation became a rational choice—emerge specifically during Operation Car Wash?

This dynamic emerged in Operation Car Wash largely because of the existence of a dedicated task force, which created what might be described as a *probative siege*—a situation in which the body of evidence began to close in from all directions. In addition, the use of pre-trial detention—while never imposed to compel cooperation—had a significant impact. It gave those under investigation a very real perception that the justice system was functioning and that consequences were likely to follow. Importantly, when a defendant is held in custody, legal proceedings tend to advance much more rapidly. A case involving someone who remains at liberty can take ten, even twenty years to reach a final judgement. But for those in detention, cases are often resolved within two or three years. This temporal difference has a major influence on how individuals under investigation assess their options and decide whether to cooperate.

The precedent set by the Mensalão[78] case also played a significant role. Just a few years before Operation Car Wash, the Federal Supreme Court sentenced Marcos Valério to forty years in prison for his involvement in a scheme that bore striking similarities to what Car Wash would later uncover—kickbacks used to finance political campaigns and, in part, for personal enrichment. That case served, in many ways, as a model.

When individuals saw that the judicial system was capable of delivering substantial prison sentences, that proceedings were moving at a faster pace, and that mounting evidence surrounded them, they became far more inclined to cooperate. It was the convergence of rigorous investigative work, tangible legal consequences, and an institutional environment that, for the first time in many years, appeared capable of delivering justice.

Why has the use of plea bargaining declined in recent years? Why are individuals no longer choosing to cooperate with the justice system?

It really began in 2019, when the Federal Supreme Court reversed its earlier position on the enforcement of prison sentences following second-instance convictions. That ruling fundamentally altered the legal landscape. From that moment onwards, particularly in cases still under investigation or awaiting trial, the expectation of meaningful punishment all but disappeared. And without the credible threat of enforcement, there is little incentive for individuals to cooperate with the justice system through plea agreements.

At this stage, pre-trial detention is no longer being applied in the remaining Operation Car Wash cases—partly because a significant amount of time has passed since the alleged offences took place. As a result, proceedings have slowed considerably, and the sense of urgency or procedural pressure that once characterised the investigation has largely disappeared. The prevailing strategy among defendants has shifted: many now rely on prolonged appeals, aiming either to delay the proceedings until the statute of limitations expires or to secure a dismissal on procedural grounds. This marks a broader return to a scenario of impunity. And it is precisely this change in the legal and institutional environment that helps explain the absence of new plea bargain agreements.

To make matters worse, changes to the Law on Criminal Organisations were introduced as part of the so-called Anti-Crime Package.[79] While the original proposal contained robust measures aimed at strengthening the fight against corruption and organised crime, much of its substance was diluted during the legislative process. By the time it was passed by Congress, several provisions had been weakened, and new amendments imposed restrictions that further limited the use of pre-trial detention and made it more difficult to negotiate plea bargain agreements.

As a result, we are now faced with a scenario in which a tool that was already difficult to employ has become nearly unworkable. Regrettably, plea bargaining—an instrument that could be of great value to society—is no longer a viable option in the remaining corruption cases linked to Operation Car Wash, particularly those involving offences committed many years ago.

To what extent does the system of privileged jurisdiction ("foro privilegiado" in Portuguese) for certain public officials contribute to the persistence of structural impunity in Brazil's justice system?
Absolutely. Privileged jurisdiction simply does not function effectively in practice. Let me explain why. Imagine an ongoing investigation in which promising leads are actively being pursued. When judicial intervention is required at the first-instance level, decisions are typically issued within two, three, or at most five days. That speed is essential. Investigations depend on maintaining momentum—time works against the process. Evidence deteriorates, memories fade, and witnesses become less reliable. Judicial responsiveness is therefore critical to the success of any complex investigation.

We simply cannot afford to lose critical evidence due to procedural delays. Now consider a situation in which, during the course of an active investigation, indications emerge that an individual with privileged jurisdiction may be involved. What happens next? The entire investigation is suspended and must be referred to the Federal Supreme Court. That transfer process alone can take one, two, or even five months. In practical terms, we often lose a year navigating bureaucratic procedures—only for the Supreme Court to eventually conclude, "Yes, you may proceed." But why was the investigation forced to stop in the first place? Because under the rules of privileged jurisdiction ("foro privilegiado" in Portuguese), every single investigative step must receive prior authorisation. That requirement severely slows the process. In the meantime, the investigation's most effective chance to recover assets and ensure justice may be irreparably undermined.

The fundamental problem is this: when individuals with privileged jurisdiction are not held accountable, they remain in office. In many cases, they continue to misuse public resources and exercise authority far beyond the bounds of the public trust they were meant to uphold. They remain in positions of power—governing the very institutions they are accused of exploiting. This raises an unavoidable truth: unless the system of privileged jurisdiction is reformed or abolished, impunity for the powerful will persist as the norm. And if that remains the case, those who have plundered the country will simply continue to do so.

What viable alternatives to privileged jurisdiction exist for ensuring accountability and effectively addressing impunity among high-ranking public officials in Brazil?

Well, one option would be to completely overhaul the system of privileged jurisdiction—but to be honest, I think that might be even harder than scrapping it altogether. From a practical standpoint, I just do not see any justification for keeping it in place when it clearly does not work. From a utilitarian perspective, the cost–benefit analysis simply does not support its retention. There are numerous arguments in favour of abolishing privileged jurisdiction—and none that convincingly justify maintaining it.

Here is a challenge for journalists: ask the Supreme Court justices how many arrest warrants their chambers have issued. Each Justice's office has investigated dozens—sometimes hundreds—of parliamentarians for serious corruption offences. And yet, very few have ever issued a warrant for someone's arrest. That says a lot, does not it? The first time the Supreme Court enforced a prison sentence was back in 2013.[80] That alone shows just how dysfunctional this system is. It is not about isolated decisions—it is a deeper, structural problem. It is about institutional design, the machinery of justice. If we are serious about building a better country, about making justice truly effective, then we need to change those gears. We need a system that can properly hold people to account—especially those in power who have strong evidence against them suggesting they've abused the public trust and stolen money they were supposed to protect.

Thanks to privileged jurisdiction, hardly any politicians were arrested during Operation Car Wash. And yet, despite that, the public still felt like something had shifted. At least in the case of businesspeople, there was this strong perception that impunity was finally being addressed. Yet one can only imagine how much further the investigation might have advanced had that barrier not been in place.

To what extent has the relationship between Brazil's private and public sectors been reshaped in the wake of Operation Car Wash? There are two main schools of thought when it comes to understanding corruption—specifically, what drives or discourages people from engaging in corrupt practices.

The first is rooted in economic theory and the law. It suggests that before someone commits a corrupt act, they weigh up the costs and benefits—comparing the potential financial gain against the risk of being caught and punished. This theory goes back to Gary Becker,[81] and was later developed in the context of corruption by Robert Klitgaard,[82] who was the first to bring the idea to this area in a widespread way and which was also adopted by another great scholar, Susan-Rose Ackerman.[83] The second line of thinking comes from behavioural science. This one's growing in influence and draws heavily on psychology—people like Dan Ariely[84] have been leading figures here. The idea is that corruption does not always come from cold, calculated decisions. Often, people want to gain some benefit—but just enough that they can still see themselves as fundamentally honest. So, it is about this little bit of dishonesty that people can justify to themselves. And what is particularly interesting is that if someone sees a peer behaving dishonestly and getting away with it, that behaviour tends to spread. It becomes normalised within that group.

Now, looking at it from either of these perspectives, Operation Car Wash had a real impact. It changed the risk-reward equation and challenged the social norms that previously enabled corruption. It sent a strong message that there could be consequences—and that helped to curb corrupt behaviour.

As for the corporate world specifically, I think Car Wash sparked a real transformation. One of the biggest changes was the rise of compliance departments. We saw a huge wave of investment in compliance across Brazil. Companies that did not have any controls in place began developing entire departments to promote integrity and prevent misconduct. And for those that already had something in place, there was a noticeable shift in focus and seriousness around compliance. It was not just box-ticking anymore—it became a genuine priority.

So, yes, there was a clear change in how companies related to the state. But the challenge now is keeping that momentum going. If the integrity culture that Car Wash helped build starts to erode—if the perception is that corruption is once again tolerated—the risk, then, is a regression into cynicism, scepticism, and a resurgence of entrenched patterns of behaviour.

Could the recent setbacks in Brazil's anti-corruption agenda, under scrutiny by a special OECD committee, jeopardise the country's bid for OECD membership?

I believe that recent setbacks in the fight against corruption can harm the country's entry into the OECD. The thing is, it is not just Brazil that is acknowledging these setbacks—they're being recognised internationally. And that has serious implications, not just for Brazil's potential accession to the OECD, but also for the country's attractiveness to foreign investors.

Anyone considering investing in a Brazilian company will, quite naturally, assess the risks and benefits from an economic perspective. And in that assessment, the risk of corruption plays a significant role. The more corrupt a country is—or the less effective it is in tackling corruption—the greater the risk that a company might end up embroiled in a scandal. That does not just bring local consequences; it can also trigger international penalties. Take the FCPA, for example—the Foreign Corrupt Practices Act in the United States.[85] If a company has any ties to the United States, like a branch or even just a transaction that passes through the American financial system, it could face serious legal consequences if it is caught up in bribery or corruption.

So, from an investor's point of view, a country that is perceived to be regressing in its fight against corruption becomes a much riskier bet. That should be a concern for all Brazilians. If the current backsliding is not halted, there is a real risk of undoing two or three decades of hard-won progress. It would amount to turning back the clock on the fight against corruption—a profound setback for Brazil as a whole.

Was the failure to approve the 10 Measures against Corruption[86] a turning point—marking the beginning of institutional resistance from entrenched interests against the anti-corruption agenda in Brazil?

The way I see it, the rejection of the 10 Measures against Corruption speaks volumes. You simply cannot change a country where corruption is systemic without changing the laws. And that is exactly what the 10 Measures aimed to do—introduce legal reforms to make corruption more difficult and accountability more likely.

But here's the thing: you cannot change the laws without changing the people who make them. And when those people—many of whom were under investigation themselves—sit in Congress, it is hardly surprising that they pushed back. What is more, you cannot change those parliamentarians without changing the civic consciousness of the population. We tried to go for a shortcut: change the laws first, in the hope that this would trigger a domino effect—less corruption, fewer corrupt officials elected, and a cleaner political environment overall. Even with massive public support—millions of people backing the initiative—Congress still voted it down. And that says a lot. It reflects a broader pattern: in countries where corruption is deeply rooted, it is incredibly hard to pass significant anti-corruption reforms. Why? Because the very people who'd need to approve those reforms either benefit from the current system or could be personally harmed by changing it.

To answer your question directly, I do not see the rejection of the 10 Measures as the start of the backlash. Rather, I think it was the first real obstacle to the progress we were trying to make. At that point, I believe the 10 Measures may have held back an even greater backlash, because while Operation Car Wash was advancing, resistance was already building behind the scenes.

Even though the Measures weren't approved, they had several positive outcomes in my view. One of the most important was that they raised public awareness. They got people talking seriously about corruption, about the flaws in our legal and political systems, and about the urgent need for reform. I am not saying the 10 Measures were perfect or the only solution, but they were certainly the kind of changes we needed to make the law more effective in the fight against corruption. Beyond that, broader electoral reform is also urgently needed. The system found it much easier to resist the 10 Measures and the investigations because those initiatives were pushing for real change—and that made them a threat. But in resisting them, the system also exposed itself, and that in turn helped awaken civic awareness.

In the end, yes—the rejection of the 10 Measures was a setback, but it was also a turning point. It showed just how deep the resistance runs, but it also made clear to citizens what we are up against, and how important it is to stay engaged in the fight for a cleaner, fairer political system.

How has the application of the statute of limitations influenced the outcomes of major anti-corruption cases—such as Operation Car Wash and Banestado—and what broader consequences has it had for Brazil's ability to combat corruption effectively?

The statute of limitations—or "prescription", as it is referred to in the Brazilian legal context—is a sound legal concept in theory—but the way it works in Brazil is completely dysfunctional. It is an important institution, meant to bring stability to social relations. The basic principle is this: if the State does not act on a crime—say, one committed in 2005—and remains inactive for years, there comes a point where it is no longer fair or sensible to pursue punishment. The idea is that legal certainty matters, and society needs some closure. But in Brazil, that logic gets turned on its head. Here, the statute of limitations can still apply even if the State has done everything right. Imagine the State investigates thoroughly, brings charges, goes through trial, appeals, all of it—and yet, because of how slowly the judicial system works, the case still expires. It is irrational.

Take the *Propinoduto*[87] case, for example. This was a huge scandal in the late 1990s and early 2000s, involving millions diverted through the Rio de Janeiro tax office. In 2003, a group of auditors were charged with corruption and money laundering. They had Swiss bank accounts stuffed with bribe money, according to the investigations. That same year, the first judge ruled and convicted them quickly. Then came the appeals. The Federal Court of the 2nd Region reviewed the case in 2007, and then the Superior Court of Justice in 2014. But the process dragged on so long that, in the end, many of the crimes were declared time barred. The defendants walked free—not because the State did nothing, but simply because of delays in the system. At the Superior Court of Justice, the defence even filed three motions for clarification. One crime—money laundering—was still pending, but there was still another step: the Federal Supreme Court. Most likely, by the time that was resolved, that too would have prescribed. I haven't revisited the case recently, but it is worth checking whether even the money laundering charges eventually expired.

And then there is something even more bizarre: Brazil's concept of retroactive prescription. When this is explained to foreign prosecutors, the response is often one of bafflement. And once they understand it, they find it absurd. Basically, the statute of limitations is not fixed at the time the crime was committed or charged—it gets recalculated backwards based on the sentence eventually handed down, after years of litigation. So, the State spends years investigating, prosecuting, going through endless appeals, only to find that—because the final sentence was below a certain threshold—everything done up to that point becomes invalid. The whole case collapses retroactively.

It is a deeply irrational system. One that does not serve justice, does not serve society, and only serves impunity. If Brazil is serious about fighting corruption, this is one of the first things that needs urgent reform.

How critical has international cooperation been to the outcomes of Operation Car Wash, and how essential is it to the broader global fight against corruption?

Serious crimes that involve large amounts of money naturally become transnational. That is because the management and movement of major financial assets have gone global alongside globalisation itself. People who receive bribes or are laundering money tend to seek out international channels to do so more discreetly, distancing themselves from national jurisdictions—especially from Brazilian justice and the risk of facing consequences here. Blanco Cordeiro,[88] one of the leading experts on money laundering, highlights three main features of modern money laundering: complexity, professionalisation, and, crucially, internationalisation. So, if corruption funds are being laundered across borders, international cooperation becomes essential—to gather evidence and to recover those misappropriated assets. In this context, international cooperation is not just important—it is vital. That is why Operation Car Wash relied so heavily on it, setting a historic record for international collaboration. Over 500 cooperation requests were sent and received, involving around 60 countries. To put that into perspective, the previous record was set during the *Banestado* case with the CC5 task force—another milestone in the development of anti-corruption and anti-money laundering practices in Brazil—which involved around 180 cooperation requests, mostly with the United States.

It is not just about official cooperation channels either. Informal cooperation is also extremely important. There is been some criticism lately around using informal channels, as though it is somehow illegal—but that is not the case. It is never been illegal. The Department of Asset Recovery and International Legal Cooperation (DRCI), Brazil's central authority in these matters, recognises that the official channel—sending or receiving requests via the DRCI—is just one available route. It is a valid and necessary one, but not the only one.

Let me give you an example. Imagine that Brazil, Portugal, and the UK are monitoring a vessel suspected of carrying drugs. The police forces of these countries are in constant communication—exchanging calls and updates in real time. They discuss how to intercept the boat, where it is, the best time and method to act, whether the suspects are armed, how much drug is on board, and so on. Now, if this boat is expected to be seized on a Saturday, the Brazilian Federal Police cannot simply say, *"Please send this information by letter to the* Department of Asset Recovery and International Legal Cooperation, *and I will have a look on Monday when the office opens."* By then, the drugs could be long gone, and the vessel docked in another country. Clearly, real-time cooperation must happen through more agile, informal channels—during both the investigative and judicial phases—not just through Department of Asset Recovery and International Legal Cooperation.

So, when is it essential to use the official route via Department of Asset Recovery and International Legal Cooperation? Whenever the information or evidence is going to be formally used—either as part of an investigation or in court. Why? Because of the chain of custody. You need to prove, for instance, that a bank statement from Switzerland was requested and received properly—from one legally recognised authority to another—so that the defence can challenge it if necessary. That chain of legitimacy is what gives the evidence weight in court.

But prior to that stage—before it becomes formal evidence—it is enough that the exchange of information is lawful in both countries. And yes, this was something observed during Operation Car Wash. Information was received by e-mail and used, for example, to justify the arrest of Renato Duque[89] in one of the cases. This use of e-mailed information was upheld by the courts: both the trial court and the appeals court accepted the legitimacy of using that material for precautionary measures. Then, when it came time to formally produce that evidence, the documents were routed through the proper official channels between the central authorities.

To what extent did Operation Clean Hands[90] (*Mani Pulite*) influence the design, strategy, or institutional approach of Operation Car Wash?

It served as both an inspiration and a cautionary tale. Clean Hands was always seen as a model, but not just in terms of what should be done. It also highlighted what shouldn't. On the one hand, it showed how the Italian authorities were able to uncover and dismantle a vast network of corruption that spanned across multiple political parties. That was incredibly valuable. But at the same time, it also demonstrated how powerful systems can push back—how the establishment can respond in ways that ultimately stall investigations and even roll back anti-corruption progress.

That experience was examined from both perspectives. The successes were taken into account, but careful attention was also given to the pitfalls. One of the most significant lessons was the intense backlash that struck Operation Clean Hands only a few years after its inception. For instance, its leading figure, Di Pietro,[91] stepped down merely two years into the operation. What followed in Italy was a decade-long wave of resistance. With that in mind, it became clear that involving society was essential—to keep the public engaged and informed, thereby helping to prevent a similar backlash and establishing a degree of protection around Operation Car Wash. And to a large extent, that worked. Instead of just two years of meaningful progress, as was the case in Italy, Car Wash managed to maintain momentum for nearly six years—from 2014 through to 2019.

The level of transparency adopted by the Car Wash Task Force—particularly its close relationship with the media—represented a significant departure from traditional practices within the Brazilian justice system. What explains this strong emphasis on transparency and public disclosure? To what extent was it seen as essential for securing public support and mobilising societal engagement?

The progress achieved in the fight against corruption endured—if it endured at all—largely because of sustained public support. Some critics argued that Operation Car Wash was overly focused on the media. But to be candid, the crimes under investigation were themselves driven by media attention. A press conference about someone forging a student ID, for example, would have drawn no interest whatsoever. It is not the press conference that draws the media in—it is the nature of the crime. The same prosecutors, the same police, the same format—but completely different impact depending on the case.

Car Wash attracted so much attention because of the scale and seriousness of the corruption involved, and the power of the individuals implicated. When you are dealing with that level of influence—people with enormous political and economic reach—a group of judges, police officers, and prosecutors in Curitiba has very little protection or power by comparison. So, what do you do? You go for full transparency. You put everything on the table, make your work visible, and invite public scrutiny. That was how confidence was built in the work being carried out, and how the operation was shielded from interference. It also served as a means of avoiding what occurred in Italy. Operation Car Wash endured for nearly six years largely because of that transparency. It was always clear who was involved, what had been done, what had not, and which cases remained open. Proceedings were made public. In contrast, consider the current situation within the Federal Supreme Court: how many cases are ongoing? What are the details? Which have been adjudicated, and which remain pending? Although Justice Fachin does publish some reports, a far more systematic approach is urgently needed—at the Federal Supreme Court, the Superior Court of Justice, the courts in São Paulo, and in other states that received cases linked to Car Wash.

There is been a lot of criticism aimed at Curitiba, sometimes overly focused on details or looking to discredit the effort. Meanwhile, very little attention is paid to the fact that much of the corruption uncovered is likely to go unpunished. Why? Because at a certain point, the Superior Court of Justice stripped Curitiba of many cases involving strong evidence of corruption in other public bodies and passed them to other states. Those investigations were scattered across the country—but the only place outside Curitiba where things really moved forward was Rio de Janeiro.

So, maybe the real question is not what went wrong in Curitiba—but what is going on in all the other places? Why haven't those cases gone anywhere? It might not even be the fault of individual actors in the justice system. Maybe it is the system itself—the way it is structured. Maybe it's built not to work when powerful people are involved. And in that sense, demanding results from other states highlights those systemic flaws.

Transparency—public access to what happened, what did not, the data, the facts, the outcomes—is not just about public trust. It is also about accountability. People had the tools to follow the progress, form their own opinions, and decide whether to support or question what was being done. That was one of the great strengths of Car Wash, and it should be seen as a model to build on—not something to silence or suppress. Now, of course, when you do something new, it is going to be criticised. And that is fair. Openness to critique and a continual search for improvement are essential. However, a model that proved effective should not be discarded merely because it deviated from established norms.

What is your assessment of the backlash against Operation Car Wash? Do you see it as a natural response to institutional overreach, or as a deliberate attempt to undermine anti-corruption efforts?
The reaction against Car Wash is not just about disagreeing with the outcomes of the operation itself. It is deeper than that—it is a push-back that affects the entire legal and institutional framework used to fight crime in Brazil. And more than that, it weakens the country's ability to tackle corruption effectively.

Take, for example, changes that prevent imprisonment after a second-instance conviction. Or the Abuse of Authority Law,[92] which in some cases ends up restricting legitimate investigations, especially those involving powerful individuals. Add to that new rules that complicate the use of pre-trial detention or plea bargains, or decisions that send political corruption cases to electoral courts—which, frankly, aren't equipped to handle these types of investigations—and what you get is a serious weakening of Brazil's justice system when it comes to fighting corruption.

It is not just about protecting individuals; it is about reducing the effectiveness of the system. And that is dangerous, because the fight against corruption is something the Brazilian public cares about deeply. So, when we see these kinds of changes, it is not just a legal debate—it is a step backwards in something the population sees as essential to justice.

To conclude, are there any final thoughts you would like to share regarding the impact of Operation Car Wash and the ongoing challenges in Brazil's fight against corruption?

If I may, I would like to take this opportunity to offer a broader reflection on the matter. Operation Car Wash led a series of investigations and legal proceedings backed by solid evidence, and all its decisions were reviewed across four judicial instances—something quite unique, as Brazil is the only country in the world with such an extensive system of appeals. Every action taken during the operation was grounded in facts, evidence, and the law. These decisions weren't just legally sound—they were consistent, transparent, and reviewed repeatedly. And let's not forget the results: Operation Car Wash disrupted one of the largest corruption schemes in our history. According to the Federal Police, just within Petrobras alone, diversions reached up to forty billion reais—and that is not even counting other public institutions. Beyond stopping this massive haemorrhaging of public funds, the operation achieved what was once thought impossible: it held extremely powerful individuals to account. It recovered around fifteen billion reais—five billion of which has already been returned to the public coffers, with the rest in the process of recovery. By enforcing the law equally—over everyone and for everyone—Operation Car Wash reinforced the very idea of the rule of law in Brazil. It also helped to strengthen our democracy, which had been eroded by the injection of illicit funds into political campaigns, across the spectrum, aimed at keeping certain groups in power.

The backlash currently unfolding is not the result of failure—it is, in fact, the consequence of success. The operation exposed networks sustained by the pursuit of power and wealth through illicit means. It disrupted these alliances and struck at the core of impunity. Unsurprisingly, those whose interests were threatened have responded. There must be no naïveté: this pushback is not merely an attempt to discredit Operation Car Wash; it poses a real risk of reversing decades of progress in the fight against corruption. If left unchecked, it could also compromise the capacity to conduct similar operations in the future. Nonetheless, many of the gains achieved by Car Wash are irreversible.

One of the most important outcomes was the diagnosis it provided. As someone once said: "You cannot unsee what is already been seen." There is now a clear understanding of the extent to which systemic corruption is embedded in Brazil. And once a disease is diagnosed, treatment must follow. That diagnosis awakened something in Brazilian society—it sparked action. You cannot treat a disease without first understanding it, and Car Wash made the illness visible. It stopped the bleeding. It brought powerful people to justice. It recovered billions. And it awakened a new level of civic awareness. Brazilians began to engage more deeply with issues that, for a long time, felt distant or out of reach. Just think of the 2019 election for President of the Federal Senate. It was followed by the public like a World Cup final—people knew it mattered. They understood the real impact of political leadership.

Today, most Brazilians can name Supreme Court justices and have an opinion on their positions. That simply did not happen before Car Wash. Journalists, thought leaders, and everyday people now have a solid understanding of how corruption investigations work. I recall that, back in 2014, it was necessary to explain even the most basic aspects of large-scale corruption investigations to journalists. Yet that knowledge has not been lost. Although this may be a period marked by setbacks, the fight against corruption is generational in nature. It is a continuous endeavour—and meaningful progress has been made. There is a genuine hope that these setbacks are temporary, that further regression can be halted, some of the damage reversed, and momentum regained. For unless structural reforms are pursued—reforms that address the root causes of corruption in Brazil—elevated levels of corruption will persist, irrespective of who holds power or which party is in office.

I would also like to say that, regardless of the outcome, there are causes worth fighting for—causes that stand on their own, independent of any result. I often draw a parallel with an existential truth: even though death is an inevitable part of life—something none of us can escape—that does not mean the fight should cease. The instinct to persevere is immediately recognisable when a loved one—a child or close family member—is confronted with a serious or even irreversible health condition. Even when told that no cure exists, the response is not to surrender. Every effort is made: time, energy, and spirit are devoted to that person's well-being. Second opinions are sought, every possible avenue is pursued—because love compels action, even in the face of unfavourable odds.

And that is the reflection I would like to leave with each listener: imagine if your child, your partner, the person you love most in the world were gravely ill, and someone told you there was nothing that could be done. Would you just walk away? Or would you pour every ounce of strength into trying to save them? Most of us would not think twice—we would fight with everything we had.

The truth is some causes are worth that kind of dedication. These causes matter not because success is guaranteed, but because they are simply too important to abandon. And Brazil is one of them. Fighting for the country means fighting for those most deeply loved—family, community, and future generations.

The message that I want to leave is one of perseverance: we must not give up on Brazil. I will conclude with a quotation from Cecília Meireles[93] who once said: "I did not win all the battles I fought, but I certainly lost all those I failed to fight." That resonates deeply. It is essential to keep pushing forward, to remain committed to this civic effort, and to continue the fight against corruption. For if the struggle is abandoned, the battle is already lost.

This is a generational struggle. It is about building civic awareness, nurturing a sense of responsibility and purpose that does not disappear with one setback or one lost battle. It reminds me of the movements against racial discrimination in the United States or the fight against apartheid in South Africa—changes that did not occur overnight, but were achieved through resilience, conviction, and collective effort. I like to think of it as a gathering of raindrops—each drop representing one person who becomes aware, who decides to take a stand. As more and more drops fall, they come together to form a stream, and eventually a river. And once a river gains momentum, it is hard to stop.

I believe in that river. I believe in this civic movement in Brazil. And I believe that if we stay the course, we will overcome corruption—and we will build the country we dream of.

Deltan Dallagnol was born in Pato Branco (PR). He was a federal prosecutor and coordinator of the Federal Public Prosecutor's Office Task Force of Operation Car Wash. He is a federal congressperson for the State of Paraná (2023–2026). His testimony was recorded on 8 April 2021 via the Zoom virtual platform and lasted 1 hour and 34 minutes. The transcript was subsequently reviewed by the interviewee on 7 May 2022.

Testimony of Orlando Martello Junior

Abstract

This testimony provides a first-hand account from a senior Brazilian federal prosecutor, Orlando Martello Junior, who played a pivotal role in two of the country's most significant anti-corruption investigations: Operation Banestado and Operation Car Wash. The narrative traces the interviewee's professional trajectory—from early legal training and diverse prosecutorial assignments across Brazil to leadership roles within complex, high-profile task forces. Particular attention is given to the evolution and institutionalisation of the task force model, the development of transnational investigative practices, and the legal innovation surrounding plea bargaining and international cooperation.

Drawing comparisons between Banestado and Car Wash, the testimony highlights key structural weaknesses in Brazil's justice system, especially the challenges posed by the statute of limitations, privileged jurisdiction, and procedural delays. It also offers a critical reflection on the backlash against anti-corruption efforts, the erosion of legal tools such as plea bargaining, and the broader implications for public accountability. The interviewee argues that Car Wash exposed not only systemic corruption across political parties and state institutions but also the enduring institutional tolerance for impunity.

In addition to recounting operational details, the testimony reflects on the social, political, and legal legacies of Car Wash. It emphasises the investigation's impact on business-state relations, the development of compliance practices, and shifting public expectations. Ultimately, the testimony underscores the importance of equal application of the law, timely enforcement of sanctions, and international cooperation as indispensable elements in combating large-scale corruption.

Could you share some reflections on your academic background and professional trajectory, particularly as they relate to your work in the Federal Public Prosecutor's Office?

I am currently a regional prosecutor, which corresponds to the second tier within the career structure of Brazil's Federal Public Prosecutor's

Office, comprising first, second, and third levels. I work before the Federal Regional Court of the 3rd Region. I obtained my law degree from the Pontifical Catholic University of São Paulo, later specialising in Tax Law, and subsequently completed a master's degree in public policy.

I was born in São José do Rio Preto. After graduating in 1993, I began my career at law firms in São Paulo, primarily dealing with tax and corporate matters. In 1997, I joined the Federal Prosecutor's Office, where I have remained for the past twenty-five years. My first post was in Ribeirão Preto, and I have since worked in various regions of the country—including Goiânia, Brasília, Marabá (in the state of Pará), Campinas, and ultimately Curitiba—gaining experience with a diverse range of legal and institutional contexts. Over the course of my career, I have worked across multiple domains: civil, criminal, electoral, and the protection of collective rights.

Between 2011 and 2012, I served as head of the Prosecutor's Office in Curitiba. I was later promoted by merit to the position of regional prosecutor. My first assignment in this new capacity was at the Regional Prosecutor's Office in Brasília.[94] Shortly thereafter, I transferred to the São Paulo office,[95] where I have been based ever since, focusing on criminal cases before the Federal Regional Court.

In 2014, I was assigned to support the Car Wash task force in Curitiba. During that period, I concurrently carried out my duties as a regional prosecutor in São Paulo while contributing to the task force's work in Paraná.

In brief, that is the trajectory of my academic and professional journey to date.

How does the task force model operate within the Brazilian legal system, particularly in the context of combating corruption?

In Brazil—or more specifically, within the Federal Public Prosecutor's Office—one of the first structurally organised task forces was the Banestado-CC5[96] operation. Prior to that, the task force model had not yet been consolidated within the institution. To the best of my recollection, Banestado was the first occasion on which prosecutors from different regions engaged in coordinated collaboration, working alongside the Federal Police and the Federal Revenue Service. The Central

Bank also became involved in certain aspects of the investigation. This model introduced a new level of institutional integration, allowing for a more comprehensive and effective approach to complex financial crimes.

Although these agencies were not necessarily operating from the same physical location, they worked in an integrated and coordinated manner with the prosecutors. This is one of the key advantages of the task force model: it enables far more comprehensive and wide-ranging investigations. Each institution contributes within its specific area of expertise, drawing on its own tools, databases, and technical capabilities. Through the systematic exchange of information, the task force is able to construct a fuller, more accurate picture of complex criminal schemes.

Banestado was launched circa 2003 and reached its conclusion in 2007; I joined the investigation in 2005. Notably, the core team involved in the Banestado investigation would later constitute the nucleus of the Car Wash task force. One of the principal defendants in Banestado, Alberto Youssef, also reappeared as a central figure in Car Wash—highlighting the extent to which these major corruption investigations are interconnected.

The task force model proved to be very effective and was widely adopted across the country by the Federal Prosecutor's Office—until it was replaced by the Special Action Group to Combat Organized Crime under the current administration. Even before this change, senior leadership within the Federal Prosecutor's Office had already been discussing ways to improve and institutionalise these collaborative models, whether through structural adjustments or terminological revisions. At one point, there were proposals to establish a National Anti-Corruption Unit, but the initiative failed to gain approval from the Superior Council of the Federal Prosecutor's Office.

That said, regardless of whether it is called Special Action Group to Combat Organized Crime, task force, or something else entirely, the effectiveness of an investigation ultimately depends on three key factors. First, those involved must have the independence necessary to carry out investigations without undue interference. Second, they need to be able to dedicate themselves exclusively—or at least predominantly—to the case. And third, they must be supported by adequate institutional infrastructure: specialised advisers, appropriate investigative tools, and sufficient operational resources.

Those elements are what truly drive the success of an investigation—far more than the name or formal structure of the model. And that is precisely what Operation Car Wash had during the tenures of Prosecutors General Rodrigo Janot and Raquel Dodge, which helps to explain the unprecedented results it achieved.

Could you explain the circumstances under which you joined the Banestado task force and what led to your involvement in that operation?

I requested a transfer to Curitiba for personal reasons, as my wife is originally from the region. At the time, the only available position at the Prosecutor's Office was within the task force—there were no alternative postings—so I accepted the role. In a sense, I boarded a moving train.

Task force work is not typically seen as desirable; it often involves highly complex cases and an intense workload. However, it ultimately became the most professionally rewarding experience I have had during my career at the Federal Prosecutor's Office.

Although I already had solid experience in the criminal field—having worked for several years on a wide range of cases across different parts of the country—I was still lacking in the international side of things. Banestado really pushed me to learn how to conduct transnational investigations effectively. I had to understand in depth how the dollar-cable system used by black-market money dealers worked, how offshores were used to make illicit payments through the international banking system, and how to quickly obtain evidence from abroad. Professionally, it was a huge period of growth for me—and a lot of that was thanks to the colleagues who came before me. By the time I joined the *Banestado* operation, they had already done a lot of the groundwork. They'd wrestled with complex issues, developed legal strategies specific to these types of investigations, and I was able to build on all that.

Notably, several of the individuals who had worked on the Banestado operation later became part of the Car Wash team. This continuity of personnel allowed for the preservation and transfer of institutional knowledge and investigative experience, which proved invaluable when confronted with even greater challenges in the subsequent operation.

Could you reflect on the key similarities and distinctions between the Banestado and Car Wash investigations, particularly in terms of their structure, legal tools, or institutional impact?

Banestado was, in many respects, the first operation in which effective international legal cooperation was successfully achieved. Information from foreign jurisdictions was obtained with relative speed—something that was highly unusual at the time. Direct channels of communication were established, particularly with United States authorities, which greatly improved understanding of the types of evidence available abroad. This, in turn, made it possible to draft formal requests for cooperation with far greater precision and efficiency.

Several visits were made to the United States to examine banking records, clarify the underlying facts, and facilitate the exchange of knowledge regarding the respective legal systems. These efforts contributed to a much more efficient process of obtaining international evidence.

The Banestado operation also resulted in a significant asset recovery—approximately thirty million, which, at the time, represented a record amount in cases involving corruption and money laundering. In general, operations of this kind rarely succeed in recovering substantial sums, if anything at all. That has long been the prevailing pattern. Historically, Brazil's criminal justice system has struggled to retrieve assets derived from illicit activities. Few cases prior to Banestado or Car Wash achieved this level of recovery, due in large part to the complexity and protracted nature of such proceedings. By the time a case reaches its conclusion, it is often on the verge of prescription. In this regard, Banestado stands out as relatively successful. For that period, the amount recovered was highly significant—and, in many respects, marked a turning point.

Banestado also marked the early use of what are now referred to as plea bargain, or "colaboração premiada" agreements. At the time, however, these arrangements lacked a clear legal foundation. What existed was a bold and systematic interpretation of various provisions within the legal framework, allowing prosecutors to offer contractual benefits to individuals who chose to cooperate. This approach was entirely novel in Brazil at the time. Because those involved felt sufficiently secure to confess and disclose the mechanics of the illicit schemes, these agreements began to pose a genuine threat to individuals who had long remained beyond the reach of criminal investigations. Gradually, the legal foundations for these agreements began to solidify. Some of the earliest arrangements were upheld by the courts, including the Federal Supreme Court, thereby lending legitimacy to the model. Eventually, in 2013, this model was formally codified with the passing of Law on Criminal Organisations (Law No. 12.850).[97] That law became the legal cornerstone of the Car Wash operation, and its impact was substantial. Unfortunately, it has since been diluted, making the negotiation of such agreements considerably more difficult. In Brazil, it is a recurring pattern that mechanisms which prove too effective—particularly when they target powerful individuals—tend to be swiftly dismantled.

The experience gained from plea bargain agreements and international cooperation during the Banestado investigation laid an essential foundation for the Car Wash operation. The task force did not begin from scratch; it was able to build upon an existing institutional and legal framework. As soon as indications of offshore accounts emerged in Car Wash, international cooperation requests were submitted without delay. This swift action enabled the identification of tens of millions of dollars held abroad by a former Petrobras executive—leaving him with little option but to cooperate. From that point forward, the investigation began to unravel rapidly, revealing the extent of the scheme. It remains regrettable, however, that the process was not permitted to reach its full conclusion.

In what ways did your experience with the Banestado investigation shape your contributions to the Car Wash task force and the development of its institutional practices?

At the outset of the Car Wash operation, the Banestado case was revisited to assess the outcomes for those who had been prosecuted. Of the more than 200 individuals charged—an even greater number than in Car Wash—only a small fraction ultimately served any form of sentence. This reality is indicative of the broader dysfunction within Brazil's criminal justice system. Some of those proceedings remain unresolved to this day. In fact, just a few months ago, one of the Banestado cases—pending for over a decade—was annulled by one of the Chambers of the Federal Supreme Court.[98] Legal arguments that had long been dismissed were unexpectedly revived and accepted, more than fifteen years after the fact.

This has become a recurring pattern in criminal proceedings involving powerful or well-connected individuals in Brazil: such cases rarely reach a definitive conclusion. The justice system has consistently proven ineffective in achieving its fundamental aims. It fails to deliver closure or a sense of justice to society, does not contribute meaningfully to the rehabilitation of offenders, and has shown limited capacity to recover misappropriated public assets.

When Operation Car Wash was launched, there was a clear determination to avoid repeating the shortcomings observed in Banestado. That earlier experience had exposed the extent to which the justice system could fail in practice. One of the most troubling aspects was that individuals who chose to cooperate with authorities—by confessing, returning assets, paying fines, and accepting penalties—often faced harsher consequences than those who remained silent and prolonged proceedings in court. The aim in Car Wash was to shift this dynamic and create a framework that would ensure meaningful accountability.

How did your appointment to the Car Wash task force come about, and what factors influenced your selection?
My involvement in the Car Wash task force stemmed directly from prior experience with the Banestado investigation. The case had initially been assigned to my colleague José Soares Frisch, who, recognising the scale and complexity of the proceedings—which already involved dozens of searches and seizure warrants as well as arrests—formally requested that the Office of the Prosecutor General establish a dedicated team to support the investigation. At the time, Deltan Dallagnol[99] was already based at the Prosecutor's Office in Curitiba and became the lead prosecutor assisting Frisch. From there, a specialised team was assembled, composed of colleagues with relevant expertise.

It was not easy, though—the operation had already been launched by the Federal Police a few weeks earlier, meant that time was already running out. Some of the defendants were in custody, and the deadline for filing charges was fast approaching—it would hit right during the Easter holiday in 2014. In the end, Deltan took over the office handling the operation and became the lead prosecutor on the case.

Initially, the task force was expected to operate for just three months—this was considered sufficient time to file the necessary charges and review the seized materials. Unexpectedly, the Prosecutor General at the time, Rodrigo Janot,[100] authorised an extension to five months, though he made it clear that no further prolongation would be granted. The early stages of an investigation of this magnitude are invariably the most challenging. The information arrives in a disorganised and often overwhelming state—documents, data, and investigative leads emerge from multiple directions. The first major task is to make sense of it all: to identify the structure of the criminal scheme and to draft the initial charges, often involving suspects already in pre-trial detention, which adds significant time pressure. Once those first charges are filed, the investigation typically transitions into a more structured and manageable phase. In most operations, this is the point at which the task force disbands, and the case is handed over to the local prosecutor's office. In the case of Car Wash, however, that transition never occurred. The deeper the investigation progressed, the more serious and widespread the crimes that came to light—there appeared to be no endpoint.

How many members were part of the Car Wash task force initially?
At the beginning, the task force comprised six federal prosecutors. Alongside Deltan and myself, the team included Carlos Fernando[101], Januário,[102] Diogo Castor,[103] and Andrey Borges.[104]

When you joined the Car Wash task force, did you anticipate that it would grow to become the largest anti-corruption operation in the world?
No, I did not. The real turning point came with the plea bargain of Paulo Roberto Costa.[105] At the very outset of the negotiations, he made a remark that immediately caught our attention: he stated that the scheme was vast. It was at that moment that it became clear the corruption did not stop at the International Directorate of Petrobras—where he had been employed—as initially assumed. Instead, it ran far deeper; it was embedded within the company itself. At first, the suspicion was that the

wrongdoing might be relatively limited—perhaps a luxury vehicle here, or a few irregular contracts. What had not been anticipated was the extent to which the corruption permeated multiple directorates within Petrobras.

Subsequent revelations demonstrated that this was not an isolated episode but rather a deeply entrenched and systematised form of corruption. Moreover, the scheme was not confined to Petrobras. Similar mechanisms were found to be operating in other public institutions as well, across all levels of government—not only at the federal level. It had become a method for politicians to raise funds—ostensibly for campaign financing, but also for personal gain. The investigation uncovered everything from luxury apartments and high-end vehicles to offshore trusts and undisclosed accounts abroad—merely a few of the more commonly encountered assets. Importantly, this was not a scheme confined to one or two political parties; it was a systemic mechanism employed by the principal political groups across the country.

Operation Car Wash is frequently cited as a paradigmatic case of grand corruption[106]. What surprised you most—the scale of the wrongdoing, the individuals involved, or some other aspect? What left the most lasting impression?

Both the scope of the wrongdoing and the standing of those implicated were exceptional. It was striking to observe that individuals who had embezzled less than one million dollars often faced significant obstacles to prosecution, while, in contrast, the investigation was uncovering a Petrobras employee who had diverted nearly one hundred million dollars. In this context, Banestado appeared comparatively modest—both in terms of the sums recovered and the overall volume of funds illicitly transferred abroad.

The level of political involvement was equally surprising. We were not just dealing with minor players—it was top-tier figures in national politics, from the biggest political parties in the country. And it was not just politicians. The largest companies operating in Brazil—both domestic and foreign—were caught up in it. This scheme had been running for years, possibly even decades.

What was most striking, however, was the absence of any meaningful institutional response. Despite the investigation implicating a huge number of sitting congressmen, governors, former governors—and even former presidents—no serious parliamentary inquiry commission was ever set up to get to the bottom of it. It was not even seriously considered. Congressional ethics committees barely moved, and political parties did not bother with internal investigations either. It felt like the country missed a golden opportunity to really examine the roots of this system, understand how it had been allowed to flourish, and take proper steps to prevent something similar from happening again. And the reason for that seems clear to me: this was a scheme that was widely known and quietly accepted within political circles. Had decisive institutional measures been taken after the Mensalão scandal, it is conceivable that the scale of corruption later uncovered by Operation Car Wash might have been significantly curtailed. Instead, Congress responded swiftly—not by addressing the underlying issues, but by enacting legislative changes that effectively made future investigations considerably more difficult to pursue.

How would you evaluate the role of the plea bargain agreement in the overall effectiveness and outcomes of Operation Car Wash?
Plea bargain agreement was essential to the success of Operation Car Wash. In fact, it is a key tool in any complex criminal investigation. When someone from within the organisation agrees to cooperate, they can provide insights that really help move things forward. Of course, this does not imply that investigators can afford to be passive—every statement made by a cooperating witness must still be independently verified. Nonetheless, the process becomes significantly more efficient as a result.

A cooperating witness can pinpoint the amount of money that changed hands, explain when, where and how it was paid, name everyone involved, and even identify the banks and accounts used. That kind of detail allows investigators to reconstruct the entire scheme and build strong, independent evidence to back up the testimony.

A common misconception persists that individuals were charged or arrested solely on the basis of a collaborator's testimony. This is simply inaccurate. Formal investigations or inquiries were not even initiated unless there was already independent evidence available that supported and lent credibility to the collaborator's account.

Plea bargain also played a major role in helping us recover stolen funds. Once the foreign financial institutions and offshore accounts had been identified, international cooperation requests could be promptly submitted, enabling the rapid freezing or seizure of assets.

The level of detail provided by cooperating witnesses made it exceedingly difficult for those implicated to deny the substance of the allegations. Confronted with such comprehensive evidence, many defendants were limited to advancing what are often referred to as "peripheral defences"—arguments that avoided engaging with the core of the accusations. These included, for example, contesting the court's jurisdiction, alleging political persecution, or challenging the legality of international cooperation mechanisms. In some instances, defendants even went so far as to hire private firms to investigate the personal lives of prosecutors and investigators in an effort to discredit them—precisely because they lacked any substantive defence grounded in the facts.

How do you assess the mechanism of international cooperation in Operation Car Wash?

Comparable to the role of plea bargaining, international legal cooperation constituted a fundamental pillar of the investigation's effectiveness. Its contribution was indispensable to uncovering transnational financial flows, securing documentary evidence from foreign jurisdictions, and facilitating asset recovery.

To give you an idea of the scale, one Brazilian company involved in the scheme created over two dozen offshore entities just to make illicit payments. The whole thing was incredibly sophisticated—the corruption deals were made in Brazil, the projects tied to the corruption were in Brazil, the people involved were Brazilian—but the bribes were paid overseas. The money came from the company's operations abroad or through one of its foreign subsidiaries, so it never even touched Brazilian soil, nor did it appear in the company's Brazilian financial accounts. That made it impossible to track through traditional means. Since a lot of the evidence was outside the country, international cooperation was the only way to piece it all together. A substantial portion of the documents used in criminal proceedings came from abroad. The information provided by cooperating witnesses enabled investigators to identify precisely what evidence was being sought. Moreover, by establishing prior and direct contact with authorities in the requested jurisdictions, it was possible to tailor mutual legal assistance requests to the specific requirements of their legal systems and to direct them to officials already familiar with the matter.

When international cooperation requests were submitted, the names of the offshore companies were already known, along with the bank accounts holding illicit funds—and even the real beneficiaries behind them. That level of detail made it far easier for other countries to respond quickly. Normally, this type of international legal cooperation can take several years to materialise. In this case, however, the combination of compelling evidence and clear, pre-established lines of communication significantly expedited the process—allowing the investigation to progress at a notably accelerated pace.

And just to clarify something important: every single piece of documentary evidence obtained abroad and used in Brazil came through official channels. Hundreds of requests were submitted, each in accordance with the protocols set out in international manuals and recommendations—those of the General Comptroller Office, the Financial Action Task Force, the UN Office on Drugs and Crime, the Council of Europe, and guidance from our own Secretariat for International Legal Cooperation.

Contrary to the assertions made by certain commentators in the media, all measures undertaken in the realm of international cooperation were firmly grounded in a robust legal framework and aligned with internationally recognised best practices. The procedures adopted by Operation Car Wash in this regard adhered fully to established global standards.

Did you anticipate the significant level of public support that Operation Car Wash ultimately received? To what extent was this response unexpected?

Given our extensive experience with investigations and legal proceedings involving political figures and influential business actors, there was a clear awareness from the outset that the operation might face significant obstacles. Unfortunately, this reflects a recurrent pattern in Brazil: in complex cases of this nature, it is not uncommon for new legal interpretations to emerge—often contradicting well-established jurisprudence of the higher courts. Matters such as jurisdiction and the legality of wiretap evidence, even when initially validated, are frequently re-examined and subsequently overturned.

In the light of this, the high level of public interest in the operation was regarded as a positive development. Public institutions are, after all, accountable to society, and transparency plays a vital role in reinforcing that accountability. With this in mind, a decision was made to create an official website dedicated to Operation Car Wash,[107] with the aim of making key information accessible and facilitating public understanding of the investigation's progress.

That move gave the operation more visibility and, as a result, I believe it helped garner public support. And that support proved to be vital—not just as a sign of approval, but also for keeping the investigation alive and in the public eye. In the absence of public engagement, there was a genuine risk that an initiative such as Operation Car Wash could have quietly receded into obscurity.

Do you believe that Operation Car Wash disrupted the prevailing structure of corruption and brought an end—however temporarily—to the long-standing impunity historically enjoyed by the country's political and economic elites?

The investigation certainly had a positive impact in that regard. It reached individuals who, until then, had never even come close to facing trial—people who, for reasons that were never entirely clear, seemed to enjoy a kind of "criminal immunity" in Brazil. Leading engineering and construction firms, along with their senior executives—who had long leveraged their dominant market position with impunity—were, for the first time, being held to account. In parallel, prominent political figures, many of whom had never previously faced criminal charges, were prosecuted and, in several cases, convicted.

From the outset, there was a commitment to applying the same legal standards to Operation Car Wash as were applied in the routine handling of other cases. Interestingly, much of the criticism directed at the operation focused on the number of arrests. However, those arrests occurred precisely because the jurisprudence of Brazil's higher courts was followed to the letter. By way of example, the Superior Court of Justice has long held that if an individual commits one or two non-violent offences—such as theft or fraud—pre-trial detention is not necessarily warranted. However, upon the commission of a third or fourth offence, it is considered reasonable for that individual to be held in custody. By the fifth or sixth offence, pre-trial detention is almost certain. This is the standard legal approach—even in cases involving comparatively minor crimes. The same legal reasoning was simply extended to the Car Wash cases, with the key distinction being the gravity and repetition of the offences involved. These included serious crimes such as corruption, money laundering, financial fraud, and organised criminal activity—committed not sporadically, but consistently over many years, if not decades. The financial sums at stake were extraordinary, frequently surpassing one million dollars. In that context, the application of existing judicial standards was not only appropriate but arguably more necessary. If pre-trial detention is considered reasonable for repeat offences of minor severity, it must logically be even more justified in the face of large-scale and systemic corruption.

That said, if society ultimately deems that those legal standards ought to be revised, I would not oppose such a development—in fact, I might well be in favour. However, any reform must be applied uniformly, without exception, and not selectively for the benefit of those with influence or power. In my view, one of Operation Car Wash's greatest strengths was its unwavering commitment to the principle of equality before the law. It conveyed a clear and unequivocal message: white-collar criminals are not beyond the reach of justice.

Unfortunately, with the recent wave of legal revisionism and the re-examination of decisions that were already final, many convictions—despite overwhelming evidence—are being overturned. And that, once again, threatens to erode the principle of equality before the law in Brazil.

In your view, has the relationship between Brazil's public and private sectors evolved meaningfully in the context of combating corruption?
I think so. You can really sense it when speaking to businesspeople—whether or not they were directly involved in the Car Wash Operation. A lot of them simply do not want to do business with the State anymore, or at the very least, they've started reassessing the cost–benefit of going down that path. They've come to realise that it is just not worth it—risking the entire history of the company, their own freedom, their reputation—all for the sake of a contract, even if it seems lucrative, if that contract was obtained through dodgy or illegal means. So, in that sense, I believe both the legislation and especially the investigation played a key role in accelerating the development of compliance in Brazil. And not just in theory or on paper, but in how it is applied—in the way business leaders now engage with the public sector. It is been a real wake-up call, and I think that is a positive legacy.

To what extent do you consider the institutional culture of the Public Prosecutor's Office to have been a decisive factor in the success of Operation Car Wash?
Combating corruption has always been one of the core missions of the Federal Public Prosecutor's Office—especially when it comes to high-level wrongdoing involving public officials and the wealthy. And for that very reason, at least under the two administrations prior to the current one, the necessary resources were made available—both in terms of staff and infrastructure—to really carry out this kind of work properly.

But it was not just about resources. Everyone involved—prosecutors, staff, interns—shared the same vision. There was a prevailing belief in contributing to something greater—something capable of leading to a fairer and more equitable society. People truly felt they were doing something innovative and meaningful for the country—whether that was recovering stolen public funds or holding powerful figures accountable.

So yes, in that sense, the institutional culture of the Public Prosecutor's Office was instrumental in making the investigation what it was.

Brazil ratified the OECD Convention against Corruption,[108] and more recently, the OECD established a special committee to examine the setbacks in the country's anti-corruption efforts. In your view,

had Brazil already been a full member of the OECD, would it have been more difficult to implement the recent legislative and judicial changes[109]?

Perhaps a statement from the OECD—or from one of its committees or member countries—might have instilled a degree of caution or humility among Brazilian public officials. However, to be frank, I do not believe that this kind of external pressure would have been sufficient to meaningfully influence our domestic political dynamics or the conduct of the legislature and other branches of government.

Right now, I see the legislature as being quite detached from reality—from the concerns and expectations of society. It is difficult to imagine that events would have unfolded differently, even if Brazil had already been a member of the OECD. That said, joining the OECD is, in my view, the right course of action—an essential step. And perhaps, in doing so, there may be an opportunity to regain momentum and reorient the fight against corruption.

How do you view the role of privileged jurisdiction[110] and the requirement that convictions are only enforced after a second-instance ruling[111]? Do you believe these factors had an impact on Operation Car Wash, and might they pose a broader challenge to anti-corruption efforts moving forward?

Privileged jurisdiction complicates investigations. Typically, investigations start at the first-instance level, and as soon as there's any indication that someone with privileged jurisdiction might be involved, the entire case must be sent to the relevant higher authority. When that happens, the investigation almost must start over again. In many instances, newly appointed authorities are unfamiliar with the case and may not have access to the same investigative resources as their predecessors. When a plea bargain agreement is underway, for example, the process often has to be suspended until the competent authority is able to assume jurisdiction or formally approve the agreement. This occurred in one of our cases involving cooperation with Switzerland. While giving testimony, the collaborator mentioned new facts involving someone who had jurisdiction before the Federal Supreme Court. The hearing had to be suspended to inform the General Prosecutor and request authorisation to proceed. Fortunately, at the time, Rodrigo Janot was serving as Prosecutor General and promptly authorised the continuation of the proceedings under his designation. However, that was far from typical. In most cases, proceedings are interrupted and reassigned to prosecutors with no prior familiarity with the facts, resulting in significant delays. Moreover, such disruptions often create fertile ground for procedural challenges.

This creates an opportunity for defence teams to argue, retrospectively, that the investigation should have been conducted by a higher court from the outset—an inherently subjective claim, but one that can nonetheless lead to the invalidation of the entire proceeding. A similar line of reasoning appears to have been used to annul part of Operation Monte Carlo,[112] which involved former senator Demóstenes Torres.[113] Privileged jurisdiction, therefore, presents considerable obstacles: it slows down proceedings, introduces additional layers of bureaucracy, and creates avoidable legal risks.

With regard to the rule that sentences are only enforced after a final decision—it significantly undermines public trust in the justice system. It creates a widespread sense of impunity and takes away any immediate consequence for wrongdoing. When individuals are aware that—even if convicted—they are unlikely to serve a sentence for ten or fifteen years, there is little incentive for genuine reflection, let alone remorse or a willingness to make amends.

In Brazil, especially in corruption, money laundering, and financial crimes involving politicians and influential businesspeople, there is often a belief that someone will eventually come up with a new legal interpretation to get them off the hook. On the other hand, when the justice system acts swiftly—as we've seen in the 4th Region,[114] where a corruption case might be tried in the first instance within a year or so, and the appeal finalised in another year or two—then people start paying attention. They realise there are real consequences and that they might serve their sentence sooner rather than later. That makes them more likely to cooperate, to reflect, and to take responsibility. And society sees that too. That is why enforcing sentences after a second-instance conviction has such a powerful educational and deterrent effect.

According to Gary Becker's rational model of crime,[115] if individuals know they are likely to be caught, punished, and compelled to return the proceeds of their offence, they are more likely to reconsider before engaging in illicit conduct. How do you assess the relevance of this framework in the context of anti-corruption efforts?
I completely agree with this reasoning. Of course, for the punishment to serve as an effective deterrent, it must be imposed within a reasonable timeframe. If criminal actions go unpunished because the time limits expire, or the illicit wealth remains hidden, and the individual is not held accountable, the message sent is the opposite: that it is possible to commit crimes like corruption, rigging tenders, and so on, without facing consequences.

To deter criminal behaviour, you do not necessarily need to impose an exemplary punishment or even jail time. Personally, I am not a fan of punitive measures that involve deprivation of liberty. What is important is that punishment is swift—or at least happens within a reasonable period. It could involve community service or being placed in an open or semi-open regime. The key point is that once the sentence is handed down and begins to be served, the person realises that they were in the wrong path. Recovering illicitly acquired assets also plays an important role in reinforcing the deterrent effect and conveying a broader educational message.

In conclusion, how would you assess the principal positive and negative outcomes of Operation Car Wash for Brazil?
That is a question that calls for a more considered response. In my view, the task force left two major legacies.

The first was its exposure of a deeply entrenched system of corruption—one that involved not only businesspeople and public officials, but an entire political structure that operated in close alignment with them. Operation Car Wash brought to light how this system functioned to generate illicit funds, frequently for electoral purposes. Of course, not all of the money was directed towards campaigns; everyone involved stood to gain. Businesspeople secured contracts worth millions—or even billions—along with guaranteed market share and inflated profits. Public officials received substantial bribes. And politicians? They not only obtained campaign financing but often diverted a portion of those funds for personal enrichment. This arrangement proved mutually advantageous for the perpetrators yet profoundly detrimental to society. Furthermore, its scope was not confined to Petrobras but extended to several other state-owned enterprises and public agencies, including the National Department of Infrastructure and Transport, Federal Saving Bank ("Caixa Econômica Federal"), and the Ministry of Health.

The second positive outcome was the equal treatment of all individuals involved. The same criminal laws and judicial standards were applied uniformly, irrespective of the person's position or influence—as I noted earlier.

On the negative side, one reflection that was never fully undertaken concerns the political system itself. This form of corruption had been entrenched for decades, spanning the entire political spectrum, and was a regular feature of Brazil's major parties. Taken to its logical conclusion, this suggests that Brazil arguably never experienced fully free and fair elections. Why? Because elections are dependent on financial resources. Campaign strategists know the precise amount required to elect a congressperson, senator, or president. Those with money are elected; those without it seldom stand a chance—exceptions aside.

This gave rise to a self-perpetuating scheme. Politicians appointed loyal allies to senior positions in state-owned companies and public agencies. These individuals, in turn, selected which firms would win inflated public contracts. In return, the companies paid bribes to public officials and channelled illicit funds to politicians—both personally and through their parties. These politicians, beyond enriching themselves, also gained influence within their parties due to the financial resources they secured. According to investigative findings, approximately 60% of the money circulating through this corrupt network ultimately reached politicians and their political parties. And it was these same actors who later determined electoral outcomes, by selecting candidates to represent the party and financing their campaigns with illicit funds. The figures involved amount to hundreds of millions of reais, year after year—creating an uneven playing field and reinforcing structural inequality in the electoral process. It was, and in many ways remains, a vicious cycle that is extremely difficult to dismantle.

Operation Car Wash, at least temporarily, disrupted this flow of illegal financing. The institutional response, however, was swift: the introduction of a billion-real public electoral fund. In essence, billion-real corruption was replaced by a billion-real state-funded mechanism—arguably in equivalent annual amounts. Nevertheless, Brazilian society now has the opportunity to engage in an open debate about whether this is the model it wishes to sustain. It is regrettable that Congress failed to initiate a proper parliamentary inquiry. Such an inquiry might have shed light on the full extent of the problem, enabled a deeper understanding of the mechanisms involved, and perhaps paved the way for safeguards to prevent a recurrence of past errors.

Orlando Martello Junior was born in São José do Rio Preto (SP). He is a regional prosecutor of the Federal Prosecutor's Office and was part of the Federal Prosecutor's Office task force of Operation Car Wash. His testimony was given on 30 March 2021 via the Zoom platform and lasted 57 minutes. The transcript was reviewed by the interviewee on 29 July 2022.

Testimony of Rafael Vela Barba

Abstract

Rafael Ernesto Vela Barba, Senior Prosecutor within the Public Ministry of Peru, offers a comprehensive account of his legal career and his leadership in the Peruvian strand of Operation Car Wash. Drawing on his background as a former anti-corruption judge and current National Coordinator for money laundering and organised crime, Vela Barba situates the Car Wash case within a broader institutional and political context, outlining its systemic challenges and transformative potential. His testimony traces the evolution of the investigation—from its fractured beginnings to the establishment of a unified prosecutorial task force under his direction—and highlights the role of international cooperation, particularly with Brazil, in securing key evidence.

He reflects on how earlier experience in the Fujimori-Montesinos trials shaped his understanding of political corruption as a form of organised power, requiring a legal response equally structured and resilient. Central to his strategy was an unprecedented level of transparency: public hearings, media engagement, and a deliberate effort to counter disinformation. These measures, he argues, were essential to sustaining legitimacy in the face of institutional resistance, media manipulation, and political interference.

Vela Barba also details the use of plea bargain agreements ("colaboración eficaz") as a pivotal tool in uncovering the financial and operational networks behind Odebrecht's corrupt practices in Peru. His testimony underscores the deeply embedded nature of political corruption, spanning all major parties, and cautions against both politicisation of the justice system and institutional fragility. He concludes with a reflection on the enduring tension between autonomy and hierarchy within prosecutorial work, the lessons drawn from Brazilian setbacks, and the importance of maintaining public trust and international solidarity in the fight against grand corruption.

To begin, could you outline your professional trajectory and personal background, particularly as they relate to your role in the Car Wash investigation?

I am currently a senior prosecutor, which is just one step below the highest rank within the Public Prosecutor's Office of Peru—the supreme prosecutors. It is a very structured, pyramidal career path, and at the moment, there are only six supreme prosecutors in the entire country. I belong to the group of senior prosecutors who are in line with the career progression framework established by the institution. I have held this position for about nine years now. Since 2015, alongside my work as a senior prosecutor, I have also served as the National Coordinator for the system that tackles money laundering and organised crime. So, it is my role to lead and oversee the national efforts in that area.

In addition to those responsibilities, since July 2018, I have been leading the special team responsible for investigating what is referred to in Peru as the Car Wash case—more widely known as the Odebrecht case. This involves both Brazilian and Peruvian companies that conspired to commit a range of crimes, including offences linked to transnational and domestic organised crime. Due to the complexity and scale of the case, it required a specialised team—a task force, if you will—with the flexibility and expertise to handle such a high-profile investigation. I am the only senior prosecutor in that task force, and as such, I lead the entire operation and bear direct responsibility for the investigations. I work alongside prosecutors who are lower in the hierarchy, but I personally oversee and steer the legal strategy. I am also involved as a litigating prosecutor at the appellate level, handling cases on appeal and defending the decisions made by our first-instance prosecutors. So, in practical terms, I supervise and guide the team investigating the Car Wash case, ensuring a proper system of checks and balances through a "double degree of review."

Before joining the Public Prosecutor's Office, I worked as an anti-corruption judge with national jurisdiction, solely dedicated to that field. I handled investigations into the administration of former President Alberto Fujimori.[116] Here, it is referred to as the Fujimori-Montesinos case.[117] I served as both a first-instance judge and a judge in the court of appeal, dealing exclusively with corruption-related matters. It was during that period that the new Criminal Procedure Code of 2004 was implemented, which introduced an accusatory system designed to more effectively combat organised crime and corruption involving public officials.

Beyond the courtroom, I have also been a university lecturer for over fifteen years, teaching Criminal Law and Criminal Procedural Law. I have taught at the Academy of the Magistracy, which is the national training body for judges and prosecutors.

In terms of international representation, I currently serve as Peru's commissioner to the Mechanism for Follow-up on the Implementation of the Inter-American Convention against Corruption (MESICIC), part of the Organisation of American States. I am also a member of the Group of Experts for the Control of Money Laundering—which works within the OAS framework to address money laundering, terrorist financing, and drug trafficking.

These various roles connect me with both national and international organisations. Much of our work involves international cooperation, particularly when it comes to cases with transnational elements. Peru maintains ongoing partnerships with key institutions such as the US Department of Justice, as well as with countries like Switzerland and, of course, Brazil. These collaborations are crucial for moving forward with major corruption cases, where mutual legal assistance and solidarity between nations make all the difference.

To what extent did your involvement in the Fujimori–Montesinos case shape your approach to the Car Wash investigation in Peru? In your view, are there substantive parallels between the two cases in terms of structure, actors, or legal strategy?
Absolutely—without question. My experience as an anti-corruption judge, both at first instance and on appeal, provided me with a clear view of how criminal organisations operate from within power structures. This aligns closely with the current investigations, which concern allegations of serious corruption and money laundering involving political figures operating within organised structures of power. There is a clear political element—political influence being used as a tool to commit crimes. It was, without question, a vital learning experience for me. Back then, under the old system, I served as an examining magistrate—which, before the 2004 reforms to the Peruvian Criminal Procedure Code, meant that I carried out the investigative acts myself. Interestingly, that is now essentially my role as a prosecutor—though today, in a sense, oversight is exercised by guarantor judges. For certain procedural steps, such as the authorisation of specific measures, judicial approval must be obtained. But from a strategic and procedural standpoint, everything I gained during that earlier period has been invaluable in shaping the current approach to handling highly complex and often unconventional cases involving powerful networks. What is being confronted today is not business as usual—it is the exercise of organised criminal power. The response also needs to be structured, legal, and adapted to that reality. For instance, transparency has been prioritised through the public disclosure of information, within the limits established by law. This has been particularly relevant in the light of the profile of those under investigation, which includes high-ranking public officials, current and former presidents, business executives, and figures from the financial sector.

These are individuals with significant economic and media influence. Public scrutiny has played a central role, enabling greater transparency in prosecutorial actions, facilitating regular reporting on the progress of investigations, and fostering sustained engagement from civil society. This has been especially important in a world so dominated by media. Criminal organisations are often quick to defend themselves by occupying media space, while traditionally the prosecution remained silent. It became clear, however, that this approach needed to change. It was no longer viable to allow one-sided or misleading narratives to dominate public discourse. A deliberate effort was therefore made to engage with the media and to correct false or inaccurate claims with factual information—always within the limits of institutional responsibilities.

Another measure adopted was the use of public hearings. This gave visibility to the process and allowed people to see what was going on. Hearings from the Car Wash case were even broadcast on Justicia TV—the judiciary's official channel, which had previously attracted limited viewership. But when these hearings were aired, they got ratings comparable to football matches! People started tuning in. Other channels—news outlets and even some entertainment networks—also began to broadcast the hearings. And in those hearings, prosecutors present their evidence, live. It created a level of societal involvement that we'd never seen before, and helped prevent abuses of power. Without that transparency, the narrative would have been completely one-sided—driven by defence lawyers in the media.

And let's be honest: it is no surprise to see lawyers out there defending their clients publicly. They had always done so—and with considerable skill. However, there was now also a prosecutor speaking publicly, stating, "*That is simply not true—here is the evidence.*" That shift unsettled them, as they were no longer the sole actors shaping public perception. The truth became something supported by real data, real documents, and society could judge for itself.

Naturally, these actions have not been without consequences. Numerous prominent defence lawyers submitted complaints, and there has also been pressure from within the institution itself. On several occasions, efforts to clarify information publicly or to counter misinformation resulted in formal reports being filed. Disciplinary proceedings were initiated, and the potential sanctions included removal from specific cases—or, in more severe scenarios, dismissal from our positions altogether. It is a kind of internal censorship, designed to stop information from circulating and to maintain a partial truth. But the more truth comes out, the harder it is to sustain false narratives.

Unfortunately, some of the backlash originated from the highest levels of the institution. At one point, our immediate superior in the Car Wash investigations—Prosecutor Pedro Gonzalo Chávarry[118]—formally dismissed us. This occurred at 9 p.m. on 31 December 2018, an apparent attempt to avoid public scrutiny. However, the move provoked a strong public reaction: many citizens interrupted their New Year's Eve celebrations to protest in the streets. The pressure was such that Chávarry was ultimately compelled to reverse his decision. He was later removed from office by the newly established National Board of Justice, a body created through constitutional reform. Another prosecutor, Tomás Aladino Gálvez Villegas[119]—who had also sought to obstruct our work—was likewise removed.

These internal tensions have left the institution somewhat fragmented. There are individuals within the Prosecutor's Office who have not expressed support for the work of the investigative team. It is an unusual position to be in, feeling like you are not supported by your own institution. On numerous occasions, there was a sense of operating in isolation.

Operation Car Wash in Peru implicated some of the most prominent figures in national politics. Could you elaborate on the impact of the investigation within the Peruvian context, particularly regarding Odebrecht's role and involvement?

From a sociological perspective, the Car Wash case in Peru significantly increased public awareness of systemic corruption. For a long time, it was only suspected that politics was plagued by criminal practices and links to organised crime—but there was little proof. With the developments of the Car Wash investigations, what was once mere speculation became undeniable reality. In short, it confirmed what many had already feared about the Peruvian political class: that high-level corruption was not the exception, but the norm.

Peru was deeply entangled in the Odebrecht scandal. Following the company's admission of wrongdoing in Brazil and its entry into a plea bargain agreement—referred to locally as "effective collaboration"—it was obliged to cooperate not only with Brazilian authorities, but also with authorities in other jurisdictions where criminal conduct had occurred. This is where Peru became directly involved. Given that both the Peruvian and Brazilian legal systems permitted this form of cross-border cooperation, Odebrecht's agreement in Brazil entailed corresponding obligations in Peru as well. Essentially, the company became a kind of whistleblower ("colaborador eficaz" in Spanish) which meant it had a duty to provide information and evidence to Peruvian authorities as part of its reparations. In fact, Peru became one of the main focal points for their disclosures, because in many instances it had served as a hub for corrupt payments. Odebrecht channelled money through Peruvian operators, often using complex schemes involving offshore accounts, fake contracts, and cash deliveries to circumvent anti-money laundering systems.

In the Peruvian context, the corruption exposed through Car Wash involved politicians at the highest levels, with serious accusations of money laundering, organised crime, and other related offences. These investigations relied heavily on the mechanism of plea bargaining—or effective collaboration, as it is referred to here.

It is important to note that the plea bargain process (effective collaboration) is inherently complex. These are individuals who have admitted to unlawful conduct, and as such, their testimonies must be substantiated by evidence. The statements of those who have committed criminal acts cannot be accepted at face value; they only acquire probative value when supported by documentation, financial records, or other forms of corroborating data. This evidentiary foundation is essential for constructing a robust case.

In most of the investigations, the claims made by executives are backed by financial trails—how the money was moved, where it came from. In Odebrecht's case, much of it stemmed from their Department of Structured Operations, which was essentially a secret slush fund, completely off the books, used to finance bribes and illicit payments. The funds were laundered through a range of methods, including the use of offshore companies, fictitious consultancy contracts, and, in some instances, the physical transfer of cash. These were instances of highly sophisticated financial crime.

One of the greatest challenges in investigations of this nature is the need to maintain complete impartiality. Everyone has to be investigated equally, regardless of political leaning. Politicians from across the political spectrum—left, centre, and right—have been subject to charges. When proceedings were initiated against Ollanta Humala,[120] the investigation was criticised as being politically motivated by right-leaning interests. Subsequently, when charges were brought against Keiko Fujimori[121] and Pedro Pablo Kuczynski,[122] similar accusations were made, this time suggesting an alignment with centrist forces. In the case of Susana Villarán,[123] associated with the centre-left, yet another narrative emerged. Ultimately, however, the evidence demonstrated that corruption transcended political ideologies. That is the reality we encountered. Understandably, this has had a significant impact on public perception. It is shown to the Peruvian people that many of their top politicians were involved in money laundering and organised crime. And yes, that might have a sociological effect—it might discredit the political class—but that is not our concern. The role is that of a prosecutor—not a politician. Our responsibility is to investigate when there is evidence—nothing more, nothing less.

Some argue that these investigations have harmed the economy. But we always ask: "In what way? Is it acceptable to allow individuals to escape accountability for criminal conduct merely to safeguard the economy?" That is not how the rule of law works. Our constitutional duty is to investigate wrongdoing. The alternative—turning a blind eye or entering into a tacit pact of silence—would be far more damaging. That is not a course of action that can be afforded. The Public Prosecutor's Office cannot, and will not, abandon its responsibilities in the face of evidence. Our commitment is to legality, not convenience.

Could you elaborate on the institutional design and operational dynamics of the Peruvian task force model in addressing systemic corruption?

Our structure is based on the Organic Law of the Public Ministry, which authorises the creation of special teams in exceptional circumstances. This model is broadly comparable to what common law systems refer to as task forces. When dealing with large-scale and complex cases involving multiple lines of investigation, it is necessary to establish dedicated teams to ensure focused and coordinated efforts. It is essential to have individuals with experience, specialised knowledge, and the capacity to divide tasks efficiently. Most importantly, a shared strategic approach is required. In the absence of a common strategy, each prosecutor may pursue their own interpretation of the case, which can result in contradictions, confusion, and procedural disarray.

That is why having a shared strategy is essential. Members of a task force need to be able to coordinate and share information, because often, cases are interconnected. Evidence initially uncovered in case A may surface again in case D. When both prosecutors belong to the same team, they are able to share such findings and coordinate their strategies, thereby enhancing consistency and strengthening the overall pursuit of the truth. In the absence of such coordination, there is a risk of adopting contradictory approaches to the same issue—an outcome that ultimately serves only the interests of the individual under investigation.

The creation of a special team is, in essence, a response to the need for effective coordination. Naturally, the establishment of such a team is ultimately a political and institutional decision. It is up to the National Public Prosecutor's Office—essentially, the General Prosecutor. This is where a certain irony emerges. I have previously commented on the often difficult—and at times openly antagonistic—relationships experienced with certain superiors. Take Pedro Gonzalo Cháverry, for example—he was the one who appointed us, and the one who tried to remove us when the investigations started gaining traction. Perhaps he thought he'd have more control over the process once the appointments were made. In practice, our work is not governed by hierarchical authority, but by the evidence. Each prosecutor functions with a degree of autonomy. For example, while I serve as a senior prosecutor and lead the special team—also coordinating national efforts related to money laundering prosecutions—the first-instance prosecutors within the team maintain their independence. A shared strategic framework is followed, and I provide support in that regard; however, each prosecutor ultimately conducts their work independently.

There is a constant tension between hierarchical structure and prosecutorial autonomy, and I believe that my experience as a judge has been instrumental in helping me navigate that dynamic. Judges must be independent, and I have carried that principle into my role as head of the team. In situations where hierarchy and autonomy clash, I always err on the side of autonomy. It is not about issuing orders—it is about supporting and complementing their work. I might suggest corrections when needed, but fundamentally, role is to provide support, enabling them to stand firm in the face of the powerful individuals under investigation—high-level politicians, businesspeople, people with significant influence.

Now, consider the implications if prosecutors lacked that autonomy—if they were merely executing directives from above. That kind of dependency is simply unworkable in complex investigations like these. So, yes, while the decision to form a special team is political in nature, functionally it shouldn't create a chain of dependency. That is been a guiding principle of my leadership.

I have enormous respect for the autonomy of each prosecutor. My role is to support them, to help when things need adjusting, and to trust that those selected for the team were chosen for their competence, experience, and integrity. Of course, mistakes happen—we all make them. No system is free from error, and it is only natural that learning occurs along the way, and that adjustments are made in the process. But what is unacceptable is dishonesty or deliberate wrongdoing. That simply cannot be tolerated in our work.

Indeed, these teams are structured with autonomy as a fundamental principle. All actions are subject to judicial oversight. No steps are taken based on impulse or assumption; proceedings are grounded in what can be substantiated before a judge. It is ultimately the judge who determines whether sufficient grounds exist to grant any request submitted.

The position of prosecutor—does it require a formal application, is it subject to election, or is it awarded through a competitive selection process? Could the appointment procedure in Peru be explained?

It is a public selection process—a merit-based competition. The interesting thing is that in Peru, under our Judicial and Prosecutorial Career Law, a stability regime is in place, specifically designed to ensure independence and autonomy. In essence, once appointed, the position is held for life—until the age of seventy years old—provided, of course, that no misconduct or criminal offence is committed. Every seven years, though, there is a process of homologation overseen by the National Board of Justice, which is the body currently responsible for appointing, confirming, or dismissing judges and prosecutors. Before this, it used to be the National Council of the Magistracy. But here's the issue—organised crime managed to infiltrate that previous council. It became a tool to undermine the autonomy and independence of the justice system.

This ties directly into the Car Wash investigations. For instance, in the case against Keiko Fujimori—who at the time was running for president—there was evidence showing she sought to align herself with a group known as *Cuellos Blancos del Puerto*[124] in order to influence judicial appointments in her favour, especially regarding investigations linked to Car Wash. It becomes evident that these cases are closely interconnected.

One of the major outcomes of the Car Wash and *Lava Juez*[125] scandals was a constitutional reform. The National Council of the Magistracy was dissolved and replaced by the National Board of Justice. This new body was the one that removed Pedro Gonzalo Cháverry, the former Prosecutor General, and Supreme Prosecutor Tomás Aladino Gálvez Villegas—both of whom were implicated in *Lava Juez* and *Los Cuellos Blancos del Puerto*. The newly established board is now responsible not only for our reappointment every seven years, but also for promoting transparency in the selection of new judges and prosecutors. As a result of these reforms, many individuals previously implicated or compromised are being removed from their positions. This has led to a renewal of Peru's Supreme Court and the Superior Council of the Public Prosecutor's Office.

But of course, there is a lingering concern: what if someone like Keiko Fujimori, who has already tried to manipulate the system, returns to power? What would happen then? If she were able to once again infiltrate key institutions like the Supreme Court or the Public Prosecutor's

Office, all this progress—this massive effort to clean up and renew the system—could be undone. If that were the case, it would suggest that our efforts have not resulted in meaningful or lasting change. It is therefore not merely a matter of removing those who were unfit for office, but of ensuring that their successors are genuinely qualified and committed to upholding integrity.

Was Keiko Fujimori among the individuals who received payments from Marcelo Odebrecht[126] as part of a broader corruption scheme? Yes, that has been definitively confirmed—not only by Marcelo Odebrecht himself, but also by the broader leadership of Odebrecht in Brazil. What is particularly noteworthy is that Marcelo Odebrecht would not typically have been aware of the specific details surrounding a payment to a presidential candidate in Peru. That level of operational detail was generally managed by his designated representative—or "viceroy"—in the country, Jorge Henrique Simões Barata,[127] who led Odebrecht's operations in Peru.

But what happened was rather unusual. Former Brazilian Minister Antonio Palocci[128]—nicknamed "the Italian"—got in touch with Marcelo Odebrecht. Palocci told him, "I have an order from Lula da Silva.[129] Lula wants you to give money to Mr Ollanta Humala Tasso, his candidate in Peru. He wants to support him financially. We think a decent contribution would be three million dollars." Marcelo had a long-standing relationship with Palocci, so he took the request seriously. He became involved in the Peruvian campaign thereafter, despite typically refraining from direct engagement in such matters. Marcelo subsequently contacted Antonio Mameri[130]—one of Odebrecht's top executives—and said: "Mameri, I have got a task. Humala must get this money; Lula himself is asking. Tell Barata to pay the three million." The funds were to be taken from an account nicknamed "Italian" in Odebrecht's internal spreadsheets—essentially Palocci's slush fund—managed by the Department of Structured Operations in Brazil, which handled bribes.

So, Mameri passed the message on to Barata: "You have to pay three million dollars to Humala." Barata was furious. He replied, "How can we pay Humala? He is a leftist, a communist. If he wins, it'll ruin the country—and us along with it." He categorically refused.

Mameri then contacted Marcelo to inform him, "Barata will not pay." Marcelo, understandably frustrated, demanded an immediate teleconference. During the meeting, he addressed Barata directly, stating: "You will pay the three million—I gave you a direct order." But Barata pushed back: "Marcelo, the man is a communist! He is aligned with Chávez, with Maduro. If he wins, our business here will suffer." Then Marcelo asked, "Do you have another candidate in mind?" And Barata said, "Yes, actually—I'd prefer Keiko Fujimori to win. In fact, I have already given her some money. But listen, Marcelo, three million is far too much for Peruvian politics. I would not give them more than five hundred thousand dollars." Marcelo replied, "It is not up to me. This is Lula's dirty money—we are just carrying out his request. I do not care about ideology. Just do as you are told. The money comes from the "Italian" account. If you're having a moral crisis, fine—give another five hundred thousand to Keiko, but do not call me again. And pay Humala."

Marcelo even wrote a note in his diary: "increase Keiko to 500 and make a visit." Later, when the task force in Curitiba arrested Marcelo and seized his records, both the diary and the spreadsheet were discovered. And there it was—clear evidence of the three million to Humala and the five hundred thousand to Keiko Fujimori. These were payments that, under normal circumstances, Marcelo would likely not have been aware of.

That is indeed a fascinating account—I was not previously aware of it. Did Odebrecht also maintain a payment spreadsheet in Peru, similar to the one used in Brazil?

Yes, such a spreadsheet existed; however, all data was stored on a central server, part of a system referred to as "IB". What is particularly striking—and somewhat ironic from the Brazilian perspective of Operation Car Wash—is that the server was located in neither Peru nor Brazil. It was based in Switzerland. The authorities succeeded in seizing the server during the course of the investigation.

In fact, during the Brazilian phase of Car Wash, the person who led the effort to secure the server was an Odebrecht employee named Fernando Migliaccio.[131] The operation itself was overseen by Brazil's prosecutor at the time, Orlando Martelo.[132] He coordinated what came to be known as "the Migliaccio operation", which resulted in the servers being seized in Switzerland.

Now here's the bit people often find quite ironic: Odebrecht had been engaging in this kind of behaviour for over thirty years. But it was only when Marcelo Odebrecht began taking a more active role in the company—the older generation like his father, Emílio, having started to step back—those things became more organised. Marcelo had been groomed to run a massive corporation, and he was also fully aware of the company's long history of corruption. So, what was his response? He introduced structure to the entire operation—he systematised it. However, in doing so, he also created a traceable record, something that had not previously existed. And that is the anecdote people tend to recall: "Why is there suddenly evidence for everything?".

This occurred because Marcelo, in his attempt to apply corporate-style efficiency to both the lawful and unlawful operations of the business, ended up documenting everything. Despite the use of encrypted systems and coded language, the Structured Operations Department inadvertently generated a detailed digital trail of every bribe it paid.

Operation Car Wash is considered an example of what legal doctrine defines as grand corruption. When you assumed responsibility for the investigation in Peru, did you anticipate that it would reveal such a vast network of corruption, involving such significant sums and high-level political figures—not only in Brazil, but also in Peru and across other Latin American countries?

To some extent, yes—as information had already begun to emerge about what was unfolding in Brazil. And if it was happening in Brazil, it was likely that similar dynamics were at play here as well…

How did the Car Wash investigation first take shape in Peru, and what factors triggered its initial development within the Peruvian context?

In Peru, it began somewhat indirectly in 2015, through a special prosecutorial team—though not the one I was part of at the time. It was led by someone who was handling cases connected to Brazil, with a focus on what became known as Operation Sandcastle (*Castelo de Areia*),[133] which, to be honest, did not progress particularly well—even in Brazil.

The investigation was based on a lead that ultimately proved to be something of a dead end. Operation Sandcastle gradually lost momentum, whereas Car Wash gained real traction, largely due to the work of the task force in Curitiba. Everything changed when Marcelo Odebrecht was sentenced to prison. That marked the turning point when the company finally chose to make use of Brazil's plea-bargaining mechanism. From that moment onwards, the operations of Odebrecht, both in Brazil and in other countries where criminal conduct may have occurred, began to come to light.

Officially, Operation Car Wash in Peru began in January 2017, when a dedicated team was formally established. Prior to that, some prosecutors had been working indirectly on the case through Operation Sandcastle, although they were unable to obtain much information. It is important to acknowledge this—there was simply no meaningful progress during that earlier phase. Then Marcelo Odebrecht came forward with information that had not been available to Peruvian prosecutors, which suddenly required a complete rethinking of the investigative strategy.

In fact, the situation became so strained that cooperation between Peru and Brazil was on the verge of collapse. It was at that point, in July 2018, that our team assumed responsibility for coordinating the Peruvian phase of Operation Car Wash. From then onwards, all efforts were consolidated under a unified strategy. Rather than passively awaiting information from the company, a decision was made to engage directly with the primary source in Brazil. This marked a significant shift in approach—one that ultimately proved effective. Strong support was received from the Brazilian Public Prosecutor's Office, and as the strategy demonstrated its effectiveness, continued leadership of the operation was entrusted to the team. The mandate included restoring damaged channels of cooperation and advancing the investigations. This transition occurred in July 2018.

What has been the role of plea bargain agreements in advancing anti-corruption efforts within the context of Operation Car Wash?

Plea bargain agreements proved to be essential. In Peru, the turning point in the investigations occurred with the signing of these agreements and the flow of information received from Brazil through international cooperation. A significant portion of the evidence was in the possession of the defendants themselves. Without their collaboration, or the use of international legal channels, it would have been impossible to access certain materials such as servers located abroad.

However, formal legal procedures require time, and time was not on our side. It became necessary to establish a more direct line of communication with the Brazilian authorities. This approach enabled a more agile and continuous flow of information, while also helping to overcome certain bureaucratic delays. This system of effective collaboration has been key to our progress. It allowed us to move forward with solid evidence, not just suspicions. It also encouraged other companies and individuals to trust the process. Individuals began coming forward with documents to which only they had access, or with information indicating where and how such materials could be located. These agreements have been groundbreaking. The evidence shared through them has enabled the construction of investigations based on fact rather than speculation. A broader ripple effect is now evident. Major companies—particularly in the construction sector—are now seeking to cooperate, express a willingness to come clean, implement compliance programmes, and reintegrate into the formal economy. It is not just about punishment—it is also about rebuilding. Many of these companies left major public works unfinished, which has a real impact on society. So corporate reintegration is also a social and economic necessity.

Naturally, this approach is not without its challenges. Defendants directly impacted by the information disclosed through these agreements often resist. Many seek to delegitimise the process, as they have no interest in seeing collaboration succeed. They advocate for a model based solely on retribution, excluding the possibility of social or corporate reintegration. This poses a serious problem, as a framework focused exclusively on punitive outcomes discourages companies from coming forward and cooperating with the authorities. There is no incentive to collaborate, no reason to blow the whistle. Without collaboration, the authorities might succeed in confiscating some assets or even driving the offending companies out of the country. However, the full truth would remain elusive, and the broader context of systemic corruption would likely be lost. When properly structured, plea bargains provide access to witnesses, material evidence, and a clearer pathway to uncovering the truth. They also make it possible for reparations to be paid, within reasonable limits, particularly in the light of the severe financial difficulties many of these companies now face. This is not a matter of showing sympathy, but rather a recognition of legal and economic realities.

There are international precedents for this. Look at Volkswagen and Siemens, both of which faced serious allegations but went on to implement compliance programmes and took steps towards reintegration. And yes, critics will say, "You cannot negotiate with criminals; they should be banned entirely." But of course they would say that. It is in their interest. If there are no agreements, there is no investigation, and they avoid standing trial altogether. That is impunity.

These agreements are undoubtedly challenging. They require engaging directly with individuals who have committed crimes. However, they are fully grounded in the law, which provides a clear framework for achieving reparations and justice. This is not a legal grey area. It involves the application of established legal instruments to uncover the truth and, ultimately, to strengthen institutional integrity.

To what extent was international cooperation instrumental in the development of Operation Car Wash in Peru?

It was absolutely vital. The Peruvian Public Prosecutor's Office was likely the one that made the most extensive use of international cooperation agreements. Special recognition is due to those who led these efforts, particularly public prosecutor Orlando Martelo, who played a key role. From a statistical and institutional perspective, both the Brazilian and Peruvian Public Prosecutor's Offices set a strong example through their collaboration in Operation Car Wash in Peru. Hundreds of requests for cooperation from the Brazilian justice system were fulfilled, and, in return, information was provided to various countries that submitted similar requests. This cooperation has been fundamental to the advancement of our investigations.

Naturally, no formal public consultation was held. Instead, efforts have centred on informing the public and promoting a broader understanding within civil society regarding the scale and seriousness of the case. The investigation has involved individuals and entities with significant political and economic influence, including political authorities, major business groups, senior public officials, and, at times, internal resistance within the institution itself.

The strategy, therefore, has been to engage consistently in public discourse. The current context is marked by the rapid circulation of both accurate information and misinformation, making it essential to ensure that credible narratives reach society. The Public Prosecutor's Office needs to have a clear, authoritative voice to counter the fake news and half-truths that often come from defence lawyers or others trying to blur the facts. The decision to engage publicly has been deliberate. As a result, there has been significant civic engagement and close scrutiny of the work undertaken. The objective has never been to gain popularity or public approval, but rather to ensure transparency and accountability. Regular communication of institutional actions has enabled society to remain informed and, in turn, exercise a form of civic oversight. This dynamic is a constructive element in any democratic context.

All actions undertaken remain subject to judicial review. Legal procedures are followed rigorously, and decisions issued by the courts are fully respected. The objective is not to seek public approval, but to foster meaningful societal engagement, particularly in a case of such scale and significance. This approach contributes to the prevention of abuses of power, regardless of their source.

In Brazil, many viewed Operation Car Wash as a potential turning point in the country's fight against corruption. Was there a comparable sense of expectation or public sentiment in Peru?
Absolutely. It was undoubtedly a watershed moment. For some, it was as if their eyes had been opened for the first time. For others, it confirmed long-standing suspicions—namely, that a concealed system had been operating in the shadows, unchecked and largely unexamined until then. What is certain is that passivity was never an option. There was full awareness that pursuing the investigation could entail both personal and professional consequences. People say—and they may be right—that once you take the lead on a case of this magnitude, your career gets frozen. That no further progress will be possible, despite individual merit.

That one might remain precisely where one is, solely for having dared to confront something so powerful.

Even so, the decision was made to proceed, supported by a group of committed and principled prosecutors who refused to remain on the sidelines. The work was carried out without fixed hours, often extending into weekends and holidays, and involved frequent travel, frequently at the expense of time with family. All of this was undertaken in order to confront some of the most powerful legal teams that financial resources can secure in the country—while receiving the same salary as any other public prosecutor. So, there was no financial gain, no personal reward—just a firm commitment to doing our job, to fulfilling our duty with integrity.

In your view, what have been the main positive outcomes and the principal limitations or challenges of Operation Car Wash?

One clear positive outcome is that the operation established, unequivocally, that there are no untouchables. That alone represents a fundamental shift. Once it becomes clear that no individual is above the law, behaviour begins to change—whether on the part of someone tempted to accept a bribe or someone considering offering one. In my view, this is a genuine achievement. There is now a visibly greater respect for the rule of law. Of course, there are always some cynical voices saying things like, "Well, before, things worked—with a little bribe, the wheel kept turning. Now, officials are too scared to sign anything, fearing they'll be investigated later, and businesspeople feel the same. " I regard that perspective as somewhat narrow. The role was to uncover the truth—and that was accomplished. If one of the consequences is that individuals now think twice before engaging in unethical practices, then that should not be viewed as a drawback. On the contrary, it reflects precisely the intended outcome. It signals a healthy shift in behaviour.

That said, there is always a strategic balance to be maintained. On the one side, there is public support and the oversight exercised by civil society. On the other, there is the influence of financial power—major law firms, prominent public figures, and business actors who do not always operate ethically. This tension is real, and the balance is inherently fragile. It can shift significantly in response to political developments or pragmatic decisions that lie entirely beyond our control.

Put simply, if an individual sentenced to thirty years for corruption can still ascend to the presidency under the constitutional order, this underscores just how precarious and conditional that balance truly is.

To conclude, is there any final reflection you would like to share regarding Operation Car Wash and the broader fight against corruption in Brazil?

I would simply like to emphasise the essential role played by the Brazilian Federal Public Prosecutor's Office, particularly through the efforts of prosecutor Orlando Martello, among others. The support received was substantial, and the information provided throughout the process proved immensely valuable. For that, there remains a deep sense of gratitude.

At the same time, it is important to acknowledge that developments in Brazil had a considerable impact on the progress of the Car Wash investigations. From our perspective, the dissolution of the task force sets a precedent that raises concern. Although the hope is that a similar situation will not arise in Peru, the possibility cannot be ruled out. Although our work is conducted with full institutional autonomy, that does not entirely shield it from external pressures.

Above all, I wish to express our solidarity, respect, and sincere gratitude to the Brazilian Federal Public Prosecutor's Office. I have mentioned Prosecutor Orlando Martello by name because it is important to humanise this type of institutional cooperation and to recognise the individuals behind it. Of course, his work has been part of a broader collective effort, supported by a team of prosecutors and dedicated professionals whose contributions have had a meaningful impact. We are deeply appreciative of that support.

Rafael Ernesto Vela Barba was born in Lima, Peru. Senior Prosecutor and Coordinator of the Specialised Prosecutor's Office for Money Laundering and Organised Crime. Head of the special team investigating the Car Wash—Odebrecht—case in Peru. His testimony was given on 12 May 2021 via the Zoom virtual platform and lasted 1 hour and 5 minutes of recording. The text was revised by the interviewee on 15 March 2023.

Testimony of Stefan Lenz

Abstract

In this testimony, Stephan Lenz, former Federal Prosecutor at the Swiss Office of the Attorney General, reflects on his personal and professional trajectory and his involvement in major international corruption cases, particularly Operation Car Wash. Tracing his career from private legal practice in Germany to his leadership role in Switzerland's white-collar crime division, Lenz highlights the structural and operational challenges of transnational anti-corruption enforcement.

He details the evolution of Swiss involvement in Operation Car Wash, beginning with suspicious activity reports linked to Petrobras and expanding into what became Switzerland's largest prosecutorial task force in a corruption case. Lenz offers insights into the mechanics of international cooperation, underscoring the decisive role of informal communication and spontaneous information-sharing in advancing complex financial investigations. He contrasts the Car Wash case with earlier experiences, such as the Alstom investigation, noting significant differences in prosecutorial commitment and institutional resolve.

Lenz identifies the unprecedented scale, organisational sophistication, and systemic nature of the corruption revealed by Car Wash as both surprising and instructive. He emphasises that the case not only disrupted entrenched patterns of impunity but also demonstrated how public transparency and prosecutorial determination can alter expectations around accountability. Drawing comparisons with Italy's *Mani Pulite*, Lenz argues that Car Wash's openness to public scrutiny was a key factor in its initial success and international impact.

While praising the professionalism and moral resolve of his Brazilian counterparts, Lenz also expresses concern over the dismantling of the task force and the resurgence of political resistance. He frames this reversal as a missed opportunity for Brazil and a discouraging signal to prosecutors across Latin America. Concluding on a personal note, he describes Car Wash as the most significant case of his career and a rare example of meaningful international legal cooperation against systemic corruption.

Could you describe your personal and professional background, particularly the experiences that led you to specialise in white-collar crime and international corruption cases?

I grew up in a small town, in a family with three brothers, and completed my primary and secondary education there. I later moved to Berlin to study law, which marked the beginning of my professional journey in the legal field. On the personal side, I have four daughters, which has always brought a special balance to my life.

After graduating from law school, I worked as a clerk for five years. Eventually, I decided to become a practising lawyer and joined a small law firm as a partner—we were just five lawyers, and I had the opportunity to work on a wide range of legal matters. After a decade in private practice, I began to feel the need for change and new challenges, so I applied for a position at the Swiss Office of the Attorney General.

I was appointed congressperson Federal Prosecutor and, after five years, became a Federal Prosecutor. Throughout my time there, I worked in the white-collar crime division, focusing on cases involving money laundering, international corruption, and other forms of economic crime.

Based on your professional background and experience, how do you view the role of international cooperation in combating corruption and money laundering?

In my view, international cooperation is absolutely essential in the fight against corruption and money laundering. Corrupt individuals often rely on large, highly specialised international networks to carry out their schemes. When they need to move illicit funds across borders, multiple jurisdictions become involved. These crimes are, by nature, transnational. I honestly believe that there is no other area of criminal law where international cooperation plays such a critical role. Without it, many of these cases would simply be impossible to investigate or prosecute effectively.

How did the Swiss authorities, particularly the Office of the Prosecutor General, handle the Car Wash operation? And what was your personal involvement in the case?

My first experience with Brazil was through a different case—the Alstom case.[134] I travelled to Brazil at the time and met with Brazilian prosecutors. Later, I noticed several connections between the Alstom case and the Car Wash investigation. While following international media coverage of corruption cases, I came across names I recognised from the Alstom files. I reached out to a colleague at the Attorney General's Office in Lausanne, who had just begun working on the Car Wash case in Switzerland. I informed him, "I know some of these companies; I dealt with them in a previous case." My contribution was welcomed, and that is how I joined the Car Wash team in Switzerland. The Swiss investigation began with Suspicious Activity Reports concerning accounts held by Mr. Costa,[135] a director at Petrobras. From there, the team expanded significantly. At its peak, up to 30 professionals—including investigators, prosecutors, financial experts, and police officers—were involved in the case.

Is the task force model also used in Switzerland for handling cases of this nature?
Indeed. In the white-collar crime division, major cases usually require the formation of an investigation team. As far as I know, the team working on the Car Wash case was the largest ever assembled at the Swiss Office of the Attorney General. Car Wash is a classic example of grand corruption, and many even consider it the largest corruption investigation ever conducted worldwide.

Did you expect the Car Wash case to reach the scale it eventually did when you first got involved?
Swiss banks are required to file Suspicious Activity Reports with the Office of the Attorney General whenever they detect accounts involving potentially illicit funds. As the Car Wash case gained momentum in Brazil and received increasing media attention, the number of such reports submitted by Swiss banks rose significantly. After the first year, the thought had already emerged: "This is a major case." Yet it continued to expand. In total, there were close to 500 suspicious activity reports linked to Car Wash. Eventually, the volume became so great that a thorough assessment of every report was no longer feasible, due to insufficient resources.

What surprised you most about the Car Wash operation? Was it the scale of the corruption, the amount of money involved, the profile of the key actors, the duration of the investigation, or even the sheer number of suspicious activity reports—considering that 500 reports is an exceptionally high figure?
All of the aspects you mentioned were striking, but what surprised me most was the level of sophistication of the system. It was highly structured and well-organised. What stood out was the fact that bribes occurred at every level—not just among top executives, but throughout the entire chain. They bribed those responsible for awarding contracts, but corruption extended far beyond that. In the cases I had worked on before, bribes were usually limited to high-level decision-makers. In Car Wash, however, the systemic nature of the corruption, reaching all levels, was unprecedented in my experience.

Do you believe that the Car Wash operation succeeded in disrupting the long-standing equilibrium between corruption and impunity in Brazil?
I believe it did. As mentioned earlier in reference to the Alstom case, there was solid evidence by the time I arrived in Brazil. Yet, for reasons that remain unclear, no criminal proceedings were initiated. I am not certain why. My impression was that the Brazilian prosecutor in charge genuinely wanted to pursue the case, but something—or someone—prevented him from doing what he was supposed to do. So, when Car Wash began, I was initially concerned that the same thing might happen again. But then I met the Car Wash team, and I was truly impressed by their energy and determination. The spirit of that prosecutorial team in Brazil was extraordinary. And I deeply appreciated that, because I share the same passion for fighting corruption—I put my whole self into it. And I could feel that my Brazilian colleagues were doing the same.

In my view, legislative **reforms** and the legal tools available to combat corruption are essential, but they are not sufficient on their own. The effectiveness of such frameworks ultimately depends on the individuals responsible for implementing them—particularly prosecutors. I have visited many countries where comprehensive legal reforms were introduced, yet no meaningful change occurred, simply because the right people were not in place to enforce the laws. In Brazil, however, both elements came together: there was a strengthened legal framework, and there were professionals genuinely committed to fighting corruption.

Could you highlight the main similarities and differences difference between the Alstom Case and the Car Wash operation?
The prosecutors did not seem to share the same sense of purpose or determination to move the investigation forward. In the Alstom case, I had the impression that some prosecutors may have been more hesitant—perhaps due to political pressure or internal dynamics within their own institutions. What struck me most was a noticeable difference in the overall spirit of anti-corruption efforts. There was a different mindset at every level of the investigative teams, including among judges. In contrast, the Car Wash team operated with a high level of professionalism and commitment.

In your opinion, did the Mani Pulite[136] Operation in Italy share any similarities with the Car Wash Case in Brazil?
Yes. I read some of judge Moro's[137] rulings, and I noticed that he referred the Mani Pulite several times. In my view, the key difference—and what ultimately made Car Wash so successful—was the decision by Judge Moro and the prosecutors to make as much information public as was legally permissible, rather than keeping it confidential. In contrast, the lack of transparency in Mani Pulite ultimately undermined the investigation. The investigating judge in Italy retained much of the knowledge himself, and when he was no longer involved, that information was lost, as others working on the case did not share the same level of insight or overview. I would say the most important aspect of Car Wash was precisely this openness. Once key details of the investigation became public, a response was observed from Swiss banks, particularly through the filing of Suspicious Activity Reports. It was thanks to this public exposure that proceedings were initiated in Switzerland. The more information was shared publicly, the broader the case became, as additional banks and investigative teams were able to act on the published material from Brazil. This transparency played a central role in the success of Car Wash—unlike what occurred with Mani Pulite.

When I look at what has happened in Brazil over the past two or three years, I cannot help but think of Mani Pulite. Back then, powerful individuals who came under pressure eventually fought back. And now, I see something very similar unfolding in Brazil—powerful actors pushing back. How this will end, I do not know. We'll have to wait and see.

How do you assess the role of international legal cooperation in the fight against corruption? More specifically, how would you evaluate the effectiveness of the cooperation frameworks between Brazilian and Swiss prosecutorial authorities in the context of the Car Wash case?
In the context of international cooperation, I believe it is important to distinguish between the exchange of evidence and the exchange of information. In my view, international investigations are only truly effective when there is a relatively free flow of information. That means, for instance, that if I come across something relevant, I can pick up the phone and call my colleagues in Brazil to share what I have found. This type of communication constitutes information, not evidence—and in Switzerland, it is entirely legal. Legislation explicitly permits what is referred to as "spontaneous information", allowing it to be shared without a formal request. In practice, communication was not limited to phone calls; messaging platforms such as Telegram were also used to exchange information. From my perspective, this was entirely within the bounds of the law. Now, the controversy surrounding Car Wash in Brazil is something I find difficult to fully understand. Perhaps it stems from differences in how the role of the investigating judge is defined in Brazil compared to Switzerland. In our legal system, the judge who oversees the investigation is not permitted to preside over the trial itself. It may be that the structure of the Brazilian system contributed to how the issue has been perceived or treated.

Switzerland froze assets in connection with the Car Wash case. Would you say this followed standard procedures, or was the process expedited compared to other similar cases?
When banks detect accounts that seem suspicious, they're required to freeze them and report the case to the Money Laundering Reporting Office, or MROS, which is part of the Federal Police. If the suspicion

looks justified, the report is then sent to the Office of the Attorney General or to a cantonal prosecutor, who decides whether the freeze should be maintained. In the Car Wash case, a decision was taken at a very early stage to keep the assets frozen, leaving it to the account holders to initiate court proceedings if they wished to challenge the measure. Many did—almost all of them, in fact—some more than once. Yet none succeeded, as the evidence presented was sufficiently robust to persuade the courts. Nonetheless, these repeated legal challenges required substantial effort, with considerable resources devoted to ensuring that the asset freezes were upheld.

In your opinion, what were the main positive and negative aspects of the Car Wash case?
The negative aspect, as I mentioned earlier, has already been addressed. As for the positive aspect, I would highlight the people involved in the case. They were highly qualified professionals; driven by a remarkable spirit I had not encountered in other investigations. They worked as a true team, demonstrating strong cohesion and excellent organisation throughout the process.

Would you like to share any final thoughts or reflections on your involvement in the Car Wash investigation?
During my time at the Office of the Attorney General in Switzerland, Car Wash was by far the most significant case I had the opportunity to work on. I have a true passion for investigation—it is something I genuinely enjoy. Finding colleagues who shared that same commitment was particularly meaningful for me. I learned a great deal from my Brazilian counterparts, and I believe important progress were made together. It was truly a valuable experience in managing a case of such magnitude. There was indeed a meaningful exchange of information, within the limits of what was legally and practically possible, between investigators in Brazil and in Switzerland, as well as with some US prosecutors. I believe this level of cooperation was truly unique. Had I remained in the Public Prosecutor's Office, I am certain I would never have encountered another a case like this. For me, it was an extremely successful investigation. That is why I feel somewhat frustrated with the current developments in Brazil. I am frustrated to see people I deeply

admired—individuals who did an outstanding job—being so harshly criticised, with the media often portraying them in an unfairly negative light. In many ways, I find this hard to accept. So yes, I feel both frustrated and saddened. I also believe it is a lost opportunity for Brazil—not only to combat corruption, but more importantly, to address the deeper issue of impunity. I fear that things are now on a downward trajectory, and I sincerely hope this changes soon. It must not be forgotten that Operation Car Wash served as a powerful example for many young Brazilian prosecutors in their fight against impunity, and also inspired prosecutorial efforts across other Latin American countries. When I look at the current developments in Brazil, I see a turning point—unfortunately, in the wrong direction, and that deeply saddens me. I know other prosecutors across Latin America who are disheartened by what they currently see happening in Brazil. It undermines their hope of successfully combating impunity in their own countries.

Stefan Lenz was born near Bern, Switzerland. He is a lawyer and was a federal public prosecutor in the General Office of the Attorney General of Switzerland. His testimony was given on 1 July 2021 via the virtual platform Zoom and lasted 43 minutes of recording. The text was reviewed by the interviewee on 31 January 2023.

Conclusion to Chapter 1

Chapter 1, "The Car Wash and the Prosecutor's Office", offers an incisive and comprehensive examination of the prosecutorial dimension of Operation Car Wash, the most significant anti-corruption investigation in Brazil's history. By drawing exclusively on interviews with prosecutors, this chapter provides a rich repository of first-hand accounts that illuminate the strategies, challenges, and institutional dynamics underpinning the operation. The narratives presented here transcend the abstract domain of legal processes, offering critical insights into their application in one of the most politically and economically complex environments in the world: corruption.

The chapter underscores the central role of the Federal Public Prosecutor's Office in orchestrating and advancing the Car Wash investigation. Through the testimonies of key prosecutors, it becomes evident that innovative legal instruments such as plea bargains and leniency agreements were pivotal in unravelling deeply entrenched corruption networks. Meticulously deployed, these mechanisms, not only incentivised cooperation among implicated individuals but also triggered a cascading effect, allowing the investigation to expand across various sectors and jurisdictions. The evolution and refinement of these tools during Car Wash not only redefined Brazil's approach to anti-corruption law but also set new benchmarks for prosecutorial practice.

The collaborative nature of the operation emerges as a recurring theme throughout the chapter. The interviewees emphasise the strategic use of interdisciplinary task forces, which brought together prosecutors, law enforcement agencies, and international partners. This innovative investigative model allowed for a holistic approach to tackling corruption, integrating financial intelligence, forensic expertise, and legal acumen. Furthermore, the chapter highlights the indispensable role of international cooperation, particularly with jurisdictions such as Switzerland and the United States, whose financial oversight systems were instrumental in tracing illicit capital flows and dismantling global corruption networks.

However, the chapter is not confined to an uncritical celebration of Car Wash's accomplishments. It adopts a reflective and nuanced tone, addressing the ethical, procedural, and institutional dilemmas confronted by prosecutors throughout the operation. These include the tension between safeguarding due process and ensuring the efficacy of investigations, as well as navigating the backlash from political actors and entrenched institutional resistance. Such candid reflections underline the precarious and often contested nature of deploying legal mechanisms to challenge systemic corruption within a politically fraught context.

A further dimension explored in the chapter is the relationship between the investigation and public perception. The prosecutors reflect on the strategic use of transparency and public communication to foster trust and legitimacy. While such openness strengthened public confidence in the investigation, it also subjected the operation to heightened scrutiny, with accusations of overreach and politicisation. This duality underscores the intricate interplay between legal processes and public opinion, a theme of considerable relevance to contemporary discussions on accountability and governance.

From an academic perspective, this chapter offers a profound case study in the exercise of prosecutorial power within a democratic framework. It invites critical engagement with questions concerning the boundaries of legal authority, the judiciary's role in addressing systemic corruption, and the broader implications of employing innovative legal instruments in politically charged investigations. The interviews underscore the operational complexities of large-scale anti-corruption efforts, particularly the trade-offs between efficiency, transparency, and procedural fairness.

The historical context provided in the chapter further enriches its academic value. The interviewees draw explicit connections between Car Wash and earlier investigations, such as the Banestado case, illustrating how institutional memory and past experiences shaped the methodologies employed in this landmark operation. This continuity underscores the importance of institutional capacity-building and the incremental evolution of anti-corruption frameworks in Brazil.

In conclusion, Chapter 1 transcends its function as a mere documentation of Car Wash's prosecutorial core; it constitutes a critical reflection on the role of law in confronting systemic corruption. The prosecutors' testimonies offer a rare and invaluable window into the ethical, institutional, and political intricacies of such a monumental undertaking. For scholars, practitioners, and policymakers, this chapter is an indispensable resource for understanding how legal institutions can navigate the complexities of entrenched corruption and function as agents of accountability. By situating Car Wash within a broader historical and institutional context, it contributes to a deeper understanding of the interplay between legal innovation, institutional resilience, and the pursuit of justice in Brazil and beyond.

Notes

1. The CC5 Accounts were created in 1969, by Circular Letter 5, from the Central Bank of Brazil. These "special accounts" were held in Brazil by Brazilians living abroad. The aim was to allow the holder to deposit money in national currency when in Brazilian territory and, upon returning abroad, could withdraw the money in foreign currency. Later, other people, besides Brazilians living abroad, could use the CC5 accounts, as long as they were identified. This facilitated the sending of foreign exchange abroad through a system that became known as "rented belly." Given the large amount of resources that left the country, the government decided, from 1996, to limit cash deposits in CC5 accounts to 10 thousand reais. In 2005, after the *Banestado* scandal, the government further restricted the use of CC5.
2. Banestado is a well-known corruption scandal, from the 1990s, involving illegal remittances of foreign exchange abroad, through the Brazilian public financial system.
3. Fernando Henrique Cardoso. ***Entry***. FGV CPDOC. He is a sociologist, professor, writer, and Brazilian politician. He was the 34th President of the Federative Republic of Brazil (1995–2003). He is president of the Fernando Henrique Cardoso Foundation and honorary president of the Brazilian Social Democracy Party. http://www.fgv.br/cpdoc/acervo/dicionarios/verbete-biografico/cardoso-fernando-henrique.
4. Marcela Moraes Peixoto, a prosecutor in the Federal Public Prosecutor's Office, was appointed Chief Prosecutor of the Republic in Paraná in 2003.
5. Nazareno Jorgel Wolff, a prosecutor in the Federal Public Prosecutor's Office.
6. Geraldo Brindeiro was a lawyer, jurist, and member of the Federal Public Prosecutor's Office and Prosecutor General, from 1995 to 2003.
7. Alberto Youssef is a Brazilian black-market currency dealer, well known after the corruption scandal at Banestado. He was arrested in 2014 as part of Operation Car Wash.

8. Deltan Martinazzo Dallagnol was a federal prosecutor and coordinator of the task force of the Public Ministry of Operation Car Wash in Curitiba.
9. Orlando Martello Júnior is a Prosecutor of the Republic of the Federal Public Prosecutor's Office and was part of the task force of Operation Car Wash in Curitiba.
10. Januário Paludo is a Prosecutor of the Federal Public Prosecutor's Office and was part of the task force of Operation Car Wash in Curitiba.
11. He is a Ph.D. and a Federal Police officer. He worked on the Banestado operation and led the initial investigations of Car Wash.
12. Érica Marena is a Federal Police officer, known for her work in Operation Car Wash. She also worked in the division of repression of financial crimes and in the division of combating corruption and embezzlement of public funds. She headed the Department of Asset Recovery and International Legal Cooperation.
13. Luciana Flores de Lima is a Federal Police officer and Head of the Americas Coordination Office of Interpol.
14. Roberto Leonel de Oliveira Lima is a consultant and instructor in AML (anti-money laundering). He was a tax auditor of the Federal Revenue and President of the Council for Control of Financial Activities.
15. Sergio Fernando Moro Entry. FGV CPDOC. http://www.fgv.br/cpdoc/acervo/dicionarios/verbete-biografico/sergio-fernando-moro. He was a former federal judge and judge of Operation Car Wash in Curitiba. He was a former Minister of Justice and director of Alvarez & Marsal. He is a lawyer and Brazilian politician. He is currently an elected Senator for the state of Paraná.
16. Vladimir Aras is a Prosecutor of the Federal Public Prosecutor's Office; he holds the position of Regional Prosecutor of the Republic in Brasília.

17. Rodrigo Janot Monteiro de Barros is a Brazilian jurist. He was a member of the Federal Public Prosecutor's Office and Attorney General of the Republic from 2013 to 2017.
18. In Brazil, "doleiros"—often translated as black-market currency dealers—operate outside the formal financial system, facilitating unregulated currency exchanges. Frequently involved in money laundering schemes, they play a central role in the concealment and international transfer of illicit funds. During the Car Wash investigations, "doleiros" were intermediaries in the financial structures used to move and disguise proceeds of corruption.
19. Law No. 12.850, of 2 August 2013, which defines criminal organisation and provides for criminal investigation, means of obtaining evidence, related criminal offences, and the procedure criminal. http://www.planalto.gov.br/ccivil_03/_ato2011-2014/2013/lei/l12850.htm.
20. The *Eletronuclear* case, an offshoot of Operation Car Wash, exposed corruption in Brazil's nuclear energy sector. Former Rio de Janeiro Governor Sérgio Cabral was implicated for receiving bribes linked to contracts awarded by Eletronuclear, highlighting the operation's reach beyond oil and construction into the energy sector. Cabral was sentenced to nearly 430 years in prison across multiple cases but was released in December 2022 following rulings by the Federal Supreme Court that questioned the legality of certain pre-trial detentions and procedural aspects of his convictions.
21. Sérgio de Oliveira Cabral Santos Filho is a journalist and politician. He was a state congressperson, senator, and governor for the state of Rio de Janeiro. He was arrested by Operation Car Wash for passive corruption, money laundering, and currency evasion. He remains imprisoned in the Bangu 8 pavilion of the Gericinó Penitentiary Complex. He was sentenced to more than 300 years in prison.
22. João Pedro Gebran Neto is a federal judge promoted in 2013 to judge of the Federal Regional Court of the 4th Region, joining the 8th Chamber.

23. Felix Fisher is a Justice of the Superior Court of Justice since 1996, nominated on the shortlist, by his peers in the Public Ministry.
24. Teori Albino Zavascki. ***Entry***. FGV CPDOC. https://www18.fgv.br/CPDOC/acervo/dicionarios/verbete-biografico/teori-albino-zavascki. He was a jurist, professor, magistrate, and Justice of the Superior Court of Justice and Justice of the Federal Supreme Court, from 2012 to 2017. He was the rapporteur of Operation Car Wash until his death.
25. Luiz Edson Fachin. ***Entry***. FGV CPDOC. https://www18.fgv.br/CPDOC/acervo/dicionarios/verbete-biografico/luiz-edson-fachin. He is a Brazilian jurist and Justice of the Federal Supreme Court, since June 2015. He was a lawyer and titular professor of civil law at the Law School of the Federal University of Paraná. He is the current rapporteur of Operation Car Wash in the Supreme Court, replacing Justice Teori Zavascki.
26. Gilmar Ferreira Mendes is a Justice of the Supreme Court, since 2002.
27. Before the Clean Company Act formally introduced plea bargaining into Brazilian law, the Federal Supreme Court had already applied similar agreements in at least two contexts. One was the Mensalão case and the other involved earlier cases related to organised crime and drug trafficking, in which the Supreme Court recognised the validity of cooperation agreements under existing legislation such as the Anti-Money Laundering Law.
28. Mensalão was a corruption scandal, which occurred through the purchase of votes from deputies by the Executive, during the government of Luiz Inácio Lula da Silva, in 2005. This illegal practice was thus known behind the scenes as it referred to a monthly payment made to deputies to vote in favour of projects of interest to the Executive.
29. Antonio Fernando Barros e Silva de Souza is a jurist and lawyer. He was Federal Prosecutor General from 2005 to 2009. When he was in the Prosecutor's Office, he presented the Mensalão complaint.

30. Antonio Palocci Filho is a doctor and politician. He was a member of the Workers' Party. He was Minister of Finance, in the government of President Luiz Inácio Lula da Silva, Chief of Staff in the government of President Dilma Rousseff. He was arrested and convicted in Operation Car Wash.
31. Marcelo Bahia Odebrecht is a Brazilian engineer. He was president of Odebrecht during the Car Wash scandal, having been arrested and convicted, having celebrated a plea bargain agreement for reduction of his prison sentence.
32. Pedro Barusco is an engineer and former service manager of Petrobras, becoming known due to his involvement in the Car Wash scandal. He was arrested in Operation Car Wash and was sentenced to 18 years and four months in open regime, with ankle monitor, in addition to performing community service. He made a plea bargain and, in exchange for a reduced sentence, returned R$ 182 million reais, illicit resources that had been sent abroad.
33. Marcelo Paranhos de Oliveira Miller was a Prosecutor of the Republic in the Federal Prosecutor's Office. He was a member of the Car Wash task force in the Federal Attorney General's Office. He left the Federal Prosecutor's Office to join, as a partner, a large law firm. He was indicted for having assisted in the leniency and plea bargain agreements of the executives of JBS.
34. Sérgio Machado is a Brazilian politician and businessman. He was President of *Transpetro* during the governments of Presidents Lula and Dilma Rousseff. He was involved in the Petrobras scandal, after he left the presidency of *Transpetro* in 2014. In May 2016, he made a plea bargain agreement with the General Prosecutors Office, in which he details his participation in the state-owned company's corruption scheme.
35. José Sarney de Araújo Costa, better known as José Sarney, is a lawyer, writer, and Brazilian politician. In the 1985 presidential election, he is a candidate for Vice-President, on the winning ticket headed by Tancredo Neves. With the death of Tancredo, he assumes the presidency of the country, from 1985 to 1990.

36. José Renan Vasconcelos Calheiros, better known as Renan Calheiros, was the president of the Senate. He is a Brazilian politician affiliated with the MDB and is currently serving his fourth term in the Senate, elected by the state of Alagoas.
37. Romero Jucá is a businessman and Brazilian politician affiliated with the Brazilian Democratic Movement. He was a Senator for the State of Roraima and was leader of the Senate, congressperson Leader of Congress and Minister of State during the government of Michel Temer. He was also Minister of State during the government of Luiz Inácio Lula da Silva.
38. Nestor Cuñat Cerveró is an engineer and was the international director of Petrobras from 2003 to 2008 and financial director of BR Distributor from 2008 to 2014, when he was dismissed because of the investigations of Operation Car Wash. He was convicted in the Car Wash for passive corruption and money laundering.
39. The JBS case refers to a major corruption scandal involving JBS S.A., one of the world's largest meat processing companies. In 2017, executives from JBS, including Joesley and Wesley Batista, entered into a leniency agreement with the Brazilian Federal Public Prosecutor's Office. As part of the deal, they admitted to extensive bribery schemes implicating numerous political figures and agreed to pay a record fine of R$10.3 billion (approximately US$3.2 billion at the time). The case gained national and international attention after Joesley Batista secretly recorded then-President Michel Temer allegedly endorsing payments to silence former House Speaker Eduardo Cunha, who had been imprisoned for corruption. The disclosure of this recording by Brazil's top newspaper, *O Globo*, led to a significant political crisis, investigations against the sitting president, and further scrutiny of Brazil's plea bargaining system.
40. Law No. 12.529, of 30 November 2011, structures the Brazilian System of Defence of Competition, as well as provides about which conducts are infractions to the economic order and their respective penalties.

41. The 5th Chamber of Coordination and Review of the Public Prosecutor's Office (Fight against Corruption) is dedicated to the fight against corruption and acts in cases related to acts of administrative improbity.
42. Valor Econômico, 4 January 2016.
43. City of God is a highly successful Brazilian film, having received four Oscar nominations. The film portrays the growth of organised crime in the City of God favela, one of the most dangerous places in the city of Rio de Janeiro, in the early 1980s.
44. About the 10 Measures against Corruption, see the website https://dezmedidas.mpf.mp.br/apresentacao/conheca-as-medidas.
45. Eduardo Consentino da Cunha Entry. FGV CPDOC. http://www.fgv.br/cpdoc/acervo/dicionarios/verbete-biografico/cunha-eduardo. He is an economist, radio broadcaster, and politician. He was a federal congressperson and president of the Chamber, between 2003 and 2016, when he had his mandate revoked by the Chamber of Deputies for breach of parliamentary decorum, resigning from the position on 7 July 2016. As president of the Chamber, he was the protagonist of the political crisis that ended in the impeachment of Dilma Rousseff. He was investigated in Operation Car Wash and denounced for passive corruption and money laundering by the Federal Attorney General's Office to the Supreme Court and sentenced to 15 years and four months in prison.
46. Jair Messias Bolsonaro **Entry**. FGV CPDOC. Army captain in reserve, he was a federal congressperson for seven terms. He was elected President of Brazil in 2018. http://www.fgv.br/cpdoc/acervo/dicionarios/verbete-biografico/jair-messias-bolsonaroé.
47. Budget Dwarfs was the name given to a group of Brazilian congressmen, involved in frauds in the resources of the Union Budget, in the 80s–90s. They were discovered and investigated in a Parliamentary Inquiry Commission, in 1993. The word "dwarfs" used in this corruption scandal is because these congressmen did not have a great repercussion in the national

territory and were "power dwarfs" within the National Congress itself.

48. The "grasshopper" scheme consists of paying the salaries of several legislative assembly employees into the bank account of just one person, generally the account holder was linked to a congressperson. In the "ghost" scheme, several people are indicated to be included in the government's payroll without providing any service in the state assembly.
49. Banestado is a well-known corruption scandal, from the 1990s, involving illegal remittances of foreign currency abroad, through the Brazilian public financial system.
50. Operation Curaçao began when the Federal Public Prosecutor's Office received information from the authorities of the Netherlands that there were Brazilian clients of the First Curaçao International Bank, closed by the Dutch Central Bank, under suspicion of money laundering in the tax haven of Curaçao.
51. CC5 Accounts were created in 1969, by Circular Letter 5, from the Central Bank of Brazil. These "special accounts" were maintained in Brazil by Brazilians living abroad. The aim was to allow the holder to deposit money in national currency when in Brazilian territory and, upon returning abroad, could withdraw the money in foreign currency. Later, other people, besides Brazilians living abroad, could use the CC5 accounts, if they were identified. This facilitated the sending of foreign currency abroad through a system that became known as "rented belly". Given the large amount of resources that left the country, the government decided, from 1996, to limit cash deposits in CC5 accounts to ten thousand reais. In 2005, after the Banestado scandal, the government further restricted the use of CC5.
52. Law No. 12.850, of 2 August 2013, which defines criminal organisation and provides for criminal investigation, the means of obtaining evidence, related criminal offences, and the criminal procedure. http://www.planalto.gov.br/ccivil_03/_ato2011-2014/2013/lei/l12850.htm.

53. Januário Paludo is a Prosecutor of the Federal Public Prosecutor's Office and was part of the task force of Operation Car Wash in Curitiba.
54. Orlando Martello Junior is a Prosecutor of the Federal Public Prosecutor's Office and was part of the task force of Operation Car Wash in Curitiba.
55. Carlos Fernando dos Santos Lima is retired from the career of the Public Prosecutor's Office. He was part of the task force of Operation Car Wash in Curitiba, as well as the task forces of Operation Banestado and CC5, when he was a Prosecutor of the Federal Public Prosecutor's Office.
56. Roberto Leonel is a Tax Auditor of the Federal Revenue and head of the research and investigation office in the 9th Fiscal Region, in Curitiba.
57. Érica Marena is a Federal Police Chief, known for her work in Operation Car Wash. She also worked in the division of repression of financial crimes and in the division of combat against corruption and diversion of public funds. She headed the department of Asset Recovery and International Legal Cooperation.
58. Rodrigo Janot was the Attorney General at the time.
59. Vladimir Aras is a Prosecutor of the Federal Public Office, serving in the position of Regional Prosecutor of the Republic in Brasília.
60. Andrey Borges de Mendonça is a Prosecutor of the Federal Public Office and was part of the task force of the Car Wash operation in Curitiba.
61. Diogo Castor de Mattos is a Prosecutor of the Republic of the Federal Public Prosecutor's Office and was part of the task force of the Car Wash operation in Curitiba, being the youngest member of the Car Wash task force.
62. The name Boi Barrica refers to a folkloric group of boi-bumbá from Maranhão, whose godparents are the Sarney family. The Boi Barrica Operation later became known as Operation Faktor, due to complaints from the folkloric group. It is a Federal Police operation that investigated Fernando Sarney, suspected of off-the-books campaign financing in the campaign of Roseana Sarney, for the dispute of the government of Maranhão in 2006.

63. The Operation Sand Castle (Castelo de Areia) was a Federal Police operation in 2009 that investigated crimes of corruption and money laundering, involving the construction company Camargo Corrêa. Many consider that this operation was the precursor of the Car Wash Operation because it dealt with a case of corruption involving well-known politicians in the Brazilian scene and construction companies.
64. The Operation Flood ("Operação Dilúvio") was a Federal Police operation that in 2006 investigated, in eight Brazilian states and in the United States, cases of tax evasion, currency evasion, ideological falsehood, among other crimes. The frauds occurred, in general, with the participation of a businessman in Paraguay, who registered dozens of companies to use them to circumvent tax legislation and "shield" the real importer of the goods.
65. The Operation Satiagraha was a Federal Police operation to combat the diversion of public funds, resulting from corruption and money laundering, initiated in 2004 and which resulted, later, in 2008, in the arrest of politicians, businessmen, black-market currency dealers, bank directors, and investors.
66. Paulo Roberto Costa is an engineer and was a career employee of Petrobras, being appointed to the position of director of Supply, between 2004 and 2012, during the government of Luiz Inácio Lula da Silva. He became known due to his involvement in the corruption scheme of the Car Wash operation. He was sentenced to 12 years of house arrest with an ankle monitor, due to his plea bargain.
67. Paulo Roberto Costa returned 26.9 million dollars, as part of his plea bargain. Hudson Corrêa. In agreement Paulo Roberto Costa commits to return millions of dollars. Época, 30th September 2014. https://epoca.oglobo.globo.com/tempo/noticia/2014/09/paulo-roberto-costa-mantinha-bu-28-milhoes-nas-ilhas-caymanb.html.
68. Teori Albino Zavascki Entry. FGV CPDOC. http://www.fgv.br/cpdoc/acervo/dicionarios/verbete-biografico/teori-albino-zavascki. He was a Justice of the Superior Court of Justice (and of the Federal Supreme Court), having been chosen by draw as the

rapporteur of the Car Wash operation in the Supreme Court, examining cases involving people with privileged jurisdiction, approving plea bargains and leniency agreements. He approved the plea bargain agreement of the seventy-seven executives of Odebrecht. He died on 19 January 2017 in a plane crash, in the region of Paraty, Rio de Janeiro.

69. The Brazilian Federal Constitution (Articles 53 and 102, particularly) assigns competence to some specific courts to prosecute and judge occupants of political and functional positions. Today, the privileged forum covers almost 60 thousand occupants of 40 types of different positions in the spheres of federal, state, and municipal government and in the three powers: Executive, Legislative and Judiciary.
70. Sergio Fernando Moro Entry. FGV CPDOC. http://www.fgv.br/cpdoc/acervo/dicionarios/verbete-biografico/sergio-fernando-moro. He was a former federal judge and judge of the Car Wash operation in Curitiba. He was former Minister of Justice and director of Alvarez & Marsal. He is a lawyer and Brazilian politician. He is currently an elected Senator for the state of Paraná.
71. On 17 March 2017, the 1st phase of the Car Wash operation, four black-market currency dealers were arrested: Nelma Kodama, Raul Srour, Alberto Youssef and Carlos Habib Chater. Federal Prosecutor's Office website, Know the timeline. http://www.mpf.mp.br/grandes-casos/lava-jato/linha-do-tempo.
72. Nelma Mitsue Penasso Kodama worked with a black-market currency dealers in the Car Wash operation, having been arrested while trying to board for Milan, Italy, with 200 thousand euros hidden in her underwear. Renato Onofre, Lava Jato: Black-market currency dealers caught with money in her underwear is convicted. O Globo. 22nd October 2014. https://oglobo.globo.com/brasil/lava-jato-doleira-flagrada-com-dinheiro-na-calcinha-condenada-14327667
73. Pedro da Silva Corrêa de Oliveira Andrade Entry. FGV CPDOC. http://www.fgv.br/cpdoc/acervo/dicionarios/verbete-biografico/pedro-da-silva-correia-de-oliveira-andrade-neto. He is a medical

doctor and politician affiliated with the Progressistas Party. In 2006, his mandate was revoked by the plenary of the Chamber of Deputies, due to his involvement in the Mensalão scandal. In 2013, he was sentenced by the Supreme Court to 9 years and five months in prison and a fine of over 1 million reais in the Mensalão trial.

74. Brazilian law and the Supreme Court interpretation have consistently held that a collaborator's statement must be backed by at least one independent piece of evidence (be it documentary proof, intercepted communications, bank-transaction records, or testimony from other witnesses) to sustain a conviction.
75. In every high-profile case arising from Operation Car Wash, plea-bargain testimony opened the inquiry but was always followed by the seizure of documents, expert analyses of financial flows, wiretaps, and paper trails.
76. Imprisonment in the second instance is the possibility of the defendant convicted to a custodial sentence starting the serving of the sentence after the judicial decision rendered in the second instance, even if there are still pending appeals to the higher instances, Superior Court of Justice (and Federal Supreme Court). In February of 2016, the ruled, by seven votes to four, a judgement confirmed by a new decision in October 2015, by six votes to five, that it was possible to imprison the defendant, after a decision rendered in the second instance. The defendants can appeal to the higher courts, but imprisoned. However, in November 2019, the Supreme Court decided by six votes to five that the serving of the prison sentence should only start after all appeals have been judged, before the higher instances, Superior Court of Justice and Federal Supreme Court.
77. BATNA (*Best Alternative to a Negotiated Agreement*) is a concept developed by Roger Fisher and William Ury at the Harvard Negotiation Project. It refers to the best outcome a party can pursue if negotiations fail.
78. Mensalão was a corruption scandal, which occurred through the purchase of votes from deputies by the Executive, during the government of Luiz Inácio Lula da Silva, in 2005. This illegal

practice was thus known behind the scenes as it referred to a monthly payment made to deputies to vote in favour of projects of interest to the Executive.

79. The Anti-Crime Package was amended by Congress and resulted in the enactment of Law No. 13.964, of 24 December 2019 which refines criminal and criminal procedural legislation. http://www.planalto.gov.br/ccivil_03/_ato2019-2022/2019/lei/L13964.htm.
80. Gil Alessi, for the first time, orders the arrest of a convicted congressperson. UOL. 26 June 2013. https://noticias.uol.com.br/politica/ultimas-noticias/2013/06/26/pela-primeira-vez--manda-prender-deputado-condenado.htm.
81. Gary Stanley Becker was an economist and professor at University of Chicago, having received the Nobel Prize in Economics in 1992. In 1968, he published the work Crime and punishment: an economic approach, in the Journal of Political Economy, Vol. 76, No. 2, pp. 169–217. https://webarchiv.ethz.ch/soms/sociology_course/Lecture6/becker1968.pdf, in which he explains, based on economic reasoning, the variables that are previously considered in the decision of illicit practices by individuals.
82. Robert Klitgaard is a professor at Claremont Graduate University and author of the book Controlling corruption, Berkley: University of California Press, 1991 where he describes a formula to explain corruption, as follows: $C = M + D - A$, where C = corruption; M = monopoly; D = discretion and A = accountability.
83. Susan-Rose Ackerman is a law professor at Yale University. She has several published works related to corruption, being considered a reference in the field.
84. Dan Ariely is a psychologist, economist, educator, and university professor. Author of several books and articles that influenced the design of integrity promotion policies in organisations.
85. The Foreign Corrupt Practice Act (FCPA) is the anti-corruption legislation of the United States of America, enacted in 1977. The Unites States was the first country in the world to enact anti-corruption legislation. FCPA, 1977 (15 U.S.C. §§ 78dd-1, et

seq). https://www.justice.gov/sites/default/files/criminal-fraud/legacy/2012/11/14/fcpa-english.pdf. Available in Portuguese https://www.justice.gov/sites/default/files/criminal-fraud/legacy/2012/11/14/fcpa-portuguese.pdf.

86. About the 10 Measures against Corruption, see the website https://dezmedidas.mpf.mp.br/apresentacao/conheca-as-medidas.
87. The Propinoduto was a political scandal that happened in Rio de Janeiro, during the government of Anthony Garotinho and discovered during the government of Benedita da Silva, which involved state revenue inspectors, among them the undersecretary of Tax Administration of Garotinho's administration, Rodrigo Silveirinha, suspected of diverting more than US$ 33 million to accounts in Switzerland.
88. Isidoro Blanco Cordeiro. Bachelor and doctor in law by the University of the Basque Country. Masters in criminology by the Basque Institute of Criminology. Full Professor of Criminal Law at the University of Alicante. He collaborated with the Organisation of the United Nations in the development of model legislation on money laundering. He was a consultant to the Organization of American States on money laundering matters. Curriculum. University of Alicante. https://cvnet.cpd.ua.es/curriculum-breve/es/blanco-cordero-isidoro/9593.
89. Renato de Souza Duque is an engineer and former director of services at Petrobras, between 2003 and 2012. He was arrested in March 2015 in Operation Car Wash and convicted of corruption crimes.
90. Operation Clean Hands, *Mani Pulite*, was an investigation into corruption cases in Italy, centred in Milan, which involved the Italian political class, political parties, the state oil company (ENI—*Ente Nazionale Idrocarburi*), and large contractors in the overpricing of works and the diversion of public money.
91. Antonio di Pietro was a public prosecutor, having been part of Operation Clean Hands, *Mani Pulite*. In 1996, he began his political career in Italy.

92. Law No. 13.869, of 5 September 2019, which provides for crimes of abuse of authority. http://www.planalto.gov.br/ccivil_03/_ato2019-2022/2019/lei/L13869.htm.
93. Cecília Meireles, Cecília Benevides de Carvalho Meireles, was a Brazilian poet, painter, teacher, and journalist.
94. The Regional Prosecutor's Office of the 1st Region covers the judicial sections of the Federal District, Acre, Amapá, Bahia, Goiás, Maranhão, Mato Grosso, Minas Gerais, Pará, Piauí, Rondônia and Tocantins.
95. The Regional Prosecutor's Office of the 3rd Region covers the judicial sections of São Paulo and Mato Grosso do Sul.
96. Banestado is a well-known corruption scandal, from the 1990s, involving illegal remittances of foreign currency abroad, through the Brazilian public financial system.
97. Law No. 12.850, of 2 August 2013, which defines criminal organisation and provides for criminal investigation, the means of obtaining evidence, related criminal offences and criminal procedure. http://www.planalto.gov.br/ccivil_03/_ato2011-2014/2013/lei/l12850.htm.
98. On 27 December 2020, the Second Chamber of the published judgement that annulled a conviction in the case of the Banestado operation, handed down by then judge Sergio Moro. The case that was annulled was that of the black-market currency dealers Paulo Roberto Krug, also a target of Operation Car Wash. Ag. Reg. in the Ordinary Appeal in Habeas Corpus 144.615—Paraná, of 25 August 2020.
99. Deltan Martinazzo Dallagnol was a federal prosecutor and coordinator of the task force of the Federal Prosecutor's Office of Operation Car Wash in Curitiba. He was elected federal congressperson for the state of Paraná (2023–2026) but had his term of office revoked by the Superior Electoral Court in May 2023.
100. Rodrigo Janot Monteiro de Barros is a Brazilian jurist. He was member of the Federal Prosecutor's Office and Attorney General from 2013 to 2017.

101. Carlos Fernando dos Santos Lima is a retired prosecutor of the Federal Prosecutor's Office. He was part of the task force of the Operation Car Wash in Curitiba, as well as the task forces of the *Banestado* and CC5 operations.
102. Januário Paludo is member of the Federal Prosecutor's Office and was part of the task force of the Operation Car Wash in Curitiba.
103. Diogo Castor de Mattos is member of the Federal Prosecutor's Office and was part of the task force of the Operation Car Wash in Curitiba, being the youngest member of the Car Wash task force.
104. Andrey Borges is member of the Federal Prosecutor's Office and was part of the task force of the Operation Car Wash in Curitiba.
105. Paulo Roberto Costa was an engineer and career employee of Petrobras, being appointed to the position of Director of Supply, between 2004 and 2012, during the government of Luiz Inácio Lula da Silva. He became known due to his involvement in the corruption scheme of Operation Car Wash. He was sentenced to 12 years of house arrest with an ankle monitor, because of his plea bargain.
106. Grand corruption is defined as corruption that occurs at the highest levels of government, causing a major negative impact on political, legal, and economic systems.
107. The Federal Prosecutor's Office website related to Operation Car Wash can be accessed at the link.
108. The OECD Convention on Combating Bribery of Foreign Public Officials in International Business Transactions was concluded in Paris on 17 December 1997 and promulgated in Brazil by Decree No. 3.678 of 30 November 2000.
109. The OECD, Organisation for Economic Co-operation and Development, is an international body that brings together the world's largest economies and aims to develop guidelines and standards for public policies, with its Decisions being mandatory for its Member States, unlike its Recommendations and Declarations, which represent the political will of its members.
110. The Brazilian Federal Constitution (Articles 53 and 102 of the Constitution, in particular) assigns jurisdiction to certain

specific courts to prosecute and judge occupants of political and functional positions. Today, privileged jurisdiction covers almost 60,000 occupants of 40 different types of positions in the federal, state, and municipal spheres and in the three branches of government: Executive, Legislative, and Judiciary.

111. Imprisonment after a second-instance conviction refers to the possibility of a defendant sentenced to deprivation of liberty beginning to serve the sentence following a decision by a court of second instance, even if appeals are still pending before higher courts—namely, the Superior Court of Justice and the Federal Supreme Court. In February 2016, the Federal Supreme Court ruled, by a vote of seven to four (a decision reaffirmed in October 2016 by six votes to five), that imprisonment was permissible after a second-instance conviction. Defendants retained the right to appeal to higher courts but would do so while in custody. However, in November 2019, the Court reversed this position, ruling by six votes to five that imprisonment could only begin once all appeals had been exhausted before the higher courts—the Superior Court of Justice and the Federal Supreme Court.
112. Operation Monte Carlo, carried out by the Federal Police, aimed to dismantle the exploitation of slot machines and gambling in the state of Goiás. Federal Police recordings show that information about the progress of this operation was passed on to then Senator Demóstenes Torres.
113. Demóstenes Torres Lázaro Xavier Torres is a Brazilian politician and a lawyer. He was a Senator from 2003 to 2012, when he was expelled by the Federal Senate for breach of parliamentary decorum. He is a retired prosecutor of justice from the Public Ministry of the state of Goiás.
114. The Federal Regional Court of the 4th Region comprises the judicial sections of Rio Grande do Sul, Paraná, and Santa Catarina.
115. Gary Stanley Becker was an economist and professor at the University of Chicago, having received the Nobel Prize in Economics in 1992. In 1968, he published the work crime and

punishment: an economic approach, in the *Journal of Political Economy*, Vol. 76, No. 2, pp. 169–217, in which he explains, based on economic reasoning, the variables that are previously considered to the decision of illicit practices by individuals.

116. Alberto Kenya Fujimori was president of Peru, for almost a decade. He was convicted of human rights violations, corruption, and bribery with the maximum sentence in the country of 25 years, since in Peru the sentences are not cumulative, remaining the longest sentence.
117. Vladimiro Ilich Lenin Montesinos Torres was a politician and former Peruvian military man. In fact, he was head of the National Intelligence Service of Peru and special advisor to then President Alberto Fujimori. He was sentenced to 25 years in prison for violation of human rights, corruption, payment of bribes, arms trafficking, illicit enrichment, and kidnappings.
118. Pedro Gonzalo Chávarry Vallejos is a Peruvian lawyer. He was Attorney General and Chief Prosecutor of the Superior Council of Prosecutors of the Peruvian Public Ministry until his dismissal by the National Council of Justice in February 2021, due to alleged contacts with the criminal organisation "Los Cuellos Blancos", apparently linked to Keiko Fujimori, as well as, in view of his actions against the Prosecutors in charge of the investigation of the Car Wash Case in Peru, which involves Keiko Fujimori, daughter of Alberto Fujimori.
119. Tomás Aladino Gálvez Villegas was the Prosecutor of the Supreme Prosecutor's Office but was dismissed from office. Currently, he is a lawyer and university professor.
120. Ollanta Moisés Humala Tasso is a Peruvian politician, leader of the *Peruvian Nationalist Party*, of the left. He was president of Peru, defeating Keiko Fujimori, daughter of former President Alberto Fujimori, in the elections.
121. Keiko Sofía Fujimori Higuchi is a business administrator and politician, daughter of former President Alberto Fujimori. She was the spokesperson for Fujimorism, which is a right-wing populist movement. She is part of the Party *Fuerza Popular*. She

was arrested in the Car Wash Operation Peru, accused of money laundering and obstruction of justice.

122. Pedro Pablo Kuczynski Godard, known by the abbreviation PPK, is a centre-right economist and politician. He was Prime Minister of Peru and President of the Country, defeating Keiko Fujimori. He resigned from the presidency, after the opening of impeachment proceedings, due to allegations of receiving bribes for his consulting companies from Odebrecht.
123. Susana Villarán is a centre-left Peruvian politician, former candidate for the presidency of the country. In the 2010 municipal elections, she became the first woman to be elected mayor of Lima. She was accused of money laundering in a case linked to the Odebrecht corruption scandal in Peru.
124. Los Cuellos Blancos del Puerto is a criminal organisation formed by three corruption networks. The first network was composed of judges and court officials. The second by lawyers and businessmen. And the third, by appellate judges and former members of the defunct National Council of the Judiciary.
125. The Lava Juez case was an investigation that revealed in detail the deep corruption at the highest levels of the justice system in Peru, shaking the nation and forcing a process of substantial reforms that exist to this day. This investigation took place parallel and convergent with an older investigation and one of the largest corruption cases in the history of Peru: The Car Wash. The discovery of the Lava Juez case carried out by the *IDL-Reporteros*, facilitated the advancement of the Peruvian Car Wash by substantially weakening the corrupt judicial cover-up mechanism intended to exonerate those involved in corruption cases.
126. Marcelo Bahia Odebrecht is a Brazilian engineer. He was president of Odebrecht during the Car Wash scandal, having been arrested and convicted, having agreed to a plea bargain to reduce his prison sentence.
127. Jorge Henrique Simões Barata was a director of Odebrecht in Peru and the main orchestrator of bribes to the Congress and Executive in that country.

128. Antonio Palocci Filho is a medical doctor and politician. He was a member of the Workers' Party. He was Minister of Finance, in the government of President Luiz Inácio Lula da Silva, Chief of Staff in the government of President Dilma Rousseff. He was arrested and convicted in the Car Wash Operation.
129. Luiz Inácio Lula da Silva is a popular Brazilian politician, affiliated with the Workers' Party. He was president of Brazil from 2003–2006 (first term) and from 2006–2010 (second term). He is the current president of Brazil (2023–2026).
130. Luiz Antonio Mameri, former director of Odebrecht, led the operations of bribe payments through the Structured Operations Sector, in Latin America and in Angola.
131. Fernando Migliaccio da Silva is a former executive of Odebrecht and was convicted of money laundering, with a sentence of imprisonment of 7 years and 6 months, according to the terms stipulated in a plea bargain.
132. Orlando Martello Júnior is a Prosecutor of the Republic of the Federal Public Prosecutor's Office and was part of the task force of the Car Wash operation in Curitiba.
133. The Sandcastle Operation was an operation of the Federal Police that in 2009 investigated crimes of corruption and money laundering, involving the construction company Camargo Corrêa. Many consider that this operation was the precursor of the Car Wash Operation as it dealt with a corruption case involving well-known politicians in the Brazilian scene and construction companies.
134. Brazilian federal prosecutors and authorities in France and Switzerland investigated Alstom for alleged payments of bribes to win contracts for metro equipment between 1995 and 2003 in the state of Sao Paulo.
135. Paulo Roberto Costa is an engineer and a career employee of Petrobras. He was appointed Director of Supply from 2004 to 2012, during the administration of Luiz Inácio Lula da Silva. He became widely known for his involvement in the corruption scheme uncovered by the Car Wash operation. He was sentenced

to 12 years of house arrest with an electronic ankle monitor as part of a plea bargain agreement.

136. Operation Clean Hands (*Mani Pulite*) was a far-reaching political corruption investigation conducted in Italy, primarily based in Milan. It unveiled systemic collusion involving the Italian political establishment, major political parties, the state-owned oil conglomerate ENI (*Ente Nazionale Idrocarburi*), and prominent construction firms, exposing a widespread scheme of inflated public contracts and large-scale misappropriation of public funds.

137. **Sergio Fernando Moro. Entry. FGV CPDOC.** http://www.fgv.br/cpdoc/acervo/dicionarios/verbete-biografico/sergio-fernando-moro. He is a former federal judge and presiding judge in the Operation Car Wash (*Lava Jato*) case in Curitiba. He also served as Minister of Justice and was a director at Alvarez & Marsal. Moro is a Brazilian lawyer and politician. He is currently a Senator elected for the state of Paraná.

2

The Car Wash and the Criminal Lawyers

Introduction to Chapter 2

The second chapter of this narrative sheds light on the perspectives of criminal lawyers entrusted with the defence of individuals and companies implicated in the Car Wash investigations and subsequent legal proceedings. It unfolds as a compelling exploration of the multifaceted role of criminal lawyers within the intricate realm of the Car Wash operations, the nation's most significant corruption investigations.

Looking into the experiences, challenges, and strategic manoeuvres employed by these legal experts as they navigate the intricate terrain of representing clients caught up in the most significant corruption investigation in the country. As the Car Wash investigations involve a complex web of allegations and legal intricacies, the testimonies of these criminal lawyers provide an important window into the multifaceted aspects of their roles, offering readers a deeper understanding of the challenges faced within this high-stakes legal landscape.

In this chapter, the testimonies of distinguished criminal lawyers, representing clients—companies and individuals—accused of corruption in the Car Wash, take centre stage. These accounts provide invaluable insights into the complexities and challenges confronted by the

L. M. Costa, *Brazil's Biggest Corruption Scandal*, Crime Prevention and Security Management, https://doi.org/10.1007/978-3-031-99078-6_2

defence. The legal experts who have shared their experiences include Alberto Zacharias Toron, Alexandre Knopfholz, Antonio Carlos de Almeida Castro (Kakay), Antônio Sérgio Altieri de Moraes Pitombo, and Pierpaolo Bottini.

Alberto Zacharias Toron, a highly skilled criminal lawyer, brings a wealth of experience to the table. Renowned for his legal acumen, his testimony offers a robust defence for his clients and a unique perspective on the intricacies of representing individuals entangled in the Car Wash corruption investigations.

Distinguished criminal lawyer Alexandre Knopfholz, alongside the late and esteemed jurist and Professor Rene Dotti, served as legal counsel for Petrobras—a role that entailed the responsibility of representing the company as a victim of corruption. In this capacity, they defended Petrobras against individuals implicated in corrupt acts during the Car Wash investigation. Alexandre Knopfholz, in particular, has earned recognition for his adept handling of the legal complexities associated with white-collar crimes.

Antonio Carlos de Almeida Castro, affectionately known as Kakay, is a prominent figure in the field of criminal defence within the Brazilian legal landscape. Widely respected for his legal prowess and unwavering commitment to defending constitutional prerogatives, he has been a steadfast advocate for upholding the rule of law, safeguarding individual liberties, and ensuring a fair and impartial judicial process. His testimony provides invaluable insights into the defence strategies employed during the Car Wash investigations.

Antônio Sérgio Altieri de Moraes Pitombo, a notable criminal lawyer, has demonstrated a keen understanding of complex legal matters. His testimony explores the challenges and nuances involved in defending clients entangled in the complexities of the Car Wash investigation.

Pierpaolo Bottini, a seasoned criminal lawyer, adds an important perspective to the chapter through his testimony, shedding light on the defence strategies and legal considerations that shaped the course of the Car Wash investigations.

In this chapter, you will explore each lawyer's testimony, gaining deeper insights into their roles, challenges faced, and contributions to the intricate legal landscape of defending high-profile individuals and large companies in the Car Wash corruption investigations. As the legal tapestry of the Car Wash investigations weaves together a myriad of allegations and intricate legal nuances, the testimonies of these criminal lawyers serve as a necessary window, providing a nuanced perspective on the intricate demands and high-stakes challenges they face.

Testimony of Alberto Zacharias Toron

Abstract

In this testimony, prominent Brazilian criminal lawyer Alberto Zacharias Toron reflects on his intellectual, academic, and professional trajectory, and offers a critical assessment of the legal and political dimensions of Operation Car Wash. Drawing on his early involvement in São Paulo's student movement, his legal education at Pontifical Catholic University of São Paulo and University of São Paulo, and his extensive experience as a defence attorney in high-profile cases, Toron contextualises his engagement with Car Wash within a broader debate on due process, judicial impartiality, and the rule of law in Brazil.

Toron offers detailed reflections on the procedural shortcomings of Car Wash, particularly the fragmentation of indictments, the abuse of pre-trial detention, and the strategic use of public pressure to coerce confessions. He contrasts these practices with constitutional guarantees, stressing the role of habeas corpus as a safeguard against arbitrary detention and judicial overreach. Toron also highlights the controversial expansion of jurisdiction by former judge Sergio Moro, which later led to key annulments by the Supreme Federal Court. Drawing parallels with Italy's *Mani Pulite* and Brazil's Mensalão case, he argues that Car Wash, despite revealing serious corruption, was ultimately compromised by its politicisation and excesses.

Toron defends the ethical and institutional role of criminal lawyers, pointing to significant habeas corpus decisions that exposed judicial irregularities and resulted in the dismantling of investigations such as Operation Sandcastle and aspects of Car Wash. He underscores the importance of legal defence in upholding democratic principles, even in unpopular or politically sensitive cases. The testimony concludes with a warning against punitive populism and the erosion of due process, calling instead for structural reform, institutional maturity, and public education on the role of legal defence in a democratic society.

Could you describe your educational background and personal trajectory, in order to provide context for your professional perspective?

During my early years, up to middle school, I studied at a Jewish school in São Paulo, located in the Bom Retiro district—a neighbourhood known at the time for its vibrant communities of Jews, Greeks, and Italians. I later attended Rio Branco School, which was considered a traditional institution at the time. Following that, I pursued a degree in Law at the Pontifical Catholic University of São Paulo. Shortly thereafter, I sat the university entrance exam once again and began studying Social Sciences concurrently with Law. At the time, my aspiration was to become a sociologist. I had little interest in continuing with Law, which I found too rigid and overly formal. I was deeply involved in the student movement and, in 1978, served as director of the Pontifical Catholic University of São Paulo's clandestine student union.[1] In my final year of university, I began an internship with Márcio Thomaz Bastos,[2] who was, at the time, the vice-president of the São Paulo chapter of the Brazilian Bar Association, and who would further be elected its president. I remained in his office for five years, gaining valuable practical experience. During that period, I also became actively involved with the São Paulo chapter of the Brazilian Bar Association, contributing to the Department of Studies and Research and participating in the Bar examination process. I eventually became coordinator of the criminal law section of the exam. I became the coordinator of the exam in the criminal part. After completing my undergraduate studies, I enrolled in a master's programme in the philosophy of law at Pontifical Catholic University of São Paulo, where I remained for five or six years, taking a range of courses. During that time, I had the privilege of studying under Tercio Sampaio Ferraz Júnior,[3] a distinguished legal philosopher. His teaching opened up an entirely new intellectual perspective—one that transcended conventional ideological divisions between left and right. It was an intellectually enriching and formative period.

Later, I left Pontifical Catholic University of São Paulo and enrolled at the Faculty of Law of the University of São Paulo, commonly known as "São Francisco" (Saint Francis). At the time, admission for external candidates was highly competitive, but I was accepted into the master's programme. I subsequently completed both my master's and doctoral degrees there, successfully defending my theses in accordance with the faculty's academic standards.

Throughout this period, I was also teaching criminal law at Pontifical Catholic University of São Paulo. In addition, I undertook several short academic courses abroad, including programmes in Salamanca and Toledo, Spain, as well as in Göttingen, Germany. I often say that studying is something to which I am happily condemned for life. Professionally, I lead a very active practice in my criminal law firm, where I currently work alongside twenty-five colleagues, all of whom specialise exclusively in criminal law. That, in broad terms, represents the core of my academic and professional background.

At what point did you first take on a case connected to Operation Car Wash?

The first case I worked on was back in 2014, representing a major businessman, who owned one of the largest assembly companies in the oil sector. The first thing that caught my attention at the outset was how the press appeared to have access to information before the investigative team. News reports on the case were constant, often referring to "leaks". When an attempt was made to request access to the case files from the former judge Moro,[4] and I had a personal audience with him in 2014, he said: "This is not my job, you have to ask the Supreme Court". As a result, I did not get access. At some point, I believe in October, a new phase of the Car Wash Operation was triggered, and several businessmen were arrested. That was the beginning of my involvement in the Car Wash Operation.

How would you characterise your perspective on Operation Car Wash, particularly in the light of its scope, methods, and legal implications?

I initially expected this operation to follow the usual pattern: a beginning, a middle, and an end. However, what unfolded was quite different. It extended far beyond initial expectations, not only in terms of duration but also in the breadth of its reach.

Former judge Moro, for example, came to occupy a position that resembled that of a "national judge." Virtually, any matter with even a remote connection to Petrobras was, often on questionable jurisdictional grounds, assigned to the 13th Federal Court in Curitiba under his authority. This practice was eventually challenged, and jurisprudence began to shift. Courts started to affirm that the mere fact that a plea bargain originated from the Car Wash Operation did not, in itself, justify the automatic competence of that particular court. As a result, a process of decentralisation emerged. Certain cases were transferred to other jurisdictions, including Rio de Janeiro, São Paulo, Brasília, and, if memory serves, even Recife. More recently, this jurisdictional reassessment culminated in the annulment of President Lula's[5] cases, on the grounds that the 13th Federal Court of Curitiba[6] lacked the proper competence to adjudicate them.

In all honesty, I did not anticipate that the operation would continue for such an extended period or that it would ultimately have the level of impact it came to exert.

In the context of anti-corruption efforts, how do you assess the dismantling of Operation Car Wash, particularly given that it was authorised by the very body that had previously taken a different position in the Mensalão case[7]? Would you regard this development as positive or negative?

I addressed the issues surrounding Operation Car Wash in an article published in the *Brazilian Journal of Criminal Sciences* in August 2016, entitled *The Right of Defence in the Car Wash Operation*,[8] in which I offered a critical perspective on how the investigation was conducted. My principal criticism was that, whereas in the Mensalão case the events were consolidated into a single accusation, which allowed for a comprehensive understanding of the facts, in Operation Car Wash the charges were fragmented, either by individual defendant or by company. This procedural choice hindered the ability to grasp the full context and interconnections of the alleged conduct.

Allow me to clarify. At that time, I was representing the businessman Ricardo Pessoa, from the company UTC, which is a matter of public record,[9] who was identified as the leader of the so-called Club of 16.[10] In the beginning, the term "Club" was often used as a euphemism for cartel. It is important to note that no one was charged with being part of a cartel, although there was a lot of talk about one, and Ricardo Pessoa was portrayed as its head. However, the largest companies in the Club were Odebrecht, Andrade Gutierrez, and Camargo Corrêa. These were the true giants, not UTC. UTC was a large company with an estimated workforce of around 35,000 employees. Nevertheless, its size and operational scope were considerably smaller than those of Odebrecht. When Ricardo Pessoa was charged, the allegation was that bribes were arranged with a certain Márcio, from Odebrecht; but Márcio was not indicted. This created a situation in which individuals A, B, and C were all alleged to have participated in the same criminal conduct, yet only A and B were charged, while C was not, and no justification for this disparity was provided. More than a year later, a significant number of Odebrecht executives were eventually indicted. However, at the time of Ricardo Pessoa's indictment, the prosecutorial strategy appeared inconsistent and difficult to comprehend. The selective nature of the charges, combined with the procedural fragmentation of the case, significantly impaired the ability of the defence to respond adequately.

An investigation had begun several months earlier, at either the end of 2013 or the beginning of 2014, and by October, involvement had commenced mid-stream. Individuals were suddenly being taken into custody, and defence lawyers were permitted to communicate with their clients only via an intercom system. Once the indictment was issued, the defence was granted only ten days to respond. This timeframe was clearly insufficient and, in practice, severely compromised the right to a full and proper defence.

Even though it is fair to say the Car Wash Operation had its own particularities when compared to the Mensalão case, the fragmentation made it very hard to grasp the full picture. Accessing the full body of evidence also proved to be extremely difficult. The very definition of the jurisdiction of the judge of the 13th Federal Criminal Court was obscured within a complex web of legal proceedings to which timely access was not available. In fact, it was Federal Judge Fabiana Alves Rodrigues,[11] her master's dissertation at the Faculty of Social Sciences at the University of São Paulo, she later demonstrated not only how Sergio Moro's broad jurisdiction had been artificially constructed, but also the significant political connections underlying the operation. These connections ultimately contributed to his appointment as Minister of Justice. It was, in my view, a deeply regrettable development.

How do you assess the use of pre-trial detention in the context of Operation Car Wash?

Prior to 2011, Brazil operated under what was commonly referred to as the prison–freedom binary. There was no intermediate solution: a defendant either faced legal proceedings while in custody or remained at liberty. However, beginning in 2011, reforms to the Brazilian Code of Criminal Procedure introduced alternative precautionary measures to imprisonment. These reforms provided judges with a broader set of tools to monitor individuals under investigation or prosecution without the need for pre-trial detention. For instance, they could impose an ankle monitor, forbid contact with witnesses or co-defendants, or require the person to remain at home, among other things.

Despite the availability of alternative measures, Operation Car Wash was marked by what I view as the abusive and indiscriminate use of both forms of pre-trial detention, namely temporary and preventive custody. To illustrate this, in the case of Ricardo Pessoa, one employee of UTC was arrested and spent ten days in jail. He was not charged, nor was he formally accused of any crime. Why, then, resort to such measures? The objective appeared to be to compel confessions. In practice, detention was used as an instrument of pressure. And this pressure was not limited to incarceration. Assets were frozen, names were widely publicised in the media, and a broader strategy of suffocation was employed to encourage cooperation with the authorities.

The Public Prosecutor's Office now asserts that the majority of confessions in Operation Car Wash were made while individuals were not in custody. While this is factually accurate, it does not capture the full picture. In many cases, individuals were only released after they had begun to confess. What emerged was a discernible pattern: arrest, followed by confession, subsequent release, and finally, the formalisation of a plea agreement.

Pre-trial detention, in principle, ought to be an exceptional measure, applied with restraint and only when strictly necessary. In practice, however, it continues to be employed far too frequently. Moreover, it is evident that many judges adopt an overly punitive approach when assessing whether such detention is warranted.

You have become widely associated with the use of habeas corpus, with *Época* magazine[12] even referring to you as the "King of Habeas Corpus." Several of your petitions have become leading cases, both in the *Castelo de Areia* (Sandcastle) Operation[13] and in Operation Car Wash. How do you view this association and its significance within your legal practice?

In fact, there were two habeas corpus petitions filed in connection with the Sandcastle Operation. The one I submitted was on behalf of Kurt Paul Pickel,[14] a man I remember with great affection. He was portrayed as a black-market currency dealers, but he was a Swiss economist who had even a spoken at the Central Bank of Brazil. The other *habeas corpus* was filed by my dear friend and great lawyer Celso Vilardi.[15] So, there were two petitions, and together they led to the dismantling of the Sandcastle Operation—which many see as the forerunner of the Car Wash Operation, since it also dealt with contractors, bribery, etc.

In the Sandcastle case, the judge[16] at the time, now a magistrate, made a big mistake: he took invasive measures based on an anonymous tip-off. The *habeas corpus* was granted by the 6th Chamber of the Superior Court of Justice[17]. The Superior Court of Justice, in a well-reasoned judgement delivered by Justice Maria Thereza de Assis Moura,[18] granted the order saying: "This is absurd, illegality does not comply with the rule of law".[19] There was an extraordinary appeal to the Supreme Court and Justice Luís Roberto Barroso[20] denied it. A decision absolutely covered by legality. In Operation Car Wash, I filed *Habeas Corpus* N. 127.186, the first *habeas corpus* that was granted, with the aim of revoking the pre-trial detention of Ricardo Pessoa, and, by extension, other businessmen were released.[21]

The granting of habeas corpus in the case of Aldemir Bendine[22] has been described by some as the first major setback for Operation Car Wash. As the lawyer involved in that case, how would you describe your experience and perspective on its legal and broader implications?

I am not certain that it constituted a major blow to Operation Car Wash. That is not how I view it. The media framed it in that way, and the narrative took hold. Perhaps the revocation of the pre-trial detention was more significant. However, when viewed from a legal standpoint, the decision represented a routine occurrence in judicial proceedings: the annulment of a trial due to a clear and identifiable breach of due process. In this particular case, the procedural violation was especially evident.

The argument presented was that the reasoning applied by the judge, which involved interrogating cooperating defendants before those who had been implicated by them, should also be extended to the order of final submissions. That is, the informants should submit their memorials first, followed by the others. But the former judge Moro completely ignored that. As journalist Elio Gaspari observed it, "Moro believed he had the authority to act as he did, but the reckoning came later."[23]

An appeal was submitted to the Regional Federal Court of the 4th Region, but it was unsuccessful. A subsequent appeal to the Superior Court of Justice also failed. The case was then brought before the Federal Supreme Court, where Justice Edson Fachin summarily denied the habeas corpus request. Following this, an appeal was lodged, and the matter proceeded to virtual judgement by the 2nd Chamber of the Federal Supreme Court. Justice Gilmar Mendes[24] requested that the case be given special attention, which led to its transfer to an in-person session.

Although it was a regimental appeal, I was granted the opportunity to present oral arguments. The court granted the habeas corpus by a majority of three votes to one, affirming that the defendant who had been informed upon should have the right to submit their final arguments after the cooperating defendant.[25]

This matter, today, is provided by law. The Anti-Crime Package, Law No. 13.964, of 24 December 2019, inserted paragraph 10-A in article 4 of the Organised Crime Law, which states: "At all stages of the process, the defendant who was informed upon must be guaranteed the opportunity to speak after the deadline given to the defendant who informed."[26]

Would you consider this decision to have represented a significant setback for Operation Car Wash?

I would not characterise Habeas Corpus No. 157.627 as a major blow to Operation Car Wash. It was significant in the specific context of the proceedings involving Bendine, but nothing beyond that. In my view, it was simply a procedural ruling within a criminal case. The true significance of the decision did not lie in the recognition that the cooperating defendant should submit final arguments first, but rather in the affirmation of habeas corpus as a legitimate mechanism for reviewing the legality of criminal proceedings and upholding due process. In my view, this decision exposed the arbitrariness of the former judge Moro. The Regional Federal Court did not dispute that the informed party had the right to speak last. However, it held that this was a procedural matter that should be addressed through an appeal, rather than by means of habeas corpus. The Fifth Chamber of the Superior Court of Justice adopted the same position, and Justice Fachin[27] likewise stated: "Habeas corpus is not the appropriate means to deal with this issue." The Second Chamber of the Federal Supreme Court, on the other hand, the court concluded: "The use of habeas corpus in this matter is both admissible and procedurally appropriate." In fact, this issue forms the central theme of my book *Habeas Corpus and the Control of Due Process Law*,[28] now heading into its fourth edition. In a democratic society, wrongdoing must be punished, whether it involves rape, corruption, or other serious offences. However, judicial arbitrariness cannot be accepted under any circumstances. It is essential to have mechanisms in place to safeguard due process. In my view, that is the fundamental issue raised by Operation Car Wash.

From a legal, political, or economic perspective, what changes do you believe are necessary to more effectively combat corruption? Would stronger punitive measures be part of the solution?

Allow me to take a brief detour in order to respond. What follows is more of a reflection than a direct answer. In 1985, the general part of Brazil's Criminal Code was reformed. It was a markedly liberal reform.

Under the new provisions, individuals could move from a closed to a semi-open regime after serving just one-sixth of their sentence. This created a structural imbalance. Consider the example of robbery followed by homicide, a crime that typically carries a sentence of fifteen years. In such cases, the offender has either killed in order to steal or committed theft and subsequently murdered to avoid identification. Under the 1940 Criminal Code, such an individual would have served nearly the entire sentence in custody. After the 1985 reform, however, the punitive framework changed substantially. Imagine someone breaking into a home, robbing a family, and killing all its members to eliminate witnesses. If sentenced to eighteen years, they might serve only three. This constitutes a disproportionately lenient punishment for an offence of such gravity.

Subsequently, Brazil experienced a wave of kidnappings for ransom—legally classified as extortion by means of kidnapping, although commonly referred to by the press simply as kidnapping. This surge in violent crime created a perceived need to strengthen the criminal justice system. In response, the Heinous Crimes Law (Law No. 8.072 of 25 July 1990[29]) was enacted. It sought to counter the prevailing perception that "the police arrest, and the judge releases." Under the new law, judges were no longer permitted to grant provisional release in cases involving heinous crimes, such as aggravated homicide, rape, or other offences deemed equally serious, including drug trafficking.

This was followed by a wave of kidnappings for ransom, legally classified as extortion by means of kidnapping, although commonly referred to by the press simply as kidnapping. This context generated a perceived need to strengthen the criminal justice system. In response, the Heinous Crimes Law (Law No. 8.072 of 25 July 1990) was enacted. Its objective was to counter the widespread perception that "the police arrest, and the judge releases." The law prohibited judges from granting provisional release in cases classified as heinous crimes, such as aggravated homicide, rape, and other offences considered of equivalent gravity, including drug trafficking. Judges were no longer permitted to authorise release, but the sentences themselves were still considered too lenient. As a result, penalties were increased, and the law established that sentences would have to be served in full under a closed regime. The underlying rationale was that by making the criminal, procedural, and penal enforcement frameworks more severe, crime rates would decline. However, while kidnapping rates have decreased in recent years, this was not the case at the time of the law's enactment, and the reduction cannot be attributed directly to the legislation.

Individuals engaged in offences such as robbery or drug trafficking are typically not concerned with whether the sentence is three, five, or ten years, nor with whether it will be served in a closed or semi-open regime. What tends to influence their decision-making is the likelihood of being apprehended. That is the critical factor.

This brings us back to an observation made as early as the late nineteenth and early twentieth centuries,[30] and reiterated more recently by the Spanish jurist Muñoz Conde[31]: "criminal law is an important tool of social control, but it is not very effective on its own. It only works when supported by other aspects of society."

What does this mean in practical terms? If a child is born in a favela without a stable family structure to instil values, and lacks access to a school environment capable of reinforcing them, the severity of the criminal justice system becomes largely irrelevant. It will have little to no deterrent effect. This, in essence, is the core of the issue. What, then, can be done? Is legislative reform sufficient? The answer is no. As long as state-owned enterprises exist in combination with politically motivated appointments to public office, often made with the expectation of personal or political return, conditions that foster corruption will continue to prevail. The moment privatisation occurs, a significant avenue for bribery is removed. This argument is often contested by left-wing parties, particularly those aligned with statist economic models, but it reflects an institutional reality that cannot be ignored. If the intention is to confront corruption meaningfully, then it is essential to reform the underlying structures that facilitate it.

Gary Becker[32] developed an economic theory suggesting that individuals engaged in criminal conduct make rational decisions based on a cost–benefit analysis. A central premise is that offenders weigh the likelihood of being caught against the potential gains. For example, a person may choose to park illegally if the financial

penalty is minimal and the probability of enforcement is low, particularly when the cost of missing a high-stakes meeting is significantly greater.

Applying this logic to a context such as Operation Car Wash: if the perceived risk of detection is low, the legal consequences are limited, and the recovery of illicit funds is unlikely, then the rational choice might be to pay a bribe, secure the contract, and accept the marginal risk. How do you respond to this line of reasoning? Do you find it convincing in explaining corrupt behaviour.

I would disagree with the broader application of that logic. It may hold true in more trivial contexts, such as traffic violations. I have, for instance, used a bus lane myself in order to avoid missing an important meeting. In that context, paying a fine of one hundred dollars was preferable to facing the consequences of being late. In such cases, the logic of a cost and benefit calculation is understandable.

However, when considering corruption—particularly forms that entail potential imprisonment and public humiliation, including the social impact on one's family, such as children being subjected to stigma at school—the situation is entirely different. And such circumstances occurred frequently. These are not factors individuals typically account for in a calculated decision-making process. More often, the immediate concern is: "If I want to do business here, I have no choice." One frequently cited example was: "If I do not pay off the Petrobras agent, I am out." The more appropriate question to ask is: "How can a businessperson participate in the market without engaging in corruption?" In truth, I do not believe most businesspeople are inclined to pay bribes. They do so because without doing so, they are excluded from opportunities. This reflects a different rationale altogether. I heard this sentiment expressed repeatedly by the businesspeople I spoke with. As they often put it: "If I did not pay, they'd find a way not to pay me for the work I'd already done." Many described feeling almost compelled to cooperate in order to sustain their operations.

I recall my father, a Jewish immigrant, often saying: "If everyone else evades and I comply, what is the problem? The problem is that my competitor will be able to offer lower prices, and I will be pushed out of the market." That, ultimately, is the core issue. If the systemic conditions remain unaddressed, individual ethical conduct becomes marginal. People are not generally engaging in detailed calculations about whether they might be arrested, publicly humiliated, or have their assets frozen.

The sanctions are in place and that is one of the lessons of the Car Wash Operation. However, corruption in other sectors persisted despite these measures which is a source of considerable frustration.

The asset recovery achieved during the Car Wash Operation was substantial, not only in terms of the recovery of stolen funds but also due to the scale of the amounts involved. How would you assess the effectiveness and impact of these recovery efforts?

I have some reservations regarding the accuracy of the asset valuations, yet I acknowledge the importance of asset recovery for the national economy. I consider this to be a significant and necessary undertaking, about which I have no doubt.

How would you characterise the parallels and divergences between the Clean Hands Operation (Mani Pulite)[33] in Italy and Operation Car Wash in Brazil, particularly in terms of their legal strategies, institutional impacts, and sociopolitical consequences?

The late Ada Pellegrini Grinover[34]—of Italian descent and daughter of a minister who served under Mussolini, once observed that the Clean Hands Operation was colloquially known as the "Easy Handcuffs" operation—a characterisation she found equally applicable to Operation Car Wash[35] as well. Sergio Moro has a text, which was written before the Car Wash Operation, in which he praises the methods of the Clean Hands Operation.[36] In my opinion, he tried to replicate this method during Car Wash, including the use of the media. There are parallels to be drawn, but I think the most striking one is that Italy, at the end of the Clean Hands, ended up with Berlusconi,[37] and Brazil, at the end of Car Wash, got Bolsonaro.[38] And, funnily enough, both names start with "BI" would contend that Berlusconi exhibits a greater degree of political decorum than Bolsonaro; however, that is a separate matter warranting its own discussion.

Are there any positive aspects or achievements of Operation Car Wash that you would highlight?

Indeed, I believe Operation Car Wash succeeded in exposing a deeply entrenched corruption network within the public sector, which was imperative to bring into the public eye. Whether this exposure will lead to a definitive end to such practices remains uncertain; however, the operation undeniably disrupted the established system in a profound and meaningful way, and that in itself was a significant achievement.

However, I would draw a parallel with the *Mensalão* scandal. That case resulted in the conviction of numerous individuals, yet no one was subjected to pre-trial detention. What distinguishes the two cases is essentially the pace of proceedings. I believe that former judge Moro could have attained similarly positive outcomes without resorting to such heavy-handed measures. Although the process might have been lengthier, it is likely that the same results could have been achieved with greater legitimacy. By adopting a more aggressive approach, I believe he ultimately undermined his own position. This was evident, for instance, in the illegal disclosure of the wiretapped conversation between Dilma[39] and Lula, which effectively accelerated Dilma's impeachment process. Furthermore, the public release of Palocci's plea bargain[40] immediately prior to the first round of the election caused significant damage to the Workers' Party candidate. These actions culminated in his subsequent appointment as Minister of Justice in Bolsonaro's administration. Such developments raise clear concerns regarding impartiality, concerns that have been acknowledged by the Supreme Court.[41] Additional serious issues emerged, notably the politicisation of the operation with the apparent objective of toppling the government. In my view, this is wholly unacceptable. The evident political bias, resulting in the downfall of a democratically elected government and followed by Moro's alignment with the opposition's administration, is profoundly troubling.

Operation Car Wash is well regarded by public opinion—perhaps because, finally, rich and powerful people were arrested. That is the favourable view public opinion tend to have of it. Given this perception, have you, as a criminal lawyer, come to be disliked for defending powerful individuals accused in Car Wash cases?

That is an interesting question. When I acted as counsel for Judge Nicolau, it was the most significant case in the country—it dominated public attention at the time. Nowadays, scandals seem to emerge constantly, with one breaking on Monday, another on Thursday, and perhaps a third by Sunday. Consequently, there is a continual succession of cases, each quickly overshadowing or overlapping the previous one.

Back in 2000, things were different. Boris Casoy[42] was talking on the news about the Regional Labour Court—169 million reais embezzled—and suddenly, my face was on screen. At law school, training on how to engage with the media is limited. On one occasion, a journalist came to conduct an interview. While discussing various topics, including amenities, there were moments of laughter, which the cameraman recorded. During the interview, I responded to the journalist's questions with a serious demeanour. Later, a news segment aired featuring Boris discussing the embezzlement of 169 million reais and the public services that could have been financed with those funds, such as nurseries, hospitals, and schools. However, the footage showed me laughing in the background, creating a misleading impression that I was dismissive of the issue. This portrayal adversely affected public perception of the role of legal defence.

At that time, I encountered unusual reactions in everyday places such as bakeries and supermarkets, similar to how an actor portraying a villain in a soap opera might be unable to separate the character from the individual. Later, during the *Mensalão* case, I continued to receive occasional curious or disapproving looks. Some people in my social circle were generally anti-Worker's Party, but I also had friends in business who were being arrested. The atmosphere was highly ambiguous. I recall one quiet Sunday morning near Ibirapuera, where I reside, when I was out for a walk or possibly buying bread—I cannot recall precisely. Suddenly, someone shouted "Thief!" Startled, I looked around and inquired, "What is happening?" The individual responded sharply, "It is you! A lawyer who defends a thief is himself a thief." He then rode away on his bicycle and disappeared. I chose not to respond.

To me, the fundamental essence of the legal profession lies in the willingness to undertake unpopular causes. Reflecting historically, consider the defence of Captain Alfred Dreyfus in France at the close of the nineteenth century, a period marked by intense anti-Semitism. Dreyfus was accused of betraying military secrets to the enemy, specifically Germany or more precisely the Austro-Hungarian Empire. It was extremely serious. In the end, he was acquitted, and it was proven that evidence had been forged. But it took a long struggle to get there, and his defence lawyer faced moral lynching. That, to me, is the real face of the legal profession.

Another case is the Base School ("Escola de Base").[43] Imagine being falsely accused of "messing with children"—an accusation of extraordinary gravity. To act as counsel for such individuals, who were ultimately proven innocent, poses profound challenges. This situation raises a fundamental question: what is the social function of the lawyer? It is to provide a robust defence. Society must comprehend—and be educated to comprehend—that for justice to be served, the prosecution must prosecute, the judge must adjudicate, and the defence must be both vigorous and sincere. Absent this balance, a fair trial cannot be ensured.

But I must say, in many of the accusations, he was innocent. That is another matter, of course, but the point stands: it is my job. And people need to understand that, just as I respect those who bring the accusations. Take the case of João de Deus, whom I also represented. Friends would ask: "How can you defend someone like that?" However, I must emphasise that, in many of the allegations, he was innocent. That is a separate issue, of course, but the central point remains: it is my professional duty. People need to understand this, just as I respect those who bring the accusations.

As this testimony draws to a close, would you wish to offer any final reflections or concluding remarks?

I would like to thank you for the opportunity to contribute to this discussion. I hope that our conversation has been of some value and relevance to your work.

Alberto Zacharias Toron was born in São Paulo (SP). Criminal lawyer. Master and Doctor in law. Author of several books and articles. His testimony was given on 17 August 2020 via the Zoom virtual platform and lasted 54 minutes of recording. The text was subsequently reviewed by the interviewee on 3 May 2021.

Testimony of ALEXANDRE KNOPFHOLZ

Abstract

Alexandre Knoppholz provides an insightful testimony on his extensive experience working at the law firm of Professor René Dotti, which represented Petrobras during Operation Car Wash, the largest and most complex anti-corruption investigations in Brazil's history. Knoppholz reflects on how the investigation exposed systemic corruption deeply embedded within Petrobras and its extensive ramifications across Brazil's political, economic, and legal systems.

He contextualises the inception of the investigation within a broader sociopolitical environment marked by public discontent and the introduction of new legal frameworks such as the Clean Company Act, which facilitated leniency agreements and plea bargaining. The testimony underscores the firm's efforts, led by the late Professor René Dotti, who accepted Petrobras' defence out of a strong sense of national duty, despite more lucrative offers from other clients implicated in the scandal. Knoppholz highlights the unique challenges faced by Petrobras' legal defence team, tasked with overturning public misconceptions of the company's complicity and instead asserting its position as a victim of orchestrated criminal conduct perpetrated by corrupt individuals exploiting the company's structure.

The testimony details the extensive litigation experience accumulated by Knoppholz, including hundreds of hearings and petitions, which culminated in Petrobras being formally recognised as an assistant to the Public Prosecutor's Office, enabling the company to actively participate in prosecutions and seek reparations. He provides critical insight into the plea bargaining and leniency mechanisms' pivotal roles in recovering billions of reais, despite acknowledging the inherent difficulties posed by the involvement of multiple government entities and the magnitude of financial losses.

Knoppholz also addresses significant procedural issues such as jurisdictional controversies, the controversial use of pre-trial detention, and the implications of recent judicial rulings affecting the criminal justice process in Brazil. He offers a nuanced discussion on the role of prescription in corruption cases and underscores the critical importance of compliance programmes in preventing corporate wrongdoing, linking their growing adoption to the broader legacy of Operation Car Wash.

Furthermore, Knoppholz evaluates the indispensable role of task forces in modern complex criminal investigations, affirming their necessity in confronting sophisticated financial crimes and dismantling entrenched networks of corruption. He draws comparisons between Operation Car Wash and previous high-profile investigations, notably the Mensalão scandal and Italy's Clean Hands Operation, highlighting procedural differences and the more enduring social and legal impact of Car Wash.

Throughout his testimony, Knoppholz maintains a balanced perspective, acknowledging both the operation's significant achievements in combating impunity and the challenges posed by legal setbacks and political interference. He concludes with a cautiously optimistic outlook, emphasising that despite attempts to undermine or discredit the operation, its tangible legal, economic, and social outcomes represent a watershed moment in Brazil's fight against corruption.

Could you please reflect on your educational background and personal journey, and explain how these experiences have influenced and shaped your professional perspective?

I have been practising law since 2002, having graduated from the Faculty of Law of Curitiba. I pursued specialisation studies at Cândido Mendes University in Rio de Janeiro and completed my master's degree at the Faculty of Law of Curitiba. Since 2004, I have served as a professor at the same faculty. Additionally, I have been affiliated with Professor René Dotti's law office since graduation, beginning as an intern and continuing to the present day as a partner.

What aspects struck you most profoundly when you first began representing Petrobras in the context of Operation Car Wash? Was it the unprecedented scale of the investigation, the vast sums of illicit funds involved, or the high-profile nature of the political figures under scrutiny?

Before addressing your question directly, it is important to clarify how our involvement commenced. Professor René Dotti,[44] who sadly passed away earlier this year, was head of the firm at the time. Owing to his extensive experience, he was invited by Petrobras to represent the company's interests in the Car Wash proceedings, which were still in their nascent stages in 2014. At that time, no one fully anticipated the eventual scope of the investigation. Professor René accepted the invitation—and I emphasise the term deliberately—out of a sense of patriotism. Although he had received other offers from individuals and construction firms implicated in Operation Car Wash, some of which promised higher fees than those offered by Petrobras, he chose to undertake Petrobras's defence from a genuine commitment to national service. He understood that a company of such strategic significance was being unfairly maligned and was suffering substantial financial losses. When we began representing Petrobras—and later Transpetro, which is a separate legal entity—we gradually started to unravel the full extent of what was happening. We were, of course, aware from the outset that the situation was serious and that Petrobras was confronting a challenging period. However, as the months progressed, it became evident that the circumstances were far more severe than initially anticipated. The harm inflicted upon the company was not only extensive but also deeply entrenched.

To address your question more directly, what struck us most profoundly was the realisation that this was not an isolated incident. Rather, it was a systemic problem. Petrobras was not simply confronting a single scandal; it was a corporation being eroded from within.

How would you assess the political, economic, and legal context in Brazil at the inception of Operation Car Wash in 2014? To what extent do you believe the prevailing environment was conducive to, or resistant against, the progression of such a comprehensive investigation?

Believe so. Reflecting on that period—although I may not recall the exact dates—there was, as I remember, a general atmosphere of public unrest and widespread dissatisfaction with those in positions of power.

This prevailing sentiment, I think, served as a catalyst for Operation Car Wash. It appeared to be the result of a convergence of various factors. The year was 2014, shortly after the Clean Company Act had been enacted,[45] which introduced leniency agreements and a new framework for plea bargain agreements. The legal system was already undergoing reforms that enabled investigations of this nature. Concurrently, the political and economic context, coupled with widespread social discontent, created a conducive environment for such an operation to unfold. Nevertheless, it is important to emphasise that the true justification for Operation Car Wash lay in the evidence of criminal activity, much of which was subsequently corroborated through thorough investigations.

Professor René Dotti's firm was engaged in approximately seventy criminal cases associated with Operation Car Wash. To clarify, Petrobras retained us specifically to handle cases in Curitiba and appeals before the Federal Regional Court of the Fourth Region in Porto Alegre, encompassing both first and second-instance proceedings. The Car Wash cases in Rio de Janeiro, São Paulo, and Brasília were managed by a separate legal firm.

Over the course of those six or seven years, we took part in well over 600 hearings and filed more than 500 petitions. It was a Herculean task. And I believe that, through our work, our major contribution—perhaps even our greatest merit—was demonstrating that Petrobras was not a perpetrator, but a victim of these crimes. Legally, Petrobras came to be recognised as such. At the beginning of the Car Wash Operation, the general perception—perhaps due to a lack of understanding—was that Petrobras had been complicit in the corruption scheme. But that simply was not the case. Petrobras was the target of wrongdoing, harmed by poor managers and unscrupulous businesspeople who exploited its structure for criminal purposes. In this context, Petrobras asserted its role as a victim and was formally qualified as an assistant to the Public Prosecutor's Office. It became an active party in the proceedings, calling for the conviction of those responsible and, most importantly, seeking the reparation of damages.

What is your evaluation of the plea-bargaining mechanism within the Brazilian legal system? To what extent do you consider it to have

been an effective instrument in furthering the aims of Operation Car Wash?

A final criminal conviction operates as a judicial enforcement instrument, analogous to a cheque, which can be utilised in civil court proceedings. Thanks to leniency agreements and plea bargains,[46] Petrobras has recovered over three billion reais. From the company's perspective, the plea-bargaining mechanism has proven to be an indispensable tool.

Although it was not possible to recover the full extent of the losses—given the magnitude of the damage and the structural limitations of the system, even after the 2013 legal reforms—the mechanism did facilitate the return of a substantial portion of the diverted fund.

Could you please provide an estimate of the financial impact regarding asset recovery? While approximately three billion reais have been successfully recovered, the total value of the losses sustained was considerably greater, is that correct?

Assessing the total damage to the company is highly complex. This complexity arises from the technical nature of crimes such as money laundering and corruption, which do not always produce a direct financial loss that can be easily quantified by the victim—in this instance, Petrobras. The question then arises: by what methods do judges determine the extent of such losses? Broadly speaking, the contracts were subject to overpricing in the range of two to three per cent, with these excess funds being diverted to various political parties. Consequently, the courts have based their calculations on the difference between the amounts Petrobras actually paid and the amounts it should have paid, effectively focusing on the inflated sums. While I would need to verify the precise figures to ensure complete accuracy, my understanding is that Petrobras currently estimates its quantifiable loss to be approximately six to seven billion reais. Of this amount, around three billion reais have been recovered to date, representing just under half of the total. The prevailing expectation is that a greater proportion will be recovered in due course, largely owing to the existence of final convictions. Although three billion reais constitutes a substantial sum, it remains relatively modest when compared to the full extent of the damage incurred. The process is now progressing to a phase where focus shifts to the amounts linked to these final convictions, with a significant portion of additional funds still pending recovery through ongoing judicial proceedings.

In your view, to what extent were the leniency agreements effective? Did they contribute positively to the defence of Petrobras? Additionally, what were the primary challenges encountered during their implementation?

Leniency agreements follow a logic quite like plea bargains. They also emerged in 2013, with the enactment of the Clean Company Act, and form part of the same broader legal framework. It became common for the Federal Public Prosecutor's Office to put together a sort of "package," combining the individual's plea deal with the company's leniency agreement.

Now, what is the main difficulty when it comes to leniency agreements, particularly in this context? Unlike plea bargain agreements, which basically involve just two parties—the accused and the Public Prosecutor's Office, followed by the judge's approval—leniency agreements bring in additional players: the Federal Court of Accounts, the Office of the Comptroller General, and the Federal Union itself. Consequently, the involvement of multiple stakeholders renders the negotiation and finalisation of leniency agreements inherently more complex.

It is also important to reiterate that Petrobras is formally acknowledged as a victim in both plea bargain and leniency agreements. A portion of the sums paid by collaborators or lenient companies is allocated to Petrobras, while the remainder is directed to the Union and other public entities identified as having incurred losses as a result of corruption.

To respond directly, leniency agreements played a significant role within the broader asset recovery process for Petrobras. The principal challenge lay in the multiplicity of entities involved, which complicated and prolonged the completion of these agreements.

What are the implications of the recent change whereby a conviction in the second instance no longer results in imprisonment, particularly regarding the fight against corruption in Brazil?

In the case of defending Petrobras, within the context of Operation Car Wash, this discussion was not relevant. The main objective was the recovery of losses. The debate around the provisional execution of the sentence—that is, whether someone should start serving their sentence after a conviction in the second instance—is tied to the issue of deprivation of liberty, of imprisonment. Under the current legal framework, a defendant may be convicted at the second instance yet remain free pending the exhaustion of all appeals until the sentence becomes final. However, in the context of enforcing judgements for the purpose of recovering damages, specifically when the victim, in this case Petrobras, seeks to execute the sentence in civil court, the sentence must be final irrespective of the criminal enforcement status. Therefore, from the standpoint of asset recovery for the company, whether the convicted individual commences serving their sentence following a second-instance conviction is largely immaterial.

From the perspective of criminal enforcement, this change holds greater significance. I believe that the Federal Supreme Court's revised interpretation, which now mandates a final judgement before an individual may commence serving their sentence, has the potential to foster a perception of impunity both among the general public and, perhaps more troublingly, among the accused themselves. Nevertheless, it is important to acknowledge that there are well-founded legal arguments supporting the Court's current position, despite the broader implications that give rise to concern.

The statute of limitations is an important legal concept in Brazilian law, but in several corruption cases, it appears to have facilitated impunity. In the specific context of Operation Car Wash, how do you assess the role and impact of the statute of limitations?

The principle of the statute of limitations has, in many respects, been weakened in Brazil. Historically, in criminal law and criminal procedure, it held considerable influence, with numerous cases being dismissed solely due to the expiration of the legally prescribed time period. Indeed, the 1990s are often referred to as the decade of the statute of limitations. This context motivated the enactment of laws establishing special courts designed to expedite judicial proceedings.

Nowadays, it is increasingly uncommon for cases to be dismissed solely due to judicial delays. In the context of Operation Car Wash, for example, there were very few instances in which the statute of limitations was applied. This is largely because the crimes involved carried severe penalties; they were serious criminal offences often committed continuously or repeatedly. To be candid, I cannot immediately recall any cases at first instance or even on appeal to the Regional Court of the Fourth Region in which the statute of limitations was recognised. Therefore, at both the first- and second-instance levels, the statute of limitations did not have a significant impact on the overall outcome of the operation.

What can trigger the statute of limitations, however, is when the Federal Supreme Court recognises a procedural nullity, effectively invalidating all legal acts performed up to that point. This situation can give rise to a genuine risk of the statute of limitations expiring, as the entire case must be restarted from the beginning.

Many view compliance as a trend in Brazil following Operation Car Wash. Companies without compliance programmes established them, while others improved existing ones, moving beyond mere "compliance for show," where codes of ethics are ignored. In your opinion, is there a genuine commitment to integrity and ethics, or has this concern waned due to recent setbacks in tackling corruption?

I would argue that one of the most significant legacies of Operation Car Wash, despite its various challenges, has been the heightened recognition of the importance of implementing truly effective compliance programmes within companies. From my perspective as a criminal lawyer, there has been a marked increase in companies engaging criminal and administrative law specialists to develop robust compliance frameworks within their organisations. I consider this to be a lasting and positive outcome of the operation. Former judge Sergio Moro even used the term "compliance for show" and emphasised that what Brazil really needed was real compliance—not just a superficial one. He often cited the example of Volkswagen in Germany, which faced a major investigation and scandal. The company responded by putting in place a serious compliance programme. Moro referred to this in his rulings, saying: "Look, we need this kind of serious compliance in our companies." And from a practical standpoint, compliance has become important even for individuals facing criminal charges. It has been observed that when a businessperson commits an offence but has an established compliance programme in place, this factor is often taken into account favourably during sentencing. On the other hand, if it is clear that the company only had a "compliance for show", this can lead to a harsher sentence. The logic behind compliance is that the State acknowledges it does not always have the capacity to dig into the inner workings of every company. Consequently, it distributes part of the responsibility by expecting companies to assume their role. This has become the prevailing approach.

Compliance has emerged as an effective tool, and it is important to acknowledge that Operation Car Wash played a significant role in this development. Although the concept of compliance was introduced with the 2013 Clean Company Act, it was from 2014 onwards, following Car Wash, that integrity programmes began to be adopted more widely, including by medium and small companies.

Is the task force model a critical component in combating corruption? Specifically, what role did it play in the success of Operation Car Wash?

Certainly. Although the term "Republic of Curitiba" is often used to imply that the task force was confined to the city of Curitiba in Paraná, this is not accurate. Numerous task forces participated in Operation Car Wash, each playing a crucial role in the investigation.

In the past, when dealing with more traditional crimes, a simple "Sherlock Holmes" approach—a classic detective-style investigation—was often sufficient. However, with the rise of modern criminality, that approach no longer suffices. Currently, the focus is on crimes perpetrated within companies, frequently lacking a clear individual or identifiable responsible party. The legal entity itself can serve as a kind of shield for impunity. To uncover crimes of the scale we saw in Car Wash, you need a whole new investigative system—more brains working together, new investigative tools, breaches of financial and communication secrecy, telephone intercepts, and so on. Without that, it is nearly impossible to identify these complex crimes.

A task force was necessary—a dedicated team working collaboratively within both the Public Prosecutor's Office and the Federal Police. It is important to note that such arrangements have been standard practice for at least the past fifteen years. I personally worked on cases involving task forces as early as 2009, 2010, and 2011.

Therefore, the task force was not an innovation exclusive to Car Wash. It was an established practice—and, in my opinion, it ought to be a permanent feature. The scale of Car Wash would not have been achievable if the investigation had been conducted by a single prosecutor or an individual federal agent.

With regard to operations preceding Car Wash, such as Banestado[47], which also involved Curitiba along with figures like former judge Sergio Moro and several prosecutors, as well as the Mensalão scandal,[48] do you consider that these cases helped establish a foundation for more effective efforts in addressing impunity among Brazil's wealthy and influential?

Indeed, these operations were instrumental. Specifically, in Operation Banestado, the firm I represent defended some of the accused. Broadly speaking, the success of that operation was significantly attributed to the deployment of task forces. The same applies to the Mensalão case. Therefore, it can be argued that, regarding complex investigations, a point of no return has been reached in Brazil's approach to combating high-level impunity. That is simply the reality of modern criminal law. Unfortunately, throughout history, there is always been the so-called white-collar criminals, something that became widely recognised thanks to Sutherland's[49] work. The long-standing perception that wealthy individuals and business elites often evade criminal accountability began to change well before Operation Car Wash, with task forces playing a significant role in driving this transformation.

Banestado marked an important turning point. I remember once, during an oral argument in Porto Alegre, a rapporteur judge remarked: "I am not dealing with a simple homicide case here, I am dealing with a crime against the national financial system." That illustrates how these kinds of crimes are now being taken seriously treated with the same gravity as more "traditional" crimes like homicide.

Whether that comparison is appropriate or not is a separate debate. What I'd emphasise, though, is that people from wealthier backgrounds are entitled to the same rights and guarantees as any other defendant in the criminal justice system. We shouldn't demonise businesspeople, for example. But, objectively speaking, I do see today that both businessmen and politicians are increasingly becoming the focus of major investigations and criminal proceedings for these types of offences.

During the Mensalão trial, the very defendants involved were simultaneously accepting bribes linked to what would later emerge in Operation Car Wash. This scenario suggests a pervasive sense of impunity; the Mensalão defendants appeared confident that their actions would go unpunished, as evidenced by their continued engagement in the same criminal conduct under scrutiny. In your assessment, to what extent did Operation Car Wash succeed in addressing this culture of impunity, particularly concerning white-collar crime in Brazil?

I believe the explanation lies largely in procedural differences. What was the principal distinction between the Mensalão and Operation Car Wash? In both instances, businesspeople and politicians enjoyed prerogative of jurisdiction, allowing them to be tried directly by the Federal Supreme Court. In the Mensalão case, under the guidance of Justice Joaquim Barbosa,[50] a provision from the Code of Criminal Procedure was used that brought all the defendants—regardless of whether they held prerogative—under the Supreme Court's jurisdiction. So virtually every one of the dozens of defendants in the Mensalão was tried by the Supreme Court, with perhaps one or two exceptions.

Currently, it is understood that, for various reasons, criminal proceedings in the Supreme Court tend to progress at a significantly slower pace. Unfortunately, there exists a prevailing presumption—frequently confirmed in practice—that such cases will result in impunity. When comparing the number of convictions or rulings issued in Operation Car Wash, whether by first-instance judges or Supreme Court justices, the contrast is quite pronounced. In Car Wash, the late Justice Teori Zavascki[51] took a different approach. He decided that only those with prerogative jurisdiction should be tried in the Supreme Court, while the others were to be tried at first instance. That development surprised many observers, as the prevailing expectation was that little action would occur at the lower judicial levels. However, arrests, asset freezes, and other substantive measures were in fact implemented.

In my view, the prevailing sense of impunity following the Mensalão case was largely influenced by the procedural approach adopted by the Federal Supreme Court at that time. In contrast, with Operation Car Wash, progress was made—whether rightly or wrongly is a separate matter—but the undeniable fact remains that concrete actions were taken. That is the key procedural difference: in the Mensalão, there were charges, but virtually no precautionary measures like pre-trial detention. In Car Wash, those measures were indeed applied.

How do you assess the significance of the pre-trial arrests implemented during Operation Car Wash within the broader context of anti-corruption efforts?

I will address this both from the perspective of a professor of criminal procedure and as a legal practitioner involved in Operation Car Wash. Pre-trial detention must be predicated upon specific legal grounds, including the protection of public order, the preservation of the economic order, the safeguarding of the integrity of the investigation, or the assurance of the enforcement of criminal law.

I believe that the arrests made in Car Wash, when they were based on the need to protect the investigation—for example, when there was evidence that the accused was threatening witnesses or destroying documents—or on the risk of flight, were entirely valid and legal. From a procedural standpoint, those were sound decisions.

From an academic standpoint, I harbour significant reservations regarding the use of pre-trial detention justified by the vague notion of the "guarantee of public order." Why? Because no one really knows what "public order" means—it is a vague and indeterminate legal concept. Over time, case law has stretched this notion to include things like public outcry, the credibility of the judiciary, or simply the gravity of the offence. More recently, it is been extended to cover the risk of repeat offences. This vagueness bothers me, particularly when we are dealing with something as serious as taking away someone's liberty. While

I personally harbour doubts about arrests justified exclusively on the grounds of protecting public order, I do not believe that this constituted the principal rationale for the majority of pre-trial detentions in Operation Car Wash.

In general, those detentions were grounded in solid procedural needs—protecting the investigation and ensuring the law could be enforced—and in that regard, I think they were appropriate. Regarding detentions justified on the grounds of public order, I maintain personal reservations from an academic perspective. However, it is important to observe that, even in such cases, the "victim"—if one may refer to the State as such in this context—typically does not adopt a stance either supporting or opposing the arrest.

In your view, how can companies be effectively protected against corruption risks? What measures can be implemented to prevent a recurrence of the issues that affected state-owned and state-controlled enterprises?

If compliance is important for private companies, it is even more so for state-owned and state-controlled companies, as Petrobras. From a personal perspective, I believe that the inherent nature of these companies entails significant public oversight and involvement. The risk of systemic issues will only really start to diminish when these companies become more professional and less politicised. A shift towards a more professional and business-oriented management—rather than one primarily influenced by political interests—may not completely eradicate corruption, as that is unlikely in any context, but it can significantly reduce the risk of these companies being involved in corruption schemes similar to those revealed by Operation Car Wash.

How would you evaluate the strengths and weaknesses of the Car Wash Operation?

On the positive side, I would highlight several points. And here, I am not speaking as a lawyer for Petrobras—whether people like it or not, accept it or not, or choose to criticise it—the fact is that Operation Car Wash was a watershed moment. That fact is unequivocal.

It uncovered a corruption scheme worth billion, systemic and endemic, and not confined to any one political party. There is often talk of it targeting Party X, Y, or Z, but that is simply not true. What has been observed, strictly speaking, was that corruption resulted from an unhealthy relationship between political figures—regardless of their party—and state-controlled companies, managed through political appointments.

Many of the challenges that Operation Car Wash has encountered, including the annulment of convictions, have not stemmed from determinations that no crime was committed or that individuals were wrongfully convicted. Rather, these issues have been procedural in nature, involving questions of jurisdiction, possible judicial bias, or other legal technicalities. At no time has the judiciary declared that "Operation Car Wash failed because criminal conduct did not occur." More recently, either Justice Carmen Lúcia[52] or Justice Gilmar Mendes[53]—though I cannot recall precisely which—expressed a view along the lines of: "I and not asserting that no crime took place, but rather that there exists a legal defect."

In my view, the true merit of Operation Car Wash—something that cannot be taken away from it—is that it marked a turning point in the fight against corruption. Perhaps I am being naïve or unduly optimistic, but I do believe that, in cases such as the one involving Petrobras, individuals will now think two, three, four, or even five times before engaging in similar wrongdoing. The weight of Car Wash's legacy will always have a positive side.

Naturally, errors may have occurred along the way—an inevitable consequence given the scale and complexity of the operation. Nevertheless, if I were to assess the overall balance, I would argue, even as a citizen, that the benefits significantly outweigh the drawbacks. The impact extended beyond the legal realm, producing tangible economic and social gains as well.

One may criticise the conduct of judges, the decisions of the courts, or the actions of prosecutors. Nonetheless, while acknowledging that certain missteps may have occurred, these appear relatively minor when weighed against the significant legal achievements of the operation, as well as its wider societal and economic effects.

That is why I find comparisons between Operation Car Wash and Italy's Mani Pulite (Clean Hands) Operation[54] somewhat regrettable.

Such comparisons can be misleading, as Car Wash had a considerably broader social impact and did not conclude in the same disillusioning manner.

Could you draw a parallel between Operation Car Wash and Italy's Clean Hands (Mani Pulite) operation, highlighting both their similarities and key differences in terms of legal strategy, institutional impact, and long-term outcomes?

Strictly speaking, yes, there are similarities—both operations sought to tackle endemic corruption. In Italy, it was closely linked to the mafia; here, we were dealing with something that could also be described as "mafioso" (mob person) in nature. But I would say the most striking similarity lies in the procedural aspects, in particular the central role of plea bargain agreements. In both cases, these agreements played a key part. There was also the creation of a task force there, although with fewer prosecutors involved than in the Car Wash Operation.

The most significant point of divergence, in my view, lies in the outcome. In Italy, the aftermath of the Clean Hands operation was marked by tragic consequences: one prosecutor was assassinated, another killed in a car bombing, and organised crime—most notably the mafia—continues to exert substantial influence, arguably retaining as much power today as it did at the height of the investigations. In the Brazilian context, I am genuinely persuaded—not merely by conviction, but by observable evidence—that we are on a different trajectory. There is a tangible possibility of a more constructive outcome, and I would argue that the early signs of such progress are already apparent.

Consider, for instance, the setback involving President Lula[55] and potentially other co-defendants. That was a specific judicial development. Yet, it is frequently invoked as though it somehow undermines the entirety of Operation Car Wash—an interpretation I regard as overly reductive. The operation resulted in the conviction of over two hundred individuals, with final judgements rendered, sentences served, and substantial efforts made to recover misappropriated public funds. These are not symbolic gestures; they represent a significant institutional accomplishment. To suggest that Car Wash concluded in a manner analogous to Italy's Mani Pulite is, in my view, misleading. It is methodologically unsound to extrapolate from a procedural outcome in a single case to dismiss the broader impact of a complex, years-long anti-corruption effort. While there may be procedural similarities, I would nonetheless argue—whether out of optimism or perhaps lack of full detachment—that the substantive outcomes diverge in meaningful ways.[56]

Before we conclude, is there any final observation or reflection you would like to share?

I am grateful for the opportunity to participate in this conversation, but I must underscore that the person who truly ought to be here is Professor René Dotti. He was the one originally approached for this interview, and I firmly believe he would have brought far greater depth and insight to the discussion. Professor René was a singular figure—an outstanding and principled jurist, and a true guardian of the rule of law. He stood in defence of those subjected to political persecution, actively opposed the military dictatorship, and consistently represented his clients with integrity, irrespective of their social class, profession, or political beliefs. He embraced the cause of Operation Car Wash with pride and with a deep conviction that it served Brazil's broader interest. I have no doubt that, where he still with us, he would remain steadfast in defending Petrobras' interests, while also upholding the rights and legal guarantees he so vigorously championed.

As for my concluding reflections on Operation Car Wash, I would like to express a sense of cautious optimism. The operation has been idolised, later criticised, and now, in some quarters, there are efforts to consign it to oblivion. I do not share that view. I never believed it ought to be idolised—after all, it was a judicial process, like many others. It encountered legal obstacles, and as Petrobras' legal representatives, we frequently had to appeal adverse decisions. That is the nature of litigation. However, I strongly disagree with those who now declare the operation defunct or portray it as having led to a "scorched-earth" scenario simply because certain proceedings were annulled. Such conclusions, in my view, overlook the broader institutional and societal gains that Operation Car Wash brought to light.

I would like to reiterate that we were involved in approximately seventy criminal proceedings as part of Operation Car Wash, which led to numerous convictions. To claim that the operation ended in failure is a gross oversimplification—it is simply inaccurate. Operation Car Wash continues to produce both legal and social outcomes. Significant amounts of embezzled funds have already been partially recovered from Petrobras, and I am confident that further results—both judicial and societal—will follow. For this reason, I view comparisons with Italy's Mani Pulite (Clean Hands) Operation as somewhat problematic. Operation Car Wash yielded concrete outcomes; it remains impactful and will continue to do so in the years ahead.

Alexandre Knopfholz was born in Curitiba (PR). He is a partner and coordinator of the criminal law department at Professor René Dotti's Office. He is a criminal procedure professor at the Curitiba University Centre. His testimony was given on 26 April 2021 via the Zoom virtual platform, with a total duration of 53 minutes. The transcript was reviewed by the interviewee on 18 January 2023.

Testimony of Antonio Carlos de Almeida Castro (Kakay)

Abstract

This testimony by Antonio Carlos de Almeida Castro, widely known as Kakay, offers a unique and critical perspective on Operation Car Wash, Brazil's most extensive anti-corruption investigation. A seasoned criminal defence lawyer, Kakay traces his personal and professional trajectory—from his formative experiences as a law student during the Brazilian military dictatorship to his long-standing career representing high-profile clients before the country's highest judicial authorities. His testimony offers rare insight into the inner workings of Operation Car Wash from its inception in 2014, particularly through his legal representation of key defendants, such as Alberto Youssef, one of the operation's pivotal figures.

Throughout the interview, Kakay provides a detailed and incisive critique of the investigation's conduct, highlighting the problematic use of pre-trial detention as a coercive tactic, the systemic pressure exerted on defendants to enter into plea bargains, and the active role of the media in shaping public perception and judicial outcomes. He argues that these practices reflected a broader departure from fundamental legal principles, raising serious concerns about violations of due process and the erosion of constitutional safeguards.

Drawing parallels with Italy's Mani Pulite (Clean Hands) investigation, Kakay contends that both operations, despite their ostensible commitment to fighting corruption, became vehicles for political manipulation. In his view, the instrumentalisation of legal processes for political ends undermined the legitimacy of judicial institutions and contributed to a wider crisis of democratic accountability. His testimony further explores the unintended political consequences of Car Wash, suggesting that its trajectory—marked by selective enforcement, legal excesses, and media-driven narratives—helped create the conditions that enabled the rise of Jair Bolsonaro.

By offering a first-hand account of the entanglement between law and politics, Kakay's testimony provides a powerful lens through which to examine legal overreach, institutional fragility, and the contested legacy of Operation Car Wash. It invites broader reflection on the limits of anti-corruption efforts in contexts marked by structural inequality, politicised justice, and fragile democratic norms.

Could you describe your personal and professional background to provide some context?

I come from the interior of Minas Gerais and have always had a strong desire to study law—particularly criminal law, which has been a passion of mine from early on. There were no lawyers in my family, so I knew I would face certain challenges, given that the legal profession in Brazil tends to be quite exclusive. At the time, there was no law school in my hometown, Patos de Minas, so I moved to Brasília and passed the entrance exam for the University of Brasília to study law.

This was still during Brazil's military dictatorship, and Institutional Act Number Five (AI-5)[57] was in force. I became involved in student politics, though never in partisan politics. In order to support myself, I began working at a law firm that practised before Brazil's higher courts. It was a small, recently founded firm, run by two young lawyers—José Eduardo Rangel de Alckmin and Carlos Eduardo Caputo Bastos—who were close friends and played a major role in introducing me to the legal profession.

I started working with them on my very first day at university and remained at the firm for four and a half years, until I graduated. Upon graduation, I became a partner and realised that my true calling was in criminal law. I have now been a criminal defence attorney for nearly 40 years, primarily practising before Brazil's higher courts. Today, I lead a small firm, which allows me to maintain greater control over the cases I accept. Around thirty to forty per cent of my work is pro bono. Out of every fifteen to twenty cases that reach the office, I choose only one to handle personally, so I can dedicate myself fully to it. Over the years, I have represented four Presidents of the Republic, more than ninety state governors, dozens of ministers and senators, and I have participated in several landmark cases—including Declaratory Action of Constitutionality 43, which dealt with the presumption of innocence.[58]

What was the first case you worked on in Operation Car Wash?

I have been involved in Operation Car Wash since its very beginning—17 March 2014—when Alberto Youssef[59] and another money launderer from Brasília were arrested. I was contacted to represent both individuals. I travelled to Curitiba and began working on Youssef's defence.

As I was entering the Federal Police headquarters in Curitiba, my nephew Pedro[60]—who is also a lawyer and a friend of the lead investigator in Car Wash at the time—called me. He told me that his friend had said something to the effect of, "This is going to be a major operation. Kakay just walked into the police building to visit one of the detainees." That was the atmosphere from the outset.

I reached an agreement with Alberto Youssef: I would not handle the case at the trial court level in Curitiba—I would not attend hearings or proceedings—since my firm is small and I could not manage the case logistically. However, once the case reached the higher courts, I would represent him.

What was your relationship with Alberto Youssef like?

I had an interesting relationship with Youssef. Early on, I realised that he was at the centre of an investigation with enormous potential—particularly if he decided to cooperate with the authorities. Of course, I had no idea the case would grow to the scale it eventually did. From a distance, I followed the progress of the investigation and quickly understood that Youssef was going to become a state's witness. While plea bargain agreements are undeniably important tools in the fight against organised crime, I had serious concerns about how his cooperation was being managed.

Why do you believe Youssef's state's witness agreement was being mishandled?

There was a great deal of pressure on Youssef to cooperate. But the foundation of any plea bargain—whether in Brazil or elsewhere—is voluntariness. That principle is fundamental. I simply do not tolerate coercion. I do not work under pressure, and I would not allow the Federal Police, the Public Prosecutor's Office, or the presiding judge to pressure my client into cooperating.

To protect Youssef's rights, I filed a *habeas corpus* petition before the Superior Court of Justice, where I often practice, along with the Supreme Court. The legal argument I advanced at that time could have led to the annulment of the entire Car Wash operation. I had previously succeeded in a similar case—the Sundown Operation, also from Curitiba—in which I managed to annul the entire investigation due to procedural overreach by the same judge and prosecutors involved in Car Wash.

Can you talk about the *habeas corpus* you filed on behalf of Alberto Youssef?

When I filed the *habeas corpus*[61] for Youssef, there was considerable internal panic because the legal theory I had developed was quite strong. To this day, as a citizen, I am actually relieved that the petition did not succeed in nullifying the operation—because Car Wash did, in fact, produce important results for the country. At the time, I was in

Paris—where I have clients—when I received a phone call informing me, upon learning about the *habeas corpus*, the prosecutors had begun pressuring Youssef to withdraw it, suggesting that if he did, negotiations or a plea agreement could move forward. I was outraged. Pressuring a detainee to abandon a *habeas corpus* petition—one that could potentially result in their release—is absolutely unacceptable. I remember going to a café, visibly upset, and writing an angry petition to withdraw the *habeas corpus*. I was not obligated to do it, but I could not, in good conscience, continue if it would harm my client. I withdrew from Youssef's defence and formally withdrew the petition. When I returned to Brazil, I visited Youssef in Curitiba and told him that it was his right to cooperate, but I could not be part of it because I do not work with clients under pressure. However, it is worth asking: "In Brazil, have most state's witnesses been free?" The Public Prosecutor's Office claims so, but that is false. Most of the agreements were made with defendants in prison or because of their imprisonment. Take Odebrecht, for example—seventy-seven people cooperated. Why? Because their boss was imprisoned.

Did you have other clients involved in Operation Car Wash?

I had almost 30 clients in Operation Car Wash. Here's an interesting story: I never attended a hearing with former Judge Sergio Moro, nor with Prosecutor Deltan Dallagnol or any members of the task force. That is not a criticism—none of them personally harmed my clients. In fact, none of my clients were convicted or imprisoned as a result of Car Wash. Not a single one. My experience was very different from that of many of my colleagues who worked in Curitiba, where judge Moro routinely ordered preventive detentions. Most of my cases were handled in the higher courts—either before the Federal Supreme Court, the Superior Court of Justice, or the regional appellate courts.

Could you draw a comparison between Operation *Mani Pulite* (Clean Hands)[62] in Italy and Operation Car Wash?

Operation Clean Hands became a kind of marketing model—just like Car Wash. One of the strategies used by the Federal Police, the Public Prosecutor's Office, and the judge, with the full support of major media outlets, was to present Car Wash as the Brazilian equivalent of Clean Hands, as if the Italian operation had been the greatest anti-corruption effort in the world. From a communications standpoint, it was highly effective—but it was only part of the story. Those who truly understand what happened in Italy know that Clean Hands was deeply flawed. In fact, I would go so far as to say it was a farce. And what we experienced in Brazil, with Car Wash, was in many respects a farce within a farce.

On what basis do you regard Operation Clean Hands as a farce?

In Italy, at least thirty-three people committed suicide because of being wrongly accused. That fact alone is a scandal of enormous proportions. The cornerstone of any legitimate criminal justice system should be the dignity of the human person. What happened during Clean Hands was that certain groups began to realise they could use plea bargain agreements as a way to destroy their rivals. It became a tool of political and institutional warfare. And what was the end result of Operation Clean Hands? It paved the way for Silvio Berlusconi[63] to come to power.

Is there a parallel between Brazil's Operation Car Wash and Italy's Operation Clean Hands?

Indeed, the parallel is unmistakable. In Brazil, Operation Car Wash ultimately contributed to the election of Jair Bolsonaro.[64] Perhaps due to cultural and temperamental differences, Brazil did not experience the same number of suicides as Italy, although there was at least one suicide connected to the methods employed by Car Wash. I was deeply moved when I was invited to speak in southern Brazil about the suicide of a university rector. While the case was not formally part of Car Wash, it reflected the same operational style, especially considering that the federal police commissioner involved had ties to the task force of the Car Wash. In Brazil, Car Wash was used as a tool to dismantle companies and economic sectors, much like what happened in Italy. In Italy, the Mafia even turned itself—because for them, it was a matter of organisational survival. The similarities are striking. At first, people liked to compare the two operations, but once the implications became clearer, they stopped. The comparison eventually became too revealing—and, frankly, embarrassing.

Did you act as defence counsel in the Big Monthly Payment (Mensalão) case before the Supreme Court?

I was represented Duda Mendonça's[65] (or only Duda) lawyer during the Mensalão case, which, at the time, was the largest corruption trial in Brazil. I spent five or six months at the plenary sessions of the Supreme Federal Court. My defence of Duda was entirely technical. In my oral argument, noted that I could have argued that the Mensalão scheme did not exist, but for Duda's case, that question was irrelevant. His defence did not depend on whether the broader allegations were true or not—it was strictly a legal argument. Both Duda and his business partner Zilmar Fernandes da Silveira[66] were acquitted. Nearly everyone else indicted in that case was convicted. Yet, despite the acquittal, Duda remained condemned in the public imagination. I remember him telling me he was moving to Portugal to start a new business because, in Brazil, he would forever be seen as a "mensaleiro"—a corrupt political operative in the Mensalão scheme. That is a serious issue. It reveals a profound disregard for the dignity of the individual. The State has every right—and obligation—to investigate and prosecute alleged crimes. But the sensationalism that began with Mensalão escalated dramatically during Operation Car Wash. And dealing with that level of media spectacle is extremely difficult.[67]

To what extent do you believe media coverage shaped the handling and outcome of the Mensalão case? How, in your opinion, did media coverage affect the course of justice?

The Mensalão trial served, in many ways, as a rehearsal for how the media would later be used during Operation Car Wash. From the very beginning of my career in criminal law, I have been a vocal critic of sensationalism. When TV Justiça was launched in Brazil, I remember telling Justice Marco Aurélio[68]—though he may not recall, I certainly do—that I would oppose the idea. Sensationalism is dangerous because it turns Supreme Court justices into demigods, and vanity can corrupt even the most serious institutions. We are all vein, after all. You put on a black robe, stand in front of the cameras, and suddenly the entire country is watching—how can one not be affected by that? Brazil is the only country I know of where the Supreme Court has its own television channel. In cases involving issues of broad societal relevance—such as same-sex marriage or land demarcation—I do believe public broadcast makes sense. Transparency, in those instances, serves democracy. But in criminal law, we are dealing with facts and with people's lives. The public exposure of criminal proceedings, which began with Mensalão, put enormous pressure on the judiciary and seriously undermined the dignity of defendants. When Car Wash began, I immediately recognised that the same strategy—using media coverage to shape public perception—was being deployed to criminalise politics.

In your view, how did the Mensalão case reflect broader challenges in the intersection between law and politics in Brazil?

I haven't spoken much about this publicly, but when the Mensalão case began, José Dirceu[69] approached me to represent him. He was expected to be the central figure in the trial, and I was already handling several high-profile cases at the time. We had dinner at my home, and I told him, "José, we are good friends, but I think you should choose another lawyer." He looked surprised and asked, "Why, Kakay?" I explained, "This case is going to be politicized. You need a lawyer who is aligned with the centre-right—someone from the Brazilian Social Brazilian Social Democracy Party,[70] someone respected by that political circle." I recommended José Carlos Dias,[71] one of my mentors in criminal law, who was already representing the owner of Banco Rural.[72] I also suggested his nephew, Juca, an excellent attorney. That was the strategy. The so-called *theory of control of the act—teoria do domínio do fato*[73] was invoked to justify convicting José Dirceu and, in effect, , to convict others as well. There were two kinds of people involved in this process: those who did not understand the theory, and those who understood it but used to secure outcomes they deemed necessary—because, in their view, Brazil *needed* those convictions. This formed part of a broader strategy to criminalise politics.

How would you define the strategy of criminalising politics, and how do you believe it has been implemented in Brazil?

The strategy to criminalise politics culminated in the election of Jair Bolsonaro. To challenge this approach from a legal standpoint, I turned to two Brazilian legal scholars living abroad—Alaor Leite[74] and Luís

Greco[75]—and requested a legal opinion on the criminalisation of politics. We submitted that opinion to the Supreme Federal Court during the indictment proceedings against Senator Romero Jucá[76]. He had been accused of corruption involving the Brazilian businessman Jorge Gerdau.[77] The allegation was based on the exchange of technical information between the senator's office and Gerdau's team regarding a specific project. That correspondence was interpreted as evidence of corruption. The e-mails in question dated from October 2014. What I found astonishing was that, around the same period—October and November 2014—the then Prosecutor General of the Republic, Rodrigo Janot,[78] was also exchanging e-mails with Senator Jucá's office, requesting budget allocations for the Public Prosecutor's Office headquarters. Jucá, at the time, was chair of the Budget Committee. In other words, the Prosecutor General was doing exactly what he accused the senator of doing. In my oral argument before the Supreme Court, I said, "Dr. Janot, if you are consistent, you should indict yourself for corruption." Ultimately, the Court did not accept the indictment against Senator Jucá—but by then, the reputational damage had already been done.

The same logic applied during the Mensalão case. The Public Prosecutor's Office recognised the political capital embedded in the anti-corruption narrative—especially with the support of major media outlets. That narrative became its exclusive domain. Whenever I argued in court, saying, "I am not discussing whether my client did or did not commit a crime; I am defending their constitutional right to due process and legal representation," nobody listened.

Constitutional guarantees were systematically ignored, and the ends were seen to justify the means. It took years for the consequences of those abuses to come to light. In defending clients targeted by that strategy, I was frequently accused—by both prosecutors and the press—of being against the fight against corruption. In reality, there was a calculated effort not only to criminalise politics, but also to delegitimize legal defence itself.

Of course, politicians must be investigated. But you cannot have an investigation that lasts three or four years, because that paralyses Congress. That is why I often say: "no judge, prosecutor, or investigator has a greater commitment to fighting corruption than I do—or than any lawyer, law student, or citizen". But the fight must take place within constitutional limits.

To what extent do you believe the legal mechanisms employed in Operation Car Wash were used to advance a political project under the guise of anti-corruption enforcement?

The fight against corruption was—and is—necessary. But in the case of Car Wash, the methods used to pursue that fight revealed a broader political agenda. I wrote about this in an article titled *Que País Queremos?* (What Country Do We Want?).[79] Of course, we all want to battle corruption—I do, you do, everyone does. But how we choose to do so makes all the difference.

At the time, I did not fully grasp the extent of the political project behind the operation, but I could sense its direction. I was listening carefully—talking to people, to detainees, to sources—and the pattern became evident. When due process is bypassed in the name of a greater goal, we begin to descend into a darker version of the country. There must be full respect for legal procedure, for the right to be heard, and for the right to a proper defence.

We could have fought corruption just as forcefully—but with constitutional safeguards intact. That would have left us with a stronger, more just, and more democratic society. I never imagined the outcome would be so destructive. At the time, no one foresaw Bolsonaro. But today, I am convinced that the excesses of Operation Car Wash created the conditions that allowed for the rise of authoritarianism in Brazil.

From the beginning, I was critical of those excesses. Over time, after repeating the same warnings again and again, those criticisms began to resonate more widely. The Car Wash task force was legally fragile composed of young prosecutors who had little time to study and were driven by a desire for power and personal visibility. I doubt whether many of them ever read literature. If they had read, for example, Fernando Pessoa,[80] they might have remembered the line: "Ugh, I am fed up of demigods. Where are the real people in this world?".[81]

If there had been no political agenda, Car Wash could have been extremely beneficial for the country. But it overreached. When the

Supreme Federal Court blocked a three-billion-real fund—followed by another fund of six billion—that was supposed to be controlled by the Car Wash task force itself, it became clear: they had a political project, and they needed money to fuel it. More money than political parties or traditional media ever dreamed of managing. The game is far from over.

The constitutional guarantees set forth in the 1988 Constitution—such as the presumption of innocence and the right to a proper defence—were simply ignored. There is a poet from Maranhão whom I admire deeply who once wrote: "The fate gives, denies, and takes away."[82] I carry a similar phrase with me, one I repeat all over Brazil: "We must ensure that those who violated due process and the Constitution are now given every right that was denied to others." They, too, must be prosecuted—but within the law, with constitutional guarantees, with full defence, and without the spectacle of media trials. If they are found guilty, they should be imprisoned—only after due process has been fully exhausted.

You referred to the concept of institutional corruption. Could you elaborate on your definition and theoretical understanding of this concept?

To illustrate what I mean, I will refer to the case of Raul Schmidt,[83] a Brazilian national living in Portugal, whom I represented. His arrest had been ordered by former Judge Sergio Moro. My office succeeded in suspending the extradition process[84]—a case that was so significant that it became the subject of academic theses in both Portugal and Brazil.

When I obtained an injunction in Brazil to suspend the extradition, former Judge Moro simply ignored it—just as he had ignored the injunction issued by Judge Rogério Favreto,[85] who had ordered the release of former President Lula.[86] What was even more troubling was that the regional court lacked the institutional courage to respond appropriately and hold him accountable for this open defiance of judicial authority.

In Schmidt's case, however, Judge Ney Belo[87] of the 3rd Panel of the Federal Regional Court of the 1st Region[88] issued a clear and principled ruling, stating: "What is this? A judicial ruling must be respected." The ruling was a turning point, affirming that judicial orders cannot be disregarded without consequence.

Was there any coordination among defence attorneys in Operation Car Wash similar to the collaborative legal strategies reportedly adopted during the Mensalão trial?

There may have been some coordination among defence attorneys in certain respects. When I filed the Declaratory Action of Constitutionality 43[89], a case that deeply divided both the country and the Supreme Court, *Veja* magazine ran an extensive article alleging that I represented specific individuals and that twenty of my clients stood to benefit from a change in legal interpretation. In reality, not a single one of them benefited from Declaratory Action of Constitutionality 43—none.

At that point, Lula had not even been arrested, let alone convicted. Later, he was indeed arrested, but because the Supreme Court took years to rule on Declaratory Action of Constitutionality 43, he was convicted—and only later released as a result of the Court's decision in that same case. My dear friend José Dirceu was also released as a consequence of the ruling, but again, none of my clients derived any benefit from it.

I had three clients who were preventively detained during Operation Car Wash. One was arrested in the afternoon, and by that same evening, I had already secured his release through a *habeas corpus*. Another, André Esteves,[90] was the victim of what I consider the most serious judicial error ever committed by the Supreme Court. He spent over twenty days in prison—which, for someone in pre-trial detention, is an eternity—but we succeeded in having him released. A third client remained in custody a little longer but was also released shortly thereafter.

In your professional experience, have allegations of corruption—particularly in major operations like Car Wash—ever posed challenges to your role as legal counsel in terms of public perception or personal conviction?

I travelled across Brazil discussing the excesses of Operation Car Wash. Before the pandemic, I gave two, three, sometimes even four lectures a month throughout the country. I once spoke to four thousand people in Cuiabá, and on another occasion to three hundred people in the interior of Minas Gerais. I have travelled extensively across Brazil, and I have never been harassed—not once.

It is worth highlighting one exception to this. In the state of Espírito Santo, during a lecture with about a thousand people in the audience, someone stood up and said, "You are defending a corrupt person." The university professors who had invited me tried to stop him from speaking, but I said, "Let him speak—it is his right." The room fell completely silent. He continued, "All you do is defend corrupt people." I calmly took the microphone and replied, "You are a scoundrel," and added, "You do not understand what I am defending here. I am defending the Constitution—not corrupt people. You do not know how to listen." The audience gave me a standing ovation and escorted him out of the room. Later, I even tried to find him to apologise—calling someone a scoundrel is a strong insult.

When I give interviews on television or in the press, I never read the comments. About twenty days ago, a Bolsonaro supporter named Allan[91] published an article that drew considerable attention in Brazil. In it, he claimed that I—alongside North Korea and China—had a suitcase for spying on Bolsonaro.[92] I remember waking up at 6 a.m. to a phone call from a television network, and it took me a moment to grasp what was going on. I laughed—mostly at the absurdity of being compared to two nuclear powers.

I also wrote a long article for a widely read magazine in Brazil titled *The Anti-Hero of Lava Jato*. Despite all of this, I do not feel harassed at all. I know that many people criticise me—and they're entitled to. But overexposure is unpleasant. Justice Gilmar Mendes[93] was nearly assaulted in Lisbon,[94] and Justice Ricardo Lewandowski[95] was humiliated in public.[96] I do not know why, but thankfully, that has never happened to me. I know there are people who dislike me and speak ill of me, but to me, it means absolutely nothing. I prefer to recall the words of Mário Quintana[97]: "They will pass…; I, little bird."

What is your assessment of the role that plea bargain agreements played in the development and conduct of Operation Car Wash?

A federal prosecutor, in an act of what I would call brutal honesty—*sincericídio*—stated in a filing before the Superior Court of Justice that preventive detention had in fact been used as a tool to secure plea bargain agreements.[98] If we had a judiciary with genuine self-respect, all of those agreements would have been annulled immediately. Why did not the Public Prosecutor's Office initiate an investigation against that prosecutor? Today, many acknowledge that this was indeed used as a strategic practice.

When Palocci's[99] plea bargain agreement was revealed, I happened to be with André Esteves, and he said, "Kakay, this is all a fantasy, complete madness." He is a brilliant individual, and he added, "I am recognizing old news stories that had been planted by my enemies—Palocci simply retrieved them from the internet to construct a house of cards that will eventually collapse, causing immense damage." And today, what is said about Palocci's statement? That it was indeed built from online searches.[100]

I also recall being in London when I was informed that, on that same day, three of my clients had been targeted for arrest: the President of the Senate,[101] former President José Sarney,[102] and then Minister Romero Jucá. The arrest warrants were issued based solely on the testimony of Sérgio Machado[103]. I returned to Brazil immediately. Shortly thereafter, the Public Prosecutor's Office itself submitted a request to void Machado's plea agreement, acknowledging that it lacked evidentiary support[104]—much like the case brought against André Esteves.

Another example: I served as legal counsel for Alberto Youssef, as I mentioned earlier. In his initial testimony, he accused then Governor Roseana Sarney[105] and former Senator Edison Lobão.[106] His account, however, conflicted with that of Paulo Roberto Costa, who stated that he had delivered money to Roseana Sarney, while Youssef claimed he had never given her any money. When two cooperating witnesses offer contradictory accounts, it stands to reason that at least one of them should forfeit the benefits of their plea agreement. A journalist published a report highlighting this inconsistency, after which the federal police investigator conducted a confrontation between the two. As a result, both the cases involving Lobão and Roseana Sarney were dismissed.

Could you elaborate on your perspective regarding the effectiveness and implications of leniency agreements?

Brazil needs to approach corruption differently. It is impossible to have a meaningful discussion on leniency agreements when oversight is fragmented across three, four, or five different agencies. Although I do not practice directly in this area, I follow its criminal aspects closely, and the current situation is a complete disaster. A company enters into an agreement with one government agency, only to have it questioned later by the Federal Court of Accounts or the General Comptroller's Office. There is neither maturity nor stability in this arrangement. Brazil urgently requires legal stability.

How do you assess the use of pre-trial detention in Brazil, particularly in terms of its legal justification and its impact on due process [107]?

Throughout Operation Car Wash, I never found myself rushing because a client had been arrested, except for the day André Esteves was detained. That was an interesting episode. I was at home when the phone rang at six in the morning—it was Renan, the President of the Senate. He said, "Kakay, they've just arrested Delcídio,[108] the first time a sitting Senator has been arrested. Can you come here?". I replied immediately, "Right away." As I was preparing to leave, the phone rang again—this time it was André Esteves' lawyer, who informed me, "They have just arrested André Esteves in the same operation." I called Renan back and explained, "Renan, I am sorry, but I must attend to André." I went directly to handle André's arrest and accompanied the case at the Supreme Court.

Later that afternoon, following the Supreme Court session, I visited the Senator at his home. I remember that moment clearly—it was around three in the afternoon, and I had not yet eaten lunch. About fourteen or fifteen Senators were present, including José Sarney, Romero Jucá, and Edison Lobão. Among them, six were my clients. Delcídio's arrest was one of the legal absurdities arising from Operation Lava Jato. I distinctly recall telling the Senators, "This arrest is absurd; the Constitution explicitly empowers you to release him immediately. You must convene today and ensure this Senator is freed." I further warned them, "If you fail to act, you will effectively transfer immense power to the judiciary and Operation Lava Jato—and soon five or six of you will be next." Renan Calheiros then replied, "You can inform Delcídio." Although I was not Delcídio's lawyer, I knew his counsel personally and thus was able to assure him, "Tonight, he will sleep at home." However, at the last minute, under mounting media pressure, the Senators lacked the courage to proceed. They had every constitutional authority to secure Delcídio's immediate release yet chose not to exercise it.

To what extent do you think Operation Car Wash transformed the dynamics between the private sector and the Brazilian State?

Today, companies have established compliance departments, which have become integral and strategically critical components of their organisational structure. Historically, Brazil had large construction firms capable of competing effectively in global markets; however, these companies lacked the preventive safeguards and compliance mechanisms commonly implemented by their international counterparts. Undoubtedly, Brazilian firms needed to confront systemic corruption, and as a result, compliance practices have significantly strengthened. Nevertheless, these critical advancements could have been accomplished without inflicting severe financial damage on the companies involved. From my perspective, Operation Car Wash unquestionably played an important role in reshaping corporate and institutional practices. However, this fight against corruption could have been carried out just as rigorously while still preserving constitutional guarantees and safeguarding the economic viability of prominent businesses. Clearly, some revisions and reforms were necessary—no one disputes this reality. That is precisely why I often emphasise: "You will never hear me criticize Operation Car Wash without first acknowledging its profound importance."

In your view, what have been the main institutional and societal consequences of Operation Car Wash in Brazil?

Operation Car Wash had a profound impact across various sectors. I clearly remember watching television at home when I saw Pedro Barusco[109] returning hundreds of millions of reais. Until that moment, I had never even heard his name—he occupied a third or fourth-tier position within Petrobras. At that point, I thought to myself, "This level of corruption is something we must urgently confront." Undoubtedly, Car Wash had several positive aspects and contributed significantly to progress. Of course, deeply entrenched corruption existed between government officials, political administrations, and major corporations—that was simply how things had been done for a long time. However, when someone from the fourth tier of a public company is able to return a hundred million reais, it clearly signals that something is fundamentally wrong. As a citizen, I could not help but feel compelled to address this issue. Yet, as Lord Acton[110] famously stated, "Power *tends* to corrupt, and absolute power corrupts absolutely."

What do you mean by "power *tends* to corrupt, and absolute power corrupts absolutely"?

Former Judge Sergio Moro assumed jurisdiction of national scope, an extraordinarily serious development. There was a clear rationale behind creating a national-level judicial authority. Today, I hesitate even to fill my car with fuel at a Petrobras station in Minas Gerais, fearing that if I had an accident, jurisdiction might somehow be assigned to Curitiba. Former Judge Moro selectively chose the cases he wished to preside over. This was his first fundamental mistake: an abuse of judicial power. Why was the Atibaia ranch case tried in Curitiba? Why was a triplex apartment located in Guarujá adjudicated by a Curitiba court?[111] Even a first-year law student would recognise the underlying issue—a political structure of power was in operation. The fight against corruption could and should have proceeded without becoming entangled in a political agenda. It is unacceptable to target a former President, especially a leading presidential candidate, and then deliberately leak his deposition to influence electoral outcomes. Former Judge Sergio Moro accumulated excessive power, resulting in institutional corruption. Had the investigation been pursued without severely damaging Petrobras and had traditional legal safeguards been respected, the outcomes would have differed substantially. Operation Car Wash ultimately lost itself in its excesses, driven from behind by an unmistakable political agenda.

Would you characterise your position as opposed to Operation Car Wash, or is your criticism focused primarily on the methods employed during the investigation?

Operation Car Wash is undeniably significant. It exposed a deeply entrenched level of corruption that had been entirely unknown—not only to the public, but also to the Public Prosecutor's Office, the police, investigative journalists, the legal community, and even the judiciary itself. Had this operation not been transformed into a political agenda—a project for power—it would have produced unequivocal benefits. My stance towards Operation Car Wash is largely neutral, despite widespread claims that I am passionately opposed to it. However, since none of my clients were incarcerated, my advocacy was not personal, but rather focused on protecting constitutional rights and legal guarantees that were being systematically undermined. Some legal measures I proposed were unfairly portrayed in the media as attempts "to end Operation Car Wash." Yet ending the operation was never my objective; Car Wash is much broader than that.

When we filed Declaratory Action of Constitutionality, the narrative emerged—and still persists—that these were moves against Operation Car Wash. They were not. At the time I filed these actions, former President Lula was not even under investigation. Nevertheless, I frequently encountered scepticism, with people questioning me: "Aren't you against Car Wash?" No, I am not against Operation Car Wash itself; rather, I oppose its excesses. I oppose the trivialisation of preventive detention, its use as coercion to secure plea bargains, sensationalist criminal proceedings, and the criminalisation of politics and the legal profession.

Other questionable tactics were also deployed. A Federal Police operation would be conducted, and immediately the following day, details would be published prominently in major Brazilian newspapers. GloboNews,[112] for instance, would broadcast coverage for hours, presenting a selective, biased interpretation of seized material—phone records, wiretaps, and other evidence. At the time, I openly criticised these practices, stating, "This is about undermining individuals' morale to obtain an early guilty verdict or force a plea deal, while simultaneously generating political visibility and enabling certain individuals to profit from public lectures across Brazil, transforming themselves into national heroes." They failed to understand that a country does not need heroes. I often quote Fernando Pessoa, "Ugh, I am tired of demigods. Where in the world are real people?" Had they internalised Pessoa's words, perhaps they would have been less inclined to view themselves as demigods or heroes.

Before we conclude, are there anything any final reflection or considerations you would like to share?

Criminal law is an area in which I have long worked and one that I find intellectually and professionally rewarding. For a considerable period, I spoke out—often in solitude—about the excesses committed during Operation Car Wash. Today, those concerns have become widely acknowledged and are no longer controversial. In this period of relative isolation, I have taken to hosting two, sometimes three, live broadcasts each day. What strikes me is the shift: whereas my earlier critiques were largely ignored, they are now being heard and recognised. It is a necessary confrontation. In a sense, that is what this has always been—a struggle I have taken up and one I continue to pursue.

Antonio Carlos de Almeida Castro (Kakay) was born in Patos de Minas (MG). He is a criminal lawyer and a partner at Almeida Castro, Castro and Turbay Associated Lawyers. His testimony was given on 17 August 2020, via the Zoom virtual platform, totalling 1 hour and 5 minutes of recording. The text was revised by the interviewee on 10 March 2023.

Testimony of Antônio Sérgio Altieri de Moraes Pitombo

Abstract

This testimony by Antônio Sérgio Altieri de Moraes Pitombo offers an incisive legal and academic reflection on the trajectory and implications of Operation Car Wash, one of Brazil's most consequential anti-corruption investigations. A criminal defence lawyer with a distinguished academic background—ranging from his legal education at the University of São Paulo to a postdoctoral fellowship in Democracy and Human Rights at the University of Coimbra—Pitombo situates his analysis within both professional experience and doctrinal inquiry. He recounts his early engagement with Car Wash, noting his initial shock at the scale of judicial arbitrariness and the emergence of what he terms a "people-grinding machine" in Curitiba, marked by coercive pre-trial detentions and a breakdown of constitutional safeguards.

Pitombo draws a historical and structural comparison between Operation Car Wash and earlier investigations such as Operation Satiagraha, arguing that both exemplify forms of judicial activism incompatible with the Brazilian rule of law. His testimony highlights the collusion between prosecutors, police, and judges, the instrumental use of plea bargains under psychological duress, and the complicity of the media in reinforcing punitive narratives and marginalising defence advocacy. He reflects critically on the failure of higher courts—including the Federal Supreme Court—to contain procedural abuses, attributing part of this failure to the politicisation of anti-corruption discourse.

Throughout the interview, Pitombo defends the constitutional validity of plea-bargaining agreement when properly regulated, while denouncing the distorted and imbalanced negotiation practices adopted during Car Wash. He also offers a Law and Economics perspective on systemic corruption in Brazil, pointing to the structural flaws of state-owned enterprises, the absence of compliance cultures, and the dysfunctional campaign financing system as drivers of endemic misconduct. He advocates for institutional reform—particularly regarding the public–private interface, corporate governance, and political accountability—arguing that criminal law alone cannot address the deeper economic and political roots of corruption.

By drawing parallels with Italy's Operation *Mani Pulite*, revisiting the doctrine of judicial impartiality, and offering reflections on legal education, Pitombo's testimony presents a multidimensional critique of legal overreach and institutional fragility. While condemning the excesses of Car Wash, he remains cautiously optimistic, seeing in the legal and academic responses to the operation a renewed commitment to procedural fairness, critical legal scholarship, and professional excellence in criminal defence. His account provides a compelling window into the tensions between legality and populism, activism and restraint, and punitive spectacle and constitutional order in contemporary Brazil.

Could you reflect on your educational background and personal trajectory, to help contextualise your professional perspective?

In brief, here's what my journey has looked like over the years: I graduated from Largo São Francisco in 1993, at the Faculty of Law of the University of São Paulo, known as "São Francisco" (Saint Francis). I then specialised in civil procedure at the University Extension Centre, followed by a master's and a doctorate in criminal law—also at the Faculty of Law of the University of São Paulo. Later on, I completed a post-doctorate in Democracy and Human Rights at the University of Coimbra.

Throughout these years, I have primarily worked as a lawyer. For a time, I also taught at "São Francisco", in the postgraduate programme, and then for nearly ten years at the Getulio Vargas Foundation. Nowadays, my academic activity is mostly focused on writing books and running the school, I have set up within my office—it is a school dedicated to training the professionals who work here. That is what I do, and that is what I have done.

Upon accepting your first Car Wash-related case, what elements of the operation did you find most striking or concerning?

Without a doubt, the degree of arbitrariness. I had already seen a certain model of activist judges in São Paulo, but I had never seen anything like that people-grinding machine they set up in Curitiba. That really shocked me. I joined the case exactly when the contractors were being arrested; I was representing one of them. And that is when I realised it was essentially a machine of psychological torture, created at the first-instance level of jurisdiction.

Could you clarify which operation in São Paulo you consider comparable to the approach used in Operation Car Wash?

It was Operation Satiagraha,[113] which followed a model of judicial activism. But it was halted by the Federal Supreme Court, through a decision by Justice Gilmar Mendes.[114] Subsequent rulings from the Superior Court of Justice (and even from the Federal Regional Court of the 3rd Region) re-established a veil of legality. That kind of judicial activism had already revealed itself to be incompatible with due process and the principle of strict legality. People often misunderstand the purpose of criminal procedure. It is not a tool for persecution—it exists to safeguard individual legal freedoms. At every stage of the process, those freedoms remain intact. The individual is still a subject of rights. That is the very essence of criminal procedure. Of course, there is the punitive and social weight that comes with it, but still—legal safeguards must remain in place. Judicial activism like that breaks with both legality and the Constitution.

In the case of Satiagraha, the then-judge[115]—now sitting as Appellate judge—was misled by a corrupt police structure. That is something not many talks about, but it was a police operation based on fabricated facts and false scenarios, created specifically to justify the investigation. It misled the judiciary. What we expect, naturally, is that police operations happen within the boundaries of the law. That is the bare minimum in a country that claims to uphold the rule of law. That is what we should all be aiming for.

The sad thing is the same model I first saw in São Paulo with *Satiagraha* was later adopted in Curitiba—but on a whole other level. There, it became a kind of coordination between the Federal Public Prosecutor's Office, the Federal Police, and the judge. And that was unprecedented. It was a people-grinding machine. Yes, I would call it a model of psychological torture.[116] Arresting people purely to extract statements, in my view, is a form of psychological torture. That article, written in tribute to Professor René Dotti,[117] explores how international conventions on torture do not permit such practices. And yet, that is exactly what was done.

What shocked me most in the context of Car Wash was not the judicial activism at first instance. "I had already encountered similar patterns in São Paulo and Mato Grosso, where criminal court judges often displayed a pronounced pro-prosecution bias." However, this case was markedly different. In Curitiba, the judge operated with the full support of the local Federal Prosecutor's Office and faced virtually no judicial oversight. There existed a comfortable and unchallenged relationship between the abuses of power committed by the judge and the Regional Federal Court of the 4th Region, which effectively acquiesced to those violations—clear and flagrant breaches of legality.

Regrettably, the Superior Court of Justice failed to articulate a clear and consistent standard to curb such practices. To some extent, the Federal Supreme Court was also carried along by the political momentum generated under the banner of combating corruption. Certain justices endorsed the direction Operation Car Wash had taken, despite its evident departure from the rule of law and the fundamental principles of criminal procedure. Unfortunately, for a time, even the Supreme Court itself became complicit in this deviation.

How would you compare Operation Car Wash to the Mensalão[118] case and other major anti-corruption investigations in terms of legal strategy, institutional impact, and political consequences?

Criminal lawyers from my generation did not have much experience dealing with corruption cases—it is quite curious. I have always worked as a lawyer for executives and company controllers; in other words, I come from a background in economic criminal law. The clients I took on—often public figures—were usually connected to me somehow, through their children, relatives, or friends. Fundamentally, I have always represented businesspeople and companies.

I hadn't really dealt with corruption cases, apart from a few involving tax inspectors, where I acted as assistant to the prosecution. That was the extent of it in my practice—until Car Wash. That operation marked a turning point. It exposed systemic corruption within Petrobras, but this must be understood within its broader historical and political context. What distinguishes it, then?

At that particular moment, the federal government exercised substantial control over Petrobras—and that control was, in significant ways, abused. The company's objective was no longer just to operate and generate results—it also became a mechanism to fund a political party's electoral campaigns and to provide political posts for its support base. Smaller allied parties were given positions in Petrobras so they could finance themselves. It was a major arrangement—a different way of exercising power compared to what we saw in the Mensalão case. It followed a different model altogether.

Mensalão was about keeping the Legislative under control. The Brazilian political model places the Executive, at the federal level, at the mercy of Congressional coalitions. Our presidential system, as it stands, is seriously flawed—and it needs reform. But that is not my area, I am no expert, so I will stick to what I do know.

In the Mensalão case, it was relatively straightforward: parliamentarians were paid to secure the government's political base in the Chamber of Deputies. That was the set-up. Later on, Petrobras became one of the sources of money used for that sort of illicit activity. That government[119] had a long-term plan—it intended to stay in power for fifty years and use Petrobras as a never-ending campaign fund. The company became a financial pillar supporting the party's hold on power.

If asked whether it was valuable for Operation Car Wash to have uncovered this illegal political scheme, I would say yes. The investigation brought to light a deeply problematic structure. The manner in which political alliances are forged in Brazil is fundamentally flawed—so much so that corruption becomes embedded in the very foundations of governability.

What factors, in your opinion, contributed to the continuation of corrupt practices despite the visibility and scale of Operation Car Wash?

I have consistently approached these issues through the lens of Law and Economics. In my view, interpreting criminal law solely within a traditional, insular framework is unduly limiting—particularly when assessing its practical effectiveness and systemic impact. Many criminal lawyers are sceptical about this approach, often dismissing it because the American model—being common law—is supposedly too different from ours to apply. But that is simply not true.

Corruption is fundamentally an economic issue—it is political too, of course, but at its core, it's about how resources and power are distributed and controlled. In the Brazilian context, here's what happens: the party in power has direct control over state-owned and state-controlled companies. Now, how is it that a company like Petrobras—a publicly traded company, no less, with a high level of legal, economic, and international engagement—ends up being controlled by a government that happens to win an election? That same government brings its political objectives into company decisions. And that is precisely what we are witnessing once again today, albeit driven by different motivations.[120] Just take the President of the Republic intervening in petrol prices. Indeed, it is legitimate to pursue public or economic policy objectives in such matters; however, this often swiftly devolves into an abuse of state control. Understandably, investors in these companies grow increasingly uneasy in the face of persistent governance deficiencies. The ongoing debates around who should lead Petrobras are clear signs that something is not right.[121] The first point that must be addressed is economic: this level of governmental control over companies of such scale is deeply troubling.

The second issue is political campaign financing. Politicians still need money to run campaigns—even if they're now mostly digital and cheaper, they still cost. And then there is the matter of building a government coalition. To govern at even a basic level, the President needs to form alliances with multiple parties. He might be able to control the actions of his own team, but he cannot control the corruption of the broader support base he has forced to bring on board. If he tried, nothing would get passed—no legislation, no public policy. And it is always the same faces returning to the scene: the same opportunistic parties getting tangled up in corruption.

There are questions we simply must tackle. How do we reform the electoral system? What do we do about presidentialism? And how do we address the ongoing issue of state control over major companies—companies that remain vulnerable to the personal or political agendas of whoever's in power? If this set-up continues, corruption will follow. Criminal law alone won't fix it. And again, this ties back to Law and Economics. The contractors who struck deals with Petrobras signed contracts without even properly evaluating whether they'd yield a profit or a loss—it did not matter. And Petrobras, which positioned itself as a victim in these criminal cases, was legally miscast, in my opinion. I say this with great respect, especially since the company was represented by someone I held in very high regard—Professor René Dotti, who sadly passed away. But the truth is, Petrobras should never have acted as assistant to the prosecution because, from a civil standpoint, it bore responsibility for many of those acts. That is how I see it.

What is your assessment of the use of pre-trial detention during Operation Car Wash, particularly in terms of its legal basis and broader implications for due process?

Pre-trial detention is a recognised component of criminal proceedings. In recent years, the legal system has evolved towards a more mature approach, in which such measures are generally reserved for cases involving violence or serious threats. The Brazilian Code of Criminal Procedure, under Article 312, provides a general framework for precautionary detention, outlining the legal criteria for its application: (i) ensuring the integrity of the criminal investigation—for instance, when someone is obstructing the inquiry, destroying evidence, or intimidating witnesses; (ii) preventing flight, to guarantee enforcement of the law; and (iii) protecting public and economic order. These last two are rather vague concepts—I have never found them convincing as grounds for imprisonment, either in case law or in legal theory.

In my view, nowadays the most pertinent basis for precautionary detention is when the concrete facts involve violence or a serious threat. Even in such cases, it is important to recall that detention should remain the exception rather than the rule. From a legal standpoint, exceptions must be interpreted narrowly, in accordance with the principle of legality.

Criminal procedure and criminal law—this is not my phrase, it is my father's,[122] and I find it quite amusing—"are only easy for those who do not understand them." The rules of interpretation in criminal law are not arbitrary. A judge is not a poet or a literature teacher. The judge must abide by strict legality. The arrests that were ordered under Operation Car Wash were opportunistic, media-driven, and lacked a sound legal basis.

What stands out to me most in relation to the defence against those pre-trial detentions is that, at that particular political juncture, there was an effort to align the interests of the contractors with those of the government. This initial attempt at conciliation ultimately weakened the coherence and effectiveness of the defence strategy. It was the Minister of Justice, Márcio Thomaz Bastos,[123] who proposed a solution meant to appease both sides. On the one hand, he had his political connections—he had served as a minister under President Lula[124]—on the other hand, he was also the lawyer for the contractors, and he appointed many of the initial defence lawyers for them. He wanted to pull a rabbit out of the hat, a solution that would suit everyone. But in trying to do so, everything was delayed. A critical error occurred at the very outset: the assertion of jurisdiction by the Curitiba court over matters involving Petrobras. This marked the beginning of the legal complications. The pre-trial detentions continued for an extended period, and initially, there was a lack of a more robust legal strategy—one that should have directly challenged the judge's evident lack of impartiality. From the start, it was clear that pre-trial detention was being used as a means of coercion against those under investigation, a practice inconsistent with the rule of law. The judge in question had studied Italian legal doctrine, particularly the prosecutorial strategies employed during Operation Mani Pulite (Clean Hands).

As it happens, I had known Judge Sergio Moro[125] well before Operation Car Wash. Due to my academic work, I regularly attended conferences on money laundering, where he, still a judge at the time, was also frequently present. I authored the first academic study on money laundering in Brazil[126] and maintained professional contact with several judges from specialised criminal courts.

What became evident was that the arrests had a specific purpose—he was copying the Italian model of arbitrary criminal prosecution. He failed to grasp the broader historical and institutional lessons. Specifically, he did not consider that the trajectory of Antonio Di Pietro[127] could also mirror his own. And, indeed, that parallel ultimately materialised—he too transitioned from the judiciary into political life, following a path remarkably similar to that of Di Pietro. But Moro's standard was one of blatant partiality—poorly reasoned decisions, rulings without factual support. And he had a court that was far too close to him, offering no checks or balance. The pre-trial detentions were used as leverage to push plea bargains.

With regard to the pre-trial detentions, I have no doubt: those imprisonments were not justified in the manner in which they were carried out. The defendants ought to have been released by the courts, in accordance with the fundamental principles of due process and proportionality.

Everything that happened should now be the subject of state compensation, because those individuals should never have been detained like that, nor under such conditions. It was primitive. The operations were absolutely degrading. People weren't just arrested—they were humiliated.

Their photos had to appear in the newspapers. There was a toxic relationship between the press, the judiciary, and the Public Prosecutor's Office—no one talks about this. It was appalling. There was a quid pro quo: the press gave fame to the "heroes of Curitiba" in exchange for privileged access to information. That became a kind of currency.

No one wants to talk about how the media really behaves in this country. Why did Car Wash take on such proportions? Because it had full backing from the media, which in turn placed pressure on the higher courts—especially on those judges who do not exactly have a clean record. Those who have acted improperly are often the first to align themselves with sweeping punitive agendas and adopt a staunchly prosecutorial stance. The unfortunate reality of growing older is that one has witnessed such patterns repeatedly—eventually, they cease to shock.

What is your assessment of the plea bargain agreements implemented during Operation Car Wash? In your view, did they represent a positive development or a problematic departure from established legal principles?

I cannot speak objectively about every plea bargain agreement that was reached. I came across some that contained inaccuracies or were incomplete—but those are individual cases. What I believe warrants deeper reflection is the overall methodology adopted during Operation Car Wash, which, in my view, was fundamentally flawed. Pre-trial detention was used as a coercive instrument to pressure individuals into entering plea agreements—a practice that was, in my assessment, unmistakably clear and deeply troubling. Judge Moro appeared to treat it as an objective in itself—drawing on the Italian experience, which he had studied, and seemingly regarding such practices as standard or legitimate. He knew the media would play an important role too, putting pressure on the families of the imprisoned to encourage them to agree to a deal. What emerged, then, was a model of psychological coercion that effectively disregarded the rights of the accused. That said, I wish to be clear: I am not opposed to plea bargaining as an institution in and of itself. In fact, I am launching a new book now on procedural plea bargain agreements.[128] It is a systematic analysis of procedural collaboration, written by the entire team at my office—forty people were involved in the project. The book is a mix of academic insight and practical experience, particularly drawn from the Car Wash period. We cover how we dealt with clients, how we approached the Federal Prosecution Office, and how we navigated the system.

Now, I believe the constitutionality of plea bargaining in Brazilian law rests on one key point: it is a defence tool. A person in prison has the right to say, "Enough—I do not want to keep fighting, I want to get this over with. I want to see my children, my wife, I want to return to my life. Yes, I committed a crime, and I want to tell the truth—how I did it, with whom, what kind of crime it was, who was involved." That is a personal decision, an exercise of self-determination. It is part of a person's right to choose how to live their own life. So, constitutionally, I see plea-bargaining agreement as part of the broader right of defence. That means it has a legitimate place in our legal system—if certain rules are followed, especially those that protect the dignity of the human person.

But the model we've adopted here in Brazil is very much a "Terra Brasilis" version. The negotiation process is completely unbalanced—there is no real parity between defence and prosecution. The defence lawyer is negotiating with a client stuck in prison, often with limited communication. The family does not really understand what is going on and cannot speak privately with the accused.

Many of the contractors involved could execute large infrastructure projects—but most had very low managerial capacity. I was quite shocked, to be honest. They all clung to Petrobras like it was some kind of seal of quality. It was as if just working with Petrobras made a project extraordinary. And yes, some of the projects were technically impressive, even exciting—but they were far from being models of sound management, let alone financially viable. There was no proper economic analysis of the relationship between these companies and Petrobras.

One of the hallmarks of Car Wash was that it was the period in which I heard more legal nonsense than at any other time in my life. In the plea agreements from the prosecutors and contractors, people were commenting on contracts they did not even understand. It was a circus of criminal law absurdities. These arguments made headlines every day, echoing nonsense. And all the while, there was a political project at play, which is problematic. The issue of corruption was used as a flag, a moment for the Public Ministry to try to dominate the Brazilian criminal process. We even saw prosecutors entering dubious plea deals[129]—I won't go into detail because some of these cases are still ongoing. But we had an Attorney General, like Rodrigo Janot,[130] who was particularly poor at managing the institution. There were disturbing movements within the Attorney General's Office, clearly driven by political aims.

If the spurious relationships between judges and prosecutors hadn't later come to light, Operation Car Wash might have succeeded in its power project—among other goals, they wanted to reshape the criminal process, effectively creating a court of instruction. Congress only pulled back because the tide started to rise, and it reached them too. In the end, populism won out in the speeches supporting arbitrary criminal processes.

That said, I need to be fair. I was involved in some significant plea agreements, and they worked out because there were excellent, principled federal prosecutors leading the negotiations. Interestingly, the ones who were truly effective remained somewhat anonymous. The public does not know who they are—but they were highly skilled legal professionals. I must give credit where it is due. I had experiences with federal prosecutors who were exceptionally well-prepared and conducted themselves with integrity. The "stars"—as always—were often more about spectacle than substance.

Brazil is a country of the unusual. Things get resolved—sometimes for the better, sometimes for the worse—but almost always in the wrong way. Even when we arrive at something good, we seem to take the wrong path to get there. I say this thinking, for example, of Judge Moro's Anti-Crime Package.[131] It was an attempt to introduce an authoritarian model of criminal procedure. But then Congress outmanoeuvred him, reworking the bill. Someone in Congress had the insight to say: "Right, let's turn this into something that actually strengthens individual rights." That is what I mean: in Brazil, even when something positive emerges, it usually does so by completely unconventional means.

Could you draw a parallel between Italy's Operation Clean Hands[132] and Brazil's Operation Car Wash, particularly in terms of their legal strategies, institutional dynamics, and political outcomes?

In a public lecture, Judge Moro openly acknowledged that he had drawn inspiration from the Clean Hands operation, particularly with regard to its media strategy. He explicitly stated that he understood the media could be employed as a tool of pressure. What is striking, however, is that the outcomes were remarkably similar. The central figure in Italy's Clean Hands, Antonio Di Pietro, also became entangled in politics. In other words, Italy ultimately repeated many of the same missteps that would later characterise the Brazilian experience. From an academic standpoint, it is quite interesting. Italy was heavily influenced by the American approach to criminal prosecution. The Italian criminal process was shaped by the American system. And this American pragmatism ultimately influenced Western legal systems. For me, it was a positive influence because, throughout my academic research—whether it was my master's, doctorate, or post-doctorate—I always worked within the American system. I have always enjoyed analysing American models. Operation Car Wash really demonstrated how much the American criminal process has permeated Western law, particularly here in Brazil.

There was a marked division within the legal community between those who, on moral grounds, opposed the use of plea bargaining and those who engaged with it directly. Some lawyers would declare, "I do not engage in such practices," while discreetly referring clients to colleagues who did—whose identities, it must be said, were widely known. These kinds of inconsistencies, in my view, are unacceptable. The circumstances made it evident that it was necessary to establish a clear constitutional and legal foundation for plea bargaining. The human drama was evident, but only those who see their clients incarcerated can truly understand it. That immense humiliation—when the person says, "I want to end this, I committed this crime, it is pointless, my life is over, I just want to see my children again, I want to take my child to school." And then, the lawyer would respond, "No, I am too noble for that. I cannot defend those who enter plea bargains." Give me a break! It is like a doctor having a life-saving technique available but saying, "Let's die together. I am an ethical person, and I will stay by your side until the end." However, what was needed was a more technical and dogmatic approach to understanding the concept of plea bargain agreements. Once you have the constitutional basis, once you have the right vision, it gives you the correct framework to interpret and apply criminal procedural law.

I feel sorry for the lawyers who made such claims back then. Some still do, but they've become increasingly irrelevant. I always joke that they're driving a 1977 Opala along the Bandeirantes highway, thinking they're flying high. The problem is the client is in the back seat. That is the person I truly feel sorry for.

How do you evaluate the stance and engagement of criminal lawyers in relation to Operation Car Wash, in terms of both legal strategy and public positioning?

Some of my colleagues continue to hold prominent positions, while others no longer do. Márcio Thomaz Bastos[133] left behind a group of followers—lawyers who sought to carry forward his legacy. However, his style of advocacy does not reflect my own. It is not how I engage with clients or structure legal defences. While I do not deny that he was a highly capable lawyer—indeed, a significant figure in his time—he is not a professional model I personally identify with. His contributions were substantial, but they belonged to a specific historical and professional context. However, he left behind many who tried to replicate his approach to law. They want to do things the way Márcio did, but they do not have the same calmness, the same political respectability, or the same ability to work behind the scenes as he did.

What we saw during Car Wash were many brave lawyers taking on criminal proceedings. Kakay,[134] for example, is one of the most skilled lawyers in the country—he has extraordinary sensitivity and great influence in political circles. But he is unique; he is Kakay, and only he can operate in that way. If I tried to do what Kakay does, it would be a farce and a failure. I cannot imitate Kakay; it would not work. He has that way of being, dressing, and speaking. Everyone likes him within our circle of colleagues because he is a sensitive lawyer who truly understands strategic thinking.

What has emerged, however, are many people trying to make a name for themselves in the name of defence but lacking the intellectual depth to push these projects forward—many doing so simply for personal promotion. Car Wash lasted if it did because of a lack of articulation. There was fear—fear of going against the tide, of opposing the anti-corruption narrative. People often confuse defending A, B, or C with who you are. I have been questioned in my career for defending certain individuals. I have always been polite about it, but I maintain my distance. I explain that I defend who I believe in, and that is that.

To what extent do you believe that criminal lawyers who defended those accused of corruption during Operation Car Wash were stigmatised by public opinion?

That was part of the broader approach associated with Judge Moro. There were instances of lawyers being investigated, and in some cases, even subjected to surveillance. While such actions were not always formalised, I am aware of situations in which defence counsel were clearly monitored. There was, one might say, a persecutory stance—particularly on the part of the media. And the media itself, it must be acknowledged, had been compromised in this process. Corrupted by this improper exchange of information with the Public Prosecutor's Office and with the judicial police. It carried a clear agenda against the accused, against the defendants. And obviously, that had a huge impact on the public image of defence lawyers.

For a long time, the Public Prosecutor's Office had a very active communications team, releasing statements on the eve of major trials, deliberately aiming to tarnish the image of the client. There is a whole game behind the scenes, and once you know how to look, it is all very clear. But again, none of this surprised me—I'd studied similar cases in the United States. I'd seen the same kind of malice at play there.

Lawyers were individually targeted. They had no real platform. Their voice was confined to the courtroom. What was really missing was a front line—institutions like the Bar Association, legal institutes, professional bodies—they did not step up. The Bar lost its once-prominent role in Brazilian civil society. That is the new reality. It lost its footing in history. The Bar today no longer speaks on behalf of civil society, nor does it truly represent it.

What the Federal Council of the Brazilian Bar Association[135] may or may not think—regrettably—has little impact on public opinion. It does matter to me, of course, as a practising lawyer who holds deep respect for the Bar. But in terms of its broader societal influence, the institution no longer carries the weight it once did. The influence it once wielded—the historical authority it held in the 1980s, particularly during the "Diretas Já" movement—has since diminished. As for why this loss of relevance occurred, I must admit that I do not have a clear explanation.

In your book, *In Search of the Lost Justice,*[136] you raise several critical points about Operation Car Wash. Among the various issues you have raised, which do you regard as the most critical in assessing the legacy of Operation Car Wash?

In the five years leading up to the publication of that book, I wrote around fifty articles. It was my way of communicating with young lawyers, of telling people what I was dissatisfied with. And what was I dissatisfied with? The arbitrariness of Operation Car Wash. I wanted to highlight the judge's lack of impartiality, the absurdity of the precautionary arrests, the use of coercive measures that denied people the time to properly prepare a defence—because apparently speaking to a lawyer was seen as hindering the exercise of criminal jurisdiction.

I also wrote about the excessive use of precautionary seizures, the damage caused by arrest as a supposed means of reparation, the judicial police overstepping their role, and the part played by the Federal Public Prosecutor's Office in those operations.

I was writing in short, digestible pieces—pills, really—because the young lawyer is busy trying to pay the bills, often working in small firms, dreaming of the day their name is on the door. And then they're faced with cases with seventy attachments… there is no time to read, they're up all night, no time to study. So, I wanted to offer something useful: a little tip here, a bit of advice there—"Look, do not accept this, do not do it like that, try it this way instead." These short articles were published on legal websites and eventually came together in *In Search of the Lost Justice*. It was my way of reaching out to other lawyers; to show them that yes, a lot of things were wrong. Very wrong. That is where my writing came from—every month something would happen that left me shocked.

There are also tributes in the book—to people who've passed away, like Arnaldo Malheiros Filho,[137] Professor Rogério Lauria Tucci,[138] and more recently Professor René Dotti. They were all true role models in law and as people. For me, the ideal lawyer was Arnaldo. He was ahead of his time—already thinking in terms of economic criminal law, already aware of the American influence. I had some rich intellectual exchanges with him. That is why I say there are different ways of seeing the law. He was a very special lawyer.

Over the years, I ended up producing so many articles because I was deeply outraged. Outraged at the Federal Supreme Court, too. From a doctrinal perspective, so many things were simply wrong. There was—and still is—a misunderstanding of what criminal procedure means. These ideas are being poorly taught. We are working with a distorted model of legal education, and that affects the profession in practice.

Of course, there is another side to it—if Judge Moro had been an intellectually rigorous professional, if his training had been solid, maybe Operation Car Wash would have held up better. But his dogmatic mistakes, his misguided views, his desire to act as an accusing judge—all of that made it clear something was seriously off.

Could you draw a parallel between your work *Impartiality of Jurisdiction*[139] and the developments observed during Operation Car Wash, particularly in terms of legal doctrine, procedural guarantees, or institutional dynamics?

When Operation Satiagraha took place, the theme of judicial impartiality first came to mind. Sometimes, even with the best intentions, a judge can be influenced—especially when a case has huge public repercussions. I wanted to explore this academically, putting aside my perspective as a lawyer, and really analyse it with some distance.

Judges today are under enormous pressure. They are in a kind of pressure cooker, really. There is social media, constant public scrutiny, people sending WhatsApp messages directly—it is non-stop. The old nineteenth-century image of the judge working in solitude, quietly making decisions in their chambers, simply does not exist anymore.

Traditionally, the sentencing process is understood to involve three sequential stages: the judge assesses the facts, applies the relevant legal provisions, and then issues a ruling. However, this is increasingly no longer the case. In contemporary practice, it is often the reverse—the judge forms a preliminary opinion and subsequently constructs the reasoning to support a predetermined outcome. That book *Thinking, Fast and Slow*[140] illustrates this way of thinking quite well. It is the same pattern we see in judicial processes today.

The question I wanted to explore in my book was this: is the criminal judge, in the current context, at risk of losing impartiality? I thought it was worth investigating academically.

There is also another aspect: the so-called exception of suspicion, which, in theory, is something that damages the judge's honour or the image of the judiciary—it is like a hammer blow to the crystal, right? But in practice, impartiality can be compromised for reasons that have nothing to do with personal bias or bad faith. Sometimes it's simply about the conditions under which the judge is placed.

Let me give an academic example, but one that occurs: when a criminal judge encounters illegal evidence. Once a court declares a piece of evidence to be illegal, every public official involved—be it the police, the prosecutors, or the judiciary—should be removed from the case. Because their exposure to that evidence, even if unintentional, can affect the impartiality of the proceedings.

What I tried to show in *Impartiality of Jurisdiction* is that the concept has evolved. It is no longer just about whether a judge is personally pursuing someone or showing bias. There are now objective situations—structural, procedural—that can undermine a judge's ability to remain impartial. And this applies across the board: to criminal proceedings, civil cases, even labour disputes.

Do you believe that Operation Car Wash led to significant changes in the relationship between the private and the public sector in Brazil?

I believe it did. Companies began to take compliance far more seriously, and there was a noticeable increase in caution regarding contractual practices. However, compliance cannot be approached as a mere mechanical process; it must be intelligent, grounded in critical thinking, and supported by robust and well-structured models.

This idea that someone under police investigation cannot engage in a commercial or financial transaction is, frankly, a bit absurd. Any one of us could end up involved in a police inquiry—have a traffic accident, for example, and there you are. And when it comes to entrepreneurs, Brazilian tax legislation is full of pitfalls. There are thousands of ways you can get caught out without any bad faith involved.

How would you assess the main benefits and drawbacks of Operation Car Wash for Brazil, in terms of both strengthening accountability and its broader consequences for the rule of law?

I tend to be an optimist—I believe that even negative experiences can lead to constructive outcomes. One of the more concerning aspects of the operation, in my view, was the way it highlighted the risks of placing excessive trust in so-called heroic judges or prosecutors. It underscored the need for constant vigilance and a case-by-case assessment of legal proceedings. In retrospect, it became evident that several aspects of the operation were deeply problematic and did not unfold as they should have.

On the positive side, Operation Car Wash showed that to handle large-scale investigations, the branches of law must work together. A lawyer could not just be a criminal lawyer or a civil or tax lawyer—they had to understand all of it. The plea bargain agreements generated during the operation are intellectually rich and have great academic value. The themes that emerged from Operation Car Wash have inspired extraordinary academic theses and dissertations.

That period also showed us something very important: the power of managing information. They had American software that allowed them to handle criminal data across thousands of cases at once. That database management, that ability to cross-reference information, left everyone speechless. I was so impressed that I started researching data analysis myself. From that perspective, Operation Car Wash became a model of more modern criminal prosecution, especially for the Federal Police and the Public Prosecutor's Office.

Another positive point is that it highlighted the need to change the relationship between the public and private sectors in Brazil. This idea that you can only win public contracts through favours—well, it is a risky and frankly outdated strategy. Is it worth it? I have my doubts. Being arrested, having your assets frozen, going through public humiliation—all based on political shifts—is a huge gamble. For a young entrepreneur, it might be safer to work with derivatives or the stock market. High risk, yes, but at least you are not dealing with the legal jeopardy that comes from shady relationships with mayors, governors, ministers, and the like.

I will tell you a story I find quite revealing. I was in Switzerland during the height of Operation Car Wash—working on a case completely unrelated to it, thank God, because that operation could be incredibly draining and frustrating. You knew exactly what would happen from the start: the client would lose in the first instance, then at the Regional Federal Court, then at the Superior Court of Justice, and the Supreme Court was not doing much better when it came to upholding individual rights. The death of Justice Teori[141] was a real setback—he was starting to bring some balance. After his death, things lost their way. Among lawyers, there was a prevailing sense of futility—proceedings became highly predictable, and the higher courts did not always extend to the defence the level of respect and consideration that the legal profession warrants.

Anyway, back to Switzerland—I was at the gym early in the morning when someone approached me and asked, "Are you Brazilian? Where are you from?" I said I was, and he replied, "I am Swiss. You Brazilians are making a big mistake." I asked, "What mistake?" And he said, "You are talking too much about corruption. Stop it. France has corruption, we have it here, the whole of Europe has it. The world has corruption. You need to learn how to deal with it, but you do not have to advertise it constantly. That is your big mistake." That conversation really stuck with me. We do need to think about how our internal problems affect our image abroad, especially in terms of international business.

Another point worth emphasising is that companies need to fundamentally reconsider their relationship with the State. In several instances I observed, the effort expended to engage in corrupt practices was considerable. Had that same energy been channelled into developing lawful and sustainable business models, the outcomes would likely have been far more advantageous—both economically and in terms of legal security.

I remember reading an article some thirty years ago, I think it was from PWC[142] in the UK. It said that companies with low ethical standards experience higher levels of fraud. If you investigate Operation Car Wash carefully, you'll see not just public corruption, but also a shocking amount of internal fraud against the companies themselves. When corruption is tolerated at the top, it gives the green light to people below to commit even more fraud. In a way, Operation Car Wash confirmed what that economic criminal theory had been predicting for decades.

Indeed, I believe corporate behaviour must evolve. While compliance practices today may at times appear excessive or overly formalistic, they remain essential to fostering integrity and mitigating legal and reputational risks. *Know Your Customer*[143] is not just a banking requirement anymore—it applies even in a law office. During Operation Car Wash, several politicians approached me, and I had to say, "I cannot take your case—there is no legitimate way for you to pay me."

The nature of these relationships has shifted—one hopes for the better. My perspective has been shaped significantly by the Law and Economics school of thought, which highlights the limitations of relying solely on legislation. Imposing severe sentences, such as a hundred years for corruption offences, is not a sufficient solution. What is needed is a new legal and institutional framework capable of addressing the structural complexities inherent in the public–private interface.

There is also an urgent need to engage in a serious and substantive discussion on campaign financing, as numerous aspects of the current model require re-evaluation. Additionally, Brazil's political structure itself warrants critical reflection. Should we persist with a form of presidentialism that effectively places the President of the Republic at the mercy of Congress? In practice, where does power truly reside—in the hands of the President, the Speaker of the Chamber of Deputies, or the President of the Senate? While these are long-standing questions, they remain central to understanding the structural roots of corruption in the country.

On top of that, the Brazilian State continues to be a major economic player, and that role needs to be redefined. The way we treat the State's role in the economy must evolve.

By way of conclusion, is there any closing thought or additional observation you would like to share?

What I would like to emphasise, in closing, is that I remain fundamentally optimistic. Despite its numerous flaws, Operation Car Wash provided important lessons for all of us. It was a period of significant personal and professional growth—I was compelled to deepen my studies and evolve in my practice. In the face of arbitrariness, the lawyer has only one meaningful response: to be better prepared. That means drafting more thorough submissions, managing cases with greater care, being more detail-oriented, and investing in training their team. Everyone had to become sharper.

I believe that is one of the positive takeaways from the Car Wash experience. From an academic standpoint, it opened countless areas of inquiry—so many topics have emerged from the overlap between different branches of law, many of which are already proving capable of offering meaningful solutions.

There is a great deal to explore in the intersection between law and economics. There is still so much to produce, intellectually speaking. Honestly, if I had more time, I would have a long list of books to write—but now, life does not quite allow for it.

Antônio Sérgio Altieri de Moraes Pitombo was born in São Paulo (SP). He is a partner of the law firm Moraes Pitombo Lawyers. He holds a master's and doctorate in Criminal Law from the Faculty of Law of USP, post-doctorate in Democracy and Human Rights from the University of Coimbra. His testimony was given on 15 August 2022 via the Zoom virtual platform and lasted 1 hour and 11 minutes of recording. The transcript was subsequently reviewed by the interviewee on 13 March 2023.

Testimony of Pierpaolo Bottini

Abstract

In this testimony, criminal lawyer and professor Pierpaolo Cruz Bottini reflects on the institutional, legal, and political implications of Operation Car Wash, drawing from his dual experience as a practitioner and academic. Tracing his professional trajectory from his legal studies at the University of São Paulo to his work alongside Márcio Thomaz Bastos[144] at the Ministry of Justice during the first Lula administration, Bottini offers a critical, insider-informed view of Brazil's anti-corruption efforts. He highlights how the operation, initially perceived as a legitimate investigation into business irregularities and public procurement fraud, gradually revealed itself as a politicised endeavour, often prioritising convictions of specific political figures over evidentiary rigour.

Bottini contrasts Operation Car Wash with the Mensalão case, noting that while both involved prominent political actors, they were structurally and procedurally distinct—particularly in their use of plea bargaining and their relationship with the press. He argues that the unequal flow of information during Car Wash, deliberately managed by authorities, fostered a biased media narrative, and undermined procedural fairness. Drawing on his academic background and experience coordinating high-profile plea agreements, Bottini offers a nuanced view of plea bargaining, acknowledging its legitimacy as a legal instrument while sharply criticising its instrumentalisation in Car Wash, especially in cases lacking corroborative evidence.

He further critiques the overuse of pre-trial detention and coercive measures, which he considers to have fostered a culture of arbitrariness. Bottini also identifies structural deficiencies in Brazil's public procurement system and campaign financing framework as root causes of corruption that were left unaddressed by the operation. His co-edited volume on money laundering and financial crimes is cited as an attempt to bridge academic and practical legal discourse—a gap he sees as particularly damaging in the context of Car Wash, where he identifies a pervasive lack of doctrinal depth among legal actors, including judges and prosecutors.

Bottini draws a cautious parallel between Operation Car Wash and Italy's Operation Clean Hands, noting their shared institutional consequences, including the weakening of national industries and the destabilisation of political parties. He argues that Car Wash inflicted lasting damage on public trust in Brazil's judicial institutions, especially after prominent figures in the operation—such as Judge Sérgio Moro—entered politics. In his view, what began as a promising legal initiative devolved into political theatre, eroding its legitimacy and weakening the criminal justice system.

Concluding on a forward-looking note, Bottini calls for a more coherent regulatory framework for both international and domestic cooperation in criminal investigations. He stresses the urgent need for better institutional coordination, intelligence-sharing, and legal reform to address the systemic issues that operations like Car Wash merely exposed but failed to resolve. His testimony contributes a critical, yet constructive, voice to the debate over the operation's legacy, highlighting the tension between legal effectiveness, procedural integrity, and democratic accountability.

Could you describe your educational background and personal trajectory, in order to provide context for your professional perspective?

I studied Law at the University of São Paulo, at "São Francisco". When I began my criminal law classes, I absolutely fell in love with the subject—that is when I realised it was what I wanted to do with my life. At the time, there was no such thing as economic criminal law with all the glamour it has today; criminal law was more focused on harsher, more violent, and serious crimes. Still, I was drawn to it.

After graduating, I opened a small office, and about a year or two later, Márcio Thomaz Bastos[145] invited me to work with him at the Ministry of Justice. This was during the first Lula administration.[146] He had been appointed Minister of Justice and asked me to serve as Secretary for Judiciary Reform. I was part of what they called "Márcio's nursery", because nearly all the secretaries were under 30.

It was a fascinating time. I lived in Brasília, got to know the workings of the Judiciary from the inside, and followed the approval of new legislation. That experience in Brasília was extremely valuable to me—on a personal, intellectual, and professional level. It gave me insight into how things really function behind the scenes. When Márcio decided to leave the Ministry, I stepped down as well. Four years later, I returned to legal practice and re-established my office, this time with my partner Igor Tamasauskas.[147]

I never gave up on academia, so I went on to do a master's and a doctorate and sat the public examination to teach at USP. I passed in 2008, and since then I have balanced legal practice with academia. I have taught both undergraduate and postgraduate law at USP. Eventually, I found myself involved in high-profile cases like the *Mensalão*[148] and Car Wash. These were complex cases that allowed me to blend legal practice with academic insight, as they required well-structured legal strategies and sophisticated argumentation. The academic background really helped in that sense.

So, in essence, that is my story—a career that combines the academic world with legal practice.

Upon accepting your first case related to Operation Car Wash, what aspects of the investigation or its context most surprised you?

The first case came in 2014. At that time, we noticed there were elements suggesting business irregularities, possible money laundering—and we understood that the most suitable path for our client was to pursue a plea bargain.

Back then, there was this belief that the Car Wash team was genuinely focused on collecting evidence to tackle crimes related to public tenders, cartels, and corruption within state-run companies. But we soon realised that the operation had a political agenda. It was clearly geared towards securing convictions against specific politicians, even when there was no solid evidence.

Initially, it seemed like Operation Car Wash was genuinely in pursuit of the truth. Later, it became evident that it was more of a political project.

In your view, was the Mensalão case a precursor to Operation Car Wash, or should the two be regarded as entirely distinct in nature and scope?

They are two distinct things, but there are points of connection. I would not say that Operation Car Wash was a continuation of the Mensalão—the facts involved were quite different. In the Mensalão, there was no plea bargaining, whereas plea bargains formed the very foundation of Operation Car Wash.

The entire Mensalão case was heard in the Federal Supreme Court, in a fully public trial. Operation Car Wash, on the other hand, began in the lower courts, in proceedings that were not public. That difference alone shaped a very different relationship with the press.

In the Mensalão, public officials could not trade information in exchange for media support. In Operation Car Wash, this sort of exchange did take place. So yes, while there are overlaps—some of the same figures appeared in both cases—the settings were quite different: where the events took place, how the investigations were conducted (one relying heavily on plea deals, the other not), and especially how the media was involved.

The relationship with the press during the Mensalão was much healthier. Journalists followed the case live at the Federal Supreme Court. They sat through the entire process and really understood what was going on. They were experienced, well-informed reporters who weren't racing each other for exclusive scoops, because everyone had access to the same information. As a result, the reporting had more depth and less bias—you heard both the prosecution and the defence.

That was not the case with Operation Car Wash. There was an openly admitted strategy—on the part of public authorities themselves—to manage the press through an unequal flow of information. This created and reinforced a biased narrative, which was intentional and, unfortunately, accepted. So yes, they're two quite different contexts.

The *Mensalão* case was, from a historical standpoint, a landmark in the fight against corruption. Nevertheless, the corrupt practices later exposed by Operation Car Wash were already taking place during

the Mensalão proceedings, suggesting a kind of never-ending political drama. In your view, why did such practices persist? Would you attribute this continuity primarily to structural features of the political system, the economic system, or both? What do you believe can be done to change this reality and to ensure that corruption offences, particularly those supported by substantial evidence, are properly investigated and punished?

That is a very important question. In Brazil, there is a tendency to turn everything into a spectacle. As you rightly noted, the *Mensalão* became a kind of soap opera, and the same happened with Operation Car Wash. However, at no point does the public debate pause to ask the fundamental questions: "*why are these events occurring, and where does the underlying problem truly lie*".

In the end, the *Mensalão* case exposed a fundamental flaw in Brazil's political structure, while Operation Car Wash brought to light systemic problems within the public procurement and bidding processes. When one examines the *Mensalão*, it becomes clear that the core issue was the urgent need for political reform. In contrast, Operation Car Wash should have prompted a thorough reform of the mechanisms governing public tenders in Brazil.

However, no one paused to say, "Let us set the characters aside and really examine the facts." Why is this happening? What is the root cause? Where, precisely, does the weakness in the bidding process lie? Why does a public authority request money from a contractor? Why does the contractor agree to pay? What lies beneath these practices?

And once one begins to examine the situation more closely, recurring patterns emerge. In many cases, contractors paid bribes simply to receive what was already contractually owed to them. If they refused to pay, they would not be paid. This reflects a broader institutional failure to implement a reliable system for certifying work and ensuring timely payments—one in which clear deadlines are established, and contractors are remunerated upon fulfilling their contractual obligations.

Why did all of this occur? Merely arresting individuals is insufficient. If the underlying structures remain unchanged, the same problems will inevitably recur. What was truly needed was a serious effort to understand the root causes of these illicit practices and to implement reforms that address the system at its foundation. However, that was not undertaken.

Once again, a genuine opportunity for institutional reform was missed, and in its place came yet another instance of turning the issue into public spectacle.

How do you evaluate the role and impact of plea bargain agreement within the context of Operation Car Wash?

The plea bargain agreement is a legitimate legal mechanism. Nonetheless, its use encounters understandable cultural resistance. In Dante Alighieri's *Divine Comedy*,[149] the person condemned to the deepest circle of hell is Judas—a collaborator[150]. In Brazil, we have the figures of Joaquim Silvério dos Reis[151] and Cabo Anselmo.[152] Plea bargain agreement, notably, generates considerable discomfort and controversy.

But today, it is a legitimate legal instrument and can be used as part of a defence strategy—provided the collaborator presents evidence and proves the truth of what they're claiming. The issue is not with plea bargaining itself, but rather how it was used during Operation Car Wash. On some occasions, it was employed without supporting evidence and became a tool for steering investigations in a particular direction.

I was involved in two plea bargain agreements during Operation Car Wash, that of the president[153] of Camargo Corrêa[154] and the president[155] of Braskem,[156] and in both cases there were supporting evidence. That, however, was not always the prevailing practice. A plea bargain agreement that lacks spontaneity, is unsupported by clear evidence, or is employed for purposes of revenge or political gain becomes a highly problematic and potentially dangerous legal instrument.

Following the 2019 Anti-Crime Package,[157] I believe the framework became somewhat more structured and institutionally grounded. Current legislation provides that no criminal charge, search and seizure, or arrest may be grounded solely on a plea bargain agreement. Other supporting evidence is required. This contributed to placing plea bargaining within a more coherent and properly regulated legal framework.

The problem was that, at one stage, the sole testimony of a collaborator was sufficient to justify a search and seizure. And we all understand the impact such measures can have on an individual's life. A collaborator might simply allege, "Person X committed a crime and there is evidence at their flat," and a warrant would swiftly follow. In effect, collaborators were granted the power to determine whether someone would be subject to a search or even arrested—an extraordinary level of influence, in my view. This created opportunities for the mechanism to be misused to settle personal scores or advance private interests. Justice Celso de Mello[158] frequently addressed this issue. After all, a collaborator is someone directly involved in the facts—someone with a vested interest. With the new legal framework, plea bargain agreement is once again a valuable investigative tool, but now one that is properly regulated and legally appropriate.

What is your assessment of the use of provisional arrests during Operation Car Wash?

Initially, some of these arrests may have been justified by concerns over the potential destruction of evidence or risk of flight. However, in most instances, they were carried out without any solid legal foundation. Once again, the Anti-Crime Package played an important role in addressing this issue. It introduced a clear requirement that no one may be held in preventive custody without current and contemporaneous evidence to support such a measure. Preventive detention can no longer be based solely on actions committed in the past. Under the provisions of this new legal framework, the majority of the arrests made during Operation Car Wash would likely not have been sustained. At the time, individuals were being arrested for acts committed years earlier. In my view, there was indeed a clear abuse—an excessive use of preventive detention and coercive measures, which I have always regarded as entirely unlawful. The courts later acknowledged this as such. Coercive measures, temporary detentions, and preventive arrests were often employed without adequate legal grounds, frequently leading to plea bargain agreements. This gave rise to a cycle of procedural misuse, contributing to a broader climate of arbitrariness within the country's criminal justice system.

In the volume you coordinated, *Money Laundering, Legal Opinions, Selected and Commented Jurisprudence,*[159] various issues are

addressed, including money laundering, corruption, electoral donations, tax evasion, and even the limits of the Council for Financial Activities Control.[160] The backdrop to the work includes recent corruption scandals in Brazil, such as the Mensalão case and, most notably, Operation Car Wash. In your view, what is the main contribution of the book, and what is its principal critique?

I would suggest that the principal lesson, and perhaps the most relevant criticism, lies in the general lack of rigour in the doctrinal analysis of the law. By this, I mean that legal actors often engage in cases and debates without adequately studying the applicable legal framework, whether national or international. There is insufficient reflection on the legal definitions of money laundering, the elements that constitute corruption, the proper handling of evidence, or the procedural contours of a plea bargain. This concern applies not only to lawyers but also to public prosecutors and, importantly, to members of the judiciary.

The discussion ends up being very ad hoc and quite precarious. We felt there was a need to bring some of that academic debate into practice—that is the whole idea behind this work. That is why we included legal opinions and judicial votes, to show that there are deep and meaningful legal discussions to be had, and they can—and should—inform legal practice.

The aim is not to be pedantic or to intellectualise matters unnecessarily. On the contrary, the objective is to apply legal knowledge in addressing complex problems in real-world contexts. The difficulty lies in the current gap between academia and legal practice. Academic institutions often appear reluctant to engage with the practical realities of the legal system, while practitioners are frequently unwilling to draw on insights from academic research. As a result, there is a noticeable lack of dialogue between the two spheres.

This work was intended to demonstrate the value of fostering dialogue between academia and legal practice. It highlights the significant contribution academic research can make to the legal field, while also showing how legal practice can inform and challenge academic perspectives. It represents a step towards building a more coherent and resilient legal culture. In many ways, the project sought to bridge the divide between these two spheres. It has helped to dismantle some of the long-standing prejudice against academic discourse within the legal profession, just as academia has begun to move beyond its traditional scepticism towards practical application.

An article published in the newspaper *Folha de S. Paulo* carried a rather striking headline: *Pierpaolo Bottini: The Exaggerations of Car Wash Do Not Tarnish the Operation.*[161] Could you elaborate on what is meant by these exaggerations?

To be honest, I believe the headline took my remarks somewhat out of context. What I said was that, in its initial stages, some of the actions associated with Operation Car Wash appeared serious and seemed to indicate genuine illegal conduct. The problem, however, was that it soon became evident that much of this was merely superficial. Many of the accusations lacked the evidentiary basis required to sustain them. This, in itself, significantly undermined the credibility of the operation.

If Car Wash had carried out the investigations properly, with the seriousness required, it could have provided an important service to the country. But once the operation became politicised—once it started targeting specific individuals regardless of whether there was real evidence—we began to see its downfall. That was made even more evident in those Telegram messages[162], where it became clear that people were being identified first, and only afterwards was evidence sought to support a case.

In my view, Operation Car Wash ultimately lost its way. The issue was not merely one of exaggeration, but rather a fundamental lack of rigour in the accusations, in the conduct of legal proceedings, and in the overall approach. That, in my opinion, is what truly undermined the operation's credibility.

The two most well-known anti-corruption operations in recent history are Operation Clean Hands[163] and Operation Car Wash. Could you draw a parallel between the two?

I do not claim to be fully familiar with all the details of Operation Clean Hands. However, from what I have read, it is evident that Judge Sergio Moro[164] drew considerable inspiration from that operation in shaping his approach to Car Wash, particularly in his relationship with the media and in the way he conducted himself during the proceedings.

In the end, both Operation Car Wash and Operation Clean Hands produced a similar outcome: they had a profound impact on the national industrial and business landscape. In my view, both in Brazil and in Italy, these operations contributed to a kind of dismantling—or hollowing out—of the national industrial base. The political consequences were also significant. What we witnessed, in effect, were operations that went beyond the legitimate aim of sanctioning individual wrongdoing under criminal law and ultimately led to the destabilisation of entire companies. National businesses were deprived of the conditions necessary for their survival. There was no meaningful effort to ensure that these companies could continue to operate within a framework of compliance and transparency. That crucial step was simply overlooked.

In Italy, the impact was arguably even more pronounced, as one of the major political parties effectively disappeared from the political landscape. In Brazil, the shock was also profound, with several parties seriously affected. However, they ultimately managed to retain a presence on the political scene.

That is about as far as I can go with the comparison, as I am not fully acquainted with the finer details of Operation Clean Hands.

In your view, has the relationship between Brazilian private companies and the Brazilian public sector changed in the aftermath of Operation Car Wash?

Yes, I do. I think the relationship between private companies and the public sector had long been marked by systemic dysfunction. A framework had developed in which certain public officials and corporate actors engaged in unduly close and ethically questionable interactions. Such a configuration required institutional recognition, rigorous scrutiny, and deliberate dismantling.

The issue is that, due to flaws in our regulatory framework, we failed to tackle the problem while still maintaining the operational viability of these companies. What could have happened, for instance, is the development of a more effective leniency system—one in which companies could reach agreements, pay the necessary fines, and continue operating within legal and ethical boundaries. But that did not happen.

What we saw instead was that many companies—especially contractors—that had a strong dependency on the State, either disappeared or were seriously weakened. So, I believe there was not enough care or strategy around how to shift the nature of that relationship, which is what I mentioned earlier. No proper effort was made to identify the root of the problem, change the level of engagement, and allow companies to evolve while holding individuals accountable. That care simply was not taken. Once the process shifted into the realm of spectacle, the focus seemed to be on dismantling the companies altogether. And I think that was one of Car Wash' most serious failings.

During the period of Operation Car Wash, serving as a criminal defence lawyer for individuals accused of corruption must have presented particular challenges, especially in the light of prevailing public opinion. How did you experience that period, given that criminal lawyers are frequently called upon to represent individuals and companies accused of serious offences?

Such circumstances are inherent to the practice of criminal law. By choosing this profession, one accepts the fundamental duty to defend those accused of criminal conduct. It is an essential role within the justice system. In many cases, the criminal defence lawyer stands as the sole advocate for the accused—particularly when public opinion, social circles, and even family members have withdrawn their support. And that, in many respects, is the profound dignity of the profession. I cannot recall who first said it, but there is a quotation I find particularly resonant: the role of the criminal lawyer is "to sit beside a person at the worst moment of their life." That, to me, encapsulates the essence of what we do.

One becomes accustomed to this dynamic. From the moment we graduate and take on our earliest cases, we begin to cultivate a professional approach to the work. It is, ultimately, a vocation. Just as a doctor might perform surgery on an individual accused of a serious offence and thereby save their life, fulfilling their ethical duty, so too does a lawyer perform a vital role when defending an individual's rights. At the end of the day, every person—regardless of whether the accusations against them are ultimately upheld or dismissed—requires and deserves a proper legal defence.

When confronted with the question, "How can you defend such a person?", I typically respond that this is precisely the function of the criminal defence lawyer. The rule of law requires that every individual, regardless of the nature of the accusation, be afforded the right to a proper defence. And one must remember that, should the roles ever be reversed, anyone may find themselves in need of the same protection. In that sense, people should be grateful that there are professionals willing to take on this role. It is fundamental for upholding the Rule of Law. Without it, the prosecuting state has no limits. And a state without limits is dangerous for everyone.

The criminal defence lawyer plays a fundamental role in establishing necessary limits, in holding the State to account, and in erecting safeguards where they are required. I recall—though I cannot say with certainty that it was him—that Judge Sergio Moro once remarked that lawyers made the work of the prosecution more difficult. If that is the case, then quite rightly so. That is our job: to make things difficult for the state. Because the state has the power, the resources, and the prerogatives to invade people's lives and privacy. Someone must push back—to create a system of checks and balances, and to ensure there is at least a degree of balance between the accuser and the accused.

The dismantling of Operation Car Wash was authorised by the Federal Supreme Court. In your view, what effect did this decision have on the ongoing investigations at the time?

In my view, the dismantling of the operation was something that should have occurred from the outset. As I have mentioned previously, in the early stages of Operation Car Wash, the higher courts upheld all decisions issued in Curitiba. However, they later continued to validate those decisions in a manner that, in my opinion, was misguided—many of the cases being adjudicated in Curitiba bore no substantive connection to the city. There was no legitimate basis for those proceedings to be conducted there.

In Brazil, we often take far too long to recognise procedural nullities—things that, had they been acknowledged earlier, could have spared us a great deal of damage. There were cases that were almost completed, only to be entirely annulled because the judge was not competent to preside over them.

And again, this highlights the importance of defence lawyers. From the very beginning, lawyers were raising concerns about jurisdiction. I myself challenged Curitiba's jurisdiction back in 2015, and I am certain many of my colleagues did the same arguing that the cases should have been under the jurisdiction of the Electoral Courts. But it took four or five years for this to be acknowledged, which meant a huge waste of time, resources, and public money.

In the end, I believe there was an avoidable loss—something that could have been prevented if the nullity had been recognised right from the start.

In your view, should Operation Car Wash have been treated as a single, centralised proceeding, similar to the approach adopted in the Mensalão case?

No, because the situations were fundamentally different. Although we refer to it as Operation Car Wash, in reality it comprised a series of distinct cases—Petrobras, Transpetro, Angra, the refineries, the triplex apartment, among others. There were numerous parallel investigations and proceedings. In my view, it was a mistake to group such a wide range of matters under the single label of Operation Car Wash, as they involved markedly different facts and circumstances.

In the beginning, in that first stage, the investigation was focused on a cartel of companies involved in Petrobras bidding processes—companies that paid bribes to Petrobras employees in order to maintain the cartel. That is already quite specific. So, it does not make sense to lump everything together under one umbrella, especially when the cases involved such distinct issues, and some individuals had special legal prerogatives, while others did not.

Could you provide your overall assessment of Operation Car Wash and its broader implications?

Certainly. In my view, Operation Car Wash lost its way. In seeking to target political figures without a solid evidentiary basis, it ultimately undermined any aspects of the investigation that may have been properly conducted. The initial body of evidence could have been managed with greater care and competence. However, the operation deviated from its proper course when the presiding judge began to harbour political ambitions—something that, in my view, also occurred in the case of the prosecutor. In the end, the greatest adversary of Operation Car Wash was the operation itself. It ultimately compromised its own legitimacy. The moment it became politicised, when it started to pursue political aims, it put everything at risk.

What, if any, enduring institutional or civic lessons can be drawn from Operation Car Wash?

It is difficult to offer a definitive assessment, but if I were to place it on a scale, I would conclude that, ultimately, Operation Car Wash did more harm than good. The principal reason for this view is that it cast a long shadow of doubt over the Judiciary. We witnessed a judge resign from the bench to assume the role of Minister of Justice, later pursue the Presidency, and eventually stand for election to the Senate. Such a trajectory inevitably prompted questions regarding the impartiality and political neutrality of the judiciary[165]. Prosecutors followed a similar trajectory. Over time, Operation Car Wash came to be perceived less as a legal undertaking and more as a political movement—at times resembling the dynamics of a political party. This perception inevitably contributed to the erosion of public trust. The unfortunate reality is that Brazil has thousands of judges and prosecutors who perform their duties with integrity and professionalism. Yet the conduct of a few individuals inflicted significant institutional damage, revealing a degree of politicisation that is simply incompatible with the principles that should govern both the Judiciary and the Public Prosecutor's Office.

Ultimately, when considered from a broader perspective, I am of the view that Operation Car Wash did more harm than good. The political posturing—what became known as "jet politics"[166]—undermined what might otherwise have evolved into a far more serious and institutionally significant operation. What began with genuine promise was gradually eclipsed by ambition and spectacle, leaving behind a legacy that is, at best, ambivalent.

In your view, what were the principal positive and negative aspects of Operation Car Wash?

What I regard as positive—particularly in the early stages—was the organisation of the evidentiary system, which was relatively robust, as well as a certain procedural agility that allowed the proceedings to advance efficiently. The structuring of plea bargain agreements into annexes was also an innovative and effective method.

As for the negative aspects, several stand out: the abusive application of coercive measures; the excessive reliance on pre-trial detention; and the distortion of jurisdictional rules—particularly the notion of a "universal judge of Curitiba" who failed to respect the authority of the electoral courts and the principles of territorial jurisdiction. There was also the overuse, and in some cases misuse, of plea bargains. When plea bargains become the sole basis for searches, arrests, or the launching of criminal proceedings, it opens the door to abuses—collaborations used for revenge or personal agendas—which ended up undermining the credibility of the entire system. So yes, Operation Car Wash brought with it a number of serious issues that ended up damaging important legal tools, tools that could have been used much more responsibly and effectively.

What is your assessment of the international cooperation that took place in the context of Operation Car Wash?

The international cooperation during Operation Car Wash—at least in the cases in which I was involved—clearly demonstrated the extent to which more precise regulation is still needed in this area. A wide range of questions remained unresolved. For example, when seeking a breach of confidentiality in another jurisdiction, what is the appropriate legal procedure to follow? If a country—Switzerland, for instance—decides to close a case against an individual, as occurred on several occasions, is it permitted to share the entire case file with another jurisdiction, rather than limiting cooperation to the evidentiary material alone?

These are technical yet important questions, and it became clear that Brazil still possesses a rather rudimentary legal framework for addressing them. There is Article 7 of the Penal Code[167] and a few provisions in the Code of Criminal Procedure, but honestly, we lack comprehensive legislation to properly regulate international cooperation. As a result, many of the issues that came up during Operation Car Wash were simply brushed aside because the evidence being brought in was seen as so significant. People focused on the substance of the evidence and ignored the procedural aspects—but those arguments were relevant, and many of them, in my opinion, pointed to serious nullities. I believe a lot of that could have been avoided with clearer, more coherent legislation.

If I may add a further observation on this point: I recently attended an event in Rome hosted by the Superior Court of Justice, where the focus was on international cooperation. What stood out to me was how far the debate on cross-border evidence and data exchange has progressed. At the same time, it became strikingly apparent how limited cooperation remains within Brazil itself. We still lack adequate mechanisms for data sharing even between state-level civil and military police forces.

This is not to suggest that international cooperation should be neglected—on the contrary, it is essential. However, before we move too far in that direction, we must ask ourselves: how can we seriously combat organised crime if we are unable to share data effectively within our own borders? Brazil still lacks a coherent national intelligence and information-sharing system. Just to give you an idea—when someone made a plea deal with, say, fifty annexes, those annexes were approved and sent all over the country, and each judge took one, without any coordination. Nobody spoke to each other. The structure was completely fragmented.

Without an effective internal system of communication, intelligence, and data exchange, the capacity to confront criminal organisations is seriously compromised such as the PCC[168] or dismantle large-scale corruption networks. If someone in Amazonas is not in touch with someone in Rio Grande do Sul, a company engages in the same questionable practices across multiple states and the connections between these actions are not identified, the broader picture risks being entirely overlooked.

While it is certainly important to strengthen international cooperation, it is equally imperative to reflect on domestic shortcomings. Fundamental elements remain underdeveloped, and in many cases, essential steps are being overlooked. In my view, this is the most concerning aspect.

All the more so given the continental dimensions of Brazil.

Indeed—and it is also a federation.

To conclude, would you like to share any final observations or reflections?

In discussing Operation Car Wash, it is important to recall that, at the outset, the investigation conveyed an appearance of institutional seriousness—even in the view of the higher courts—which enabled it to move forward. Over time, however, the politicisation and instrumentalisation of the operation became increasingly evident. This ultimately undermined the credibility and legitimacy it had initially projected or might otherwise have achieved.

Pierpaolo Cruz Bottini was born in São Paulo (SP). Lawyer, partner of Bottini & Tamasauskas Lawyers. He is a professor at the Faculty of Law of USP. He was Secretary of Judiciary Reform of the Ministry of Justice. Author of several books and articles in the field of criminal law. His testimony was given on 9 September 2022 via the Zoom virtual platform and lasted 47 minutes of recording. The transcript was subsequently reviewed by the interviewee on 17 February 2023.

Conclusion to Chapter 2

Chapter 2, "Car Wash and the Criminal Lawyers", offers a compelling and indispensable perspective on the role of criminal defence lawyers during Operation Car Wash, Brazil's landmark anti-corruption investigation. Through detailed interviews with prominent defence attorneys, the chapter explores the interplay between prosecutorial power and the safeguarding of fundamental legal principles. By shifting the narrative focus from prosecutors to defence counsel, it enriches our understanding of the adversarial system within the context of one of the most consequential legal and political investigations in Brazilian history.

A central theme emerging from the interviews is the tension between the zealousness of the Federal Public Prosecutor's Office and the constitutional rights of the accused. Defence lawyers repeatedly highlight the controversial use of pre-trial detention and the extensive reliance on plea bargain agreements. While these tools were instrumental in accelerating the investigation and uncovering intricate networks of systemic corruption, their use raises significant concerns about due process and the erosion of the presumption of innocence. The testimonies in this chapter illustrate how coercive measures—particularly the strategic use of pre-trial detention to secure plea bargain agreements—created an environment in which defence counsel faced extraordinary challenges in mounting an effective defence, especially in the face of extensive evidence of corruption.

The lawyers interviewed in this chapter also critique what they describe as an asymmetrical system that disproportionately favoured the prosecution. They point to the immense public and political pressures surrounding Car Wash, which they argue compromised judicial impartiality and led to an alignment between the judiciary and the prosecutorial agenda. The pervasive media coverage, combined with a public perception of guilt before trials had even begun, added an extra layer of complexity to the work of the defence. This environment, they argue, frequently blurred the line between justice and public spectacle—creating what some termed a "trial by media". Such reflections offer a sobering critique of the procedural dynamics of Operation Car Wash, indicating that its outcomes may have been secured at the expense of long-standing legal safeguards. They also expose a broader discomfort within segments of the criminal defence community, which at times appeared hesitant to confront the structural and evidentiary realities of systemic corruption.

Moreover, this chapter critically examines the broader implications of Car Wash for Brazil's legal system. Defence attorneys underscore how the operation redefined fundamental legal practices, including plea bargain agreements and leniency deals, which were extensively employed as prosecutorial tools. While these agreements were praised for their efficiency in dismantling corruption networks, the chapter raises concerns about their long-term impact on the adversarial system. Criminal lawyers have argued that the broad discretion granted to prosecutors in negotiating plea agreements, combined with limited judicial oversight, created a power imbalance that undermined the principle of equality of arms between prosecution and defence. However, such claims often overlook the scale and consistency of the evidentiary material uncovered during the investigations. In this context, appeals to procedural imbalance risk deflecting attention from the substantive findings of wrongdoing, particularly in cases involving politically and economically powerful defendants implicated in white-collar crime.

A key critical dimension of this chapter lies in its examination of the ethical dilemmas encountered by defence lawyers operating within the context of a politically charged investigation. The attorneys reflect on their dual role—both as advocates for their clients and as actors within a legal system struggling to address systemic corruption. They highlight the stigma associated with defending individuals accused of corruption, particularly in an environment where public opinion often conflates legal defence with complicity. These reflections bring into sharp relief the difficulty of upholding professional ethics and the right to a rigorous defence in a climate dominated by demands for severe punitive measures.

While the chapter presents reflections by defence lawyers on the ethical tensions they claim to have faced, it is important to critically assess these narratives. The claim that the defence function was unduly stigmatised or ethically compromised often obscures the fact that many of these lawyers operated in cases supported by substantial and consistent evidentiary records. Assertions of procedural imbalance or professional hardship, while rhetorically powerful, risk deflecting attention from the systemic nature of the corruption uncovered. The fight against corruption is a legal and democratic imperative, and efforts to prosecute such crimes must be recognised as legitimate—provided they are conducted within the bounds of due process and constitutional guarantees.

The chapter also contributes to a broader academic discussion on the rule of law and its resilience under extraordinary circumstances. Car Wash, as a case study, highlights the inherent tensions between the imperative to combat systemic corruption and the need to safeguard constitutional guarantees. The reflections of the criminal lawyers interviewed in this chapter reveal the fragility of legal principles when subjected to intense public and political pressures. They caution against allowing expedient measures, however effective they may seem, to erode the foundational principles of justice, such as the presumption of innocence, the right to a fair trial, and the independence of the judiciary.

From an academic perspective, this chapter raises profound questions about the limits of legal pragmatism in the face of systemic corruption. It invites critical engagement with the broader implications of Car Wash for the Brazilian legal system, particularly its legacy for criminal procedure and the balance of power within the justice system. It also highlights the importance of maintaining a critical lens on the role of defence counsel as a counterweight to prosecutorial and judicial authority, especially in politically sensitive cases. The interviews underscore the need for systemic reforms to ensure that the pursuit of justice does not compromise the very principles upon which the justice system is built.

In conclusion, the Car Wash and the Criminal Lawyers offers a necessary counterpoint to the prosecutorial narratives that have dominated public discourse on Operation Car Wash. It presents a critical—though at times strategically constructed—perspective on the role of criminal defence in cases of systemic corruption. While the accounts provided by defence lawyers raise important questions about procedural justice, they also reveal attempts to reframe the legal process in ways that obscure the gravity of the offences involved. Assertions of ethical dilemmas and professional hardship must be read with caution, as they risk minimising the overwhelming evidentiary record and the broader institutional harm caused by corruption. For proponents of prosecutorial accountability, the chapter serves as both a critique and a cautionary reminder: anti-corruption efforts must be conducted within the bounds of legality, but they must also be protected from narratives that seek to erode their legitimacy under the guise of procedural concern.

Ultimately, this chapter constitutes an essential resource for scholars, practitioners, and policymakers concerned with the complex interplay between efforts to combat grand corruption, the operation of criminal law, and the preservation of constitutional guarantees. By exposing the tensions and dilemmas inherent in high-profile investigations, it contributes to a more nuanced and critical understanding of justice in contemporary Brazil. Chapter 2 challenges readers to engage with one of the most difficult questions confronting modern democracies: how to pursue the urgent and legitimate goal of fighting systemic corruption while simultaneously safeguarding the rule of law and protecting individual rights.

It is important to acknowledge that, notwithstanding criticisms raised by segments of the defence bar, the rule of law remained operative throughout the course of these proceedings in Brazil. While concerns regarding procedural safeguards were voiced, many of these claims appear difficult to substantiate when considered against the magnitude of the corruption uncovered. Operation Car Wash revealed an extensive and deeply rooted network of illicit practices involving high-ranking officials, major corporations, and vast sums of public money. In this context, assertions of systematic procedural violations must be weighed carefully, particularly when they risk overshadowing the gravity and scale of the misconduct exposed.

Notes

1. The Central Directory of Students is an entity responsible for representing the student body to the rectorate and governments. In 1978, Brazil was living under a military dictatorship (the period from 1968 to 1978, under the enforcement of AI-5—Institutional Act Number 5, was called the Lead Years) and student movements were clandestine.
2. Márcio Thomaz Bastos was a well-known Brazilian criminal lawyer. He was president of the Federal Council of the Brazilian Bar Association, from 1987 to 1989, Minister of Justice during the first term of Luiz Inácio Lula da Silva's government and advocated for several construction companies in Operation Car Wash, but only in the beginning, as he died in 2014.
3. Tercio Sampaio Ferraz Júnior is a famous Brazilian jurist, retired full professor from the Department of Philosophy of Law at the University of São Paulo Law School.

4. Sergio Fernando Moro ***Entry***. FGV CPDOC. http://www.fgv.br/cpdoc/acervo/dicionarios/verbete-biografico/sergio-fernando-moro. He was a former federal judge and judge of Operation Car Wash in Curitiba. He was former Minister of Justice and director of Alvarez & Marsal. He is a Brazilian lawyer and politician. He is currently an elected Senator for the state of Paraná.
5. Luiz Inácio Lula da Silva is a popular Brazilian politician, affiliated with the Workers' Party. He was president of Brazil from 2003 to 2006 (first term) and from 2006 to 2010 (second term). He is the current president of Brazil (2023–2026).
6. The Plenary of the Federal Supreme Court decided on the incompetence of the 13th Federal Court of Curitiba to process and judge the cases involving former President Lula related to the triplex in Guarujá (SP), the Atibaia (SP) site, and the two actions involving the Lula Institute.
7. Mensalão was a corruption scandal, which occurred through the purchase of deputies' votes by the Executive, during the government of Luiz Inácio Lula da Silva, in 2005. This illegal practice was thus known behind the scenes as it referred to a monthly payment paid to deputies to vote in favour of projects of interest to the Executive.
8. Alberto Zacharias Toron, the right of defence in Car Wash, *Brazilian Journal of Criminal Sciences*, n. 122, 2016, pp. 15–41.
9. Ricardo Ribeiro Pessoa, better known as Ricardo Pessoa, is a Brazilian businessman and former president of the company UTC Engineering. He was indicted for corruption in Operation Car Wash and convicted of corruption. In 2015 he celebrated a plea bargain agreement with the then Prosecutor General, Ricardo Janot, being obliged to indemnify the amount of R$ 51 million.
10. To defraud the bids, the construction companies involved in Operation Car Wash formed a cartel, closing themselves into a group that became known as the "Club of 16".
11. Fabiana Alves Rodrigues, *Operation Car Wash: institutional learning and strategic action in criminal justice*. Master's Thesis.

Faculty of Philosophy, Letters and Human Sciences of the University of São Paulo, 2019.

12. Dimitrius Dantas and Cleide Carvalho, "King of habeas corpus": how Alberto Toron became one of the most sought-after lawyers of the Car Wash operation. *Época Magazine*. 4 October 2019. https://epoca.globo.com/brasil/rei-dos-habeas-corpus-como-alberto-toron-tornou-se-um-dos-advogados-mais-concorridos-da-lava-jato-23994065.
13. The Operation Sandcastle was an operation of the Federal Police in 2009 that investigated corruption and money laundering crimes, involving the contractor Camargo Corrêa. Many consider this operation to be the precursor of the Car Wash Operation because it deals with a corruption case involving well-known politicians in the Brazilian scenario and the contractors.
14. Kurt Paul Pickel is a Swiss citizen, naturalised Brazilian, who was pointed out as the operator of an alleged scheme of frauds in tenders, overpriced public works and evasion of currency in the Operation Sandcastle.
15. Celso Vilardi is a well-known Brazilian criminal lawyer. He holds a master's degree in criminal procedural law, graduated in law from Pontifical Catholic University of São Paulo.
16. The judge of the 6th Federal Criminal Court of São Paulo was Fausto Martin De Sanctis, today a judge of the TRF of the 3rd Region. He specialises in combating white-collar crimes and money laundering, being responsible for the trial and imprisonment of well-known personalities, such as former banker Edemar Cid Ferreira, businessman Ricardo Mansur, black-market currency dealers Toninho da Barcelona, investor Naji Nahas, among others. He was one of the first Brazilian magistrates to proceed with the early sale of criminals' assets, to carry out award-winning collaborations, and to allocate the resources recovered from white-collar crimes and money laundering to philanthropic associations, as a form of compensation to society.
17. There was a tie among the justices of the 6th Chamber of the Superior Court of Justice and, for this reason, two external judges

to the Superior Court were called to decide the matter. The two called judges voted for the annulment of the operation.

18. Maria Thereza de Assis Moura is a justice of the Superior Court of Justice. She is a doctoral professor at São Francisco in the chair of criminal procedural law. She was Vice-President of the Superior Court of Justice and General Inspectorate of the Federal Justice, from 29 August 2018 to 27 August 2020. She holds a doctorate, master's, and bachelor's degree in law from São Francisco, with a specialisation in criminal procedural law from Pontifical Catholic University of São Paulo and in economic and European criminal law from the Faculty of Law of Coimbra, Portugal.
19. HC 137.349 and HC 159.159. 6th Chamber Superior Court of Justice. 5th April 2011. https://www.stj.jus.br/websecstj/cgi/revista/REJ.cgi/ITA?seq=1002984&tipo=0&nreg=200901010385&SeqCgrmaSessao=&CodOrgaoJgdr=&dt=20110530&formato=PDF&salvar=false.
20. Luís Roberto Barroso is a jurist and justice of the Federal Supreme Court. He holds a bachelor's degree in law from the State University of Rio de Janeiro, a master's degree from Yale University, and a Ph.D. from the same University, with post-doctorate from Harvard Law School. He is a full professor of constitutional law at State University of Rio de Janeiro.
21. Habeas Corpus 127.186 decided in a tight vote—three votes in favour and two against—by the 2nd Chamber of Supreme Court on 28 April 2015.
22. Aldemir Bendine is a business administrator. He was president of Banco do Brasil and Petrobras. He was arrested in the Car Wash Operation, suspected of having received a bribe from Odebrecht and was sentenced in the first instance to 11 years in prison in 2018. This conviction was overturned by the regimental appeal in HC 157.627, on 27 August 2019. On 11 May 2020, he was again sentenced to six years and eight months in prison by Judge Luiz Antonio Bonat, of the 13th Federal Criminal Court of Curitiba, successor to the former Judge Moro in Operation Car Wash.

23. Elio Gaspari, Moro's hell, a Brazilian tragedy. *Folha de S. Paulo*, 1 September 2019.
24. Gilmar Ferreira Mendes ***Entry***. FGV CPDOC. http://www.fgv.br/cpdoc/acervo/dicionarios/verbete-biografico/mendes-gilmar. He has been a Justice of the Federal Supreme Court since 2002.
25. Regimental Appeal in HC 157.627. 2nd Chamber of the Federal Supreme Court. 27 August 2019. http://portal..jus.br/processos/detalhe.asp?incidente=5472232.
26. Law No. 12.850, of 2 August 2013, which defines criminal organisation and provides for criminal investigation, the means of obtaining evidence and the criminal procedure. http://www.planalto.gov.br/ccivil_03/_ato2011-2014/2013/lei/l12850.htm.
27. Luiz Edson Fachin is a Brazilian jurist and Justice of the Federal Supreme Court, since June 2015. He was a lawyer and full professor of civil law at the Law School of the Federal University of Paraná. He is the current rapporteur of Operation Car Wash in the Federal Supreme Court.
28. Alberto Zacharias Toron. ***Habeas corpus and the control of due legal process***. 3rd ed. São Paulo: Revista dos Tribunais, 2020.
29. Law No. 8.072, of 25 July 1990, which provides for heinous crimes. http://www.planalto.gov.br/ccivil_03/leis/l8072.htm.
30. David Émile Durkheim was a French sociologist, anthropologist, political scientist, psychologist, and philosopher, considered the "father" of social science and sociology.
31. Francisco Muñoz Conde, ***Criminal law and social control***. (trans.). Rio de Janeiro: Forense, 2005.
32. Gary Becker was an economist and professor at the University of Chicago. He won the Nobel Prize in economics in 1992, for extending microeconomic analysis to human behaviour. In 1968, he published the article titled "*Crime and punishment: An economic approach*" in the *Journal of Political Economy*, vol. 76, no. 2, pp. 169–217, https://www.nber.org/system/files/chapters/c3625/c3625.pdf in which he uses economic reasoning to explain the rational variables that are considered by individuals before deciding to commit illicit acts, the so-called *Simple Model of Rational Crime*.

33. Operation Clean Hands, *Mani Pulite*, was an investigation into corruption cases in Italy, centred in Milan, that involved the Italian political class, political parties, the state fuel company (ENI—*Ente Nazionale Idrocarburi*) and large contractors in the overpricing of works and in the diversion of public money.
34. Ada Pellegrini Grinover was an Italian Brazilian jurist and lawyer. She was a professor of civil procedure at Largo São Francisco and a prosecutor for the State of São Paulo.
35. Ana Bonchristiano. Law will toughen against organised crime. *Folha de S. Paulo, Daily Life*, 11th September 1994. https://www1.folha.uol.com.br/fsp/1994/9/11/cotidiano/3.html.
36. Sergio Fernando Moro. Considerations on the operation mani pulite. *CEJ Magazine*. vol. 8, n. 26, Jul./Sep. 2004, pp. 56–62. https://revistacej.cjf.jus.br/cej/index.php/revcej/article/view/625/805.
37. Silvio Berlusconi is an Italian politician and businessman. He was Prime Minister (President of the Council of Ministers) between 1994 and 1995, from 2001 to 2005, between 2005 and 2006 and from 2008 to 2011.
38. Jair Messias Bolsonaro is a retired captain and Brazilian politician. He was President of Brazil, from 1 January 2019 until 31t December 2022.
39. Dilma Vana Rousseff is an economist and Brazilian politician, affiliated with the Workers' Party. She was President of Brazil from 2011 to 2014 (first term) and from 2015 to 2016 (second term), when she was removed by an impeachment process.
40. Antonio Palocci Filho is a Brazilian doctor and politician. He was affiliated with the Workers' Party, having been a Minister in the government of Luiz Inácio Lula da Silva and in the government of Dilma Rousseff. He was convicted by Operation Car Wash, in 2017, to twelve years of imprisonment in a closed regime, which were converted into semi-open imprisonment, due to his plea bargain agreement in 2018.
41. The 2nd Chamber of the Federal Supreme Court, by majority of votes, granted in HC 164,493 the recognition of the suspicion of the former judge Moro in the conduct of the criminal action

that convicted the former President Lula for passive corruption and money laundering related to the triplex in Guarujá (SP). On 22 April 2021, the plenary of the formed a majority to maintain the decision of the 2nd Chamber of the Court that declared the suspicion of the former Judge Moro to judge the former President Lula in the case of the triplex in Guarujá.

42. Boris Casoy is a Brazilian journalist and popular news presenter in the country.
43. "Escola Base" was a private school located in São Paulo, SP, whose owners (Icushiro Shimada and Maria Aparecida Shimada), a teacher and the driver (Paula Milhim Alvarenga and Maurício Monteiro de Alvarenga) were accused of sexual abuse, but which in the end turned out to be a false accusation.
44. René Ariel Dotti was one of the greatest Brazilian criminal lawyers, professor at the Federal University of Paraná, co-author of the draft laws N. 7.209/84 (reform of the General Part of the Penal Code) and Law N. 7.210/84 (Penal Execution Law). He passed away in early February 2021. He agreed to give an interview for this book but passed away before the date scheduled for the interview.
45. Law No. 12.846, of 1 August 2013, which provides for the administrative and civil liability of legal entities for the practice of acts against public administration, national or foreign. http://www.planalto.gov.br/ccivil_03/_ato2011-2014/2013/lei/l12846.htm.
46. Today, Petrobras managed to recover a little more than six billion reais.
47. Banestado is a well-known corruption scandal from the 1990s, involving illegal remittances of foreign currency abroad, through the Brazilian public financial system.
48. Mensalão was a corruption scandal, which occurred through the purchase of votes from deputies by the Executive, during the government of Luiz Inácio Lula da Silva, in 2005. This illegal practice was known behind the scenes as referring to a monthly payment made to deputies to vote in favour of projects of interest to the Executive.

49. In 1939, the sociologist Edwin Sutherland, appointed president of the American Association of Sociology, mentions in his inaugural speech, for the first-time, white-collar crimes. The speech was published in the *American Sociological Review, with the title White collar criminality* ("White collar criminality"), v. 5, n. 1. 1940, p. 9.
50. Joaquim Benedito Barbosa Gomes. ***Entry***. FGV CPDOC. https://www18.fgv.br/CPDOC/acervo/dicionarios/verbete-biografico/barbosa-joaquim. He was a Justice of the Federal Supreme Court. He is a jurist and lawyer. He was a member of the Federal Public Prosecutor's Office. In 2006, he took over the role of rapporteur of the *Mensalão*, his performance being of fundamental importance in the conviction of corrupt politicians for the first time in the country.
51. Teori Albino Zavascki. ***Entry***. FGV CPDOC. https://www18.fgv.br/CPDOC/acervo/dicionarios/verbete-biografico/teori-albino-zavascki. He was a jurist, professor, magistrate, and Justice of the Superior Court of Justice and Federal Supreme Court, from 2012 to 2017. He was the rapporteur of Operation Car Wash until his death.
52. Cármen Lúcia Antunes Rocha. ***Entry***. FGV CPDOC. https://www18.fgv.br/CPDOC/acervo/dicionarios/verbete-biografico/lucia-carmem. She has been a Justice of the Federal Supreme Court since 2006. She was a prosecutor and Attorney General of the state of Minas Gerais.
53. Gilmar Ferreira Mendes ***Entry***. FGV CPDOC. http://www.fgv.br/cpdoc/acervo/dicionarios/verbete-biografico/mendes-gilmar. He has been a Justice of the Federal Supreme Court, since 2002.
54. Operation Clean Hands, *Mani Pulite*, was an investigation into corruption cases in Italy, centred in Milan, which involved the Italian political class, political parties, the state-owned fuel company (ENI—*Ente Nazionale Idrocarburi*), and large contractors in the overpricing of works and the diversion of public money.
55. Luiz Inácio Lula da Silva is a popular Brazilian politician, affiliated with the Workers' Party. He was president of Brazil from

2003 to 2006 (first term) and from 2006 to 2010 (second term). He was arrested as part of Operation Car Wash. He is the current president of Brazil (2023–2026).

56. Unfortunately, despite the scale and achievements of Operation Car Wash, nearly all high-level executives and political figures who were convicted have since been released, primarily due to rulings by the Brazilian Supreme Federal Court. These decisions were largely based on procedural arguments—such as jurisdictional challenges and questions of due process—and nulifying evidences rather than on determinations of innocence. This development has reinforced a prevailing perception of impunity among Brazil's political and economic elite and has fuelled public scepticism regarding the resilience and credibility of the country's anti-corruption framework. It is important to note that, at the time this testimony was given, such an outcome would have been regarded as almost unthinkable, highlighting the extent to which the political and institutional landscape has shifted since then.
57. Institutional Act Number Five (AI-5) was the fifth of seventeen acts issued during the military dictatorship following the 1964 coup. AI-5 was the harshest of all the Institutional Acts, and it was promulgated by President Artur da Costa e Silva on December 13, 1968.
58. The National Ecological Party, the Federal Council of the Brazilian Bar Association, and the Communist Party of Brazil filed Declaratory Actions of Constitutionality 43, 44, and 54, respectively, before the Federal Supreme Court, opposing imprisonment after conviction in the second instance, a jurisprudence then adopted by the Supreme Court. In a closely contested decision on 7 November 2019, by a narrow majority (six votes to five) the decided to prohibit the possibility of imprisonment for those convicted in the second instance, overturning the previously adopted understanding.
59. **Alberto Youssef** is a Brazilian "doleiro" (black market dollar dealer), widely known after the *Banestado* corruption scandal. He was arrested in 2014 because of his involvement with the Car Wash Operation.

60. Pedro Machado de Almeida Castro is a criminal defence attorney and partner at the law firm Machado de Almeida Castro & Orzari.
61. *Habeas corpus*, in Latin language "you shall have the body". It refers to a legal writ or order that is employed to bring a person before a court or judge, particularly to determine whether that person's detention or imprisonment is lawful. It is a fundamental safeguard against unlawful or arbitrary detention, requiring that the authority holding the person must justify the detention. If the detention is found to be unlawful, the person must be released.
62. Operation *Mani Pulite* (Clean Hands) was a large-scale investigation into cases of corruption in Italy, centred in Milan. It implicated the Italian political class, political parties, the state-owned oil company (ENI—*Ente Nazionale Idrocarburi*), and major contractors in the overpricing of public works and the embezzlement of public funds.
63. Silvio Berlusconi is an Italian politician and businessman. He served as Prime Minister (President of the Council of Ministers) from 1994 to 1995, from 2001 to 2005, from 2005 to 2006, and from 2008 to 2011.
64. Jair Messias Bolsonaro is a retired army captain and Brazilian politician. He served as President of Brazil from 1 January 2019, to 31 December 2022.
65. José Eduardo Cavalcanti de Mendonça, known as Duda Mendonça, is a Brazilian advertising executive famous for leading successful political advertising campaigns. He worked on several elections for various political parties. In 2005, he was implicated in the *Mensalão* scandal alongside his business partner Zilmar Fernandes da Silveira.
66. Zilmar Fernandes da Silveira is a Brazilian advertising professional and business partner of Duda Mendonça. Their firm specialized in political marketing and contributed to the election of numerous political figures. In 2005, she was indicted in the Mensalão scandal alongside her partner, Duda Mendonça.

67. Operation *Mani Pulite* (Clean Hands) was a large-scale investigation into cases of corruption in Italy, centred in Milan. It implicated the Italian political class, political parties, the state-owned oil company (ENI—Ente Nazionale Idrocarburi), and major contractors in the overpricing of public works and the embezzlement of public funds.
68. **Marco Aurélio Mendes de Farias Mello** is a Brazilian judge who served as a Justice of the Supreme Court from 1990 to 2021. He was appointed by then-President Fernando Collor de Mello, his cousin. Additionally, he held the positions of Minister and President of the Superior Electoral Court and Justice of the Superior Labor Court.
69. José Dirceu de Oliveira e Silva is a Brazilian politician affiliated with the Workers' Party. He served as both a state and federal congressperson for the state of São Paulo and as Chief of Staff during the government of President Luiz Inácio Lula da Silva. In 2012, he was convicted by the Federal Supreme Court for the crime of active corruption and imprisoned in 2013. A year later, he was released to serve the remainder of his sentence under house arrest. He was arrested again in 2015 as part of Operation Car Wash and convicted in 2017. In 2019, he was released following the Supreme Court's shift in understanding regarding imprisonment after conviction in the second instance, based on the decisions in Declaratory Action of Constitutionality 43, 44, and 54.
70. The Brazilian Social Democracy Party is a centrist political party in Brazil.
71. José Carlos Dias is a well-known Brazilian criminal lawyer. He served as Minister of Justice during the administration of President Fernando Henrique Cardoso.
72. Kátia Rabello was the controlling shareholder and CEO of Banco Rural. In 2005, Banco Rural ranked among the forty largest banks in Brazil. It became widely known to the public for having bank accounts that were used in corruption schemes, including the Mensalão case.

73. The "theory of control of the act" ("*teoria do domínio do fato*" in Portuguese) is a legal doctrine that determines the distinction between the principal offender (main author) and an accomplice in criminal cases. Developed by German jurist Claus Roxin, this theory posits that the principal offender is the one who exercises control over the execution of a criminal act, as opposed to an accomplice who merely participates in it. The concept centres on whether an individual has dominance over the crime's occurrence and outcome, as opposed to simply contributing to it indirectly.
74. Alaor Leite is an assistant lecturer at the Chair of Criminal Law, Criminal Procedure, Foreign Criminal Law, and the Theory of Criminal Law at the Faculty of Law of Humboldt University in Berlin. He holds a PhD and an LL.M. in Law from Ludwig Maximilian University of Munich.
75. Luís Greco is Full Professor and Chair of Criminal Law, Criminal Procedure, Foreign Criminal Law, and the Theory of Criminal Law at the Faculty of Law of Humboldt University in Berlin. He holds a PhD and an LL.M. in Law from Ludwig Maximilian University of Munich.
76. Romero Jucá is a Brazilian politician and businessman affiliated with the Brazilian Democratic Movement (MDB). He has served as Senator for the state of Roraima, Senate Majority Leader, Congressperson Leader of the National Congress, and Minister of State under President Michel Temer. He also previously held a ministerial position during the administration of President Luiz Inácio Lula da Silva. Jucá was implicated in investigations related to Operation Car Wash (Lava Jato), accused of accepting bribes connected to contracts involving Transpetro and alleged corruption schemes linked to Odebrecht. However, in May 2024, Supreme Court Justice Edson Fachin dismissed an inquiry against Jucá and Senator Renan Calheiros, concerning allegations of receiving illicit funds from Odebrecht. Currently, there are no publicly available reports of ongoing investigations or legal proceedings against Romero Jucá related to the Car Wash operation. See Martins, L. (2024, May 3). Fachin arquiva inquérito da Lava Jato

contra Renan e Jucá. *CNN Brasil*. Retrieved March 23, 2025, from https://www.cnnbrasil.com.br/blogs/luisa-martins/politica/fachin-arquiva-inquerito-da-lava-jato-contra-renan-e-juca.

77. Jorge Gerdau Johannpeter is a Brazilian businessman and Chairman of the Board of Directors of the Gerdau Group, the largest steel producer in Brazil.
78. Fundação Getulio Vargas (FGV) CPDOC. (n.d.). *Janot, Rodrigo* [Biographical entry]. In *Dicionário histórico-biográfico brasileiro* [Brazilian historical-biographical dictionary]. Fundação Getulio Vargas. https://www18.fgv.br/CPDOC/acervo/dicionarios/verbete-biografico/rodrigo-janot-monteiro-de-barros. He was a member of the Federal Public Prosecutor's Office and served as Attorney General of Brazil from 2013 to 2017.
79. Almeida Castro, A. C. (2015, September 9). *Queremos* [What country do we want]. *Folha de S.Paulo*. https://www1.folha.uol.com.br/opiniao/2015/09/1679124-que-pais-queremos.shtml.
80. Fernando Pessoa (1888–1935) was a Portuguese poet, essayist, and literary critic, widely regarded as one of the most important literary figures of the twentieth century. Known for writing under numerous heteronyms, his work explores themes such as identity, introspection, and the fragmentation of the self.
81. Reference to Fernando Pessoa, writing under the heteronym Álvaro de Campos, in the poem *Saudação a Walt Whitman* [Salutation to Walt Whitman]. The poem is a tribute to Walt Whitman and expresses a rejection of idealized figures in favor of real, ordinary people.
82. Reference to Brazilian poet Trasíbulo Ferraz Moreira (1870–1895), in the poem "A Orgulhosa" (The Proud Woman) where he writes: "*A sorte dá, nega e tira*" ("Fate gives, denies, and takes away"). The poem reflects the author's critical view of social inequality and the fleeting nature of fortune and privilege in modern society.
83. Raul Schmidt is a Brazilian businessman with dual Portuguese citizenship who was targeted by Operation Car Wash. He resided in Portugal during the investigation, and Brazilian authorities

requested his extradition based on corruption allegations related to contracts in the oil and gas sector.

84. Extradition is an act of international cooperation whereby a person under investigation, prosecution, or conviction for a crime is surrendered by one country to another that requests the individual's return and where the crime was allegedly committed.
85. Judge Rogério Favreto, from the Federal Regional Court of the 4th Region, during a judicial duty shift, granted an injunction ordering the release of former President Lula in a decision made in a *habeas corpus* filed by Workers' Party deputies Wadih Damous, Paulo Pimenta, and Paulo Teixeira. This injunction was highly controversial and short-lived. After Favreto granted the injunction for Lula's release in July 2018, there was a swift legal dispute among various judges from the Federal Regional Court of the 4th Region and the Supreme Court. The president of the Federal Regional Court of the 4th Region, Judge Carlos Eduardo Thompson Flores, ultimately intervened, suspending Favreto's decision and ordering that Lula remain in prison. Flores argued that Favreto's ruling lacked the proper legal basis, as Lula's imprisonment had been determined by earlier judicial processes and rulings from higher courts.
86. Luiz Inácio Lula da Silva was a union leader, metallurgist, and Brazilian politician. He served as Brazilian President from 2003 to 2011. He is currently the President of the country.
87. Judge Ney Bello is a federal appellate judge at the Federal Regional Court of the 1st Region in Brazil. He is known for his rulings on high-profile criminal and constitutional cases, particularly those involving procedural guarantees and due process.
88. The Federal Regional Court of the 1st Region has jurisdiction over the judicial sections of the states of Acre, Amapá, Amazonas, Bahia, the Federal District, Goiás, Maranhão, Mato Grosso, Minas Gerais, Pará, Piauí, Rondônia, Roraima, and Tocantins.
89. The Declaratory Action of Constitutionality is a legal mechanism intended to establish the constitutionality of a federal law or normative act.

90. André Santos Esteves is a Brazilian businessman listed by Forbes among the World's Billionaires. In 2015, he was accused of obstruction of justice. The Federal Prosecutor's Office requested his acquittal in 2017, and in 2018 he was acquitted by the Federal Court due to lack of evidence.
91. This refers to Allan dos Santos, a far-right blogger and founder of the pro-Bolsonaro blog Terça Livre. Since 2020, he has been under investigation in an inquiry opened ex officio by the Brazilian Supreme Federal Court for spreading fake news and organizing pro-dictatorship demonstrations.
92. On 30 July 2020, pro-Bolsonaro blogger Allan dos Santos, during a livestream organized by federal congresswoman Bia Kicis, claimed—without evidence—that Justice Luís Roberto Barroso, then President of the Superior Electoral Court, had information about wiretaps allegedly originating from the embassies of China and North Korea, as well as from the home of criminal defence attorney Kakay, aimed at annulling President Jair Bolsonaro's mandate. The blogger's statement is available at: https://www.youtube.com/watch?v=-C1aUxnPUhU.
93. **Fundação Getulio Vargas (FGV) CPDOC. (n.d.).** *Mendes, Gilmar Ferreira* [Biographical entry]. In *Dicionário histórico-biográfico brasileiro.* Fundação Getulio Vargas. https://www.fgv.br/cpdoc/acervo/dicionarios/verbete-biografico/mendes-gilmar. He has been a Justice of the Supreme Court since 2002.
94. Justice Gilmar Mendes was approached by Brazilian citizens on several occasions while walking in Lisbon, the capital of Portugal, where he owns an apartment.
95. **Fundação Getulio Vargas (FGV) CPDOC. (n.d.).** *Lewandowski, Enrique Ricardo* [Biographical entry]. In *Dicionário histórico-biográfico brasileiro.* Fundação Getulio Vargas. http://www.fgv.br/cpdoc/acervo/dicionarios/verbete-biografico/lewandowski-ricardo. He has been a Justice of the Supreme Court since 2006.
96. Justice Ricardo Lewandowski was insulted in public on more than one occasion, including during a flight from São Paulo to Brasília.

97. Mário de Miranda Quintana was a Brazilian poet, translator, and journalist, widely regarded as one of the greatest figures in Brazilian literature. One of his most popular works is the short poem "*Poeminha do Contra*" (*Little Poem of Defiance*), composed of just four lines, including the well-known verses: "*Eles passarão... / Eu passarinho*" ("They will pass... / I, little bird" or more freely as *"They will pass; I will soar"*).
98. This refers to Manoel Pastana, the Federal Prosecutor for Brazil's 4th Region, who issued legal opinions during Operation Car Wash in support of using pre-trial detention as a means of encouraging suspects to cooperate with investigations. See: Pastana, M. (2014, December 1). Porque sustento prisão preventiva para corroborar delação premiada [Why I argue in favor of pre-trial detention to support plea bargaining]. *Consultor Jurídico*. https://www.conjur.com.br/2014-dez-01/manoel-pastana-sustento-prisao-preventiva-lava-jato.
99. Antonio Palocci Filho is a Brazilian physician and politician who was affiliated with the Workers' Party (PT). He served as a minister under both Presidents Luiz Inácio Lula da Silva and Dilma Rousseff. In 2017, he was convicted as part of Operation Car Wash and sentenced to twelve years in a closed prison regime. In 2018, the sentence was converted to semi-open confinement following a plea bargain agreement. He ran for federal congressperson in São Paulo in 2022 but was not elected. In 2023, Supreme Court Justice Dias Toffoli annulled the evidence obtained through Palocci's plea bargain, asserting that it had been used improperly, without judicial oversight, and for political purposes. The decision was met with significant criticism in legal and political circles, particularly given the relevance of Palocci's testimony to multiple high-profile corruption cases.
100. Antonio Palocci's plea bargain was subject to criticism for allegedly lacking substantive evidentiary support. *According* to the legal team representing former President Luiz Inácio Lula da Silva, portions of Palocci's testimony were based on previously published news reports rather than original evidence. This claim was submitted in court filings and reported by major Brazilian

media outlets. In 2023, Supreme Court Justice Dias Toffoli annulled the evidence obtained through Palocci's cooperation agreement, asserting that it had been used improperly, without judicial oversight, and for political purposes. The decision was met with domestic and international criticism. In 2024, the Inter-American Commission on Human Rights (IACHR), part of the Organization of American States (OAS), formally requested clarification from the Brazilian government, questioning whether the ruling posed an obstacle to anti-corruption accountability. See: ***Folha de S.Paulo. (2020, June 22).*** *Defesa de Lula diz que delação de Palocci se baseia em notícias antigas e pede que ela seja inutilizada [*Lula's defence argues Palocci's plea deal was based on old news reports and requests that it be disregarded*]*. Folha de S.Paulo. https://www1.folha.uol.com.br/poder/2020/06/defesa-de-lula-diz-que-delacao-de-palocci-se-baseia-em-noticias-antigas-e-pede-que-ela-seja-inutilizada.shtml; ***Gazeta do Povo. (2024, March 11).*** *OEA contesta o Brasil sobre decisão de Toffoli na Lava Jato [OAS challenges Brazil over Toffoli's decision in the Car Wash case].* Gazeta do Povo. https://www.gazetadopovo.com.br/republica/oea-contesta-brasil-decisao-toffoli-lava-jato/.

101. In 2016, José Renan Vasconcelos Calheiros, better known as Renan Calheiros, was President of the Brazilian Senate. He is a politician affiliated with the Brazilian Democratic Movement and is currently serving his fourth term as Senator, elected by the state of Alagoas.
102. José Sarney de Araújo Costa, better known as José Sarney, is a Brazilian lawyer, writer, and politician. In the 1985 presidential election, he ran as Vice President on the winning ticket headed by Tancredo Neves. Following Tancredo's death, Sarney assumed the presidency and served as President of Brazil from 1985 to 1990.
103. Sérgio Machado is a Brazilian politician and businessman. He served as President of Transpetro during the administrations of Presidents Lula and Dilma Rousseff. He became involved in the Petrobras corruption scandal after leaving Transpetro in 2014.

In May 2016, he entered into a plea bargain agreement with the Office of the Prosecutor General, in which he detailed his involvement in the corruption scheme within the state-owned company. In 2021, the PGR formally closed the investigation into Machado, citing the statute of limitations (*prescrição penal*) as the primary legal basis for the dismissal, along with a lack of sufficient evidence to justify criminal prosecution.

104. Although Sérgio Machado's plea bargain included audio recordings of private conversations with prominent political figures—such as José Sarney, Romero Jucá, and Renan Calheiros—these recordings were not sufficient to sustain criminal charges. Under Brazilian law, particularly Law 12.850/2013 on criminal organizations and plea agreements, a conviction cannot be based solely on the statements of a cooperating witness (§16). In this case, the recorded conversations were considered ambiguous and lacked corroborating evidence such as financial records, documents, or testimony from other witnesses. While politically impactful, the material failed to meet the evidentiary threshold required for prosecution. In 2020, the Office of the Prosecutor General (PGR) formally requested the dismissal of investigations against Sarney and Jucá, citing the absence of concrete proof of criminal conduct. The case exemplifies the tension between public perception and the demands of due process and legal certainty in corruption prosecutions.
105. Roseana Macieira Sarney Murad is a sociologist and politician affiliated with the Brazilian Democratic Movement. She is the daughter of former President José Sarney. Roseana served four consecutive terms as Governor of the state of Maranhão and has also held office as a Federal Congressperson and Senator for the same state.
106. Edison Lobão is a Brazilian businessman and politician affiliated with the Brazilian Democratic Movement (MDB). He has served as Senator, as Governor of the state of Maranhão, and as a Cabinet Minister under Presidents Luiz Inácio Lula da Silva and Dilma Rousseff. He was named in several investigations related to Operation Car Wash. In 2021, a federal judge in Curitiba

dismissed one of the criminal cases against him and his son, citing insufficient evidence to proceed. However, he remains a defendant in a separate case before the Federal Court in Rio de Janeiro, where he has been charged with passive corruption and money laundering in connection with contracts for the Belo Monte hydroelectric plant. See G1. (2020, September 10). MPF denuncia Edison Lobão e filho por lavagem de dinheiro e corrupção na Lava Jato [Federal prosecutors charge Edison Lobão and son with money laundering and corruption in Operation Car Wash]. https://g1.globo.com/politica/noticia/2020/09/10/mpf-denuncia-edison-lobao-e-filho-por-lavagem-de-dinheiro-e-corrupcao-na-lava-jato.ghtml; G1. (2021, October 4). Juíza tranca ação contra Edison Lobão e filho na Lava Jato [Judge dismisses Operation Car Wash charges against Edison Lobão and his son]. https://g1.globo.com/politica/noticia/2021/10/04/juiza-tranca-acao-contra-edison-lobao-e-filho-na-lava-jato.ghtml.

107. Preventive detention is a term is used to describe the detention of a defendant before trial to prevent them from fleeing, tampering with evidence, or posing a threat to public safety. It is a precautionary measure taken by the court when there is reasonable belief that releasing the defendant before trial could compromise the legal process or public safety. *See:* **Folha de S.Paulo. (2020, November 25).** PGR pede arquivamento de investigações contra Sarney e Jucá [Prosecutor General's Office requests dismissal of investigations against Sarney and Jucá]. *Folha de S.Paulo.* https://www1.folha.uol.com.br/poder/2020/11/pgr-pede-arquivamento-de-investigacoes-contra-sarney-e-juca.shtml.

108. Delcídio do Amaral Gómez, known simply as Delcídio do Amaral, is an engineer and politician. He served as Minister of State during President Itamar Franco's administration and as Senator for the Workers' Party (PT). In 2015, he was arrested in flagrante delicto for obstruction of justice, accused of attempting to impede a plea-bargain agreement by a former Petrobras executive as part of Operation Car Wash. In 2016, his Senate mandate was revoked, and his plea-bargain agreement was ratified by the

Supreme Court. In 2018, he was acquitted by the Federal Court. In 2024, Delcídio ran unsuccessfully for mayor of Corumbá, Mato Grosso do Sul, finishing last in the elections. He declared a financial loss of nearly R$ 2 million between 2022 and 2024. In September 2024, the Supreme Court suspended the payment of a R$ 1.5 million fine established in his plea-bargain agreement, ruling that such a fine would only be enforceable upon final conviction. See Supremo Tribunal Federal (2024, September 17). STF suspende pagamento de multa de ex-senador Delcídio Amaral. *Notícias STF*. https://noticias.stf.jus.br/postsnoticias/stf-suspende-pagamento-de-multa-de-ex-senador-delcidio-amaral/.

109. Pedro Barusco is an engineer and former Petrobras executive who became widely known du9 to his involvement in the Operation Car Wash corruption scandal. He was arrested during Operation Car Wash and sentenced initially to 18 years and four months in prison. However, under the terms of a plea-bargain agreement, his sentence was reduced to 15 years served in an open regime with electronic monitoring, community service, and other restrictions. As part of his collaboration agreement, he returned approximately R$ 182 million in illicit funds previously held abroad. In 2018, after fulfilling several obligations outlined by the agreement, Barusco was permitted to remove his electronic ankle monitor. Nevertheless, he remains legally required to submit biannual activity reports and to notify judicial authorities of any change of address until 2031.
110. Lord John Dalberg-Acton is described as "the magistrate of history" and was one of the great figures of the nineteenth century, considered among the most erudite personalities of his time. The history of liberty was his life's work.
111. The judicial jurisdiction of Judge Sergio Moro and the 13th Federal Court of Curitiba for the Atibaia ranch and Guarujá triplex cases was initially established by Moro himself and subsequently confirmed by the Regional Federal Court of the 4th Region (TRF-4). The Superior Court of Justice, upon reviewing defence appeals, did not challenge this jurisdictional arrangement and upheld Moro's competence for several years. Only in

March 2021—approximately seven years after the start of Operation Car Wash—the Supreme Court overturned these decisions, declaring Curitiba's jurisdiction invalid due to insufficient direct connection between the cases and Petrobras corruption schemes. The delay of nearly seven years by Brazil's highest court to determine jurisdictional competence in such high-profile corruption cases has been subject to significant legal criticism, as this prolonged uncertainty affected the integrity and stability of Brazil's judicial process.

112. **GloboNews** is a Brazilian 24-hour news television channel owned by Grupo Globo, one of the largest media conglomerates in Latin America.
113. Operation *Satyagraha* was an operation against the diversion of public funds, initiated in early 2004, carried out by the Federal Police and ordered by the 6th Federal Court of São Paulo. In 2011, the operation was annulled by the Superior Court of Justice (due to illegality). In 2015, the Federal Supreme Court ratified the Superior Court of Justice's decision.
114. Gilmar Ferreira Mendes ***Entry***. FGV CPDOC. https://www18.fgv.br/CPDOC/acervo/dicionarios/verbete-biografico/mendes-gilmar. He has been a Justice of the since 2002.
115. The judge was Fausto Martins de Sanctis, who is now a judge of the Federal Regional Court of the 3rd Region.
116. Antonio Sergio Altieri de Moraes Pitombo. Prisoner's dilemma: pre-trial detention and torture. *In search of the lost just*. São Paulo: Ed. Singular, 2021, p. 15–20.
117. René Ariel Dotti was one of the greatest Brazilian criminal lawyers, professor at the Federal University of Paraná (UFPR), co-author of the draft laws No. 7.209/84 (reform of the General Part of the Penal Code) and Law No. 7.210/84 (Penal Execution Law). He passed away in early February 2021.
118. Mensalão was a corruption scandal, which occurred through the purchase of votes from deputies by the Executive, during the government of Luiz Inácio Lula da Silva, in 2005. This illegal practice was known as such behind the scenes because it referred

to a monthly payment made to deputies to vote in favour of projects of interest to the Executive.
119. The reference here is made to the Workers' Party, which was the government at the time, as well as to the parties that made up the base of that government.
120. The reference is made to the government of former President Jair Bolsonaro.
121. During the government of Jair Bolsonaro, Petrobras had five presidents, including an interim president.
122. Sergio Marcos de Moraes Pitombo was a lawyer, Judge of the Criminal Court of Appeal and Judge of the Court of Justice of the State of São Paulo. He was a Professor-Doctor in Criminal Procedural Law at the Law School of Largo de São Francisco (USP) and a member of the Commission of Jurists that drafted the Penal Reform of 1984.
123. Márcio Thomaz Bastos was a well-known Brazilian criminal lawyer. He was president of the Federal Council of the Order of Lawyers of Brazil, from 1987 to 1989, Minister of Justice during the first term of the government of Luiz Inácio Lula da Silva and advocated for various contractors in Operation Car Wash, but only in the beginning, as he died in 2014.
124. Luiz Inácio Lula da Silva is a popular Brazilian politician, affiliated with the Workers' Party. He was president of Brazil from 2003 to 2006 (first term) and from 2006 to 2010 (second term). He is the current president of Brazil (2023–2026).
125. Sergio Fernando Moro ***Entry***. FGV CPDOC. http://www.fgv.br/cpdoc/acervo/dicionarios/verbete-biografico/sergio-fernando-moro. He was a former federal judge and judge of Operation Car Wash in Curitiba. He was former Minister of Justice and director of Alvarez & Marsal. He is a lawyer and Brazilian politician. He is currently an elected Senator for the state of Paraná.
126. Antônio Sérgio Altieri de Moraes Pitombo. *Money laundering: the typicality of the preceding crime*. São Paulo: Revista dos Tribunais, 2003.

127. Antonio di Pietro was a public prosecutor and was part of the operation Clean Hands. In 1996, he began his political career in Italy.
128. Antônio Sérgio Altieri de Moraes Pitombo (Coord.). *Plea bargaining and other agreements—systematic analysis and critical study*. São Paulo: Singular, 2022.
129. Marcelo Paranhos de Oliveira Miller was a Federal Prosecutor, close to the Attorney General Rodrigo Janot, and negotiated some plea bargains, among them those of the executives of J&F. He left the Prosecutor's Office to join a law firm, which represented J&F. The plea bargains made by the partners and executives of J&F began to be questioned after recordings of conversations of Joesley Batista that revealed the then Prosecutor's proximity at the time with the executives of J&F.
130. Rodrigo Janot Monteiro de Barros is a Brazilian jurist. He was a member of the Federal Public Prosecutor's Office and Attorney General of the Republic from 2013 to 2017.
131. The Anti-Crime Package was amended by Congress and resulted in the promulgation of Law No. 13.964, of 24 December 2019 which improves criminal and criminal procedural legislation. http://www.planalto.gov.br/ccivil_03/_ato2019-2022/2019/lei/L13964.htm.
132. Operation Clean Hands, Mani Pulite, was an investigation into corruption cases in Italy, centred in Milan, which involved the Italian political class, political parties, the state oil company (ENI—Ente Nazionale Idrocarburi), and major contractors in the overpricing of works and in the diversion of public money.
133. Márcio Thomaz Bastos was a well-known Brazilian criminal lawyer. He was president of the Federal Council of the Brazilian Bar Association, from 1987 to 1989, Minister of Justice during the first term of Luiz Inácio Lula da Silva's government and advocated for several construction companies in Operation Car Wash, but only in the beginning, as he died in 2014.
134. Antônio Carlos de Ameida Castro, known as Kakay, is a prestigious criminal lawyer.

135. The Federal Council is the highest body in the structure of the Brazilian Bar Association. It is made up of representatives from the 27 Sections. It is responsible for defending the interests of the legal profession.
136. Antônio Sérgio Altieri de Moraes Pitombo. *In search of the lost justice*. São Paulo: Singular, 2021.
137. Arnaldo Malheiros Filho was a respected Brazilian criminal lawyer.
138. Rogério Lauria Tucci was a great criminal lawyer and professor at the Law School of the University of São Paulo.
139. Antônio Sérgio Altieri de Moraes Pitombo. *Impartiality of jurisdiction: Contemporary problems of the criminal process*. São Paulo: Revista dos Tribunais, 2022.
140. Daniel Kahneman. *Thinking, Fast and Slow*. Rio de Janeiro: Objetiva, 2012.
141. Teori Albino Zavascki. ***Entry***. FGV CPDOC. https://www18.fgv.br/CPDOC/acervo/dicionarios/verbete-biografico/teori-albino-zavascki. He was a jurist, professor, magistrate, and Justice of the Superior Court of Justice and the Federal Supreme Court, from 2012 to 2017. He was the rapporteur of Operation Car Wash until his death.
142. PWC was known as PricewaterhouseCoopers. It is one of the largest consulting and auditing firms in the world.
143. "*Know Your Customer*" (KYC) is understood as a process of *due diligence*, initially typical of financial institutions, to verify the identity of customers and assess potential risks of money laundering, financing of terrorism or other illicit activities. The aim is to protect financial institutions against financial crimes, as well as ensure compliance with laws and regulations, relating to banking secrecy, money laundering, and combating terrorism.
144. Márcio Thomaz Bastos was a well-known Brazilian criminal lawyer. He was president of the Federal Council of the Brazilian Bar Association, from 1987 to 1989, Minister of Justice during the first term of Luiz Inácio Lula da Silva's government and advocated for several construction companies in Operation Car Wash, but only in the beginning, as he died in 2014.

145. Márcio Thomaz Bastos was a well-known Brazilian criminal lawyer. He was president of the Federal Council of the Brazilian Bar Association, from 1987 to 1989, Minister of Justice during the first term of the government of Luiz Inácio Lula da Silva and advocated for several construction companies in Operation Car Wash, but only in the beginning, as he died in 2014.
146. Luiz Inácio Lula da Silva is a popular Brazilian politician, affiliated with the Workers' Party. He was president of Brazil from 2003 to 2006 (first term) and from 2006 to 2010 (second term). He is the current president of Brazil (2023–2026).
147. **Igor Sant'Anna Tamasauskas** is a lawyer graduated from the Law School of the University of São Paulo, partner of Bottini & Tamasauskas Lawyers. He was the city attorney of São Carlos and congressperson chief of the Civil House of the Presidency of the Republic for Legal Affairs.
148. Mensalão was a corruption scandal, which occurred through the purchase of votes from deputies by the Executive, during the government of Luiz Inácio Lula da Silva, in 2005. This illegal practice was so named in the corridors because it referred to a monthly payment made to deputies to vote in favour of projects of interest to the Executive.
149. Dante Alighieri was born in Florence, Italy. He is considered one of the greatest writers of all time. In addition to being a writer, he was a poet and philosopher in the Middle Ages. Many consider *The Divine Comedy*, his masterpiece.
150. In the book *The Divine Comedy*, by Dante Alighieri, the subject who is in the last circle of hell is Lucifer or Satan. Judas Iscariot, on the other hand, is in the ninth circle of hell, together with significant traitors.
151. Joaquim Silvério dos Reis was a military and political Brazilian of the eighteenth century, best known for having denounced the leaders of the Minas Gerais Conspiracy ("*Inconfidência Mineira*") to the Portuguese colonial authorities and for betraying the movement for Brazil's independence. He is considered one of the greatest traitors in the country's history.

152. José Anselmo dos Santos, known as *Corporal Anselmo*, was a Brazilian military and unionist. He was one of the leaders of the armed resistance movement against the military regime, but he became a government infiltrator in the resistance movement. His collaboration with the military authorities led to the arrest and death of several members of the armed resistance.
153. Dalton dos Santos Avancini was an engineer and president of the construction company Camargo Corrêa, during Operation Car Wash. He was arrested in 2014 and convicted for involvement in the bribery scheme in contracts with Petrobras. He made a plea bargain, then moving to house arrest. In 2016, he died in a plane crash.
154. Camargo Corrêa is one of the largest Brazilian construction and engineering companies. Founded in 1939, it operates in construction civil, as well as in the infrastructure, energy and public service concessions sectors. Camargo Corrêa participated in the construction of several important projects, such as the Itaipu Power Plant and the Rio-Niterói Bridge. The company was involved in Operation Car Wash, accused of paying bribes to Petrobras. It was the first construction company to close a plea bargain in Car Wash.
155. José Carlos Grubisich is a Brazilian businessman. He was president of Braskem, during Operation Car Wash. And, in 2015, he refused to participate in the collective plea bargain of 78 executives from Odebrecht, understanding that it was not the case, despite having been informed by Odebrecht's lawyers that his name appeared in other plea bargains awards. In 2019, he was arrested upon landing at JFK airport, in New York, United States. He remained in custody until he paid a bail of US$ 30 million. In 2021, he was sentenced to 20 months in prison. The process in the United States results from a plea bargain agreement signed by Odebrecht with American and Brazilian authorities, within the scope of Operation Car Wash.
156. Braskem is a Brazilian petrochemical company, being one of the largest in the world in the sector. The controlling stake of

Braskem is held by Odebrecht and Petrobras. In 2016, it celebrated leniency agreement with Brazilian, American, and Swiss authorities, within the scope of Operation Car Wash.

157. The Anti-Crime Package, proposed by then Minister of Justice Sergio Moro, was altered by Congress and resulted in the promulgation of Law No. 13.964, of 24 December 2019 that perfects criminal and criminal procedural legislation. http://www.planalto.gov.br/ccivil_03/_ato2019-2022/2019/lei/L13964.htm.
158. José Celso de Mello Filho. ***Entry***. FGV CPDOC. https://www18.fgv.br/CPDOC/acervo/dicionarios/verbete-biografico/jose-celso-de-melo-filho. He is a jurist and Brazilian magistrate. He was a Justice of the Federal Supreme Court (1989–2020), being recognised for his work in the defence of human rights and the Rule of Law.
159. Pierpaolo Cruz Bottini and Ademar Borges (Coord.). *Money laundering, legal opinions, selected and commented jurisprudence*. São Paulo: Revista dos Tribunais, 2021.
160. The Council for Financial Activities Control is Brazil's financial intelligence unit, responsible for receiving, analysing, and forwarding reports on suspicious financial activities to the competent authorities. It plays a central role in anti-money laundering efforts and the prevention of terrorism financing.
161. Rogério Gentile and Wálter Nunes, Pierpaolo Bottini: exaggerations of the car wash do not tarnish the operation. *Folha de S. Paulo*, 26th March 2017. https://www1.folha.uol.com.br/poder/2017/03/1869737-pierpaolo-bottini-exageros-da-lava-jato-nao-maculam-a-operacao.shtml.
162. The operation *Spoofing* is a Federal Police operation to investigate invasions of Telegram accounts of Brazilian authorities and people related to the Car Wash Operation.
163. The Clean Hands Operation, *Mani Pulite*, was an investigation of corruption cases in Italy, centred in Milan, which involved the Italian political class, political parties, the state fuel company (ENI—*Ente Nazionale Idrocarburi*), and major contractors in the overpricing of works and the diversion of public money.

164. Sergio Moro wrote, in 2004, an article about the Clean Hands Operation, whose title is Considerations about the mani pulite operation. *CEJ Magazine*. vol. 8, n. 26, Jul./Sep. 2004, pp. 56–62. https://revistacej.cjf.jus.br/cej/index.php/revcej/article/view/625/805.
165. Reference is made to the former judge Sergio Moro, now Senator of the Republic, for the State of Paraná.
166. The expression "jet politics" (*política de jatinho*, in Portuguese) refers to the use of private air travel by public officials as a symbol of prestige, power, and media visibility. In the context of Operation Car Wash, the term became associated with the perceived politicisation and personal promotion of some of its leading figures.
167. Article 7 of the Penal Code: "Are subject to Brazilian law, even if committed abroad: I—crimes: (a) against the life or freedom of the President of the Republic; (b) against the patrimony or public faith of the Union, the Federal District, a State, a Territory, a Municipality, a public company, a mixed economy society, an autarchy or a foundation established by the Public Power; (c) against public administration, by those who are at its service; (d) of genocide, when the agent is Brazilian or domiciled in Brazil; II—crimes: (a) that, by treaty or convention, Brazil has undertaken to repress; (b) committed by Brazilian; (c) committed on Brazilian aircraft or ships, merchant or private property, when in foreign territory and are not judged there. § 1º—In the cases of item I, the agent is punished according to Brazilian law, even if acquitted or convicted abroad. § 2º—In the cases of item II, the application of Brazilian law depends on the concurrence of the following conditions: (a) the agent enters the national territory; (b) the fact is also punishable in the country where it was committed; (c) the crime is included among those for which Brazilian law authorises extradition; (d) the agent has not been acquitted abroad or has not served the sentence there; (e) the agent has not been pardoned abroad or, for another reason, the punishment is not extinct, according to the most favourable law. § 3º—Brazilian law also applies to the crime committed by a

foreigner against a Brazilian outside Brazil, if, meeting the conditions provided for in the previous paragraph: (a) extradition was not requested or was denied; (b) there was a request from the Minister of Justice."

168. The First Command of the Capital, named PCC, is the largest criminal organisation in the country, with operations mainly in the State of São Paulo, but with branches throughout the national territory, as well as in some South American countries. It was created within the prisons of São Paulo, in 1993. The PCC is known for its violence, hierarchy and for its punishments to those who disobey the leadership.

3

The Car Wash and the Judiciary

Introduction to Chapter 3

In the third chapter of this compelling narrative, titled "Car Wash and the Judiciary", you will explore the intricacies of the Brazilian judicial system. This chapter focuses on judges from the first instance and appellate courts, as well as those in the higher courts in Brasília—the Superior Court of Justice (and at the Federal Supreme Court)—who bring their unique perspectives to the forefront of the Operation Car Wash.

This chapter presents important testimonies that reveal the views and experiences of renowned adjudicators during the agitated period of Operation Car Wash.

Sergio Moro, a federal trial judge, opens the curtains of this chapter. As a central figure in the conduct of the Car Wash investigation, he shares his insightful analysis of the challenges faced, key decisions made, and the impact of legal actions from his standpoint in the fight against corruption.

Following Moro, João Pedro Gebran Neto, an appellate court judge, takes the stage. A key figure within the appellate body, his testimony offers a unique perspective on the role of the appeals court and the legal

L. M. Costa, *Brazil's Biggest Corruption Scandal*, Crime Prevention and Security Management, https://doi.org/10.1007/978-3-031-99078-6_3

nuances involved in interpreting case law related to corruption investigations such as Car Wash. His reflections provide a deeper understanding of the complexities encountered in higher judicial instances.

Eliana Calmon, a Justice of the Superior Court of Justice, provides a singular perspective, offering insights into the internal dynamics of the Superior Court of Justice before and during Operation Car Wash. Her experience enriches the narrative, highlighting the critical role of the court in adjudicating high-profile corruption cases.

Marco Aurélio Mello, a Justice of the Federal Supreme Court, concludes this chapter with his reflections on the decisions of the country's highest court in the context of both Operation Car Wash and the earlier Mensalão case (the "Big Monthly Payment"), another major corruption scandal judged by the Federal Supreme Court. Having served as a Justice during both investigations, his testimony offers a profound understanding of the legal and political considerations that shaped the deliberations during this historic period.

Readers can prepare for an immersion into the corridors of the Brazilian judiciary, where the intersections between law and politics are profound. The destinies of many individuals and corporations, as well as the destiny of the country in the ongoing battle against corruption, intertwine with the pivotal decisions that shaped the nation's anti-corruption history.

Testimony of Eliana Calmon

Abstract

In this landmark testimony, Eliana Calmon—former Minister of Brazil's Superior Court of Justice and the first woman to hold that position—offers a rare and unflinching account of institutional transformation, political resistance, and judicial responsibility in Brazil across five decades. Her trajectory, from a law professor and Federal Prosecutor during the military regime to a reform-minded federal judge and ultimately a national leader in judicial oversight, provides unique insight into the evolution of the Brazilian justice system under the 1988 Constitution and the rise and fall of Operation Car Wash.

Calmon reflects on her formative experiences within a structurally weak and politicised Public Prosecutor's Office, her early reform efforts to create the first federal judicial training school, and her later work at the Office of the Inspector General, where she oversaw the judiciary during the early phases of Car Wash. She defends the operation's legal and institutional foundations, denounces the political and judicial backlash that led to its erosion, and identifies the systemic complicity of Brazil's elites in sustaining a culture of impunity. With remarkable candour, she describes the political dynamics behind her own appointment, her encounters with figures such as Sergio Moro and Joaquim Barbosa, and her disillusionment with the Federal Supreme Court's reversal of anti-corruption gains.

The testimony also engages with wider questions: How did Car Wash expose the contradictions within Brazil's democratic institutions? What role did the judiciary play in both enabling and undermining the operation? And what does the backlash against Car Wash reveal about the endurance of political patronage and impunity in Brazil? In her closing reflections, Calmon expresses deep concern over the institutional regression that followed the operation, while still affirming the transformative potential of principled judicial action. Simultaneously personal and institutional, Calmon's testimony is an important source for understanding the internal contradictions of Brazil's judicial system, the high-stakes struggle against grand corruption, and the risks posed by institutional decay. Her testimony stands as both a historical document and a call to preserve the integrity of public institutions in the face of persistent political interference in contexts of entrenched corruption.

Could you describe your educational background and personal trajectory, particularly how your early academic and professional experiences shaped your entry into the judiciary and informed your later institutional role within Brazil's legal system?

My academic background is in Law; I graduated in 1968 and began my professional life working at a small law firm. Shortly thereafter, I transitioned into academia. Following a competitive public examination, I was appointed as a professor at the Federal University of Rio Grande do Norte, where I remained for four years. My academic career formally began in the role of teaching assistant, a position that, at the time, also required a rigorous selection process.

At the time, I was married to a military officer who served as the commander of the Naval Base in Natal. During our time there, I developed a close professional relationship with the Federal Prosecutor, who also lectured at the university. It was he who encouraged me to sit the entrance examination for the Federal Prosecution Service—a suggestion I accepted. I passed the examination, but due to the absence of vacancies in Rio Grande do Norte, I was appointed to a post in Pernambuco. My husband remained stationed in Natal, and we maintained this arrangement for several months until his eventual transfer to Pernambuco. I served as a Federal Prosecutor there for two years.

Initially, I found the experience somewhat disconcerting. The Federal Prosecutor's Office was strikingly disorganised. Having sat a highly rigorous examination in Brasília, I had developed a strong impression of the institution: the professionalism of the Prosecutors, the stature of the General Prosecutor, and the seriousness with which the prosecutors carried out their duties all suggested a highly structured and purposeful organisation. However, once I assumed my post in Pernambuco, the day-to-day realities proved markedly inconsistent with those expectations. Despite the institutional shortcomings, I remained committed and continued in my role.

In due course, my husband was transferred to Brasília, and I assumed a position at the Office of the General Prosecutor. This was still during the period of military rule. I dedicated myself fully to my professional duties—my husband, an intellectual by temperament, had little interest in social engagements, and as we did not have children, I was able to devote myself entirely to my work. I quickly established a strong reputation within the Office and was received with great collegiality, including by the Attorney General of the Republic. I felt a genuine sense of belonging in that institutional environment.

At that time, the role of the Federal Prosecutor resembled that of legal counsel for the Federal Government more than that of an autonomous representative of the Public Ministry. The prevailing orientation among senior prosecutors was to prioritise the defence of the Union's interests, often at the expense of the broader constitutional mission of the Public Ministry. I, however, consistently positioned myself as an institutional member of the Public Ministry. One example of this divergence concerned our handling of writs of mandamus. While some colleagues argued that, as representatives of the Union, we were obliged to defend the coercive act in question, I maintained that the Federal Prosecutor's role in such cases should be that of a guardian of legality and justice. Our duty was to defend what was right—not merely to legitimise state action. This stance occasionally generated institutional friction, but I was never overruled. I earned respect by grounding my positions in consistent and well-reasoned legal argumentation.

Over time, however, the situation became increasingly untenable. A formal directive was issued prohibiting Federal Prosecutors from issuing opinions that opposed coercive acts by the state. I recall vividly the day the military intervened at the University of Brasília. The General Prosecutor requested to know who had authored the opinion in response to the university's writ of mandamus. It was mine. He then conveyed that he wished to review my submission before it was formally filed. I refer to this episode as it marked a turning point—one that would ultimately lead to my decision to leave the Public Prosecutor's Office and pursue a career in the judiciary.

I went to see him with my written opinion in hand. He received me graciously—he was a courteous and thoughtful man. After our initial conversation, he said, "Leave your opinion with me. I will read it, and please come back tomorrow." So, I did. When I returned the next day, he said, "Your opinion is excellent—I have accepted all the preliminary arguments. However, regarding the merits, I took the liberty of making a few modifications. I believe we cannot support this act We cannot endorse an action that involves the invasion of a university."

I replied: "Dr. Henrique Fonseca de Araújo,[1] I understand and respect your political position—that is entirely legitimate." However, my stance is a technical one. I joined the Public Prosecutor's Office through a competitive examination, and regardless of which government is in power, my role and responsibilities remain the same. I responded, "For that reason, I would prefer not to submit a revised opinion. Of course, I have no objection if you choose to reassign the case to a colleague." He looked at me and asked, "Are you certain about this?" I replied that I was and added that I fully understood how difficult his position must have been. Then I left. That was the moment I fell out of favour—he was furious. Yet, at the same time, he seemed to respect my integrity. Sometime later, during another entrance examination for the Federal Prosecutor's Office, he stated that he wanted me to serve as secretary of the selection committee, as he was confident that I would carry out the task with absolute rigour.

I have always valued clarity—both in how I express myself and in the positions I take. I view myself, above all, as a legal technician. However, that particular episode raised serious concerns for me about the lack of institutional independence within the role of a Federal Prosecutor. In time, a formal directive was issued prohibiting the issuance of opinions that challenged coercive acts by the state. It became clear to me that I no longer had the professional autonomy necessary to act in accordance with my convictions. As a result, I decided to sit for the Federal Judiciary entrance examination—which ultimately marked my transition to the bench.

Indeed, upon becoming a judge, I experienced a significantly greater degree of professional autonomy. I was appointed before the 1988 Constitution came into force. Naturally, even at that time, judicial discretion was bounded by legal norms and institutional protocols. However, with the promulgation of the 1988 Constitution—a remarkably modern and democratic charter—I was promoted to the Federal Regional Court. By then, I had served for ten years as a federal judge in Bahia. The Court itself was established by the new Constitution, and with its creation, I transitioned to this new role within the federal judiciary.

I was, however, often perplexed by the conduct of judges—particularly following their elevation to higher courts. After spending a decade as a first-instance judge, I had been actively involved in the judges' association and regularly participated in its assemblies. During that period, I had been outspoken in my criticism of appeal court judges, especially in relation to practices such as nepotism, the use of public office for personal benefit, and the appropriation of institutional functions for private interests.

However, upon arriving at the Court, I realised that my colleagues were also former first-instance judges—some older, certainly, but largely from similar professional backgrounds. Despite this commonality, there was a noticeable shift in their outlook once they assumed higher positions. I found this transformation deeply puzzling. During administrative sessions, I would often remark, "But you did not used to think this way," *to which they would respond*, "Yes, but now it is different—now we have a political responsibility to manage the Court, and that requires a different attitude."

That left a lasting impression on me. I began to question why judges, once promoted, so often adopted a markedly different stance. In time, I came to realise that the issue did not lie with individuals, but with the system itself. If meaningful change is to occur, it is not enough to replace the people—you must transform the institutional structure. The system must be fractured. Yet that is an extraordinarily complex task, as one cannot simply bring the judicial process to a halt.

In response, I began to adopt a different approach, directing my efforts towards supporting first-instance judges. I proposed the establishment of a judicial training school. At that time, the Federal Judiciary had no such institution—only the State Judiciary had begun to discuss the concept. The proposal was met with scepticism. "Why would judges need a school?" some asked. "They've already passed a very difficult exam." But in my view, that was not sufficient.

As the idea of a judicial training school was considered too forward-thinking at the time, I proposed—during an administrative meeting—the creation of a support nucleus for first-instance judges. The initial reaction was one of confusion: "But what would that be for?" I explained that it would serve as a resource to assist judges by providing jurisprudential support and guidance on complex cases. After all, we were appointing very young judges to remote regions such as Acre, Rondônia, and Roraima—locations that lacked adequate libraries and, at the time, had no internet access. It was clear that we needed someone based in Brasília, at the Court, to offer institutional support. To implement the idea, I said all I needed was a fax machine, a telephone, and a computer. That modest support nucleus would later evolve into the first federal judicial training school in Brazil.

I came to realise that the trajectory of a magistrate often follows a pattern marked by abrupt transformation. A young law graduate, having succeeded in an exceptionally competitive examination, is dispatched to a distant and often under-resourced regional capital. Frequently, these individuals come from modest backgrounds and view the judiciary not only as a vocation, but as a means of social and economic stability. Upon assuming office, they are immediately vested with authority: they become the head of the local court, participate in electoral proceedings, and are quickly integrated into the city's institutional and social fabric. By the time they reach Brasília, their outlook—and even their bearing—has changed. One can observe a subtle yet unmistakable shift in posture and presence, shaped by the authority they have grown accustomed to exercising.

I witnessed first-hand how the judiciary can, at times, distort a young judge—someone newly appointed, often driven by strong ideals—simply by virtue of the power suddenly entrusted to them. Upon arriving in smaller cities—Amapá, for instance, where I was responsible for establishing the judicial section during its transition from a territory to a state—these judges are quickly targeted by political actors. Local politicians seek to influence those who hold decision-making authority, particularly in matters of electoral justice, where judicial discretion can have significant political ramifications.

It was at that point that I began advocating for a new protocol: every judge who passed the entrance examination should first come to the support nucleus, prior to taking office, in order to begin their training. The initiative was modest—I had very limited resources, and the structure was rudimentary. Nonetheless, the work began to attract attention at the Superior Court of Justice, as no comparable project had been attempted before. One of the Justices, Sálvio,[2] had a particular interest in the development of judicial schools and requested a meeting with me. "Did you really create this school? How does it operate?" he inquired. I explained its structure and objectives, and he then asked, "Would you be willing to serve as my secretary at the National School of Magistracy?"

At that time, the school operated under the auspices of the Association of Brazilian Magistrates, with Justice Sálvio serving as its director.

I accepted the role of his secretary and was entrusted with work of real substance. Over time, Justice Sálvio came to hold me in high regard. In that capacity, I began accompanying him to various events organised by the Judicial School, which significantly increased my visibility within the legal community. This, in turn, created the opportunity for my appointment as the first woman to serve on the Superior Court of Justice. I wish to emphasise, however, that none of this was motivated by personal ambition. Quite the opposite—my involvement arose from a sincere commitment to the mission of the school and to the broader goal of improving judicial training in Brazil.

I continued to engage actively with the issue of judicial training, while also reflecting critically on the structural shortcomings of the judiciary. I published articles, gave interviews, and spoke openly about the weaknesses I observed within the system. Over time, I came to believe that, in order for the judiciary to earn the respect of the society it serves, magistrates must uphold the highest ethical standards. When a judge errs, the consequences extend far beyond the individual—the damage to the institution itself can be significant. For this reason, internal mechanisms of self-correction are essential. If accountability is left solely to external forces, the resulting consequences are likely to be far more severe and traumatic.

When I decided to stand for a seat on the Superior Court of Justice, some of my colleagues asked, "Do you really think the Justices will vote for you, given the way you criticise the judiciary?" I replied, "I do not know. But if I do not run, I will never know. After all, they've never voted for a woman before." What I wish to emphasise is this: my way of speaking the truth—of openly criticising what I believe to be wrong—has never worked against me. On the contrary, it has always resulted in something constructive. I have therefore never seen a reason to change. And when I left the judiciary, I did so with the same conviction: I had no reason to alter my approach, as this way of being had always served me well.

My arrival at the Superior Court of Justice was, in many respects, quite remarkable. I do not claim to serve as a model—each person navigates these paths in their own way—but I do believe there is a lesson to be drawn from my experience. The President of the Republic had nominated me to the Superior Court of Justice, and by the time I was summoned for the Senate confirmation hearing, I had already contacted several politicians to request their support. I was consistently well received—even by those whom we now refer to as the so-called rotten ones. Today, their reputations are well known, but at that time, they were my political sponsors: Jader Barbalho,[3] Edison Lobão,[4] and Antônio Carlos Magalhães.[5] When people learn who my political sponsors were, they often assume that I must have been deeply compromised—after all, these are individuals now widely associated with the misappropriation of public funds. Yet the truth is that they provided me with substantial support. I recall visiting Jader Barbalho in his office. He looked at me and said, "I know who you are. You are very strict. You ruled against me in that case concerning the Polygon of the Chestnut Trees.[6]" Then he added, "That does not concern me. I have great respect for judges who take their work seriously."

At the Senate confirmation hearing, one of the senators asked what I thought of the process for selecting Justices to the Superior Court of Justice. I replied, "Formally speaking, it is the most correct system. The Judiciary prepares a shortlist, the President—representing the Executive—makes the nomination, and you, as the Legislative, conduct the confirmation hearing. In theory, all three branches participate in the decision." I then added, "What complicates matters is that everyone acts politically—not necessarily selecting the most qualified candidate, but the one with the strongest backing." The senator followed up: "Did you have a political sponsor?" I responded, "If I did not, I would not be sitting in this chair." When he asked who they were, I said, "Edison Lobão, Jader Barbalho, and Antônio Carlos Magalhães—in that order." The room fell completely silent. I must have appeared incredibly naïve—after all, no one publicly names their political sponsors. That simply is not done. But I spoke on impulse.

When I returned to the Tribunal, my colleagues were appalled. "Are you mad? How could you do such a thing?" they asked. "That is not how it is done, Eliana—you've really messed up." I left the hearing with the impression that perhaps I had indeed committed a serious misstep. Yet, in truth, it turned out to be one of the best decisions I ever made. The political sponsors were pleased—they felt flattered to have been publicly named as supporting my nomination. And I gained complete freedom. Throughout my fourteen years at the Superior Court of Justice, I never adjudicated any case involving any of them—I was legally barred from doing so. I was formally and publicly recused, which meant I owed nothing to anyone. And, notably, none of them ever approached me to request a favour.

That was the context in which I arrived at the Superior Court of Justice: entirely independent. I assembled my team from the ground up and did not appoint anyone on the basis of personal recommendations. I selected staff based on merit and organised everything myself. At the Superior Court of Justice, I gained a broader view of the magistracy and the training of judges—everything I'd already been working on, but now from a much wider perspective. I also continued working with Justice Sálvio at the School.

I made some very meaningful choices. Becoming Chief Inspectorate ("corregedora" in Portuguese) was a way of changing the system—but without causing open fractures, doing it in a more constructive way. Then came the National Council of Justice, which really impressed me. That was in 2004, with the judicial reform brought by Constitutional Amendment 45. I worked diligently, delivering lectures in support of the proposal—even though the idea of a national inspectorate was widely unpopular at the time, I defended it without reservation. In 2010, I was ultimately appointed Chief Inspector. But that is a story for another time.

Could you elaborate on your role within the Office of the Inspector General, particularly in view of the position you held at the time Operation Car Wash was initiated?

I was in the Office of the Inspector General from 2010 to 2012, that is when I met Sergio Moro.[7]

Was your first encounter with him connected to your institutional responsibilities within the Office of the Inspector General?

Yes, I met him briefly. The Office of the Inspector General included both federal and state judges within its structure. One of them, who served as a direct advisor to me, was from the state of Paraná.[8] This judge and I would often have lunch together. At the time, former Minister Sergio Moro was serving as an advisor to Justice Rosa Weber.[9] He frequently had lunch at the same restaurant. On one occasion, the judge from Paraná invited him to join us, as Moro—then serving as an advisor without a team—was often alone. He came over to our table and stayed with us for the meal. He was very quiet, very reserved; he has always been that way.

The information shared with me by the auxiliary judge, Erivaldo, was entirely positive. He described Moro as an excellent and highly regarded judge, with a specialisation in financial law. Moro had completed a course in the United States and was presiding over a federal court in Curitiba that dealt specifically with money laundering cases. At that time, however, he was serving as an advisor to Justice Rosa Weber. That was the context in which I first met him.

How would you evaluate the legal, political, and economic context in Brazil beginning in 2014, when Operation Car Wash was launched? In your view, were there structural conditions or institutional developments that enabled an investigation of such magnitude to take place?

Certainly. The origins can be traced back to the 1988 Constitution, which granted the Judiciary both administrative and financial independence. This institutional autonomy made the system more open—more permeable, one might argue. Around the same period, and particularly following the events of 2001 and the attacks on the Twin Towers, there was a marked shift in global concern towards terrorism. Among the key issues identified at the time was the network of support structures facilitating terrorist activity, with corruption increasingly viewed as one of its principal enablers.

At that point, all civilised countries felt the growing threat of terrorism and began to turn their attention to combating corruption. Prior to that, in negotiations with Brazil, there had been an unspoken assumption that corruption was merely a cultural trait—something ingrained and tolerated. There was little real commitment to addressing it. That was simply how Brazil was perceived, and the issue was largely dismissed.

A shift gradually began to take place. From 1988 onwards, there was a genuine institutional effort to transform the Federal Police into an intelligence-led agency. At the time, I was serving as a federal judge, having previously worked as a public prosecutor, which meant that I collaborated closely with the Federal Police. Their operational focus at that stage was primarily directed towards smuggling, embezzlement, and the misappropriation of public funds by lower-level officials—what might be described as "minor bosses" within government departments. There was little sustained attention to white-collar crime or systemic corruption, whether during my time at the Public Prosecutor's Office or subsequently on the bench.

But following the enactment of the new Constitution, the Federal Police began to evolve, and the Public Prosecutor's Office was also significantly strengthened. One key development was the institutional separation between the Prosecutor General's Office and the Public Prosecutor's Office. The latter assumed a clearly defined role as the guardian of the law, with responsibility for initiating and leading criminal prosecutions.

These developments unfolded gradually, beginning around 1989–1990, but their effects only became fully visible during the Mensalão case. That marked a decisive turning point: by then, both the Federal Police and the Public Prosecutor's Office had undergone significant transformation.

One key figure at that time was Márcio Thomaz Bastos,[10] who had been Minister of Justice and was known for defending some of the most notorious corrupt individuals in Brazil. He was brilliant—highly intelligent and very competent. Ironically, he was also the one who really gave the Federal Police the structure it needed. Under his leadership, the institution grew more than ever. He got everything he wanted from ministers and presidents alike, perhaps because of his close ties with powerful clients.

That was the moment when Brazil began to awaken to the seriousness of the issue. Other countries also began to exert pressure, urging Brazil to adopt a more robust stance against corruption. This was followed by the adoption of the Inter-American Convention Against Corruption, signed in Caracas, through which Brazil formally committed to combating corruption within public institutions and services.[11] The 1992 Money Laundering Law[12] was also a key development. It led to the creation of the Council for Financial Activities Control and later the National Strategy for Combating Corruption and Money Laundering.[13] All these changes paved the way for what would become something extraordinary—the Mensalão.[14] Mensalão was an outlier. Until then, we consistently encountered major institutional barriers at the Federal Supreme Court. To be candid, the Supreme Court at that time did not support the fight against corruption. I can say this with confidence: in every operation I participated in that involved members of audit courts or the judiciary, the moment the case reached the Supreme Court, it was effectively brought to a standstill—arrests were overturned, and rulings reversed. The situation was chaotic. I devoted myself tirelessly to these cases, only to witness all that work systematically undone by the Supreme Court. Gilmar Mendes[15] was largely the same as he is today, although at that time he exhibited a somewhat more restrained demeanour.

I always had a strong connection with the Federal Police. It is simply not realistic to claim that a judge should have no contact with either the police or the Public Prosecutor's Office—how else is an investigation supposed to be conducted? Take, for instance, a search and seizure warrant. The judge who issues it has no way of knowing how the operation will unfold in practice. Sometimes, a team of fifty officers is deployed early in the morning. Are we to assume that the judge should have no communication with them? That is not how judicial operations function—anywhere in the world. A judge must ensure that their order is properly executed and must actively monitor the process. On days when operations were being carried out, I would not sleep at all. I would be awake, waiting for six o'clock in the morning, when officers would call to report, "They're not letting us into the administrative office. What should we do?" And I would respond, "Break down the door and go in. The warrant is on its way to support you—just secure everything."

By six o'clock in the morning, I already had staff in my office preparing the documentation for forced entry and issuing the necessary warrants.

This level of communication and direction must come from the judge—it cannot be left entirely to the discretion of the police. I would also inform the Public Prosecutor's Office, as it holds responsibility for leading the criminal proceedings.

Therefore, when people today suggest that Moro's communication with the Public Prosecutor's Office was in some way scandalous, such claims are, quite frankly, unfounded.

The Mensalão case marked a true turning point—an exceptional outlier—because it originated in the Federal Supreme Court, and few believed it would progress. I often refer in lectures to a particular photograph published in *Estadão* on the day the case was opened. It captured many of Brazil's most prominent lawyers—what I often call the "Avenida Paulista lawyers," who have since migrated to Faria Lima—gathered in the plenary chamber, conversing before the session began. They were laughing, clearly expecting little more than a theatrical display. But they had not accounted for two key figures.

The first was Justice Ayres Britto,[16] who was President of the Court at the time and really pushed for the case to be heard. He practically insisted that Joaquim Barbosa,[17] the rapporteur, schedule the trial. And Joaquim Barbosa was incredibly serious—he'd come from the Public Ministry, and he was deeply committed.

Thus, contrary to all expectations, the Mensalão case moved forward—and became a true watershed moment in Brazil's legal and political history. It was at that point that the broader landscape began to shift, and Brazilian society started to take serious notice, particularly with Justice TV ("TV Justiça" in Portuguese) broadcasting the proceedings live. The revelations were striking. The case initially targeted businessmen, bankers, bank owners, and several high-profile politicians from across the political spectrum—individuals such as José Dirceu[18] and Genoíno.[19] Initially, few truly understood the magnitude of what was unfolding. It was difficult to believe.

I remember asking Justice Fux[20]—he and I were colleagues at the Superior Court of Justice, working together in the First Section—"Fux, explain it to me, why did the Mensalão work?" And he said, "Eliana, the evidence against them was so overwhelming it surfaced just by flipping through the case files." Because the Federal Supreme Court had never handed down a conviction of that kind before, no one truly believed it would happen—so much so that no one even made a serious effort to conceal the evidence. As a result, the evidence was so clearly laid out that conviction became inevitable. From that point onwards, a significant shift began to occur in Brazil. The legal community felt reinvigorated, as did the Public Prosecutor's Office. The case was widely perceived as a victory—for them, for the Federal Police, and for the justice system more broadly. Judges became not only more willing but increasingly enthusiastic about confronting corruption. Public discourse also began to change: the country started to engage seriously with themes such as ethics, compliance, corporate conduct, and the imperative of transparency—issues that had not, until then, featured prominently in the national conversation.

Therefore, Operation Car Wash was not a spontaneous development, nor was it solely the product of Sergio Moro or Deltan Dallagnol's initiative. Rather, it was the natural outcome of a broader institutional evolution that began with the 1988 Constitution. I witnessed that trajectory first-hand—closely following its unfolding, first as a judge, then as a justice, and participating in police operations such as Operation Dominoes ("Dominó" in Portuguese),[21] Operation Octopus ("Polvo" in Portuguese),[22] and Operation Folding Knife ("Navalha" in Portuguese)[23] all of which carried serious political implications. It was through these cases that I came to understand where the true root of the problem lies: the Legislative Branch. That is where it all begins. I can state with confidence that everything originates with parliamentary amendments. That is the serpent's egg—precisely there. And this is not something I gleaned from books or second-hand accounts; I witnessed it first-hand. That, I can affirm without hesitation.

In your view, in what ways did the Judiciary contribute to—or influence—the course and outcomes of Operation Car Wash?

I regard it as genuinely significant. For the first time in many years, judges began to feel that their work carried real purpose—and few things are more demoralising for a magistrate than the perception that their decisions lack practical effect. When a judge is able to carry out their duties and see a case through to its conclusion, producing a tangible impact on society, it generates a rare and meaningful sense of professional fulfilment. Operation Car Wash offered precisely that.

Sergio Moro embodied the image of a judge genuinely committed to the pursuit of justice—someone who was part of a team determined to combat corruption, understood as one of Brazil's most entrenched and destructive evils. From that point forward, corruption ceased to be viewed as merely part of the national culture. Before Operation Car Wash, people would often respond with resignation: "It is always been like this, even in my parents' and grandparents' time," or "He steals, but he gets things done—so He is a good politician." I even saw this mindset reflected in court, when Justice Lewandowski[24] remarked during the trial that Car Wash had only harmed Brazil because certain companies went bankrupt. It reflected the same familiar logic: "Yes, he steals, but at least he delivers"—as if public service achievements could somehow justify corruption. Within that rationale, some steal and achieve nothing, so the one who "delivers" is perceived as the lesser evil.

However, that narrative began to shift. Brazilians started to assert that corruption could no longer be tolerated. There is no place for it in a modern society committed to transparency and effective compliance mechanisms. I often stress this point: the global environment now demands it. Even banking—arguably the most traditional and conservative sector of the economy—has long embraced compliance as a core operational principle.

Indeed, a change of course had become urgently necessary. The broader push for transparency—and the global demand for integrity—also began to take root in Brazil. It could be felt among the public and within the judiciary. Justice itself began to shift—though not entirely, as there has always been a quiet and persistent effort to dismantle Operation Car Wash. The Legislature never truly accepted it, and the Federal Supreme Court merely gave the appearance of doing so.

I am now convinced that the Supreme Court merely feigned acceptance—allowing events to unfold to observe how far they might go. The Car Wash task force followed a very deliberate strategy: to start from the bottom. The investigation began with a single money launderer. It was as if they had cast a line and, unexpectedly, hooked a whale. And that whale was corruption—not limited to criminals or dubious entrepreneurs but entrenched in the very fabric of political power.

Corruption is sustained by criminal acts such as fraud, forgery, theft, and embezzlement. However, what Operation Car Wash revealed was that these offences were not being committed with guns or knives. No—the weapon of choice was the official pen. That was how power was both exercised and abused. In my view, this was one of the most striking revelations of Operation Car Wash. Even so, I believe that Operation Car Wash contributed to demystifying the Federal Supreme Court. In truth, the Court has never been anything other than what it is today—and that, too, forms part of the operation's legacy.

Could you elaborate on what you mean by "demystifying" the Federal Supreme Court? In what way did Operation Car Wash alter public perceptions of the institution?

In the sense that the Supreme Court has long been regarded as the guardian of the Constitution, the pinnacle of the Judiciary. And at a time when the entire country was rallying against corruption, the Supreme Court appeared to join that movement, signalling, "We are part of this effort too." In fact, many of the decisions handed down by former judge Sergio Moro and others were initially upheld by the Federal Supreme Court. That trend continued—until the investigations began to reach political figures. That is when resistance truly set in. **Fighting corruption in Brazil necessarily entails** confronting political power directly—and that power does not tolerate opposition. To do so is, in effect, to challenge the very system that sustains it.

I often refer to a statement once made by Zé Padilha[25]: "Brazilian democracy is a farce. What holds it together is corruption. The entire electoral machine runs on the back of political rot." And that, in essence, is what Operation Car Wash exposed. It revealed that the Federal Supreme Court does not necessarily act as the guardian of the Constitution. Rather, it defends a version of Brazilian democracy that has been created and maintained by the very political actors who remain entrenched in power. One only has to look at the most recent Parliamentary Inquiry Committee[26] election to see this dynamic at work. In the end, the Supreme Court serves to safeguard the very system that allows Brazil to continue functioning as it always has.

Reflecting on Operation Car Wash, what did you find most striking: the scale of the financial crimes, the involvement of corporate and political actors, the unprecedented nature of the investigation, or the systematic efforts that have since emerged to dismantle its legacy?

It was, in truth, a combination of factors. Operation Car Wash surprised me on a daily basis. I often found myself at a loss for words to express my admiration for those involved. With each passing day, new revelations emerged—another layer exposed, another hidden connection brought to light. For example, the investigation initially centred on construction firms and, for some time, did not reach Odebrecht. I found this difficult to understand. Being from Bahia, I was well aware of what that company was capable of. How could it possibly remain untouched?

At the time, I was told, "Odebrecht will be dealt with separately." I could not understand the rationale—why should it be treated differently? It only began to make sense later—it only began to make sense later—once the so-called whale had been caught. Only then did I fully grasp the strategy behind it. And when the investigation finally reached Odebrecht, I was genuinely astonished, but in the most positive sense. It was the kind of revelation that made one want to stand and applaud. That moment was powerful. It affirmed that everything I had done throughout my career had not been in vain—that real change might finally be on the horizon. It restored my belief that meaningful transformation could be achieved.

As for the dismantling of Operation Car Wash, the greatest surprise—by far—was the conduct of the Federal Supreme Court. Initially, I was genuinely surprised in a positive sense: the Court was upholding the convictions arising from Operation Car Wash. That initially caught me off guard—but in the best possible sense. However, over time, the Court began to reverse course. And that was the real shock. I could never have imagined that it would go as far as it ultimately did. By that point, I was already aware that Brazil no longer had a functioning system of criminal justice; the Supreme Court had, in effect, dismantled the Code of Criminal Procedure. But now, the situation has deteriorated even further:

the Constitution itself has been disregarded. For me, that was the most devastating and disillusioning surprise.

I was among the most enthusiastic voices—saying things like, "Brazil has changed! Things are different now!" The world had shifted, and I truly believed we were evolving as well. But now, looking back at what happened to Operation Car Wash, I feel deceived. I feel as though I was lying—not intentionally, but still. Everything I used to say in lectures no longer holds. It feels hollow now. Quite frankly, Brazil is now experiencing a reality more commonly associated with the developing world. While other Latin American countries continue to prosecute Odebrecht, here we have witnessed the complete dismantling of the operation. So yes—those have been the most striking and disheartening surprises for me.

In your view, what were the principal contributions and limitations of Operation Car Wash in the Brazilian context?

There were undoubtedly both political and economic ramifications. On the political front, certain consequences were perhaps inevitable. Economically, the construction sector suffered significant disruption. Yet I interpret these effects as intrinsic to the process of dismantling a structurally corrupt system: it is simply not possible to undertake genuine reform without dislocating the entrenched order. While institutional integrity must be safeguarded, the prevailing economic architecture demanded rupture. Established firms had to be unsettled to make room for the emergence of new, more accountable frameworks.

In that sense, the process was undeniably disruptive, and errors were made along the way. Such outcomes are, to some extent, unavoidable in an operation of that scale, involving numerous actors—many of whom were young and lacked substantial institutional experience. Naturally, there were instances of excess, and elements of personal vanity began to emerge. When I began to detect signs of personal vanity, I felt a profound sense of unease. Having witnessed numerous institutional cycles over the course of my career, I could tell that the trajectory was beginning to shift in a troubling direction. For me, those were the most disheartening aspects of the process.

But the positive outcomes were quite real. Several NGOs dedicated to anti-corruption conducted research and surveys, and their findings indicated a genuine shift in public perception. The private sector also began to change its mindset. Suddenly, there was a real concern with compliance—companies started to take it seriously.

Consider my own experience: I currently manage a law firm, and in recent months, several major companies—ones I would never have anticipated—have approached me. The very first question they ask is, "Do you represent anyone linked to Operation Car Wash?" If I respond affirmatively, they promptly withdraw. There is an international stigma attached to those involved in Car Wash, and these companies are deeply concerned with reputational risk. This is particularly true for those linked to multinational firms, which are acutely aware of how they are perceived abroad.

Smaller companies, on the other hand, often continue to play by the old rules. If they are involved in a complex case with five judges, they will hire five lawyers—each with some form of connection to a different judge—to influence the outcome. That is still how many smaller firms, or those accustomed to operating through fraudulent means, navigate the justice system: by relying on personal ties and exploiting their networks of influence.

Clients often seek me out because of my prior institutional experience. They assume I might be able to exert influence on their behalf—but I put an immediate end to such expectations. That entire mentality, that way of operating, was precisely what Operation Car Wash sought to dismantle. It marked the beginning of a new model, a new institutional culture. But when the Supreme Court adopts positions that appear to be shaped by personal ties—by friendships, affinities, or questionable connections with lawyers—then all of that progress, achieved through immense effort and sacrifice, begins to erode. I am genuinely concerned. There is a growing sense of disillusionment among principled professionals in both the Judiciary and the Public Prosecutor's Office. Some are considering leaving their careers altogether. Others are simply counting the days until retirement. But there are also those who are walking away without any retirement benefits—because they can no longer endure the institutional environment. The atmosphere within the Public Prosecutor's Office is deeply troubling—truly demoralising—and many prosecutors are struggling to come to terms with what is unfolding.

Has silence become the price one must pay to survive within the institution?

It increasingly resembles a witch hunt. A pervasive atmosphere of fear has taken hold—fear of speaking openly, of engaging in frank discussion, even of publishing critical reflections. The institutional environment has grown stifling. It is an immensely challenging—and profoundly disheartening—moment.

In closing, how do you reflect on the legacy of Operation Car Wash, and what prospects do you see for Brazil moving forward?

Given the current state of affairs, I find myself deeply pessimistic. I see no light at the end of the tunnel. The only notion I continue to hold onto is that perhaps we have reached rock bottom—because, in truth, little remains in which to place hope. There is, quite simply, nothing left to grasp. Is there? The oversight institutions have been dismantled, the branches of power are compromised, and those currently in charge are precisely the individuals who, in any functioning democracy, should have been publicly repudiated.

I no longer believe there is time to construct what some call a "third way." The expectation that a political saviour might appear—arriving on a white horse to restore order—is, quite frankly, a fantasy. The polarisation currently afflicting the country is profoundly corrosive. And yet, I continue to hold onto the possibility that something may still emerge—if only because, once a nation has reached rock bottom, some form of transformation often follows. What shape that transformation might take, however, remains uncertain.

What can be stated with confidence is this: a military coup is not on the horizon. The armed forces are neither prepared nor inclined to engage in such an undertaking; they lack the necessary leadership, organisation, and institutional cohesion. On the contrary, recent signs suggest a deliberate distancing from the current administration.

My hope—though cautious—is that institutional recovery may gradually take root. However, this will be a slow and arduous process. The damage inflicted over the past two or three years cannot be undone overnight; rebuilding what has been systematically dismantled will require sustained effort. Indeed, it would not be an exaggeration to suggest that even a decade may prove insufficient.

Eliana Calmon Alves was born in Salvador (BA). She is a jurist, professor, and magistrate. She was a Justice of the Superior Court of Justice. Her testimony was given on 26 April 2021 via the Zoom virtual platform and lasted 1 hour and 31 minutes of recording. The transcript was subsequently reviewed by the interviewee on 22 August 2022.

Testimony of João Pedro Gebran Neto

Abstract

This testimony by Judge João Pedro Gebran Neto—Federal Appellate Judge of the Regional Federal Court of the 4th Region and the reporting judge for Operation Car Wash—offers one of the most comprehensive and authoritative insider accounts of Brazil's most consequential anti-corruption investigation. Drawing on his pivotal judicial role throughout the operation, Gebran provides a detailed reconstruction of the legal, institutional, and procedural architecture that supported the Car Wash cases, many of which involved some of the most powerful political and corporate actors in Brazilian history. He outlines how existing legal frameworks, particularly those governing plea bargaining, cooperation agreements, and preventive detention, were tested and in some instances redefined under the pressure of unprecedented volumes of evidence, cross-border transactions, and systemic criminal conduct.

In this highly technical yet accessible reflection, Judge Gebran walks the reader through the structure and reasoning of his decisions, the methodological rigour of evidence assessment, and the challenges of navigating judicial responsibility amidst intense public scrutiny. He offers critical insights into the mechanisms of judicial control over prosecutorial conduct, the evolving jurisprudence on leniency agreements, and the importance of ensuring procedural integrity even when facing crimes of enormous social impact.

Beyond the strictly legal realm, the testimony engages with broader institutional and political dynamics. Gebran discusses the transformation of public perception of the Judiciary, the intense polarisation generated by the operation, and the organised backlash that ultimately sought to delegitimise and dismantle its legacy. He strongly defends the constitutional legality of Car Wash and repudiates the accusations of political bias that later surfaced—particularly in relation to coordination between judges and prosecutors, which he argues were both lawful and necessary within the framework of complex criminal litigation.

This testimony also speaks to the personal and professional toll of presiding over such a high-profile operation. With measured clarity, Gebran reflects on the solitude of judicial decision-making, the ethical burden of impartiality in a deeply divided nation, and the corrosive effects of attempts to rewrite the past through media campaigns and selective outrage. In so doing, his testimony emerges as both a legal document and a philosophical meditation on justice, democratic accountability, and the limits of institutional resilience.

Ultimately, this testimony not only illuminates the inner workings of Car Wash from the appellate bench but also contributes to a more textured understanding of how the Brazilian legal system responded—albeit imperfectly—to the challenge of grand corruption. It raises fundamental questions about the Judiciary's role in transitional moments, the dangers of institutional rollback, and the enduring tension between law, politics, and public morality.

Could you describe your educational background and professional trajectory, to provide context for your subsequent judicial experience and perspective?

In brief, I have served as a federal appellate judge at the Federal Regional Court of the 4th Region[27] since 2013, serving in the 8th Chamber, which is responsible for adjudicating criminal matters. I entered the federal judiciary in 1993, initially assigned to the city of Cascavel, where I was responsible for establishing the newly created federal court. Before that, I practised law for a short time and then served as a state prosecutor in Paraná for four years. Academically, I specialised in criminal and procedural criminal sciences at the Federal University of Paraná. I graduated from the Law School of Curitiba and later completed a master's degree in constitutional law, also at the Federal University of Paraná. I have authored several books—two in the field of criminal law and others focusing on health law, an area in which I am actively engaged both professionally and academically. At present, I collaborate with the National Council of Justice[28] through the National Health Forum,[29] contributing to institutional efforts aimed at improving access to and governance of public health services.

In your view, how would you characterise the legal, political, and economic context in Brazil beginning in 2014, when Operation Car Wash was launched? Were there any structural conditions or institutional dynamics that, in your assessment, made an investigation of such magnitude possible?

It is no simple task to summarise the period from 2014 to 2021, particularly in relation to Brazil's political and economic developments. However, from a legal perspective, some observations can be made. This period witnessed notable progress in the country's anti-corruption efforts, despite certain setbacks. Brazil made advances by reinforcing critical legal instruments such as plea bargaining, enhancing mechanisms for the repatriation of illicit assets held abroad, and by recognising crimes such as corruption, money laundering, and procurement fraud as serious offences—serious enough, in some instances, to warrant pre-trial detention. Overall, I would say the balance of the past seven years is still positive, despite some worrying reversals in the past year or two. One example is the Law of Abuse of Authority.[30] A close reading of the changes introduced by that law reveals a striking imbalance: nearly all provisions were aimed at judges, prosecutors, and police officers, as though only these actors within the state apparatus were capable of overstepping their bounds. The reform conspicuously failed to address potential abuses by other branches of government, particularly the Legislative and Executive. This selective approach gave the impression of a targeted response, which, in my view, is regrettable.

Another example of this regressive trend was the significant dilution of the so-called Anti-Crime Package.[31] Originally conceived as a comprehensive set of measures to enhance the efficiency and integrity of the criminal justice system, it was substantially watered down during the legislative process. Key provisions that would have bolstered investigative and prosecutorial tools were removed or weakened, thereby undermining the initiative's intended impact. The title "Anti-Crime Package" lost much of its meaning and original intent.[32] While the final version of the Anti-Crime Package retained certain positive elements, the overall result represented, in my assessment, a step backwards. Equally concerning was the Federal Supreme Court's reversal of its earlier position permitting imprisonment following a second-instance conviction. This doctrinal shift marked a significant retreat from previous jurisprudence and contributed to the perception of weakening institutional resolve in the fight against corruption.

Equally noteworthy is the Federal Supreme Court's reversal of its jurisprudence on the possibility of imprisonment following a second-instance conviction—a doctrinal shift that constitutes a significant regression in the enforcement of criminal accountability. If I may add, with all due respect, I personally disagree with several decisions issued by the Court in recent years, particularly the ruling that declared Operation Car Wash procedurally incompetent. That decision, in my view, lacked a sound legal basis and undermined the integrity of extensive judicial proceedings already concluded. At the time, Justice Fux[33] stressed that even if incompetence existed, it would only justify a relative nullity and should be declared only if specific harm could be proven. None of that was considered.

The past seven years have indeed brought meaningful progress, but they have also been marked by significant setbacks. One particularly concerning development has been the emergence of new jurisprudence applied retroactively, affecting cases that had already been adjudicated—even in instances where judgements had become final. This retrospective reinterpretation is highly unusual within the Brazilian legal system. A notable example is the rule requiring cooperating defendants to be questioned before other accused parties—a procedural safeguard introduced after several cases had already progressed. Nevertheless, this change was applied retroactively, calling into question the stability of earlier convictions.

In your view, what parallels can be drawn between Operation Clean Hands ("Mani Pulite" in Italian)[34] and Operation Car Wash, particularly with regard to their legal frameworks, institutional impacts, and political repercussion?

In 2021, I published an article in *O Estado de S. Paulo* titled *Era Uma Vez na Itália* (*Once Upon a Time in Italy*),[35] in which I examined not only the trajectory of Operation Clean Hands ("Mani Pulite"), but also the earlier "maxiprocessi". Although these judicial efforts occurred in distinct historical and political contexts, I believe they reveal important parallels—not only between themselves, but also in relation to Brazil's Operation Car Wash. Each of these initiatives emerged as responses to deep-rooted systemic corruption and relied on judicial innovation and prosecutorial coordination to pursue accountability at the highest levels of power. Their commonalities underscore the transnational nature of anti-corruption challenges and the institutional dilemmas they often provoke.

When examining Operation Clean Hands and Operation Car Wash, one cannot help but note the almost umbilical connection between them, particularly in the light of the striking parallels in their origins. Both investigations were triggered by corruption schemes involving major state-controlled oil companies—ENI in Italy and Petrobras in Brazil. And both started from what seemed like minor or isolated cases, with the evidence gradually snowballing into something much larger. There is that famous expression: "They tugged at a single thread—and the whole fabric came undone." In these cases, it was not just a thread—it unravelled the entire tapestry of corruption.

In Italy, Clean Hands led to the exposure of illegal political party financing and even the dissolution of some parties. The ones that were not dissolved often changed their names. Similarly, in Brazil, we saw various political parties recently rebranding, distancing themselves from names or acronyms associated with past scandals. Operation Car Wash also revealed the diversion of public funds for campaign financing and illicit personal enrichment—another strong parallel. But it is when we consider the *maxiprocesso* that we start to understand how the response to such investigations can shift. Initially, there is public support, but over time, especially when powerful interests are affected, there is political backlash and a progressive dismantling of the investigations. The *maxiprocesso*, which targeted the Italian Mafia, became known internationally, particularly because two prosecutors were murdered by the Mafia. These events were portrayed in films like *Excellent Cadavers*[36] and in books, one of which was translated into Portuguese as *Morte ao Excelentíssimo Senhor (Death to Your Excellency)*.[37] They offer a clear picture of how the narrative can be deconstructed, and how bias can influence judicial outcomes—something that book addresses quite accurately.

I brought these reflections into the article because, to some extent—certainly not in every detail—there are similarities between the Italian and Brazilian experiences. Sadly, the final outcome in Italy was disheartening. Much of what had been achieved in the fight against corruption and organised crime was eventually undone. The whole effort ended with very little to show for it in the long run, and the battle against corruption nearly went back to square one.

I also like to refer to a piece published in *Piauí* magazine, titled *The Untouchables*,[38] which provides a richly detailed account of what prosecutors and judges from Clean Hands experienced, and how things unfolded in Italy. In my view, these insights are profoundly relevant and merit careful reflection.

In your view, is there a significant risk that Operation Car Wash could ultimately follow the same trajectory as Operation Clean Hands in Italy?

It is difficult to make any definitive prediction, but I remain deeply optimistic—perhaps incorrigibly so. There is still a strong belief that Brazil can overcome its current challenges and recover from recent setbacks. Despite the backlash that is presently unfolding, there is hope that the course can be corrected and that, ultimately, the truth will prevail.

Prior to Operation Car Wash, there were earlier efforts to address corruption and organised crime in Brazil, including Operations Banestado[39] and Sandcastle.[40] In your view, what was the significance of these investigations for the emergence of Car Wash? Would

you consider them to have had a substantial influence on its development?

Alongside Operations Banestado and Sandcastle, I would also include Satiagraha[41] and Mensalão.[42] These four major investigations—each with its own complexities and limitations—undoubtedly laid the groundwork for what would later become Operation Car Wash. The connections are numerous, ranging from recurring individuals, whether as investigators, suspects, or defendants, to striking similarities in procedural dynamics and outcomes. Take Banestado, for instance: there is a direct connection through the money launderer Alberto Youssef,[43] who reappears in Car Wash. Banestado faced several setbacks, but in terms of results and contribution to the fight against corruption, I see it as more positive than Sandcastle or Satiagraha. The Mensalão, out of all of them, was probably the most successful. It resulted in convictions, final judgements, people actually serving sentences. It stands as a milestone in Brazil's anti-corruption efforts.

I look at these earlier operations from two perspectives. First, particularly with Sandcastle and Satiagraha—and to an extent, Banestado—I see them as missed opportunities. The Brazilian State was able to uncover and investigate illicit practices, even prosecute them, for various reasons—and I do not intend to critique judicial decisions here—those investigations did not progress as they ideally should have. Whether due to procedural mistakes or perhaps an overly broad recognition of nullities, many major cases were annulled. This is hardly a novelty in Brazil: cases involving high-ranking individuals frequently end in dismissal or lapse due to statutes of limitation. It remains one of the most persistent challenges in combating organised crime.

Nonetheless, a more constructive perspective also emerges: those earlier operations were instrumental in shaping institutional approaches to anti-corruption efforts. These investigations contributed to the development of task force models, improvements in plea-bargaining mechanisms, and the strengthening of international legal cooperation. Important lessons emerged regarding the tracing and recovery of assets, both domestically and abroad. Above all, such cases highlighted the critical need for coordination between the police and the Public Prosecutor's

Office, particularly when dealing with complex and concealed criminal networks that extend far beyond isolated acts or individual defendants.

For better or worse, those earlier efforts contributed to the evolution of Brazil's justice system, laying the groundwork for more structured operations such as Car Wash. Combined with international pressure, these experiences also played a role in driving significant legislative advancements. Bodies like the FATF,[44] the Palermo Conventions[45] and Mérida,[46] the OECD[47] pushed Brazil and other countries to take a stronger stand against money laundering—a growing global concern.

Even countries once known as untouchable tax havens started cooperating with major investigations, so as not to risk the credibility of their financial systems. Brazil, in turn, took important steps, particularly from a legislative standpoint. One highlight is Law No. 12.850/2013, which addresses organised crime.[48] Several other legislative developments have since contributed to a more robust legal framework in Brazil—one that is notably stronger than during the initial waves of anti-corruption investigations.

Given your reference to the OECD,[49] to what extent do you consider Brazil's accession process to the organisation a potential counterbalance to the institutional regressions witnessed in recent years—particularly in the areas of anti-corruption enforcement, judicial independence, and the rule of law?

I would hesitate to offer a definitive judgement. Nonetheless, it is reasonable to question whether Brazil's ongoing exclusion from the OECD reflects, at least in part, a perceived erosion of its long-term commitment to anti-corruption efforts. In this light, the failure to secure accession and the broader dismantling of integrity frameworks may be seen as two interrelated facets of the same institutional regression.

Operation Car Wash was remarkable in many respects—from the sheer scale of the financial crimes to the number of cases, and the range of companies, executives, and political figures implicated. In your view, was there a single aspect that stood out as most significant, or should the operation be understood as a convergence of equally important elements?

Let me give a bit of context first. Operation Car Wash officially began in March 2014, though investigations had already been underway before then including some that led to a pre-assignment of the case to the rapporteur at the Regional Federal Court of the 4th Region. March 2014 marked the first arrest related to the operation, which was essentially the start of its public phase. From then on, we saw a series of ongoing surprises and increasing public astonishment.

The first surprise came when it was discovered that Alberto Youssef—who had already been involved in the Banestado case—had returned to the illegal exchange market, again acting as a black-market currency dealer. That was a shock for the federal police, the Public Prosecutor's Office, and the judiciary, because Youssef had signed a plea bargain and was not just breaching it—he had resumed criminal activity. The next surprise was the level of power he had become involved with. This time, he was not simply laundering money—he was linked to a director of Petrobras, Paulo Roberto Costa,[50] as well as to politicians and political parties.[51] This connection came to light quite quickly, when it was discovered that Costa had received a car as a gift. Until then, although some may have suspected it, most of society could not have imagined that Petrobras—Brazil's largest and most respected company—was so deeply entangled in corruption. It was a huge shock for everyone.

From these two initial characters—and the back-and-forth jurisdictional issues, as the case moved from the 13th Court in Curitiba to the Supreme Court and then back again—the operation expanded to include other black-market currency dealers involved in laundering money, even for drug traffickers. That is a core element of the operation's origins, and it also justified some of the arrests that followed.

Then came the plea bargains—first from Youssef, which were controversial given his previous breach, and then from the Petrobras director, which stunned the country. Another shocking moment was the plea bargain of a Petrobras manager—not a top executive, but someone at the second level—who returned roughly one hundred million US dollars.[52] It's hard not to be amazed by that figure. The money was held abroad, and he not only confessed but agreed to repatriate the funds.

But the case that struck me most—and that had countless ramifications—involved a loan of twelve million reais from Banco Schahin to José Carlos Bumlai.[53] That money was used for two things: to pay off campaign debts and to make an improper payment to a well-known businessman from Santo André, who had apparently demanded the favour.[54] The basis for his so-called credit remains unclear; what is certain, however, is that he not only received the funds but did so through a series of laundering schemes.

This led to three criminal cases—one against the businessman, another against Bumlai, and a third against the directors of Banco Schahin. But what is truly surreal is not just that this businessman acted as a front to distribute millions. It is how the debt was eventually repaid. Initially, there was an attempt to resolve the loan quickly, but it failed. The bank's management began to worry, as the Central Bank was set to inspect them, and they had this massive outstanding debt. First, the businessman refinanced it using his lands as collateral. Then, a string of fraudulent contracts and fake settlements were created, leading to even more Car Wash-related cases.

And the most astonishing part? The bank was ultimately reimbursed via a contract with Petrobras—a contract worth one and a half billion dollars—awarded to a company in the Schahin Group, which also owned the bank. What began as a twelve million real loan to cover a political party's[55] campaign debt ended up as a multi-year contract worth billion. That, to me, is an incredibly disturbing example of how things were operating—how these illicit schemes escalated into cascading losses for the Brazilian state. Even more, this entire story is intertwined with the creation of Sete Brasil,[56] the appointment of O executives, and public funds from state pension schemes being used to set up the company. One simple loan led to all of this. And honestly, I do not think even the most imaginative Hollywood screenwriters or Netflix creators could come up with something so complex and criminal.

I speak openly about this not as a matter of opinion, but based on direct judicial experience. I presided over these cases. What I recount here is drawn from the evidentiary record and substantiated through numerous plea bargain agreements—among them, confessions from Banco Schahin executives, black-market currency operators, and senior officials at Petrobras.

The Car Wash cases, at the first instance in Curitiba and at the Regional Federal Court **of the 4th Region, were moving quickly. On the other hand, at the Federal Supreme Court and at the Superior Court of Justice, the pace was different. Is there a reason for the slowness in the higher courts? What could be done to change that?**

Once again, I will take a bit of time to answer. First, I will speak about the Regional Federal Court of the 4th Region,[57] about our Court, because I feel it is important to give due credit to the judges who worked on Operation Car Wash—not to myself, of course, but to my colleagues, who were extremely dedicated. There were four of us in the 8th Chamber, along with the judges from the 4th Section of the Regional Federal Court of the 4th Region, who handled these cases. Everyone involved felt the responsibility and the duty to act with depth, speed, and quality.

I would also like to highlight the exceptional contribution of the court staff. They quickly grasped the magnitude and complexity of the Car Wash cases, recognising that such proceedings could not be managed by a single individual. These cases demanded collective effort—multiple minds and skilled hands—to handle everything from drafting decisions to conducting meticulous analyses of documents and evidence. This included deliberations on authorship, materiality, legal classification, sentencing, and other fundamental aspects of criminal adjudication. The work in my office was very intense. There were regular debates—both on the facts and on legal points. I am deeply grateful to the team: those who worked directly on Car Wash, and those who did not but who took on the rest of the caseload so we could focus on it. So, I want to express my public thanks to all the court staff—especially those in my own office. In addition, it is important to acknowledge the role played by our electronic case management system, e-proc. This digital platform has been instrumental in streamlining judicial proceedings by allowing all parties involved to access case information simultaneously. It marks a decisive shift away from the traditional paper-based model, where files would circulate sequentially between offices, often resulting in significant delays. At the Federal Regional Court of the 4th Region, that outdated model has been replaced by a far more efficient and transparent system. Today, the digital process is very agile—it allows simultaneous access across different offices. Even before I release my vote, the other judges can see everything that is been done in the case, both at first and second instance—they get a complete view. The e-proc system is widely recognised across Brazil—by lawyers and even by the Federal Court of Accounts report[58]—as the best electronic legal system in the country.

And why else did proceedings move swiftly at the Federal Regional Court of the 4th Region? Because there were defendants in custody. Cases involving individuals in pre-trial detention are routinely prioritised—not only in Operation Car Wash, but as a matter of standard judicial practice. Unsurprisingly, the intricate and high-stakes nature of the Car Wash cases necessitated sustained efforts, with work frequently extending into Saturdays, Sundays, holidays— whatever was required— to address what I often refer to as the "Amazonian scale" of Operation Car Wash.

As for the higher courts, I would not characterise the Superior Court of Justice as slow; in my view, it responded within a reasonable timeframe. What is being dealt with involves numerous procedural incidents. There is the special appeal, and if that is not admitted by the vice-president of the court, the matter proceeds to the Superior Court of Justice, which then determines whether the appeal should advance. The Superior Court of Justice rules on that, and if disagreements arise, additional mechanisms may follow—such as appeals for breach of precedent, motions for clarification, or other forms of review. It is a complex sequence of procedures and represents a substantial workload. Considering the circumstances, the response from the Superior Court of Justice was appropriate, in terms of both timing and content. I am unable to comment on the original jurisdiction cases at the Superior Court of Justice, as I do not recall whether any were directly related to Operation Car Wash. However, in terms of appellate review, many decisions were handed down quite promptly.

It is also important to bear in mind that the Superior Court of Justice functions as a national court, receiving appeals not only from the five Federal Regional Courts but also from all State Courts and the Federal District. And this refers solely to its appellate jurisdiction. The volume of work facing each Justice is immense, and that context must be taken into account when assessing the pace at which cases are processed.

As for the Federal Supreme Court, I do not know whether there are any extraordinary appeals related to the merits of Car Wash awaiting judgement there. What I do see are several original jurisdiction cases connected to the operation. And those do not appear to have moved quickly, at least from what I can observe. The Supreme Court has a very broad range of responsibilities, and what we see most are *habeas corpus* cases—over and over again.

The truth is that higher courts in general—including all of them—are not institutionally structured to handle the evidentiary phase of criminal proceedings. This became particularly evident during the Mensalão case, where the concentration of jurisdiction under the privileged forum highlighted the challenges of conducting complex criminal proceedings in higher courts. There were some efforts to eliminate or at least reduce the privileged forum for public officials, so that cases would not be tried in a single bloc, as happened in the Mensalão case.

Nonetheless, the reality is that conducting criminal proceedings in higher courts remains a difficult and complex task. The considerable temporal and factual distance from the events under investigation tends to slow the process significantly. This structural limitation may well warrant reconsideration—perhaps even at the legislative or constitutional level.

How would you assess the role of pre-trial detention in addressing corruption and organised crime? To what extent can it serve as an effective legal instrument without undermining fundamental rights?

It is essential to emphasise that pre-trial detention should remain an exceptional measure. This principle must be clearly understood as a rule, individuals ought to respond to legal proceedings while at liberty. However, this concept is frequently misunderstood—particularly in a country like Brazil, where elevated crime rates and a pervasive sense of insecurity and impunity lead to widespread public pressure for pre-trial incarceration. Yet it must be reiterated that pre-trial detention is the exception, not the norm. The standard is that individuals face trial and begin serving their sentence only upon conviction, ideally after judgements at both first- and second-instance levels.

One of the most significant positive outcomes of Operation Car Wash was the paradigm shift it introduced. It established a clearer understanding that certain corruption-related offences—particularly those involving the co-optation of state agents by criminal interests, the operation of structured criminal organisations, or transnational money laundering schemes involving concealed illicit assets—constitute continuing crimes. This reconceptualisation enabled a more robust legal response by acknowledging the persistent and systemic nature of such conduct.

These crimes—corruption, money laundering, criminal association—are extremely serious. They cause significant harm to society and are just as damaging as violent street crime, which naturally shocks us all. Both types of crime deserve a serious and timely response from the justice system. Pre-trial detention should not only be used in cases of homicide, drug trafficking, or sexual offences—although those certainly warrant it too—but also in cases where criminal organisations are still active, still reaching out to commit further crimes.

These groups divert public resources—money that should be going to healthcare, education, infrastructure, even public security itself. To dismantle such entrenched structures within the State, pre-trial detention was ordered at first instance, upheld at second and third instance, and even by the Federal Supreme Court. There was a real need to interrupt the criminal cycle and break up organisations that had essentially taken over the State. In that sense, pre-trial detention became a key tool in dismantling these networks. That said, it must be emphasised once again that pre-trial detention cannot serve as a form of anticipatory punishment. Its purpose is not to substitute or pre-empt a criminal sentence—it must always be based on necessity, in line with the requirements of Article 312 of the Code of Criminal Procedure.[59] And I believe that is precisely how it was applied in Operation Car Wash: as an exceptional measure, grounded in legal criteria, rather than as a tool for prematurely enforcing punishment.

I would also highlight a particularly illustrative case in which an individual, after being placed in pre-trial detention and subsequently released, proceeded to transfer assets abroad in a renewed attempt to conceal their illicit origin. That led to a second pre-trial detention. It is a clear example of how Operation Car Wash tried to strike a balance—keeping key members of these criminal organisations in custody, when it was truly necessary.

How do you evaluate the legal and procedural aspects surrounding the pre-trial detention and subsequent release of former Congressman Eduardo Cunha[60]?

Everything I mentioned earlier applies to the case of congressperson Eduardo Cunha. He was preventively arrested—and I want to emphasise that again—because there was strong evidence of his involvement in a criminal organisation that aimed to cause harm to Petrobras and the Brazilian state. The arrest was necessary to interrupt that ongoing activity. This was clearly demonstrated during the proceedings: funds held abroad, illicit payments—there was, frankly, an abundance of evidence. Otherwise, of course, a conviction would not have been possible.

What happened next, however, was a shift in the Federal Supreme Court's stance, which ruled that imprisonment could no longer occur after a second-degree conviction. In my view, this effectively meant imprisonment could only happen after a final judgement at the fourth degree of jurisdiction. This change reinforced the perception of impunity within Brazilian society and made Brazil one of the few countries that require such an extensive appeals process before sentence execution.

There is now a delay of ten—and in some cases, even twenty—years between the commission of the offence and the final conviction with effective enforcement of the sentence. I recently read a book by Professor Virgílio Afonso da Silva, where he explains that most countries do not treat the concept of "final judgement" the way we do here in Brazil. In many jurisdictions, the process does not drag on to the extent we are used to—where the final decision only comes after the very last appeal has been heard and ruled upon in the Supreme Court. That is a very telling insight.

In the case of Eduardo Cunha, pre-trial detention was initially ordered on the basis that the legal requirements were clearly satisfied. He had long maintained—and arguably continues to maintain—undisclosed financial assets abroad. But as time went on and he remained in custody, no further assets were discovered beyond those already identified. That either points to a failure in the state's investigative efforts or suggests he truly does not possess additional resources.

Eventually, the case reached the Federal Regional Court of the 4th Region, where a *habeas corpus* was granted. Since he'd already been convicted in both the first and second instances, but no longer had any other ongoing proceedings, and because the rules now no longer allow for sentence execution after a second-degree conviction, his release became inevitable—simply because the legal grounds for continued pre-trial detention were no longer present.

This highlights a serious flaw in our system: we do not allow for the provisional enforcement of a sentence before final judgement. His release, in the end, was a lawful decision, but it points to a broader issue in how our legal system handles cases like this.

Plea bargaining has been a key mechanism in the fight against corruption, both in Brazil and internationally. To what extent might recent legislative changes affect the structure and application of plea agreements, such as those implemented during Operation Car Wash[61]?

I always find it useful to begin by providing some context. First and foremost, it is important to understand the nature of the crimes that typically give rise to plea bargains. These are offences committed under a veil of secrecy—often more so than other types of crime. They involve covert arrangements, carefully orchestrated to avoid leaving any trace.

This is often the case with drug trafficking, where negotiations and communications are typically carried out using technology in ways that are deliberately obscure and cautious. One might think of the Italian Mafia and its code of *omertà*—a culture of silence in which no one speaks out, and no one betrays their associates. The same principles apply to corruption and money laundering. These are crimes that try to leave no trail, no clue, no sign of wrongdoing. And that is exactly why plea bargains are such a vital tool—not just in Brazil, but around the world—for tackling these kinds of offences.

Only someone who is embedded in that world, someone who's part of the organisation or who has taken part in the crime, has the ability to bring in real evidence, to connect the dots, to interpret cryptic notes in a diary, or to explain the meaning behind complex financial transactions. For instance, why does a particular action in one context trigger consequences elsewhere? Why is the appointment of a specific individual to a given position significant in terms of political campaign financing? Why was that drillship allocated to a certain company, and how does this connect to a bank loan? These are the kinds of links that only a cooperating witness is in a position to reveal.

Nonetheless, beyond the intrinsic value of the plea bargain as a legal instrument, it is essential to acknowledge the necessity of offering the collaborator a meaningful incentive. Few people agree to cooperate out of pure remorse—although theoretically, it is possible that someone might collaborate for ethical reasons. Still, in most cases, they want something in exchange. Traditionally, this has been a reduced sentence, which is well established in our legal system. But with recent developments, collaborators now expect more—more tangible benefits.

Until the Anti-Crime Package legislation came into effect, the benefits offered in plea bargains were relatively flexible, guided by case law and existing legal provisions. There was more room for negotiation, depending of course on the quality and effectiveness of the cooperation.

It is actually quite interesting, from a practical perspective, to see how plea bargain agreement with the police or the Public Prosecutor's Office unfolds. A potential collaborator will want to signal what they could reveal—but without laying all their cards on the table. They'll only divulge specific facts and evidence once there is a guarantee of what benefits they'll receive in return. Meanwhile, the authorities will indicate what they might be able to offer, but without revealing what they already know. So, it becomes a kind of game—an exchange of hints and cautious offers. Each side assesses the cost–benefit of the negotiation. There is a legal incentive, a sort of structured agreement, where what the authorities need—facts, names, clarity—has to be matched with what the collaborator is willing to give.

After several rounds of meetings and hearings, once all sides are aligned, the agreement is formalised and signed. But now, with the changes brought by the Anti-Crime Package and, more importantly, the Federal Supreme Court's shift in position regarding the execution of a sentence after a second-degree ruling, things have changed significantly. I return to this point because I believe it is central to the conversation about impunity in Brazil. It's central to building the country that society expects—one where justice is not endlessly delayed.

What these legislative changes have done is limit the range of benefits the police and the Public Prosecutor's Office can offer. And when you combine that with the fact that prison sentences can no longer be enforced after a second-degree conviction, we've essentially removed some of the key incentives that once drove people to collaborate. These two changes, in practice, have made plea bargaining far less attractive and, in my view, have undermined the effectiveness of this crucial legal instrument.

I must underscore that this instrument is not simply important; it is indispensable in confronting complex forms of criminal conduct. I am not only talking about corruption and money laundering. This also includes crimes such as drug trafficking, terrorism, arms smuggling, and human trafficking—these are all extremely serious crimes. In many of these cases, it is the collaborator who provides the evidence that enables justice to be served. In my view, the recent legislative changes represent a setback in our efforts to combat impunity.

What led you to characterise Operation Car Wash as "Amazonian" in scale?

I like to describe it as "Amazonian"—vast, intricate, and difficult to map—yet not always accompanied by widespread public information. Operation Car Wash, however, stood out for its scale and impact. It captured the public's attention in a significant way, much like other major investigations, such as the Mensalão scandal. Society's perception of the fight against crime is fragile. I am currently reading a very interesting book by a Swedish health professional, which talks about something called "factfulness"[62]—it is about how society tends to perceive the world through a negative lens. We are bombarded with far more negative news than positive, and that affects how we interpret reality. For instance, launching a high-profile operation makes headlines, but the actual trial or sentencing process hardly gets the same attention. Preventive arrests grab the spotlight much more than someone quietly beginning to serve a sentence. So, society ends up developing a skewed, sometimes mistaken, perception of impunity in Brazil—not that impunity does not exist; it certainly does.

Take the Federal Regional Court of the 4th Region, for instance: it has already ruled on more than two thousand cases related to Car Wash, including both main proceedings and procedural incidents. For the sake of clarity, my references to Operation Car Wash pertain specifically to cases involving Petrobras and its subsidiaries. I am not talking about the cases unfolding in Rio de Janeiro, São Paulo, Brasília, Recife, and elsewhere—although these are often referred to as part of Car Wash or "Car Wash Brazil", they are separate strands that do not directly link back to Petrobras. This Petrobras connection is even the line the Supreme Court has drawn to determine what falls under the jurisdiction of the 13th Federal Court in Curitiba—namely, the cases involving damage to Petrobras and those original ones involving currency dealers who operated in the parallel foreign exchange market. That in itself was no small matter, even though it did not receive as much media attention.

So, within this narrower definition of Car Wash, we've had more than two thousand cases and incidents judged. Beyond that, the broader numbers are also impressive: once hundred and seventy-four people convicted across first and second instances, seventy-nine different stages of Operation Car Wash up until May 2021, and two hundred and nine individuals signing plea bargain agreements. The Court has already ruled on over fifty cases on the merits—the first on 22 September 2015, and the most recent on 10 November 2021. More than four billion reais have been returned to Petrobras' coffers, although it is estimated the actual damage was nearly three times that. Approximately one-third of the embezzled funds has been recovered to date—and while further recovery remains a goal, it is by no means an easy task.

The Federal Regional Court of the 4th Region increased several sentences compared to those handed down at first instance. About fifteen per cent of first-instance acquittals were overturned on appeal, and in many cases, first-instance convictions were reversed by the second instance to acquit the defendants. In short, the Federal Regional Court of the 4th Region has truly acted as a second-instance court should—reviewing the facts, the appeals, the evidence, and the law, and applying it under the principle of collegiality, with panels of three judges, or up to six or seven when dealing with appeals that seek to overturn earlier rulings.

It is an enormous undertaking—and Car Wash-related cases are still being addressed on a weekly basis. Yet, returning to the beginning of my response: what most captures public attention are the arrests and convictions of high-profile individuals. By contrast, when many of those involved are relatively unknown, they fail to attract the same level of media attention or public interest.

The fragmentation of Operation Car Wash—across jurisdictions such as Curitiba, São Paulo, Rio de Janeiro, Brasília, and others—led to markedly different outcomes. Among these, the Rio de Janeiro cases most closely resembled those of Curitiba. How do you evaluate this fragmentation? Was it beneficial or detrimental to the broader fight against corruption in Brazil?

To begin with, I believe this fragmentation was, in fact, quite natural—and I have consistently defended it. In my view, it was entirely appropriate. There needs to be a clear dividing line. When you are dealing with an investigation as complex and wide-ranging as Operation Car Wash in the 13th Federal Court in Curitiba—involving multiple collaborators, contractors working on public infrastructure projects across Brazil, money launderers tied to various kinds of crimes, from drug trafficking to corruption—it is inevitable that you'll face a massive spread of facts and actors.

Admittedly, attempting to keep everything under a single umbrella does offer certain advantages, particularly in terms of consolidating information—which may appear beneficial at first glance. However, it also presents a significant challenge in terms of managing and processing the sheer volume of material involved. More importantly, Brazilian procedural law requires the existence of a legal nexus—a proper connection—that justifies the consolidation of such case.

Broadly speaking, the main connection that allowed for that grouping—and this was almost unanimously accepted—was Petrobras.

That was the thread tying most of the Curitiba cases together. But when a collaborator worked not only for Petrobras but also on unrelated projects elsewhere—say, highways or energy infrastructure in another state, where bribes were paid to entirely different beneficiaries—then the link becomes weaker. There is no longer that close evidentiary connection. Among all the forms of procedural linkage, evidentiary connection is perhaps the most flexible—but even then, sometimes cases need to be split off and sent to the appropriate jurisdiction.

Take the Eletronuclear cases, for instance—they were sent to the competent court. And what connection exists between Eletronuclear and Petrobras? Virtually none. Maybe a money launderer was involved in both, but that is a thin link. The same goes for a highway concessionaire in Paraná—what do they have to do with Petrobras-related investigations? Not much, if anything. It makes perfect sense to draw that procedural distinction, sever the case, and refer the information to the court with jurisdiction over the relevant facts.

In fact, the Federal Regional Court of the 4th Region followed precisely that approach in several cases. Personally, I view this fragmentation as quite positive: it meant that a greater number of judges, federal prosecutors, and police officers became involved in the investigations. It spread the workload and allowed for a broader application of the law. In theory, this should lead to quicker and better-quality rulings.

Naturally, this has not always held true in practice. In some cases, due to a lack of initiative from the police or prosecutors, or because of limited resources or infrastructure, proceedings did not advance as swiftly as society might have hoped. That really has to be evaluated on a case-by-case basis, region by region. But what I can say with confidence is that here, in the Federal Regional Court of the 4th Region and particularly in the 13th Federal Court of Curitiba, matters progressed efficiently and effectively—at least until quite recently.

Could you describe the episode involving the habeas corpus granted by on-call judge Rogério Favreto of the Federal Regional Court of the 4th Region, in favour of President Lula?

That episode is rather unique in the history of the Court. Judge Rogério Favretto,[63] considering himself competent to rule on the matter while on duty—even though it was already being handled by the 8th Panel—granted an injunction on a Sunday to release the then former president. Lula was in prison at the time, based on an earlier decision by the 8th Panel itself, which had ordered his detention following a second-instance conviction, in line with the legal understanding of the Supreme Court in force at that time.

The then former president was, at that point, serving a custodial sentence, and Judge Favretto received a *habeas corpus* request late on a Friday afternoon. Subsequently, on Sunday morning, under the assumption of urgency, he granted the *habeas corpus*—not only going against a decision of the 8th Panel, but in a case originally directed against the first-instance judge. He believed he had the authority to make that decision—I won't comment on the merits—but the fact remains that it was a monocratic ruling issued while on duty, and one that could have been reviewed the following Monday.

Given that the matter had remained unresolved from Friday to Sunday, a further 24-hour delay would hardly have resulted in any prejudice. There was no risk of irreparable damage in those next 24 hours—not from Friday, and certainly not from Sunday to Monday. But the order was granted, nonetheless.

What is particularly striking is that this monocratic decision, rendered while the judge was on duty, effectively overturned a prior ruling issued by the competent collegiate body. There were a series of back-and-forth developments in that process—which I do not think are worth going into here—but in the end, on Monday, I issued a ruling that essentially confirmed, almost word for word, the decision I had already drafted on Sunday, revoking Judge Favretto's injunction.

The matter then went to the 8th Panel, which upheld my decision and denied the *habeas corpus*. It is important to understand that President Lula's imprisonment was not pre-trial detention—it was the result of a conviction sentence being enforced. There was no new element presented, even though the petitioners claimed there was. Nothing justified the urgency, let alone the granting of the order. Indeed, the 8th Panel upheld the original decision at the time. At the end of 2019, the Federal Supreme Court changed its reasoning—about the execution of a sentence following a second-instance conviction ruling. As for the rest of the facts surrounding that episode, I imagine that one day, someone will study the matter in greater depth. Perhaps a historian will be able to delve further and truly uncover what transpired.

How do you assess Operation Spoofing and its impact on Operation Car Wash and, more broadly, on the fight against corruption in Brazil[64]?

I am not in a position to comment on Operation Spoofing, as it did not pass through the Federal Regional Court of the 4th Region. What I do know about it comes from the media—primarily newspapers. In any case, it is not a matter I have ever examined in depth. The only observation I can offer is that all the material in question stems from illicit evidence—criminally obtained by a hacker—and, in my view, is entirely inadmissible in any criminal proceeding. Beyond that, I do not have much to add regarding this operation, simply that the evidence is illegal and should be treated as such.

In your view, to what extent might the recent setbacks experienced by Operation Car Wash undermine the structural reforms it introduced in Brazil's anti-corruption framework?

As I mentioned at the beginning, I am fundamentally an optimist. I believe we are moving forward—towards the future and, ultimately, towards improvement. If we consider the course of Brazilian history, or indeed global history, despite recurring doubts and uncertainties, tomorrow tends—more often than not—to be better than today. People may not believe that straight away, but when you step back from the heat of the moment, from the emotion of current events, it becomes clear that progress is being made.

We are living through the longest democratic period in Brazil's history. Despite the horrors of the pandemic and some extremely serious challenges, we now have a public health system—the SUS—that is the only thing holding things together. That did not even exist before 1988. Is SUS perfect? No. Is it ideal? Certainly not. Does it fulfil all our expectations? Not yet. Nonetheless, it represents far more than we have ever had in the past—and that, in itself, is deeply significant.

And I think this applies to other areas too—education, democracy, our institutions in general. Going back to the book I mentioned earlier, *Factfulness*, this is precisely the kind of outlook it confirms. The book points out that we currently live in a world with fewer wars, less hunger, more women engaged in public and political life, more girls completing secondary school, and longer life expectancy—both in Brazil and globally. We have progressed and recognising that helps people face life in a more hopeful and positive way.

Within that broader context, I view Operation Car Wash as a development that brought tangible progress and institutional improvements to Brazil. Compliance, for example, is now a reality. Companies working with public authorities—or even those that do not—are increasingly committed to integrity programmes. And this is not merely because the law requires it; many international companies are unwilling to engage in business with Brazilian firms unless they can demonstrate a robust and credible compliance framework. None of this was simply handed to us—it was earned. Even if through some hard and uncomfortable processes, Brazil evolved. It exposed its corruption and, in doing so, showed both its worst and its best.

Brazil's position on the Transparency International Index[65] may initially appear disheartening. However, this ranking arguably reflects, above all, the country's commitment to transparency as a guiding principle. Brazil dared to show its corruption to the world. Many other countries have similar problems, but they simply do not come to light. The corruption was not merely exposed; it was confronted, investigated, and the process of holding individuals accountable was set in motion. That, to me, is a very positive step. What Operation Car Wash revealed was precisely what is described in the book *Crime.gov*[66]—that the Brazilian state itself had been co-opted. Not just its institutions, but the very machinery of the state, which is far more serious. The entire federal public structure was, at some point, compromised. And I am not making a political or ideological point here; this is just the reality we saw. Look at the pension funds, for example—outside of Car Wash's scope. Reckless investments left them in such a state that members now have to make additional contributions to ensure they'll even receive their pensions in future. That is not a theory—that is a recognised fact.

Nonetheless, Brazil is confronting the issue. At times, holding up a mirror reveals uncomfortable truths—but such recognition is the necessary first step towards meaningful change. Precisely because there is a desire for improvement, I regard this as a positive development. As previously noted, progress is seldom linear and often accompanied by setbacks. I like a quote from Justice Luís Roberto Barroso[67]: "There are those who want to leave their past behind and, from this point forward, build a society that is more just, freer, more humane and more solidary, as laid out in the Constitution." Sadly, some do not want that—however, society as a whole—and the Executive, Legislative, and Judiciary branches in particular—must recognise that those who continue to refuse to act honestly must be held accountable.

The overwhelming majority of society demands honesty—not only moving forward, but, ideally, from the very beginning.

To close, may I invite you to share any concluding thoughts?

Yes, I would like to leave a message of hope—a reminder that the present moment is only a fragment of a larger narrative. This is not a mere snapshot but part of an unfolding story. Today's image may not be the one I would have chosen, nor the one many would prefer—but the broader trajectory, at least since 1988, remains fundamentally positive in my view.

I firmly believe that in future, with the benefit of hindsight, it will be possible to recognise not only the difficulties and setbacks but also the progress made. Brazil's advancement over time will be seen—reflected in the evolution of society, the strengthening of democracy, and increased civic and political engagement. That is the message I wish to leave: progress is inevitable, and the challenges faced will be overcome. Brazilian society must both believe in this and, more importantly, actively participate in making it a reality.

João Pedro Gebran Neto was born in Curitiba (PR). He is a federal judge. Since 2013, he has been a judge of the Federal Regional Court of the 4 Region, integrating the 8 Chamber. His testimony was given on 19 May 2021 via the Zoom virtual platform and lasted 1 hour and 15 minutes of recording. The transcript was subsequently reviewed by the interviewee on 21 March 2022.

Testimony of Marco Aurélio Mello

Abstract

This testimony by Marco Aurélio Mello, former Justice of the Federal Supreme Court of Brazil, offers a deeply insightful and comprehensive reflection on his extensive judicial career alongside the broader evolution of Brazil's legal and political landscape. Mello recounts his early motivations and aspirations, illustrating the formative experiences that shaped his commitment to the rule of law and judicial independence. Throughout his tenure at the nation's highest courts, he provides a nuanced first-hand perspective on the judiciary's critical role in upholding constitutional principles and fostering democratic governance in a country marked by complex political dynamics and long-standing challenges.

Central to Mello's testimony is a detailed examination of Operation Car Wash (Lava Jato), widely regarded as one of the most significant anti-corruption investigations in Brazil's history. He traces the operation's origins to earlier political corruption scandals such as the Mensalão, highlighting the continuity in efforts to confront entrenched illicit practices. Mello underscores the instrumental role played by Curitiba's 13th Criminal Court, which became a symbol of judicial activism and determined anti-corruption enforcement. While recognising the undeniable importance of Operation Car Wash in exposing systemic corruption and advancing public accountability, Mello does not shy away from critiquing procedural inconsistencies, judicial overreach, and shifts in legal interpretation that ultimately led to the annulment of key convictions.

Mello reflects critically on the legal principles implicated in these controversies, particularly the presumption of innocence, the appropriate use of pre-trial detention, and the imperative of legal certainty. These principles, he argues, must remain sacrosanct even in high-profile corruption cases to preserve the legitimacy and credibility of the judiciary. He expresses concern that deviations from these fundamental safeguards have contributed to setbacks in Brazil's broader anti-corruption agenda, including the political rehabilitation of figures such as former President Luiz Inácio Lula da Silva.

Importantly, Mello questions the fragmentation and eventual disbandment of Operation Car Wash's task force, suggesting that its dissolution weakened coordinated efforts to combat corruption across multiple institutions. He warns that institutional backsliding has ensued, undermining the structural reforms achieved and eroding public confidence in the justice system. Drawing instructive parallels with Italy's Operation Mani Pulite, Mello cautions against the risks posed by judicial overreach, politicisation, and interference, emphasising the delicate balance required to maintain the independence of the judiciary while vigorously pursuing accountability.

Throughout his testimony, Mello reiterates that the fight against corruption is indispensable for Brazil's democratic consolidation and socio-economic development. However, he insists that such efforts must never compromise due process, legal stability, or the integrity of democratic institutions. His reflections serve as a sober reminder of the tensions inherent in anti-corruption endeavours and a call for a judicious, principled approach that respects both justice and the rule of law.

Could you please elaborate on your educational background and personal trajectory to provide greater context for your judicial career?

I initially planned to follow in my father's footsteps and become a lawyer—perhaps even pursue a career at Banco do Brasil, where he worked as a legal advisor. I passed the civil service exam for a position as a prosecutor with the INSS, but in the end, I did not take up the post. I also applied for a role as a labour inspector. Around that time, an interim opportunity arose for the position of Acting Labour Prosecutor, which allowed me to keep practising law. I worked at the Labour Public Prosecutor's Office from 1975 to 1978.

When two vacancies opened at the Regional Labour Court (TRT) of the 1st Region—one for a Public Prosecutor and one for a lawyer—I applied for the position allocated to the legal profession. At that time, the Federal Council of the Brazilian Bar Association did not yet compile lists of nominees, and I ended up being appointed to the TRT during President Geisel's administration. I served as a judge there for three years, and in 1981, having reached the minimum age requirement, I was appointed to the Superior Labour Court.

I completed 35 years of public service on 12 July, and my retirement paperwork was sent to the Senate on 15 July. My family and I moved to Brasília, where we settled in quite well. Eight years later—despite never having held the presidency of any tribunal—I was appointed to the Supreme Court, becoming the first labour judge to take on that role. I was warmly received by what I affectionately call the "old guard", and I actively contributed to debates and took my responsibilities very seriously.

Later on, in 2002, I became President of the Supreme Court, and it was during my term that the TV Justiça project was launched from within my office. I succeeded President Fernando Henrique Cardoso in that role and was involved in facilitating the enactment of the relevant legislation.

Currently, I am serving my fourth term at the Superior Electoral Court. Some colleagues chose to step down before completing their terms, which are typically two years long. Personally, I have never turned down work, and I have always had a strong appreciation for Electoral Justice, especially because of its focus on real, tangible legal matters—often involving mandates—which I find deeply rewarding as a judge. I have served three terms as President of the TSE and am currently a substitute justice on the same court. That is been my journey. I have never actively sought appointments—they happened naturally, and I believe I have lived up to the trust that others placed in me. The judiciary is a calling; it demands full dedication, spontaneity, independence, and the daily exercise of virtue—above all, courage.

Given your central role at the inception of Operation Car Wash, how would you characterise its origins? Would you consider it

primarily the product of institutional maturity, or rather a response to specific circumstances and conditions that converged at that particular moment in time?

Operation Car Wash has its roots in the *Mensalão* scandal.[68] It is important to consider the role of the 13th Criminal Court in Curitiba. Judge Sergio Moro, however, is not a figure who can be universally applied to the entire operation. The first criminal case involving Petrobras, a mixed economy company, was in Paraná. Attempt to launder money in Londrina was redirected to the 13th Court in Curitiba, which specialised in money laundering. Some argue that this caused a national disruption, but I view it differently.

When you analyse both the positive and negative aspects—something inherent in any action and that can be addressed through appeal—the judicial efforts of the 13th Court in tackling corruption were undeniably valuable. It is surprising how a figure who was once celebrated as a national hero for imprisoning powerful individuals could, in turn, be regarded as suspect, as the 2nd Panel of the Supreme Court suggested—this was a severe blow to a judge's reputation. That said, Operation Car Wash represented a cultural advancement by addressing the issue of impunity among public officials, which is deserving of recognition. It also had significant economic and financial repercussions, aiming to establish standards that must be upheld in a democracy, especially in public matters. For these reasons, I view Operation Car Wash positively.

As a Justice of the Federal Supreme Court during the Mensalão trial—a case widely regarded as a watershed moment in Brazil's fight against corruption—you witnessed first-hand a significant instance of institutional affirmation. Yet, as subsequent events have shown, the illicit practices uncovered by Operation Car Wash were already in motion during that same period. How do you explain the persistence of such systemic corruption despite the Supreme Court's rulings and the convictions rendered in the Mensalão case?

It boils down to a misguided sense of invulnerability, driven by a belief in impunity. I believe the significant merit of these operations was in raising awareness—both among citizens and public officials—about the importance of the law. The law applies to everyone, and any deviation from proper conduct must be sanctioned to deter further breaches. We've made undeniable progress, but even during the *Mensalão* proceedings, Operation Car Wash was already underway. This is astonishing.

I emphasise that holding a public office should never be about serving personal or familial interests; it should be dedicated solely to the public good. A shift in mindset among public officials is crucial for the system to work properly. For instance, I did not understand the political "resurrection" of former President Luiz Inácio Lula da Silva, and I voted against it. To me, it represented a step backwards. Why? Because judicial processes had proceeded normally through various levels, including the Superior Court of Justice. Then, suddenly, a *habeas corpus* petition—without proper adversarial proceedings or state prosecutor input—reverted the situation to square one. This was detrimental to the progress made through Mensalão and Operation Car Wash. It reflects a tendency in Brazil to undo progress. Cultural advancement does not work this way. I was a dissenting vote throughout, and I also disagreed with the declaration of territorial jurisdictional incompetency, which is relative and could have been extended.

Legal coherence, particularly in procedural matters, must be upheld. The process should move forward unless there is clear nullity. The goal is to reach a conclusion in a reasonable timeframe, restoring social peace that was temporarily disrupted by conflicting interests. Today, I remain sceptical about this perspective, and despite re-examining the matter, I am unconvinced that I was wrong. History will, in due course, provide greater clarity.

Operation Car Wash involved a significant number of pre-trial detentions. How do you assess the use and impact of these measures within the broader context of due process and the presumption of innocence?

Pre-trial detention has very specific requirements. It is used to avoid interference with an investigation or when there is a real threat to public order. Currently, it is limited to ninety days, and it can be renewed for the same period, and so on—but if these limits are not respected, the detention becomes unlawful.

Now, the provisional execution of a sentence does not align with the Federal Constitution. The principle behind provisional execution is that the situation may be reversible; however, when it involves the deprivation of an individual's liberty, such harm cannot genuinely be undone. That is why the principle of non-culpability is so important.

Even though the number of people in provisional detention has reached record levels, we must remember that detention should only happen once guilt has been established, and the sentence is final. Pre-trial detention should be the exception, not the rule. Procedural integrity must always be maintained—especially in criminal cases.

As the Justice rapporteur for Declaratory Action of Constitutionality 43 concerning the presumption of innocence, could you elaborate on your reasons for opposing imprisonment following conviction at the second instance?

The fight against corruption is essential—but we cannot pursue it through excessive or disproportionate measures. It is imperative to avoid vigilantism and the subversion of the established criminal justice process. The correct sequence is investigated, determine guilt, and only then apply a sentence involving imprisonment.

The presumption of innocence is not something people usually think about in daily life—but it is fundamental for those facing criminal charges. Guilt should only be confirmed once all appeals against a conviction have been fully exhausted. This is clearly established in the core list of constitutional guarantees, specifically in Article 5. In other words, the starting point must always be the presumption of innocence—not guilt.

Throughout my judicial career, I have consistently opposed the idea of provisional execution of a sentence. It is not a true execution—it is premature. Some argue it benefits the accused by giving them more time. But how can anyone benefit by losing their freedom? That argument does not hold.

I have always sought consistency in my position. It is troubling when colleagues change their views without any change to the constitutional text. Given that the Supreme Court is the final interpreter of the law, these fluctuations can seriously undermine legal certainty.

Procedural law exists to outline how the process should unfold and to safeguard the right to defence. In this case, the decision was a close one—if I recall correctly, six votes to five. But ultimately, the principle of non-culpability was upheld. Under the Federal Constitution, provisional execution of a sentence simply is not permissible. This was a step forward in our commitment to the rule of law—which, of course, applies to all branches of government, including the judiciary and even the Supreme Court itself.

In your assessment, did the fragmentation of Operation Car Wash—originally based in Curitiba—have a positive or negative impact on the fight against corruption in Brazil?

If I remember correctly, the saying "divide and conquer" is often attributed to Napoleon—or perhaps General Ney. Honestly, I never fully understood the fragmentation of Operation Car Wash. At the start, any federal judge could handle the case. Things progressed under the jurisdiction of the 13th Criminal Court in Curitiba.

Rolling back to an earlier stage in a criminal proceeding compromises legal certainty. The Court reached a different conclusion, which was rather surprising. When the 13th Court was declared territorially incompetent—a relative, not absolute incompetency—there was debate over where jurisdiction should lie. Justice Alexandre de Moraes argued for São Paulo; others leaned towards Brasília.

This created uncertainty, which ended up benefiting the accused through delays and the risk of cases becoming time barred. It felt like we were starting from scratch again. What about the acquittals handed down by the 13th Court? Our constitutional principles demand equal treatment. One cannot simply reopen a case that followed all due process just because it involves a political figure who had already started serving a sentence. Decisions must respect prior rulings—even if some remain unconvinced.

In the light of recent setbacks in Brazil's anti-corruption agenda, do you consider the country to be at risk of regressing to the entrenched systems of corruption that Operation Car Wash and related initiatives sought to dismantle?

The prevailing sentiment is one of impunity. The recent setbacks have fostered a perception that judicial delays and the mere passage of time can be relied upon to evade accountability. Skilled lawyers have presented compelling arguments, resulting in criminal proceedings that, in some cases, have undermined anti-corruption efforts.

In the light of the Spoofing Operation, which involved unauthorised hacking, how do you evaluate its implications for the integrity and administration of justice in Brazil?

The Spoofing operation had a major impact on public confidence in the judiciary and the integrity of legal proceedings. The interception of messages among members of the judiciary revealed serious vulnerabilities and raised questions about how procedures were being conducted. It highlighted the urgent need for strong security systems and greater transparency to protect the judicial process and maintain trust in legal institutions.

To what extent is legal certainty fundamental to the effective fight against corruption?

Legal certainty is absolutely essential. The roles of the state—as legislator, prosecutor, and judge—must be carefully considered, adhering strictly to established rules. This is the foundation of genuine progress. Combating corruption is imperative; however, it must be pursued with rigour rather than recklessness.

What parallels can be drawn between Italy's Operation *Mani Pulite* and Brazil's Operation Car Wash in terms of their scope, impact, and challenges faced?

The regression witnessed—where earlier progress appears to have been undone—is deeply concerning. Lessons should be drawn from positive examples, rather than repeating paths that lead to distortion. Italy experienced such a regression, and unfortunately, a similar pattern is emerging here. The case of former President Luiz Inácio Lula da Silva is illustrative: he benefited from the statute of limitations, which, due to his age, was effectively halved. This circumstance is highly revealing.

What do you consider to be the primary strengths and limitations of Operation Car Wash within the broader context of Brazil's fight against corruption?

The right to a defence and adherence to due process must always be safeguarded—they are fundamental pillars of a democratic state governed by the rule of law. It is unthinkable, in certain cases, to disregard the organic nature of the legal process.

At the moment, the fight against corruption feels weakened. The setbacks in decision-making we've seen recently have opened the door to practices that stray from legal norms—and that is harmful. Believing that there will be no consequences for this undermines efforts to hold people accountable. In my view, the Supreme Court's recent rulings have clearly represented a step backwards in the fight against corruption.

Do you have any final remarks you would like to make in conclusion?

Judges—particularly those serving on the Supreme Court, as the ultimate guardians of citizenship—must adopt a long-term perspective. It is essential to reflect on the kind of Brazil that will be left to future generations? Every decision made in the Supreme Court sends ripples well beyond its chambers and affects public life on multiple levels.

As I often say, the example must come from the top. The Court has a powerful pedagogical role, and each of us, when donning the judicial robe, must recognise the weight of that role. The Supreme Court is not a place for public relations exercises—allowing such a situation to develop risks sliding into widespread disorder. Progress must continue, with the understanding that, whether welcomed or not, the Supreme Court holds the ultimate authority over both legal matters and broader societal processes. Each Supreme Court Justice must be fully conscious of the profound responsibility inherent in serving on the nation's highest judicial body.

Marco Aurélio Mendes de Farias Mello was born in Rio de Janeiro (RJ). A jurist, Justice of the Federal Supreme Court (1990 to 2021), and President of the UniCeub Citizenship Institute. His testimony was recorded on 8 July 2021 via the Zoom virtual platform and lasted 43 minutes of recording. The transcript was subsequently reviewed by the interviewee on 6 May 2022.

Testimony of Sergio Fernando Moro

Abstract

This testimony by Sergio Fernando Moro—former federal judge, Minister of Justice, and current Senator—provides a comprehensive and candid narrative of his legal career and his pivotal role in Brazil's fight against corruption. Offering rare insight into landmark cases such as Banestado and Operation Car Wash, Moro traces the evolution of anti-corruption efforts within the Brazilian judicial system and reflects on the challenges and achievements that have defined his tenure.

Moro recounts his early judicial work, highlighting his engagement with complex financial crime investigations and the development of specialised judicial bodies, most notably the 13th Federal Criminal Court of Curitiba. This court became the epicentre of Operation Car Wash, a far-reaching investigation that uncovered an extensive bribery scheme involving Petrobras and reshaped Brazil's approach to systemic corruption. The testimony revisits the Banestado case of the 1990s—a sprawling money laundering operation centred on clandestine CC5 accounts—illustrating the long-standing difficulties in prosecuting white-collar crime in Brazil, from investigative hurdles to legal loopholes and procedural delays.

Detailing the innovative investigative techniques and the critical role of dedicated task forces, Moro draws instructive parallels with Italy's Mani Pulite (Clean Hands) operation, emphasising the necessity of specialised, coordinated teams in dismantling entrenched corrupt networks. His reflections underscore the transformative impact of Operation Car Wash on Brazilian law, including significant legal reforms and the integration of international cooperation for asset recovery.

Moro defends the use of plea bargains as indispensable tools in uncovering complex criminal structures, while also critically analysing the legal setbacks that have undermined key convictions, particularly the judicial reversal of imprisonment following second-instance rulings. He voices concern over the weakening of Brazil's anti-corruption framework and the troubling resurgence of impunity resulting from recent judicial decisions.

Despite these setbacks, Moro remains resolute in his conviction that Operation Car Wash established a historic precedent: that systemic corruption in Brazil is prosecutable and punishable. His testimony serves as both a detailed chronicle of a transformative period in Brazilian justice and a sober warning about the fragility of anti-corruption progress, offering crucial lessons for future efforts to uphold accountability and the rule of law.

Could you describe your education and personal trajectory to provide context?

I was born in Maringá, Paraná, into a family of educators. My schooling encompassed both private and public institutions, after which I pursued legal studies at the State University of Maringá. Upon graduation, I practised law briefly before successfully passing the civil service examination to become a federal judge.

I pursued my judicial career while also completing both a master's and a doctoral degree. In 2002, I began serving in one of the three criminal courts in Curitiba. Before that, I had worked in a role with full jurisdiction. Around that time, the Federal Justice Council[69] decided to specialise one criminal court in each state of the Federation to handle financial crimes and money laundering. In Paraná, the court where I was working was selected for that specialisation.

From then on, I began working primarily with two categories of cases: financial crimes and money laundering. Although it may have seemed that judges in these specialised courts would only handle white-collar crime, the reality was a bit different. In practice, we often had to deal with serious drug trafficking cases as well—since the related money laundering brought them under our jurisdiction.

Not long after this shift, we encountered the Banestado[70] case (Banco do Estado do Paraná), which was a particularly large and complex case originally being tried in Foz do Iguaçu. Due to limitations in the infrastructure of the courts there, and because of the court's new specialisation, the case was transferred to Curitiba. That is the broad outline of my background.

Could you describe your involvement in the corruption scandal known as Banestado?

The so-called Banestado case unfolded as follows: between 1996 and 1998, the main legal mechanism for sending money abroad was through CC5 accounts.[71] However, billions of reais were moved irregularly by individuals seeking to conceal the true ownership of the funds. This triggered a series of investigations aimed at tracing these transfers overseas.

The investigations uncovered the participation of black-market currency dealers, banks, and bank agents who knowingly facilitated the fraudulent scheme, along with the actual holders of the funds. These cases involved a wide range of crimes: corruption, drug trafficking, and, more commonly, tax evasion and fraud in import and export operations. There were also cases where individuals sent money abroad legally but were unaware, they were being used as part of a wider illicit scheme.

I was one of the judges assigned to handle these cases. At the time, each court had two judges,[72] and it was agreed that I would deal with half of the caseload while my colleague, the substitute judge, took on the other half. Due to the size and complexity of the case, the Public Prosecutor's Office set up a task force, and the Federal Police did the same to carry out the investigations.

Given the limitations we faced at the time—both legal and practical—I'd say the results were relatively successful, especially when compared with other white-collar crime cases in Brazil. Criminal convictions were secured; some individuals were imprisoned, while others served sentences. That said, the punishments did not always reflect the gravity of the crimes committed.

Regarding the dimensions of the Banestado operation you described as having relative success, could you elaborate on what these dimensions entailed? Furthermore, did these aspects evolve or cease altogether during the course of Operation Car Wash?

Globally, prosecuting white-collar crime is extremely difficult. Effective institutional responses to these types of crime are rare, though it depends on the country and the period in question. It is often challenging to ensure those involved are actually prosecuted and held accountable.

In Curitiba, the strategy adopted by the Public Prosecutor's Office and the Federal Police was to focus on the core perpetrators—the black-market currency dealers and bank agents. As for those who had sent the funds abroad, there were simply too many, and they were scattered across the country. The decision was made to refer the investigative material to the Federal Revenue Service, multiple federal oversight agencies, and the local courts within the respective jurisdictions of the individuals involved. The idea was for those entities to handle the cases from the standpoint of tax evasion or, where applicable, more serious offences.

One of the notable developments in Curitiba was an operation called Operation Beacon Hill ("Farol da Colina" in Portuguese).[73] At the time, it was quite unusual: it involved multiple search and seizure actions and the arrests of several major black-market currency dealers. The operation Banestado attracted a lot of public attention and even led to the creation of a Parliamentary Inquiry Commission. Unfortunately, the commission did not make much headway.

There were some convictions, including of bank agents and directors at Banco Banestado. But it is not entirely accurate to speak of the Banestado case as a single case—it actually involved several financial institutions, including Banco do Brasil, Banco Meridional, and Banespa, among others.

In many cases, convictions were eventually annulled or expired due to endless procedural appeals. For example, in the Banestado leadership case over which I presided, certain defendants were held in pre-trial detention, while others were not. In several instances, even those partially convicted ended up not serving sentences due to the statute of limitations. Although the Appeals Court and even the Superior Court of Justice upheld the convictions, full enforcement was never achieved.

How do you evaluate the effectiveness of task forces in combating corruption?

The task force model has been applied around the world with considerable success. The general understanding is that, in large-scale cases, it is simply not feasible for a single prosecutor or police officer to handle everything. Effective investigations require adequate human and financial resources.

This model is slightly different when it comes to the judiciary, where it is not really possible to form a task force made up of multiple judges. Instead, the judicial response has been the creation of specialised courts. The benefit here is that a judge can focus solely on more complex cases. Specialisation helps to eliminate the common excuse among judges that managing such cases is unfeasible due to the volume of their dockets.

There is often a natural inclination to prioritise simpler cases—ones that are quicker to deal with and boost statistics—rather than the more demanding ones. In courts of general jurisdiction managing thousands of cases, only a small proportion are complex, and such cases often risk being sidelined. Specialised courts exist to ensure that complex matters receive the dedicated attention necessary.

Task forces have long been a feature in the United States, and Italy later adopted a similar model—combining prosecutors, investigative judges, and police officers—to tackle the mafia. The structure unites the appropriate personnel and resources and, perhaps most importantly, consolidates critical information.

It is well known that you are a leading expert on the Mani Pulite (Clean Hands)[74] operation. Is it possible to draw parallels between Italy's Mani Pulite Operation and Brazil's Operation Car Wash?

A long-standing interest in comparative law has consistently informed my approach and perspective. Italy has a serious problem with organised crime—probably even more so than Brazil—though, given the different ways these organisations operate, it is hard to make direct comparisons.

That said, Italy has seen some major criminal cases that, in many respects, echo what we've experienced here.

The Mani Pulite operation in Milan is often confused with the anti-mafia effort in Sicily. There is some overlap, but they're actually separate cases. I have engaged extensively with the subject, including reading an excellent book—albeit one bearing a rather sombre title—*Excellent Cadavers: The Mafia and the Death of the First Italian Republic*,[75] written by an American journalist. It tells the story of Judges Giovanni Falcone[76] and Paolo Borsellino[77] and their efforts to dismantle the mafia.

I have long-held great admiration for the work of Falcone and Borsellino. Although Falcone tends to get most of the recognition, their success was the result of teamwork. For instance, one judge in Palermo might be dealing with a mafia-related case, while another judge in a more rural area of Sicily is handling a different case with links to the same organisation. Each judge holds a piece of the puzzle, but without communication between them, the full picture is never seen.

That is where the task force model becomes essential bringing together not just people and resources, but also information. When that information is centralised and shared, it becomes possible to build a far more solid case. And beyond efficiency, it adds a layer of protection—if one person is targeted, others can carry on the work, so the case does not fall apart.

Back in 2004, I wrote an article titled *Considerations on the Clean Hands Operation.*[78] I was already a criminal judge at the time, and the topic really intrigued me. The piece was largely descriptive—it summarised what I had read and heard about Mani Pulite, and included several excerpts from other works, all properly quoted and cited.

Later on, people began attributing certain statements in the article to me, even though they were clearly marked quotations. It is important to clarify that the paper was never intended as a roadmap for what would later happen with Operation Car Wash. It was simply a factual account of events in Italy. Any similarities between the two—particularly in terms of using a task force or uncovering systemic corruption—are purely coincidental.

Did you participate in the Mensalão[79] case as a member of the legal team?

In 2012, I was invited to serve as an assistant judge to Justice Rosa Weber[80] at the Federal Supreme Court, focusing specifically on criminal matters. The second half of that year was almost entirely devoted to the Mensalão case. It was an invaluable learning experience.

The Mensalão case was a major criminal trial, involving prominent figures from the Republic who were tried directly before the Supreme Court. The Court handed down very severe penalties, particularly to the corruptors and those involved in money laundering schemes—individuals like operator Marcos Valério,[81] his associates, and members of Banco Rural.

For some of those who were corrupted, the sentences were less harsh, but even so, within an institutional context where white-collar crime often went unpunished, the trial marked a step forward—a sign of progress, at least symbolically.

At the onset of Operation Car Wash, what were your initial expectations regarding its scope, the financial sums involved, and the individuals implicated?

Operation Car Wash expanded significantly as new evidence emerged, revealing a far more intricate web of corruption than initially anticipated. In the beginning, there was not a clear overall strategy, nor a full grasp of the scale of the criminal network.

Initially, the investigation concentrated on professionals engaged in money laundering—commonly referred to in Brazil as *doleiros*, or black-market currency dealers—but the operation soon expanded as new evidence began to emerge. At one stage, there was even talk of shelving the investigation, as it was not producing substantial results.

In 2013, for example, there was a wiretap involving two suspects speaking Arabic, and it proved difficult to find an Arabic translator within the Federal Police. Even so, the team chose to continue, and gradually new elements began to surface—not only through surveillance but also through financial and banking data.

At first, the investigation centred on four money laundering professionals. Then came Paulo Roberto Costa,[82] a director at Petrobras, whose involvement expanded the case considerably—though, at that stage, the full magnitude of the operation was still unclear.

Interestingly, some of the first real indications of the case's broader implications came not from the investigation itself, but from media reports. Stories began to circulate that major construction firms were worried, politically mobilising, and hiring top-tier legal teams. That marked the point at which the operation began to expand considerably.

However, it was not until the plea bargain agreements with Paulo Roberto Costa and Alberto Youssef,[83] towards the end of 2014, that a broader appreciation of the operation's potential impact began to emerge. Even at that stage, no definitive roadmap existed. The extent to which the investigation would unfold remained uncertain, as the full scale of the corruption scheme was only partially comprehended.

A substantial segment of Brazilian society holds that Operation Car Wash transformed the country's anti-corruption landscape. Would you agree with this assessment?

The answer is not a simple yes or no—it requires further explanation. In Brazil, there has long been a pervasive perception of widespread corruption. However, acknowledging the existence of corruption is one matter; possessing concrete evidence is quite another.

Operation Car Wash did more than merely confirm this perception; it exceeded societal expectations, revealing a scale of corruption that was truly staggering. In this regard, Car Wash merits considerable recognition for exposing this extensive body of evidence.

My impression is that, over time, the quality of public affairs declined. As crimes went unpunished, criminal behaviour intensified, following the well-established logic of risk and opportunity. I use the term "systemic corruption" because what we saw was a routine practice of paying bribes in public contracts. This was not limited to Petrobras—it extended to other state-owned companies and eventually to other areas of government.

That practice was interrupted, although there had already been a partial break with the Mensalão case—just not on the same level or scale as Car Wash. It cannot be Brazil's destiny to live side by side with corruption and impunity.

Car Wash showed that it is indeed possible to have convictions, trials, and serious investigations into grand corruption. Many people were indicted, tried, and served prison time. It proved that large-scale corruption does not have to go unpunished.

It brought about significant changes, though in recent years those gains have been eroded. A clear example is the reversal of the rule allowing imprisonment after a second-instance conviction. That principle, which had been influenced by Car Wash and approved by the Federal Supreme Court in February 2016, was overturned by the same court in November 2019.[84]

How do you assess the prohibition on imprisonment following conviction at the second instance?

One illustrative case is Habeas Corpus 84.078 from 2009,[85] when the ruled that a final judgement had to be awaited before imprisonment. This involved an attempted murder: a man shot another person five times. Thankfully, the victim survived—but the attacker went unpunished.

With all due respect to the Federal Supreme Court, from a legal precedent and crime deterrence perspective, that decision was a disaster—and that is without even getting into its impact on anti-corruption efforts. The accused had been convicted in both the first and second instances, but the Supreme Court granted *habeas corpus*, allowing him to remain free.

The case then moved to the Superior Court of Justice (and dragged on until it expired due to the statute of limitations). It took nearly a decade for it to reach a conclusion, and by then, the crime was time barred. That is a clear picture of impunity for the powerful: the offender was a wealthy landowner, able to sustain a lengthy legal battle through every appeal available.

It is the system enabling the powerful to escape justice. To be clear, I am not suggesting that individuals should be punished solely on account of their wealth or influence. Far from it. When a law is violated or a crime committed, the identity of the person should be irrelevant. While I hold the Federal Supreme Court in the highest regard, I regard this particular ruling as profoundly unfortunate.

Are you referring to the Declaratory Actions of Constitutionality 43, 44, and 54[86]?

Certainly. When I was Minister of Justice, I tried to prevent that outcome—I spoke with some of the Justices. But what had started as a seven-to-four majority quickly shifted to a six-to-five majority the other way. In my view, Supreme Court Justices changed their positions without solid legal justification. There was also a disregard for precedent, which, let's not forget, was quite recent. I do not consider the shift to have been justified.

This created a great deal of legal uncertainty—and, more importantly, impunity. With all due respect, the reasoning supporting that decision is unconvincing. No other legal system experiences the sheer volume of appeals found in Brazil.

So, what has been done since? Despite going against the Supreme Court's ruling, there have been efforts to reintroduce imprisonment after conviction in the second instance—either through legislation or a constitutional amendment. But whether such measures will be approved remains unclear. The strongest resistance comes from the upper echelons of Congress. At one point, there was some optimism around it, but then the pandemic hit and changed the political landscape. I am not entirely sure that, even without the pandemic, it would have been possible to pass a constitutional amendment. The issue clashes with many entrenched interests.

Do you believe Operation Car Wash has altered the relationship and conduct between private companies and the Brazilian state?

Operation Car Wash deserves credit for changing the way people see anti-corruption efforts. The tools to tackle corruption are now in place, and despite some setbacks, promising signs remain evident. For instance, in the private sector, the whole discussion around compliance and integrity took a huge leap forward during the Car Wash period. There is a KPMG study[87] involving a fairly significant group of Brazilian companies, which shows how investment in compliance and integrity skyrocketed at the start of Car Wash and continued to grow throughout the operation.

More recently, we saw the enactment of the new Public Procurement Law—Law No. 14.133 of 1 April 2021—which includes provisions that actively promote compliance and integrity programmes. Therefore, it is clear that a substantive change has indeed occurred.

That said, these gains represent human achievements and, like all human constructs, they remain vulnerable to reversal. I sincerely hope such a regression does not occur. Have there been setbacks? Undoubtedly. However, I do not believe the situation has reverted to its previous state. Corruption persists, naturally, and is not always easily detected—but I do not perceive it as reaching the magnitude revealed during Operation Car Wash.

How do you assess your relationship with the media during Operation Car Wash?

While I was serving as a judge, I gave very few interviews to the press—perhaps one or two at most. I recall the first was in 2016, to *Estadão*, where I reflected on two and a half years of Operation Car Wash, and another came in 2017.[88] Things were quite different, of course, once I became Minister of Justice.

How do you assess the high level of transparency in Operation Car Wash?

The Federal Constitution states that court proceedings must be public. In practice, though, even when there is no confidentiality order, it can be quite difficult to access court records due to bureaucratic obstacles. Journalists—or any third parties, really—often need to schedule a visit to the registry, navigate red tape, and deal with difficulties making copies and so on.

From the start, I made the decision to ensure maximum transparency. The Car Wash cases were digital, and decisions were published online, which made a huge difference. It allowed the public to access both the rulings and the proceedings themselves. Most of the cases were open to the public.

Now, it is important to say this was not about trying cases in the court of public opinion. Public opinion is not a reliable basis for judicial decisions. Much misinformation has circulated regarding the transparency of Operation Car Wash—for example, allegations that it was employed as a tool for exerting pressure. At least in my case, my commitment was always to judge based on the law and the evidence. That said, I also made sure to act transparently—which, after all, is a constitutional duty.

Do you think Operation Car Wash criminalised politics?

The focus was on addressing grand corruption—not on criminalising politics. If an individual accepts a bribe, how else can that be characterised but as a crime? The ones who criminalised politics were the politicians who got involved in corruption—and those who paid them off.

This was not about imposing a moral agenda on society. No one in Car Wash was debating things like skirt lengths, for example—that is the kind of absurd argument you hear now and again, particularly when people criticise the Public Prosecutor's task force: "Oh, the prosecutors wanted to impose a moral code on the Republic." It is just not true. Car Wash was not about moral codes—it was about legal ones. Is it moral not to take or offer a bribe? Certainly. But, more importantly, it is illegal. To suggest otherwise is, frankly, laughable.

What is the importance of pre-trial detention in combating corruption in Operation Car Wash?

Pre-trial detention is a measure that should be used sparingly, as it carries certain risks. However, Operation Car Wash involved exceptional circumstances. There was a bribery scheme that had been running for years, and the proceeds from the crimes were still in the hands of the criminals, creating a risk of those assets being dissipated. There were clear and specific reasons justifying such exceptional measures.

Take the case of Paulo Roberto Costa, for example. Initially, I did not order pre-trial detention. However, a situation later arose—one that was even filmed—where he instructed relatives to hide and remove documents from a location that was about to be searched. It was also revealed that he had millions of dollars in Swiss bank accounts. Should he have been allowed to remain free while holding those funds abroad? How could it be ensured that funds would neither be concealed nor dissipated? These were serious concerns.

For years, construction companies had been systematically paying bribes, with one even going so far as to create a special department solely dedicated to this purpose. These individuals had grown accustomed to such practices—it had become part of their way of doing business. So, it was not merely about uncovering an isolated crime; it was about exposing a deeply ingrained criminal operation that required a severe response—in this case, pre-trial detention.

Later, we discovered that the president of Odebrecht, who eventually confessed, had even bribed the new CEO of Petrobras,[89] who had taken over after Graça Foster[90] was replaced by President Dilma[91] in early 2015. Even during the investigation, with its vast scope, the new CEO was still receiving bribes! He was prosecuted, too[92], although the case remains under appeal, and thus the outcome cannot yet be confirmed—particularly in the light of the prevailing legal uncertainty in Brazil.

The Mensalão case is another example. Some individuals convicted in Mensalão were still receiving bribes from new sources, as revealed by Car Wash. One individual, in particular, was even involved in a media campaign against then Supreme Court Justice Joaquim Barbosa[93] while also being convicted for corruption in Mensalão. It later came to light that this person had been receiving bribes in the same year they were on trial for Mensalão. In cases of repeated criminal behaviour, pre-trial detention is often the only remedy available. It was crucial in these cases. I do not regret any of the pre-trial detentions I authorised. If anything, the error may have been in not ordering more, notwithstanding the exceptional nature of such measures.

How do you evaluate the role of plea bargaining in the progress and outcomes of Operation Car Wash?

Plea bargain agreement fits into the broader context of the need for special investigative methods when tackling complex crimes like grand corruption. Today, methods such as wiretapping, environmental surveillance, undercover operations, controlled actions, and plea bargaining are widely employed both in Brazil and internationally. Plea bargaining is one of several techniques aimed at gathering insider information. However, Brazil continues to face certain regulatory deficiencies in this area.

Which method is most effective? The answer largely depends on the specific circumstances. In the case of Operation Car Wash, plea bargaining was crucial because it allowed for extensive financial and asset tracing. Plea bargaining often provides context for other forms of evidence and helps to interpret the investigation in a more comprehensive way. It is carried out by the Public Prosecutor's Office with the collaborators and their lawyers. As a judge, I reviewed plea agreements during the homologation process.

Some have criticised the large number of collaborators, but I understand the rationale behind the Public Prosecutor's approach. It was a highly complex criminal scheme. Take a bank robbery, for example one of the perpetrators may need to cooperate to identify the others. Now, imagine one hundred bank robberies, which gives you a sense of the scale of the systemic corruption we were dealing with in Operation Car Wash. It was not just one isolated event of corruption, but dozens, even hundreds.

There has been criticism of Odebrecht's plea bargain agreement, but it revealed bribery payments in foreign countries, exposing a wave of corruption abroad, as well as within Brazil. Complaints have also been voiced regarding the perceived leniency of sentences under plea agreements; however, this reflects the realities of the Brazilian institutional context. In a system where harsher penalties prevailed—where offenders might face twenty-year sentences—a plea bargain could result in a sentence reduced to ten or five years. In Brazil, where institutional weakness prevails and impunity for major corruption is the norm—except for during Operation Car Wash—plea deals could not afford to be overly harsh, given the context. This explains why the Public Prosecutor's Office was, so to speak, "generous" in some of these agreements, as the circumstances left little alternative.

A collaborator does not become a friend of the law; such an individual remains inherently untrustworthy. Their testimony must always be corroborated. Plea bargaining can be a powerful tool for uncovering criminal schemes and proving crimes. One of the prosecutors[94] involved in Italy's Operation Clean Hands stated: "Corruption involves both the payer and the recipient. If they remain silent, we will never uncover anything."[95] If silence prevails, the truth remains concealed, as there are no witnesses to corruption offences. Someone within the criminal scheme is needed to reveal the facts.

What is your assessment of the current obstacles and institutional challenges facing Brazil in its continued efforts to combat corruption?

Setbacks have undoubtedly occurred—an unfortunate development, as such reversals may lead some individuals to reconsider entering into plea agreements. Was it worth it? Should those individuals have chosen to collaborate, or would it have been better for them to withdraw? Many individuals who committed similar crimes but did not collaborate remain at liberty. This absurdity is a direct result of these setbacks. Of course, the responsibility does not lie in the stars, but in institutions, including the Federal Supreme Court, which have contributed to these setbacks. This is not to suggest a lack of respect for the Federal Supreme Court, Congress, or the Executive branch; however, it is evident that the anti-corruption agenda must be realigned and advanced.

In your view, did the business leaders implicated in Operation Car Wash express genuine remorse for their actions?

In the course of questioning numerous individuals, it became apparent that the conduct in question was often approached with a striking sense of normality. Participation in the criminal scheme was widespread, with decisions often framed as a calculation of risk versus opportunity. Some individuals claimed to have been extorted. At the same time, many business leaders who were paying bribes were also socialising—playing golf, for instance—with Petrobras directors. How can one claim extortion in such circumstances? Extortion is something very different. I refrain from moral judgement, yet it is evident that the prevailing context enabled these crimes to occur with ease and with little ethical scrutiny—of that, there can be no doubt. Nevertheless, it was still wrong. There is no justification for it, and business leaders had responsibilities.

Given that illicit funds derived from corruption frequently cross-national borders, to what extent is international cooperation essential for the effective recovery of asset?

Reciprocity is the foundation of cooperation. When I began in criminal court in 2002, and in 2003 with the specialised commission on money laundering, I worked on several cases involving international judicial cooperation. This led to the development of an international legal framework that has significantly helped in asset recovery. Even when a country has the necessary legal tools, natural mistrust between nations can present a challenge. During Operation Car Wash, the Federal Public Prosecutor's Office and the Federal Police built strong relationships with their counterparts in other countries, such as Switzerland and the United States. This development played a key role in enhancing the effectiveness of international cooperation.

International cooperation involves both formal documentations being returned to the country and informal communications. Some claim these informal communications were irregular, but such opinions often come from those who do not understand how international cooperation works. I am surprised by how some speak with such ignorance, unaware of how the system functions. Informal communications are entirely natural. Formal procedures are frequently required, given the need to understand the other country's legal framework and to articulate requests in a form likely to be granted. The exchange of information is quite natural.

Another phenomenon is extraterritorial jurisdiction. With globalisation and the rise of international transactions, we will increasingly see cases involving extraterritorial jurisdiction. In Operation Car Wash, there were cases in Switzerland and the United States that involved individuals and companies in Brazil. The Foreign Corrupt Practices Act (FCPA) is highly significant in this context. Brazil now has its own Clean Company Act[96] with certain extraterritorial effects. The world is becoming smaller, and this is a positive development for investigations into corruption and money laundering, which are often transnational in nature.

During your tenure as Minister of Justice, Brazil faced the risk of being blacklisted by the FATF/GAFI as a jurisdiction deemed insufficiently committed to combating money laundering and the

financing of terrorism—an outcome that could have triggered significant economic, political, and diplomatic consequences, particularly from the United States and European Union member states. How do you assess the seriousness of that risk at the time?

In my experience as Minister of Justice, when dealing with the Financial Action Task Force (FATF), or GAFI, as it is known in French, Brazil was at risk of suspension due to certain past incidents. The consequences would have been severe, not just in terms of reputational damage, but also because international financial transactions and foreign investments could have been jeopardised. Investors tend not to invest in countries that are not compliant with FATF standards; sometimes, they are even prohibited from doing so by their own funds' compliance rules. Thankfully, the risk of FATF suspension was eventually overcome.

To what extent could Brazil's accession to the OECD have mitigated the recent setbacks in its anti-corruption efforts?

It is unclear to me whether OECD membership would have made a significant difference in practice; however, Brazil is actively pursuing accession, and the Organisation undoubtedly plays a vital role in promoting good governance. The process of joining the OECD is significant because it requires the country to implement reforms to align its governance with OECD standards and rules. There is no violation of sovereignty here. However, these rules and standards are not an absolute guarantee of integrity and anti-corruption. Despite the importance of OECD membership, a number of member countries continue to grapple with entrenched problems such as systemic corruption, impunity, and even cases of grand corruption. That being said, there is pressure from the OECD's anti-bribery group in response to the recent setbacks in Brazil. I see this pressure as positive. The benefits are ultimately for Brazil itself—provided that the country fulfils its responsibilities and commitments.

What, in your view, are the broader legal, ethical, and institutional implications of the unauthorised access to prosecutors' mobile communications?

There was a criminal intrusion into the mobile devices of federal prosecutors, and an attempt was also made to compromise my own communications. First and foremost, this constitutes a criminal offence, and it is inherently problematic to respond to matters arising from an unlawful act. Moreover, questions persist regarding the authenticity of the communications in question. Although I did use Telegram, I ceased doing so in 2017 due to concerns about Russian interference in the US elections, given that the application originates from Russia. Consequently, I discontinued use of the application, and all content previously stored there was automatically deleted after six months. I therefore have no means of verifying the authenticity of the communications, nor of determining whether any alterations or insertions were made. That said, I do not regret any of the actions undertaken in the context of Operation Car Wash. All actions were carried out in accordance with the law and grounded in the available evidence. Naturally, anyone is capable of making mistakes; however, with the benefit of hindsight, I do not identify any errors in my conduct—at least to the best of my own judgement. My position on the matter is unequivocal. The allegation of partiality is a farce rooted in a criminal act, as all proceedings were conducted with full respect for due process and the rights of the accused. All trials were public, and most of the decisions were confirmed by the Regional Federal Court of the 4th Region, the Superior Court of Justice, and even the Federal Supreme Court, up to a certain point. It is evident that this criminal episode has been instrumentalised to discredit Operation Car Wash and those associated with it, driven by vested interests' intent on restoring the status quo—one in which impunity prevails, and accountability is systematically avoided.

As we draw to a close, is there any final comment or insight you would wish to offer?

I sincerely hope that Brazil will soon be able to resume a robust and credible anti-corruption agenda. This remains a considerable challenge, given the strength of entrenched interests and the inertia that often hampers institutional reform. Nonetheless, Operation Car Wash stands as a period of meaningful progress in combating impunity for grand corruption. It is important to recognise that the fight against corruption cannot rely solely on punitive measures. On the contrary, prevention, transparency, and education are essential components of a comprehensive approach. In this regard, the conduct and example of the highest authorities play a fundamental role. Still, punishment remains an inherent and necessary element of the legal system—not as a form of vengeance, but as a clear affirmation that the law exists and must be applied equally to all. Raising the costs for those inclined to engage in corrupt practices may prove necessary. Punishment, ultimately, is part of the broader legal and institutional process. That is, in essence, my position.

Sergio Fernando Moro was born in Maringá (PR). He is a former federal judge, former Minister of Justice, and lawyer. He served as a director at Alvarez & Marsal and is currently a Senator of the Republic for the state of Paraná. His testimony was given via the virtual platform Zoom, with a total recording time of 1 hour and 4 minutes.

Conclusion to Chapter 3

In conclusion, "Car Wash and the Judiciary" underscores the judiciary's indispensable role in the success of Operation Car Wash, with Judge Sergio Moro emerging as a central figure and symbol of judicial courage and integrity. Moro's leadership in Curitiba exemplified a steadfast commitment to justice, showcasing how a determined and principled judiciary can confront deeply entrenched corruption within a political and economic system that has historically been marked by impunity. His approach, characterised by decisive action and a refusal to yield to political or public pressures, represents the ideal of judicial resolve that many hoped would set a precedent for future anti-corruption efforts in Brazil.

The chapter also draws attention to the stark contrast between the effectiveness of the lower courts, particularly in Curitiba and Rio de Janeiro, and the increasingly contentious role of the Federal Supreme Court in shaping the trajectory of Car Wash. While Moro and his colleagues worked tirelessly to dismantle corruption networks, the Supreme Court's more recent decisions—especially those that have invalidated key convictions and allowed many convicted individuals to regain their freedom—highlight a troubling regression in Brazil's fight against corruption. These rulings, often framed as a defence of procedural individual rights, risk undermining the accountability mechanisms that Operation Car Wash sought to establish and have provoked widespread public disillusionment with the judiciary's capacity to serve as a bulwark against impunity.

From an academic perspective, the chapter raises profound questions about the judiciary's institutional coherence and its long-term impact on the rule of law in Brazil. The sharp contrast between the decisiveness of Moro's lower court rulings and the the Supreme Court's subsequent interpretations reveals a troubling inconsistency within the judiciary, with the latter widely perceived as contributing to impunity in Brazil. The Supreme Court's justification for its rulings—often based on technicalities and procedural arguments—has been criticised for prioritising formalism over substantive justice. This approach risks eroding public confidence in the judiciary and may embolden corrupt actors by signalling that systemic accountability can be circumvented through legal manoeuvring and political influence.

The chapter also invites deeper reflection on the Supreme Court's broader role in the fight against corruption. While its function as a guardian of constitutional rights is critical, its recent actions have arguably undermined the foundational principles of justice and accountability that Operation Car Wash championed. By overturning convictions and limiting the scope of anti-corruption measures, this has inadvertently enabled a return to the status quo of impunity for powerful political and economic elites. This shift not only undermines the achievements of Car Wash but also jeopardises future efforts to combat systemic corruption in Brazil, sending a message that even the most significant investigations can be undone by institutional reluctance or political pressure.

In stark contrast, Moro's approach during Car Wash exemplified the potential of judicial leadership in addressing systemic corruption. By emphasising efficiency, transparency, and the strategic use of legal tools such as plea agreements, Moro demonstrated how judicial resolve could effectively dismantle corruption networks and hold even the most powerful individuals accountable. His dedication to ensuring that justice prevailed, despite enormous political and institutional pressures, underscores the importance of judicial independence and integrity in the fight against corruption. For many, Moro represents a hero who proved that the judiciary could act as a transformative force for accountability and reform.

Ultimately, "Car Wash and the Judiciary" serves as both a tribute to the achievements of judges like Moro and a stark warning about the dangers of judicial complacency or overreach at higher levels. For scholars, practitioners, and policymakers, the chapter underscores the need for institutional reforms to safeguard the progress made during Car Wash, ensuring that judicial efforts to combat corruption are not undermined by higher courts or political interference. It also raises broader questions about the role of the judiciary in democratic governance, particularly in contexts where entrenched corruption threatens the foundations of the rule of law. By highlighting both the triumphs and setbacks of Car Wash, the chapter provides a critical and timely reminder of the ongoing struggle for justice and accountability in Brazil.

Notes

1. Henrique Fonseca de Araújo was Attorney General of the Republic from 1975 to 1979, during the government of General Ernesto Geisel.
2. Sálvio de Figueiredo Teixeira was a professor, lawyer, judge, and magistrate. He was a Justice of the Superior Court of Justice, appointed during the presidency of José Sarney.
3. Jader Fontenelle Barbalho ***Entry***. FGV CPDOC. http://www.fgv.br/cpdoc/acervo/dicionarios/verbete-biografico/jader-fontenelle-barbalho. He is a lawyer, politician, and senator. He was a councillor, state congressperson, federal congressperson, senator, and governor for the state of Pará. He was also a minister during the presidency of José Sarney. He was the target of several accusations of passive corruption, money laundering, and gang formation. He was accused by Operation Car Wash, based on the accusations

of Nestor Cerveró and Delcídio do Amaral, but the investigation was archived.

4. Edison Lobão ***Entry***. FGV CPDOC. http://www.fgv.br/cpdoc/acervo/dicionarios/verbete-biografico/lobao-edison. He is a businessman and politician, affiliated with the MDB. He was a Senator, Governor of the state of Maranhão and Minister of State in the governments of Luiz Inácio Lula da Silva and Dilma Rousseff. He was accused by Operation Car Wash of passive corruption and money laundering.
5. Antônio Carlos Peixoto de Magalhães. ***Entry***. FGV CPDOC. http://www.fgv.br/cpdoc/acervo/dicionarios/verbete-biografico/antonio-carlos-peixoto-de-magalhaes. He was a doctor, politician, and immortal in the Brazilian Academy of Letters. He was a federal congressperson, senator and governor for the state of Bahia.
6. Popular action no. 93.000.84526, 15th Federal Court, referring to the purchase of an area by Jader Barbalho in the "Polygon of the Chestnut Trees", in Pará.
7. Sergio Fernando Moro ***Entry***. FGV CPDOC. http://www.fgv.br/cpdoc/acervo/dicionarios/verbete-biografico/sergio-fernando-moro. He was a former federal judge and judge of Operation Car Wash in Curitiba. He was a former Minister of Justice and director of Alvarez & Marsal. He is a lawyer and Brazilian politician. He is currently a Senator elected for the state of Paraná.
8. The judge's name is Erivaldo Ribeiro dos Santos. He is a federal judge and professor. He was an auxiliary judge of the registry of the National Council of the Judiciary.
9. Rosa Maria Weber Candiota da Rosa ***Entry***. FGV CPDOC. http://www.fgv.br/cpdoc/acervo/dicionarios/verbete-biografico/rosa-maria-weber-candiota-da-rosa. She is a magistrate and Justice of the Federal Supreme Court. She was president of the Superior Electoral Court and former Justice of the Superior Labor Court.
10. Márcio Thomaz Bastos was a well-known Brazilian criminal lawyer. He was president of the Federal Council of the Brazilian Bar Association, from 1987 to 1989, Minister of Justice during

the first term of Luiz Inácio Lula da Silva's government and advocated for several construction companies in Operation Car Wash, but only in the beginning, as he died in 2014.

11. Inter-American Convention against Corruption, signed on 29 March 1996, promulgated by Decree No. 4.410, of 7 October 2002. http://www.planalto.gov.br/ccivil_03/decreto/2002/d4410.htm.
12. Law No. 9.613, of 3 March 1998 on crimes of money laundering or concealment of assets, rights, and values and creates the Financial Activities Control Council. http://www.planalto.gov.br/ccivil_03/leis/l9613.htm.
13. The National Strategy for Combating Corruption and Money Laundering was created in 2003, on the initiative of the Ministry of Justice, it is the most important network for articulation and joint discussion among various bodies of the Executive, Legislative, and Judiciary, at the federal and state levels and, even cases, for the formulation of public policies to combat corruption.
14. The Mensalão was a corruption scandal, which occurred through the purchase of votes from deputies by the Executive, during the government of Luiz Inácio Lula da Silva, in 2005. This illegal practice was known in the backstage as it referred to a monthly payment made to deputies to vote in favour of projects of interest to the Executive.
15. Gilmar Ferreira Mendes ***Entry***. FGV CPDOC. http://www.fgv.br/cpdoc/acervo/dicionarios/verbete-biografico/mendes-gilmar. He has been a Justice of the Federal Supreme Court, since 2002.
16. Carlos Augusto Ayres Britto ***Entry***. FGV CPDOC. http://www.fgv.br/cpdoc/acervo/dicionarios/verbete-biografico/brito-carlos-aires. He was a Justice of the Supreme Court from 2003 to 2012, President of the Supreme Court in 2012, Justice of the Superior Electoral Court (2006–2010), President of the Superior Electoral Court (2008–2010), and President of the National Council of Justice (2011–2012). He is a Brazilian lawyer, professor, and legal opinion writer.
17. Joaquim Benedito Barbosa Gomes ***Entry***. FGV CPDOC. http://www.fgv.br/cpdoc/acervo/dicionarios/verbete-biografico/barbosa-joaquim. He is a lawyer and jurist. He was a member of the

Public Ministry and appointed to the Federal Supreme Court as a Justice from 2003 to 2014.

18. José Dirceu de Oliveira e Silva is a Brazilian politician, affiliated with the Workers' Party. He was a state and federal congressperson for the State of São Paulo and Chief of Staff during the government of President Luiz Inácio Lula da Silva. In 2012, he was convicted by the Federal Supreme Court for the crime of active corruption, imprisoned in 2013. A year later he was released to serve the remainder of his sentence at home. He was arrested in 2015 involved in Operation Car Wash, being convicted in 2017. In 2019 he left prison, due to the change in the Supreme Court's understanding of prison in the second instance, in the decision of the Declaratory Action of Constitutionality 43, 44, and 54.
19. José Genoíno Neto was president of the Workers' Party and federal congressperson for the state of São Paulo. He was indicted in the Mensalão for the crimes of active corruption and formation of gang and convicted for active corruption.
20. Luiz Fux ***Entry***. FGV CPDOC. http://www.fgv.br/cpdoc/acervo/dicionarios/verbete-biografico/luis-fux. He is a Justice of the Federal Supreme Court. He was a professor, lawyer, member of the public ministry and magistrate. He was appointed in the government of Fernando Henrique Cardoso as Justice of the Superior Court of Justice.
21. Operation Dominó (Dominoes) as an operation of the Federal Police to dismantle the diversion of resources in the Legislative Assembly of the state of Rondônia.
22. The Octopus Operation, conducted by the Brazilian Federal Police in 2006, investigated a network of fraudulent public procurement schemes and embezzlement of federal funds in the state of Amapá. The operation targeted local government officials, civil servants, and private contractors engaged in systemic corruption. The name "Octopus" refers to the multi-branched nature of the scheme, which extended across various public institutions, reflecting the diffuse and entrenched structure of subnational corruption in Brazil during the early 2000s.

23. Operation Octopus was an operation of the Federal Police started in Bahia to investigate frauds in bidding procedures, in the execution of public works, and in the provision of services. Due to leaks within the Federal Police itself, the operation had its name changed to Operation Razor.
24. Enrique Ricardo Lewandowski Entry. FGV CPDOC. http://www.fgv.br/cpdoc/acervo/dicionarios/verbete-biografico/lewandowski-ricardo. He has been a Justice of the Federal Supreme Court since 2006.
25. José Bastos Padilha Neto is a filmmaker and film producer His first fiction film, Elite Squad, won the Golden Bear. The film portrays the daily life of the Special Operations Brigade of the Military Police of Rio de Janeiro. A captain needs to find a replacement and two rookie candidates come across the rot of corruption in the police force, while trying to provide security for the Pope's visit to the city.
26. It is the COVID-19 Parliamentary Inquiry Committee.
27. The Federal Regional Court of the 4th Region comprises the judicial sections of Rio Grande do Sul, Paraná, and Santa Catarina.
28. The National Council of Justice is a Brazilian administrative body, established by Constitutional Amendment No. 45 of 2004, responsible for overseeing the administrative and financial operations of the judiciary and ensuring that judicial actors perform their duties with transparency, efficiency, and accountability.
29. The National Health Forum is a permanent body within the National Council of Justice that promotes dialogue between the judiciary and health sector actors to improve the handling of health-related legal claims and support public health governance.
30. Law No. 13.869, of 5 September 2019 (Abuse of Authority Law) on the crimes of abuse of authority. Article 1: "This Law defines the crimes of abuse of authority, committed by a public agent, servant or not, who, in the exercise of their functions or under the pretext of exercising them, abuses the power that has been attributed to them."
31. The Anti-Crime Package was amended by Congress and resulted in the promulgation of Law No. 13.964, of 24 December

2019 which improves criminal and criminal procedural legislation. http://www.planalto.gov.br/ccivil_03/_ato2019-2022/2019/lei/L13964.htm.

32. Law No. 13.964/2019, widely referred to as the Anti-Crime Package ("Pacote Anticrime" in Portuguese), was originally proposed by then Minister of Justice Sergio Moro with the objective of strengthening Brazil's criminal justice framework in the fight against organised crime, violent offences, and corruption. The initial draft included measures such as streamlined procedures for plea bargain agreement, stricter sentencing for repeat offenders, and improved asset recovery mechanisms. However, during its passage through Congress, the legislative text was substantially weakened. Key provisions were removed, diluted, or reinterpreted in ways that curtailed their effectiveness. The final version of the law, rather than reinforcing institutional capacity to combat corruption, introduced new procedural obstacles and has been widely criticised by legal practitioners and scholars for hampering enforcement efforts.
33. Luiz Fux ***Entry***. FGV CPDOC. http://www.fgv.br/cpdoc/acervo/dicionarios/verbete-biografico/luis-fux. He is a Justice of the Federal Supreme Court. He was a professor, lawyer, member of the public ministry and magistrate. He was appointed in the government of Fernando Henrique Cardoso as Justice of the Superior Court of Justice.
34. Operation Clean Hands, *Mani Pulite*, was an investigation into corruption cases in Italy, which involved the Mafia, the Vatican Bank and the masonic lodge. It led to the end of the so-called First Italian Republic (1948–1994) and brought about profound changes in the political party framework.
35. João Pedro Gebran Neto, Once upon a time in Italy. *The State of São Paulo*, 26 April 2021. https://politica.estadao.com.br/blogs/fausto-macedo/era-uma-vez-na-italia/.
36. Alexander Stille. *Excellent cadavers: the mafia and the death of the first Italian republic*. New York: Pantheon Books, 1995.

37. Alexander Stille. *Death to your excellency. Understand the true story of the judge who challenged and shook the mafia*. Porto Alegre: Citadel, 2020.
38. Rafael Cariello, The untouchables. How a group of prosecutors fought corruption in Italy—and ended up defeated. *Magazine Piauí*, ed. 116, May 2016.
39. *Banestado* is a well-known corruption scandal from the 1990s, involving illegal remittances abroad, through the Brazilian public financial system.
40. Operation Sandcastle was an operation of the Federal Police in 2009 that investigated corruption and money laundering crimes, involving the contractor Camargo Corrêa. Many consider this operation to be the precursor to Operation Car Wash because it deals with a corruption case involving well-known politicians in the Brazilian scenario and the contractors.
41. Operation *Satiagraha* was an operation of the Federal Police to combat the diversion of public funds, resulting from corruption and money laundering, started in 2004 and which resulted, later in 2008, in the arrest of politicians, businessmen, black-market currency dealers, bank directors, and investors.
42. Mensalão was a corruption scandal, which occurred through the purchase of votes from deputies by the Executive, during the government of Luiz Inácio Lula da Silva, in 2005. This illegal practice was known in the backstage as it referred to a monthly payment paid to deputies to vote in favour of projects of interest to the Executive.
43. Alberto Youssef is a Brazilian black-market currency dealer, very well-known after the corruption scandal in *Banestado*. He was arrested in 2014 as part of Operation Car Wash.
44. Financial Action Task Force, FATF.
45. United Nations Convention against Transnational Organized Crime, promulgated by Decree No. 5.015, of 12 March 2004. http://www.planalto.gov.br/ccivil_03/_ato2004-2006/2004/decreto/d5015.htm.
46. United Nations Convention against Corruption adopted by the United Nations General Assembly on 31 October 2003, in force

since 14 December 2005. http://www.planalto.gov.br/ccivil_03/_ato2004-2006/2006/decreto/d5687.htm.

47. The Convention on Combating Bribery of Foreign Public Officials in International Business Transactions of the OECD was concluded in Paris on 17 December 1997 and promulgated in Brazil by Decree No. 3.678 of 30 November 2000. http://www.planalto.gov.br/ccivil_03/decreto/d3678.htm.
48. Law No. 12.850, of 2 August 2013, which defines criminal organisation and provides for criminal investigation, the means of obtaining evidence, related criminal offences, and the criminal procedure. http://www.planalto.gov.br/ccivil_03/_ato2011-2014/2013/lei/l12850.htm.
49. OECD, Organisation for Economic Co-operation and Development (in English acronym OECD) is an international body that brings together the world's largest economies and aims to develop guidelines and standards for public policies, its Decisions being mandatory for its Member States, unlike its Recommendations and Declarations, which represent the political will of its members.
50. Paulo Roberto Costa is an engineer and was a career employee of Petrobras, being appointed to the position of Director of Supply, between 2004 and 2012, during the government of Luiz Inácio Lula da Silva. He became known because of his involvement in the corruption scheme of the Car Wash operation. He was sentenced to 12 years of house arrest with an ankle monitor, because of his plea bargain agreement.
51. Progressive Party, whose acronym is PP.
52. The manager of Petrobras is Pedro Barusco. He was arrested in the Car Wash operation and sentenced to 18 years and four months in an open regime, with an ankle monitor, in addition to performing community service. He made a plea bargain agreement and, in exchange for a reduced sentence, returned illicit resources that had been sent abroad.
53. José Carlos da Costa Marques Bumlai, better known as José Carlos Bumlai, is an engineer and cattle rancher. He was arrested and convicted by the Car Wash operation.

54. The businessman was Ronan Maria Pinto, owner of the *Diário do Grande ABC and Viação Expresso Santo André*. He allegedly received around 6 million of the 12 million from the loan from Banco Schahin.
55. The political party is the Workers' Party.
56. Sete Brasil is created by pension funds, banks, Petrobras for the management of asset portfolios for the exploration of Pre-Salt.
57. The Federal Regional Court of the 4th Region comprises the judicial sections of Rio Grande do Sul, Paraná, and Santa Catarina.
58. Federal Court of Accounts, TCU.
59. Article 312 of the Code of Criminal Procedure: "Pre-trial detention may be decreed as a guarantee of public order, economic order, for the convenience of criminal instruction or to ensure the application of criminal law, when there is evidence of the existence of the crime and sufficient indication of authorship and danger generated by the state of freedom of the accused. § 1º Pre-trial detention may also be decreed in case of non-compliance with any of the obligations imposed by other precautionary measures (art. 282, § 4o). § 2º The decision that decrees pre-trial detention must be motivated and based on fear of danger and concrete existence of new or contemporary facts that justify the application of the adopted measure." http://www.planalto.gov.br/ccivil_03/decreto-lei/del3689.htm.
60. Eduardo Consentino da Cunha ***Entry***. FGV CPDOC. http://www.fgv.br/cpdoc/acervo/dicionarios/verbete-biografico/cunha-eduardo. He is an economist, radio broadcaster, and politician. He was a federal congressperson and president of the Chamber, between 2003 and 2016, when his mandate was revoked by the Chamber of Deputies for breach of parliamentary decorum, resigning from the position on 7 July 2016. As president of the Chamber, he was the protagonist of the political crisis that ended in the impeachment of Dilma Rousseff. He was investigated in the Car Wash operation and indicted for passive corruption and money laundering by the Federal Prosecutor General to the and sentenced to 15 years and four months in prison.

61. The legislative changes were made by the Anti-Crime Package, Law No. 13.964, of 24 December 2019 which perfects the criminal and criminal procedural legislation. http://www.planalto.gov.br/ccivil_03/_ato2019-2022/2019/lei/L13964.htm.
62. Hans Rosling, Ola Rosling and Anna Rosling Rönnlund. *Factfulness: the liberating habit of only having opinions based on facts* (translation from English of Factfulness: ten reasons we are wrong about the world—and why things are better than you think). 1 a ed. Rio de Janeiro: Record, 2019.
63. Rogério Favreto, magistrate and judge of TRF-4.
64. The operation *Spoofing* is a Federal Police operation to investigate invasions of Telegram accounts of Brazilian authorities and people related to Operation Car Wash. The *hacker* responsible for stealing the information from the Brazilian authorities, Walter Delgatti Neto, already had an extensive criminal record, including crimes of fraud and forgery.
65. Transparency International. *Corruption Perception Index*. https://www.transparency.org/en/cpi/2021/index/bra, 2021.
66. Jorge Pontes and Márcio Anselmo. *Crime.gov: when corruption and government mix*. Rio de Janeiro: Objetiva, 2019.
67. Luís Roberto Barroso ***Entry***. FGV CPDOC. http://www.fgv.br/cpdoc/acervo/dicionarios/verbete-biografico/luis-roberto-barroso. He is a jurist and Justice of the Federal Supreme Court. He holds a law degree from the State University of Rio de Janeiro (UERJ), a master's degree from Yale University, and a doctorate and free lecturer from UERJ, with post-doctorate from the *Harvard Law School*. He is a full professor of constitutional law at UERJ.
68. Mensalão (Big Monthly Payment) was a corruption scandal involving the buying of votes from congressmen by the Executive branch during the government of Luiz Inácio Lula da Silva in 2005. This illegal practice, informally known as Mensalão in political circles, referred to the monthly payments made to congressmen to secure their support for projects of interest to the Executive.
69. The Federal Justice Council is the foundational body for systemic activities within the Federal Justice system. It is responsible

for administrative and budgetary supervision, with disciplinary powers, whose decisions are binding on all first- and second-instance units of the Federal Justice system, pursuant to Article 105, sole paragraph, item II, of the Federal Constitution and Article 3 of Law No. 11,798, dated 29 October 2008.

70. *Banestado* refers to a well-known corruption scandal from the 1990s, involving the illegal transfer of foreign currency abroad through the Brazilian public financial system.
71. CC5 accounts were created in 1969 by Circular Letter 5 of the Central Bank of Brazil. These "special accounts" were maintained in Brazil by Brazilians living abroad. The objective was to enable the account holder to deposit money in the national currency while in Brazilian territory and, upon returning abroad, to withdraw the money in foreign currency. Later, other individuals, beyond Brazilians living abroad, were permitted to use the CC5 accounts, provided they were identified. This facilitated the transfer of funds out of the country through a system that became known as the "surrogate mother" scheme. Due to the large volume of resources leaving the country, the government decided, as of 1996, to limit cash deposits into CC5 accounts to 10,000 reais. In 2005, after the *Banestado* scandal, the government further restricted the use of CC5 accounts.
72. Bianca Georgia Cruz Arenhart was Judge Sergio Moro's colleague at the court at that time.
73. Beacon Hill or in Portuguese Operation *Farol da Colina* is an offshoot of the Banestado scandal. *Farol da Colina* was a Federal Police operation conducted in 2004, which investigated billions of dollars transferred out of the country irregularly between 1999 and 2002 through undeclared bank accounts held by black-market currency dealers (*doleiros*) and offshore companies.
74. Operation *Mani Pulite* (Clean Hands) was a large-scale investigation into cases of corruption in Italy, centred in Milan. It implicated the Italian political class, political parties, the state-owned oil company (ENI—Ente Nazionale Idrocarburi), and major contractors in the overpricing of public works and the embezzlement of public funds.

75. Alexander Stille. *Excellent cadavers: The Mafia and the death of the first Italian republic.* New York: Pantheon Books, 1995.
76. Giovanni Falcone was a judge in Italy who became renowned for prosecuting the leaders of the Cosa Nostra, the Sicilian criminal organisation. In 1992, Falcone was assassinated in a mafia terrorist attack. He became a symbol of the fight against the mafia and organised crime.
77. Paolo Borsellino was a judge in Italy who, alongside Giovanni Falcone, presided over judicial proceedings against the Cosa Nostra. He was assassinated by the mafia (Cosa Nostra) in 1992 in an attack in Palermo, Sicily. Known for his determination to confront the mafia, he became a symbol of resistance in the fight against corruption and organised crime.
78. Sergio Fernando Moro. Considerações sobre a operação mani pulite (*Considerations on the Clean Hands Operation*). *Revista CEJ*, vol. 8, n. 26, jul/set, 2004, pp. 56–62.
79. Mensalão (Big Monthly Payment) was a corruption scandal involving the buying of votes from congressmen by the Executive branch during the government of Luiz Inácio Lula da Silva in 2005. This illegal practice, informally known as Mensalão in political circles, referred to the monthly payments made to congressmen to secure their support for projects of interest to the Executive.
80. Rosa Maria Pires Weber. Entry. FGV CPDOC. http://www.fgv.br/cpdoc/acervo/dicionarios/verbete-biografico/rosa-maria-weber-candiota-da-rosa. She is a judge and former Minister of the Federal Supreme Court. She previously served as a Minister of the Superior Labour Court before assuming her position at the Supreme Court.
81. Marcos Valério Fernandes de Souza, commonly known as Marcos Valério, is a Brazilian businessman and advertising executive, widely known for his involvement in the Mensalão scandal. Through two advertising companies in which he was a partner, he secured substantial loans from several private banks, such as Banco Rural and BMG. These funds were then channelled to

the Workers' Party and other allied parties supporting the government of former President Luiz Inácio Lula da Silva. The guarantees provided to the financial institutions for these loans were contracts between Marcos Valério's advertising firms and public agencies. His partners in the advertising companies were Cristiano Paz and Ramon Hollerbach. Marcos Valério was sentenced by the Federal Supreme Court to 37 years, 5 months, and 6 days in prison.

82. **Paulo Roberto Costa** is an engineer and was a career civil servant at Petrobras, having been appointed to the position of Director of Supply between 2004 and 2012 during the government of Luiz Inácio Lula da Silva. He became known for his involvement in the corruption scheme uncovered by Operation Car Wash. He was sentenced to 12 years of house arrest with an ankle monitor because of his plea bargain.
83. Alberto Youssef is a Brazilian black-market currency dealer (*doleiro*), who became widely known following the corruption scandal involving Banestado. He was arrested in 2014 as part of Operation Car Wash.
84. Imprisonment after conviction in the second instance refers to the possibility that a defendant sentenced to a custodial penalty begins serving their sentence following a judicial decision at the second instance, even if appeals are still pending before higher courts, namely the Superior Court of Justice and the Federal Supreme Court. In February 2016, the Supreme Court ruled by a majority of seven to four—confirming a prior decision from October 2015, which was decided by six to five—that imprisonment after a second-instance conviction was permissible. Defendants could still appeal to the higher courts but would remain in custody during the process. However, in November 2019, the Supreme Court reversed this stance, ruling by six votes to five that custodial sentences should only commence after all appeals before the Superior Court of Justice and the Federal Supreme Court have been adjudicated.
85. Habeas corpus No. 84,078, Plenary Session, 5 February 2009. Available at: https://redir.stf.jus.br/paginadorpub/paginador.jsp?docTP=AC&docID=608531.

86. A Declaratory Action of Constitutionality is a judicial measure aimed at affirming the constitutionality of a federal law or normative act. The National Ecological Party, the Federal Council of the Brazilian Bar Association, and the Communist Party of Brazil filed Declaratory Actions of Constitutionality 43, 44, and 54, respectively, before the Federal Supreme Court, challenging the jurisprudence then adopted by the Supreme Court that allowed imprisonment following conviction at the second instance. In a decision rendered on 7 November 2019, by majority vote, the Supreme Court ruled to prohibit imprisonment of individuals convicted at the second instance, thereby reversing its previously established understanding.
87. KPMG. Pesquisa maturidade da compliance no Brasil. 4 ed., 2019. https://assets.kpmg/content/dam/kpmg/br/pdf/2019/10/br-pesquisa-de-maturidade.pdf.
88. Two interviews were conducted since the inception of Operation Car Wash in 2014. The first, in 2016, is titled I would never enter politics ("Jamais entraria para a política"), by Fausto Macedo and Ricardo Brandt, published in *Estadão* on 5 November 2016. Available at: https://politica.estadao.com.br/blogs/fausto-macedo/jamais-entraria-para-a-politica-diz-sergio-moro/. The second interview, conducted in 2017 by Gerson Camarotti, is entitled Operation Car Wash, privileged jurisdiction, imprisonment after second-instance conviction ("Lava Jato, foro privilegiado, prisão após 2ª instância"), published on G1 on 17 October 2017. Available at: http://g1.globo.com/politica/blog/blog-do-camarotti/post/lava-jato-foro-privilegiado-prisao-apos-2-instancia-veja-integra-da-entrevista-com-sergio-moro.html.
89. The new president of Petrobras, succeeding Graça Foster, was Aldemir Bendine. He is a business administrator and has served as president of both Banco do Brasil and Petrobras.
90. Maria das Graças Silva Foster, commonly known as Graça Foster, is a chemical engineer and a career executive at Petrobras who assumed the presidency of the company on 13 February 2012. She resigned from the presidency on 4 February 2015.

91. Dilma Vana Rousseff. Entry. FGV CPDOC. http://www.fgv.br/cpdoc/acervo/dicionarios/verbete-biografico/dilma-vana-rousseff. She is an economist and politician affiliated with the Workers' Party (PT). She served as President of Brazil from 2011 to 2014 (first term) and from 2015 to 2016 (second term), when she was removed from office through an impeachment process.
92. Aldemir Bendine was arrested as part of Operation Car Wash, suspected of having received bribes from Odebrecht. He was initially sentenced in first instance to 11 years' imprisonment in 2018. This conviction was annulled by a regimental appeal in Habeas Corpus 157,627 on 27 August 2019. On 11 May 2020, he was again sentenced to six years and eight months' imprisonment by Judge Luiz Antonio Bonat of the 13th Federal Criminal Court of Curitiba, Moro's successor in Operation Car Wash.
93. Joaquim Benedito Barbosa Gomes. Entry. FGV CPDOC. http://www.fgv.br/cpdoc/acervo/dicionarios/verbete-biografico/barbosa-joaquim. Commonly known as Joaquim Barbosa, he is a jurist and served as a member of the Public Prosecutor's Office before being appointed Minister of the Federal Supreme Court (2003 to 2014). He was the rapporteur in the Mensalão trial.
94. The prosecutor in Italy's Operation Clean Hands was Piercamillo Davigo.
95. Pedro Simon (ed.), *Operation "Clean Hands": Public hearing with Italian magistrates* (Operação "mãos limpas": audiência pública com magistrados italianos) Brasília: Federal Senate, 1998, p. 27.
96. Law No. 12.846, of 1st August 2013, which provides for the administrative and civil liability of legal entities for the practice of acts against public administration, national or foreign. http://www.planalto.gov.br/ccivil_03/_ato2011-2014/2013/lei/l12846.htm.

4

Car Wash and the Civil Society

Introduction to Chapter 4

In the fourth chapter of this book, you will turn your focus to the intersection of the Car Wash corruption investigations and Brazilian civil society, examining testimonies of key figures who play pivotal roles in the nation's fight against corruption. Each person in this chapter represents a unique perspective and contributes significantly to the comprehensive understanding of this complex undertaking. Their insights shed light on the broader impact of the Car Wash investigations on the societal foundation, revealing the intricate dynamics between legal proceedings and the collective consciousness and ethics. The esteemed figures whose testimonies are presented in this chapter include Hermes Magnus, Jorge Pontes, Marcelo Zenkner, Maria Cristina Pinotti, Michel Temer, Modesto Carvalhosa, Roberto Livianu, and Rodrigo Chemim. The paragraphs that follow offer a glimpse into their unique contributions and reflections, enriching the reader's appreciation of the multifaceted nature of Brazil's anti-corruption efforts.

Hermes Magnus, a pivotal figure in the Car Wash operation, distinguished himself not only through his commitment to transparency and accountability but also as a courageous whistleblower. By coming

L. M. Costa, *Brazil's Biggest Corruption Scandal*, Crime Prevention and Security Management, https://doi.org/10.1007/978-3-031-99078-6_4

forward with valuable information, he demonstrated an unwavering dedication to upholding ethical standards and uncovering the truth. Magnus's decision to blow the whistle marked the Car Wash operation, contributing to the unveiling of systemic corruption and initiating a chain of events that reshaped the narrative around anti-corruption efforts in Brazil. His act of courage underscores the importance of individuals within civil society actively participating in the fight against corruption, highlighting the impact one person's commitment to truth and justice can have on a broader societal scale.

Jorge Pontes is a distinguished professional, having graduated from the FBI National Academy and combined with nearly three decades of experience within the Brazilian Federal Police. He has not only battled environmental crimes throughout his career but has also emerged as one of the foremost advocates against corruption. Pontes co-authored the book *Crime.gov* showcasing his commitment to combating corruption within government institutions. His testimony brings a unique perspective from the front lines of the fight against illicit activities, providing a first-hand account of the challenges faced by those working to uphold justice.

Marcelo Zenkner assumed the role of Director of Governance and Conformity at Petrobras after the Car Wash operation emerged. As a key figure during this transformative phase, Zenkner's insights into navigating corporate governance in the aftermath of the Car Wash operation contribute significantly to the broader understanding of the challenges faced by organisations implicated in major corruption investigations.

Maria Cristina Pinotti stands out as a prominent voice in civil society, recognised for her significant contributions. She authored the well-known book titled *Corruption: Car Wash* and Mani Pulite (*Corrupção: Car Wash e Mãos Limpas*). Her work has been instrumental in shedding light on corruption and advocating for clean governance in Brazil. In this chapter, her testimony draws insightful parallels between *Mani Pulite* and Car Wash, offering valuable perspectives on the commonalities and unique aspects of anti-corruption efforts in different contexts.

Drawing on his deep political experience, Michel Temer's testimony, the former President and Vice-President of Brazil for a significant portion of the Car Wash corruption investigation, offers a unique perspective on the challenges faced by political figures during the Car Wash investigations. His insights offer a nuanced understanding of the complexities inherent in reconciling political governance with the imperative to combat corruption.

Modesto Carvalhosa, a distinguished jurist, lawyer, and legal scholar, has published several books addressing the complex issue of corruption. Through his extensive literary contributions, he explores the legal and social dimensions, challenges, and intricacies surrounding corruption, providing valuable insights and contributing to the broader discourse on this critical societal issue. His testimony in this chapter reflects a deep commitment to understanding and addressing corruption from a legal, economic, and social standpoint.

Roberto Livianu is a fervent advocate for legal integrity and ethical conduct. Serving as a prominent member of the Public Prosecutor's Office of the State of São Paulo and presiding over the NGO Do Not Accept Corruption institute (*Instituto Não Aceito Corrupção*), Livianu's testimony goes beyond legal expertise to underscore the paramount importance of ethical considerations within the legal system. His insights significantly contribute to a broader understanding of the ethical dimensions that form the bedrock of the ongoing fight against corruption.

Rodrigo Chemim is a key figure in civil society actively engaged in the anti-corruption discourse. Serving as the Public Prosecutor of the State of Paraná, his testimony, derived from his book about the Car Wash and the *Mani Pulite* corruption investigations, illustrates the profound societal implications of corruption. It underscores the crucial role played by civil society in advocating for accountability and the need for collective efforts in the fight against corruption.

Together, these testimonies form a compelling narrative that captures the dynamic interplay between legal proceedings, civic engagement, and the individual leadership in Brazil's ongoing struggle with corruption. They remind us that while legal mechanisms are essential, it is the commitment and courage of individuals—within and beyond institutions—that truly drive change.

Testimony of Hermes Magnus

Abstract

In this testimony, Hermes Freitas Magnus, a Brazilian businessman in the technology sector and pioneer in product certification, recounts his unwitting involvement in one of the financial laundering schemes connected to Operation Car Wash. His narrative provides a first-hand account of the mechanisms by which legitimate entrepreneurial ventures were co-opted by corrupt networks operating in and around Petrobras and political circles in the late 2000s. Initially seeking investment to expand his company, Magnus was drawn into a business arrangement with figures later central to the Car Wash investigation, including former congressperson José Janene and operator Alberto Youssef.

Magnus describes in detail the coercive and manipulative strategies used to capture his company, Dunel, turning it into a front for illicit financial flows. His account reveals how project finance, political influence, shell companies, and cash transactions were used to construct an appearance of legitimacy while facilitating large-scale money laundering. Over time, Magnus recognised the criminal nature of the operation and took significant personal risks to report the scheme, including anonymously contacting the Federal Police and later becoming a whistleblower. He and his partner Maria Teodora were subjected to intimidation, surveillance, and psychological pressure, ultimately fleeing the country out of fear for their lives.

The testimony sheds light on the broader ecosystem of corruption in Brazil, where political power, private enterprise, and institutional complicity converge. It underscores the systemic nature of grand corruption, and the vulnerabilities of individuals caught between legitimate enterprise and illicit networks. Magnus offers a critical reflection on Operation Car Wash, acknowledging both its historical significance and its limitations, especially in the light of the institutional fragilities that ultimately undermined its outcomes. His final remarks express disillusionment with the failure to complete the mission of institutional reform, but also a conviction that accountability must remain a collective and ongoing pursuit.

Could you elaborate on your educational background and professional trajectory to provide contextual grounding for your testimony?

I am an entrepreneur in the technology sector and was among the pioneers in Latin America in developing testing equipment for compliance and product certification. I have always worked in the technical field—mechanical, electrical—I even had a stint in conventional aviation. I started out as a machine and equipment designer until the Dunel company project came about in 2001, in Santa Catarina. From that point on, I became a businessman in this area and was even recognised as a pioneer in the field of product certification in Brazil by *Gazeta Mercantil*, in their 2003 national edition.[1]

Would you outline how your first involvement with matters related to Operation Car Wash came about?

In 2008, the company was experiencing unusually rapid growth relative to its size, which made the search for external investment a necessity.[2] This step was encouraged by major international clients—particularly one based in Sweden—who observed that the product was well received and urged expansion. Although exports were already substantial, it was clear that the company needed to professionalise its production processes and obtain certification. A detailed business plan was therefore prepared, and efforts commenced to identify suitable investors in the market. Unfortunately, during this search, my partner, Maria Teodora Silva, and I ended up getting involved with a project finance company,[3] based in the Itaim neighbourhood in São Paulo. This company turned out to be a headquarters—a sort of meeting point—for the corrupt group that was looting Petrobras and the pension funds.

Could you explain the factors that influenced your and your partner's decision to engage with this specific project finance company?

The business plan was shared with a small number of acquaintances within our professional network. Unfortunately, through a childhood friend of my partner,[4] the plan ended up in the wrong hands. The document had been entrusted to a friend of my partner's, and within 24 hours it had reached an individual from Paraná—the son of José Muggiati Filho,[5] founder of the Brazilian Democratic Movement[6] in Paraná. From there, it made its way to Janene,[7] from CSA Project Finance Ltda.

A meeting was then arranged by the intermediary, at a restaurant near Congonhas. He told us, "They liked the project and want to meet you tomorrow at ten in the morning. Here is a voucher for the Transamérica Hotel, right in front of our office. It is on us." I was used to travelling to Europe for business, with expenses covered by clients, so I did not see anything wrong with it—I even thought it was a nice gesture. Sure enough, I arrived at the Transamérica Hotel, my name was on the reservation as promised, and I checked in.

The next morning, my partner joined me for the first meeting. Present were Alberto Youssef[8] and José Janene. Both individuals were unfamiliar, and at the time, there was no awareness of their involvement in illicit activities. The meeting was brief. Due to limited experience with fundraising, the rapid pace did not immediately raise any red flags. It was assumed that this was simply how the financial market operated—that such proceedings were "standard procedure". There was even a sense that "the right people had been impressed" and that "everything was falling into place". Maria Teodora, my partner, is a journalist who graduated from Federal University of Paraná. She worked at Jornal do Brasil, O Globo, Correio Braziliense, and had interviewed political figures like Fernando Henrique Cardoso,[9] Maluf.[10] She had covered Ministries in Brasília and knew how to navigate situations like this. I, on the other hand, was a technician—I was not used to that kind of environment. I had begun outlining the business plan when Janene abruptly interrupted, likely due to the length of my exposition. He said, "I have seen enough, I like the business. I am not well, I have got young kids, and a technology company is exactly what I want to leave them. It is a beautiful project." That sort of talk had me over the moon. He went on, "If you want to open a branch from Espírito Santo upwards, we have access to Banco do Nordeste—there are no limits. However, given your prior difficulties with banks, an alternative would be to establish a branch in Londrina. We would sign a memorandum of understanding, conduct six months of due diligence, and subsequently designate a company to act as our partner in your business. The proposal is a 50/50 partnership—you retain 50%, and we take the remaining 50%." Maria Teodora immediately responded, "Very well, we will submit the proposal to our legal counsel." However, he abruptly retorted, "No—it is take it or leave it." Faced with uncertainty, a decision had to be made, and ultimately, I agreed to the terms. That was unequivocally my error. Maria Teodora opposed the arrangement from the outset, and to this day, she holds me responsible for that decision. Ten minutes later, one of them—Carlos Costa,[11] who was later arrested in Operation Car Wash—left through one door and came back in through another with the memorandum of understanding already printed. We agreed on one million in cash for cash flow and setting up the factory, and another million in equipment and machinery. There was even a clause that said "not limited to this"—so the laundering operation was right there in front of us, but we were completely unaware.

This was on a Wednesday. Then Janene said, "I want you in Londrina on Saturday, eight in the morning, at my office. We'll start organising things and look for a warehouse to set up the factory. How much do you need to handle the paperwork and begin preparations?" I said, about 30 thousand reais. Alberto Youssef then left through one door, came back through another with an envelope, and handed me the money in cash, saying, "Money is not an issue here." I took the money and got started on sorting things out with the company and preparing the move.

Could you describe your trip to Londrina for the purpose of establishing the factory?

I arrived in Londrina at eight o'clock on Saturday morning—and, quite frankly, the only thing missing was a marching band to mark the occasion. The atmosphere was overtly political: luxury vehicles lined the area, and it was clear that appearances had been carefully orchestrated. Janene, adopting the posture of an experienced politician, presented me as a kind of trophy to his electoral base. His words were, "I have brought a businessman to the region," and put me in his car. Following that, we embarked on a tour of the surrounding municipalities.

He took me around all the small municipalities, introducing me to the mayors and asking, "Do you have a warehouse? Here is the businessman who wants to set up a factory." The poor mayors did their best, offering options, but in the end, he would say things like, "This warehouse is not good enough." I actually liked some of the warehouses! Then he had turn to the mayor and say, "Do not say I never try. I bring people here, but you lot do not deserve it," and off we'd go to the next town. In every one of those municipalities, he was selling me as the businessman who was bringing development to the region. I honestly felt sorry for the mayors.

Finally, late in the afternoon—and now I realise the whole thing had been staged—someone called him, and he said, "I have found the perfect warehouse in Londrina, in the Aeroporto neighbourhood." It turned out to be the old Skol brewery. Later, I found out from the Federal Police that the warehouse owner was a former campaign donor of Janene's—someone already tangled up in investigations. The contract was sorted in no time. Everything I requested for setting up the factory was suddenly available.

At what point did you come to the realisation that your business associate was the former Federal Congressman José Janene?

From the very beginning, everyone referred to him only as "Mr José." I had not yet made the connection that this "Mr José" was the politician involved in the Mensalão scandal.[12] I did know that there was someone from Paraná involved in that case, who was supposedly ill and kept dodging court summons. He was being sought at the time, but no one ever called him Janene around us—it was always just "Mr José", or "Mr José this" and "Mr José that". Maria Teodora insists it was mentioned early on that he had been a congressman, but I honestly do not recall that. I was caught up in the adrenaline of solving our company's production issues, so for me, I thought I was simply dealing with a businessman—an investor.

When did you first begin to sense that something was amiss with your prospective business partner?

As the factory inauguration in Londrina drew closer, things started to feel a bit strange. They even asked me to bring clients from Sweden for the opening—two actually came: the accountant and the manager from a Swedish client company. But while the date approached, the most expensive piece of equipment—the CNC robot—still had not been delivered.

The company responsible for delivering it was from Rio Grande do Sul, Ferramentas Gerais S.A.[13]—a company I had personally recommended. Their compliance is impeccable, and it was actually one of their employees who opened my eyes and ended up saving me.

Janene always assigned me two "bodyguards" who were former advisers of his from Brasília. One of them, Roberto Brasiliano,[14] arrested in Operation Weak Flesh,[15] came up to me and said, "Mr José wants to know why the big machine, the robot, the star of the factory, hasn't arrived yet. Call the company and find out what is going on, everything's already been paid for."

Feeling confident, I called Ferramentas Gerais: "Why has not it been delivered? What is the issue? Is there a delay with some imported part?"—essentially, I was asking, "What is the excuse?" The person on the other end responded, "Would you like to come here in person?" I replied, "No, just tell me what is going on." And then came the shock: "Well, here is the thing—it was not Dunel, your company, that paid for the equipment. I have got records here of multiple payments from different CNPJs based in Brasília and various CPFs. If those individuals do not authorise your company to collect the machine—via written declarations—we will have to reverse the payments and cancel the deal."

It was a complete mess—around fifteen individuals and companies involved. I hung up the phone, and Roberto, the so-called bodyguard, asked, "So? What did they say?" I explained the situation, and he just blurted out, "They have messed it up"—well, not quite in those words—"the congressman's going to lose it." So, I asked, "Congressman? Which congressman?" And he said, "José Janene, the congressman who is your partner."

It was at that point that the full extent of the situation became clear. He stepped away for a moment, and I went online. The first thing that popped up was an article linking Alberto Youssef, José Janene, and the

Mensalão scandal. I had been completely disconnected from politics, so when I read that, I trembled.

They did not even try to hide it. Suddenly, declarations came pouring in from everyone involved. They quickly mobilised the whole group. My secretary received all the paperwork—documents that later formed part of the Car Wash investigations. Ferramentas Gerais also received everything. That is when I found out Janene even had his own "notaries." I began reaching out to people. One of them was my uncle—a retired lawyer, former priest, and an extremely rational, principled man. He said, "You are laundering money for someone. If you are fine with that, stay. But do not ever contact me again." He is radically against any form of corruption, completely unyielding on that front. I spoke with others, and they all told me the same thing: "You are in serious trouble." I spoke to my partner, Maria Teodora, and she started reaching out to her network to find a lawyer. Unfortunately, the first contact she managed to make was a journalist who—unbeknownst to her—was also involved in the Mensalão. He had received money and was on Marcos Valério's infamous list.[16] He even recommended a lawyer to help with the company's dissolution. I tried to speak to Janene about ending the partnership, but he said, "No. I made a one-year deal, and you will stay until the end—otherwise, things will get complicated for you." That is when everything became very clear.

Eventually, the robot arrived at the factory, and production could begin. They started hiring people—whether they had experience or not did not seem to matter. What mattered was just getting bodies into the building. The payroll was always paid in cash. Someone would go to the head office and come back with bundles of money. And here's something I still question to this day: the money was brand new, still with banking labels—Itaú, Banco do Brasil, and so on. It was not drug or gambling money; it was clean cash, withdrawn from banks. They paid everyone in full and always on time—just always in cash.

Stock lists were routinely requested, and all materials were paid for either in cash or through the same convoluted network of payments. No invoice was ever required.

That is when I realised: If I produce a single screw in this factory, I am laundering money.

So, the only thing I could do was sabotage. Which was not hard, since Janene had not hired anyone truly qualified to run the place. The management team was made up of his former advisers from Brasília. When he left politics, he simply brought them all with him to Londrina. None of them had any technical knowledge, yet they were in charge of hiring and operations.

At that point, Maria Teodora and I had no real control over the company anymore. Danielle Janene[17]—his daughter—was acting as the general director. She started off in the commercial department and soon took over everything. Faced with the circumstances, I took the only course of action available to me: I began deliberately sabotaging the production process.

Could you describe the day-to-day conditions at the factory, particularly in the light of the control exerted over you and your partner by those involved?

It was a distressing experience. The so-called gunman advisers spoke openly and without any apparent shame about criminal activities and corruption in Brasília. There were endless stories. Janene had a company in the public lighting sector, and they racked up debts in dozens of municipalities by handling public lighting projects all over Brazil. They openly shared how the crimes were committed—how they extorted mayors, how they bribed judges and police officers—and I was just sitting there, eyes wide, absolutely terrified.

There were two employees I trusted, who had been with me since my previous company, and one would say, "Did you see that?" one would ask, and the other would reply, "I am scared." Yet there was little that could be done. They were aware of how much I was suffering. It felt as though I were living in a private prison—within the confines of my own company. The house I was living in was in a condominium in Londrina. It was rented by Janene—the rent was in my name, but the guarantor was his brother. I was under constant surveillance, from home to work and back again. It was dreadful—real imprisonment. If I went to a restaurant, the "hired gun" would come with me.

It resembled something straight out of the film The Firm[18]?

It was, in truth, a harrowing experience. On one occasion, I managed to escape briefly to visit my daughter, but a flood in Santa Catarina left me stranded. Once it became apparent that I was beyond their reach, my phone was inundated with calls—almost to the point of collapse. Now and then, I would find ways to sneak away in Londrina. I would say, "I am just popping out for a haircut," and I'd actually go into the Federal Revenue Office to try and make a complaint. I was desperate—doing crazy things—but I kept trying. I spoke to one person, then another, left messages on the Federal Police's answering machine. I was trying to report what was happening, in any way I could.

What led you to the decision to become a whistleblower and provide information to the authorities?

I believe it ultimately comes down to personal character, more than anything else. There was just so much crime, such a heavy, toxic energy around everything. It is not about being self-righteous—not at all. I was simply a fish out of water. Reporting it became a matter of survival, almost life or death. I did not belong in that world.

It undoubtedly demanded a great deal of courage.

It may have appeared courageous, but in truth, I was rather reckless.

Was there a defining moment that compelled you to take the courageous step of becoming a whistleblower?

The situation was deteriorating rapidly. I must say, Janene treated me "like a son". But during the week, his "hired guns" … my God. It was relentless. I was constantly being watched and manipulated. They sabotaged me, turned me against the factory workers. They'd say things like, "This guy is incompetent, he deceived us, he does not know what he is doing."

I even had to sabotage my own technology. Creating a device that does not work—it is horrible. But I had no choice. It was eating me up inside. They treated me terribly. In meetings, they would humiliate me in front of everyone. They even went so far as to bring in university professors solely to discredit me and demonstrate that I was at fault. That was profoundly destabilising—it was breaking me.

Then Janene would come at the weekend to calm me down. He had a hot potato in his hands. I had not yet signed the loan documents, and both Maria Teodora and I needed to sign them to formalise the money he'd put into the company. But we did not.

Since Maria Teodora is a journalist, he even tried to entice her with a radio station he owned in the interior of Paraná. Most of the shares were in her name, while I had a second company in Londrina undermine. The structure was divided between two entities—one overseeing export operations, and the other holding the rights to the Dunel brand.

One day, Maria Teodora came to me absolutely desperate. She had discovered there was no accounting for anything that had been done. Since she was legally responsible for Dunel, she went to speak with the outsourced accountant—Mr Simões, at an office in Londrina. She asked him, "Mr Simões, please, tell me what is going on." And he said, "My dear, there is no bookkeeping, nothing has been integrated."

But as soon as he told her that, he rang Janene to let him know she had been there. Strangely enough, that accountant died later that same year. Some individuals died; others disappeared without explanation. When we inquired, "What became of so-and-so?", the answer was often stark: "He died." Shortly after her visit to the accountant, Janene scheduled a meeting with us. It was a Saturday—employees only worked the morning shift. He waited for everyone to leave, then locked us in a room around noon. He took a stack of contracts from a folder and started shouting: "Sign here! Your software supplier must immediately hand over all the passwords!".

I refused. He yelled, and I broke down—I started crying. All the hired guns were standing by the door, armed. He did horrible things to Maria Teodora—called her all sorts of vile names—but she held firm. She is incredibly strong. But I crumbled. I said, "Please, can I go to the bathroom?" I really just wanted to call the Federal Police. I turned my back to leave, and Janene grabbed my shirt: "No one turns their back on me!" I said, "I just want to go to the bathroom." While I was in there, Teodora was trying to calm him down, speaking softly. She managed to de-escalate things.

In the bathroom, I was trying to ring the Federal Police when suddenly one of the hired guns appeared at the window and shouted, "Get back in there!" Then Danielle Janene—who was later acquitted in Operation Car Wash—came to me and said, "Magnus, go back in there, or my father's going to lose it—and I will kill you." That girl was acquitted. That is why I cannot forgive those acquittals. I really cannot. So, I went back. And when I returned, he was a completely different person. The same man who had just exploded with rage was now calm. Janene said, "I have got this contract here, Gois[19]"—his lawyer in Londrina—"drew up this loan agreement and wants you to sign it."

I have always been a quick reader, and I spotted right away that the contract was dated two years earlier. I said, "Mr José, this date is wrong." He immediately rang Gois and started scolding him. Then someone called, inviting him somewhere. He said, "Let's stop here. We will finish this another day." Someone had arrived at his house. He turned to Danielle and said, "Go to the steakhouse at the airport and have lunch with Magnus and Maria Teodora, because I will not be able to make it. Treat them well—lunch is on me."

In a striking display of cynicism, they invited us to lunch; immediately after the meal, we were let go. The hired gun drove Danielle home, and I headed to mine. On the way, I stopped at a phone booth, rang the Federal Police answering machine, and poured everything out. I begged them, for God's sake, to raid that place.

Over those months, I left message after message. I had no idea of the risk I was running, considering Janene had "his own" delegates within the Federal Police.

The six-month due diligence period was coming to an end, and after that we would have to officially associate. Every day I kept thinking: How do I get out of this? How do I escape? There was no light at the end of the tunnel. That same afternoon, Maria Teodora had to go to hospital—her blood pressure had gone through the roof.

What information did you convey when leaving a message on the Federal Police's answering machine?

One day, they were hit with a major blow. It was the day Enivaldo Quadrado[20] was arrested at the airport with euros hidden in his underwear, coming from Portugal. They took one of the company's cars and headed to Guarulhos to collect him. I did not suspect anything at the time, because they often used the company cars for all sorts of things—distributing Christmas hampers, food baskets, doing political errands. It was routine. Maria Teodora did not approve, of course, since she was legally responsible for the company, and those cars were not meant for that sort of thing. But still, on weekends, off they would go with the company vehicles.

Later, I learned that they had taken a van to São Paulo to retrieve this man—Enivaldo. But things went awry: he was arrested. When they returned to Londrina, they were completely shattered—no sleep, barely able to curse. They looked defeated, and I thought, "What on earth happened to them?" Then I saw the newspaper article: "Enivaldo Quadrado arrested at the airport." I knew Enivaldo was connected to Janene. The office I worked in had a vent for the air conditioning, and one day I overheard a phone conversation between Janene and his then-wife, Stael.[21] He was unbelievably cruel to her. I never saw him physically hurt her, but the way he spoke to her was appalling. I remember him trying to calm her down, saying things like, "Relax, it has gone wrong… the money did not arrive… everything is a mess, it has been seized." And that is when I connected the dots. I went to a phone booth and passed all that information along to the Federal Police's answering machine. That whole week, Janene and his "hired guns" were completely off their game—they were reeling.

Was there a particular officer or contact within the Federal Police with whom you communicated directly?

No, it was always anonymous. The tip-offline was just an answering machine. I'd leave my messages, but I never got any sort of signal back. Some days, I would sit there thinking, "Will they come today?", but no one came. Once, a tax inspector did show up. He came because of one of the complaints I'd filed. He asked a bunch of questions, looked me straight in the eye, and then left. I honestly would've preferred to be arrested right then, if it meant it would all just end. But there was never any indication—no idea if the Federal Police were doing anything, if they were even listening. Still, I kept at it.

Did you confide in anyone about what was taking place at Dunel?

Just one person: the owner of a hotel who ended up helping me when I fled. It was late November, maybe early December. I told two of the employees closest to me—Luiz and Alan—"I have got to take this car to Rio, get it registered, and I will leave it there." I took them with me, both of them were from Rio, and we drove there. I left the car and came back to Londrina by bus.

When I got off at the bus station, my mobile rang. It was Janene: "Did you have a good trip to Rio, Magnus?" He knew everything. Later, I found out it was because of "Sem Parar" (a car tag). He had a shop in the shopping mall in Londrina, right across from a Sem Parar franchise.

I replied: "Yes, I did. Took the car to get serviced and registered, it was acting up." And he said, "Those Ford cars are rubbish. I will be arriving on Wednesday with the contracts—everything's ready now." By then, Alberto Youssef had already set up the offshore. I am not sure if it was called Dunel Bahamas or Dunel Cayman. In fact, I do not even know if the company ever truly existed. All I know is, the plan was always to have three layers of companies—one inside the other. They used to brag about the OAS[22] set-up, saying that when prosecutors reached OAS Cayman, it belonged to OAS Bahamas, and when they got there, it belonged to another OAS in yet another tax haven. There were up to five layers of offshores at OAS. And when São Paulo's prosecutors finally reached the last one, there were no assets left to seize. They told this story with such pride. That whole offshore architecture took about six months to build—hence the six months of due diligence.

In the end, Janene told me: "To show that I still trust you, despite everything—despite production not working—I am buying you a Hilux truck." Upon hearing that, I immediately thought: "This marks the end—this is the kiss of death."

Given everything that had transpired, what course of action did you take?

I went straight to my friend's hotel and said, "For the love of God, I need to get out of here." She went to Localiza with one of her employees, rented a car, and had it delivered to the condominium where I lived.

I packed the car with as much as I could, preparing for a midnight escape—before the "gunmen" showed up.

On Monday night, I left earlier than usual and told people at the factory, "I am going to get a haircut." Then, in the middle of the night, I fled in a state of absolute desperation. I have never driven so fast in my life. Somewhere along the way, I actually crossed paths with the "gunmen" heading towards Londrina. But I believe that, because they were accustomed to seeing me in a black Ranger, they did not even register that I was in a different vehicle. Still, I froze when I saw them.

Once I crossed the São Paulo state border and arrived in the city, Maria Teodora and I grabbed a few things and headed straight for the airport. Our destination was Sweden—we had money to collect there, and I also needed to apologise to the Swedish company for everything that was going on. When I got to São Paulo airport, I went to the Federal Police and officially reported what was happening. I told them, "I am leaving, but I am not running from the police." The officer logged the report on the Federal Police intranet. Later, when the Federal Police eventually made official contact with me for the first time, they were furious. They said, "You should not have done that. We have no idea where that complaint might have ended up. This is not a reliable way of doing things. And our colleague should never have uploaded it to the intranet". And here is the miracle: the moment I landed in Sweden, all of our Banco do Brasil credit cards were cancelled overnight. Account limits? Zeroed. I was terrified. Thankfully, I still had a bit of money in hand. We had initially planned to stay longer but ultimately cut the trip short and returned. Upon our return, we went into hiding in São Paulo for a time. Later, we relocated to Santa Catarina, where we were forced to sleep in a different hotel each night. It was an utterly harrowing experience. The year 2009 was, quite simply, a nightmare.

At what point did you first engage directly with the Brazilian authorities to disclose the facts you had observed?

I managed to schedule a meeting with a Federal Police task force in Londrina. They promised me an escort. I brought two witnesses with me—two employees from Rio who'd seen everything. That was the first time I gave a video testimony. Present at the meeting were members of the Civil Police, the Federal Police, the state Public Prosecutor's Office, Special Action Group to Combat Organized Crime, the Federal Public Prosecutor's Office—and overseeing everything was Gerson Machado,[23] who later retired. He is the one portrayed as "Ruffo" in the series The Mechanism.[24]

They began at the very beginning—examining my past in its entirety—and I told them everything. It was three or four hours of testimony, and I withheld nothing.

The truth is—and I have stated this previously, albeit without much attention being paid—my principal concern was never Alberto Youssef or the network, which by the onset of Operation Car Wash had already begun to lose strength. What genuinely alarmed me was the broader environment surrounding them. The "gunmen", the fixers, the people who kept the machine running: from the guy carrying the little bag of cash to the professional hitman. It included people who bribed judges and others who got their hands dirty with the real dirty work.

I requested police protection for myself and my employees. That same afternoon, we left Londrina in a small convoy—me in my truck and an unmarked Federal Police car. We have recorded several videos beforehand, even some for Federal Police officers, because Janene was making serious threats against Gerson Machado. By the time we reached the Curitiba metro area, in Campo Largo, it was late afternoon. Normally, I would have pushed through to Santa Catarina in one go, but the police decided to stop: "We are tired, let's stay the night, it is safer." Panic set in when I saw a truck belonging to Janene parked at the hotel. I told the officers, and they said, "No, it is just in your head." I slept there that night, but only just. The next morning, when we continued the journey, the truck had vanished. After that, I never received any further police protection.

Following your testimony, is it accurate that a fire occurred on one of your properties?

A few days after giving my statement to the police, I got an invitation from José Muggiati Neto—the one who had taken the business plan. Janene was still trying everything he could. Muggiati said to me, "Magnus, Janene wants to return your things, your machines. You just need to sign some receipt, and he'll give everything back. But you have to make a statement saying that, if you've made any complaint so far—and he knew I had—it was only done to favour his political rival. Just say that, and he'll return your things."

I had that conversation with him in a shopping centre in Joinville, around seven in the evening. I went back home. That night, I had a guest staying with me—an American friend. I went to bed and locked the door. My American friend usually stayed up late. Around eleven o'clock, he knocked on my door: "Magnus, someone just called to say the building on Emidio de Souza Street is on fire"—the place where Dunel had started. This was only three hours after I had seen Muggiati in Joinville.

I immediately called him—he had wanted to meet me in Curitiba, then go on to São Paulo, where I was supposed to cancel the contract with Janene. I was not about to go along with that madness, no way. I said to him, "Muggiati, how do you explain this? We spoke three hours ago, and now the place where I kept the documents—the closed files—is on fire. How do you explain that?" He hinted that it was not Janene, but rather the Federal Police. "This is counterintelligence," he said. I told him: "I am not going with you to São Paulo." I did not want to go anyway, and after everything that had happened, I made up my mind for good. I recorded that conversation and even handed it over to the Federal Police. Nothing ever happened to him.

In the aftermath of this episode, what course of action did you choose to take?

I was living in a state of panic—I had no idea who to trust anymore. I kept working, though. A friend of mine in Santa Catarina lent me a factory, and I started producing equipment again, just to keep things going and build a small reserve. I managed to earn around a hundred, maybe a hundred and fifty thousand reais over the course of 2009.

At the beginning of 2010, I travelled to the United States to see what I could do there and ended up staying until 2012. After Janene's death,

I thought it was all over. My complaints had not gone anywhere, and he was dead. We came back to Brazil and opened a company in Rio Grande do Sul. For me, none of the complaints I had made ever led to anything—that is what I believed. In early 2012, I started a new company, with a different name but the same technology. By the time Operation Car Wash began in 2014, that company was already making over a million reais.

Were you ever in direct communication with then-Judge Sergio Moro during that period[25]?

As with many others, I first became aware of Operation Car Wash through television coverage. When I saw Youssef, I immediately recalled Judge Moro. Why? Because Gerson Machado had once asked me to send an e-mail to someone—it turned out to be Sergio Moro's e-mail address. Maria Teodora and I put together a chronological account of everything that had happened to us and sent it to him. He replied to thank us. This was back in 2009. But for me, nothing ever came of it.

Then, in 2014, I was doing well in Brazil. I had built a company that was profitable, I had even bought a pick-up truck. I was happy with my clients, supplying to large companies. When I saw all those people being arrested on the news, I instantly remembered Moro. And honestly, today I say—I wish I had not seen that news report and that my life had just carried on as it was.

But when I saw it, I thought of Moro and sent him a new e-mail. The original message I'd sent with the complaint was still in my inbox. I wrote, "Judge Sergio, I think the people being arrested now have something to do with my company back in 2008, 2009." He replied, "I know not everything turned out as you had hoped, but the information you gave to the authorities was of great importance to what is happening now. I am updating your contact with the current Federal Police officer in charge of the case."

At any point, did you engage with the media to disclose what had occurred to you and your partner?

When Operation Car Wash was just beginning, Cláudio Dantas[26]—back then with *IstoÉ* in Brasília, and now with *O Antagonista*—sent me a message on Facebook Messenger. That marked the beginning of our dialogue and the development of our friendship. He said, "I want to interview you about Operation Car Wash." I did not even know what that was—I replied, "Sorry, I do not know what you are talking about." He said, "I am going to send you a document from the Public Prosecutor's Office—it includes your name." He e-mailed it to me, and as soon as I read it, it was like a film playing in my head. That is when everything started again—all the torment—because my life completely changed.

At first, people began distancing themselves from me. Within just a few days, I lost around five employees. The fear of travelling returned—if I needed to go to São Paulo to meet a client, I was gripped by anxiety. The threats resumed, and unsettling incidents began to occur. Everything became intensely stressful. It was a dreadful experience, truly. Eventually, I asked for police protection again—it was denied. I shut down the company, sold off the equipment, the machinery—almost gave it away like scrap—and left Brazil.

Where did you go in the aftermath of those events?

I had a company registered in Portugal and thought, "I will go there for a bit. If things get worse in Brazil, I will apply for residency." I arrived in Portugal, but the persecution followed me. After I appeared on a television programme about corruption, the show aired on a Saturday night, and by Monday morning, I had an expulsion letter in my hands. It said that "after contact with Brazilian authorities, it was determined that my participation in Operation Car Wash was neither important nor relevant." In Portugal, I became a liar. I was expelled and had nowhere to go. I got back in touch with the people from Operation Car Wash and said, "I cannot take this anymore. I am going to a third country, and if someone in Brazil keeps spreading false information about me, I will be expelled again." It was at that point that Prosecutor Paludo[27] issued a statement clarifying who I really was. That is when Operation Car Wash began acknowledging my role. Since I only had a tourist visa for Canada, I went there. And another ordeal began. The first year was spent proving who I was. They treated me with great suspicion. Only after two years did I begin to have anything resembling a normal life.

There were other consequences too. For instance, the assets that backed the leasing contracts with the Bank of Brazil were stolen. Every single lawyer involved in the case failed to request a reduction for the excessive seizure of assets—even though the initial debt was 135 thousand reais and the value seized was already over a million. All the lawyers missed their deadlines—every one of them, as if by some miracle. The remaining properties are now going to auction. The Banco do Brasil, which had previously proposed a settlement, ultimately withdrew. It was profoundly frustrating—there was no one to turn to. No one at all.

How do you assess the political and economic landscape in Brazil beginning in 2014, when Operation Car Wash was launched? At the time, did you, like many Brazilians, believe that the operation could transform the country's systemic corruption? And what is your perspective on this today?

At times, I find myself reflecting on the Car Wash operation. Had it genuinely succeeded in addressing systemic corruption in Brazil, then the personal hardship I experienced might have carried some purpose. However, to endure such an ordeal only to see its outcomes unravel has been profoundly disillusioning.

The greatest flaw in Operation Car Wash, as I see it, was that in attempting to confront a far greater evil, it relied on fragile institutional support—support that ultimately proved unreliable, as it belonged to the very system the operation sought to dismantle. Ultimately, their very strategy turned against them—both the prosecutors and the judge. There were missteps, some of which were undeniably grave, evident even to those without legal training. But to my mind, the deeper reality is that the system managed to reassert itself and take its revenge on those who sought to disrupt it. This happened through poorly constructed plea bargains—"I will tell you this, but you leave that out"; "I will name this person but protect that one." And those individuals who were spared, the ones left out of the operation, were the very people who ended up conspiring to bring the judge down first—and then the whole Car Wash operation. I have no doubt about that.

Would you like to share any closing reflections or a final message for future generations?

If I may, I would like to revisit the earlier question concerning the economic context, as I view it as fundamentally connected to Operation Car Wash. It constitutes a key component of the systemic framework in which corruption operates: the system feeds on it, and many players in the economy thrive on it. Corruption fuels both the formal and informal economies in Brazil. That is one important point.

The second point is that, with the collapse of that particular government, it has become quite clear that ideology has nothing to do with corruption. The mechanism of corruption cuts across almost all parties—it is embedded in the whole political structure of Brazil. Car Wash should have been the rallying cry for all well-intentioned prosecutors. All institutions should have seized the moment to push for sweeping change, to scrutinise all politicians and public figures involved in corruption. That would've been the only way to truly honour what was good about Car Wash.

It should have become a nationwide standard—it was an operation involving the Public Prosecutor's Office, task forces, and the Federal Police—bringing everything to light and making the public fully aware of who was involved and in what capacity. And to keep at it relentlessly, until society itself began to support the honest authorities in their mission. Quite simply, there is no other way forward.

The message I wish to leave is this: in my view, Operation Car Wash failed because it did not complete its mission. It was unable to do so, as the judge was removed before the process reached its conclusion. Certainly, there were errors, and these played a role. However, the most significant failure was the inability to bring the operation to its intended end. That, for me, is what remains. That is the message.

Hermes Freitas Magnus was born in Torres (RS). He is a businessman and was responsible for the first complaints to the Justice that led to the beginning of the Car Wash Operation. His testimony was given on 4 March 2021 via the Zoom virtual platform and lasted 1 hour and 20 minutes of recording. The transcript was subsequently reviewed by interviewee on 5 March 2023.

Testimony of Jorge Pontes

Abstract

This testimony presents the professional trajectory and reflections of Jorge Pontes, a former high-ranking Federal Police officer in Brazil, whose career has spanned environmental enforcement, internal affairs, and anti-corruption leadership. Trained initially in biology and later in law, Pontes narrates his early work combating environmental crimes in the Amazon and his creation of Brazil's first specialised police division for environmental offences. His tenure in internal affairs, particularly in Rio de Janeiro, exposed him to entrenched institutional dysfunction and the corrosive impact of internal corruption.

Pontes became an early and active interlocutor in Operation Car Wash, offering strategic and evidentiary support to investigators, notably Márcio Anselmo. His testimony describes a direct connection to Petrobras whistleblowers and details his role in facilitating early investigative breakthroughs. As a co-author of *Crime.gov*, Pontes conceptualises "institutionalised crime" as an entrenched, adaptive criminal ecosystem embedded within Brazil's democratic structures—one that thrives on the complicity of political elites, legislative manoeuvring, and selective judicial appointments.

He offers a critical analysis of the systemic nature of political corruption, describing it not merely as a set of illicit acts, but as a deliberate architecture designed to perpetuate impunity. While acknowledging the institutional evolution of the Federal Police and its role in large-scale anti-corruption operations, he laments the backlash against Car Wash, characterising recent judicial and political actions as a counteroffensive by the very structures the operation sought to dismantle.

Despite institutional setbacks, Pontes asserts that Car Wash holds enduring symbolic value as a watershed moment in Brazil's democratic maturity. His testimony is both a personal account and a broader institutional critique, highlighting the tension between enforcement efforts and political resistance, and calling for structural reform rooted in the deconstruction of entrenched impunity

To begin, could you provide an overview of your academic background and the key milestones in your professional and personal trajectory?

I began studying Biology at the Federal University of Rio de Janeiro. I have always had a deep interest in science and nature—particularly fauna, and especially mammals, which tend to be the most affected. I have always had a scientific streak—an ideal of science, of protecting nature, of understanding animal life, of classifying, discovering new species. I wanted to be a naturalist. And I think I became one—still am, really, even if just as a hobby now.

That was the path I set out on, but I left it behind when I got married in my early twenties. I felt that Biology would not offer the financial stability I needed, so I started preparing for public service exams. I sat the entrance exam and was accepted into State University of Rio de Janeiro, where I studied Law. I enjoyed it, and shortly after graduating, I passed the exam to become a federal police agent. My first post was in Amazonas, which brought together all the strands of environment, nature, crime, and corruption in a very raw way. Corruption is at the heart of environmental issues in the Brazilian Amazon and the northern states—beneath every pressure that nature suffers, there's systemic political corruption running through it all.

Eventually, I left Amazonas and returned to Rio, where I passed another exam and began my career as a police chief. I decided to create something that did not yet exist in the Federal Police: a dedicated unit to investigate environmental crimes. I drafted a proposal while working in internal affairs, and today that unit has grown into a major division with twenty-seven police stations across the country.

Working in internal affairs is a kind of hell. There is even a philosopher who says that no creation—no music, no drawing, no work of art—comes from someone who is not trying to escape some kind of hell. And I agree. Internal affairs are the kind of job where you never really win, because you are going after your own colleagues. But when I caught a corrupt officer, I felt an even greater sense of justice than I would if it were a civilian criminal. Because internal rot damages the whole system more deeply. Still, it is heavy. You are not popular, the pressure is immense, and the workload is intense.

I worked in the Rio de Janeiro internal affairs department at a time when the city had even bigger problems than today. Despite the Federal Police being, in general, a very correct institution, there were vulnerable spots—historically, Rio, São Paulo, and Foz do Iguaçu.

So, the environmental crimes unit was created. I spent years building it up—creating the general coordination, the police stations—I really threw myself into the environmental area. I led operations and investigations and took part in several Interpol conferences to improve our model. I was, in a way, the architect of this effort in Brazil. I still work in that area today.

Later, I was invited to take on a leadership role. A director told me, "Pontes, if you do not go into management, you will spend your whole career in the environmental unit." Over the course of my career, I advanced to the position of superintendent, later served as general coordinator, and ultimately concluded my professional trajectory as a Federal Police *attaché* in France and as a member of Interpol's Executive Committee. I was elected to the Committee for the 2009–2011 term during the General Assembly held in Singapore.

My work in combating environmental crimes gradually brought me into international arenas. Whereas Brazil was once primarily associated with football, global interest has shifted. Today, what truly captures the attention of forums such as the G7 and G20 is our environmental wealth—particularly the Amazon. It has become our most strategic asset and a central point of international curiosity and concern.

While serving as superintendent in Pernambuco, in Brazil's Northeast, I began to grasp how the institutional machinery truly operated. My previous years in the Federal Police, dedicated to confronting organised crime—particularly drug and arms trafficking—had offered only part of the picture. Over time, I came to understand that the gravest threat to Brazil was not external criminal networks alone, but rather a deeply rooted, systemic form of criminality embedded within the State itself. This structural corruption extended across all three branches of government, though it was most pervasive in the Executive and Legislative branches, and somewhat less so in the Judiciary. What I witnessed was not merely the failure of institutions, but their instrumentalisation for illicit purposes.

When the Judiciary is appointed by corrupt politicians, particularly to the higher courts, the system becomes vulnerable. This is institutionalised crime, operating across all levels of government—municipal, state, federal. Brazil is now facing a new kind of criminal entity—a megastructure with tentacles in every area, appointing people to cover up fraud, creating a feedback loop where corruption funds political campaigns, and power is used to generate more wealth. It is a vicious, perfect, and deeply troubling circle.

I have been a police officer since my early twenties. Over the years, I worked across Brazil—in Amazonas, Brasília, Rio de Janeiro, Pernambuco, and São Paulo—and also built an international career. I served as Interpol Director for Brazil and had the unique opportunity to observe the system from the inside out. I was later nominated for a position at the Organization of American States, with plans for a direct transition from France to Washington. Everything had been arranged; all that remained was the issuance of the plane ticket. But the ticket never came.

At the time, my children were still young, and I had already met the conditions for retirement. When I began to notice repeated delays, I sensed that something was off—it felt like a message. I went to Human Resources, formally requested my retirement, and asked for it to be processed without delay. Shortly thereafter, it was official—and the move to the United States never materialised. I have no patience for conspiracy theories, but the situation was undeniably unusual. It felt as though fate was intervening.

After that, I was invited to help organise the Rio 2016 games.[28] I was originally appointed to serve from 2012 to 2016, but I chose to leave at the end of 2014 after witnessing situations that, in my view, possibly involved corruption. I submitted a formal letter outlining the reasons for my decision to step away. It was during that period that everything truly crystallised for me: the scale of the scheme was vast—so deeply entrenched that it appeared almost indestructible.

In what capacity were you involved in Operation Car Wash, and how did that experience shape your understanding of corruption and institutional dynamics in Brazil?

I published an article called *The Scourge of Institutionalised Crime* in 2013.[29] Márcio Anselmo,[30] who was the Federal Police Chief of Car Wash, sent me a message by e-mail: "Pontes, what you are describing is exactly what is happening." Just a few days later, the first phase of Operation Car Wash made national headlines. Around that same time, something quite significant happened that unexpectedly connected me to Márcio. A childhood friend—someone I had known for years from playing football at Clube Naval in Lagoa, at Piraquê—was then a senior executive at Petrobras. He had built an international career, with postings in Chile, Singapore, and Houston, and happened to be at the company during that critical period Pasadena refinery[31] was being offered. Following our football matches, he would approach me as I was leaving the pitch and say, "Jorge, now that you have returned to Brazil, we need to talk." This was roughly two months prior to the launch of the operation.

That friend, who I later mentioned in the book I co-wrote with Márcio,[32] said: "There are massive schemes going on at Petrobras. The scheme involved constructing a comprehensive corporate architecture, exemplified by the establishment of departments like the New Business Directorate —but it is all a front to siphon off money." He mentioned names—especially Paulo Roberto Costa.[33] I told him, "You need to present something tangible." Often, when individuals raise complaints in a highly emotional state, their words lose clarity and impact. I said "You cannot throw this at me when I am just out of football, still sweaty, about to jump in the shower. I need this in writing, properly structured." I also said, "An investigation into Petrobras would be a big deal—it could shake Brazil's economy, even the political system. There will be serious pushback, so you need to give me solid evidence."

While watching the national news at home one day, I saw coverage of the initial phase of Operation Car Wash, featuring the arrest of Paulo Roberto Costa. At that moment, I realised: this was precisely the individual my friend had named. Events were unfolding exactly as he had described. Yet at that point, we were merely glimpsing the tip of the iceberg. No one could have imagined the scale it would reach or how profoundly it would shake Brazil. And now, there are efforts to dismantle it. Nonetheless, I remain confident that we will restore what has been lost. I have no doubt. I called my friend and said, "Are you watching the news?" Right after that, I contacted Roberto Troncon,[34] a Federal Police officer, and asked, "Who's in charge of this operation? Is he there with you?" He said, "It is Márcio Anselmo—He is in Curitiba." I had thought it would be São Paulo or Brasília. But no—Curitiba, working with Moro. Sergio Moro[35] was a judge the officers really respected—very proper, very serious. Everyone who had worked with him—Pontel,[36] Paulo de Tarso,[37] Paulo Lacerda,[38] Getúlio[39]—they all spoke highly of him.

I messaged Márcio Anselmo and said, "I have a friend who knows the inner workings of Petrobras." He understood the percentages involved in naval rigging contracts, tanker charters—everything. He had even tried to blow the whistle on the Pasadena deal in the past. He is an engineer from the Federal University of Rio de Janeiro, with a highly analytical, Cartesian mindset. He could explain the numbers, the accounting, and the business logic behind it all. Oil, by the way, is the most complex and weighty business sector—it underpins every other industry, with its own language, systems, and peculiarities. And he understood it thoroughly, inside and out.

I told Márcio, "You need to speak with him." So, I created a WhatsApp group for the three of us. Márcio responded, "Pontes, I am coming to Rio—let's drive there," referring to that now-infamous Land Rover that would later become emblematic of the Car Wash investigation. By then, it was already clear that the federal government under the Workers' Party in Brasília was deeply unsettled by the unfolding inquiry. Minister Cardoso[40] appeared to be hoping that information would be leaked to the press in order to undermine the operation. The Workers' Party did not take the kind of direct action against Car Wash that Bolsonaro later would—but in my view, they were aiming to derail it in more subtle ways.

Márcio came to Rio and met with my friend at my house. The meeting began at nine in the morning and lasted until ten at night—nearly twelve hours of conversation. My friend laid everything out: names of companies, structural details, and the inner mechanics of the schemes. Márcio left that day with an extraordinary amount of information. This happened between the first and second phases of the operation, around April 2014. From that point on, Márcio and I remained in close contact. I supported him in every way I could—he is an exceptionally capable investigator: highly cerebral, intellectually rigorous, and extraordinarily disciplined. At the time, he was completing his PhD while simultaneously leading one of the most complex investigations in Brazil's history. Quite remarkable, when one stops to consider it!

As the investigation progressed, I was invited by colleague officers in Rio to take part in discussions about class-related demands. Of course, I would not have objected to a salary increase—who would?—but I did not believe it was the right time, not while the police were engaged in such nationally significant work. Around then, a major anti-corruption march was being organised in Copacabana. I had already written several articles on ethics and public accountability, some of which were published in *O Globo* and *Estado de S. Paulo.* A group of younger officers approached me and said, "Join us, Pontes." I was not involved in union matters—but I went, as a citizen. As we walked past the *Vem Para a Rua*,[41] which is a social movement I identified with—there were Gabeira,[42] Marcelo Madureira,[43] Adriana Balthazar,[44] now a congressperson for *Novo*[45]—someone on the microphone announced, "Look, it is the Federal Police—let's give them a round of applause!" Then someone turned to me and asked, "Would you like to come up and say a few words?" At the time, I was speaking with Márcio daily. The younger officers beside me hesitated and said, "We cannot go up—we are still active duty." Then they looked at me: "Pontes, you go. You can speak for us." I hesitated. What was I going to say? I was not there to talk about salaries, legislation, or institutional autonomy—it did not feel like the right moment to make demands on behalf of the Federal Police. One of them encouraged me: "Just say what you wrote in your latest article." I had recently published a piece on the autonomy of the Federal Police. As I climbed onto the sound truck, I nearly froze. The crowd was enormous. I thought, "I am going to back out." But I grabbed the microphone—this was a historic moment for me—and said, "Good morning. My name is Jorge Barbosa Pontes, and I am a Federal Police officer." I spoke loudly—it echoed like a samba drum from Padre Miguel. The crowd had been buzzing, people chatting and milling about—but suddenly, everything went silent. All eyes turned towards me. When I said, "Federal Police officer", the crowd erupted in cheers. As for me—timid as a mouse until that moment—the energy suddenly took hold. It is striking how crowds and politics can influence the human psyche. I continued: "Of the Brazilian Federal Police—not this governments, nor any others, and it never will be." I grew bolder. "We are facing crime within the government. Our enemies are inside the Planalto right now, trying to sabotage this investigation. We must support the judge, the prosecutors, the Federal Police." I added, "They are saying it will be traumatic if we arrest this or that person, just because they were once president. But it will not be a trauma—it will be a test. It will be redemption. It will prove the maturity of our institutions. Because in this country, no powerful person has ever gone to jail."

When I stepped down, the reception was unbelievable. The video went viral. Overnight, my Facebook was maxed out. Suddenly I was being invited to everything. People saw me as a political activist—some thought I was going to run for office. But I was not. I am an activist in the sense of citizenship—I want to speak out, share my views—but I have no interest in joining a party or chasing votes. Some people get famous and next thing you know, they are campaigning. That is not me.

I was critical of the Worker's Party. I was harsh, yes—because of what they did. But I do not regret it. That is how my journey unfolded. I kept writing, and Car Wash kept going. In my articles, I always defended the operation—right up until Márcio called and said, "Pontes, you are the one who came up with the theory of institutionalised crime. It is catching on—people are quoting you everywhere. Let's write a book together."

As co-author of *Crime.gov: When Corruption and Government Mix*,[46] how do you characterise the functioning of political crime in Brazil—particularly the institutionalised corruption examined in your work? Could you elaborate on how these dynamics parallel or intersect with those observed during Operation Car Wash?

The phenomenon at hand cannot be adequately captured by the term "systemic corruption," which, in my assessment, fails to convey the depth and complexity of the issue. What Brazil is up against is more than a mechanism; it is a morphology, a criminal structure with its own shape and behaviour. A mechanism implies something you can turn on or off. The challenge lies in confronting a structure that behaves more like a living organism—adaptive, mutable, and constantly shifting. When pressure is applied in one area, it reorganises itself elsewhere.

And how does it function? The foundation, ironically, is democracy. That is why I often say it is a crime sanctioned by the vote—and that is the hardest kind of crime to fight. If this were a coup d'état, like we've seen in some African countries where corrupt regimes take over with machetes or rifles, the problem would be easier to reverse. Why? Whereas *coups d'etat* produce a definitive institutional rupture, Brazil has, since re-democratisation, preserved a functioning democratic framework—something of fundamental importance. That democratic continuity must not be compromised. Structural change should not come through abrupt disruptions—whether in the form of Operation Car Wash, the Bolsonaro government, or the Workers' Party—but must instead be pursued through the reform of existing institutions.

Take the Federal Supreme Court, for instance. If a court composed of eleven justices includes four, five, or even six who act more as pseudo-guarantors than impartial adjudicators, this must be addressed—not through institutional destruction, but by acknowledging it as part of a long and complex process. Reform is not instantaneous; what exists today is the result of decades of deliberate construction. In this context, institutionalised crime is not accidental—it is a system intentionally designed to operate in precisely this way. It was shaped by parts of Brazil's political elite, in partnership with sectors of the business community—a business elite stuck in a crony capitalist model, as discussed in American literature on the subject. At the heart of this organism is the Executive branch, but it is propped up by the Legislative, which plays a key role: passing laws that make it easier to commit crimes and harder to investigate them.

Any reaction from the state's repressive apparatus—prosecutors, judges, police—gets an immediate pushback from the Legislative. In a country like Germany, if something of this magnitude were uncovered, Parliament would likely shut down until the issue was resolved. Here, it is the opposite. Our politicians gather to ask, "What went wrong for these prosecutors, this little judge, these little police officers? Who do they think they are, coming after us?".

This form of institutionalised crime is especially visible at the municipal level—in the city halls. But it seeps into the states as well. State politics are often built on local patronage: appointments, favours, political deals, overt clientelism. The main difference is that mayors cannot appoint magistrates. So, while crime at the municipal level is serious, it is less metastatic. It does not usually reach the higher courts or permeate the Judiciary in the same way.

The Judiciary, in principle, should be trustworthy. Judges are career professionals who pass rigorous exams. But the appointment of appellate judges and high court justices is a political process—controlled by heads of the Executive. If the government in power behaves like a criminal organisation—as was the case with Sérgio Cabral[47]—it is obvious they won't appoint independent, serious judges. They will choose people who align with them ideologically, someone they know they can count on when needed. And that is where things fall apart. When you have a high-ranking judge overturning valid judicial decisions—because they owe their position to a political group—justice is compromised. Not always, of course; there are exceptions. But too often, the Judiciary becomes entangled in the same web it was meant to regulate.

Some Supreme Court Justices are doing a good job, I can mention Justice Barroso,[48] Justice Fachin,[49] Justice Fux,[50] Justice Rosa Weber,[51] Justice Teori[52] did a great job. At times Cármen Lúcia[53] and Justice Alexandre de Moraes[54] also performed well, though with some ups and downs. If I were a Justice, I would not even bother with pleasantries, I would do exactly what Joaquim Barbosa did.[55] He essentially gave a "Take that!" to those who nominated him and went on to convict them from the bench. It is a real pity he left—he is sorely missed.

The Federal Police is up against a criminal group that appoints its own bosses, dismisses them at will, approves the budgets for their own investigations, and even appoints the judges who will try them. They also nominate the Attorney General, who has the authority to bring criminal charges against them. Meanwhile, legislators draft laws that make life easier for politicians and actively undermine police officers, judges, and prosecutors. It is almost a lawless landscape—a dead end. That is what we are up against: institutionalised crime. And for anyone serious about tackling this level of criminality, it is a massive challenge.

Naturally, many within the Federal Police and the Public Prosecutor's Office might say, "This won't lead anywhere." I see colleagues who worked on the Car Wash operation who are now facing disciplinary and even criminal proceedings. They're trying to reverse the roles—now the criminals are running for office, and before long, it is the judge who'll be in the dock, simply for doing what judges and prosecutors always do: communicate and coordinate. They weren't conspiring to forge evidence or negotiate bribes—they were just working the way they always have. I have been a police chief my entire life—I have always spoken to judges, always coordinated with prosecutors. There has always been collaboration. Judges also speak with defence lawyers—it is how things operate. These allegations are sophisms—twisted, misleading arguments.

Obviously, I became close friends with Érika,[56] with Moscardil,[57] Mauat,[58] Márcio Anselmo, Skora,[59] friends with the entire Car Wash team. Later, when Sergio Moro took on the role of Minister of Justice, he invited me to join him. I assembled a brilliant team from the Car Wash operation. My aim was to transfer that investigative expertise to the Civil Police, because my view of institutionalised crime leads me to believe we must support the Civil Police in undergoing the same institutional strengthening that the Federal Police experienced. We need judicial police teams able to collaborate and tackle corruption in a systemic way. It is very difficult for the Federal Police to combat institutionalised crime in Brazil on their own. We need Car Wash-style teams operating at the municipal and state level.

That is why I created the Programme for Strengthening Judicial Police. The entire team was assembled—Márcio, Érika, and others. However, the project was naturally brought to a halt when Minister Moro resigned from the Ministry of Justice. At that point, I chose to step down as well; remaining within that government was no longer an option. In truth, I had already considered leaving earlier, as the direction of events had become increasingly clear. Moro delayed his resignation—arguably longer than might have been advisable. His efforts were directed at advancing institutional objectives, in the hope that reform might still be possible. In similar circumstances, such a course of action would have been entirely justifiable. He made a genuine attempt to advise the President and to promote a more constructive path. However, upon recognising that the President was acting in demonstrable bad faith, he made the decision to resign.

In your view, to what extent was the institutional role of the Federal Police instrumental in allowing Operation Car Wash to emerge as the most extensive anti-corruption initiative in Brazil's history—and potentially worldwide?

Absolutely. The Federal Police underwent a significant process of institutional maturation. I myself conducted a study mapping the various stages of this development, beginning in the 1990s. With the advent of globalisation, the institution became increasingly outward-looking—officers began to travel more frequently, undertake training abroad, and establish connections with international bodies. A whole generation of Federal Police delegates started seeing the world with new eyes, and this coincided with a similar shift within the Public Prosecutor's Office. Then came the era of major operations.

I give a lot of credit to Dr. Paulo Lacerda.[60] And there is a bit of a paradox when it comes to the Workers' Party —because it was precisely during the first Workers' Party government that the Federal Police consolidated itself as a real engine for large-scale operations. Serious, well-executed operations. Several historical factors aligned to bring about that moment, which culminated in Car Wash, in Greenfield,[61] and in all those complex investigations.

There was also a notable shift in the institutional profile. More women joined the force, more bilingual officers were recruited, and increasingly, professionals arrived with expertise extending beyond drug enforcement. This new generation began to understand and confront corruption directly. It marked a transformation in the composition of the Federal Police—from excellent officers focused primarily on drug and arms trafficking, which aligned with the system's interests at the time, to professionals engaged in complex financial and political investigations. It is not to suggest that combatting drug or weapons trafficking is unimportant—on the contrary, it remains essential. However, crime functions like a building…

Think of it this way: the ground floor is street crime, things like car theft. Then on the fifth or sixth floor, you've got drug and arms trafficking, the criminal factions. But right up there at the top, on the tenth floor, is the group of the so-called untouchables. And they need to be hit too. This is precisely why the autonomy of the Federal Police is of such critical importance.

What is required is the deconstruction of the architecture of impunity. The emphasis must be on dismantling—rather than building anew—since no meaningful reform can take place without first disassembling the structures that have long sustained systemic corruption. Because this whole system was built, engineered to function like this. So, the first step is recognising that, and then unravelling it all. There is no use trying to build something new on top of a mess—it is like being given a plot of land with a terrible, haunted castle on it and someone says, "Build your house there." Well, you cannot. You have to knock it down first. You have got to untangle every knot, because everything is connected. This remains the position I uphold, and it is the framework presented in the book.[62]

Given your long-standing engagement with Operation Car Wash, were you surprised by the magnitude of the investigation, the extent of systemic corruption it exposed, or the vast sums of illicit funds brought to light?

None of it came as a surprise, as the signs had long been evident. In the book we authored,[63] we use the metaphor of the great black sperm whale—we could sense its sheer scale because, no matter where we turned, something would obstruct the path. If you put your hand in the water here and touch something, you feel something hard and at the same time slimy. Then you cross the entire Brazilian coastline, put your hand in again, and you feel that same slimy structure—so you realise the creature is enormous. It is a huge whale. This metaphor was used because the scale of the phenomenon could be sensed—its presence was unmistakable. I went to Pernambuco and there was something there; in Amazonas, there was something too. When I set up the environmental crime police stations, it was there as well. The problem is this: if they were criminals like drug traffickers—who are marginal figures, even if they have power, weapons, and money to corrupt—it would be one thing. But they're not marginal; they're at the very core. They do things like this: "Pontes, you were supposed to be going to the south of Pará, but now you are being sent to a ceremony to plant fruit trees in a kindergarten." And you say, "But what about the operation in Pará?" And they reply, "No, there is a new priority at the kindergarten."

The biggest drug trafficker in Brazil cannot simply call the Minister of Justice and order the transfer of a Federal Police officer—they do not have that kind of power. The FBI in the United States faces challenges too, but no one there picks up the phone to the American President to say, "Transfer this agent," or "We will not release funds for this operation," or "Find out what investigation He is working on." That does not happen in the United States.

The true threat lies within—the enemy is already inside the house. It is a structure that operates from the inside out. Various manifestations emerge family ties resembling those of a mafia, political nepotism, and entrenched patronage networks. Organised crime delineates its zones of control, and in much the same manner, political parties allocate control over state-owned companies and government ministries. The criminal organisation gets mixed up with the political benches, even entire parties. The Mensalão[64] case provides clear evidence of high-level political involvement, with multiple party presidents among those implicated. It is not just one or two rogue deputies—it is benches of them. It is a broad agreement, a grand orchestration among political structures, who hold the positions and make the appointments. That is the real difficulty.

To what extent do you believe Operation Car Wash succeeded in addressing the structural roots of corruption and impunity in Brazil? Do you consider that its reach was sufficient, or that it ought to have pursued deeper institutional reform?

Operation Car Wash, in my view, represented a breakthrough unparalleled in Brazilian legal history. It succeeded in bringing cases to completion and even secured the conviction of a former Brazilian President.[65] At a certain point, Operation Car Wash genuinely broke the mould. However, it could not withstand the backlash—the mafia-style countermeasures, the waves of opposition, and the pushback from entrenched, institutionalised criminal interests. This government, in particular, delivered the most severe blow. It began by dismantling Car Wash itself: the task force was dissolved, rendering the operation incapable of producing further results. In effect, this administration took deliberate steps to dismantle the broader anti-corruption framework—it disbanded the task force, appointed a new federal police chief, and selected a General Prosecutor who is openly opposed to Car Wash.

There are still ongoing inquiries and legal proceedings, of course. But the one stronghold they haven't managed to topple is society's conscience. That is why I say Car Wash has an intangible value—something that transcends politics. People say, "They released Lula", but who genuinely believes Lula is innocent? "They are going to release Cabral; they are going to release Cunha". These setbacks are deeply discouraging and feed a sense of impunity. Still, Car Wash carries this symbolic weight, this intangible character. They can only truly destroy it if they erase our memory.

That is why it is so important to move past polarisation. I believe even Bolsonaro supporters—the so-called bolsominions—do not want corruption, at least not in principle. Though they seem to tolerate things like the "rachadinhas",[66] which, frankly, are just a stepping stone to a scandal on the scale of the Petrolão.[67] The "rachadinhas" happened because Bolsonaro and his sons were still small players—like kids playing futsal. But the day they went to Maracanã, they started playing full-pitch football.

Car Wash was under attack from the very beginning, but it endured—for a time. Back then, people mobilised; there was no pandemic, and the country was not so deeply polarised. Today, the right-wing camp that once opposed the Workers' Party is fractured. "Bolsominions" are now spreading fake news against Moro, Dallagnol[68] and the other prosecutors—it is absurd. They're starting to regret the choice they made when Sergio Moro left the government in April.

This current wave of setbacks for Car Wash, in my view, comes from a group of Supreme Court Justices who decided to dismantle the operation through technicalities—procedural issues, claims of bias, and raising suspicions about Sergio Moro. They never had the courage to do this before, but they saw that society was divided. When Sergio Moro left the

Bolsonaro government, many were disgusted with what they saw, but, surprisingly, a large group stuck with Bolsonaro and turned on Moro—criticising him for speaking out, for calling out what he did. They ended up backing the wrong man.

The core of institutionalised crime sits within the political structures of the Executive and Legislature, with some influence over the courts. I would not say the judiciary is actively involved, but some members are allies of the political figures who appointed them—and they certainly have sway when it comes to the outcome of cases. The real operators are in the Executive and Legislature—just look at the Petrolão and Mensalão scandals.

But then there are what we call, in our own terms "superstructures": entire sectors that benefit hugely from systemic corruption. In some cases, entire careers are built on this kind of privilege. This often includes segments of the judiciary, which tend to remain unaffected by legislative measures. For instance, when salary reductions are implemented, their remuneration is left intact; when broad cuts impact public servants, the military and the judiciary are frequently exempt. Then you have other sectors that profit, like some criminal lawyers who, for years, made a living not through actual defence, but through influence-peddling. There are also advertising agencies, polling firms—a whole range of peripheral players who benefit from the edges of corruption. We call them "edge dwellers".

The scale of the phenomenon is vast—truly immense. Just as the Workers' Party government refined its corruption schemes through the Civil House under José Dirceu's[69] leadership, Bolsonaro perfected the use of fake news, I mean, we'd never seen anything quite as brutal in terms of fake news until the 2014 election, when that Bahian marketer[70] of Dilma[71] destroyed Marina Silva.[72]

And Marina—she is truly remarkable. As a person, she is exceptional: kind, principled, and untainted. A woman who only learned to read and write at the age of fifteen yet rose to become a national figure—she is, without question, someone worthy of deep admiration. She was well ahead in the polls, and then came a deluge of fake news, orchestrated by the Workers' Party's propaganda machine. Now everyone is shocked by Bolsonaro's fake news, but the truth is, it was merely an evolution—a perfected version—of what the Workers' Party had already been doing.

To return to your earlier question, the impact of Operation Car Wash was unprecedented. Nevertheless, there is now a discernible effort to alter the course of its legacy. The operation has not been entirely dismantled, but its trajectory is being actively reversed. The catch is that no one has managed to do so without revealing their own contradictions in the process. Car Wash went so deep that it compelled individuals to expose themselves. There is an ongoing effort to dismantle the entire operation—to discredit it entirely—but we have still achieved two important victories. First, they cannot erase our memory. We know those schemes existed. Second, all those now shouting and pointing fingers, trying to rewrite history—it is all sophistry. Because they're doing the very same things. They meet with lawyers, they speak with defendants, they drop hints, they receive calls… There is even a case of a Supreme Court Justice showing up on a wiretap. I mean, come on—someone gets arrested and rings up a Supreme Court justice, and the minister ends up caught on tape. It is a joke.

The irony is that Operation Car Wash was, in fact, conducted with genuine technical rigour. Its findings were upheld at every judicial level: initially in the first instance, then by the Federal Regional Court of the 4th Region in Porto Alegre, followed by the Superior Court of Justice, and ultimately by the Federal Supreme Court. Justice Teori validated all the lower-court decisions. And Judge Sergio Moro—he demonstrated an extraordinary work ethic. What is currently unfolding verges on satire: there is an active effort to recast a judge who acted with integrity, along with a team of dedicated prosecutors, as if they were the wrongdoers. And this will not end with Lula—others will inevitably follow. Yet, in my view, Operation Car Wash remains untouchable. It is not merely a legal operation, but a symbol.

Jorge Barbosa Pontes was born in Rio de Janeiro (RJ). He is a retired federal delegate. Co-author of the book *Crime.Gov – when corruption and government mix*. His testimony was given on 12 March 2021 via the Zoom virtual platform and lasted 1 hour and 14 minutes of recording. The transcript was subsequently reviewed by the interviewee on 14 February 2023.

Testimony of Marcelo Zenkner

Abstract

This testimony traces the professional and intellectual journey of Marcelo Zenkner, a former Brazilian public prosecutor and compliance leader, whose career has spanned the fight against systemic corruption, the advancement of institutional reform, and the promotion of integrity within both public and corporate spheres. Beginning with a deep vocational commitment to the Public Prosecution Service, Zenkner recounts his early work in Espírito Santo at a time when the state was effectively captured by organised crime and political corruption. His pioneering efforts in anti-corruption enforcement—including high-profile arrests of municipal and state officials—positioned him at the forefront of institutional resistance, often at great personal and familial risk.

Zenkner's transition from traditional prosecutorial work to a focus on structural reform came during his doctoral studies in Portugal, where he engaged with international anti-corruption frameworks such as the OECD Convention and the UK Bribery Act. This academic and policy exposure shaped his later contributions to Brazil's compliance movement, most notably through his leadership roles in implementing the Clean Company Act in Espírito Santo and, later, as Director of Governance and Compliance at Petrobras.

His testimony offers a rare dual perspective: first, as a prosecutor confronting entrenched criminality from within the state; second, as a corporate compliance leader engaged in rebuilding institutional trust in the wake of the Operation Car Wash scandal. He reflects critically on the evolution from reactive enforcement to a more preventive, integrity-based model, distinguishing between compliance systems focused on rule enforcement and broader integrity systems rooted in values, trust, and ethical culture.

Zenkner concludes by affirming the enduring impact of Operation Car Wash on corporate governance in Brazil, while also warning against superficial reputational reforms and the risks of institutional regression. His account is both a case study in personal resilience and a blueprint for structural transformation, underscoring the belief that lasting reform depends not merely on punitive mechanisms, but on the cultivation of institutional and individual integrity—even under pressure, and especially when under scrutiny.

Could you describe your educational background and personal trajectory, in order to provide context for your professional journey?

First of all, thank you very much for the invitation. For me, it is genuinely a privilege to speak about a role I hold in high regard and to share aspects of a professional journey of which I am equally proud.

I would like to begin from the perspective of vocation, as this is something about which I have never had the slightest doubt—not at any point in my life. I always knew that I wanted to study law. From my earliest engagements with the Public Prosecution Service during university, it became immediately clear to me that this was where I wished to build my professional career. I recognised in the institution a genuine potential to promote meaningful social transformation.

What struck me most about the Public Prosecution Service was its capacity for independent initiative—and that was precisely what drew me to it. I graduated at a relatively young age, 22 and then dedicated three uninterrupted years to preparing for the entrance examination for the Prosecutors Office. In 1996, I passed the entrance examination for the Public Prosecutor's Office in the state of Espírito Santo—a state that, at the time, was entirely unfamiliar to me. I am originally from Minas Gerais and had been living in my hometown, intending to sit the exam there. However, due to political circumstances, the examinations in Minas were suspended. Given the circumstances, I turned to other states and, on my first attempt, was successful in the Espírito Santo Public Prosecutor's Office exam. On my first attempt, I passed—and I took office in April 1997.

Espírito Santo is a small state, and the career path was quite open, which meant promotions could come quickly. Because of that, I ended up deciding not to pursue exams in other states and stayed in the Public Ministry of Espírito Santo. But this lack of familiarity with the state—and at that time information did not circulate nearly as easily—led to a very interesting turning point in my career. I had no idea that the state was, at the time, essentially under the control of organised crime.

The recent history of Espírito Santo was characterised by a particularly turbulent period—most notably between 1996 and 2005—during which organised criminal groups wielded considerable influence over the state. At the time, President of the Legislative Assembly[73] was a former illegal lottery operator ("bicheiro") who had been arrested by the Federal Police. He exerted control over nearly all members of the state legislature, and in a political system like Brazil's, such influence inevitably affects the entire public apparatus. He also maintained strong ties to the executive branch and, by extension, exercised control over both the military and civil police forces. Gratz—that was his name—even managed to extend his influence to the judiciary,[74] and the leadership of the Public Ministry at the time was accused of being entangled in corruption[75] as well. The state's Court of Auditors functioned almost like an extension of the Legislative Assembly. Espírito Santo was, therefore, undergoing a period of acute institutional crisis[76]—with a very low Human Development Index[77] and alarmingly high crime rates.

To illustrate the gravity of the situation, the state of Espírito Santo recorded one of the highest homicide rates in the country. Unsurprisingly, this environment also fuelled a widespread public perception of systemic corruption, as a direct consequence of the dynamics described above. It was precisely at that juncture that I arrived in Espírito Santo—motivated by a strong sense of purpose and a commitment to advancing social transformation.

In Viana, one of the first districts where I served—early in my career and still acting as a substitute prosecutor—I worked alongside a particularly fearless colleague, Angela Abranches.[78] Corruption proved to be deeply entrenched in the municipal public administration—blatant and systemic. An investigation was initiated, ultimately resulting in the arrest of eight councillors and three high-ranking municipal officials, followed shortly thereafter by the mayor himself.[79] This was back in 1998, and at the time, operations of this kind were far from common in Brazil. The case gained such prominence that it was featured in a special report on Fantástico.[80]

Today, the arrest of a city councillor might scarcely attract media attention, given the extent to which the fight against corruption has advanced—Brazil has, after all, witnessed the imprisonment of a former President of the Republic.[81] At the time, this kind of prosecutorial work was virtually unheard of and left me highly exposed. The Public Prosecutor's Office was not accustomed to operating in such a confrontational manner, and organised crime remained extremely active—most notably through an armed group known as *Scuderie Le Cocq*.[82] I received death threats and was placed under armed escort. I had just recently married, and my wife—also from Minas Gerais—stood by me throughout, though she was unable to leave the house due to the risks we faced. The Federal Police advised that she be taken out of the state, as they could not guarantee her safety. She chose to remain, effectively living under house arrest—a profoundly challenging start to our married life.

In 1999, the Prosecutor's Office of the state of Espírito Santo established its first Group for the Repression of Organised Crime, and I was among its founding members. From then on, various other anti-corruption initiatives began to take shape in the state. The situation in Espírito Santo had deteriorated to such an extent that the then Minister of Justice, Miguel Reale Júnior,[83] formally requested that the Prosecutor General Brindeiro,[84] consider federal intervention in the state. Conditions were, quite simply, out of control.

At that point, the most consistent source of resistance to crime in the state was the Brazilian Board Association.[85] The then President of the Espírito Santo Chapter. Agesandro da Costa Pereira[86]—sadly no longer with us and was someone for whom I have immense admiration—became the leading figure in this resistance. He created a group called "Fórum Reage Espírito Santo" which began to publicly denounce cases of corruption and overt criminal activity.

However, despite what had previously been agreed, the Prosecutor General ultimately dismissed the request for federal intervention, prompting the resignation of the Minister of Justice. As a palliative measure, then-president Fernando Henrique Cardoso[87] set up a special task force[88] to operate in Espírito Santo, bringing in federal police officers from other states, as local law enforcement was deeply compromised.

This special mission began working discreetly, supporting our efforts in secret. At the time, I was still a Substitute Prosecutor, and unfortunately, the Prosecutor General—who was closely aligned with the then Governor José Ignácio Ferreira[89]—had reassigned me, against my will, to Family Court.

The situation was extremely delicate. To illustrate the severity, one of the mission's key witnesses—who had provided a detailed account of the criminal organisation operating within the state—was murdered inside the prison system. Such was the level of brutality we were confronting. Tragically, the violence culminated in the assassination of Alexandre Martins de Castro Filho,[90] who had collaborated with the mission. He was killed in March 2003, in Vila Velha, as he arrived at a gym.

At the end of 2002, Senator Paulo Hartung,[91] who was closely linked to the "Reage Espírito Santo Forum", was elected governor. From the moment he took office, things began to change for the better, with strong support from organised civil society. Conditions began to improve, supported in large part by the active engagement of organised civil society. A recently published book captures this trajectory particularly well—*Decadence and Reconstruction*[92]—which chronicles both the rise of organised crime in Espírito Santo and the efforts undertaken to reverse that reality. Naturally, many individuals contributed to this process; no transformation of that magnitude is ever the result of a single person's work. What emerged was a remarkably cohesive group, united by a profound sense of mutual trust and it chronicles the rise of organised crime in Espírito Santo and the efforts made to turn that page. Of course, such efforts were the result of collective endeavour; no transformation of that magnitude is ever achieved single-handedly. A tightly knit group was formed, marked by strong bonds of trust and shared purpose.

Espírito Santo has since undergone a profound transformation. It now ranks among the Brazilian states with the highest Human Development Indexes, reflecting substantial improvements in governance, public services, and quality of life. Its basic education is recognised by the Ministry of Education[93] for its high quality, and the National Treasury gave it an A rating for its financial management.[94] Crime levels are under control, and the state now offers a good quality of life to its population. It was even the first state in Brazil to create a sovereign fund to manage and properly allocate oil royalties. My journey in Espírito Santo is deeply intertwined with that transformation.

In 2006, I became head of the Prosecutor's Office specialising in combating administrative misconduct. Several major cases were handled during that period, including the removal of state deputies from office. The president of the Court of Auditors was also removed and faced criminal charges as a result of an investigation led by our office. In addition, numerous high-ranking military police officers, civil police agents, councillors, and other public officials were prosecuted.

That office gave me the opportunity to carry on the fight against corruption, building on the experience I had gained over time. In 2008, during Operation Shipwreck,[95] led by the Prosecutor's Office in Brasília, three judges—including the president of the Court of Justice of Espírito Santo—and a Public Prosecutor were arrested. The prosecutor involved was indicted for corruption, but on the administrative side, he only received a disciplinary suspension.[96] Curiously, he was later elected by his peers as the Public Ministry's General Ombudsman.[97]

By 2011, with a growing number of cases involving the state government, the judiciary, the Court of Auditors, and even the Public Ministry itself, I began to sense some internal instability and diminishing support for the work we were doing. I started to face internal complaints and was subject to investigations by the Inspector General's Office. That said, I was never sanctioned in any way. Nonetheless, this kind of internal pressure takes its toll, gradually eroding one's motivation. I came to the realisation that it was time to step back—not to abandon the cause, but to change strategy, to step out of the direct line of fire for a time.

In 2011, I moved to Portugal to pursue my doctoral studies at the Faculty of Law of NOVA University Lisbon, one of Europe's most respected institutions, particularly renowned in the fields of economics and business. My research focused on the prevention of corporate corruption. At the time of my arrival, Portugal had just incorporated the OECD Convention on Combating Bribery of Foreign Public Officials into its legal framework. It was during this period that I was first introduced to the concept of compliance.

The OECD Convention encourages companies to establish internal control systems to prevent corruption—a smarter, more strategic approach that focuses on the role of the briber, rather than only the one being bribed. It is similar to what we see in drug trafficking: the police may raid a favela, dismantle a drug den, arrest traffickers, and even, tragically, kill someone during the operation—and yet, the very next day, another individual takes their place, and the criminal activity continues. These operations demand enormous resources and effort yet yield limited long-term impact. The same often holds true in cases of corruption. I lost count of the number of times I was legally required to remove a public official from office, only to later prosecute their successor. Over time, it became clear to me that, despite working relentlessly, the structural impact of my efforts remained limited. If my objective was genuine social transformation, I needed to pursue a more effective path—and persisting with the traditional one was exposing me to significant personal risk.

Pursuing my doctorate in Portugal was an extraordinary experience that profoundly reshaped my perspective on the issue. As part of my research, I also spent time in London studying the UK Bribery Act, which had recently come into force and, like many contemporary anti-corruption instruments, was inspired by the OECD Convention. I returned to Brazil in 2013 with a suitcase full of books, an advanced research project, a wealth of new ideas, and a firm determination to work in the field of compliance—because it had become clear to me that this was the approach that had proven effective in countries that had succeeded in curbing corruption. It was, therefore, the strategy that needed to be pursued in Brazil.

Could you describe how your career evolved from the Public Prosecution Service to Petrobras, and how you would characterise that shift in professional focus?

The transition unfolded at a pivotal moment. Shortly after my return to Brazil in 2013, Law No. 12.846/2013—commonly referred to as the Clean Company Act and widely recognised as Brazil's counterpart to the OECD Convention on Combating Transnational Bribery—was enacted.

Brazil had lagged significantly in implementing the Convention and was under considerable pressure from the OECD to comply. In fact, the legislative process was expedited through an urgency regime. The law came into force in 2014, but at the time, very few people in Brazil had a clear understanding of how to interpret or apply it. As it happened, my doctoral research in Portugal had focused precisely on this subject, which positioned me to begin delivering numerous lectures—primarily to corporate audiences. My long-standing role as a university lecturer at the Faculty of Law of Vitória[98] also helped open many professional doors. The year 2014 proved particularly significant: it marked the beginning of Operation Car Wash, and Paulo Hartung was elected for his third term as Governor of Espírito Santo. I had previously worked with him during the 2002 government transition, at a time when organised crime posed a serious threat, and we had developed a respectful and constructive working relationship. He subsequently invited me to serve as State Secretary for Control and Transparency.

Governor Hartung has a sharp political instinct, and he could already foresee that Operation Car Wash would dramatically reshape the national landscape. I remember him telling me: "Marcelo, the anti-corruption agenda will dominate the media from now on." I asked him why he thought so, and he replied, "Because this Operation Car Wash will turn the country upside down." He wanted to position Espírito Santo in the national spotlight, and to do that, he needed bold, high-impact work. A central component of that effort would be the pioneering implementation of the Clean Company Act.

The objective was to implement the law ahead of any other state—and the effort proved successful. A dedicated institutional framework was created: the Subsecretariat of Governmental and Corporate Integrity.[99] State auditors underwent specialised training, and Espírito Santo ultimately emerged as a national leader in the area. The state launched Brazil's first administrative accountability proceeding and applied the first corporate sanction under the new legislation.[100] In parallel, the law was refined locally, and the foundations were laid for a broader public integrity system.

Espírito Santo became a national benchmark. Even today, if you check the National Register of Punished Companies, Espírito Santo is among the states that have applied the most sanctions under the law.[101] It was a meaningful and successful piece of work—especially considering the broader challenges around implementing the legislation.

Unfortunately, I had to step down as State Secretary due to an unfortunate turn of events. In 2016, President Dilma, already politically weakened, moved Minister of Justice José Eduardo Cardozo[102] to the role of Attorney General. To replace him, she appointed a member of the Prosecutors Office from the state of Bahia. The opposition, already highly mobilised, filed an Allegation of Breach of a Fundamental Precept[103] with the Federal Supreme Court, arguing that a member of the Prosecutor's Office could not take up an executive role.

The Court agreed with that view, and as a result, Dilma could not confirm the appointment. This decision also had a knock-on effect: across Brazil, seventeen State Secretaries who were Prosecutors lost their positions—including myself.

I returned to the Public Prosecutor's Office and, in 2017, was nominated by the National Council of the Public Ministry for a position within the World Bank's Vice Presidency of Integrity. This department is responsible for overseeing compliance in the Bank's financing activities with a range of stakeholders. Prosecutors from around the world serve in this capacity, and for the first time, a position had been created specifically for Brazil—largely as a result of the international impact of Operation Car Wash.

After successfully completing a personal interview in Washington, I was formally requested by the Prosecutor General at the time to take up the position. However, the head of the Espírito Santo Public Ministry opposed the nomination. She filed a representation with the National Council of the Public Ministry seeking to have the appointment annulled, but the request was rejected. Subsequently, she brought a writ of mandamus before the Federal Supreme Court, challenging Prosecutor General Rodrigo Janot's requisition on the grounds that it violated the principles of the federal pact.

Just four days before I was due to depart for Washington with my family, I received a call from Brasília informing me that my nomination would be revoked by Rodrigo Janot himself.[104]

The reasoning was that Operation Car Wash had already created enough turbulence for the Federal Public Prosecutor's Office—there was no appetite for further controversy at the Federal Supreme Court.

Naturally, I was devastated—not only because of the professional setback and significant financial loss, but above all due to the impact on my family. At the time, my two daughters were teenagers. They had withdrawn from school, said farewell to their friends, and were already enrolled in an American school. They were full of excitement and expectation. And then, quite suddenly, everything collapsed. I was the cause of that heartbreak, and it was profoundly painful.

The leadership of the Espírito Santo Prosecutor's Office regarded the outcome as a "victory", but I do not believe in victories that are achieved through the destruction of another. And matters only deteriorated from there: shortly thereafter, several disciplinary proceedings were initiated against me—including one for "institutional disloyalty", on the grounds that I had accepted the CNMP's invitation without formal authorisation.

At one point, my lawyer—who remains a close friend to this day—said to me: "Marcelo, I'm sorry, but we need to change our approach. There are so many disciplinary cases now that I'm doing nothing else but working on your defence." It was at that moment I realised that my career in the Prosecutor's Office had come to an end. It soon became evident that there was no longer a place for me within the institution, nor any motivation to remain. I set myself a clear objective: to contest every disciplinary proceeding and fully restore my reputation before formally stepping down from the Prosecutor's Office. However, I resolved only to resign if a professional opportunity arose that would allow me to uphold my family's dignity. That commitment became my personal mission. Integrity is a non-negotiable value for me—there can be no doubt about that.

Eighteen months later, in November 2018, I prevailed in the final disciplinary case. In fact, I succeeded in every single one, each requiring a distinct legal strategy. It had been a long and painful journey, but one defined by resilience and determination. I celebrated that final victory with my family—a simple certificate of good standing from the Office of the Inspector General meant everything.

Then, the very next week, I received a call from a head-hunter inquiring whether I would be interested in a position at Petrobras, focused on the Clean Company Act and internal investigations. She even asked whether I would truly consider leaving the Prosecutor's Office. I replied that I would—and that marked the beginning of the selection process.

By the end of 2018, my name had been approved by Petrobras' Board of Directors for a seat on the newly created Disciplinary Measures Committee. This committee is responsible for applying sanctions under the Corporate Clean Company Act and for enforcing disciplinary measures against employees involved in misconduct, including fraud and corruption.

On 31 January 2019, I formally resigned from the Prosecutor's Office of Espírito Santo. The very next day, 1 February 2019, I began my new role at Petrobras.

How do you assess the legal and economic landscape in Brazil from 2014 onwards, when Operation Car Wash began? To what extent did the context at the time facilitate—or perhaps hinder—the development of the Operation?

First and foremost, I wish to make it clear that I hold no political affiliation. That said, it is important to recognise that, during the administrations of former Presidents Lula and Dilma, Brazil's oversight and control institutions were, in practice, functioning effectively. The head of the Federal Prosecutor's Office was selected from a shortlist drawn up by members of the institution itself, which allowed the Prosecutor General to take office with significantly greater freedom, autonomy, and independence. The Federal Police also operated with a notable degree of institutional independence, and the Ministry of Justice did not interfere in the appointment of the General Superintendent of the Federal Police.

Indeed, the institutions were undeniably strong and functioning effectively at that time. It is no coincidence that such conditions created a favourable environment for the launch of Operation Car Wash. In turn, the Operation generated a domino effect—Petrobras being a prime example. Until that point, Petrobras did not even have its own internal compliance body. However, in response to the scandals that came to light, the company was compelled to establish the Governance and Compliance Directorate in December 2014.

There is no question that this directorate came into being as a direct consequence of Car Wash. Thus, the combination of robust institutions—characterised by genuine independence and autonomy—laid the foundation for the development of a solid anti-corruption framework in Brazil, both in administrative practice and in legislative terms.

What aspect of Operation Car Wash surprised you the most—the scale of the financial sums involved, the involvement of Petrobras, the role of business leaders, or the conduct of political figures?

What most compelled me to accept the invitation to join Petrobras was the opportunity to contribute to anti-corruption efforts within Latin America's largest company—an institution then undergoing profound upheaval in the wake of what the US Department of Justice[105] described as the largest anti-corruption investigation ever conducted globally.[106]

What most impressed me was the sheer scale—not only of Petrobras as a company, but also of the corruption itself, with misappropriated sums consistently reaching astronomical levels. From the outside, I had been following the company's efforts to rebuild, and when the opportunity arose, I saw it as a chance to take part in a historic moment. It was an opportunity to make a meaningful contribution while also learning from the extraordinary process of institutional reconstruction that was underway.

In July 2019, the Director of Governance and Compliance at Petrobras at the time stepped down from the position.[107] As I was already employed within the company, my curriculum vitae was submitted to the external consultancy tasked with overseeing the recruitment process—an obligation arising from the agreement Petrobras had entered into with the United States authorities. I proceeded through the formal selection process and was ultimately appointed to the position.

In August 2019, I assumed the position of Director of Governance and Compliance at Petrobras. The role is equivalent to that of a Chief Compliance Officer and entails responsibility for internal controls, corporate governance, the compliance framework, and internal investigations within the company.

In your view, did Operation Car Wash alter the relationship between the Brazilian state and companies—whether private, state-owned, or state-controlled, like Petrobras?

It brought about profound changes, accompanied by significant legislative developments. I often say that Brazil has experienced three distinct waves of integrity. The first wave began in 2013 and 2014, marked initially by the enactment of the Corporate Clean Company Act and subsequently by the launch of Operation Car Wash. This period had a direct impact not only on the companies implicated in the investigations but also on others—both domestic and foreign—that sought to conduct business in Brazil through the lens of integrity.

A further development came with the enactment of Law No. 13.303 in 2016,[108] which established a specific legal framework for state-owned and state-controlled enterprises. The legislation introduced clearer rules on governance, procurement, and compliance, significantly reinforcing transparency and accountability in entities such as Petrobras and other publicly controlled organisations.

At present, integrity reforms are increasingly extending to the direct public administration. This began in 2017 with Decree No. 9.203[109] and strengthened by Decree No. 10.756.[110] The federal government is actively implementing its own integrity systems, and we are seeing similar movements across states, municipalities, the National Council of Justice, and even the National Council of the Public Ministry.

It is therefore fair to say that, over the past decade, Brazil has undergone a significant transformation. This progress provides a great deal of encouragement and hope—regardless of the political leadership in place. Brazil is beginning to move away from a purely reactive, punitive approach to fighting corruption, and towards a more preventive model. This is the model that truly delivers results, as has been shown in other countries that have successfully improved their corruption perception indexes. I firmly believe this is the path forward, and I am very optimistic about the direction Brazil's anti-corruption system is taking.

What impact, in your view, did Operation Car Wash have on Petrobras' governance? To what extent has the company—and its culture—changed as a result?

The establishment of the Directorate of Governance and Compliance, as I noted earlier, was a direct consequence of Operation Car Wash. Ideally, such initiatives should originate internally within the company, rather than as a reactive measure in response to a crisis. However, this was not the case at Petrobras. In 2018, Petrobras signed an agreement with US authorities, and within that agreement were clear commitments to implement an integrity system aligned with international best practices. As a result, Petrobras found itself in the position of having to lead this movement in Brazil.

When I joined the company in 2019, I found that Petrobras already had a well-established and robust compliance system—one that was aligned with American standards. On the other hand, it did not yet have what I would call a true integrity system. And that is exactly the focus of my doctoral thesis: to draw a distinction between compliance systems and integrity systems.

A compliance system rests on the three pillars of prevention, detection, and correction. It is structured to prevent illicit acts from happening. Why does a company implement a compliance system? Because it does not want to be penalised. The consequences can be severe—sanctions, reputational damage that can seriously impact market value. In fact, one of the clearest effects of Car Wash was the significant drop in market value of the companies involved, far beyond what regular market fluctuations would explain. So, companies turn to compliance as a way to avoid that scenario, to keep themselves away from risky or questionable practices.

But no compliance system is foolproof. When irregularities do happen—whether large or small—the system needs to detect them, whether through whistleblowing channels or internal controls. And once detected, those issues need to be corrected. That means applying disciplinary measures, reporting to the appropriate authorities, and learning from the incident to improve the system.

By the time I arrived, the compliance framework was functioning effectively and was well established. However, Petrobras still lacked a comprehensive integrity system, primarily because internal and external trust had yet to be fully restored. An integrity system goes beyond rules and enforcement. It is about promoting a culture of integrity: encouraging people to do what is right because it is right, not just because they're afraid of being punished. It is about recognising and valuing ethical behaviour—not merely avoiding misconduct. And creating that kind of cultural shift, especially in a company as large as Petrobras, is no small task. But that was the challenge I set for myself.

I was deeply committed to contributing to that transformation within the company, and I believe I succeeded. I was able to implement several initiatives that significantly enhanced Petrobras' culture of integrity. A clear sign of this progress is that Petrobras, which had previously been excluded from the Norwegian Sovereign Wealth Fund—one of the strictest in the world when it comes to compliance—was readmitted to their investment portfolio thanks to the work we carried out.[111] More recently, just after the end of my tenure, Petrobras was awarded the Pro-Ethics Seal by Brazil's Office of the Comptroller General for the 2020–2021 cycle.[112]

Operation Car Wash has brought compliance into greater prominence in Brazil—a positive development, one might say. Despite recent setbacks in the country's anti-corruption efforts, do you believe that a genuine concern for integrity and ethics persists within companies as part of Car Wash's legacy?

It has become increasingly evident that companies today are more focused on attaining reputational capital through the implementation of integrity practices, rather than merely avoiding misconduct. This shift in mindset is not confined to Brazil but reflects a broader global trend. To illustrate, recent studies indicate that approximately 40% of the market value of publicly traded companies is attributable to their reputation, underscoring the tangible value that integrity confers on business.

It is therefore unsurprising that contemporary corporations are deeply committed to sustainability and social responsibility—dimensions I have long regarded as fundamental elements of an integrity system. Such a system transcends the traditional compliance framework, which it certainly includes but does not exhaust. An integrity system builds upon compliance by integrating principles of transparency, meritocracy, innovation, fair competition within sectors, social responsibility, sustainability, and reputation. In my assessment, reputation constitutes the most valuable asset a company can possess.

This was precisely the approach I sought to implement at Petrobras. I am confident that the work undertaken there generated a positive ripple effect across numerous other companies. At the end of 2021, Transparency International[113] made a statement that made our team very proud—they said the work Petrobras had done served as a beacon of integrity for the entire Brazilian business environment.[114] Petrobras is not just the largest company in Brazil—it is a national symbol. And with that comes the responsibility to lead by example. Many of the companies that work closely with Petrobras—some of which depend on it for their survival—began to follow the same path. This is particularly significant, as it demonstrates that the impact of our efforts extended beyond the company itself, exerting a tangible influence on the broader business environment.

What is your assessment of the primary outcomes of Operation Car Wash for Petrobras in particular?

For Petrobras, it truly marked a turning point. I even articulated this perspective in a recent article I published online.[115] A reader responded with criticism, asserting, "What happened in Petrobras's history has stained the company forever—you will never be able to turn that page." I felt compelled to reply, explaining: "A company's history is like a book—we read a page, absorb and learn from it, then turn the page and move forward, while never forgetting what was written. Indeed, the page has been turned—but the lessons have been fully internalised." I can say with confidence that today Petrobras possesses a robust integrity system, sufficiently strong to prevent a recurrence of past transgressions. The foundation is now fundamentally different, rooted in a culture and set of values centred on integrity.

I would like to illustrate the distinction between a compliance system and an integrity system—and how Petrobras's approach sets itself apart. Not long ago, a major financial institution[116] in Brazil publicly announced that its internal compliance controls had identified fifty employees who had applied for emergency government aid during the pandemic. Their internal controls picked it up, action was taken immediately, and all fifty were dismissed without cause. The controls worked, the company took swift action, and they made it public—which, of course, helps bolster their reputation. I am not criticising them—far from it—but I want to highlight how Petrobras handled a similar situation differently.

At the same time, Petrobras also ran internal checks for similar issues. Out of a workforce of forty thousand, only six cases were found—already a sign that the culture of integrity had taken hold. But we did not immediately dismiss anyone. Instead, we opened internal procedures to give those involved a chance to explain themselves, with all legal guarantees. None of the six had applied for the emergency aid while employed at Petrobras—they had done so before joining the company, at a time when they genuinely needed it. They continued receiving the aid afterwards, which was, of course, a mistake. But the explanations varied—one said, "I tried to cancel it on the government website but could not get through the bureaucracy," another said, "I had just moved my family from Ceará and there was so much going on, it slipped my mind."

What stood out was that none of them acted in bad faith. A new mechanism introduced during my tenure at Petrobras was the disciplinary commitment term. The employees acknowledged the irregularity, their good faith and honest mistake were recognised, and they committed to returning the funds to the federal government. Once that was formalised, the disciplinary proceedings were closed without any sanctions. It is a process that is been very successful at Petrobras. It values people, good faith, and honest error. And importantly, it avoids contributing to unemployment and losing trained, valuable employees.

To conclude, this is just one example of the numerous initiatives implemented to establish an effective integrity system. Today, the Governance and Compliance Directorate is held in high regard within Petrobras, largely owing to the excellent work continued by my successor, Salvador Dahan. It is now recognised as a genuine partner to the business units. As I often say, an integrity system should function like oil in the gears of a company—never like sand.

Would you like to offer any final reflections or leave a message?

I like to conclude interviews—especially after discussing integrity, a principle fundamental to both personal and professional life—by reflecting on a belief I hold strongly: people often do the right thing even when no one is watching. An honest individual acts rightly simply because it is the correct course of action. This, in my view, provides a solid foundation on which to build.

However, Gerry Zack, a highly respected authority in the field of compliance, once expressed a sentiment that has remained with me. He emphasised that integrity is not merely about doing the right thing when no one is watching—that alone is insufficient. True integrity involves doing the right thing even under immense pressure, when the decision is unpopular, and when everyone is observing. That, he asserted, constitutes genuine integrity.

Marcelo Barbosa de Castro Zenkner was born in Juiz de Fora (MG). He is managing director at FTI Consulting. He holds a Master's and Doctorate in law. He was a prosecutor in the State of Espírito Santo, Secretary of State for Control and Transparency and Director of Governance and Compliance at Petrobras. His testimony was given on 21 May 2021 via the Zoom virtual platform and lasted 1 hour and 3 minutes of recording. The transcript was subsequently reviewed by the interviewee on 25 January 2023.

Testimony of Maria Cristina Pinotti

Abstract

Maria Cristina Pinotti's testimony provides a rich and nuanced analysis of corruption, institutional integrity, and economic development in Brazil, informed by her extensive academic and professional background in economics and public administration. Beginning with her formative experiences during Brazil's military regime, where academic freedom to discuss constitutional and democratic principles was rare, Pinotti reflects on how these early lessons shaped her lifelong commitment to ethics and governance.

Her journey through macroeconomic analysis and consulting led her to explore corruption through the lens of economic theory, drawing on seminal international scholarship that links the quality of institutions to sustainable development. Pinotti articulates a clear distinction between public and private corruption, emphasising the profound social and economic harm wrought by the former, particularly when state capture occurs.

Pinotti situates Operation Car Wash within a historical and comparative context by drawing parallels with Italy's Mani Pulite operation, underscoring both the similarities—such as the scale of systemic corruption and initial public support—and the differences, including cultural and institutional factors that shape anti-corruption trajectories. She critically examines the political, judicial, and media challenges that both operations faced, highlighting the complex interplay of public opinion, institutional pushback, and the eventual erosion of initial gains.

The testimony discusses Brazil's evolving anti-corruption landscape, marked by legislative advances such as the Corporate Clean Company Act and Law No. 13.303 regulating state-owned enterprises, alongside the persistent institutional and cultural barriers to transparency and accountability. Pinotti highlights the dangers posed by political fragmentation, impunity, and institutional weaknesses, while remaining cautiously optimistic about the potential for civic mobilisation and reform.

Central to her analysis is the conceptual differentiation between compliance systems and broader integrity systems—where integrity encompasses transparency, meritocracy, innovation, fair competition, social responsibility, and sustainability. She stresses that reputation is a company's most valuable asset and that genuine integrity must be embedded in organisational culture rather than enforced solely through compliance.

Throughout, Pinotti advocates for systemic institutional reforms, including judicial independence, electoral and political party reform, tax system simplification, and stronger mechanisms for oversight and accountability. She warns against complacency and the risk of regression but affirms the importance of continuing to build on the legacy of anti-corruption initiatives like Operation Car Wash to achieve a more just and prosperous Brazil.

Could you please describe your educational background and personal journey to provide context for your professional trajectory?

Interestingly, after a considerable journey, I feel as though I have come full circle—returning to my origins and my alma mater. I studied Public Administration at FGV EAESP,[117] at the very beginning of my studies, a course in Constitutional Law was taught by Bandeira de Mello.[118] This occurred during the military regime, a time marked by censorship and prohibitions against criticising the government. It was a stifling atmosphere. Yet, within that class, there was complete freedom to discuss the arbitrariness imposed on the country from an institutional and constitutional perspective. Outside the university, however, student gatherings were banned. I was fascinated and nearly switched to Law. However, I was ultimately drawn to Economics, which provided a powerful and elegant explanation of human behaviour and the workings of the world. Nevertheless, those discussions about democratic values, justice, and ethics—freely debated within an academic setting amidst a dictatorship—left a lasting impression on me.

After graduating, I worked in macroeconomic analysis at Unibanco, where I had the opportunity to learn from Rubén Almonacid,[119] an Argentine economist fresh from his PhD in Chicago. Later, I returned to FGV to pursue a master's in economics. Before completing it, though, I moved to University of São Paulo to begin a doctoral programme. I wrote a thesis—*The Impact of Financial Innovations on Money Demand*—but did not end up defending it. At that time, I was balancing work, motherhood, and the excitement of discovering a vast world still ahead. One notable aspect of my life is that I have always had the privilege of working with excellent teachers—true mentors—from whom I have learned immensely and continue to learn.

Later, I moved into applied macroeconomic consulting—first at MBE consulting firm, with José Roberto Mendonça de Barros[120] and Ibrahim Eris,[121] and then at A. C. Pastore & Associates, founded by Affonso

Pastore,[122] whom I later married. What continues to attract me to Economics is how it helps us understand human behaviour—just like History, Psychology, Political Science, and Anthropology do.

Around 2015, during the Car Wash operation, I came across an article by Sergio Moro on *Mani Pulite*[123] in Italy and found it fascinating. A few months later, while visiting my daughter (who was studying Law at FGV) in Italy, I came across Gherardo Colombo[124]—*Letter to a Son on Clean Hands* (Letter to a son about Clean Hands).[125] I was struck by how similar the Italian case was to what we were seeing in Brazil. That is when I started diving into the topic more deeply, particularly from the perspective of corruption theory and its economic costs—something that is been studied by economists abroad since the 1970s. Think of names like Douglass North,[126] Daron Acemoglu,[127] and James Robinson,[128] among many others.

Their key idea is this: economic development hinges on the quality of institutions. When institutions are built for the common good, countries prosper, and corruption is low. When they're shaped to serve narrow interests, development stagnates and corruption soars. In that sense, corruption and poverty go hand in hand, as I often say. After all, corruption is the abuse of public power for private gain. When the state is captured by special interests, public services—healthcare, education, safety, transport, infrastructure—suffer. Citizens pay taxes, but the services they receive are of poor quality because some of those resources are siphoned off.

That is why I feel, in some ways, that I have returned to the same principles I learned in my undergraduate studies: the fundamentals of good public administration and the importance of ethics in managing public affairs.

One of the major distinctions in corruption theory lies between public and private corruption. My focus has always been on public corruption. Private corruption is typically a transfer of income within the private sector—say, a corrupt firm losing out in a competitive market. Of course, there are exceptions, like corruption in football, which can have a lasting impact on consumers, but that is not the same as diverting taxpayer money.

My interest lies primarily in public corruption due to its profound implications for economic and social development, income distribution, and overall societal well-being. After many years in economics, I feel as though I have returned to my roots—now integrating development theory with the imperative for ethical and efficient public administration.

As the organiser of the book *Corruption: Car Wash and Clean Hands*[129] and recognised as one of Brazil's foremost experts on the topic, could you elucidate the parallels between the Clean Hands Operation and Operation Car Wash? Which aspects do you find most striking?

There are numerous similarities, as well as some notable differences. Clean Hands was an overwhelming, brief, and intense operation, the effects of which continue to resonate across the economic, social, and political spheres of the country, even after three decades. It is important to note that it took place during a particularly dramatic period in Italian history, marked by the brutal murders of magistrates[130] and Paolo Borsellino[131] by the mafia. These killings came as a direct response to the "Maxi Trial", which, for the first time, saw the top bosses of the Palermo mafia sentenced to prison. Organised crime always relies on corruption to operate, and while there was initially strong public support for combating corruption, the mafia had already begun infiltrating the political system more deeply as a survival strategy. Both aspects played a crucial role in shaping the course of Clean Hands.

Until Car Wash emerged, Clean Hands was considered the largest anti-corruption operation of its kind. It uncovered crimes including corruption, illegal party financing, falsified accounts, and money laundering. The three most well-known figures involved were Piercamillo Davigo,[132] Gherardo Colombo, and Antonio Di Pietro.[133] In practice, the operation lasted just under three years. It began in February 1992 and formally ended in 2005, but its golden phase ran only until mid-1994, when the political system began to push back changing the rules to limit judicial action and ensure the persistence of corruption. There had been previous anti-corruption efforts in Italy, but none matched the scope and impact of Clean Hands. One of the most notorious cases before that involved the Ambrosiano Bank[134] and the Masonic lodge "Propaganda

Due", or P2,[135] in which Gherardo Colombo was also involved. Despite the extensive evidence collected, that case was swiftly buried after the change of jurisdiction from Milan to Rome.

By chance—as was the case with the start of Car Wash—Clean Hands began with the discovery of a small bribe, around five thousand euros, paid to a public official. It is that classic thing: you lift a feather and end up uncovering a nest full of dinosaurs. And they went after the dinosaurs. Nearly five thousand people were implicated in the investigations, including four former Prime Ministers, a dozen state ministers, over one hundred and fifty members of Parliament (current and former), party secretaries, regional and municipal officials, officers of the "Guardia di Finanza" (Italy's financial crime police), executives from the country's largest companies, employees of public enterprises, and even judges. Corruption was not the exception—it was the rule of the game. It had become systemic, deeply embedded in Italy's political, social, and economic structures.

The Clean Hands task force confronted immense challenges given the technological and societal conditions of the period. With no internet, communication relied on fax, photocopies, and other analogue methods. Public access to information was limited to media reports, subject to inevitable editorial filters. Unlike in Brazil, the public could not directly witness testimonies or view evidence. Nevertheless, this initial wave of investigations sparked an unforeseen phenomenon: businesspeople began voluntarily approaching magistrates to confess and cooperate. The escape of then Prime Minister Craxi[136] to Tunisia, in an attempt to evade the ten lawsuits, he faced, illustrates the profound fear that had gripped the political system. He never returned to Italy and ultimately died in exile.

What was the ultimate outcome of these events? The backlash manifested on multiple fronts. Notably, there was a sustained campaign to discredit the task force members, orchestrated by the political establishment and reinforced by a media landscape heavily reliant on state funding and advertising from large corporations. There was even an attempt to frame Gherardo Colombo by planting money in a Swiss account under his name. Di Pietro, too, was targeted—with a dossier full of falsehoods and baseless accusations, which eventually led him to step away from the operation. The slogan "criminalisation of politics" was used relentlessly, even in the face of public confessions by politicians and business leaders. And of course, the mafias played their part, discreetly but effectively, to bring down an operation that was seriously threatening their operations.

In addition to the campaign in the press, there is another aspect I find important to highlight. Tax evasion in Italy is significantly higher compared to its European peers. While the "big fish" were being arrested, the public applauded. But when the investigations started to reach the smaller accountants—those handling the books for doctors, architects, and small business owners who were dodging some of the many taxes—the mood shifted. People began to criticise the operation, saying it had gone too far. As members of the Judiciary were also implicated in corruption, the smear campaign eventually targeted the magistrates too, further fuelling public distrust.

This helped create the perfect environment for the political system to strike back, changing the laws under the pretext of ending the "persecution" of the corrupt. The Biondi Decree,[137] in 1994[138] which blocked pre-trial detention for suspects in corruption cases, was not ratified by Parliament because it was unconstitutional—but it still saved most of those who'd been arrested by Mani Pulite from staying in jail. Prescription periods were drastically shortened, evidence was scrapped, and the definition of the crime of abuse of office was rewritten, significantly lowering the penalties. Accounting fraud was no longer punishable, effectively burying many corruption cases. In short, a sense of impunity, and a culture of *omertà*, created fertile ground for corruption to carry on unchecked.

An examination of the World Bank's Rule of Law index for Italy reveals a clear and steady decline beginning in the mid-1990s—coinciding with the period when Mani Pulite was dismantled. Prior to this, Italy's trajectory closely paralleled that of the rest of Europe. At the same time, Italy's economic growth and productivity, which had also mirrored its European peers, began to diverge, leading to a long period of stagnation. Why? Because corruption corrodes economic efficiency. Public works are poorly chosen. Take, for example, MOSE[139]—the barrier system for Venice. It took nearly 35 years to complete, with countless officials, politicians, and contractors arrested during Mani Pulite and later investigations. But they always managed to escape real consequences. Public projects dragged on endlessly, contracts were renegotiated time and time again, and projected costs ballooned—sometimes by a factor of three, five, even six. High-speed trains built in Italy cost up to four times more than in Spain or France. A lot of money was spent, but public welfare was compromised, and the economy suffered.

For many reasons, the comparison between Car Wash and Mani Pulite is inevitable. To start with, consider the historical context—here in Brazil, we had the mass protests in 2013[140] which alarmed Congress and stopped efforts to curb the powers of the Public Prosecutor's Office, as proposed in the Constitutional Amendment Proposal No. 37.[141] New legal tools also emerged to support the fight against corruption, like the Organised Crime Law,[142] which formalised plea bargains, and the Clean Company Act,[143] which introduced leniency agreements for companies. While we did not have a "Maxi Trial" like in Italy, we did have the Mensalão case,[144] which may represent the peak of judicial effectiveness in punishing corruption in Brazil—particularly due to the novel use of the "domain of the facts" theory.

Another relevant factor is the deep cultural and legal connection between Brazil and Italy. Besides the strong presence of Italian immigrants in Brazil, our legal system borrowed heavily from Italian law—both its strengths and its flaws. It is well known that Sergio Moro studied Mani Pulite closely and adapted some of the strategies used in Milan. And of course, the fact that these were the two biggest anti-corruption operations in their respective countries naturally invites comparison. Learning from history is always worthwhile.

Car Wash started in a similar fashion to Mani Pulite—as a money laundering investigation that seemed small at first but soon began to uncover what had long been whispered about in the media and among the public. We'd heard stories of dodgy Petrobras projects, both here and abroad. Of political parties receiving shady funds here and there. I always make a point of stressing: corruption in Brazil did not begin with the Workers' Party.[145] It has always existed, in varying degrees, under governments from the left, right, and centre. By definition, corruption is the abuse of public power for private gain—so whoever's in power at the time is the one committing it. It is impossible to measure the exact extent of corruption, given the diffuse nature of its victims. However, institutional loosening occurred, which allowed corruption to grow and become systemic. Alongside the similarities, it is also important to acknowledge some differences between the two cases—differences that give me hope for a different outcome here in Brazil. For one, petty corruption in Brazil is very low. By that I mean the kind that affects ordinary people: paying bribes to get documents, school places, medical appointments, and so on. This kind of everyday corruption is widespread in some parts of Africa and Latin America, but not here. According to a 2019 Transparency International report, only twelve per cent of Brazilians reported paying bribes to access public services, compared to thirty-five per cent in Mexico and fifty per cent in Venezuela. Scheduling a medical appointment here might mean waiting in line, but bribery is not part of the equation.

That said, we do have a troubling issue with electoral corruption. In poorer regions, there is a sort of tacit agreement between voters and those who offer something in return for votes: "Vote for me and I will make sure your child gets a school place; if you need a doctor, I will get you an appointment; if you need an ambulance, I will arrange the transport." This is deeply concerning because it benefits candidates who spend the most and incentivises them to maintain the very scarcity of public services—schools, hospitals, ambulances—as a form of political currency. From the southern regions of the country downward, such practices appear less prevalent. With this caveat in mind, it can still be argued that petty corruption in Brazil remains relatively low, at least for the time being.

On the other hand, despite having an extremely complex, opaque, inefficient, and unfair tax system, the Federal Revenue is highly efficient, especially in collecting taxes on payroll. In other words, those in the formal sector, including small and medium-sized entrepreneurs, have no way to escape. No one can avoid the heavy burden of indirect taxes, which are highly regressive and disproportionately affect the poorest. As a result, the population bears an exception ally high tax burden, around thirty-four per cent of GDP, which exceeds that of countries with similar income levels. People are aware that they are paying a significant amount in taxes, yet the quality of the public services they receive is very poor. A large part of this imbalance is due to the misappropriation resulting from corruption.

We've always known this, but after Operation Car Wash, the population saw an apartment being rented to store suitcases filled with banknotes.[146] They saw money being smuggled out of pizzerias and taken to unknown destinations,[147] among many other examples. One of the great merits of Operation Car Wash was exposing the inner workings of grand corruption—corruption involving big businessmen and high-ranking officials in the Executive, Legislative, and Judicial branches, revolving around major public works and state-owned companies. Showing these actions is far more impactful than simply describing them; the images stick in the mind and remain there. Brazilian society, in general, does not engage in acts of corruption but suffers from its harmful effects. Therefore, they are in favour of the fight against corruption. They know they do not receive the appropriate returns for the taxes they pay, particularly in the areas of health, education, public security, and infrastructure.

I remain confident that civil society can organise itself in a way that facilitates a transition, building a more ethical and just country. Achieving this requires changing the rules that have led to the current situation. Much work remains, beginning with tax reform to simplify the system and ensure it is transparent, efficient, and equitable. The Judiciary must become more effective, and the law must be applied equally to all. The political system also needs reform, with greater transparency in party spending and a reduction in fragmentation, which remains a problem. Although improvements have been made, the system remains far from fully functional. As the country faces challenges to growth, municipal and state governments frequently act as "employers of last resort," appointing unqualified individuals, thereby inflating the public sector and contributing to rising costs and inefficiency. There is an urgent need for a public administration reform that focuses on the efficiency of spending and programmes.

Operation Car Wash exposed this scenario, and now it is up to civil society to propose changes and pressure the political class—this is one of its great legacies. It's important to note that large anti-corruption operations do not end corruption. Their role is to investigate, expose crimes, and punish wrongdoers, but corruption only decreases when institutions are reformed to prevent it from reaching such extreme levels. It is not the responsibility of Operation Car Wash, or any other operation, to eradicate corruption. Laws are needed that enable the prosecution and punishment of corrupt individuals, rather than allowing cases to end in failure and perpetuating impunity. Looking at the results, our institutional framework is not yet equipped to contain and punish corruption, as evidenced by recent events. Moving forward, the country faces the difficult task of rewriting what has failed and continues to fail, and which has allowed grand corruption to flourish.

It has been noted that corruption in Brazil did not begin with the Workers' Party. How would you characterise the current landscape of public corruption in the country?

The response began by noting that corruption did not originate with the Workers' Party; however, it undoubtedly expanded as a consequence of institutional weaknesses that developed over time. One of these weaknesses is the enormous party fragmentation that followed the fall of the party clause barrier.[148]

This was partially addressed in 2018, although there are still those who attempt to downplay the significance of that change. With party fragmentation, democracy faces a serious risk, because instead of representing the population's interests, political parties become mere facilitators of obscure, profitable ventures. Very few people benefiting from the current situation will take the initiative to change the rules unless they feel significant pressure from society. Therefore, creating majorities in Congress is difficult—and costly in terms of budgetary resources—with such majorities often being fleeting.

In this context, Operation Car Wash and the fight against corruption are undergoing a dismantling process. There are even parliamentarians who openly defend nepotism,[149] arguing that "my son cannot be harmed just because I am a parliamentarian". This argument is deeply flawed. This is the price of entering public life. If a parliamentarian's son is competent, the private sector will welcome him with open arms.

There needs to be transparency in accounting, particularly regarding the financing of electoral campaigns, which used to be handled by the private sector but has now returned to the public sector. It was good that this responsibility shifted away from the private sector, because there were no checks in place to prevent companies with connections to municipal, state, and federal governments from making donations. However, now it is up to parliament itself to decide how much it will receive from the party fund[150] and the transparency of spending remains minimal. Party Transparency[151] did manage to digitise the accounts, which is a step forward. Stacks of receipt were once sent to the Superior Electoral Court two or three years after each election. Now, it is in a reasonably understandable spreadsheet. But the accounts are still annual, with significant delays, and there are numerous loopholes for unsubstantiated expenses, such as those related to party foundations and others.

What we are seeing is an attempt to expand the privileges and protections for parliamentarians. In addition to the privileged forum,[152] there is the issue of executing sentences after a second-instance ruling[153] which was a problem during Mensalão. It was changed and later reinstated, leaving the country in the unenviable position of being the only one requiring trial in four instances before a sentence can be executed. Given the excessive number of appeals in our legal system, those who can afford good lawyers rarely face prison. This, in turn, perpetuates impunity. As a citizen, I believe justice in Brazil was designed not to work for everyone—full stop. One fact that particularly shocks me is that the number of lawyers in Brazil is double the number of doctors. I would argue that this is a very sick country. The average citizen needs doctors, not an abundance of lawyers. This reflects a bloated, sluggish, and consequently inefficient Judiciary. Such a system neither contributes to the country's development nor promotes greater fairness or civility. Amid this process, the ethical dimension has been entirely eclipsed.

In retrospect, which aspects of Operation Car Wash most surprised you or challenged your expectations?

There were several surprising aspects. While corruption had long been suspected, the sheer scale of the scheme—and the ease with which it was conducted—was profoundly shocking, as revealed through the testimonies and evidence presented. It really was like a parallel universe, where the rules of the game involved engaging in corruption without the slightest hint of embarrassment. That is why it is accurate to say that Car Wash uncovered a situation of systemic corruption. It was the norm, and whether it was right or wrong, ethical or legal, did not seem to matter in the slightest. Sergio Machado,[154] in his plea bargain testimony, described Petrobras as "the most honest madam in the cabarets of Brazil." According to him, bribes on government contracts followed a sort of price list: at the federal level, it was common to pay three per cent; at the state level, between five per cent and ten per cent; and at the municipal level, anywhere from ten per cent to thirty per cent. It is dramatic.

Another surprise was the strong public support for Car Wash—a pleasant surprise, really. From the start, the operation faced a great deal of opposition from the media, and there were several attempts to delegitimise it and discredit the judges involved. Yet, despite all that, the majority of the population consistently backed it and gave it real momentum.

More recently, I was surprised—negatively, this time—by the reaction of the political establishment. I had sincerely believed that lessons would have been learned that a sense of shame would prevail regarding the revelations, and that a significant number of our representatives retained fundamental decency and ethics. However, this was not the case. Instead of remorse, what emerged were attacks and slander. A sort of "How dare they come after us?" attitude. Many continue to behave as though above the law, steadfastly clinging to the privileges afforded by the so-called privileged jurisdiction.

It is not a matter of learning; it is a matter of interests—and for those interests to prevail, impunity is essential. Unless society demands institutional reform, insists on ethics and transparency in public life, and calls for laws that apply equally to all—regardless of individual identity or prevailing political winds—the risk remains of regressing to a pre-civilised state, where the law of the strongest prevails.

That said, some hope remains that backsliding will be limited. If ten steps have been taken forward, it is hoped that only two or three will be lost. Furthermore, it is anticipated that the next election will bring forth leaders genuinely committed to an anti-corruption agenda—individuals prepared to reform the legal system, enhance the efficiency and speed of the judiciary, and simplify the tax system and broader public administration.

In short, the negative surprise was realising just how deep and widespread the corruption was—but the positive surprise was seeing just how much support came from the Brazilian society.

Is there a shared institutional basis underlying the culture of impunity observed in both Brazil and Italy?

First of all, I believe impunity has both institutional and cultural causes. Culture is an extremely important factor, but it does not exist or operate in a vacuum. It may have a great deal of inertia—yes, that is true—but it can change. There is a constant interaction between culture and institutions—institutions shape culture, and culture, in turn, shapes institutions. The judiciary plays a key role in mediating this relationship, by applying the law and ensuring it is respected.

When it comes to cultural change, a good example is the hyperinflation we experienced in Brazil. For years, newspapers, television, and everyday conversations all repeated the idea that inflation in Brazil was a cultural issue—that nothing could ever eliminate it, because "Brazilians had a culture of inflation." But that was not the case. All it took was political will and a well-crafted economic plan—one that was solid from a theoretical perspective, backed by legal and institutional support, and clearly communicated to the public. And just like that, inflation was brought under control.

The same goes for impunity. However deeply rooted it may be, it can change. For such change to occur, clear laws and rules are required—those that serve the common good, apply equally to all, and are enforced by a judiciary that is both efficient and independent from political influence.

On the issue of judicial inefficiency, I mentioned earlier the surprising number of lawyers in Brazil. It is a similar situation in Italy. A comparison of the number of lawyers in Italy with those in countries such as France, Spain, or Germany reveals that Italy has double or even triple the number. And when it comes to the time it takes to resolve legal cases, Italy also takes twice or three times as long as its European counterparts.

In Italy, the public perception of impunity really worsened after the dismantling of Mani Pulite. And if you ask me what is happening in Brazil after Justice Fachin's decision on Monday—I honestly do not know yet.[155] It was a real shock to see an investigation the size of Car Wash, which carried out an enormous amount of work over seven years, with convictions upheld by higher courts, suddenly being called into question because, as it turns out, none of it should have taken place in Curitiba, but rather in Brasília. It is a blow to the very heart of the Brazilian judicial system.

I can only imagine what the average citizen must be thinking—someone who followed the testimonies, saw the evidence—and now it is all just... dismissed? Does that really reflect the role of justice? It is devastating. It feels like a celebration of impunity.

If no changes occur and the current trajectory continues, the country faces dark times ahead, marked by further institutional decay and the legalisation of corruption. There remains hope that some progress can be made in the coming weeks and months.

During the trials for the Mensalão scandal, many of the defendants were reportedly still receiving bribes linked to the Car Wash operation. What is your perspective on this overlap?

While the Mensalão case was still underway, some defendants continued engaging in corrupt activities, confident they would evade accountability. It bears repeating: no anti-corruption operation can eradicate corruption entirely. Such operations serve primarily to expose wrongdoing and, when possible, hold perpetrators to account. However, lasting change requires reforming the legal framework. Anti-corruption efforts are invaluable for revealing the reality of corruption, but it is ultimately the responsibility of the Legislature to enact laws that effectively prevent it. Without genuine political will, meaningful progress remains elusive. This distinction is critical.

Could you elaborate on the role that task forces played in the investigation and prosecution efforts during Operation Car Wash?

Task forces were absolutely vital, especially considering that corruption crimes have become extremely complex and increasingly global. Investigators have to piece together a massive puzzle, which often involves highly sophisticated money laundering schemes using tax havens and offshores that are notoriously difficult to access. If the work is spread out across different regions, it becomes fragmented—and in some cases, nearly impossible.

The importance of teamwork cannot be overstated. It means everyone involved can keep up with the progress of the investigation, and if someone falls ill or is transferred, others can continue the work without delay. This results in much faster, more efficient investigations.

Some people have expressed concern about concentrating too much power in the hands of a task force. But there are control mechanisms in place to deal with that. The success of the "Maxi Process" against the Palermo mafia, which I mentioned earlier, shows just how effective this type of approach can be.

If there were any excesses along the way, I cannot point them out—this underscores the essential role of oversight bodies. When corruption reaches such a scale, strategies and techniques commensurate with the challenge are required.

Operation Car Wash led to the arrest of numerous wealthy and influential Brazilian businessmen, yet comparatively few politicians faced prosecution. To what extent might this disparity have affected the operation's overall outcome?

Certainly. Where are the cases involving the politicians who were indicted? They are sitting in the Supreme Court[490], gathering dust in some drawer, waiting for the statute of limitations—or other "miracles"—to kick in. There are several things that need to be re-evaluated. As a citizen, I look at the outcomes and cannot help but notice how differently things work in other countries. Take José Maria Marin,[156] for example—he served five years in New York for corruption, while others involved in the same scandals walked freely here.

These are the twists and turns of our justice system—technicalities and loopholes that render it inefficient. Yet there are places where justice is fast and effective, and still fully respectful of the defendant's rights. Here, though, we seem to almost deify the defendant. There is a mistaken idea about the role of punishment—it is meant to deter antisocial behaviour and set an example. On top of that, income inequality influences how justice is applied, reinforcing the status quo.

Institutions—particularly written laws and rules—reflect the prevailing political balance of power at any given time. However, signs of growing friction are evident, as seen in the trivialisation of constitutional amendments. The Constitution, just over 30 years old, has already undergone more than one hundred Constitutional Amendment Proposal, with some proposals[157] effectively cancelling out previous ones. This creates the impression that the institutional framework is built not on solid ground, but on quicksand—or, worse, a tectonic fault line. Resolving these political tensions through democratic means requires political parties that genuinely represent the public interest.

How can legal certainty be assured under such conditions? Businesspeople were the ones who paid the biggest price—legally and reputationally. So why did not politicians face the same consequences?

And there is one important institutional change I haven't mentioned yet, which has caused serious harm to our democracy—the introduction of re-election. That was the first major crack in the 1988 Constitution. In fact, Fernando Henrique[158] recently acknowledged publicly that allowing re-election was a mistake. Much of the energy in a president's first term ends up being spent securing a second. The alternation of power is vital in a democracy.

This returns the discussion to the root of the problem: political parties. No one wants to demonise politics—quite the opposite, it is a noble endeavour. There is no democracy without politics and political parties. But a political party should be serious, grounded in a programme, able to engage with the electorate, and committed to the common good. The privileged forum that shields politicians from prosecution sends entirely the wrong message and should not exist.

If we start closing the loopholes that perpetuate the rule of "those in charge do not follow the rules"—as Professor Roberto Da Matta[159] puts it—we'll begin to build a path towards a more honest and prosperous nation.

Corruption, after all, is an entirely rational crime. Unlike crimes of passion or violence, corruption is carefully planned. People meet in private to figure out the best way to maximise gain, to hide and launder the money, and so on. It is all based on a calculated cost–benefit analysis. The cost is the risk of being caught and punished. The gain is how much can be made. If there is no real risk—no cost—then there is every incentive to carry on as before.

It would be encouraging if different sectors of society could come together and agree on what needs to change in Brazil, if we truly want to take the country seriously.

In conclusion, how would you assess the positive and negative outcomes of Operation Car Wash?

That really depends on what happens next. It is entirely possible that, ten years from now, we'll see an operation even bigger than this one—or worse, that we'll follow the same path as Italy: broad institutional weakening, a kind of liberalisation of corruption, and increasing difficulty in identifying and punishing wrongdoing.

Should the gates be thrown wide open to the "Centrão," and the powers of the Speaker of the Congress continue to expand unchecked, alongside the weakening of oversight bodies, the country faces a serious institutional backslide. There is a very worrying agenda in Congress: removing any kind of financial oversight from political parties, attacking the barrier clause, reversing second-instance imprisonment, even reintroducing nepotism. If that agenda goes forward, in five to ten years we could be stuck with a stagnant economy, institutions captured by narrow interests, widening inequality, and no national vision or project.

Unless civil society assumes a leading role in rebuilding the country, the nation risks sliding down the same path observed in other Latin American countries.

Operation Car Wash, by putting pressure on the system, exposed its weak points. It made clear, for instance, how essential it is to have a judiciary that is both efficient and independent from political influence. But the system of checks and balances we once had had been eroded.

Take the nomination and approval of justices to the Federal Supreme Court, for example. On paper, it sounds like a decent system: the President nominates, and the Senate reviews and approves (or not). But in practice, things get complicated. Because of the privileged forum, the senator in charge of the confirmation hearing may one day be judged by the very person they are evaluating. So, most prefer not to make waves. What you end up with is a kind of cosy arrangement, rather than a proper, objective assessment of the candidate's qualifications.

This contrasts sharply with the procedures observed in the US Congress.

Exactly. Over there, the questioning is taken seriously—several nominees have actually been rejected. Here, the whole process often feels like a foregone conclusion, a game of marked cards, driven by the wrong incentives—mainly due to the existence of the privileged forum.

Back then, Operation Car Wash exposed the symbiotic and murky relationship between the private sector and government. The dynamics between the Judiciary and Congress are now becoming increasingly apparent. What are the cracks in the system? What is not working properly in our democracy itself? These are important questions—not just in relation to corruption, but for the very survival of democracy in Brazil.

Car Wash revealed many of these weaknesses. It is now up to us, civil society, to come up with proposals and push for meaningful reform. That, I believe, is the operation's greatest legacy.

It is hard to point to negatives. Mistakes may have been made, but mistakes are part of any human endeavour. For me, a greater mistake is legitimising the profession of a hacker, for example. Or using private conversations between a judge and a prosecutor as evidence to overturn decisions. If that is acceptable, then all judges should be expected to hand over their phones for public inspection—always. It is absurd. A horror show.

From a positive perspective, Operation Car Wash laid bare the many fractures within our system. The pressing question is how this knowledge will be utilised. Will there be a commitment to progressing towards a more honest, prosperous, and just nation for future generations?

Maria Cristina Pinotti was born in Itápolis (SP). Partner of A. C. Pastore & Associates. Author of several books and articles on the theory of corruption and the history of the Clean Hands operation. Her testimony was given on 12 March 2021 via the Zoom virtual platform and lasted 1 hour and 3 minutes of recording. The transcript was subsequently reviewed by the interviewee on 15 February 2023.

Testimony of Michel Temer

Michel Temer's testimony offers a comprehensive reflection on his legal and political career and his perspectives on Brazil's fight against corruption, particularly in relation to Operation Car Wash. Tracing his journey from his education at the Law School of Largo São Francisco through roles as Attorney General and Secretary of Public Security to his tenure as President of the Chamber of Deputies, Vice-President, and ultimately President of Brazil, Temer situates his experience within the broader constitutional and institutional framework of the country.

Temer emphasises the constitutional basis for the fight against corruption, underscoring its permanence as a legal and political duty rather than a transient campaign. He addresses misconceptions surrounding the cessation of anti-corruption efforts and stresses the essential role of institutions such as the Public Prosecutor's Office and the Judiciary, highlighting their functional independence and constitutional guarantees.

Responding to controversies including his issuance of a presidential pardon and the impeachment of Dilma Rousseff, Temer clarifies his positions and attributes political dynamics and economic challenges as primary factors behind significant events. He recognises the transformative impact of Operation Car Wash on private sector conduct, particularly regarding the adoption of compliance mechanisms, while also critiquing legal excesses and judicial conduct during the operation.

Temer offers insights into the complexities of Brazil's institutional framework, including constitutional provisions, judicial processes, and political party dynamics, advocating for adherence to the rule of law as the foundation for combating corruption effectively. He reflects on Brazil's international engagements, including its pursuit of OECD membership, while maintaining that anti-corruption efforts must be rooted in domestic legal reforms and political will.

Concluding with a call for optimism amid challenges such as the COVID-19 pandemic, Temer stresses the importance of unity, democratic principles, and institutional resilience in navigating Brazil's future. His testimony provides valuable legal and political perspectives on governance, accountability, and the enduring struggle against corruption in Brazil.

To provide some context, could you please describe your educational background and personal journey?

I studied at the University of São Paulo Law School of Largo São Francisco, which means we are actually university colleagues. My decision to pursue law was influenced in part by the fact that three of my older brothers had already attended the same institution. It was at Largo São Francisco that my political journey began. In my first year, I successfully ran for the position of second treasurer of the "XI de Agosto Academic Centre", which is the student union. Later, during my fourth year, I campaigned for the presidency of the Centre, though I was not elected on that occasion.

After graduating, I became an assistant to Professor Ataliba Nogueira,[160] father of Geraldo Ataliba,[161] who had been appointed Secretary of Education. He invited me to work as an office official. I stayed in that role for about two years, then began practising law. Around that time, I also took the exam to become a State Prosecutor. I passed and became a prosecutor, but I still had the freedom to practise law, which I did.

Encouraged by Geraldo Ataliba and Celso Antônio Bandeira de Mello,[162] I pursued a doctorate in Constitutional Law at Pontifical Catholic University of São Paulo. I started teaching quite early as well—both at Pontifical Catholic University of São Paulo and later at the Law School of Itu. Eventually, Governor Franco Montoro[163] invited me to serve as Attorney General of the State. That was back in 1983 or 1984. I held that position for a year, and then I was appointed Secretary of Public Security for the State of São Paulo.

At one point, Franco Montoro said to me, "Temer, you work with Constitutional Law—why not run for the Constituent Assembly?" I followed his advice and ended up being elected. I was actually a substitute, but I soon took up a seat in the Congress as a constituent congressperson, which was a great honour. After completing that mandate from 1986 to 1990, I returned as Attorney General of the State under the Fleury government,[164] and a year later, I was once again appointed Secretary of Public Security of the state of São Paulo.

I returned to the Congress in 1994, was elected leader of my party, and later became President of the Chamber of Deputies twice—from 1997 to 1998, and again from 1999 to 2000, during the Fernando Henrique Cardoso government.[165] I chaired my party for many years while continuing my legislative work and teaching Constitutional Law—this is something I have never ceased doing. In 2009, I was elected President of the Chamber of Deputies for the third time, after which I became Vice-President of the Republic and subsequently President.

Having been Vice-President from 2010 to 2016 and subsequently President of the Republic until 2018, how would you assess the changes in the country's political, economic, and social situation since the beginning of Operation Car Wash in Curitiba in 2014?

First and foremost, it is important to clarify that "Car Wash" was the informal name given to the task force—it is not a legal term. Legally, the matter pertains to the fight against administrative misconduct and corruption. These are the legal instruments in play. Car Wash is more of a journalistic expression, but it gained traction and, without a doubt, had an impact. After all, the fight against corruption and the preservation of administrative integrity are constitutional matters.

The Constitution itself provides several mechanisms for oversight—not only through the judiciary, the Public Prosecutor's Office, and the Federal Court of Accounts, but also through internal controls within the executive branch and external controls as well. These are all tools to prevent and address administrative misconduct.

Expanding on the question, recent rulings—particularly by the Federal Supreme Court—have given rise to the notion that "the fight against corruption has come to an end". I find that quite strange. Frankly, such alarmism appears incompatible with constitutional reality and the country's actual needs. The fight against corruption, from both political and administrative perspectives, must be ongoing—not by personal decree but because it is mandated by the Constitution.

In reality, anyone who fails to combat corruption is, effectively, complicit in the crime. This form of fearmongering—if the term may be permitted—is unfortunately widespread.

For instance, when I was President, I issued a Christmas pardon—something that, according to the Constitution, falls under the exclusive competence of the President of the Republic. "Exclusive", by definition, means that no one else has the authority to do it. Yet, despite this clear mandate, a judicial action was taken, and an injunction was issued to suspend the effects of the pardon. At that time, there was a wave of statements alleging—once again, under this type of legal alarmism—that two hundred or three hundred individuals convicted of corruption would benefit from my action.

That simply was not true—not to be impolite and call it a lie. Do you know how long it took for the Supreme Court to judge this matter and declare my act absolutely constitutional? One year and two months.[166] And they only did so because the Public Defender's Office kept pointing out that thousands of poor individuals were still in prison, even though they were eligible for the pardon—all because of this unfounded fear that two hundred or three hundred convicted in the Car Wash Operation might benefit.

By the time the Court ultimately ruled the pardon constitutional, those individuals had already served over a year longer in prison than warranted—entirely due to this legally misguided opposition. And when it was eventually reviewed who exactly would have benefited among those convicted in the Car Wash Operation, there were only a few—and by then, most had already served at least a sixth of their sentence.[167] It's a curious thing. Why do I say this? Why do I give this example? Because I believe it is harmful to go around saying things like "Car Wash is over" or "the fight against corruption is over". The fight against corruption never ends. It is not optional—it is a duty, a constitutional requirement, an expression of popular sovereignty as laid out in our Federal Constitution.

How would you assess the prevailing culture of impunity in Brazil?

Impunity is not readily apparent; rather, institutions appear to be functioning. Consider the number of individuals—from both the political sphere and the business sector—who have faced consequences. These involve white-collar crimes which, historically, often went unpunished, but this is no longer the case. Many individuals have been convicted, many have been investigated, and many have faced various penalties. Some have entered into plea bargain agreements, and from those bargains came leniency agreements for companies.

So, I do not believe there is widespread impunity today. There might be the occasional manoeuvre, but it would always be a legal or judicial one—and even then, I do not see people committing crimes and walking away without consequence. Of course, this discussion refers to impunity in a broad sense. Considering the criminal justice system more generally, Brazil has one of the largest prison populations worldwide, second only to the United States. The country has over eight hundred thousand detainees.[168] This hardly suggests a nation where crime goes detainees. This hardly points to a country where crime goes unpunished—whether we are talking about so-called common crimes or white-collar offences.

Nowadays, with the internet, transparency, a free press, and the speed at which information circulates. It is difficult to understand how one could argue that impunity prevails.

Do you consider the functional independence of the Public Prosecutor's Office to have been crucial to the success of Operation Car Wash?

I think it was one of the fundamental elements. During the Constituent Assembly, as I come from a legal background, it was only natural that I was approached by people from the legal field, including those from the Public Prosecutor's Office, the judiciary, and the lawyers. I must admit, my office ended up being something of a headquarters for the work of the Public Prosecutor's Office, the judiciary, and the lawyers.

The Constituent Assembly was divided into general commissions—the commission for the separation of powers, the economic order commission, the individual rights commission, and so on. Within the separation of powers commission, there was a subcommittee dedicated to the Public Prosecutor's Office and the Judiciary. I specifically worked within that commission. I put in a lot of effort to ensure that the Public Prosecutor's Office would have the powers it gained in the Federal Constitution, just as the judiciary and lawyers did.

I was the author of Article 133 of the Federal Constitution, which guarantees the inviolability of lawyers in their practice and makes them indispensable to the administration of justice, alongside the state prosecutors. I also played a role in defining the attributes of the Public Prosecutor's Office. I clearly remember that we focused on ensuring its functional autonomy.

However, what I have observed over time is that functional autonomy was meant to refer to the functions of the Public Prosecutor's Office[169]. Over time, though, it has evolved into individual autonomy, which is a different matter altogether. The Public Prosecutor's Office is comprised of prosecutors who, as the name suggests, are there to promote justice. They are not part of the litigation process in the same way as a lawyer defending a case. Their role is to assess and verify whether justice is being served in an investigation or legal action, not to get emotionally involved as if they were a lawyer advocating for a particular cause.

There have been many occasions when members of the Public Prosecutor's Office have asked, for example, for acquittals in various cases, because their role is to promote justice, not to be on a quest to "win the case." This is not the function of the Public Prosecutor's Office, nor was it what we envisioned for it in the Constituent Assembly. I must stress, though, that it plays an absolutely an important role in defending the democratic state.

Some contend that the impeachment of former President Dilma Rousseff was a consequence of Operation Car Wash. How do you evaluate this assertion?

I do not believe that is the case. I have often said that the former president was a victim of popular mobilisation. Millions of people took to the streets because the economy was not performing well. That is the first point. The second point is that we were facing a negative Gross

Domestic Product. When I took over in May 2016, the GDP was negative at -3.6%. On top of that, there were the so-called fiscal manoeuvres. I do not think this was due to the Car Wash operation.

In fact, I have said this before: from my interactions with the former president, she always came across as a very honest person in both her personal and governmental actions. However, she did not have a good relationship with the National Congress, and without that, it is very difficult to govern. The fiscal manoeuvres and the people in the streets calling for impeachment played a far bigger role, in my view. However, it is my belief that the impeachment was not a consequence of the Car Wash operation.

Whenever Operation Car Wash is mentioned, it often implies extraordinary dishonesty or impropriety; however, in the case of her impeachment, this does not appear to be accurate.

Did Operation Car Wash result in any structural changes within Brazil?

It certainly did, particularly in the fight against corruption. There is no doubt about that. It is important to emphasise, however, that the assertion "now that Operation Car Wash is over, the fight against corruption is over" is simply not accurate. The fight against corruption is everyone's responsibility. Every public administrator, every member of the judiciary, every member of the Public Prosecutor's Office, and every member of the Federal and Civil Police—all of them have a duty to combat corruption.

The Car Wash operation played a significant role in encouraging and, more precisely, bringing visibility to the fight against corruption. However, its impact should be understood within these limits. It does not mean they are the only ones capable of fighting corruption, with all due respect to them, of course. I am not making any personal criticisms, just advocating for the continued fight against corruption and, by extension, the maintenance of administrative probity.

Did Operation Car Wash lead to changes in the relationships and conduct between private companies and the Brazilian state?

It is believed that it did. For instance, compliance has become a central focus within companies, which now commonly maintain dedicated departments or specialists tasked with ensuring appropriate conduct in both private dealings and interactions with public authorities. What I have noticed is that this has become quite beneficial for companies today. I am not just talking about large companies, which were largely sidelined due to the fight against corruption, but in general, companies now have these internal control systems, known as compliance, to oversee and regulate their relationships with both other businesses and the public sector.

I believe this effect was a direct result of the Car Wash operation. Just the other day, I heard about a large company. Years ago, its turnover was fifteen billion, but now it is down to one billion. Still, I must say that companies have significantly improved their relationships both internally and with public authorities.

Operation Car Wash is internationally recognised as a landmark anti-corruption initiative. What aspects of the operation surprised you the most? Was it the values involved, the companies implicated, or the individuals engaged? What factors contributed to its significant impact both nationally and internationally?

For those within the legal profession, such developments should come as little surprise. To slightly exaggerate, there is a strong adherence to strict compliance with the constitutional text. What happened was simply the search for adherence to the Constitution. It was a republican gesture—if I may joke, the ruler sneezed, but it was a republican sneeze. The Republic fundamentally represents the temporariness of mandates, in contrast to the monarchy, where rulers held life tenure. Furthermore, the essence of the Republic lies in the constitutional principle that public affairs belong to the people rather than the ruler. In this system, sovereignty resides with the people, who hold the original power and authority. Those in positions like president, Supreme Court Justices, governors, senators, and deputies are constituted authorities, meaning they are secondary. These developments do not come as a surprise for me, as the struggle against corruption has always been present.

As for the international acclaim, it has been amplified by media coverage. Just like other events abroad often gain regional prestige and international attention, the Car Wash operation became highly publicised, which is why it gained global recognition.

What has been the impact of the changes to Brazil's legal framework for combating corruption implemented since 2018?

Certain excesses have occurred, which, incidentally, affected me personally. On several occasions, judicial conduct and actions by the Public Prosecutor's Office directed towards me were excessive; fortunately, these are now being overturned within the judiciary. If I may add, these rulings have been overturned in a manner that is unfavourable to those who brought the accusations. The idea behind such accusations—some of them three hundred pages long—is that those making them are among the best legal professionals. But when the first-instance judge reviews them, they often say: "This accusation is absurd, it is incompetent." In such cases, there is no need for any further investigation. No need to hear from the accused, no need for witnesses, police, or documents—nothing. It is called a summary acquittal, where the accusation is so absurd that the process does not require instruction, and the person is immediately acquitted. Thankfully, that is been the case for me.

It is often stated that the Constitution encompasses all the necessary provisions for combating corruption. Equally important, it guarantees respect for individual rights, due process, and the right to a fair hearing. Article 5 of the Constitution, in particular, outlines these protections. There are seventy-eight clauses outlining individual rights. These are not exhaustive; they are illustrative, as Paragraph 2 makes clear, stating that the list does not prevent the invocation of other rights derived from the interpretation of the Constitution and international treaties Brazil is part of.

For those of us who are passionate about the Constitution and legal security, it is clear: the fight against corruption is enshrined in the constitutional text, but so too is the protection of due process. The combination of these two principles—observed historically and to be upheld henceforth—constitutes what is commonly referred to as legal security.

During your tenure as President of Brazil, significant efforts were made towards Brazil's accession to the OECD. In your view, would the fight against corruption in Brazil have benefited positively had Brazil succeeded in joining the OECD as anticipated during your term?

It would have had no impact whatsoever. Accession to the OECD is primarily an economic and diplomatic matter concerning relations between states. Naturally, it is not believed that joining the OECD would have eradicated corruption within the country. The fight against corruption is an internal matter; it depends on each country's laws. It is acknowledged that, at the time, there was a proposal to join the OECD; however, my presidency lasted only two and a half years. During that time, I was able to implement what I believe were crucial reforms for the country, such as the public spending cap, labour reform, high school reform, the recovery of state-owned companies, the reduction of inflation, and the lowering of interest rates. But, of course, it was a short term. There was not enough time to achieve everything I aspired to, including pension reform, which was ready to go to the plenary of the Congress for approval in June 2017. Unfortunately, it was not possible at that time. Nonetheless, the National Congress and the public were persuaded of the reform's importance, leading to its approval early in the Bolsonaro administration.

Brazil ratified the OECD Convention against Corruption,[170] which formed the foundation for the Clean Company Act[171]. Recently, the OECD established a special committee to assess developments in Brazil's fight against corruption since 2018. What is your assessment of this committee and its potential impact on the country?

I believe this is a standard procedure for the OECD, reflecting the need for thorough oversight of member states' administrative actions. Naturally, it has always been my view that countries with extremely high levels of corruption would face difficulties in joining the OECD. However, it must be emphasised that accession to the OECD does not, in itself, eliminate corruption within member states. Nonetheless, I regard the establishment of this committee to examine corruption with a positive outlook, recognising it as a significant and commendable initiative.

The Mensalão case was regarded as a milestone in the fight against corruption[172]. However, it is now clear that, during the trial of this case, the corrupt practices later exposed by Operation Car Wash were already occurring. In your view, why did these practices persist? What changes are necessary—political, economic, legal, or perhaps increased enforcement—to effectively address corruption?

I would answer this way: the response to this lies in strict compliance with the existing legal framework. Simply put, adherence to the law is essential. A careful reading of the Constitution reveals numerous provisions specifically dedicated to combating corruption. It is important to note that what is called the Mensalão—a term coined by the media—in fact Justice Ayres Britto,[173] called it criminal action 470,[174] if I'm not mistaken; he did not use the expression Mensalão. Even before the so-called Mensalão, there was the Budget Dwarfs,[175] which dates back to the early 1990s, around 1991, 1992, or 1993. Corruption was already being addressed at that time, was it not? And how was this fight pursued? Not due to the personal will of deputies, senators, or judges, but because it was firmly rooted in legal principles. This battle has been ongoing for a long time, and thankfully it has intensified, especially with the transparency mandated by the 1988 Constitution for all public acts. I believe this has greatly contributed to the fight against corruption.

Could you provide an assessment of the positive and negative outcomes that Operation?

I shall refrain from providing a definitive answer, as Operation Car Wash undoubtedly involved both successes and shortcomings. Furthermore, any commentary on these achievements or errors risks misinterpretation. My preference is to focus instead on the imperative of continuing the fight against corruption. It must be reiterated that this struggle is ongoing and far from concluded. The campaign encompasses both its triumphs and its failures, attracting criticism as well as commendation. Therefore, I would rather avoid an extensive discourse on this particular matter.

Is Brazilian democracy sufficiently established and resilient to withstand the challenges posed by corruption?

Corruption is not a threat to democracy, because we have a well-established and well-instituted state. The fight against corruption has been ongoing precisely because of the democratic principles that our Constitution set out. Take the issue of press freedom, which is fundamental. I always say that freedom of the press is not for the journalist or the communicator, but for the people. It is part of a broader concept called freedom of information. This widespread information helps fight corruption and preserve democracy. Democracy can be undermined if there are movements aimed at toppling the system, yes. But corruption does not bring down democracy. It is imperative to remain vigilant in preserving democratic principles. The nation is approaching thirty-two, nearly thirty-three years under the current Constitution, which, following the Empire,[176] stands as one of the longest lasting in its history. The Constitution is functioning effectively, as evidenced by the significant progress made in combating corruption. Numerous examples have been noted and commendable efforts acknowledged. Accordingly, democracy is not presently at risk. Recognition should be given to the democratic system and national institutions rather than criticism. From time to time, I see attempt to create a new constituent assembly, but a new constitution would bring enormous instability to the Brazilian state. That is why I always say: "The constituent assembly defines what the state will become; the constitution defines what the state is." We must work with the state we have today. So, I do not believe there is any immediate danger to Brazilian democracy.

To conclude, would you like to make any final comments or leave a message?

First, I want to congratulate you on your very objective, clear, and precise questions, which are undoubtedly of great interest in the fight against corruption. That is the first point. The second point is that promoting optimism is crucial, especially in the dramatic moment we are going through—the pandemic. The pandemic has caused significant economic issues and, sadly, thousands of deaths. This is a painful reality for all families and for every Brazilian. Nevertheless, we must remain optimistic. In terms of the economy, current projections indicate a negative GDP of around −4.5% to −5%. However, back in May 2016, when we assumed office, the GDP was already negative at −3.6%. One year and seven months later, we had achieved a growth rate of 1.3%. So, economic recovery is possible. Unfortunately, lives cannot be recovered. That is why, even as I try to promote a certain optimism—*optimism*, as I call it—we must prioritise the protection of human life. All leaders—from the President of the Republic to state governors and members of the National Congress—must come together in the fight against the pandemic. The guiding principle must be united and vaccinated. Only when most Brazilians are vaccinated will we be able to overcome the pandemic and, at the same time, revive the national economy. So, despite all the tragedy, I continue to advocate for a certain optimism—in both our personal and political conduct.

Michel Miguel Elias Temer Lulia was born in Tietê (SP). He served as Vice-President of the Republic from January 2011 to August 2016, when he assumed the Presidency, holding office until 2018. He is a lawyer, professor, writer, and Brazilian politician. His testimony was given on 29 March 2021 via the Zoom virtual platform and lasted 48 minutes of recording. The transcript was subsequently reviewed by the interviewee on 2 June 2022.

Testimony of Modesto Carvalhosa

Abstract

This testimony by *Professor Modesto Carvalhosa* offers a deeply personal and historically grounded reflection on the evolution of Brazil's legal and political landscape, with a particular focus on systemic corruption and institutional integrity. Drawing from his distinguished trajectory as a legal scholar, practising lawyer, and public intellectual, Carvalhosa situates his commitment to justice within the formative context of Brazil's public education system and his academic engagement at the University of São Paulo during the military dictatorship. His long-standing critique of entrenched political oligarchies and his direct involvement in landmark investigations—including the *Budget Dwarves* ("Anões do Orçamento" in Portuguese) and the publication of *The Black Book of Corruption* ("O Livro Negro da Corrupção" in Portuguese)—position him as a singular witness to the country's institutional decay and periodic attempts at renewal.

The testimony traces the emergence, impact, and dismantling of Operation Car Wash, which Carvalhosa regards as Brazil's most significant anti-corruption initiative to date, comparable in scope and consequence to Italy's Mani Pulite. He underscores the role of legislative advances, international cooperation, and the task force model in enabling Car Wash's success, while lamenting the subsequent political backlash—manifested in judicial reversals, legislative rollbacks, and executive inertia. In his assessment, the operation not only exposed the scale and sophistication of political corruption but also revealed the structural flaws of the 1988 Constitution, which he argues foster a self-serving and unaccountable political class.

Advocating for sweeping constitutional reforms—including the end of re-election for legislators, the abolition of public campaign funding, and the introduction of district-based voting—Carvalhosa contends that only a fundamental restructuring of Brazil's political architecture can prevent the resurgence of impunity. His testimony stands as both a historical account and a normative call to action, offering scholars, policymakers, and citizens a critical lens through which to evaluate the legacy of anti-corruption efforts in Brazil and the fragility of democratic institutions in the face of elite resistance.

Could you reflect on your educational background and professional trajectory, particularly in terms of how they shaped your civic and institutional commitments?

I studied in public schools throughout my life—from primary school at the prestigious Caetano de Campos School to university at the University of São Paulo. My three brothers also attended public schools and universities. Therefore, I owe my education to the Brazilian nation. I come from a time when studying in a public school was considered a privilege, as candidates for state schools had to undergo a rigorous entrance exam. I was educated with a strong sense of citizenship and the responsibility to contribute to my country. These were the old days, from the 1930s to the 1950s. Furthermore, during my university education at the University of São Paulo Law School (known as "Largo de São Francisco"), there was a strong emphasis on social justice and political nonconformity, set against the backdrop of the populist wave that dominated the period ("Getulismo", "Ademarismo", "Janismo").[177] Our professors always insisted that, just as a doctor's role is to save lives, alleviate pain, and prevent diseases, a legal professional has the mission, in any circumstance, to promote justice in the exercise of their profession, whether as a lawyer, judge, or prosecutor.

I have always been a lawyer, and from the 1960s to the 1980s, I was a professor at the University of São Paulo's Law School during the military regime. In that role, I always tried to oppose the dictatorship, both in the classroom and through the various actions I participated in, alongside professors and students at University of São Paulo, in the struggle for the return of democracy during those dark years. However, I always preserved my freedom as a citizen and avoided getting involved in party politics. I never participated in the political game, although, as a citizen, I did contribute to the Presidency of the Republic in 1994, during the time of Itamar Franco,[178] as a member of the Commission of Investigation of the Budget Dwarves scandal,[179] uncovered in 1992 during the Collor administration. Deputies and senators who made up the Joint Budget Committee extorted bribes from parliamentary amendments to the budget allocated to parliamentarians. This scandal was the subject of an in-depth investigation led by a group of seven citizens, chosen from among Justices of the higher courts, professors, academics, and professionals, including Candido Mendes de Almeida, Daniel Quintela Brandão, Emerson Kapaz, Evandro Gueiroz Leite, Francisco Batista Torres de Melo, Miguel Jeronymo Ferrante, Modesto Carvalhosa, and Romildo Canhim. I was part of this investigation as a representative of the Brazilian Bar Association. These investigations were documented in *The Black Book of Corruption*,[180] which I curated and edited. The volume was awarded the Jabuti Prize for journalistic literature in 1995, one of Brazil's most prestigious literary honours. The corruption scandals detailed in the book also revealed, within the then DNER (National Department of Roadways, now DNIT—National Department of Transport Infrastructure), a massive scheme set up between politicians, public servants, and well-known contractors—a prelude to what would later become the subject of investigations, leniency agreements, lawsuits, and convictions promoted by Operation Car Wash. It was from this experience, witnessing the systemic corruption within the Brazilian state, that I became even more interested in studying the phenomenon of public corruption in our country.

You are one Brazil's most renowned jurists, with numerous published works. Among them, it is worth highlighting *The Black Book of Corruption*;*From Kleptocracy to Democracy (2019); A Government Project, of State*[181]; and,*A New Constitution for Brazil: From a Country of Privileges to a Nation of Opportunities*.[182] How would you characterise the current state of Brazil's anti-corruption efforts, particularly in the light of recent legal, institutional, and political developments?

In addition to my work with corporate law, as both a professor and a lawyer, I ended up dedicating myself to the issue of public corruption in Brazil. Through this, I followed the legislative developments in the country, marked by Brazil's adherence to various international treaties and conventions aimed at combating corruption, such as those from the OECD,[183] the United Nations,[184] and the Organisation of American States.[185] In the early 2000s, Brazil began presenting itself as a country moving towards modernisation and internationalisation in the fight against corruption, through the introduction of appropriate legislation and institutional dialogue with international anti-corruption bodies. From 2010 onwards, we had the Money Laundering Law,[186] Law No. 12.846 of 2013, the Clean Company Act.[187] In sum, a comprehensive and coherent legislative framework was being constructed in a manner well-aligned with both domestic needs and international standards.

By the first decade of this century—and especially at the start of the second—Brazil had established a comprehensive body of national legislation on the topic. International norms and methods for combating corruption were being internalised, supported by vital tools such as the internet, high technology, and global cooperation. These efforts complemented our existing Penal Code, particularly the chapter on crimes against public administration, which remained relevant and was integrated into this new legislative structure and approach to tackling corruption.

What is the importance of the task force model in combating corruption and in particular the task force of Operation Car Wash?

What Brazil lacked at the time was the creation of task forces—a model widely adopted in American law—to combat corruption in an organic and integrated way. It was within this context that a task force was established to investigate corruption related to Banestado operations, in Paraná. As often happens in history, by sheer chance, bribes paid to a black-market currency dealers involved in the Banestado case led to the discovery of what would become the largest corruption scandal known in the Western world—the so-called Petrolão.

This investigation, which began at a humble petrol station, ended up in the hands of the most capable and courageous members of the Public Prosecutor's Office, the Federal Police, the Federal Revenue Service at the time, and the federal judiciary. The Car Wash team consisted of young professionals who not only understood the newly established national and international legislation but were also deeply committed to enforcing it. Many had studied in American universities, focusing specifically on anti-corruption practices, while others had received training in British institutions in the same field.

Thus, from the 2010s onwards, a unique historical moment emerged—a modern legislative framework coinciding with the rise of a group of prosecutors, judges, and investigators who were prepared, both nationally and internationally, to face corruption head-on.

Car Wash, therefore, is not simply the result of the competence, courage, and integrity of its members—from the Federal Judiciary, the Federal Public Prosecutor's Office, the Federal Police, and the Revenue Service—but also the product of the tools and frameworks that made this kind of operation viable, efficient, and effective. Car Wash did not invent anything. It simply made use of the instruments already available—legislation aligned with international standards—and applied them. And it did so with remarkable effectiveness.

How do you evaluate the significance of Operation Car Wash, both within Brazil and in terms of its impact on the global anti-corruption landscape?

There is a certain duality to this issue. From 2014 onwards, as the scandals unfolded and the anti-corruption efforts gained traction through Operation Car Wash, Brazil found itself under the watchful eye of the international community. On the one hand, there was the sheer scale of the corruption scheme uncovered—one of the largest the world had seen. On the other, there was a firm and determined response from federal police officers, prosecutors, and judges, which impressed observers abroad.

We had a precedent in the 1990s with Italy's Mani Pulite—Operation Clean Hands[188]—which became a historical reference in the global fight against corruption. Within that comparative framework, Car Wash received significant international support. Brazil, while exposing itself as a deeply corrupt country in terms of politics and public administration, simultaneously showed its institutional strength and readiness to confront and dismantle that corruption.

Thus, Brazil came to be viewed on the one hand, as a kleptocracy; yet on the other, as a nation possessing the institutional capacity and political will to confront—and potentially overcome—such a system. That constitutes Operation Car Wash's legacy on the global stage. It is now regarded as being at least as significant as, and arguably even more consequential than, Italy's *Mani Pulite*, owing in part to its more extensive use of digital technologies and mechanisms of international cooperation. In this respect, Car Wash went even further in exposing and prosecuting systemic corruption.

Given your involvement in prior landmark investigations—such as the Budget Dwarves scandal ("Anões do Orçamento" in Portuguese) and the Mensalão[189] case—how do you view Operation Car Wash in comparison? What continuities or departures do you observe in terms of institutional dynamics and societal repercussions?

That is a complex and far-reaching question. While the historical timeline may appear relatively brief, the events it encompasses were profoundly disruptive. Itamar Franco was one of the most decent political figures this country has known—a great president, remembered for his humility, sincerity, and public spirit. His major legacy, of course, was the Real Plan. It was in that atmosphere of renewed public confidence, under the Itamar Franco administration, that a Parliamentary Investigation Commission uncovered the stranglehold that Brazil's major construction companies had over several ministries and departments of the federal government. The mechanisms later revealed by Operation Car Wash were already at play back then.

The corruption model took shape as far back as the 1940s, with Brazil's first major infrastructure projects—the Anhanguera, Anchieta, and Dutra highways. Then came the hydroelectric boom in the 1950s and the construction of Brasília, along with a sprawling network of federal roads. With this massive wave of public works, a corrupt system took root: construction firms operated through bribes, which allowed them to deliver substandard work, inflate contracts and defraud the State—creating vast fortunes for themselves in the process.

They bribed across the board: engineers, civil servants, and the highest echelons of the political class. This culture of corruption became deeply embedded in Brazilian political life, expanding steadily over the decades. The "Budget Dwarves" scandal brought much of this to light in the 1990s, and its findings were later included in *The Black Book of Corruption.*

But it was under the Workers' Party government that corruption reached a systemic, almost pandemic scale. The Workers' Party not only participated in corruption—it organised and institutionalised it. Between 2003 and 2016, we saw the deliberate rigging of the entire federal public administration. The method was straightforward: fill thousands of commissioned positions in ministries and state-owned companies with political allies—Workers' Party militants or those nominated by the Centrão.[190] These individuals, often unqualified and inexperienced, were appointed not to manage but to collect. They operated as political agents, extorting bribes for themselves, the Workers' Party, and its allied factions.

That is what marked the Workers' Party government: the transformation of the State into a machine for plundering itself. In the past, under Getulio's time,[191] Adhemar de Barros,[192] or even the post-military governments, corruption certainly existed. But the State itself had not become a criminal organisation. Petrobras hadn't become a central instrument of systemic corruption.

What we witnessed under the Workers' Party was unprecedented: a planned, structured, and far-reaching scheme to turn the machinery of the State into a tool for political and personal gain. And it was not just the Workers' Party. They had the support of the Centrão and other major parties who, while posing as opposition—such as the Brazilian Social Democracy Party, Brazilian Democratic Movement, and the Democrats[193]—shared in the spoils and received huge sums from the same contractors.

Undoubtedly, corruption existed prior to this period. However, there had never been such a deliberate, structured, and far-reaching attempt to co-opt the machinery of the State for corrupt ends. This represents the fundamental distinction between the historically endemic corruption in Brazil and the systemic model that emerged under the Workers' Party. This criminal strategy was laid bare in 2005, during the Mensalão scandal, which came to light through the Federal Supreme Court at the time. And that is the real difference.

Operation Car Wash has been criticised by some for alleged selectivity. In your view, was the operation impartial in its application of the law, or did it exhibit any degree of selective enforcement?

What Operation Car Wash actually practised was non-selectivity. It did not choose its targets, as had so often happened in Brazil, to only go after minor public officials or small-time contractors. Instead, it went straight for the top—the real architects of corruption—including the President of the Republic, ministers, senior public servants, major contractors and operators in the criminal network, well-known money launderers, and frontmen. For the first time in Brazil's history, these figures were brought before the courts to answer for the widespread corruption that eroded the ethical foundations of the State.

What Car Wash exposed was a State completely stripped of administrative morality. Under the Workers' Party government, the State itself functioned as a criminal organisation—with the help of both the governing coalition and the so-called opposition. One could say, if anything, that there was a sort of top-down selectivity. It did not spare the most powerful players. It exposed the biggest contractors and most influential politicians in Brazil—including the President, who acted as the general commander of it all. It investigated, prosecuted, and arrested hundreds of individuals, handing down convictions with a level of functional courage rarely seen in a patrimonialism country like Brazil.

The only operation that comes close is Mani Pulite—the Clean Hands operation in Italy in the 1990s. No other operation worldwide achieved what Car Wash did. It hit the core of power, the very summit of authority, and revealed the pervasive corruption at its heart. It indicted and convicted people who, historically, would never have faced justice and who had been stealing from the country for generations.

Brazil is ruled by a sordid political oligarchy, where power is passed from father to son, to grandson, to son-in-law, to brother-in-law—a typical patrimonialism system, epitomised by the Centrão. Thanks to Operation Car Wash, it became possible to expose crimes committed by the upper echelons of this deeply entrenched political establishment, along with the contractors and suppliers who systematically diverted billions in public funds for private gain.

Given the widespread public support for Operation Car Wash, were you surprised by the intensity of the popular response? How do you interpret the significance and broader implications of that support within the Brazilian political and institutional context?

Brazilian citizens have virtually no direct access to public life. Under the 1988 Constitution, candidacy for elected office is only possible through political party affiliation. This means that no individual can run for city council, state or federal legislature, governor, or president without being tied to a political party. The result is a closed, self-preserving political class that monopolises power and systematically uses it to access and distribute public resources.

Furthermore, the 1988 Constitution adopted a system of proportional representation—an inherently flawed electoral model that has resulted in parliaments lacking genuine representativeness. True political representation tends to emerge under a district-based voting system, which is the norm in most consolidated democracies. Under proportional voting, the party-electoral coefficient often obscures the outcome: voters frequently do not even know which candidate their vote ultimately helped elect. As a result, there is little to no meaningful connection between the electorate and its representatives.

What follows, then, is a predictable outcome: the public, deprived of meaningful representation, grows increasingly disillusioned with the political class. This dissatisfaction often evolves into indignation, particularly when citizens witness their so-called representatives exploiting public office to extract vast sums from the State—whether through parliamentary amendments, party and electoral funds, allowances, perks, travel budgets, or a host of other privileges.

Each federal congressperson employs approximately thirty advisers; senators have as many as eighty. Meanwhile, the average citizen has no meaningful connection to these so-called representatives. When it then becomes evident—often with clear and documented proof—that these career politicians are receiving bribes and engaging in large-scale corruption, it is only natural that the public would rally behind those seeking to combat it.

One might suspect a local mayor of corruption based on rumours or questionable conduct, but when concrete evidence is presented—when wrongdoing is irrefutably proven—public support naturally turns to those who expose it. That is why Operation Car Wash resonated so strongly with the Brazilian population. For the first time, crimes against public administration committed by an entrenched political elite—a caste of corrupt figures occupying the highest spheres of power—were not only uncovered but publicly documented.

That is the root of this widespread public support: a nation deprived of genuine political representation, exploited by false representatives who systematically drain public resources funded by taxpayers. And since tax revenue alone does not satisfy their appetite, they generate fiscal deficits to access even more—serving personal and political interests at the expense of the public good.

Why does Brazil face a massive fiscal deficit? Is it because more resources are being allocated to education, healthcare, housing, urban development, or sanitation? Certainly not. The deficit stems from the diversion of public funds into the hands of political parties and their leadership. That is why the Brazilian public has grown increasingly disillusioned with a political elite that feeds off the State—draining its resources from within legislative chambers, ministries, and government departments. Beginning in 2014, when irrefutable evidence and confessions began to surface exposing the depth of corruption within much of the political class, public support for Operation Car Wash became overwhelming.

In the light of Brazil's current political, economic, and legal structures, what measures do you believe are necessary to strengthen institutional integrity and promote a more accountable system of governance?

What Operation Car Wash revealed is that Brazil's 1988 Constitution contains serious structural flaws. There is no real incentive or encouragement for Brazilian citizens to engage in political life. Political parties have become highly profitable businesses—run by their owners and allies who enrich themselves through substantial benefits.

Consider, for instance, a hypothetical young entrepreneur. He may contemplate establishing a business—whether in commerce, industry, or services—which inevitably entails risk: success might yield profit, but failure could lead to insolvency. By contrast, the formation of a political "enterprise"—namely, a political party—offers a radically different proposition. Upon formal registration, such an entity becomes eligible for substantial and continuous public funding via the party fund, irrespective of performance. Rain or shine, the funding flows; the venture is virtually risk-free.

And if I want to be elected, I no longer need shady donations from contractors' secret accounts. Instead, I go straight to the State's coffers. We created a second electoral fund, on top of the already guaranteed free

TV and radio campaign time under the 1988 Charter. In 2018, I helped myself to R$2 billion for campaigns. In 2020, another R$800 million—even though there was not even an election that year. Then in 2022, I pocketed R$5.9 billion more. It is a brilliant "business plan" for those founding political parties.

Once elected, using just a fraction of those billions to buy votes, I can propose budget amendments. That represents a further R$47 billion channelled into the hands of Members of Parliament under the pretext of financing minor local projects—such as the construction of a fountain here or the sponsorship of a traditional June Festiva ("festa junina")[194] there—within their constituencies. In this unrestrained distribution of public funds, federal deputies frequently align themselves with mayors, councillors, and governors, collectively diverting resources that ought to be allocated to essential public services for the taxpayers who ultimately finance the system.

The political system embedded in the 1988 Constitution was designed to attract criminals to public life. Of course, not all parliamentarians are corrupt—perhaps twenty out of eighty-one senators, and around a hundred deputies out of 513. But even those few decent ones are sidelined. They do not get appointed to committees, they're barely listened to in plenary sessions, and their colleagues openly ignore them—more interested in scrolling on their phones than hearing about public interest.

This political caste, composed largely of opportunists, is a by-product of the 1988 Constitution, which permits the unlimited re-election of federal and state legislators, as well as municipal councillors. Some have been in office for fifty years. Once they have consolidated sufficient wealth and political influence, power is often transferred to a son, son-in-law, or brother-in-law. This dynastic succession reflects a deeply entrenched and sordid form of oligarchy, in which families maintain their grip on power across generations while systematically exploiting the resources of the State.

This system simply cannot go on. If it does, Brazil will remain stuck in a cycle of economic, social, political, and institutional crises. Every year, millions more are pushed into poverty. Brazil is a country that manufactures misery—millions without access to decent food, education, or basic dignity. Functional illiteracy remains widespread. Brazil faces a significant population of so-called neither-nors—young people who are neither in education nor in employment. The country also registers one of the highest rates of tuberculosis in the world—even surpassing India in some metrics—largely due to inadequate housing conditions in informal settlements, where homes are densely packed, poorly ventilated, and lack basic sanitation. These are not mere coincidences; they are symptomatic of a political structure that is fundamentally decayed.

Electing individuals of integrity is insufficient if the underlying rules of the political system remain profoundly compromised. Structural reform is essential. This includes the prohibition of re-election for all elected offices, the adoption of a pure district-based voting system, and the legal recognition of independent candidacies. Furthermore, the abolition of the party fund, the electoral fund, and the mechanism of parliamentary budget amendments is imperative. What Brazil requires are genuine democratising reforms and the dismantling of the privileges entrenched in the current institutional framework. These ideas and many more are outlined in my book *A New Constitution for Brazil*. And yes—I am absolutely plugging the book, no shame there.

So why does not Brazil work? Why did the world's eighth-largest economy fall to thirteenth? Why have we become marginal on the global stage? It is because we have over thirty million invisible people—as Minister Guedes[195] once said—without birth certificates, documents, or even a record of when they were born. Most grow up without a father figure—just a mother, struggling alone. Brazil is a country of heroic matriarchy, where women bear the burden of family life in impoverished conditions—financially, socially, and morally. Fathers disappear. The mothers are the backbone of society in the favelas.

This is the reality of the country—a nation that continues to generate deepening misery, governed by a political class entrenched in, and sustained by, the institutional framework established by the 1988 Constitution. Right now, around fifty million Brazilians are going hungry. Whether the president is from the Workers' Party, Fernando Henrique[196]—an illustrious intellectual—or the current leader, they all end up hostage to this same gang of corrupt, professional politicians. And that is why I find it very hard to see how Brazil will ever truly improve without radically reforming the political structure imposed by the 1988 Constitution.

To what extent do you believe that the introduction of plea bargains represented a step forward for Brazil's legal system? How do you assess the role and effectiveness of plea and leniency agreements as incorporated into Brazilian law and employed during Operation Car Wash?

Indeed, without question. Plea bargains—and, by extension, leniency agreements—derive from the type of legal framework previously discussed, one that is standard across most developed democracies, particularly in the United States. In fact, the United States pioneered this approach in the fight against organised crime, including corruption. The key idea is that you do not just go after an individual criminal in isolation—you also work to dismantle the criminal organisation behind them.

Even when someone is individually responsible for a crime, investigators look into whether that person is part of a wider criminal network. If so, and if the individual is willing to cooperate, the authorities can then investigate the entire organisation—its links to third parties, its financial operations, its ties to government, business, and so on.

Modern, effective criminal investigation is not just about punishing the individual—it is about tackling the structure that enables the crime. For instance, an individual associated with an organised crime group—such as the mafia—may agree to provide evidence concerning the wider criminal network in exchange for a reduced sentence or, in certain cases, a suspended sentence, particularly if that individual occupies a relatively minor role within the organisation. This is far more beneficial for society as a whole than just locking up one person and leaving the rest of the organisation intact.

It is better, for example, that someone gets a three-year suspended sentence and witness protection—perhaps even a new identity—if that means the criminal organisation they belong to can be completely dismantled. That is exactly what Car Wash did. The operation brought to Brazil, through the skill of those involved, a deep understanding of what truly serves the public interest: dismantling criminal organisations, even if it means reducing the sentences of those who help expose them, provided it leads to the real masterminds.

Who are the heads of the mafia? Who controls the public institutions at the centre of the corruption? Which political parties built the machinery of systemic corruption in Brazil? Car Wash applied this method brilliantly, and received international recognition for it, winning several awards. The Mani Pulite operation in Italy followed a similar path, leading to the collapse of the three major political parties at the time—the Christian Democrats, the Socialists, and the Communists—all of which had been turned into corrupt machines by their own leaders.

Leniency agreements constitute a fundamental component of this approach. It is not always necessary to dissolve a corrupt company in its entirety; rather, the State may enter into a settlement that imposes substantial financial penalties, mandates structural reforms, and requires the removal of executives involved in illicit conduct. The objective is to dismantle the criminal enterprise into which the company had evolved, while allowing the entity itself to continue operating—albeit under a thoroughly restructured and legally compliant framework.

Accordingly, leniency agreements represent an extremely valuable instrument in the fight against corporate and systemic corruption. By implementing plea bargains and leniency agreements, the Car Wash operation simply made use of the excellent legislation Brazil had already enacted laws that, importantly, align with international treaties Brazil had signed to fight organised crime, terrorism, and corruption.

In your view, has Operation Car Wash led to significant changes in the relationship between private companies and the State, particularly in terms of transparency, compliance, and public procurement practices?

The relationship between the State and private companies has become more transparent. I believe that contractors are now more inclined to act appropriately, thanks to the tools provided by the Car Wash operation. However, there hasn't been a corresponding improvement on the State's part regarding institutional ethics in the public sphere. Car Wash didn't manage to prompt any public agency or department to establish a compliance programme. There is a law—the State-Owned Enterprises Law from 2016[197]—which is quite commendable. It introduces several measures to combat corruption within state-owned companies. Yet, within the central government and its direct and indirect administration, no compliance regime has been implemented. In contrast, private companies implicated in corruption have widely adopted internal control systems to prevent such criminal practices. As a result, I believe they've fostered a better relationship with public authorities.

Nevertheless, these contractors have suffered significant damage. Corruption severely tarnishes a company's reputation, which is paramount for any business. Without a good reputation, a company risks disappearing from the market. This fate befell some major contractors. Even after signing statute of limitations agreements, they experienced substantial downsizing. They might recover in the market eventually, but for now, they're paying the price for the loss of their business reputation.

How would you evaluate the overall impact of Operation Car Wash on Brazil's political, legal, and institutional landscape, considering both its achievements and its unintended consequences?

Much like Italy's *Mani Pulite* operation, Operation Car Wash in Brazil was followed by a significant political backlash, aimed at curtailing its legacy and weakening the legal instruments that had enabled its success. Following episodes of public disgrace—and, in certain cases, criminal convictions and imprisonment—established political figures mobilised to dismantle not only Operation Car Wash itself, but also the legal framework that had made such investigations possible.

In 2019, the Abuse of Authority Law[198] was enacted, stipulating that police officers, Council for Financial Activities Control agents, Federal Revenue officials, prosecutors, or judges who accuse or prosecute politicians "without evidence" could face up to four years in prison. This law is, in essence, a law of impunity. The Federal Supreme Court also played a significant role in undermining anti-corruption efforts. One of the most critical setbacks was the decision that prison sentences should only be executed after all appeals are exhausted. This interpretation, favouring major criminals, is unparalleled globally. Among the 194 UN member countries, none uphold this principle. Brazil stands alone in this regard, all to benefit corrupt politicians.

The Executive Branch, from 2018 onwards, equipped institutions like the Federal Police, the Attorney General's Office, and the General Advocacy of the Union to neutralise any anti-corruption measures within the federal administration. Consequently, the Car Wash operation was dismantled.

Furthermore, the ruled that corruption cases involving politicians without privileged jurisdiction[199] should be transferred to Regional Electoral Courts, which, besides their electoral duties, now serve as criminal courts. This arrangement is far from ideal. The Legislative Branch, meanwhile, has been actively diluting anti-corruption measures. They have disfigured the 10 Measures against Corruption,[200] and the Anti-Crime Package[201] proposed by the then Justice Sergio Moro.[202] In the view of 80% of the members of Congress, it is necessary to destroy what remains of the legislation to combat corruption. They have also weakened the Administrative Improbity Law [203] and are currently undermining the Money Laundering Law.

This has been instrumental in restoring rights to notorious corrupt politicians. For instance, five years after initial convictions, Justice Fachin[204] ruled that Sergio Moro lacked jurisdiction to judge Lula's cases,[205] as the Curitiba court was geographically incompetent. Another Justice, Gilmar Mendes, declared that Moro was biased against Lula, leading to the annulment of the process.

There is a concerted effort among the Legislative, Executive, and Judicial branches to obliterate all remnants of the Car Wash operation. This nullifies Car Wash cases and prevents new ones against corrupt politicians and their associates. The Executive equips institutions to suppress anti-corruption initiatives, and the Legislative passes laws that dismantle the legal framework supporting Car Wash.

Brazil mirrors Italy's experience in 1994, witnessing the resurgence of corruption and the rehabilitation of convicted politicians. Politicians now enjoy greater freedom to engage in corruption than before the Car Wash operation. Previously, there was legislation to combat corruption; today, there's virtually nothing left. In this endeavour to restore unchecked power to the corrupt, the Court has granted *habeas corpus* to both politicians and major criminals.

The narrative that Judge Sergio Moro convicted Lula and others for political reasons, rather than legal ones, is a falsehood. This mirrors the situation in Italy, where the Mani Pulite operation was dismantled because one of its former judges ran for parliament after retirement.[206] This served as a pretext for the triumphant return of corrupt politicians and parties. Italy remains one of the most corrupt nations in the European Union, and Brazil is following a similar path. Corruption is now more rampant than ever in our country.

In conclusion, is there any final reflection you would like to offer regarding the legacy of Operation Car Wash or the broader challenges of combating systemic corruption in Brazil?

The legacy of Operation Car Wash is quite like that of Italy's Mani Pulite. It is a historical milestone that not only exposed systemic corruption but also revealed the resilience of politicians, who have managed to return to power and resume corrupt practices—now under judicial, legislative, and administrative conditions that are even more favourable than before.

Take Italy as an example. During the Mani Pulite operation, the statute of limitations for corruption crimes was ten years. Under Berlusconi—who made it his mission to dismantle the Clean Hands legacy—that period was reduced to just one year. So, after one year and a day, a politician could no longer be considered corrupt under the law.

That is precisely the path Brazil is heading down, especially with the Supreme Court's decision that imprisonment should only occur after all appeals are exhausted—in other words, never.

Operation Car Wash leaves behind a historic legacy. It was a powerful moment of unity between society and the State, a moment in which Brazilian citizens actively engaged in demanding the restoration of political morality. But that moment has passed.

Today, we are witnessing the complete reinstatement of a culture of corruption—driven by actions of the Federal Supreme Court, legislative measures passed by Congress, and the weakening of anti-corruption institutions by the Executive Branch.

Modesto Souza Barros Carvalhosa was born in São Paulo (SP). Lawyer, consultant, arbitrator and retired professor of Commercial Law at the Faculty of Law of USP. Author of several books and articles related to the issue of corruption, as well as topics related to business law. In 2021 he published the book *A New Constitution for Brazil*. His testimony was given on 31 March 2021 via the Zoom virtual platform and lasted 1 hour and 2 minutes of recording. The transcript was subsequently reviewed by the interviewee on 13 April 2022.

Testimony of Roberto Livianu

Abstract

In this testimony, Roberto Livianu offers a critical and historically informed reflection on Brazil's anti-corruption trajectory. His testimony traverses pivotal episodes, including the Mensalão and Banestado scandals, and culminates in an incisive analysis of Operation Car Wash (Lava Jato), which he regards as a landmark in Brazilian legal history—albeit one later undermined by political resistance and institutional backlash.

Livianu outlines the evolution of anti-corruption legislation in Brazil and underscores the importance of plea bargaining, pre-trial detention, and international cooperation in confronting complex financial crime. He defends these mechanisms as necessary instruments within a democratic framework, particularly in contexts of entrenched impunity and political capture. He also addresses the role of public support in sustaining legal reforms and contrasts the trajectory of Lava Jato with that of Italy's Operation Clean Hands, highlighting striking parallels in the dynamics of reform and reaction.

Throughout the testimony, Livianu expresses concern over the erosion of legal safeguards that once empowered institutions to pursue grand corruption cases. He denounces legislative initiatives aimed at weakening prosecutorial independence and judicial accountability and warns of a broader cultural regression marked by the normalisation of corrupt practices. At the same time, he maintains that the achievements of Lava Jato should not be dismissed on the basis of its imperfections, and that the dismantling of its legacy represents a threat to the democratic rule of law.

The testimony concludes with a call to action: for institutions to remain vigilant, for civil society to reclaim its role as a democratic counterweight, and for a renewed political commitment to transparency, ethical leadership, and the long-term consolidation of integrity mechanisms in Brazil.

To provide some context, could you tell us about your educational background and personal trajectory?

I obtained my Law degree from the University of São Paulo (USP) in 1990. Subsequently, I undertook research that culminated in my doctoral thesis, which I defended in 2004, also at USP. The title of my dissertation was *Penal Control of Corruption.*[207]

The doctoral programme gave me the opportunity to study the subject in depth, particularly at a time when there was a marked absence of academic work dedicated specifically to corruption. While much was written about consumer crimes, economic offences, and tax violations, corruption itself remained largely overlooked within scholarly discourse. I chose this topic precisely because of its relevance, practical significance, and the contribution it could make to society.

From there, I became increasingly involved in the subject and started participating in public debates. I am currently a Prosecutor of Justice, which is the highest position in the career path of the Public Prosecutor's Office in the State of São Paulo. I have been working there since 1992, primarily in the criminal field. Beyond my role in the Public Ministry, I also became engaged in mobilising society around the issue of corruption, which eventually led me to found the Institute I Do Not Accept Corruption[208] in 2015.

As of July 2021, the Institute marks its sixth anniversary. It was established to promote an intelligent and *strategic* approach to combating corruption, and is structured around four core pillars: research, public policy, civic mobilisation, and education. I also have experience in academia, having lectured at the university level for approximately ten years, including positions at Paulista University and the United

Metropolitan Colleges. These days, I occasionally teach postgraduate courses and give lectures. I have authored several books on the subject, coordinated others, and contributed chapters to various additional volumes. These days, I occasionally teach postgraduate courses and give lectures. I have authored several books on the subject, coordinated others, and contributed chapters to various additional volumes, titled *Corruption in the History of Brazil*.[209] The book comprises fifteen essays that examine corruption from a historical perspective, spanning from Brazil's colonial beginnings to the era of Operation Car Wash. In short, that is the trajectory of my professional journey to date.

As a recognised scholar in the field of anti-corruption, how do you compare the Petrobras scandal with other major cases, such as Italy's Operation Clean Hands,[210] the Mensalão scandal,[211] or the Banestado case[212]? Do you see significant similarities or key differences among them?

Each of these cases has its own particular features—we could spend hours discussing them individually. But, in essence, I would say that the Mensalão case represented a historic milestone in Brazil, primarily because it marked the first time the justice system effectively held individuals in high political office to account. That had long been something of a taboo. Much of this progress was due to the determination of two key figures in the Federal Supreme Court and the Superior Court of Justice: Justices Joaquim Barbosa[213] and Ayres Britto,[214] who presided over the proceedings as a result of the privileged legal status of the accused. The Mensalão was a turning point—it showed that political elites could, in fact, be held accountable. The Banestado case also carried this idea of accountability, but I highlight the Mensalão due to its greater impact and depth.

When it comes to Operation Car Wash, however, the situation becomes even more complex. In this case, Judge Sergio Moro convicted former President Lula, which rendered him ineligible to run for office, despite his leading position in the polls at the time. This effectively excluded him from the 2018 presidential race. The winner of that election, Jair Bolsonaro—who directly benefited from Lula's disqualification—went on to appoint Moro as his Minister of Justice and Public

Security. Moro accepted the invitation and brought an end to a twenty-two-year career in the federal judiciary, as required by law when taking up a political position.

Just over a year later, Moro resigned from his position, accusing President Bolsonaro of political interference. In response, Bolsonaro publicly labelled him a traitor. Meanwhile, leaked messages published by The Intercept have since raised serious questions about Moro's impartiality. The Supreme Court may soon rule on this and potentially annul Lula's convictions—something that could seriously undermine the legacy of Operation Car Wash.

With Petrobras and everything that led to Car Wash, we saw a broadening of scope—a more ambitious attempt to deliver far-reaching results compared to the Mensalão. It did not stop at political elites who had long seen themselves as untouchable. It also targeted powerful business figures, such as Marcelo Odebrecht,[215] who symbolised Brazil's corporate elite. He was at the helm of the country's largest construction firm and was absolutely convinced that, as usual, he would be released within 24 to 72 hours through a habeas corpus ruling. But that did not happen. His prolonged detention marked a significant turning point—the system that had long all but guaranteed impunity for the elite had begun to fracture.

First the Mensalão case, and then Operation Car Wash, posed serious challenges to Brazil's entrenched culture of impunity. For the first time, those in positions of power began to feel vulnerable. The constitutional principle that all are equal before the law had long been regarded almost as a joke—more aspirational than actual. These operations began to shift that perception, demonstrating that the law could indeed reach the wealthy and powerful. And, naturally, this provoked resistance—just as it did in Italy with Operation Clean Hands. But Moro's move from the bench to the government that had benefited from his own judicial decisions understandably cast a shadow of doubt over the impartiality of his rulings—and, by extension, over the broader anti-corruption agenda in Brazil.

In Italy, Clean Hands was initially a victory for the judiciary and public prosecutors. But the political establishment soon fought back—by passing laws that restricted the powers of prosecutors and judges, essentially clipping the wings of the judiciary. Unfortunately, society remained largely passive. There was insufficient public reaction to halt these political manoeuvres, and as a consequence, many of the gains achieved by Operation Clean Hands were ultimately reversed.

I see the same script playing out in Brazil. There are numerous signs pointing in that direction. One clear example is the new Abuse of Authority Law.[216] This law contains glaring constitutional flaws—it allows for the punishment of judges and prosecutors simply for interpreting the law, which poses a serious threat to their independence. It is such a flagrant overreach that the OECD[217] sent a delegation to Brazil to investigate the situation first-hand. It was concluded that the law raised important concerns. Although the final version introduced some improvements compared to the original draft, it still conveys a message that may be interpreted as placing constraints on judges and prosecutors. The law purports to update legislation dating back to the 1965 military regime; however, its underlying purpose appears to be to place pressure on members of the judiciary and the Public Prosecutor's Office who adopt a firm stance against corruption.

The legislation is known as the Abuse of Authority Act, yet it does not contain any specific criminal provisions defining acts of abuse within parliamentary activity. Nor does it provide for the criminal classification of abusive conduct committed by members of the Executive. One illustrative example is the highly controversial case involving the Legislative Assembly of the State of Rio de Janeiro, which convened a session to decide whether to uphold the detention of three state deputies—Picciani[218] and others. Some individuals obtained a court order to ensure their access to the Assembly on the day of the vote. They arrived with the judicial order in hand, showed it to the Acting President of the Assembly, state congressperson Wagner Montes[219] who then prohibited them from entering a public building—even with a court order. Such an episode would, in any classroom setting, be presented as a textbook example of abuse of authority. Yet it is not covered under the current Abuse of Authority Act. And this is merely one instance—there are numerous others involving budgetary manipulation or typical forms of abuse within parliamentary conduct. None of these are addressed by the legislation.

Every day, individuals are stopped on the street by the police solely because they are Black—a clear example of abuse of authority. Yet there has been little progress in holding officers accountable for such conduct. Naturally, there are many outstanding police officers, but there are also those who engage in misconduct. Yet there is no sign of concern about this. The only progress we have seen from this law is in punishing the so-called abuse of status ("carteirada" in Portuguese)[220] that awful Brazilian habit of pulling rank to get special treatment.

Meanwhile, other efforts are underway that seek to undermine everything the Abuse of Authority Law should represent. There is a push to dismantle the Clean Record Law,[221] the Administrative Improbity Law[222]—our main legal tool for the Public Prosecutor's Office in fighting corruption. And this is no exaggeration—the proposal seeks to eliminate Article 11 of the Administrative Improbity Law, which provides for sanctions in cases involving harm to public funds or illicit enrichment.[223] That includes vaccine diversion, nepotism, and even the denial of information to journalists under the Access to Information Act.[224] What is more concerning is that this is accompanied by a cynical discourse—such as that of the Government leader in the Chamber of Deputies, who publicly advocates nepotism as a legitimate state policy. Nepotism! A system that may have made sense in the era of monarchies, before the Enlightenment. Ricardo Barros[225] currently under investigation for misconduct committed at the "Fim da Picada" steakhouse[226] has the audacity to defend nepotism in public—and he is applauded by both the President of the Republic and the Speaker of Brazil's lower house of Congress. And who is this Speaker of Brazil's lower house of Congress? A man facing corruption allegations, widely known by the nickname "the King of salary kickbacks" ("rachadinhas" in Portuguese)[227] in Alagoas.[228] This is the President of Brazil's lower house of Congress. That is the level to which the situation has deteriorated. Following this, there is the Money Laundering Act[229]—regarded as one of the most effective and advanced pieces of legislation of its kind worldwide. Indeed, it functioned so well that it is now facing efforts to dismantle it. Geddel Vieira Lima[230] was caught with 51 million reais in cash. Such outcomes are precisely what occur when a law functions effectively. However, when a law proves too effective—particularly in imposing sanctions—its very success is perceived by some as problematic. A commission has now been established to review it.

Ordinarily, when a commission of legal experts is formed, one expects a degree of balance—with participation from lawyers, prosecutors, and judges. But that was not the case here. This commission is dominated by people who defend individuals accused of money laundering. Its secretary is Judge Ney Bello Filho.[231] And what is he known for? Granting house arrest to Geddel. Dismissing the complaint against Michel Temer.[232] Denying the request to remove Minister Ricardo Salles.[233] These are Judge Ney Bello Filho's most notable decisions—and this is the individual now leading the process of revising the legislation. That alone offers a sense of the direction in which things are moving. And it does not stop there: discussions are now under way regarding a general law on the protection of criminal data. The General Data Protection Law[234]—a European-style piece of legislation—is meant to safeguard privacy. But in this context, the spirit of the law is being distorted to introduce procedural barriers within the criminal justice system. In other words, new mechanisms are continually being devised to dilute the law's effectiveness.

And then there is Justice Kassio Nunes,[235] the President's[236] hand-picked appointee to the Supreme Court. He has been nicknamed the "copy-and-paste" Justice due to allegations of plagiarism in both his master's dissertation and doctoral thesis—not to mention academic credentials that do not appear to exist. Very early in his tenure at the Supreme Court, he issued a decision against the Clean Record Law[237] in a case on which the full bench had already ruled.[238] He unilaterally reversed a ruling that had already been handed down by the full bench—earning public praise from the President of the Republic[239] for his actions.

And what is the Clean Record Law? It is legislation intended to prevent corrupt politicians from holding public office—a law that originated through a popular initiative. It represents one of the very few instances in which society has had a genuine opportunity to participate directly in the exercise of political power.

This collection of examples—just a few among many—I have not even mentioned the Impunity Constitutional Amendment Proposal proposed by Arthur Lira.[240] He sought to pass it without any public debate. And its final, most striking feature? A clause that would prohibit the Judiciary from removing any sitting member of parliament from office—under any circumstances. According to the terms of this proposed constitutional amendment, even if a parliamentarian were to wield an AK-47 and murder ten people in a school, they could not be removed from office by judicial decision. If a member of parliament were to kill a thousand people in the street or commit sexual violence against a thousand women, the law would still shield them from judicial accountability. That is the proposal being put forward. It contravenes every universally recognised principle of justice, including judicial independence and the separation of powers. And even so, the Speaker of Brazil's lower house of Congress. That is the proposal. It violates every universal principle of justice, including judicial independence and the separation of powers. And even so, the Speaker of Brazil's lower house of Congress—from the Centrão,[241] himself accused of corruption—tried to ram it through without any debate or constitutional review.

This is the Brazil in which we now live—where corruption, tragically, is becoming dangerously normalised. The very name of our institute, *I Do Not Accept Corruption*, is intended to serve as a constant reminder that corruption is never acceptable. It must not be tolerated, let alone treated as something natural or inevitable. Yet it remains an uphill battle.

In your view, what significance did Operation Car Wash hold for Brazil—and for the wider world?

Operation Car Wash began with promising prospects and sound principles. What struck me most was the level of institutional cooperation—something rarely seen in the day-to-day functioning of Brazil's justice system. Ordinarily, justice is administered in a highly individualised manner: each actor manages their own cases, documents, and decisions. It is not typically a coordinated or collective endeavour.

By contrast, Operation Car Wash stood out as a genuine task force, built on inter-institutional collaboration. The Public Prosecutor's Office, the Federal Police, and the Federal Revenue Service worked in close coordination—sharing the same table, jointly developing strategies, setting objectives, and pursuing outcomes collectively. That spirit of coordinated effort was its first major strength. Unfortunately, Judge Moro's later decision to join the government that had benefited from his rulings against Lula drastically changed the course of events. It lent credibility to the narrative pushed by the Workers' Party that Lula had been a selective target.

What set Operation Car Wash apart was its focus on combating corruption at the highest levels of power—a truly groundbreaking shift. Historically, Brazilian institutions have tended to treat corruption much like petty theft, as if stealing a papaya from a market or a deodorant from a supermarket were equivalent offences. Such an approach has consistently failed to produce meaningful results.

When institutions bring people together to thoroughly understand cases, analyse financial data, lift secrecy protections where appropriate, map connections, and develop coordinated strategies, genuine efficiency begins to emerge. This was one of Car Wash's key strengths: senior officials prioritised these cases, and teams engaged with full commitment. There was active collaboration across departments—from the Public Prosecutor's Office to the Federal Police and the Federal Revenue Service—all working towards concrete outcomes.

It is regrettable that Judge Moro chose to leave the judiciary in order to enter politics, accepting a position within the administration of a politician who had directly benefited from his prior judicial decisions.

Nevertheless, the results were significant. Brazil succeeded in recovering approximately one-third of the misappropriated funds—around 4.3 billion reais. By international standards, this is a remarkable achievement. For that reason, Operation Car Wash was regarded by international observers as a model of excellence in the fight against corruption. Recovering stolen assets is one of the key elements that restores a sense of justice—it is not just about sentencing individuals. Of course, there were setbacks—as expected—because those affected by the investigations would naturally push back. Powerful people do not simply accept consequences without resistance; they try to create alternative narratives.

I remember being in a debate with Congressman Wadih Damous,[242] from the Workers' Party in Rio de Janeiro. His argument was that Car Wash had destroyed Brazil's economy, bankrupted companies, and left behind economic scorched earth. With all due respect, that is not a fair interpretation. Those who work with international instruments to which Brazil is a signatory—such as the United Nations Convention against Corruption (UNCAC)[243] and the OECD Anti-Bribery Convention[244]—are aware that Article 5 of the OECD Convention is unequivocal: corruption must not go unpunished merely because enforcement could affect the productive chain.[245]

Claims such as "this will cause unemployment" or "it will harm the economy" cannot serve as justifications for tolerating corruption. On the contrary, combatting corruption purifies the system, enhances market transparency and predictability, and fosters fair competition among honest actors. Those who act dishonestly and rely on illicit funds must be held accountable. Unfortunately, the repeated use of a "scorched-earth" narrative—suggesting that anti-corruption efforts were causing widespread institutional harm—began to evoke the kind of propaganda strategies famously employed by Goebbels[246]—that reflects the idea that if a lie is repeated often enough, it begins to take on the appearance of truth. Even when the narrative is later disproven, its effects linger—many continue to be deeply influenced by it.

At one point, it seemed as though the Public Prosecutor's Office was being blamed for everything—from summer floods to droughts in the Northeast. Virtually any problem was attributed to Operation Car Wash.

This raises an important question: what, then, was the operation expected to do? Ignore the existence of corruption? Refrain from enforcement on the grounds that it might lead to job losses? Should society simply turn a blind eye? Such reasoning borders on the irrational—it is wholly indefensible. Yet this was the narrative advanced by certain segments of the political left.

Meanwhile, on the political right, then-candidate Jair Bolsonaro[247] publicly positioned himself as a staunch supporter of Operation Car Wash and a champion of anti-corruption. However, his actions in office told a very different story. One of the most striking examples was Provisional Measure No. 966,[248] which effectively sought to shield public officials from accountability for acts of corruption committed during the pandemic. Not even Lula[249] Dilma[250] or Temer[251] attempted something of the sort. Bolsonaro did. This measure was not speculative or rhetorical—it represented a concrete exercise of executive power, taking effect upon publication. And it was not an isolated case. There were multiple such initiatives: a broader offensive against transparency, political alliances with groups such as the Centrão, and promises of a "new politics" that ultimately proved to be little more than demagogic rhetoric.

The Car Wash operation achieved its objectives; however, its agenda was falsely appropriated by a right-wing political campaign. Meanwhile, the left began to demonise the Car Wash operation—all the work and the staggering results, which truly shook the foundations of the Republic. Naturally, there were reactions. The operation reached far and wide, and the impact was undeniably significant. Those who were "affected" by it started to build their own narratives.

The individuals behind the Car Wash operation are, after all, human—and humans are prone to errors. Mistakes are made every day by all of us, myself included. However, from my perspective, observing from a distance, the successes far outweigh the mistakes. The operation tackled chronic impunity and reached the powerful—that, to me, is essential. It helped restore the credibility of the justice system, and that is fundamental. Of course, there was no need to generate such extensive media hype or create so much spectacle. But scholars who study anti-corruption efforts—political scientists like Robert Klitgaard[252]—say that when dealing with entrenched corruption, as is the case in Brazil, you need to catch the big fish and show them to the public. This is a matter of the pedagogy of exemplarity. What did the prosecutors do? They adhered to the established playbook. They showcased the "big fish" so that society would have faith in the system, become engaged, and report wrongdoing—thereby helping to restore trust in justice. "But they went too far." That, of course, is a subjective judgement. Opinions vary widely regarding the now-famous presentation of the indictment against Lula—complete with PowerPoint slides. There are countless arguments on the matter. In contemporary practice, PowerPoint is routinely used as a dynamic and visual aid to support presentations. "But they should not have gone that far." Again, perspectives on this differ considerably. One could even argue that the level of detail was a sign of respect for the former President—to ensure nothing was left unclear. Interpretations vary. Much has been said about the spectacle, but the principle of publicity is enshrined in our Constitution. As the scholar Norberto

Bobbio[253] once said, democracy is the government of public power in public.[254] The exercise of power must be open. What they did was report back to society. "Was the way they did it exaggerated?" That is another matter, and not one I feel qualified to judge. What I can say is that the investigation had incredible reach, the wheels were set in motion, and an important tool for its success was plea bargaining—something used worldwide and, in Brazil, regulated under Law No. 12.850.[255] The Car Wash team utilised this tool effectively to reach the highest levels of power. Without it, their success in doing so would have been unlikely.

In my view, the Car Wash Operation was truly groundbreaking—a sharp contrast to what we had before. It was not some minor process. By contrast, under Prosecutor General, Augusto Aras,[256] the Car Wash Operation was effectively shut down, with all cases transferred to the jurisdiction of the Special Action Group to Combat Organised Crime. In other words, the system has regressed to a pre-Car Wash state, where minor offences are indiscriminately grouped together with major cases—petty crimes alongside high-level corruption.

There are no longer professionals dedicated solely to handling complex, high-stakes cases. There is no miracle solution to this problem. When such focus is lost, productivity and efficiency inevitably decline, especially in the fight against large-scale corruption. If you do not have people who are fully committed and specialised, it simply does not work. And then there is the workload—if someone has 20 cases on their desk and does not get through them on time, they face consequences from the Inspectorate. The situation is clear: effectiveness in tackling serious corruption has been lost. This is the real consequence of the termination of Operation Car Wash. In my view, this outcome was no accident. The operation was beginning to penetrate increasingly deeper layers of power, which provoked significant resistance. It is also important to acknowledge—respectfully regarding Mr Augusto Aras—that under the Constitution, Brazilian President[257] may appoint any member of the Federal Public Prosecutor's Office as Prosecutor General.

That is how the rules are written. Traditionally, however, the process involved an internal debate, followed by a shortlist of three names being submitted to the President. Choosing one of those three would ensure legitimacy—these were candidates endorsed by the Public Prosecutor's

Office itself. However, President Bolsonaro appointed someone who was not even among the top ten candidates actively engaged in debating the future of the institution. Ten prosecutors had toured the country discussing these issues, from which three were selected as leading candidates. Augusto Aras was not among them. He was simply the individual chosen by the President. Is this permissible? Yes, constitutionally it is.

Nonetheless, this appointment undermines the autonomy of the Prosecutor's Office. Several prosecutors have openly expressed their discontent, particularly in response to statements made by Augusto Aras, including his assertion that democracy in Brazil is, in some way, a matter for the Armed Forces. That left many prosecutors stunned. After all, the Armed Forces are just one institution among many—like the Public Defender's Office, the State Prosecutor's Office, and the Federal Prosecutor's Office. The Armed Forces are not superior to other institutions. Like all entities, they are subject to the Constitution. The concept of a "moderating power" in Brazil ceased to exist with Dom Pedro I and the Constitution of the Empire.

In your view, how significant was the institutional culture of the Prosecutor's Office in enabling Operation Car Wash to become such a major anti-corruption initiative?

The Prosecutor's Office has existed in Brazil since 1609. Its earliest manifestation was before the Court of Appeal in Bahia, originally established to defend the interests of the Crown. The first reference to Brazil's Prosecutor's Office was as the King's Ombudsman. For a long time, it maintained this role until the current configuration emerged, in which the Prosecutor's Office serves to defend society—even prosecuting, when necessary, the State itself. Originally, it acted as the defender of the Crown and the Kingdom. Over time, it evolved, and the 1988 Constitution enshrined its role as a steadfast defender of citizenship and society.

Professor Dalmo Dallari[258] once referred to the Prosecutor's Office as the "people's lawyer". If the Prosecutor's Office is positioned as a defender of citizenship and society, in addition to safeguarding diffuse and collective interests, it also bears the responsibility of defending the legal order and the democratic regime. From the 1980s onwards, the institution underwent a significant period of evolution, growth, and maturation—particularly in its defence of diffuse interests, such as environmental protection and consumer rights. In 1985, Law No. 7,347, known as the Public Civil Action Law,[259] was enacted. These developments culminated in the constitutional framework established in 1988.

These new roles and responsibilities shaped a new profile for members of the Public Prosecutor's Office—a new kind of prosecutor or attorney with broader responsibilities. More and more, they understood the need not just to act mechanically, but to be professionals who engage with society, who are attuned to what is happening around them, who hold public hearings to understand community priorities and to use those insights in building action plans. In short, all of this contributed to a maturation process. I would say that Operation Car Wash, and the way it was structured through collaborative dynamics and a pursuit of efficiency, was a direct outcome of this evolution.

The 1941 Code of Criminal Procedure enshrined the principle of mandatory criminal prosecution. At the time, it made sense—criminal prosecution was seen as an indisputable public good, something rigid and non-negotiable. But as the pursuit of efficiency gained importance, it became clear that punitive efficiency was not compatible with the idea of rigid, mandatory prosecution. This pursuit of greater efficiency brought about change. The Law on Special Criminal Courts—Law No. 9.099[260]—introduced a more flexible approach. The introduction of criminal agreements, settlements, and case suspensions marked a shift away from automatic and non-negotiable criminal action, ushering in an era where negotiation and efficiency gained prominence. Today, such agreements—including non-prosecution agreements, civil non-prosecution agreements, settlements, and plea bargains—have become increasingly prevalent like in the US system—which resolve eight-five to ninety per cent of criminal cases. I do not advocate overturning the entire system, but I do endorse the incorporation of negotiation and agreement within criminal justice processes.

Regarding the guarantor judge—hypothetically, this could be an interesting figure within the justice system. It might function effectively in smaller jurisdictions such as Vaduz, the capital of Liechtenstein, or

Valletta, Malta. However, in contexts like Ferraz de Vasconcelos or Cabaceiras, where hundreds of judicial districts are each served by a single judge, the concept of a guarantor judge presupposes the presence of at least two judges. Implementing such a system cannot be achieved overnight without adequate preparation. Consequently, this initiative risks facilitating impunity by introducing technicalities that may be exploited—exemplified by the case of André do Rap,[261] who famously walked free through the prison gates laughing, on the basis of a release order signed by a sole Supreme Court Justice. That was made possible by manipulating the habeas corpus distribution and relying on a rider clause ("jabuti"[262] in Portuguese means tortoise), that had been added into the Anti-Crime Package.[263] This is Brazil—where, in the middle of the legislative process, some people insert "jabutis" [rider clauses], and as the saying goes, "a tortoise that cannot climb trees—so if it is found in the branches, it is clear that someone placed it there deliberately".[264] Someone must have placed it there deliberately to produce a specific outcome. Therefore, I would suggest that all of this forms part of the same process of institutional maturation.

A good prosecutor, a good attorney, should start thinking about engaging with the press from the very first day of training. The press is an ally of the Public Prosecutor's Office. Accountability for actions is essential. Justice must never be administered behind closed doors or in secrecy. It is important to engage with the press professionally and transparently, avoiding turning such interactions into spectacles. Those seeking attention are better suited for entertainment than public service. However, knowing how to communicate openly and respectfully with journalists regarding ongoing cases is crucial. Journalists are not adversaries; rather, they uphold the constitutional right to information—an imperative that the Prosecutor's Office must safeguard.

When a President blocks information from the Ministry of Health, or when pandemic data is withheld from the Prosecutor's Office, it should be the first institution to raise its voice—because this is a violation of transparency. The right to access information is fundamental. In May, the Access to Information Law will mark its ninth anniversary.[265] By comparison, Sweden has had a similar law in place since 1766. Brazil has fallen behind. While Brazil was still abolishing slavery, neighbouring

Colombia had already enacted its own access to information legislation. There is an urgent need to make up for lost time and foster a genuine culture of transparency. Transparency is essential; it is a cornerstone of citizenship and a powerful instrument in the fight against corruption. Corruption flourishes in darkness—behind closed doors rather than in the open. Therefore, transparency serves as a critical anti-corruption strategy.

What impact did the use of plea bargain agreements and pre-trial detention have on the fight against corruption in Operation Car Wash?

That is an excellent question. To begin, it is important to clarify the concept of plea bargains—often referred to as plea bargain agreements. This is not something unique to Brazil—it is a procedural mechanism used all over the world to get results in criminal investigations. When we talk about plea bargain agreement, it is important to stress what the law itself states—in fact, a law signed by former President Dilma, which is clear and leaves no room for doubt: no one can be convicted solely on the word of an informant or collaborator. That is just the starting point for accountability. Corroborating evidence is essential. No individual can be convicted solely on the testimony of another party. This is an important principle to bear in mind.

As I have said before, and I will say again, we cannot afford to give up this tool. It played an important role in Operation Car Wash. Why? In practice, those who refused to cooperate faced significantly harsher sentences, whereas collaboration could result in a reduced penalty. This created a prisoner's dilemma: individuals, recognising the gravity of their situation and the likelihood of conviction, opted to collaborate in order to reduce their time in custody. This dynamic encouraged the disclosure of evidence, which in turn facilitated the dismantling of deeper layers of criminal organisation.

This was key to the success of Operation Car Wash. That is not to downplay the importance of other types of evidence—be it financial, telephone or tax records, witness statements, or documents. All of those play a critical role. Undoubtedly, the plea bargain agreement was central to the success of the operation. This mechanism is employed worldwide and has progressively evolved within the Brazilian legal system—starting with Law No. 7.492[266] on financial institutions, and later becoming more structured through Law No. 12.850, which provides a detailed legal framework for such agreements.

Turning now to the issue of pre-trial detention: unfortunately, unlike in much of the democratic West, Brazil permits definitive imprisonment only after four levels of judicial review—namely, first instance, court of appeal, the Superior Court of Justice, and finally, the Federal Supreme Court. In 2019, the ruled that no one can be imprisoned until all appeals are exhausted and a final decision is handed down by itself. In my view, this stance is deeply problematic when it comes to tackling impunity. Leading democratic nations—France, Germany, Spain, Italy, the United States—all allow imprisonment after conviction in the first or second instance. Unlike Brazil, these jurisdictions do not have a fourth level of appeal. The current system in Brazil creates a rather bleak scenario that undermines the administration of justice and discourages cooperation.

Simultaneously, there are cases in which, if an individual remains at liberty, they may actively obstruct investigations by concealing evidence, intimidating witnesses, and engaging in similar conduct. It is unsurprising that some may exploit their position or influence to manipulate the judicial process. That is why pre-trial detention—or temporary detention, in some cases—becomes such an important legal tool. It allows investigators to act quickly and secure key evidence before it disappears or is compromised.

Of course, this type of imprisonment must always be properly justified, as the law demands. But when it is, I see it as a vital component of a successful investigation. It is not meant to be a punishment—that only comes after a final conviction. But to ensure public order, uphold the law, and protect the integrity of the legal process, it should absolutely be used when needed. And in the case of Car Wash, it proved to be indispensable.

Was the popular support for Operation Car Wash unexpected, or was it to be anticipated given the broader context of Brazilian society's long-standing desire to combat corruption, pursue justice, and end entrenched impunity?

Transparency International[267] is the most important organisation in the world when it comes to the fight against corruption. It operates in over 110 countries and was founded in either 1995 or 1993[268]—so it has been around for more than thirty years. The organisation conducts ongoing studies, analyses, and data verification related to corruption. The best known of these is the Corruption Perception Index, or CPI,[269] which currently evaluates indicators in 180 countries.

Unfortunately, Brazil has been dropping in the rankings. In the most recent CPI, released in early 2021.[270] Brazil scored just 38 points. To put that into context, the average for Latin America is 41 and the global average is 43. Brazil came in at 96th out of 180 countries. But despite that bleak picture, another recent study by Transparency International found that a large portion of the Brazilian population—if I am not mistaken, around 80%—believes that society does have the ability to turn things around. In other words, even in the face of a serious and complex situation, there is still a sense of optimism among Brazilians that change is possible.

Corruption is undeniably a significant issue, with institutions compromised at various levels. Nevertheless, there remains a prevailing belief that societal engagement can help reverse this trend. Paradoxically, while many desire change, they often inadvertently perpetuate the cycle. Regrettably, there persists a tendency to raise children not necessarily to be honest, but to be clever—to "get ahead" by any means necessary. Integrity is not always prioritised.

To answer your question more directly, the popular support for Operation Car Wash largely resulted from the way the operation was conducted. There was a clear commitment to transparency—data was made publicly available, an accessible website was created, and it was easy for people to follow developments. This openness resonated deeply, fostering a sense of hope that justice was finally accessible to the poor and powerless. For the first time, the public witnessed the justice system confronting powerful individuals with both resolve and determination.

In my view, that was incredibly significant. As I mentioned earlier, political science often highlights the idea that you need to catch the "big fish" and make it visible—it is a sort of pedagogy of exemplarity. Car

Wash followed that script to the letter. The major figures were targeted, thereby inspiring society to engage in the fight against corruption.

Have there been changes in the relationship between the Brazilian government and public or private companies as a result of Operation Car Wash?

Indeed, there have been improvements, advances, and tangible developments resulting from the work of Operation Car Wash. It is also important to highlight the introduction of Law No. 12.846[271]—the Clean Company Act—which laid the legal groundwork for compliance in Brazil. These represent important steps contributing to progress; however, in my view, the overall improvement remains limited. Companies need to place integrity and compliance at the very core of their operations—it has to be part of their DNA. It needs to live in the heart, in the soul of the company. The process is ongoing, and although progress is being made, cultural change does not occur overnight; it takes generations. Transformation cannot be achieved solely through a single event or investigation. Operation Car Wash was undoubtedly significant, yet it has not entirely transformed the approach to combating corruption in Brazil.

In fact, part of the reason Brazil dropped in the Corruption Perception Index rankings was precisely because Car Wash lifted the rug—and a lot of hidden dirt came to light. While it was an essential step, it is insufficient on its own. What is truly required is comprehensive legal reform, including the abolition of privileged jurisdiction, the allowance of imprisonment following second-instance convictions, and the criminalisation of electoral slush funds—since current penalties, such as those stipulated in Article 350 of the Electoral Code,[272] are inadequate.

A strong proposal in this direction is the *New Measures Against Corruption*[273]—the largest anti-corruption package ever developed globally. It was created over the course of a year by Transparency International in partnership with the Getulio Vargas Foundation. They consulted hundreds of experts and institutions, and the result was a comprehensive plan containing seventy proposals across twelve thematic areas to help reshape our reality.

Was Operation Car Wash important? Undoubtedly. However, it represents only one step in a much longer journey. Far greater progress is needed, including comprehensive legislative reform. Furthermore, it is essential that citizens become more informed and exercise greater awareness when voting, thereby electing representatives who genuinely honour their mandates. Significant investment in education is also imperative; the existing deficit in this area is vast. Brazil requires a genuine educational revolution to raise public awareness and fundamentally transform the foundations of its current reality.

There is a lot that still needs to happen. I often say—and will reiterate—that corruption cannot be combated with a superhero's cape or a silver bullet. Reliance on individual heroes is misguided, and no magical solution exists to resolve the issue overnight. There is no single answer; rather, a suite of measures must be consistently implemented. Dependence on specific individuals—person A, B, or C—is untenable. Efforts must focus on reducing opportunities for corruption, strengthening institutional systems, promoting transparency, and diminishing concentrations of power. Regrettably, those in positions of authority frequently act to increase, rather than limit, opportunities for corrupt practices.

Would you like to offer a final comment on Operation Car Wash?

Despite the controversy arising from leaked conversations published by The Intercept, and Judge Moro's transition from the judiciary into politics, Operation Car Wash leaves a lasting legacy in the fight against corruption.

Car Wash played a key role—regardless of the narratives that have been constructed, or the episode involving those criminally obtained messages, which were never forensically examined, may have been edited, and whose content, while not fully confirmed, was also not denied by those involved. Despite all the attempt at deconstruction, often driven by those with vested interests, I have no doubt that Operation Car Wash made a significant contribution to Brazil—particularly in terms of tackling corruption efficiently, encouraging institutional cooperation, and placing high-level corruption at the forefront of the agenda. And prioritising the fight against high-level corruption is vital. It directly impacts the right to education, to healthcare, to sanitation, housing, security—to the implementation of all public policies. That kind of prioritisation is essential.

When reflecting on the full scope of what Operation Car Wash represented, it is essential to adopt a balanced perspective and consider the entire forest rather than focusing on a single tree. In my view, the overall impact was positive. It brought real results for Brazilian citizenship and public integrity. The fight against corruption existed before Car Wash and it continues now—but it is a real pity that the operation ended the way it did. Without a doubt, the way it was dismantled has led to a loss in both efficiency and effectiveness in combatting high-level corruption. Currently, attention appears to be concentrated on low-level, isolated cases, lacking dedicated structures or strategic focus. This represents a regression, resulting in a significant loss of momentum.

Car Wash brought a serious and firm response to corruption. If there were concerns about how individuals were portrayed in the media or about internal protocols, those matters could and should have been addressed through proper dialogue. However, encountering operational issues is not a justification for shutting down an entire institution. Much like a hospital with faulty plumbing or wiring, the appropriate response is to undertake necessary repairs to ensure continued service and effectiveness. The same principle applies to Operation Car Wash: efforts should have focused on rectifying its shortcomings while allowing it to continue serving society by protecting public assets, as it had been doing. That is my perspective.

Roberto Livianu was born in São Paulo (SP). He is a Prosecutor of Justice of the Public Ministry of the State of São Paulo and president of the Institute I Do Not Accept Corruption. His testimony was given on 5 March 2021 via the Zoom virtual platform and lasted 1 hour and 8 minutes of recording. The transcript was subsequently reviewed by interviewed on 26 February 2023.

Testimony of Rodrigo Chemim

Abstract

This section provides a detailed account of the legal, institutional, and cultural conditions that shaped the evolution of Brazil's anti-corruption enforcement capabilities, with a particular focus on the trajectory leading to Operation Car Wash. It begins by situating the transformation of the Public Prosecutor's Office within the broader context of the 1988 Constitution, which granted the institution unprecedented guarantees—such as functional, administrative, and financial autonomy—thereby enabling prosecutors to move beyond a reactive, desk-bound role and take on proactive investigatory functions. The testimony underscores the significance of this structural change, noting how it allowed the development of specialised prosecutorial branches and a new investigative culture, particularly in the area of white-collar crime.

In drawing a comparison between Italy's Operation Clean Hands (1992–1994) and Brazil's Operation Car Wash (2014–2019), the narrative highlights striking similarities, from the triggering events and use of plea bargaining to the pivotal role of the media and the eventual backlash by political institutions. While both operations temporarily disrupted systemic corruption and galvanised public mobilisation, both also encountered organised resistance that sought to reverse their gains—whether through legislative reforms, judicial reinterpretations, or political interference.

The section also provides a critical legal analysis of the Brazilian criminal justice system's structural obstacles to accountability, particularly the controversial doctrine of retroactive prescription and the excessive reliance on procedural nullities to avoid substantive rulings. These legal peculiarities, alongside political inertia and elite impunity, form a "perfect storm" that continues to undermine enforcement. Yet, the testimony maintains that the public played, and continues to play, a vital role in resisting this regression. From spontaneous civic mobilisation to electoral pressure, the population has intermittently demonstrated the capacity to influence institutional outcomes and defend democratic integrity.

Ultimately, this section offers both a diagnosis and a call to action: the fragility of the Brazilian legal system in the face of elite corruption requires not only institutional reform but also sustained civic oversight. The interview ends with a reflection on the legacy of these anti-corruption efforts, framed by the question of how future generations will judge the choices made today. The cost of corruption, the testimony reminds us, is borne not only in abstract terms, but in lives denied access to healthcare, education, and opportunity. It is this invisible suffering—diffuse, bureaucratic, and often politically tolerated—that makes the fight against systemic corruption both so urgent and so difficult.

Could you provide an overview of your academic background and professional trajectory, in order to contextualise your involvement in anti-corruption efforts?

I graduated in Law from the Federal University of Paraná in 1991, followed by a specialisation in Criminal Law and Criminal Procedure in 1993. I later earned a master's degree in public relations law in 2001 and a doctorate in State Law in 2015. I have been a member of the Public Ministry of the State of Paraná for 30 years, with more than fifteen of those dedicated to criminal investigations, particularly focusing on white-collar crimes.

Alongside that, I have also been teaching Criminal Procedural Law for over 25 years. I currently lecture on both the undergraduate and professional master's programmes in Law at Positive University, as well as on undergraduate Law courses at Unicuritiba and Franciscan University Centre, all based in Curitiba.

You wrote the book *Clean Hands and Car Wash: Corruption Looks in the Mirror*.[274] You are considered one of Brazil's leading experts on Operation Clean Hands.[275] Could you please provide an overview of Operation Clean Hands and draw a comparison with Operation Car Wash?

Although Italy and Brazil are very different countries, with distinct histories and cultures, and although these two major anti-corruption operations happened decades apart—Operation Clean Hands in Italy between 1992 and 1994, and Operation Car Wash in Brazil from 2014 to 2019—the similarities are striking.

Both operations began with seemingly minor events. In Italy, it all started with the arrest of a relatively obscure politician, Mario Chiesa,[276] who ran a public care home in Milan and was caught extorting money from the service providers—demanding a cut of the contracts. In Brazil, the trigger was news that Alberto Youssef,[277] a well-known black-market currency dealer, had gifted a Land Rover to a former Petrobras director, Paulo Roberto Costa.[278] In both cases, the investigations progressed through a series of plea bargain agreements, setting off a domino effect that eventually implicated key political figures.

Another shared aspect was the intense media coverage, which played a major role in shaping public perception. The widespread attention encouraged people to take to the streets in protest corruption. In both countries, the press effectively "appointed" national heroes: in Italy, it was the Public Prosecutor Antonio Di Pietro[279]; in Brazil, the spotlight fell on judge Sergio Moro.[280] Interestingly, both eventually resigned from their judicial posts to enter politics.

The investigations reached the very top. In Italy, former Prime Minister Bettino Craxi[281] was convicted. In Brazil, the probe eventually reached former President Lula.[282]

There is a memorable episode involving Craxi: he went to Parliament and gave a speech essentially saying that everyone there had done the same as him—implying that they should all just own up to it together. The response was silence. But that silence was powerful. It resonated so deeply with the Italian public that they took to the streets the very next day.

Craxi was staying at the Raphael Hotel in Rome at the time. When he emerged the next morning, protesters were outside waiting. They began singing a parody of Guantanamera and threw coins at him, chanting, "Bettino, vuoi pure queste?"—"Bettino, do you also want these?" It was their way of saying, "If you have sold yourself for money, here are a few more coins for you."

Such a reaction is unlikely to be witnessed again today, considering the widespread frustration resulting from the erosion of effective criminal justice responses. In both countries, the establishment ultimately found ways to dilute the outcomes of these investigations. In Italy, it was mainly through legislative reforms—decriminalising certain actions, reducing limitation periods, and creating new evidentiary hurdles. In Brazil, the backlash came more forcefully, from all three branches of government: Executive, Legislative, and Judiciary.

And the outcome? Much like in Italy, there remains a pervasive sense of collective disillusionment—a profound frustration at the persistent failure to hold those who misappropriate public funds genuinely accountable.

What underlying factors contribute to the culture of impunity in countries such as Italy and Brazil? To what extent can this phenomenon be explained?

The Brazilian people, in general, exhibit a temperament similar to that of Italians—not only because of the significant Italian immigration to Brazil but also in their character. Cheerfulness, sociability, and a fondness for festivities are common traits. In fact, these characteristics align more closely with the Italian way of life than with the Portuguese. Expressiveness, passion for football, and an enjoyment of celebration are prevalent. A cultural tendency towards joyfulness persists, even in the face of adversity.

This personality, I think, might contribute to something that Raimundo Faoro,[283] in a book called *The Owners of Power*.[284] He identifies a tendency to solve problems not through legal means, but through personal relationships. So, for those who control or influence power, the law becomes more of a detail than a determining factor. When someone becomes entangled in criminal activity, the first instinct is not to think about legal consequences, but to say: "Hang on, I know someone who knows someone who might be able to sort this out." This desire to resolve things through personal connections rather than through the justice system is very much present both in Italy and in Brazil. I believe this contributes to enabling powerful individuals to escape accountability—and perhaps explains the persistence of impunity.

However, the issue is not solely cultural; it is also legal. Legislation, even when correctly applied, significantly contributes to the difficulty of holding those in power accountable. Both Brazilian and Italian laws tend to be considerably more lenient towards the ruling class than towards the less privileged segments of society.

Taking Brazil as an example, an examination of the Penal Code and broader criminal legislation reveals that offences typically classified as "white-collar crime"—a term coined by the American criminologist Edwin Sutherland[285] in the 1950s to describe non-violent crimes involving public resources or trust—carry relatively low penalties. The highest minimum sentence for these crimes is typically just three years. I will explain why that is important.

In Brazil, penalties are set between a legal minimum and maximum, and the tradition is to start from the minimum. If the defendant is a first-time offender, has a clean record, and no aggravating circumstances—traits that are very common among white-collar defendants—then they almost always receive the minimum sentence. And what is the problem with that? Under current legislation, which sets a three-year minimum sentence, numerous benefits and alternatives to imprisonment are now available. This was not always the case, particularly at the outset of Operation Car Wash, but it is the situation today.

The so-called the Anti-Crime Package[286]—which, ironically, includes very few anti-crime provisions—introduced several measures that make it harder to prosecute elite criminality. This new law, introduced in the Code of Criminal Procedure in Article 28-A,[287] provides for the so-called non-prosecution agreement for all crimes whose minimum penalty is less than four years and are without violence or serious threat. Therefore, for all white-collar crimes, accountability is already challenging and is likely to become even more so under the current legal framework.

Prior to the 2014 commencement of Operation Car Wash and before the recent reforms, existing legislation already tended to permit cases to lapse due to statute of limitations. For clarity, an explanation follows for those unfamiliar with the concept. The State has a limited window of time to bring someone to justice, called the statute of limitations. There is a table in Article 109[288] of the Penal Code establishes the statute of limitations period based on the maximum sentence prescribed by law. For example, corruption carries a penalty of two to twelve years. According to that table, a crime with a twelve-year maximum sentence has a limitation period of sixteen years—from the date the crime occurred.

If charges are filed within this period, the limitation period resets, initiating a new sixteen-year timeframe for the trial to be conducted. Upon conviction, a further sixteen years commence for the execution of the sentence. In theory, one might argue that such extensive periods make conviction almost inevitable. However, Brazil has a distinctive feature absent even in Italy: the "retroactive statute of limitations." This provision allows the limitation period to be recalculated based on the actual sentence imposed rather than the maximum sentence permitted. Consequently, if an individual receives a sentence of, for example, two years instead of twelve, the applicable limitation period is retroactively shortened. This mechanism permits convictions to be overturned on the basis that the statute of limitations has expired, even after prolonged legal proceedings. This peculiarity is distinctly Brazilian and disproportionately benefits those already in a privileged position.

Would you consider retroactive prescription to be one of those uniquely Brazilian legal peculiarities—a sort of juridical "jaboticaba"[289] (a rare Brazilian fruit that grows exclusively in Brazil)?

It is a jabuticaba—a term denoting something uniquely Brazilian, for better or worse, a distinctly national legal peculiarity. The retroactive statute of limitations entails recalculating the limitation period based on the actual sentence imposed by the judge, rather than the maximum penalty prescribed by law. Once proceedings conclude, the judge determines a specific sentence within the prescribed minimum and maximum range. Consequently, the limitation period begins to run from the date of the actual sentence, rather than from the maximum theoretical penalty.

Take corruption, for instance. The minimum sentence is two years. If the defendant is a first-time offender with a clean record, tradition in Brazilian law says the judge will likely stick to the minimum. So, you take those two years and look at Article 109 of the Penal Code—it tells you that the crime prescribes in four years. It used to be sixteen. So, looking back in time, if more than four years passed between the crime and the conclusion of the investigation, that is it—prescription applies. Which means the sentence is pointless. The process shouldn't have even reached this stage. I do not know if you are following—it is genuinely hard to explain.

I once tried to explain retroactive statute of limitations to a German professor visiting the university in Curitiba. Dinner was underway—he spoke Portuguese, fortunately, as he was married to a Brazilian. An attempt was made to communicate, but he said, "I did not understand." A second attempt met the same response. Then, the waiter was asked for pen and paper, and everything was drawn out. He looked and said, "I did not understand. But I did understand one thing—I understand why you lost seven-one". Then he added, "You are not a serious country." That remark struck hard. Flour was requested from the waiter as a metaphorical means to swallow the criticism, for there was no defence to be made. The observation was accurate; it simply defied logic and contradicted the fundamental purpose of prescription.

The statute of limitations is intended to reflect the state's interest in administering punishment. If an excessive amount of time elapses, it is assumed that the state is no longer interested in pursuing punishment, thereby undermining the purpose of the penalty. Yet the irony lies in the fact that the state asserts, "Yes, I am punishing," while simultaneously implying, "Actually, my interest has waned." The German's bafflement was understandable: "How can that be? I do not understand." This concept can be difficult to grasp, and readers may find it challenging as well. The crucial point is that, due to this recalculation of the limitation period based on the actual sentence imposed and the retrospective nature of the analysis, effective punishment becomes virtually impossible. By the time a conviction is reached and reviewed, the offence may already have prescribed according to the imposed sentence.

In the Car Wash Operation, something interesting happened—especially early on. A legislative change in 2010 eliminated retroactive statute of limitations during the investigation phase. So now, from the date of the crime until the end of the investigation, retroactive statute of limitations no longer applies. But from the start of the trial to sentencing, it still does. That is a different phase, and the retroactive rule still holds.

After 2010, criminal defence lawyers lost one of their traditional strategies. Prior to that, when defending clients accused of white-collar crime, it was common to advise, “Relax. Conviction is likely, but imprisonment is unlikely. By the time a conviction is secured, the sentence will be minimal, and the offence will likely have prescribed.” This was a realistic approach, given the protracted duration of such cases—and the possibility of further delays only improved prospects. The strength of the evidence was often acknowledged, but the expectation remained that, while reputational damage might occur, incarceration could be avoided. This was the fallback strategy when a direct challenge to the evidence was not feasible.

And in white-collar crimes, the evidence is usually documentary and hard to dispute. Holding power of attorney for a Swiss bank account registered under the name of a Panamanian shell company with fictitious directors—used by a Brazilian contractor or politician—presents a challenge to direct explanation. When the evidence cannot be confronted head-on, legal defence often resorts to what are termed lateral attacks: either invoking prescription or identifying procedural flaws, such as nullities. Arguing the facts or documents is avoided, as they would likely result in conviction. Instead, the strategy focuses on delaying proceedings until prescription applies or capitalising on procedural technicalities. However, in May 2010, one such lateral defence—reliance on the retroactive statute of limitations—was no longer available.

Then, in 2014, Car Wash begins. Most of the crimes under investigation had taken place after May 2010. Criminal defence lawyers were left with one principal option: procedural nullity. Consequently, they sought to identify any such grounds. Early in the investigation, the focus was primarily on Alberto Youssef and Paulo Roberto Costa. A phone intercept mentioned a federal congressperson. Given that congresspersons enjoy special legal privileges and are meant to be tried by the Federal Supreme Court, the defence contended that the entire process was invalid, arguing that a lower court judge should not have presided over any matters involving a federal congressperson. However, at that stage, the congressperson was not under formal investigation; their name had surfaced incidentally within the scope of the inquiry. Nevertheless, the defence seized upon this point in an attempt to assert procedural nullity from the outset.

When the news broke, the defence lawyer's immediate thought was to seize the opportunity: argue that the first-instance judge lacked jurisdiction over the case and that it should properly be heard by the Federal Supreme Court. The strategy involved filing a complaint alleging that the authority of the Supreme Court was being usurped by a lower court judge. The complaint landed on Supreme Court Justice Teori Zavascki's [290] desk. He looked at it and said, "You are right, here's the name of the congressperson mentioned in the wiretap." So, he sent an official request to Judge Sergio Moro: "Send me everything." But before forwarding it, Moro wrote back to Teori: "Justice, I will send it, but I have a question—do I send everything?".

Of course, the lawyers did not inform the Justice of the full extent the investigation had already reached. From its inception, the Car Wash operation had a substantial investigative backstory, beginning with a drug trafficking case in Londrina. The inquiry was already extensive—a comprehensive investigation involving numerous documents and many individuals. Upon seeing the magnitude of the case, Teori Zavascki instructed Moro: "Do this—only send what refers to the congressperson. The rest stays in Curitiba." With this decision, Teori effectively preempted a legal argument that might have arisen later—that the entire process was null on the grounds that a first-instance judge lacked jurisdiction. This potential claim of nullity was resolved at the very outset.

So, what remained for the defence lawyer? The option to mount a lateral attack based on retroactive statute of limitations was no longer available. The nullity argument had failed. What was left was the forward statute of limitations—the one that begins after sentencing, based on the actual penalty imposed. This period amounts to four years, counted prospectively, encompassing the appeals process. Given Brazil's notably generous appeals system, it is, in practice, possible to file more than thirty appeals against a single decision. Even though there are only four levels of courts, each has internal procedural avenues. Altogether, it is common for cases to involve more than thirty appeals, which can prolong proceedings for ten to fifteen years.

The defence strategy shifted to relying on the forward statute of limitations. However, in 2016, the Supreme Court ruled that it was possible to commence serving a sentence following conviction at second instance, without waiting for all appeals to be exhausted. That decision by the Supreme Court triggered a wave of plea bargains. For the first time in Brazilian history, white-collar criminals faced a genuine risk of punishment.

At that point, what options remained for the defence? With the evidence unassailable, retroactive statute of limitations no longer viable, and the appeals process unable to delay sentencing indefinitely, the only recourse was negotiation—striking a deal and cooperating.

That was when Operation Car Wash escalated massively. The volume of material uncovered was sufficient to sustain investigations for another ten to fifteen years.

However, as is widely known, much of this material was ultimately lost following rulings that declared the investigations in Curitiba null on the basis that jurisdiction should have been in Brasília—and subsequently, due to the formal declaration of Judge Sergio Moro's partiality.

Which aspects of Operation Car Wash do you find most striking? Was it the scale of the illicit sums involved, the participation of high-ranking politicians, or the role played by major corporations? In your view, what was the most surprising element of the investigation?

I believe it is the amounts involved. The corrupt nature of Brazilian politics was already somewhat known—it has always been present, really. Perhaps what is most striking is that, while people had long suspected this was how things operated, it is no longer mere suspicion. Now, it is known exactly how it worked. What was once assumed has been laid bare—in detail, with names and figures—revealing precisely how the game was played.

The major construction companies were effectively running the country. There has always been some awareness of their political influence, but Operation Car Wash truly exposed the extent of it. When the same construction company donates to both politician A and politician B—who might even belong to opposing parties—it becomes clear that it is not about supporting the best candidate. It is not a matter of political ideology; it is purely business. Operation Car Wash made this crystal clear.

No one today can claim ignorance about how things have operated in Brazil for years—perhaps even decades. It is truly heartbreaking to witness how much public money has ended up in private pockets—funds that could, and should, have been invested in improving the lives of Brazil's poorest citizens.

That is what is most shocking: grasping the sheer scale of it all. For example, there was a black-market currency dealer under investigation who offered to return one or two billion reais. And let's be honest—we cannot even truly comprehend what a billion means. It is an astronomical sum, one that could solve countless problems across numerous sectors throughout the country.

One of the first individuals investigated in Operation Car Wash was Pedro Barusco,[291] a third-tier manager at Petrobras. As part of a plea bargain, he issued a cheque for over 100 million reais.

If someone at that level voluntarily returns more than a hundred million reais, just imagine how much was actually diverted—and how much remains undiscovered. Not everything will ever come to light. Stories circulate about flats stuffed with cash—suitcases containing fifty million reais inside.[292] That is not an isolated incident; it is a recurring pattern of behaviour.

Brazilian politics has developed a kind of know-how when it comes to embezzlement—it runs through all levels. I have investigated countless councillors and deputies, and I came to realise it is a learned system. There is considerable discussion about the "rachadinha" scheme[293]—that too is part of the know-how. In nearly every municipal council across the country—and numbering over five thousand—and in most legislative assemblies, similar schemes are taking place.

In Paraná, a major scandal known as Secret Diaries ("Diários Secretos" in Portuguese)[294] exposed the same mechanisms currently under investigation. Similar practices were uncovered in the Curitiba City Council. Therefore, when fifty million reais in cash is found in a suitcase in a flat in Bahia, it is not merely a bizarre incident; it is the modus operandi.

Rocha Loures[295] was caught leaving a traditional pizzeria in São Paulo carrying a suitcase containing 500,000 reais.

Exactly. That whole scenario—the suitcases, the empty flats—is part of a repeated pattern. It is reasonable to assume that several such flats exist across the country, although they have yet to be discovered. This is a systematic, replicable method of operation—a know-how of embezzlement and money laundering. Operation Car Wash is shocking from every angle. The scale of misconduct in the management of public funds is staggering. It is deeply saddening to acknowledge that this situation has been allowed to reach such proportions.

Gary Becker's economic theory of crime[296] posits that an individual's decision to engage in criminal behaviour is essentially a rational calculation aimed at financial gain. If the perceived risk of detection is low and the potential reward high, the individual is more likely to proceed. In your view, did Operation Car Wash, at least initially, succeed in shifting this paradigm of impunity by increasing the risk and reducing the financial rewards, thereby diminishing impunity? Or do you consider that it failed to bring about a fundamental change, particularly in the light of more recent legislative developments in Brazil?

I have been part of the Public Prosecutor's Office since 1992, so I lived through the changes brought about by the 1988 Constitution, when the role of the Prosecutor's Office was redefined. It is important that people understand this. The design of the Constitution, by conferring specific guarantees upon the Public Prosecutor's Office, established the foundation for the achievements that followed.

Historically, until the 1988 Constitution, the Brazilian Public Prosecutor's Office functioned essentially as an extension of the Executive Branch, remaining subordinate to it. In the states, for example, the head of the Prosecutor's Office was accountable to the governor—the chain of command ran from governor to secretary of justice, then to the General Prosecutor, who was a trusted appointee of the governor. At the federal level, the structure was similar: the president, followed by the minister of justice, and then the attorney general, who was likewise subordinate to the president.

Prosecutors at both state and federal levels lacked autonomy. They were deprived even of fundamental guarantees such as job security and immovability. What was the consequence? Widespread political interference whereby allies of those in power were simply exempt from investigation.

The 1988 Constitution brought about a fundamental change. It gave prosecutors the same guarantees as judges: immovability, irreducibility of salary, and functional autonomy. It also granted administrative and financial autonomy. So, in fact, there are three types of autonomy—administrative, financial, and functional—and that transformed the entire structure of the Public Prosecutor's Office.

For the first time, it had its own line in the state budget. Before that, it did not even appear in the annual budget law because it was not seen as an independent entity. I will give you a simple, everyday example. Before 1988, if a prosecutor working in the countryside needed to buy something as basic as paper, they'd have to go through a whole chain of requests: from the attorney general to the secretary of justice, then to the secretary of administration, who would need to get approval from the Treasury—and all of that depending on whether the governor was in a good mood. If he was not, the paper just would not be bought. It may sound trivial, but it illustrates the lack of autonomy. After 1988, that all changed. The Public Prosecutor's Office could make its own decisions, carry out its own procurement, and decide where to allocate its funds. It started defining its own priorities. It began to create internal structures with specific focus areas. That is an essential point to grasp—because this restructuring paved the way for the sense of hope we experienced during Operation Car Wash. Even though, yes, much of that has now been dismantled through legislative changes and rulings by the Federal Supreme Court, the momentum we had come from those earlier reforms.

Before 1988, prosecutors were essentially bureaucrats. Their daily routine involved arriving at the office to find a stack of police inquiries and ongoing cases awaiting review. Each case would be assessed: "This one requires formal charges; that one should be filed away." Attendance at court hearings to hear witness testimonies was part of the role, followed by returning the next day to a new batch of cases. That was the extent of the role. This remains largely the reality for many prosecutors working in criminal courts today. However, prior to 1988, this limited scope was the norm for all prosecutors.

What changed after the Constitution? With financial and administrative autonomy, the Prosecutor's Office began establishing specialised branches. For example, in Paraná—an area I am familiar with—the first office dedicated to the protection of public property was created in 1992. This was followed in 1994 by the establishment of the first criminal investigations office. This represented a significant transformation: the Prosecutor's Office became actively investigative, moving beyond its previously passive, desk-bound role. It began to pursue evidence independently—something unprecedented at the time. Prior to this, it relied solely on police investigations; if the police did not investigate a matter, it was effectively invisible to the Prosecutor's Office.

And what did the police normally bring forward? Cases of street crime—such as theft, robbery, drug trafficking, homicide, assault, and rape. What did they not bring? Financial fraud, corruption, embezzlement, procurement scams, tax evasion—essentially, white-collar crime. This was not due to the absence of such offences, but rather because these matters were not pursued by the police, nor, consequently, by the Prosecutor's Office.

This created an environment conducive to inaction, which explains why impunity prevailed in Brazil for so long—right up until 1988. Only once the Constitution began to be effectively implemented—starting around 1992 to 1994—did tangible change become apparent. Granting autonomy in the Constitution was one matter; securing respect for that autonomy from governors, legislative assemblies, and other powerholders—who stood to lose control—was quite another.

The 1988 Constitution led to the Prosecutor's Office being referred to as the so-called fourth power.

Indeed, the Prosecutor's Office was entrusted with a broad array of responsibilities. Today, it is active in numerous fields—environmental protection, consumer rights, among others—that it had not engaged with prior to 1988. This represents a rather unprecedented model on a global scale: a Public Prosecutor's Office intervening across such diverse sectors. This may largely stem from the historically limited organisation of Brazilian society—though that is a discussion for another time.

When I was a prosecutor working in the countryside, I went to the city council to present a bill to establish a Consumer Protection Agency—essentially a local consumer protection body—just to relieve myself a bit from that side of the workload. Once the city council created the Consumer Protection Agency, my involvement in consumer-related matters decreased, and I was able to devote more time to criminal issues.

The fact is, the Public Prosecutor's Office started investigating highly sensitive areas. Just to give you an example—in Paraná, which I know quite well—if you look at the number of criminal cases brought against mayors before the 1988 Constitution, I doubt it would even fill one hand. There were one, two, maybe three sporadic cases, usually triggered by some sort of political conflict. But from 1992 to 2002, in just the first ten years of the specialised office's existence in Paraná, over a thousand criminal complaints were filed against mayors—and that is just in one state. How many mayors are there in Paraná? There are three hundred and ninety-nine. Over a period of ten years—approximately two and a half terms—it is evident that a significant backlog of demand accumulated.

This even caused some discomfort in the courts at the time, because they did not have the structure to handle it. That is changed now. Twenty-five or thirty years later, the Paraná courts actually have a dedicated chamber for crimes committed by mayors. The system had to adapt. Nowadays, a mayor being convicted is not even news anymore—but at the time, it was a major scandal. Gradually, that starts to build a new culture: "It is not so easy anymore."

The high point of this structuring of the Brazilian Public Prosecutor's Office came when the Federal Public Prosecutor's Office began to catch up. When did that happen? When the new generation of federal prosecutors started moving into specialist roles.

The Federal Public Prosecutor's Office has always faced a different historical issue. If you look at the older generation of federal prosecutors—those who joined before the 1988 Constitution, including the current Attorney General of the Republic, Augusto Aras[297]—they were allowed to practise law. They acted as lawyers for the Union. At that time, there was no Attorney General's Office for the Union, so the Federal Public Prosecutor's Office played a dual role: both as legal counsel for the government and as public prosecutors. The older generation never really operated under the tradition of an independent Public Prosecutor's Office leading criminal investigations.

That only began to change with the new generation. The structure of the Attorney General's Office for the Union was created in 1988 precisely to take that legal advocacy role away from the Prosecutor's Office, so it could focus on what it is really meant to do—investigate crime. And this new generation was not influenced by that old dual identity, of being both advocate and prosecutor. They came in with a different mindset, with renewed energy. The prosecutors involved in Operation Car Wash—they were all from that younger generation.

To what extent did this institutional aspect of the Prosecutor's Office contribute to the success of Operation Car Wash?

Undoubtedly, a combination of factors contributed to the emergence of a new institutional culture within the Public Prosecutor's Office—one characterised by a proactive stance, no longer merely awaiting police action but assuming a leading role in the investigation of white-collar crime. That is what made cases like the Mensalão possible at first, and later, Car Wash. But these actions did not just begin with Mensalão or Car Wash. They started within the State Public Prosecutor's Offices. This task force model was already being used in what we call the Special Action Group to Combat Organised Crime which exists within state-level Public Prosecutor's Offices. The Special Action Group to Combat Organised Crime have their origins in the creation of criminal investigation prosecutor offices back in 1994.

This culture has gradually taken shape since the 1988 Constitution—removing prosecutors from behind their desks and, as the saying goes, from "beans with bureaucratic rice", and placing them on the front line. It has been a slow, step-by-step process. If, in 1992, upon joining the Public Prosecutor's Office, someone had said: "An investigation will be carried out, leading to the imprisonment of a former President of the Republic. A sitting governor will be arrested as part of an inquiry," the immediate reaction would have been: "Such a notion is very naïve—there is a clear lack of understanding of how things operate here. That is never going to happen." But it did happen.

Take Governor Pezão[298] of Rio de Janeiro—for the first time in Brazilian history, a sitting governor was arrested while still in office. Although a few former governors had previously been detained, this was without precedent. Naturally, a backlash followed. This forms part of a broader, gradual transformation. In retrospect, significant progress can be identified in the state's capacity to ensure accountability for misconduct in public office, with Operation Car Wash representing the pinnacle of that process. At present, however, there is a clear sense of decline in that very capacity—driven, in large part, by an intense reaction from the political establishment, including from within the Public Prosecutor's Office itself. Even its highest-ranking official, the Prosecutor General, recently issued highly inappropriate remarks, casting doubt on the work of the Car Wash task force. At the very least, these were extremely regrettable statements.

The outlook from here does not seem too promising. It is very likely we'll see a kind of pendulum effect—a reaction that drags us backwards. But if we look at things on a broader, long-term scale, the trend over the last thirty years does point towards progress. Whether that progress can hold depends on the strength of the forces now pushing back—in Parliament, in the Judiciary, within the Public Prosecutor's Office itself. We've seen multiple layers of the establishment beginning to speak with one voice against Car Wash, in a very clear effort to rewrite history.

There is, indeed, a degree of optimism when comparing the present with thirty years ago. I do, however, remain cautious, keeping both feet firmly on the ground when reflecting on the reaction already underway.

In conclusion, are there any recommendations that could be offered regarding measures considered essential to reversing the current trajectory towards renewed impunity for the rich and powerful?

Civil society plays a fundamental role in this context. Although the political class possesses considerable influence, its capacity for action is not unlimited. A reaction from the public remains a source of apprehension for many political actors. It is essential, however, to distinguish this from what occurred in January 2023, which cannot be characterised as legitimate public mobilisation, but rather as an attempted coup d'état. Even outside the exceptional context of the pandemic, there were moments when the public took to the streets—and, in some instances, these actions brought about tangible change. There were numerous attempts—I am not sure whether that remains widely recalled, as such episodes are often quickly forgotten.

For example, there was an incident on a Monday night when Congress tried to pass an amnesty law. As soon as news of this leaked on social media, there was an immediate and widespread reaction of indignation, which forced members of the Congress to back down within hours. No political actor was willing to take responsibility for the bill that would have granted a general and unconditional amnesty. The episode made it unmistakably clear how powerful the public's reaction can be. A similar attempt occurred more recently. For example, there was an effort to introduce the so-called crime of hermeneutics—a provision that ultimately was not included in the Law on Abuse of Authority.[299]

Initially, this law proposed a very dangerous provision. The idea was that if a prosecutor brought a charge against someone, and after several appeals, the Federal Supreme Court ruled that the interpretation was incorrect, the prosecutor could be charged with a crime. This was part of the Law of Abuse of Authority, but thanks to public pressure, it did not make it through. The role of the public in keeping an eye on the political class, especially during elections, is vital. People need to choose their candidates carefully, investigate their positions, and understand who they're voting for. This is key to improving the Brazilian Parliament and ensuring that people who truly grasp the importance of upholding guarantees for the Prosecutor's Office are in power.

There are risks ahead. For example, Congress has occasionally called for a Parliamentary Inquiry Commission" into Car Wash or the Public Prosecutor's Office. This is an attempt to create a climate of demoralisation. Once this objective is achieved, the Public Prosecutor's Office will be stripped of its power. And what would that mean in practice? It would mark a return to the pre-1988 status quo, in which prosecutors were confined to bureaucratic functions—precisely the scenario envisioned by those seeking to protect corrupt political interests. At present, the Prosecutor's Office is the only institution in the country that possesses genuine autonomy to act Car Wash prosecutors do not receive directives from any superior authority—not even from the General Prosecutor. There was even an attempt to remove Deltan[300] from the Car Wash task force, but ultimately, the decision to leave was his. Why was it so important to remove him? Because Deltan was someone who was acting in strict compliance with procedural requirements. His removal conveyed a clear message: "Interference is possible." In many respects, that established a dangerous precedent.

In the thirty years since the 1988 Constitution, there had never been instances of prosecutors being removed for performing their duties properly. There were a few exceptional cases involving removal due to negligence, but such circumstances cannot be attributed to those involved in Operation Car Wash. For this reason, the sustained vigilance and engagement of civil society—particularly in preventing setbacks through parliamentary initiatives—remain essential. It is strongly recommended that efforts to strengthen investigative work continue, so that in the near future, a better country may be left for future generations.

It is also fascinating to look back at Clean Hands in Italy, thirty years ago, and then compare it to the Italian public's situation today. In many respects, Italy has fulfilled its projected path. Yet, from the perspective of thirty years ago, the outcome cannot be regarded as ideal. This prompts a crucial reflection: what kind of country will exist thirty years from now? Looking back on the present, what will be said? And what questions will future generations pose? "Mum, Dad, what did you do to make sure the country turned out the way it did?".

We need to think about the future of the nation, especially for the poorer population, who suffer most from corruption. The diverted funds are the money that should be going towards education, healthcare, housing—the basic needs of the Brazilian people. It is the poor who suffer the most.

Consideration must be given to the future of the nation, particularly in relation to the most economically vulnerable, who bear the greatest burden of corruption. The funds that are diverted through corrupt practices are precisely those intended for essential public services—education, healthcare, housing, and other basic needs of the Brazilian population. It is the poorest who suffer most.

This is the fundamental problem with corruption: the victim is not visible. And when the victim is not seen, there is no compassion, no awareness of who is actually suffering. Funds are diverted—perhaps from a school, for instance—but there is no public outcry at the scene of the crime, because the offence occurs behind closed doors, through concealed and self-serving arrangements. It is an extremely difficult phenomenon to confront.

Rodrigo Régnier Chemim Guimarães was born in Curitiba (Paraná). He is a Prosecutor of Justice at the Public Prosecutor's Office of the State of Paraná and a full professor of criminal procedural law at Positive University. He is the author of several books and articles on anti-corruption efforts. His testimony was given on 19 August 2020 via the Zoom virtual platform and lasted 1 hour and 6 minutes. The transcript was reviewed by the interviewee on 29 January 2023.

Conclusion to Chapter 4

Chapter 4, the Car Wash and Civil Society, presents a rigorous and multifaceted examination of civil society's role in the trajectory of Operation Car Wash. By focusing on the perspectives of key figures from Brazilian civil society and experts in anti-corruption, the chapter highlights the profound impact of public mobilisation, media influence, and societal engagement on the success—and eventual challenges—of the operation. This analysis not only stands as a testament to the transformative power of an engaged civil society but also serves as a cautionary tale about its limitations and unintended consequences.

A central theme of the chapter is the pivotal role that civil society played in fostering and maintaining a climate of accountability during Car Wash. Public demonstrations, grassroots movements, and extensive media coverage helped to generate unprecedented pressure on political and judicial institutions to prioritise the fight against corruption. These societal forces elevated Car Wash from a technical investigation to a national—and even international—symbol of justice and transparency. The testimonies in this chapter emphasise how civil society's activism raised collective awareness of corruption as an existential threat to democratic governance and institutional integrity. This public support not only empowered prosecutors and judges to act decisively but also legitimised their efforts in the face of intense political opposition.

However, the chapter goes beyond celebrating civil society's role, offering a critical analysis of the complexities and contradictions inherent in its engagement. While public mobilisation amplified Car Wash's impact, it also created immense pressure on judicial and prosecutorial actors to deliver swift and visible results. This pressure, as the testimonies reveal, sometimes led to a prioritisation of efficiency over procedural rigour, raising concerns about due process and the potential for judicial overreach. For instance, the extensive use of pre-trial detentions and plea bargain agreements, while effective in uncovering corruption networks, became sources of contention. Critics argued that these measures, shaped partly by societal demands for accountability, risked undermining constitutional principles such as the presumption of innocence and the right to a fair trial. The chapter invites readers to critically assess whether civil society's well-intentioned demands inadvertently contributed to legal practices that blurred the line between justice and expediency.

The role of the media emerges as another pivotal, yet deeply ambivalent, dimension in the relationship between Car Wash and civil society. The media's relentless focus on corruption scandals helped to galvanise public outrage and mobilise societal support for the operation. However, as the chapter illustrates, the media's sensationalist framing often oversimplified the complexities of the legal process and reinforced a punitive rather than reformative approach to justice. By privileging dramatic narratives over nuanced analysis, the media risked fostering a polarised public discourse in which corruption became synonymous with individual culpability rather than systemic failure. This dynamic underscores the double-edged nature of media engagement: while it can amplify civil society's voice and enhance transparency, it can also distort public understanding of the legal and institutional challenges inherent in combating corruption.

From an academic perspective, Chapter 4 offers a rich and critical framework for understanding the interplay between civil society and the state in the context of anti-corruption initiatives. It challenges romanticised notions of civil society as a uniformly positive force for accountability, instead revealing the complexities and contradictions that arise when societal engagement intersects with political, legal, and institutional constraints. The chapter underscores the dual-edged nature of public mobilisation: while it can enhance democratic accountability and institutional resilience, it can also impose pressures that risk compromising the independence and impartiality of the judiciary and prosecution. This dynamic raises broader theoretical questions about the limits of public participation in legal processes and the conditions under which civil society's demands align—or conflict—with the principles of justice and the rule of law.

The chapter also invites critical reflection on the long-term implications of Car Wash for Brazilian civil society. While the operation galvanised a significant portion of the population to demand greater transparency and accountability, the eventual backlash against Car Wash—exacerbated by political polarisation, judicial controversies, and media sensationalism—reveals the fragility of these gains. The chapter cautions against conflating public mobilisation with sustainable reform, emphasising the need for structural changes that extend beyond the episodic activism triggered by high-profile scandals. It highlights the risks of over-reliance on civil society's mobilisation to sustain accountability, particularly in contexts where institutional weaknesses and political resistance undermine the durability of anti-corruption efforts.

Furthermore, the chapter critically examines the relationship between civil society's engagement and the broader political landscape of Brazil during and after Car Wash. The operation became a focal point for deep societal divisions, with different segments of civil society aligning themselves along partisan and ideological lines. While some groups viewed Car Wash as a necessary and overdue reckoning with corruption, others saw it as a politically motivated tool that disproportionately targeted certain political actors and institutions. This polarisation underscores the risks of politicising anti-corruption efforts and highlights the challenges of maintaining civil society's role as an impartial advocate for justice and reform. The testimonies reveal how this polarisation not only weakened public trust in Car Wash but also contributed to broader societal divisions that complicated Brazil's democratic consolidation.

Ultimately, Car Wash and Civil Society serves as both a tribute to the transformative potential of public engagement and a critique of its limitations and unintended consequences. The chapter underscores the need for a more nuanced understanding of civil society's role in anti-corruption efforts, one that recognises its capacity to mobilise public support while also acknowledging the risks of populism, polarisation, and institutional overreach. For scholars, practitioners, and policymakers, the chapter offers valuable insights into the complexities of state-society relations in the context of democratic governance. It challenges readers to reflect on how civil society can contribute to accountability and reform without undermining the principles of justice, fairness, and institutional autonomy.

By presenting a balanced and critical analysis, the chapter deepens our understanding of Car Wash's legacy and its implications for Brazil's political and legal systems. It highlights the importance of building institutional frameworks that can harness civil society's energy while mitigating its excesses and contradictions. In doing so, it provides a compelling and thought-provoking contribution to the broader discourse on the role of civil society in combating corruption and promoting democratic accountability in Brazil and beyond.

Notes

1. Fabiana Gitsio. The era of certification gives rise to a new market. *Gazeta Mercantil*, 18th September 2003.
2. The company was Dunel Comércio e Indústria Ltda.—EPP, a small, limited liability company, which also had Maria Teodora Silva as a partner.
3. The project finance company was *CSA Project Finance Consultoria e Intermediação de Negócios Empresariais Ltda.*, based at Rua Pedroso Alvarenga n. 1221, 5th floor, Itaim, São Paulo, SP. Its formal partners were Rubens de Andrade Filho and Carlos Alberto Pereira Costa. However, the company was run by the congressperson José Janene and the black-market currency dealers Alberto Youssef.
4. The partner was Maria Teodora Silva.

5. José Muggiati Filho was a lawyer, state congressperson, and regional president of the MDB (1972 to 1975). He had six children. The son in question was José Muggiati Neto.
6. Brazilian Democratic Movement, opposition party during the military dictatorship in Brazil. With the end of the bipartisanship during the dictatorship, PMDB, Party of the Brazilian Democratic Movement, emerged, which later gave rise to several other parties, such as the Brazilian Social Democracy Party, Democratic Labour Party, the Workers' Party.
7. José Mohamed Janene was a businessman and Brazilian politician, affiliated with the Progressive Party. In politics, he gained visibility for being one of the pivots of the *Mensalão* corruption scandal. Later, his name was involved in Operation Car Wash.
8. Alberto Youssef is a Brazilian black-market currency dealer, well known after the corruption scandal at *Banestado*. He was arrested in 2014 as part of Operation Car Wash.
9. Fernando Henrique Cardoso. ***Entry***. FGV CPDOC. https://www18.fgv.br/CPDOC/acervo/arquivo?busca=Fernando+Henrique+Cardoso&TipoUD=0&MacroTipoUD=0&nItens=30. He is a sociologist, professor, writer, and Brazilian politician. He was the 34th President of the Federative Republic of Brazil (1995–2003). He is president of the Fernando Henrique Cardoso Foundation and honorary president of the Brazilian Social-Democracy Party.
10. Paulo Salim Maluf. ***Entry***. FGV CPDOC. https://www18.fgv.br/CPDOC/acervo/dicionarios/verbete-biografico/paulo-salim-maluf. He is an engineer and Brazilian politician. He was governor of the State of São Paulo, mayor of the city of São Paulo twice, leader of five political parties. His last political position was as a federal congressperson, elected four times. He was a candidate for the presidency of the Republic. His political career is marked by several accusations of corruption, having even been on the World Bank's list of accused of corruption, as well as on Interpol's. He was sentenced to more than seven years of imprisonment for money laundering, but today he has been under house arrest for more than five years.

11. Carlos Alberto Pereira da Costa is a lawyer, and he was investigated and convicted by the Operation Car Wash, accused of being a "front man" for the black-market currency dealers Alberto Youssef in several companies. He was released after signing a plea bargain agreement.
12. *Mensalão* was a corruption scandal, which occurred through the purchase of votes from deputies by the Executive, during the government of Luiz Inácio Lula da Silva, in 2005. This illegal practice was known backstage as it referred to a monthly payment made to deputies to vote in favour of projects of interest to the Executive.
13. Ferramentas Gerais S.A. is a national leader in the sale of professional and industrial tools and equipment.
14. Roberto Brasiliano da Silva, former parliamentary advisor to Jose Janene, had a preventive arrest warrant issued due to Operation Weak Flesh and was convicted of passive corruption and criminal organisation.
15. Operation Weak Flesh is an operation by the Federal Police that investigated more than thirty food companies, among them JBS and BRF, all accused of adulterating the meat they sold in domestic and foreign markets, as well as pointing out government agents who received bribes to release these meats.
16. Marcos Valério Fernandes de Souza is a businessman and advertiser. He became nationally known because of the *Mensalão* scandal. He was a partner in two communication agencies, DNA and SMP&B, which began to provide services for political election campaigns. Marcos Valério had a very close collaboration relationship with Delúbio Soares, then treasurer of the Workers' Party, who under the orders of José Dirceu, then Minister of the Civil House of the Lula government, distributed payments, using resources from state and private companies to the parliamentarians indicated by Delúbio. Marcos Valério was sentenced in the Mensalão to more than 37 years in prison in a closed regime. In 2019, he began to serve his sentence in a semi-open regime.
17. Danielle Kemmer Janene is the daughter of Jose Janene. She was accused in Operation Car Wash of the crimes of criminal

association, money laundering, misappropriation, and fraud. The complaint against her was archived by the judge of Operation Car Wash in Curitiba, Gabriela Hardt.

18. The Firm is a film starring Tom Cruise where he plays a newly graduated lawyer who starts working in a firm in Memphis, with a salary well above standard. Soon he discovers that the firm where he works is involved in money laundering for the Mafia and that all the lawyers who left or tried to leave the firm died, mysteriously.
19. Adolfo Luís de Souza Góis was José Janene's lawyer.
20. Enivaldo Quadrado was caught when he arrived at Guarulhos airport in São Paulo, coming from Portugal with 600 thousand euros not declared, in bundles of notes stuck to his body, in his socks, and even in his underwear. This money came from an account that José Janene held at BES bank in Porto, Portugal.

    He was director of the brokerage firm Bônus-Banval, one of the channels for the transfer of resources in the Mensalão case. He was convicted in the Mensalão trial for money laundering to 3 years and 6 months in prison, in addition to a fine. The prison sentence was replaced by the alternative penalty of community service. But later he was arrested and convicted by Operation Car Wash for the crime of money laundering to five years in prison in a closed regime.
21. Stael Fernanda Rodrigues de Lima, widow of former congressperson José Janene, was sentenced to more than 7 years in prison in a semi-open regime for money laundering of resources originating from the Mensalão.
22. The OAS Group is a Brazilian conglomerate in the field of civil engineering, founded in Salvador, Bahia, with headquarters in São Paulo. It is formed by the following companies: Construtora OAS, which operates in civil and heavy construction; OAS Empreendimentos, which operates in the market real estate and OAS Investments, responsible for private investments in infrastructure and public and private service concessions. With the Car Wash operation, the Group changed its corporate name and became known as Group Metha.

23. Gerson Machado is a former Federal Police officer, considered the first officer of the investigations that preceded the Operation Car Wash. He faced several pressures from the black-market currency dealers Alberto Youssef and former congressman José Janene, after his involvement in the Mensalão scandal emerged. For medical leave reasons, he stepped away from the Federal Police and retired prematurely. He was given the nickname of "father of Car Wash," for the arrest of Alberto Youssef in the *Banestado* scandal and then for having pulled the thread of a money laundering scheme much larger than *Banestado*, the Car Wash.
24. The Netflix series "The Mechanism," inspired by the Operation Car Wash, features many characters inspired by real-life figures, one of the main ones being the officer Marco Ruffo, portrayed by actor Selton Mello, who represents officer Gerson Machado.
25. Sergio Fernando Moro ***Entry***. FGV CPDOC. http://www.fgv.br/cpdoc/acervo/dicionarios/verbete-biografico/sergio-fernando-moro. He was a federal judge and judge of the Car Wash operation in Curitiba. He was former Minister of Justice and director of Alvarez & Marsal. He is a lawyer and Brazilian politician. He is currently an elected Senator for the state of Paraná.
26. Claudio Dantas is a journalist and general director of journalism for O Antagonista. For more than two decades he covered the newsrooms of Correio Braziliense, Folha de S. Paulo, and IstoÉ. He won the Esso and Embratel awards, among others. He is considered one of the most influential journalists on Twitter.
27. Januário Paludo is a Prosecutor of the Federal Public Prosecutor's Office and was part of the task force of the Car Wash operation in Curitiba.
28. Rio de Janeiro was the host city of the 2016 Olympic Games.
29. Jorge Pontes. The scourge of institutionalised crime. *Public*, 2 June 2017. https://www.publico.pt/2017/06/02/mundo/opiniao/o-flagelo-do-crime-institucionalizado-1773553.
30. Márcio Anselmo is a Federal Police officer. He worked on the Banestado case, presided over the original investigations of the

Operation Car Wash and stayed in the task force in Curitiba for three years.

31. In 2005, the Pasadena refinery in Texas was purchased by Belgian Astra Oil for US$ 42.5 million. In 2006, Petrobras bought 50% of the shares in Pasadena from Belgian Astra Oil for US$ 360 million. In 2012, by court order, Petrobras is forced to buy the remaining 50% of the shares from Belgian Astra Oil for US$ 820.5 million, after a disagreement between the partners, as stipulated in a put option clause.
32. Jorge Pontes and Marcio Anselmo. *Crime.Gov—when Corruption and government intertwine.* 1st ed. Rio de Janeiro: Objetiva, 2019.
33. Paulo Roberto Costa is an engineer and was a career employee of Petrobras, being appointed to the position of Director of Supply, between 2004 and 2012, during the government of Luiz Inácio Lula da Silva. He became known due to his involvement in the corruption scheme of the Car Wash operation. He was sentenced to 12 years of house arrest with an ankle monitor, because of his plea bargain agreement.
34. Roberto Ciciliati Troncon Filho was the regional superintendent of the Federal Police in São Paulo.
35. Sergio Fernando Moro ***Entry***. FGV CPDOC. http://www.fgv.br/cpdoc/acervo/dicionarios/verbete-biografico/sergio-fernando-moro. He was a former federal judge and judge of the Car Wash operation in Curitiba. He was ex-Minister of Justice and director of Alvarez & Marsal. He is a lawyer and Brazilian politician. He is currently an elected Senator for the state of Paraná.
36. Luiz Pontel de Souza is a lawyer and corporate investigations consultant. He was a Federal Police officer.
37. Paulo de Tarso Teixeira, a retired Federal Police officer, was the executive director of the institution.
38. Paulo Fernando da Costa Lacerda is a lawyer and retired Federal Police officer. He was the director of the institution during the government of former President Luiz Inácio Lula da Silva.

39. Getúlio Bezerra dos Santos is a retired Federal Police officer. He was responsible for the Directorate of Combat against Organised Crime of the Federal Police.
40. José Eduardo Martins Cardozo is a lawyer and politician affiliated with the Workers' Party. He was a federal Congressperson, Minister of Justice, and Federal Prosecutor General.
41. Come to the Street is a supra-party, democratic and plural movement, emerged from the spontaneous organisation of civil society in 2014, seeking a Brazil free from corruption.
42. Fernando Paulo Nagle Gabeira. ***Entry***. FGV CPDOC. https://www18.fgv.br/CPDOC/acervo/dicionarios/verbete-biografico/fernando-paulo-nagle-gabeira. He is a journalist and writer. Politician, federal congressperson elected by Rio de Janeiro, by the Green Party, of which he is a founding member. He ran for mayor of Rio de Janeiro and for the state government but was not elected. He participated in the armed struggle against the military dictatorship and was exiled from the country, only returning after the amnesty.
43. Marcelo Garmatter Barretto, better known by the artistic name Marcelo Madureira. He is a comedian and was the host of the highly successful comedy show Casseta & Planeta, on Rede Globo, in addition to having been a commentator on Jovem Pan and BandNews and a columnist for Agamenon in O Globo, a fictional character created by him and by Hubert Aranha, also a member of Casseta & Planeta.
44. Adriana Bonow Balthazar da Silveira is a lawyer and politician, affiliated with the New Party. She is a state congressperson in Rio de Janeiro.
45. The New Party is a Brazilian political party, founded in 2011. Among its main stances is the non-use of public resources for electoral campaigns, maintaining itself from donations and contributions from its affiliates. The party's principle is economic freedom.
46. Jorge Pontes and Márcio Anselmo. ***Crime.gov: when corruption and government mix***. Rio de Janeiro: Objetiva, 2019.

47. Sergio Cabral (Sergio de Oliveira Cabral Santos Son). ***Entry***. FGV CPDOC. https://www18.fgv.br/CPDOC/acervo/dicionarios/verbete-biografico/sergio-de-oliveira-cabral-santos-filho. He is a Brazilian politician, former member of the Brazilian Democratic Movement. He was a state congressperson in Rio de Janeiro for three terms, later governor of the state from 2007 to 2014, when he resigned from office. In 2016, he was arrested by Operation Car Wash for passive corruption, money laundering, and currency evasion. His twenty-four convictions exceed four hundred years of imprisonment. In 2022, the Federal Supreme Court revoked his pre-trial detention, moving to house arrest.
48. Luís Roberto Barroso. ***Entry***. FGV CPDOC. http://www.fgv.br/cpdoc/acervo/dicionarios/verbete-biografico/luis-roberto-barroso. He is a jurist and Justice of the Federal Supreme Court. He holds a law degree from the State University of Rio de Janeiro, a master's degree from Yale University, and a doctorate and free lecturer from UERJ, with post-doctorate from Harvard Law School. He is full professor of constitutional law at UERJ.
49. Luiz Edson Fachin. ***Entry***. FGV CPDOC. https://www18.fgv.br/CPDOC/acervo/dicionarios/verbete-biografico/luiz-edson-fachin. He is a Brazilian jurist and Justice of the Federal Supreme Court, since June 2015. He was a lawyer and full professor of civil law at the Law School of the Federal University of Paraná. He is the current rapporteur of Operation Car Wash in the Federal Supreme Court, replacing Justice Teori Zavascki.
50. Luiz Fux ***Entry***. FGV CPDOC. http://www.fgv.br/cpdoc/acervo/dicionarios/verbete-biografico/luis-fux. He is a Justice of the Federal Supreme Court. He was a professor, lawyer, member of the public ministry, and magistrate. He was appointed in the government of Fernando Henrique Cardoso as Justice of the Superior Court of Justice.
51. Rosa Maria Pires Weber. ***Entry***. FGV CPDOC. http://www.fgv.br/cpdoc/acervo/dicionarios/verbete-biografico/rosa-maria-weber-candiota-da-rosa. She is a judge and current Justice of the Federal Supreme Court. She was a Justice of the Superior Labor Court, before taking up the position in Federal Supreme Court.

52. Teori Albino Zavascki. ***Entry***. FGV CPDOC. https://www18.fgv.br/CPDOC/acervo/dicionarios/verbete-biografico/teori-albino-zavascki. He was a jurist, professor, magistrate, and Justice of the Superior Court of Justice and the Federal Supreme Court, from 2012 to 2017. He was the rapporteur of Operation Car Wash until his death.
53. Cármen Lúcia Antunes Rocha. ***Entry***. FGV CPDOC. https://www18.fgv.br/CPDOC/acervo/dicionarios/verbete-biografico/lucia-carmem. She has been a Justice of the Federal Supreme Court since 2006. She was a prosecutor and Attorney General of the state of Minas Gerais.
54. Alexandre de Moraes. ***Entry***. FGV CPDOC. https://www18.fgv.br/CPDOC/acervo/dicionarios/verbete-biografico/alexandre-de-moraes. He is a Justice of the Federal Supreme Court and associate professor of the Faculty of Law at the University of São Paulo. He was a prosecutor and secretary of Justice and Defence of Citizenship of the state of São Paulo. He was Minister of Justice and Public Security in the government of former President Michel Temer.
55. Joaquim Benedito Barbosa Gomes. ***Entry***. FGV CPDOC. https://www18.fgv.br/CPDOC/acervo/dicionarios/verbete-biografico/barbosa-joaquim. He was a Justice of the Federal Supreme Court. He is a jurist and lawyer. He was a member of the Federal Public Prosecutor's Office. In 2006, he took over the reporting of the Mensalão, and his performance was of fundamental importance in the conviction of corrupt politicians for the first time in the country.
56. Érica Marena is a Federal Police delegate, known for her work in Operation Car Wash. She also worked in the division of repression of financial crimes and in the division of combating corruption and diversion of public funds. She headed the Department of Asset Recovery and International Legal Cooperation.
57. Maurício *Moscardi* Grillo is a Federal Police delegate, known for his work in Operation Car Wash. He was coordinator of Operation Weak Flesh which investigated the crime of passive corruption in the food sector.

58. Eduardo Mauat da Silva is a Federal Police delegate, having worked in Operation Car Wash between 2014 and 2016. He has worked in operations along the borders of Bolivia, Paraguay, and Argentina.
59. Frederico Skora Lieberenz is a Federal Police delegate, having coordinated Operation Car Wash in Rio de Janeiro.
60. Paulo Fernando da Costa Lacerda is a retired Federal Police delegate. He was director-general of the Federal Police during the Lula government (2003–2007).
61. *Greenfield* is an operation of the Federal Police and the Federal Public Prosecutor's Office that occurred in 2016 and investigated the diversion of pension funds (*Funcef*, *Petros*, *Previ*, and *Postalis*), from public banks and state-owned companies.
62. Jorge Pontes and Márcio Anselmo. ***Crime.gov: when corruption and government mix***. Rio de Janeiro: Objetiva, 2019.
63. Jorge Pontes and Márcio Anselmo. Op. Cit.
64. *Mensalão* was a corruption scandal, which occurred through the purchase of votes from deputies by the Executive, during the government of Luiz Inácio Lula da Silva, in 2005. This illegal practice was known behind the scenes as it referred to a monthly payment made to deputies to vote in favour of projects of interest to the Executive.
65. This refers to the conviction of the now President Luiz Inácio Lula da Silva.
66. The term "rachadinha" refers to a widespread and illicit practice in Brazilian politics whereby elected officials or their aides require staff members to return part of their publicly funded salaries—often under duress or as a condition of employment. The funds are then diverted for personal or political use. The word derives from the Portuguese verb "rachar," meaning "to split," and the scheme is commonly translated as "salary kickbacks".
67. Operation Car Wash is also commonly referred to as *Petrolão*.
68. Deltan Martinazzo Dallagnol was a prosecutor of the republic and coordinator of the task force of the Public Ministry of Operation Car Wash in Curitiba.

69. José Dirceu de Oliveira e Silva is a Brazilian politician, affiliated with the Workers' Party. He was a state and federal congressperson for the State of São Paulo and Chief Minister of the Civil House during the government of President Luiz Inácio Lula da Silva. In 2012, he was convicted by the Federal Supreme Court for the crime of active corruption, imprisoned in 2013. A year later he was released to serve the remainder of his sentence at home. He was arrested in 2015 involved in Operation Car Wash, being convicted in 2017. In 2019, he left prison, due to the change in the understanding of the Federal Supreme Court about prison in the second instance, in the decision of the Declaratory Action of Constitutionality 43, 44, and 54.
70. This is about João Santana, a Brazilian advertiser who had a strong performance in political marketing. He was arrested during Operation Car Wash, in the phase called Operation ("Operação Acarajé"). He was released after a year of imprisonment based on a plea bargain agreement.
71. Dilma Vana Rousseff. ***Entry***. FGV CPDOC. https://www18.fgv.br/CPDOC/acervo/dicionarios/verbete-biografico/dilma-vana-rousseff. She is an economist and Brazilian politician, affiliated with the Workers' Party. She was president of Brazil from 2011 to 2014 (first term) and from 2015 to 2016 (second term), when she was removed by an impeachment process.
72. Marina Osmarina da Silva Vaz de Lima. ***Entry***. FGV CPDOC. https://www18.fgv.br/CPDOC/acervo/dicionarios/verbete-biografico/maria-osmarina-silva-de-sousa. She is a politician and environmentalist. She is the current minister of the environment. She was Senator and candidate for the presidency of the republic three times.
73. José Carlos Gratz is a former state congressperson, former bookmaker, and former owner of casinos and bingos. He presided over the Legislative Assembly of the state of Espírito Santo for three consecutive terms, until 2002. After, he was imprisoned three times. Gratz was impeached by the Regional Electoral Court of Espírito Santo (TRE-ES) and imprisoned for embezzlement of

public resources and illicit enrichment, responding to more than 100 processes.

74. Daniela Falcão. ES congressperson has partners in Campinas. *Folha de S. Paulo*. 9th December 1999. https://www1.folha.uol.com.br/fsp/brasil/fc0912199907.htm.
75. Espírito Santo prosecutor archived cases against Gratz. *Estado de S. Paulo*. 22nd February 2003. https://www.estadao.com.br/politica/procurador-do-es-arquivou-processos-contra-gratz/.
76. Sandra Carvalho and Andressa Caldas. *Human rights crisis in Espírito Santo: threats and violence against human rights defenders*. React Forum Espírito Santo. Global Justice Centre Rio de Janeiro and Espírito Santo, 2002. http://www.global.org.br/wp-content/uploads/2015/09/2002-Crise-DH-ES.pdf.
77. The Human Development Index, HDI, is a statistical index composed of life expectancy, education, and per capita income used to classify countries into four different levels of human development.
78. Angela Centurion Abranches is a *retired Justice Prosecutor* in the state of Espírito Santo.
79. Nilo de Mingo. Eight councillors are arrested for embezzlement of money. *Folha de Londrina*, 7th November 1998. https://www.folhadelondrina.com.br/politica/oito-vereadores-sao-presos-por-desvio-de-dinheiro-106702.html.
80. *Fantástico* is a weekly investigative journalism and news magazine programme broadcast by TV Globo, Brazil's largest television network.
81. Reference is made to Luiz Inácio Lula da Silva, a popular Brazilian politician, affiliated with the Workers' Party. He was president of Brazil from 2003 to 2006 (first term) and from 2006 to 2010 (second term). He was arrested as part of Operation Car Wash. He is the current president of Brazil (2023–2026).
82. Natalia Bourguignon. Understand what was the scuderie le cocq and the relationship with politics in ES. *A Gazeta*, 5th October 2022. https://www.agazeta.com.br/es/politica/entenda-o-que-foi-a-scuderie-le-cocq-e-a-relacao-com-a-politica-no-es-1022.

83. Miguel Reale Júnior. ***Entry***. FGV CPDOC. https://www18.fgv.br/CPDOC/acervo/dicionarios/verbete-biografico/reale-junior-miguel. He is a lawyer, jurist, philosopher, professor of criminal law at the Law School of the University of São Paulo (USP), and politician. He was Minister of Justice in the government of former President Fernando Henrique Cardoso.
84. Geraldo Brindeiro. ***Entry***. FGV CPDOC. https://www18.fgv.br/CPDOC/acervo/dicionarios/verbete-biografico/brindeiro-geraldo. He was a lawyer and member of the Federal Public Prosecutor's Office. He was Attorney General of the Republic from 1995 to 2003.
85. Order of Lawyers of Brazil, OAB.
86. Agesandro da Costa Pereira was a lawyer, professor, and president of the Order of Lawyers of Brazil, Espírito Santo section (OAB-ES), for nine terms.
87. Fernando Henrique Cardoso. ***Entry***. FGV CPDOC. https://www18.fgv.br/CPDOC/acervo/arquivo?busca=fernando+henrique+cardoso&TipoUD=0&MacroTipoUD=0&nItens=30. He is a sociologist, professor, writer, and Brazilian politician. He was the 34th President of the Federative Republic of Brazil (1995–2003). He is president of the Fernando Henrique Cardoso Foundation and honorary president of the Brazilian Social Democracy Party.
88. Special mission obtains confidentiality breach of 55. *Folha de S. Paulo*, 30th of August 2002. https://www1.folha.uol.com.br/fsp/brasil/fc3008200206.htm.
89. José Ignacio Ferreira was a Councillor of Vitória, state Congressperson, and Senator for Espírito Santo, and he was governor of the State of Espírito Santo, having been convicted of reckless management crime in *Banestes* (Bank of the State of Espírito Santo), when running for governor.
90. Alexandre Martins de Castro Filho was a criminal judge in Espírito Santo and a symbol of justice in the fight against impunity and organised crime. He was murdered by a group of criminals he was investigating at the time.

91. Paulo César Hartung Gomes. ***Entry***. FGV CPDOC. https://www18.fgv.br/CPDOC/acervo/dicionarios/verbete-biografico/paulo-cesar-hartung-gomes. He is an economist and politician. He was a state congressperson, mayor of Vitória, federal congressperson, senator, and governor of the state of Espírito Santo from 2003 to 2010 and from 2015 to 2018.
92. Carlos Melo, Malu Delgado, and Milton Seligman. Decay and reconstruction. Espírito Santo: lessons from civil society for a political case in contemporary Brazil. São Paulo: Bei, 2020.
93. Ministry of Education, MEC.
94. ES Government achieves A grade from the national treasury again. A Gazeta, 19th of September 2022. https://www.agazeta.com.br/es/economia/governo-do-es-conquista-novamente-nota-a-do-tesouro-nacional-0922#:~:text=O%20Esp%C3%ADrito%20Santo%20recebeu%2C%20pela,bom%20pagamento%20ou%20cadastro%20positivo.
95. Operation Shipwreck investigated a corruption scheme in the Judiciary power of the state of Espírito Santo, whose accusations involved the sale of sentences, interferences in public competitions, allotment of notary offices, among others. In 2008, twenty-six people were accused in the corruption scheme (four justices, four judges, six lawyers, a state prosecutor, two businessmen, a mayor, former employees of the Court of Justice of Espírito Santo). Today, of these twenty-six people, five have died and twenty-five crimes have expired since the accusation was presented. In 2021, the Superior Court of Justice accepted the accusation against fifteen investigated.
96. Prosecutor investigated in Operation Shipwreck is suspended, in ES. *Portal G1*, 8th of December 2011. https://g1.globo.com/espirito-santo/noticia/2011/12/procurador-investigado-na-operacao-naufragio-e-suspenso-no-es.html.
97. State Public Ministry elects new general inspector and new ombudsman. *News. Espírito Santense Association of the Public Ministry*. http://www.aesmp.org.br/index.php.
98. Law School of Vitória. Faculty. https://www.fdv.br/docentes/.

99. Website of the Secretariat of Control and Transparency of the State of Espírito Santo. Undersecretariat of Governmental and Business Integrity https://secont.es.gov.br/sobre-a-subsecretaria-de-integridade-governamental-e-empresarial.
100. Adriana Aguiar. Espírito Santo is the first to apply the anti-corruption law. *Valor Econômico*, 15 January 2016. https://valor.globo.com/legislacao/noticia/2016/01/15/espirito-santo-e-o-primeiro-a-aplicar-lei-anticorrupcao-1.ghtml.
101. National survey shows Espírito Santo in 1st place in the application of the anti-corruption law. *ESGES*. https://portalesg.es.gov.br/Not%C3%ADcia/levantamento-nacional-mostra-espirito-santo-em-1o-lugar-na-aplicacao-da-lei-anticorrupcao.
102. José Eduardo Martins Cardozo. ***Entry***. FGV CPDOC. https://www18.fgv.br/CPDOC/acervo/dicionarios/verbete-biografico/cardoso-jose-eduardo. He is a lawyer and politician affiliated with the Workers' Party. He was federal Congressperson, Minister of Justice (2010–2016), and General Prosecutor until the impeachment of President Dilma Rousseff (from March to May of 2016).
103. Allegation of Non-Compliance with Fundamental Precept Action is an action proposed before the Federal Supreme Court, to prevent or repair injury to a fundamental precept resulting from an act of public power. It cannot be proposed to question the constitutionality of a law, except municipal laws or those prior to the Constitution of 1988.
104. Gabriel Mascarenhas. Prosecutor loses position on the eve of taking up post at the World Bank. *Veja*, 20th November 2017. https://veja.abril.com.br/coluna/radar/promotor-leva-banda-as-vesperas-de-assumir-posto-no-banco-mundial/.
105. DoJ (Department of Justice)—United States Department of Justice.
106. Gaspard Estrada. Operation car was no magic bullet. *The New York Times*, 26th February 2021. https://www.nytimes.com/2021/02/26/opinion/international-world/car-wash-operation-brazil-bolsonaro.html.

107. Director of governance and compliance at Petrobras resigns. *G1. Economy*, 5th July 2019. https://g1.globo.com/economia/noticia/2019/07/05/diretor-de-governanca-e-conformidade-da-petrobras-renuncia-ao-cargo.ghtml.
108. Law No. 13.303, of 30 June 2016 (State-Owned Companies Law) on the legal status of public companies, mixed economy societies, and their subsidiaries, within the scope of the Union, States, Federal District, and Municipalities. http://www.planalto.gov.br/ccivil_03/_ato2015-2018/2016/lei/l13303.htm.
109. Decree No. 9.203, of 22 November 2017 on the governance policy of the direct, autarchic, and foundational federal public administration. https://www.planalto.gov.br/ccivil_03/_ato2015-2018/2017/decreto/d9203.htm.
110. Establishes the public integrity system in the Federal Executive Power. http://www.planalto.gov.br/ccivil_03/_ato2019-2022/2021/decreto/D10756.htm.
111. Norway's sovereign fund removes Petrobras from its watch list. *G1. Economy*, 3rd December 2019. https://g1.globo.com/economia/noticia/2019/12/03/fundo-soberano-da-noruega-retira-a-petrobras-de-sua-lista-de-observacao.ghtml.
112. We won the Pro-Ethics Company Award 2020–2021. *Petrobras. Facts and Data*, 9th December 2021. https://petrobras.com.br/fatos-e-dados/conquistamos-premio-empresa-pro-etica-2020-2021.htm.
113. Transparency International is an NGO, based in Berlin, Germany; its main objective is to combat corruption. To this end, it has a series of publications, among them the Corruption Perception Index Corruption Perception Index (CPI) and the Global Corruption Barometer *Global Corruption Barometer* (GCB). The website of Transparency International Brazil is https://transparenciainternacional.org.br/.
114. Transparency International Brazil. *Twitter*. https://twitter.com/TI_InterBr/status/1318959582203576320?s=20&t=1CsxF0iD9Mq35meVGNH0cQ.

115. Marcelo Zenkner. Reputation, professional decorum and the effectiveness of corporate integrity systems. *The State of S. Paulo*, 7th April 2021. https://www.estadao.com.br/politica/blog-do-fausto-macedo/reputacao-decoro-profissional-e-a-efetividade-dos-sistemas-de-integridade-corporativos/.
116. Reference is made to Itaú Bank. Below are some articles about the fact. *Exam* https://exame.com/negocios/itau-demite-50-funcionarios-que-solicitaram-auxilio-emergencial/; *CNN Brazil* https://www.cnnbrasil.com.br/business/itau-demite-50-funcio narios-que-pediram-auxilio-emergencial/; *State of S. Paulo* https://www.estadao.com.br/economia/coluna-do-broad/itau-demite-50-funcionarios-que-pediram-auxilio-emergencial-indevi damente/.
117. School of Business Administration of São Paulo, Getulio Vargas Foundation, simply known as GV.
118. Celso Antonio Bandeira de Mello is a jurist and lawyer. Emeritus Professor at the Pontifical Catholic University of São Paulo. He is considered one of the greatest references in Brazilian administrative law.
119. Rubén Dário Almonacid was a well-known economist of Argentine nationality, PhD from the University of Chicago. He was a professor of economics at the University of São Paulo, USP.
120. José Roberto Mendonça de Barros is an economist and consultant at MB Associados. He was former Secretary of Economic Policy of the Ministry of Finance between 1995 and 1998 and former executive secretary of the Foreign Trade Chamber of the Presidency of the Republic in 1998. He was a professor at USP.
121. Ibrahim Eris. ***Entry***. FGV CPDOC. https://www18.fgv.br/CPDOC/acervo/dicionarios/verbete-biografico/eris-ibrahim. He is an economist. He was president of the Central Bank of Brazil in the government of President Fernando Collor de Mello.
122. Afonso Celso Pastore. ***Entry***. FGV CPDOC. https://www18.fgv.br/CPDOC/acervo/dicionarios/verbete-biografico/pastore-afonso-celso. He is an economist. He was president of the Central Bank of Brazil from 1983 to 1985.

123. Operation Clean Hands, *Mani Pulite*, was an investigation into corruption cases in Italy, which involved the Mafia, the Vatican Bank, and the masonic lodge. It led to the end of the so-called First Italian Republic (1948–1994) and brought about profound changes in the political party landscape.
124. Gherardo Colombo is a former Italian magistrate specialising in political corruption cases. He was a member of the Court of Cassation in Italy between 2005 and 2007. He was one of the judges of Operation Clean Hands and of P2.
125. Gherardo Colombo. *Letter to a son about clean hands*. Milan: Garzanti, 2015.
126. Douglass North was an economist. He received, alongside Robert William Fogel, the Nobel Prize in Economics in 1993.
127. Daron Acemoglu is an economist and professor at MIT (*Massachusetts Institute of Technology*), in the United States.
128. James A. Robinson is an economist and political scientist, with significant contributions in the field of political and economic development and in the relations between political power, institutions, and prosperity. He is a professor at the University of Chicago.
129. Maria Cristina Pinotti. (Org.). *Corruption: car wash and clean hands*. São Paulo: Portfolio-Penguin, 2019.
130. Giovanni Falcone was a judge in Italy and became famous for judging the bosses of the *Cosa Nostra*, a Sicilian criminal organisation. In 1992, Falcone was assassinated by the mafia in an attack. He became a symbol of the fight against the mafia and organised crime.
131. Paolo Borsellino was a judge in Italy who, along with Giovanni Falcone, presided over trials against the Cosa Nostra. He was assassinated by the mafia (Cosa Nostra) in 1992, in an attack in Palermo, Sicily. He was known for his determination to confront the mafia, considered a symbol of resistance in the fight against corruption and organised crime.
132. Piercamillo Davigo was the prosecutor of Operation Clean Hands.

133. Antonio di Pietro was a public prosecutor and was part of Operation Clean Hands. In 1996, he began his political career in Italy.
134. The Ambrosiano Bank was an Italian bank that declared bankruptcy in 1982, after the discovery of a major corruption scandal, involving accounting fraud, ghost accounts to cover financial losses, money laundering, and transactions with the mafia. The bank was controlled by the banker Roberto Calvi, a person close to the high ranks of the Vatican and who also maintained close ties with the Freemasonry.
135. P2, *Propaganda Due* or Propaganda Two was a Masonic lodge that was implicated in several crimes in Italy, including corruption and the collapse of the Vatican Bank.
136. Benedetto "Bettino" Craxi was an Italian politician, secretary of the Italian Socialist Party (PSI), from 1976 to 1993, and Prime Minister of Italy from 1983 to 1987. He was pointed out as one of the corrupt politicians of Operation Clean Hands and moved to Tunisia, to escape Italian justice. He died in 2000.
137. The Biondi Decree, also called "*Salva-Ladri*" (Save Thieves), extinguished pre-trial detention, limiting it to cases of homicide and crimes of association with the mafia or terrorism. The prosecutors of Operation Clean Hands and the massive protests of the Italian population pressured Parliament not to convert the Decree into law, which ended up expiring.
138. The Biondi Decree, of 13 July 1994, also called "*Salva-Ladri*" (Save Thieves), extinguished pre-trial detention, limiting it to cases of homicide and crimes of association with the mafia or terrorism. The prosecutors of Operation Clean Hands and the massive protests of the Italian population pressured Parliament not to convert the Decree into law, which ended up expiring.
139. MOSE, *Modulo Sperimentale Elettromeccanico* or Experimental Electromechanical Module is a project to protect the city of Venice from floods.

140. The series of mobilisations in various Brazilian cities that took place in June 2013 are known as "June Journeys." They are the clear representation of the widespread dissatisfaction of the population with politicians and with social and economic conditions in the country. They drove important changes, including the entry into force of the Clean Company Act, in record time.
141. The Constitutional Amendment Proposal 37/2011 aimed to remove the power of criminal investigation from the Public Ministry and grant it to the Federal and Civil police. It was heavily criticised by civil society, human rights defence entities, the press and various sectors of justice, and the Public Ministry itself.
142. Law No. 12.850, of 2 August 2013, which defines criminal organisation and provides for criminal investigation, means of obtaining evidence, related criminal offences and criminal procedure. http://www.planalto.gov.br/ccivil_03/_ato2011-2014/2013/lei/l12850.htm.
143. Law No. 12.846, of 1 August 2013, which provides for the administrative and civil liability of legal entities for the practice of acts against the public administration, national or foreign. http://www.planalto.gov.br/ccivil_03/_ato2011-2014/2013/lei/l12846.htm.
144. Mensalão was a corruption scandal, which occurred through the purchase of deputies' votes by the Executive, during the government of Luiz Inácio Lula da Silva, in 2005. This illegal practice was so known behind the scenes because it referred to a monthly payment paid to deputies to vote in favour of projects of interest to the Executive.
145. Abbreviation for Workers' Party, PT.
146. Reference is made to Geddel Quadros Vieira Lima, former federal congressperson for the state of Bahia, Minister of National Integration in Lula's government, Vice-President of the Federal Economic Bank, in Dilma Rousseff's government and Minister of Government, in Michel Temer's government. He was

arrested in September 2017 after more than 51 million reais were seized in cash, in an apartment in Salvador, linked to him. It was the largest cash seizure in the history of Brazil.

147. Reference is made to Rodrigo Santos da Rocha Loures, former federal congressperson for Paraná. He was an advisor to then President Michel Temer when he was filmed by the Federal Police, in Operation Patmos, with a suitcase containing 500 thousand reais leaving the Pizzaria Camelo in São Paulo. The money was delivered by Ricardo Saud, then director of JBS.
148. A barrier clause is a legal provision that restricted or prevented the operation of a party that did not achieve a certain percentage of votes.
149. Nepotism is the term used to designate the favouring of relatives to the detriment of more qualified people, in the granting of privileges or positions particularly in public service, but also in the private sector.
150. The Special Fund for Financial Assistance to Political Parties, commonly called the Party Fund, is composed of budgetary appropriations from the Union, fines, penalties, donations, and other financial resources assigned by law and passed on to political parties. For more information, see the Superior Electoral Court. https://www.tse.jus.br/partidos/contas-partidarias/fundo-partidario-1.
151. The Party Transparency Movement is an NGO that aims to change politics and political parties through the improvement of governance, renewal of leadership, and the promotion of system integrity. The movement's website is https://www.transparenciapartidaria.org/.
152. The Brazilian Federal Constitution (Articles 53 and 102 of the Constitution, in particular) assigns competence to some specific courts to prosecute and judge occupants of political and functional positions. Today, privileged jurisdiction covers almost 60 thousand occupants of 40 different types of positions in the spheres of federal, state, and municipal government and in the three powers: Executive, Legislative, and Judiciary.

153. Second-instance imprisonment is the possibility of the defendant sentenced to deprivation of liberty to start serving the sentence after the judicial decision rendered in the second instance, even if there are still pending appeals to higher instances, Superior Court of Justice and Federal Supreme Court. In February of 2016, the ruled, by seven votes to four, a judgement confirmed by a new decision in October 2015, by six votes to five, that it was possible to imprison the defendant, after a decision rendered in the second instance. Defendants can appeal to the higher courts, but imprisoned. However, in November 2019, the Federal Supreme Court decided by six votes to five that the enforcement of the prison sentence should only be initiated after all appeals have been judged, before the higher instances, Superior Court of Justice and Federal Supreme Court.
154. Sérgio Machado is a Brazilian politician and businessman. He was President of Transpetro during the governments of Presidents Lula and Dilma Rousseff. He was involved in the Petrobras scandal, after he left the presidency of Transpetro in 2014. In May 2016, he made a plea bargain agreement with the Attorney General's Office (PGR), in which he details his participation in the corruption scheme of the state company.
155. Justice Luiz Edson Fachin decided on Monday, 8 March 2021, in a *Habeas Corpus* filed by Lula's defence on 3 November 2020, that the 13th Federal Court of Curitiba, whose The title was the former judge Sergio Moro, he was incompetent to prosecute and judge the former President Lula in the cases of the Guarujá triplex, the Atibaia site, and in two other actions involving the Lula Institute. With this, Lula can run for the presidential elections of 2022.
156. José Maria Marin is a former lawyer, former sports executive, and former politician. He was governor of the state of São Paulo between 1982 and 1983. He was president of the Brazilian Football Confederation from 2012 to 2015 and president of the Local Organising Committee for the FIFA World Cup—International Football Federation—Brazil 2014. In 2015, he was arrested in Switzerland, alongside six other FIFA executives, accused of

corruption. He was banned by FIFA from any football-related activity. In 2017, he was convicted and imprisoned for six crimes by the Federal Court of Brooklyn. In 2020, he was released for humanitarian reasons.

157. Fernando Henrique Cardoso. Fernando Henrique Cardoso. ***Entry***. FGV CPDOC. He is a sociologist, professor, writer, and Brazilian politician. He was the 34th President of the Federative Republic of Brazil (1995–2003). He is president of the Fernando Henrique Cardoso Foundation and honorary president of the Brazilian Social Democracy Party.
158. Roberto Da Matta is an anthropologist, philosopher, and Brazilian newspaper columnist. He is Professor of Anthropology in the Department of Social Sciences at the Pontifical Catholic University of Rio de Janeiro and Emeritus Professor at the University of Notre Dame.
159. José Carlos de Ataliba Nogueira ***Entry***. FGV CPDOC. http://www.fgv.br/cpdoc/acervo/dicionarios/verbete-biografico/jose-carlos-de-ataliba-nogueira. He was a jurist, politician, and full professor of General Theory of the State at the Faculty of Law of Largo São Francisco. He was founder of the Social Democratic Party, federal congressperson for the state of São Paulo, and secretary of education of the same state. He is the father of José Geraldo de Ataliba Nogueira.
160. José Geraldo de Ataliba Nogueira was a full professor at the Faculty of Law of Largo São Francisco and at the Pontifical Catholic University of São Paulo, having also been rector of the Pontifical Catholic University of São Paulo. He is the son of José Carlos de Ataliba Nogueira.
161. Celso Antônio Bandeira de Mello is a jurist, lawyer, and emeritus professor of administrative law at the Pontifical Catholic University of São Paulo. He is considered one of the greatest references in administrative law in Brazil.

162. André Franco Montoro ***Entry***. FGV CPDOC. http://www.fgv.br/cpdoc/acervo/dicionarios/verbete-biografico/andre-franco-montoro. He was a jurist and politician. He was elected governor by the state of São Paulo, after twenty years of military regime, he was also a senator, state congressperson, federal congressperson and councillor for São Paulo, and Minister of Labour and Social Security during the short period of parliamentarism in Brazil.
163. Luís Antônio Fleury Filho ***Entry***. FGV CPDOC. http://www.fgv.br/cpdoc/acervo/dicionarios/verbete-tematico/luis-antonio-fleury-filho. Prosecutor, teacher, and politician, he was also Governor of the State of São Paulo.
164. Fernando Henrique Cardoso. ***Entry***. FGV CPDOC. He is a sociologist, professor, writer, and Brazilian politician. He was the 34th President of the Federative Republic of Brazil (1995–2003). He is president of the Fernando Henrique Cardoso Foundation and honorary president of the Brazilian Social Democracy Party.
165. ADin 5.874. Full Decision Federal Supreme Court. 9th May 2019. https://redir.jus.br/paginadorpub/paginador.jsp?docTP=TP&docID=754291421.
166. There were 21 people convicted in the Car Wash who would benefit from the pardon. They were: 1. Adir Assad; 2. André Gustavo Vieira da Silva; 3. André Luiz Vargas Ilário; 4. Antonio Palocci; 5. Antonio Carlos Brasil Fioravante Pieruccini; 6. Bruno Luz; 7. Carlos Habib Chater; 8. Dalton dos Santos Avancini; 9. Eduardo Hermelino Leite; 10. Elton Negrão de Azevedo Junior; 11. Gim Argello; 12. João Cláudio Genu; 13. João Ricardo Auler; 14. José Carlos Bumlai; 15. Jorge Antonio da Silva Luz; 16. Luiz Argôlo; 17. Mário Frederico de Mendonça Goes; 18. Nelma Kodama; 19. Ricardo Pessoa; 20. Ronan Maria Pinto; 21. Zwi Skornicki.
167. Brazil has 820,689 people with some form of deprivation of liberty. National Penitentiary Department. https://www.gov.br/depen/pt-br/assuntos/noticias/segundo-levantamento-do-depen-as-vagas-no-sistema-penitenciario-aumentaram-7-4-enquanto-a-populacao-prisional-permaneceu-estavel-sem-aumento-significativo.

168. In this sense, Articles 127 and 129 of the Federal Constitution. http://www.planalto.gov.br/ccivil_03/constituicao/constituicao.htm.
169. The Convention on Combating Bribery of Foreign Public Officials in International Business Transactions of the OECD was concluded in Paris on 17 December 1997 and promulgated by Decree No. 3.678 of 30 November 2000. http://www.planalto.gov.br/ccivil_03/decreto/d3678.htm.
170. Law No. 12.846, of 1 August 2013, provides for the administrative and civil liability of legal entities for the practice of acts against the public administration, national, or foreign. http://www.planalto.gov.br/ccivil_03/_ato2011-2014/2013/lei/l12846.htm.
171. Mensalão was a corruption scandal, which occurred through the purchase of votes from deputies by the Executive, during the government of Luiz Inácio Lula da Silva, in 2005. This illegal practice was known backstage as it referred to a monthly payment made to the deputies to vote in favour of executive interest projects.
172. Carlos Augusto Ayres Britto ***Entry***. FGV CPDOC. http://www.fgv.br/cpdoc/acervo/dicionarios/verbete-biografico/brito-carlos-aires. He was a Justice of the Federal Supreme Court from 2003 to 2012, President of the in 2012, Justice of the Superior Electoral Court (2006–2010), President of the Superior Electoral Court (2008–2010), and President of the National Council of Justice (2011–2012). He is a Brazilian lawyer, professor, and legal opinion writer.
173. The Criminal Action No 470 (AP 470/MG). Full Federal Supreme Court. https://www.conjur.com.br/dl/ap470.pdf.
174. Budget Dwarfs was the name given to a group of Brazilian congressmen, involved in frauds in the resources of the Union Budget, in the 80s-90s. They were discovered and investigated in a Parliamentary Inquiry Commission, in 1993. The word “dwarfs” used in this corruption scandal is since these congressmen did not have a great repercussion in the national

territory and were "power dwarfs" within the National Congress itself.

175. The Political Constitution of the Empire of Brazil was granted by D. Pedro I on 25 March 1824 and lasted for 65 years.
176. "Getulismo", "Ademarismo", and "Janismo" refer to distinct forms of populist political movements in mid-twentieth-century Brazil, each centred around a dominant political figure. "Getulismo" relates to the legacy and ideology of Getúlio Vargas, who governed Brazil as both dictator (1930–1945) and democratically elected president (1951–1954), promoting labour rights and state-led industrialisation. "Ademarismo" is associated with Ademar de Barros, governor of São Paulo, known for his clientelist style and pragmatic populism. "Janismo" refers to Jânio Quadros, an idiosyncratic populist who briefly served as president in 1961, advocating anti-corruption while cultivating a flamboyant, moralising public image.
177. Itamar Augusto Cautiero Franco was a military engineer and politician. He was Vice-President of the Republic from 1990 to 1992 (government of Fernando Collor de Mello) and President of the Republic from 1992 to 1 January 1995.
178. Budget Dwarfs was the name given to a group of Brazilian congressmen, involved in fraud in the resources of the Union Budget, in the 80s–90s. They were discovered and investigated in a Parliamentary Inquiry Commission, in 1993. The term "dwarfs" was used in reference to this corruption scandal because these congressmen had little national visibility and were considered "power dwarfs" within the National Congress itself.
179. Modesto Carvalhosa. *The black book of corruption*. São Paulo: Paz e Terra, 1995.
180. Modesto Carvalhosa. *From kleptocracy to democracy in 2019, a government project, a state project*. São Paulo: Revista dos Tribunais, 2022.
181. Modesto Carvalhosa. *A New Constitution for Brazil: From a Country of Privileges to a Nation of Opportunities*. São Paulo: LVM editora, 2021.

182. The OECD Convention on Combating Bribery of Foreign Public Officials in International Business Transactions was concluded in Paris on 17 December 1997 and promulgated in Brazil by Decree No. 3.678 of 30 November 2000. http://www.planalto.gov.br/ccivil_03/decreto/d3678.htm.
183. The United Nations Convention against Corruption adopted by the United Nations General Assembly on 31 October 2003, in force since 14 December 2005. http://www.planalto.gov.br/ccivil_03/_ato2004-2006/2006/decreto/d5687.htm.
184. The Inter-American Convention against Corruption was approved within the framework of the Organization of American States, signed on 29 March 1996, approved by Legislative Decree No. 152, of 25 June 2002 and promulgated by Presidential Decree No. 4,410, of 7 October 2002. http://www.planalto.gov.br/ccivil_03/decreto/2002/D4410.htm.
185. Law No. 9,613, of 3 March 1998 on crimes of money laundering or concealment of assets, rights, and values and creates the Council for Financial Activities Control. http://www.planalto.gov.br/ccivil_03/leis/l9613.htm.
186. Law No. 12,846, of 1 August 2013 on the administrative and civil liability of legal entities for the practice of acts against public administration, national or foreign. http://www.planalto.gov.br/ccivil_03/_ato2011-2014/2013/lei/l12846.htm.
187. Operation Clean Hands, Mani Pulite, was an investigation of corruption cases in Italy, centred in Milan, which involved the Italian political class, political parties, the state oil company (ENI—Ente Nazionale Idrocarburi), and large contractors in the overpricing of works and in the diversion of public money.
188. Mensalão was a corruption scandal, which occurred through the purchase of votes from deputies by the Executive, during the government of Luiz Inácio Lula da Silva, in 2005. This illegal practice was known in the background as it referred to a monthly payment paid to deputies to vote in favour of projects of interest to the Executive.
189. "Centrão" refers to a loosely organised bloc of centrist and centre-right parties in the Brazilian Congress, characterised less

by ideological coherence than by a pragmatic pursuit of political influence and patronage. Historically, the Centrão has played a pivotal role in supporting successive governments—regardless of party or platform—in exchange for access to budgetary amendments, appointments, and other institutional privileges. It is widely associated with clientelism and has been a central actor in Brazil's political bargaining culture.

190. Getulio Dornelles Vargas ***Entry***. FGV CPDOC. https://pt.wikipedia.org/wiki/Get%C3%BAlio_Vargas. He was a lawyer and Brazilian politician. He was President of Brazil for almost 20 years, first for 15 uninterrupted years (1930–1945) and in the second period for almost 4 years (31 January 1951 to 24 August 1954).
191. Adhemar Pereira de Barros ***Entry***. FGV CPDOC. http://www.fgv.br/cpdoc/acervo/dicionarios/verbete-biografico/ademar-pereira-de-barros. He was a doctor and Brazilian politician, mayor of São Paulo, federal intervenor and twice governor of the State of São Paulo.
192. The Democrats was a political party that merged with the Social Liberal Party (PSL) to form a new party, Union Brazil.
193. *Festa Junina* (June Festival) is a traditional Brazilian celebration held throughout the month of June, particularly in rural and northeastern regions. Originally rooted in Catholic festivities honouring saints such as Saint Anthony, Saint John, and Saint Peter, it features folk music, square dancing, costumes, bonfires, and regional food. While culturally significant, such events are often used as pretexts for discretionary public spending by politicians seeking local visibility and electoral support.
194. Paulo Guedes. He is the Minister of Economy of the Jair Bolsonaro government. He is an economist with a doctorate from the University of Chicago, was a professor and served on company boards of directors before being appointed to the ministry.
195. Fernando Henrique Cardoso. ***Entry***. FGV CPDOC. He is a sociologist, professor, writer, and Brazilian politician. He was the 34th President of the Federative Republic of Brazil (1995–2003).

He is president of the Fernando Henrique Cardoso Foundation and honorary president of the Brazilian Social Democracy Part.

196. Law No. 13,303, of 30 June 2016 (State-Owned Companies Law) on the legal status of the public company, the society of mixed economy and its subsidiaries, within the scope of the Union, the States, the Federal District, and the Municipalities. http://www.planalto.gov.br/ccivil_03/_ato2015-2018/2016/lei/l13303.htm.
197. Law No. 13.869, of 5 September 2019 (Abuse of Authority Law) on the crimes of abuse of authority. Article 1: "This Law defines the crimes of abuse of authority, committed by a public agent, servant or not, who, in the exercise of their functions or under the pretext of exercising them, abuses the power that has been attributed to them."
198. The Brazilian Federal Constitution (Articles 53 and 102 of the Constitution, particularly) assigns competence to some specific courts to prosecute and judge occupants of political and functional positions. Today, privileged jurisdiction covers almost 60,000 occupants of 40 different types of positions in the federal, state, and municipal spheres and in the three Executive, Legislative, and Judicial Powers.
199. About the 10 Measures against Corruption, see the website https://dezmedidas.mpf.mp.br/apresentacao/conheca-as-medidas.
200. The Anti-Crime Package was amended by Congress and resulted in the promulgation of Law No. 13.964, of 24 December 2019 which improves criminal and criminal procedural legislation. http://www.planalto.gov.br/ccivil_03/_ato2019-2022/2019/lei/L13964.htm.
201. Sergio Fernando Moro ***Entry***. FGV CPDOC. http://www.fgv.br/cpdoc/acervo/dicionarios/verbete-biografico/sergio-fernando-moro. He was a former federal judge and judge of the Car Wash operation in Curitiba. He was former Minister of Justice and director of Alvarez & Marsal. He is a Brazilian lawyer and politician. He is currently an elected Senator for the state of Paraná.

202. Law No. 8.429, of 2 June 1992 (Administrative Improbity Law) on the sanctions applicable due to the practice of acts of administrative improbity.
203. Luiz Edson Fachin. ***Entry***. FGV CPDOC. https://www18.fgv.br/CPDOC/acervo/dicionarios/verbete-biografico/luiz-edson-fachin. He is a Brazilian jurist and Justice of the Federal Supreme Court, since June 2015. He was a lawyer and full professor of civil law at the Law School of the Federal University of Paraná (UFPR). He is the current rapporteur of the Car Wash Operation in the Federal Supreme Court.
204. Luiz Inácio Lula da Silva. ***Entry***. FGV CPDOC. https://www18.fgv.br/CPDOC/acervo/dicionarios/verbete-biografico/luis-inacio-da-silva. He was a unionist, metalworker, and Brazilian politician. He was President of the Republic from 2003 to 2011. Re-elected President of the Republic in 2022.
205. Antonio di Pietro was a prosecutor of the Italian public ministry in the Clean Hands operation. He is now a lawyer and politician.
206. Roberto Livianu. *Penal control of corruption.* Thesis (PhD in Law). Law School, University of São Paulo, 2004.
207. The Institute I Do Not Accept Corruption (INAC) is an NGO Brazilian, whose aim is to concentrate efforts in the fight against corruption. https://www.naoaceitocorrupcao.org.br/quem-somos.
208. Rita de Castro Biason and Roberto Livianu. *The corruption in the history of Brazil*. São Paulo: Mackenzie Publisher, 2019.
209. The Clean Hands Operation, *Mani Pulite*, was an investigation of corruption cases in Italy, centred in Milan, which involved the Italian political class, political parties, the state oil company (ENI—*Ente Nazionale Idrocarburi*), and large contractors in the overpricing of works and in the diversion of public money.
210. Mensalão was a corruption scandal, which occurred through the purchase of votes from deputies by the Executive, during the government of Luiz Inácio Lula da Silva, in 2005. This illegal practice was known in the background as it referred to a monthly payment paid to deputies to vote in favour of projects of interest to the Executive.

211. Banestado (Bank of the State of Paraná) is a well-known corruption scandal, from the 1990s, involving illegal remittances abroad, through the Brazilian public financial system.
212. Joaquim Benedito Barbosa Gomes. ***Entry***. FGV CPDOC. http://www.fgv.br/cpdoc/acervo/dicionarios/verbete-biografico/barbosa-joaquim. He is known simply as Joaquim Barbosa, is a jurist, and was a member of the Public Ministry until being appointed as Justice of the Federal Supreme Court (2003 to 2014). He was the rapporteur of the Mensalão process.
213. Carlos Augusto Ayres Britto ***Entry***. FGV CPDOC. http://www.fgv.br/cpdoc/acervo/dicionarios/verbete-biografico/brito-carlos-aires. He was a Justice of the Federal Supreme Court from 2003 to 2012, President of the in 2012, Justice of the Superior Electoral Court (2006–2010), President of the Superior Electoral Court (2008–2010), and President of the National Council of Justice (2011–2012). He is a Brazilian lawyer, professor, and legal opinion writer.
214. Marcelo Bahia Odebrecht is a civil engineer and businessman. He was president of Odebrecht from 2008 to 2015, the largest engineering company in Brazil and one of the largest in Latin America. On 19 June 2015, he was preventively arrested, during the 14th phase of Operation Car Wash, named, "Erga *Omnes*". In March of 2016, he was sentenced to nineteen years and four months for the crimes of corruption, money laundering, and criminal association. On 1 December 2016, he closed a plea bargain agreement, alongside his father and seventy-seven executives from Odebrecht, having his sentence reduced.
215. Law No. 13.869, of 5 September 2019, which provides about the crimes of abuse of authority. http://www.planalto.gov.br/ccivil_03/_ato2019-2022/2019/lei/L13869.htm.
216. Organisation for Economic Co-operation and Development, OECD.
217. Jorge Sayed Picciani was a cattle rancher and politician, affiliated with the Brazilian Democratic Movement. He was President of the Legislative Assembly of Rio de Janeiro (ALERJ) from 2003 to 2010. In November 2017, he was the target of a coercive conduct

warrant issued by the Regional Federal Court of the 2nd Region (TRF-2), within the scope of the Operation Old Chain, a development of Operation Car Wash. According to the investigations, Picciani commanded a scheme of bribe distribution, alongside state deputies Edson Albertassi and Paulo Melo, in the Legislative Assembly of the State of Rio de Janeiro, known as "Fetranspor Little Box", as it aimed to protect the interests of businessmen linked to the Federation of Passenger Transport Companies of the State of Rio de Janeiro (*Fetranspor*). By thirty-nine votes in favour of the release of the imprisoned politicians and nineteen votes against, one abstention and eleven absences, Picciani, Albertassi, and Melo are released by the Legislative Assembly. In November 2017, the Regional Federal Court-2 does not recognise the authority of the Assembly's decision and again orders the trio's arrest.

218. Wagner Montes dos Santos. ***Entry***. FGV CPDOC. https://www18.fgv.br/CPDOC/acervo/dicionarios/verbete-biografico/zenobio-da-costa-e-silva. He was a lawyer, journalist, TV show juror, radio and television presenter and politician affiliated with the Republicans Party. He was a state congressperson in Rio de Janeiro and acting president of Rio de Janeiro State Legislature.
219. The term abuse of statutes, in Portuguese "carteirada", refers to the act of using one's official status—often by literally showing an identification badge ("carteira" in Portuguese)—to gain undue privileges or avoid legal consequences. It is typically associated with public officials, law enforcement agents, or members of the judiciary who abuse their position to bypass rules or obtain special treatment. Though informal, the term is widely recognised in Brazil as a symbol of entrenched hierarchical privilege.
220. Complementary Law No. 135, of 4 June 2010 (Clean Record Law) on hypotheses of ineligibility aimed at protecting administrative probity and morality in the exercise of the mandate. https://www.planalto.gov.br/ccivil_03/leis/lcp/lcp135.htm.
221. Law No. 8.429, of 2 June 1992 (Administrative Improbity Law) on the sanctions applicable due to the practice of acts of

administrative improbity. https://www.planalto.gov.br/ccivil_03/leis/l8429.htm.

222. Article 11 was amended by Law No. 14.320, of 25 October 2021 (https://www.planalto.gov.br/ccivil_03/leis/l8429.htm), having today the following wording: "It constitutes an act of administrative improbity that attacks the principles of public administration the intentional action or omission that violates the duties of honesty, impartiality and legality, characterised by one of the following conducts: I – to perform an act aiming at a purpose prohibited by law or regulation or different from that provided for in the rule of competence (revoked by Law No. 14.320); II – to delay or fail to perform, improperly, an official act (revoked by Law No. 14.320); III – to reveal a fact or circumstance of which he/she is aware due to his/her duties and which should remain secret, providing benefit from privileged information or putting at risk the security of society and the State; IV – to deny publicity to official acts, except due to their indispensability for the security of society and the State or other hypotheses established by law (amended by Law No. 14.320); V – to frustrate, in offence to impartiality, the competitive character of a public contest, call or bidding procedure, with a view to obtaining one's own benefit, direct or indirect, or of third parties (amended by Law No. 14.320); VI – to fail to render accounts when obliged to do so, provided that he/she has the conditions to do so, with a view to concealing irregularities (amended by Law No. 14.320); VII – to reveal or allow a third party to become aware, before its official disclosure, of the content of a political or economic measure capable of affecting the price of a commodity, good or service; VIII– to fail to comply with the rules relating to the celebration, supervision and approval of accounts of partnerships established by the public administration with private entities; IX – to fail to comply with the requirement of accessibility requirements provided for in the legislation (revoked by Law No. 14.320); X – to transfer resources to a private entity, due to the provision of services in the health area without the prior conclusion of a contract, agreement or similar instrument,

in the terms of the sole paragraph of art. 24 of Law No. 8.080, of 19 September 1990 (revoked by Law No. 14.320); XI – to appoint a spouse, partner or relative in a straight line, collateral or by affinity, up to the third degree, inclusive, of the appointing authority or of a server of the same legal entity invested in a position of direction, management or advisory, for the exercise of a position in commission or of trust or, still, of a gratified function in the direct and indirect public administration in any of the Powers of the Union, of the States, of the Federal District and of the Municipalities, including the adjustment through reciprocal designations (included by Law No. 14.320); XII – to practice, within the scope of public administration and with resources from the treasury, an act of publicity that contradicts the provisions of § 1 of art. 37 of the Federal Constitution, in order to promote unequivocal praise of the public agent and personalisation of acts, programmes, works, services or campaigns of public bodies (included by Law No. 14.320). § 1º Under the terms of the United Nations Convention against Corruption, promulgated by Decree No. 5.687, of 31 January 2006, administrative misconduct will only occur, in the application of this article, when it is proven in the functional conduct of the public agent the aim of obtaining undue profit or benefit for himself or for another person or entity (included by Law No. 14.320). § 2º the provisions of § 1º of this article apply to any acts of administrative misconduct typified in this Law and in special laws and to any other special types of administrative misconduct established by law (included by Law No. 14.320). § 3º the classification of functional conduct in the category referred to in this article presupposes the objective demonstration of the practice of illegality in the exercise of public function, with the indication of the constitutional, legal or infra-legal norms violated (included by Law No. 14.320). § 4º the acts of misconduct referred to in this article require relevant harm to the legally protected good to be subject to sanction and do not depend on the recognition of the production of damage to the treasury and of illicit enrichment of public agents (included by Law No. 14.320). § 5º Mere appointment or political nomination by the holders of elective mandates will not constitute misconduct, it being necessary to ascertain malicious intent with illicit purpose on the part of the agent" (included by Law No. 14.320).

223. Law No. 12.527, of 18 November 2011 (Access to Information Law) on the guarantee of access to information. https://www.planalto.gov.br/ccivil_03/_ato2011-2014/2011/lei/l12527.htm.
224. Ricardo José Magalhães Barros. ***Entry***. FGV CPDOC. https://www18.fgv.br/CPDOC/acervo/dicionarios/verbete-biografico/ricardo-jose-magalhaes-barros. He is an engineer and politician, affiliated with the Progressistas Party (PP). He is federal congressperson for the State of Paraná, for six terms. In 2017, he was denounced by Eduardo Queiroz Galvão, from the construction company Galvão Engenharia, within the scope of Operation Car Wash, for receiving bribes. In 2021, then government leader in the Chamber, he defended nepotism, saying that the "public power could be better served, possibly, with a qualified relative than with an unqualified non-relative".
225. According to the Public Prosecutor's Office of Paraná, part of the bribe received from Galvão Engenharia by the Government leader in the Chamber, Ricardo Barros, went to honour debt with the steakhouse Fim da Picada, traditional establishment in Maringá, frequented by politicians from the region.
226. The term "rachadinha" refers to a widespread and illicit practice in Brazilian politics whereby elected officials or their aides require staff members to return part of their publicly funded salaries—often under duress or as a condition of employment. The funds are then diverted for personal or political use. The word derives from the Portuguese verb "rachar," meaning "to split," and the scheme is commonly translated as "salary kickbacks".
227. Reference is made to the Speaker of the Brazilian lowest Speaker of Brazil's lower house of Congress Arthur César Pereira de Lira. ***Entry***. FGV CPDOC. https://www18.fgv.br/CPDOC/acervo/dicionarios/verbete-biografico/arthur-cesar-pereira-de-lira. He is a politician affiliated with the Progressists Party On 4 September 2015, the Prosecutor General, Rodrigo Janot presented charges

to the Federal Supreme Court against federal congressperson Arthur Lira, for involvement in the corruption scheme at Petrobras, resulting from Operation Car Wash. In 2002, he was charged by the Attorney General of the Republic for the crimes of embezzlement and money laundering for participation in a scheme known as "rachadinhas", when he was State congressperson in Alagoas between 2001 and 2007. In December 2020, Judge Carlos Henrique Pita Duarte, summarily acquitted Lira in the "rachadinhas" scheme, annulling all evidence collected against him.

228. Law No. 9.613, of 3 March 1998, on the crimes of laundering or concealment of assets, rights, and values and creates the Council for Control of Financial Activities. http://www.planalto.gov.br/ccivil_03/leis/l9613.htm.
229. Geddel Quadros Vieira Lima. He is an administrator of businessman and politician affiliated with the Brazilian Democratic Movement. Former federal congressperson for the state of Bahia. He was Justice of National Integration in Lula's government, Vice-President of the Federal Economic Bank, in Dilma Rousseff's government and Minister of Government, in Michel Temer's government. He was arrested in September 2017 after more than 51 million reais were seized in cash, in an apartment in Salvador, linked to him. It was the largest cash seizure in the history of Brazil.
230. Ney de Barros Bello Filho is a magistrate and currently a judge of the Federal Regional Court of the 1st Region. On 12 July 2017, he authorised Geddel Vieira Lima to leave the Papuda complex in Brasília to serve house arrest in Salvador, Bahia. House arrest had been denied on 6 July 2017 by the first-instance magistrate, Vallisney de Souza Oliveira.
231. Judge Ney de Barros Bello Filho was the reporter of the case involving former President Michel Temer related to the asset freeze. He authorised the unfreezing of the assets that had been frozen by the first instance.
232. Ricardo de Aquino Salles is a lawyer, administrator, and politician affiliated with the Liberal Party. He was Minister of the

Environment during the government of former President Jair Bolsonaro. He is now a Federal congressperson for São Paulo. He faced several requests for removal for administrative misconduct. On 23 June 2021, he is dismissed from the Ministry of the Environment, at his request, after accusations of involvement in a scheme of illegal export of Brazilian wood abroad. In December 2020, the Federal Police carried out a historic operation of seizure of 130,000 cubic metres of illegal woods on the border between Pará and Amazonas. It is the largest environmental operation carried out in Brazil. On 24 November 2020, Judge Ney de Barros Bello Filho denied the request for precautionary removal made by the Federal Public Prosecutor's Office of then Minister of the Environment, Ricardo Salles.

233. Law No. 13.709, of 14 August 2018, on the protection of fundamental rights related to the treatment of personal data, including digital, by a natural or legal person of public or private law. https://www.planalto.gov.br/ccivil_03/_ato2015-2018/2018/lei/l13709.htm.
234. Kassio Nunes Marques is a magistrate and current Justice of the Federal Supreme Court. He was a Judge of the Federal Court of the 1st Region.
235. Reference is made to then President Jair Bolsonaro.
236. Complementary Law No. 135, of 4 June 2010 on cases of ineligibility. https://www.planalto.gov.br/ccivil_03/leis/lcp/lcp135.htm.
237. At the end of 2020, Nunes Marques suspended a section of the Clean Record Law on the ineligibility of candidates. This decision was overturned by the Full of the Federal Supreme Court in 2022, on the grounds that this issue had already been debated and decided by the Federal Supreme Court, and that the arguments brought do not justify a new analysis of the case.
238. At the time, the President was Jair Bolsonaro.
239. Arthur César Pereira de Lira. ***Entry***. FGV CPDOC. https://www18.fgv.br/CPDOC/acervo/dicionarios/verbete-biografico/arthur-cesar-pereira-de-lira. He is a lawyer, cattle rancher, and politician, affiliated with the Progressistas. He is a federal

congressperson for the State of Alagoas and was Speaker of Brazil's lower house of Congress.

240. Centrão, in Brazilian politics, is a set of political parties, without ideological orientation, formed by parliamentarians of the so-called lower clergy, whose aim is to ensure proximity to the executive power and, with this, advantages and privileges.
241. Wadih Nemer Damous Filho is a lawyer and politician, affiliated with the Workers' Party. He was president of the Order of Lawyers of Brazil, Rio de Janeiro section, and federal congressperson for the State of Rio de Janeiro. He was the head of the National Consumer Secretariat.
242. United Nations Convention against Corruption, promulgated on 31 October 2003, came into force in Brazil on 14 December 2005. https://www.unodc.org/documents/lpo-brazil/Topics_corruption/Publicacoes/2007_UNCAC_Port.pdf.
243. OECD Convention on Combating Bribery of Foreign Public Officials in International Business Transactions was concluded in Paris on 17 December 1997 and promulgated in Brazil by Decree No. 3.678 of 30 November 2000. http://www.planalto.gov.br/ccivil_03/decreto/d3678.htm.
244. OECD Convention on Combating Bribery of Foreign Public Officials in International Business Transactions, Article 5: "Enforcement. The investigation and prosecution of the bribery of a foreign public official shall be subject to the applicable rules and principles of each Party. They shall not be influenced by considerations of national economic interest, the potential effect on relations with other States or the identity of natural or legal persons involved."
245. Paul Joseph Goebbels was a German politician and Minister of Propaganda in Nazi Germany from 1933 to 1945.
246. Jair Messias Bolsonaro is a retired captain and Brazilian politician. He was president of Brazil, from 2019 to 2022.
247. Provisional Measure No. 966, of 13 May 2020 on the accountability of public agents, for action or omission in acts related to the COVID-19 pandemic. https://www.in.gov.br/en/web/dou/-/medida-provisoria-n-966-de-13-de-maio-de-2020-256734909.

248. Luiz Inácio Lula da Silva is a popular Brazilian politician, affiliated with the Workers' Party. He was president of Brazil from 2003 to 2006 (first term) and from 2006 to 2010 (second term). He is the current president of Brazil (2023–2026).
249. Dilma Vana Rousseff is an economist and Brazilian politician, affiliated with the Workers' Party. She was president of Brazil from 2011 to 2014 (first term) and from 2015 to 2016 (second term), when she was removed by an impeachment process.
250. Michel Miguel Elias Temer Lulia is a lawyer, professor, and politician, affiliated with the Brazilian Democratic Movement. He was President of Brazil, from 31 August 2016 to 1 January 2019, following the impeachment of Dilma Rousseff.
251. Robert Klitgaard is a professor at the Claremont Graduate University in the United States and author of several books, among them *Controlling corruption*. Berkeley: University of California Press, 1988, which greatly assisted in the global movement against corruption.
252. Norberto Bobbio was an Italian philosopher, historian, and politician. He defended socio-liberal democracy and legal positivism. Author of numerous books.
253. Norberto Bobbio. *The future of democracy*. 7th ed. (Trans.). Carlos Nelson Coutinho. São Paulo: Paz e Terra, 2000, p. 98.
254. Law No. 12.850, of 2 August 2013, which defines criminal organisation and provides for criminal investigation, the means of obtaining evidence, related criminal offences and the criminal procedure. http://www.planalto.gov.br/ccivil_03/_ato2011-2014/2013/lei/l12850.htm.
255. Antônio Augusto Brandão de Aras is a professor at the Faculty of Law of the University of Brasília and the current Prosecutor General.
256. Reference is made to the government of Jair Bolsonaro.
257. Dalmo de Abreu Dallari was a jurist, lawyer, and director of the Faculty of Law of the University of São Paulo, as well as an emeritus professor of the institution.
258. Law No. 7.347, of 24 July 1985 (Public Civil Action Law), on the public civil action of responsibility for damages caused to the

environment, to the consumer, to goods and rights of artistic, aesthetic, historical, tourist, and landscape value.

259. Law No. 9.099, of 26 September 1995 (Law of Special Criminal Courts), on Special Civil and Criminal Courts. https://www.planalto.gov.br/ccivil_03/leis/l9099.htm.
260. André Oliveira Macedo, known as André, do Rap, is one of the leaders of the First Command of the Capital, a criminal faction that operates inside and outside prisons. He was released from the Penitentiary of Presidente Venceslau, in the interior of the State of São Paulo, through a *habeas corpus* granted by then Justice of the Federal Supreme Court, Marco Aurélio Mello, on 10 October 2020. The decision was suspended on the same day by the then President of the Federal Supreme Court, Justice Luis Fux. However, André do Rap had already fled and is still wanted by justice.
261. Jabuti in Brazilian political jargon means the insertion of amendments by parliamentarians, amendments that have no direct connection with the main text under discussion in the National Congress, and are true "smugglings", when put to vote. Despite the illegality of this practice, it is still used in texts of provisional measures, for the text to be voted on more quickly or to benefit someone.
262. The Anti-Crime Package was amended by Congress and resulted in the promulgation of Law No. 13.964, of 24 December 2019 which improves criminal and criminal procedural legislation. http://www.planalto.gov.br/ccivil_03/_ato2019-2022/2019/lei/L13964.htm.
263. It is an old and popular phrase in Brazilian politics: "tortoise does not climb a tree. Either it was a flood, or it was human hand".
264. The law is from 2011. Today, it would be eleven years.
265. Law No. 7.492, of 16 June 1986, on crimes against the financial system. https://www.planalto.gov.br/ccivil_03/leis/l7492.htm.
266. Transparency International is an NGO, based in Berlin, Germany; its main objective is to combat corruption. To this end, it has a series of publications, among them the Corruption

Perception Index (CPI) and the Global Corruption Barometer (GCB). The website of Transparency International Brazil is https://transparenciainternacional.org.br/.

267. It was founded on May 4, 1993, in Germany.
268. The Corruption Perception Index (CPI) was created in 1995.
269. Transparency International. *Corruption perception index 2021.* https://www.transparency.org/en/cpi/2021.
270. Law No. 12.846, of 1 August 2013, which provides for the administrative and civil liability of legal entities for the practice of acts against the public administration, national or foreign. http://www.planalto.gov.br/ccivil_03/_ato2011-2014/2013/lei/l12846.htm.
271. Law No. 4.737, of 15 July 1965, establishes the Electoral Code. Article 350: "Omit, in public or private document, declaration that should be included, or insert or make insert false declaration or different from what should be written, for electoral purposes: Penalty—imprisonment up to five years and payment of 5 to 15 days-fine, if the document is public, and imprisonment up to three years and payment of 3 to 10 days-fine if the document is private. Single paragraph. If the agent of the documentary falsity is public servant and commits the crime taking advantage of the position or if the falsification or alteration is of civil registration records, the penalty is aggravated." https://www.planalto.gov.br/ccivil_03/leis/l4737compilado.htm.
272. About the 10 Measures against Corruption, see the website https://dezmedidas.mpf.mp.br/apresentacao/conheca-as-medidas.
273. Rodrigo Chemim. Clean Hands and Car Wash: Corruption looks at itself in the mirror. Porto Alegre: Citadel. 2017.
274. Operation Clean Hands, *Mani Pulite*, was an investigation of corruption cases in Italy, centred in Milan, which involved the Italian political class, political parties, the state-owned fuel company (ENI—*Ente Nazionale Idrocarburi*), and large contractors in the overpricing of works and in the diversion of public money.

275. Mario Chiesa is an Italian politician, member of the Socialist Party. He was arrested on charges of corruption during Operation Clean Hands.
276. Alberto Youssef is a Brazilian black-market currency dealer, well known after the corruption scandal at Banestado. He was arrested in 2014 as part of Operation Car Wash.
277. Paulo Roberto Costa is an engineer and was a career employee of Petrobras, being appointed to the position of Director of Supply, between 2004 and 2012, during the government of Luiz Inácio Lula da Silva. He became known due to his involvement in the corruption scheme of the Car Wash operation. He was sentenced to 12 years of house arrest with an ankle monitor, because of his plea bargain agreement.
278. Antonio di Pietro was a public prosecutor, having been part of the Clean Hands operation. In 1996, he began his political career in Italy.
279. Sergio Fernando Moro ***Entry***. FGV CPDOC. http://www.fgv.br/cpdoc/acervo/dicionarios/verbete-biografico/sergio-fernando-moro. He was a former federal judge and judge of the Car Wash operation in Curitiba. He was former Minister of Justice and director of Alvarez & Marsal. He is a lawyer and Brazilian politician. He is currently an elected Senator for the state of Paraná.
280. Benedetto "Bettino" Craxi was an Italian politician, secretary of the Italian Socialist Party (PSI), from 1976 to 1993, and prime minister of Italy from 1983 to 1987. He was pointed out as one of the corrupt politicians of the Clean Hands Operation and moved to Tunisia, to escape from Italian justice. He died in 2000.
281. Luiz Inácio Lula da Silva. ***Entry***. FGV CPDOC. https://www18.fgv.br/CPDOC/acervo/dicionarios/verbete-biografico/luis-inacio-da-silva. He was a unionist, metalworker, and Brazilian politician. He was President of the Republic from 2003 to 2011. Re-elected President of the Republic in 2022.
282. Raimundo Faoro was a sociologist, historian, political scientist, lawyer, and Brazilian writer. He was president of the Brazilian

Bar Association (OAB) from 1977 to 1979 and a member of the Brazilian Academy of Letters.

283. Raimundo Faoro. *The owners of power*. 15th edition. Porto Alegre: Globo, 1958.
284. Edwin Sutherland was an American sociologist, considered one of the most important criminologists of the twentieth century. In the speech The *White-Collar Criminal* (The White-Collar Criminal) given on 27 December 1939, to the *American Sociological Association*, Sutherland introduces the concept of white-collar crime, as a violation of existing prejudices that aristocrats do not err.
285. The Anti-Crime Package was amended by Congress and resulted in the promulgation of Law No. 13.964, of 24 December 2019, which improves criminal and criminal procedural legislation. http://www.planalto.gov.br/ccivil_03/_ato2019-2022/2019/lei/L13964.htm.
286. Code of Criminal Procedure, Article 28-A: "If it is not a case for archiving and the investigated has formally and circumstantially confessed to the practice of a criminal offence without violence or serious threat and with a minimum penalty of less than 4 (four) years, the Public Prosecutor may propose a non-prosecution agreement, provided that necessary and sufficient for the reproach and prevention of the crime, through the following cumulatively and alternatively adjusted conditions: [...]". http://www.planalto.gov.br/ccivil_03/decreto-lei/del3689.htm.
287. Penal Code, Article 109: "The prescription, before of The final sentence, except as provided in § 1 o of art. 110 of this Code, is regulated by the maximum of the custodial sentence commensurate with the crime, as follows: I - in twenty years, if the maximum sentence is more than twelve; II - in sixteen years, if the maximum sentence is more than eight years and does not exceed twelve; III - in twelve years, if the maximum sentence is more than four years and does not exceed eight; IV - in eight years, if the maximum sentence is more than two years and does not exceed four; V - in four years, if the maximum sentence is equal to one year or, if greater, does not exceed two;

VI - in 3 (three) years, if the maximum sentence is less than 1 (one) year." https://www.planalto.gov.br/ccivil_03/decreto-lei/del2848compilado.htm.

288. *Jabuticaba* is a native Brazilian fruit often used metaphorically to refer to phenomena, especially legal or institutional, that exist only in Brazil and have no parallel elsewhere.
289. Teori Albino Zavascki. Entry. FGV CPDOC. https://www18.fgv.br/CPDOC/acervo/dicionarios/verbete-biografico/teori-albino-zavascki. He was a jurist, professor, magistrate, and Justice of the Superior Court of Justice and Justice of the Federal Supreme Court, from 2012 to 2017. He was the rapporteur of Operation Car Wash until his death.
290. Pedro Barusco is an engineer and former services manager of Petrobras, becoming known due to his involvement in the Car Wash scandal. He was arrested in Operation Car Wash, was sentenced to 18 years and four months in an open regime, with an ankle monitor, in addition to performing community service. He made a plea bargain and, in exchange for a reduced sentence, returned R$ 182 million reais, illicit funds that had been sent abroad.
291. Reference is made to Geddel Quadros Vieira Lima. He is a business administrator and politician affiliated with the Democratic Movement. Former federal congressperson for the state of Bahia. He was Minister of National Integration, in the Lula government, Vice-President of the Federal Savings Bank, in the Dilma Rousseff government, and Minister of Government, in the Michel Temer government. He was arrested in September 2017 after more than 51 million reais, in cash, were seized in an apartment in Salvador, linked to him. It was the largest seizure of cash in the history of Brazil.
292. Salary kickbacks is a corrupt practice of diverting part of the salaries of parliamentary advisers, as a prior agreement for the exercise of the function between the adviser and the parliamentarian. This practice can also occur when the parliamentarian uses ghost employees.

293. Secret Diaries is the name of an operation denounced by the Public Prosecutor's Office of the state of Paraná that involved the diversion of public resources from the Legislative Assembly of Paraná, through the hiring of ghost employees. These hires were reported in "secret diaries," i.e. in publications that should be public, but were not made available for consultation.
294. Rodrigo Santos da Rocha Loures is a business administrator and politician. He was a federal congressperson for Paraná and a member of the National Executive of the Party of the Democratic Movement (PMDB, today MDB). He was an adviser to then President Michel Temer and was filmed by the Federal Police, in Operation Patmos, with a suitcase containing 500 thousand reais, delivered by Ricardo Saud, director of JBS. On 18 May 2017, Justice Edson Fachin, of the Federal Supreme Court ordered his removal from the position of federal congressperson.
295. Gary Stanley Becker was an economist and professor at the University of Chicago, having received the Nobel Prize in Economics in 1992. In 1968, he published the work Crime and punishment: an economic approach, in the *Journal of Political Economy*, Vol. 76, No. 2, p. 169–217. https://webarchiv.ethz.ch/soms/sociology_course/Lecture6/becker1968.pdf, in which he explains, based on economic reasoning, the variables that are previously considered in the decision to engage in illicit practices by individuals.
296. Antônio Augusto Brandão de Aras is a professor at the Faculty of Law of the University of Brasília and the current Attorney General of the Republic.
297. Luiz Fernando de Souza, better known simply as Pezão, is an economist and politician affiliated with the Brazilian Democratic Movement (MDB). He was the governor of the state of Rio de Janeiro. In March of 2015, the former director of Petrobras Paulo Roberto Costa mentions, in a plea bargain, that Pezão and the former governor Sergio Cabral would have received 30 million reais for slush funds. Pezão was arrested by the Federal Police on the morning of 29 November 2018.

298. Law No. 13.869, of 5 September 2019, which provides for the crimes of abuse of authority. http://www.planalto.gov.br/ccivil_03/_ato2019-2022/2019/lei/L13869.htm.
299. Deltan Martinazzo Dallagnol was a federal prosecutor and coordinator of the task force of the Public Ministry of Operation Car Wash in Curitiba. He is currently a federal congressperson for Paraná (2023–2026).
300. Special Action Group to Combat Organised Crime, GAECO.
301. Reference is made to the Government of then President Jair Bolsonaro.
302. For more information about the React Espírito Santo Forum, see part of the text from the book by Carlos Melo, Malu Delgado and Milton Seligman. *Decay and reconstruction. Espírito Santo: lessons from civil society for a political case in contemporary Brazil*. São Paulo: Bei, 2020. https://www.terra.com.br/noticias/leia-trecho-do-livro-inedito-decadencia-e-reconstrucao,c2906ad61ea7028b07425f59a54a1573cz7emovv.html
303. Law School of NOVA University of Lisbon: https://novalaw.unl.pt/.
304. Convention on Combating Bribery of Foreign Public Officials in International Business Transactions, Organisation for Economic Co-operation and Development (OECD). https://www.gov.br/cgu/pt-br/assuntos/articulacao-internacional-1/convencao-da-ocde/arquivos/cartilha-ocde-2016.pdf
305. The *UK Bribery Act* is from 2010. It is considered the strictest legislation against corruption. https://www.legislation.gov.uk/ukpga/2010/23/contents
306. Law No. 12.846, of 1 August 2013, which provides for the administrative and civil liability of legal entities for the practice of acts against the public administration, national or foreign. http://www.planalto.gov.br/ccivil_03/_ato2011-2014/2013/lei/l12846.htm
307. Integrity Vice Presidency. The World Bank. https://www.worldbank.org/en/about/unit/integrity-vice-presidency

308. Rodrigo Janot. ***Entry***. FGV CPDOC. https://www18.fgv.br/CPDOC/acervo/dicionarios/verbete-biografico/rodrigo-janot-monteiro-de-barros. He was a member of the Federal Public Prosecutor's Office and Attorney General of the Republic from 2013 to 2017
309. Pontifical Catholic University of São Paulo, Pontifical Catholic University of São Paulo.
310. Nepotism is the term used to designate the favouring of relatives to the detriment of more qualified people, in the granting of privileges or positions particularly in public service, but also in the private sector.
311. *Plea bargain* according to Black's Law Dictionary can be understood as a criminal process in which the defendant and the prosecutor make a mutually satisfactory agreement for the case, subject to the judge's agreement. Generally, there is a confession from the defendant of a lesser offence or only some of the charges, in exchange for a lighter sentence than would be possible.

Final Conclusion

"Something is rotten in the state of Denmark."— William Shakespeare, Hamlet

Brazil's Biggest Corruption Scandal: Testimonies from Operation "Car Wash" offers an extraordinary window into the legal, institutional, and political dynamics that shaped the most far-reaching anti-corruption investigation in Brazil's democratic history. Through the voices of those who participated in or were directly affected by Operation Car Wash, this volume reconstructs a moment of rupture—an attempt to confront systemic corruption with unprecedented institutional coordination, international cooperation, and judicial innovation.

The testimonies reveal that Car Wash was more than an isolated operation: it functioned as a mirror held up to the Brazilian state. What it reflected was a political economy deeply enmeshed in illicit finance, collusive practices, and structural impunity. The investigation exposed a mode of governance in which corruption had ceased to be an anomaly and had instead become a mechanism of political viability. The revelations about public procurement cartels, party financing through slush funds, and the entanglement of public and private interests offered not

L. M. Costa, *Brazil's Biggest Corruption Scandal*, Crime Prevention and Security Management, https://doi.org/10.1007/978-3-031-99078-6

just legal cases, but a stark diagnosis of how power is exercised and preserved in Brazil.

Yet, the story told in these pages is not only one of exposure and enforcement. It is also one of institutional resistance and political backlash. The same operation that once embodied legal progress was later subjected to dismantlement through rulings by the Federal Supreme Court and legislative interventions that weakened its legal foundation. Many of these developments, as the testimonies make clear, were not the result of judicial consensus or democratic debate, but of strategic recalibrations by political elites seeking to reassert control over the instruments of accountability.

A recurring concern among contributors is the role played by the higher judiciary—notably the Supreme Court—in fragmenting investigations, weakening the coherence of jurisdictional doctrine, and, in several instances, nullifying critical evidence and plea bargains. These decisions were taken in the name of procedural guarantees but, in practice, they had the effect of reversing hard-won investigative advances. When courts shift jurisprudence retroactively or selectively, the rule of law is not affirmed—it is destabilised. That destabilisation became a key feature of the post-Car Wash environment, enabling the rehabilitation of figures previously convicted of serious wrongdoing and eroding public trust in the justice system.

Political actors, for their part, mobilised institutional tools to neutralise oversight. Legislative reforms curtailed investigative powers, weakened whistleblower protections, and reasserted the dominance of party leadership over internal accountability mechanisms. The political class—many of whom had been directly implicated in Car Wash—undertook a concerted effort to reframe anti-corruption as judicial overreach. This narrative, amplified by partisan media and facilitated by strategic court rulings, ultimately succeeded in dismantling the operation's architecture.

And yet, even in its deconstruction, Car Wash revealed something enduring. It made visible the scale of corruption; it demonstrated that institutions, even within their limits, can act; and it catalysed a public discourse on integrity, governance, and the legitimacy of enforcement. For a period, it shifted the normative expectations of the electorate, imposed consequences where impunity once prevailed, and forced elite actors—political, corporate, and judicial—to confront the possibility of accountability.

This book neither idealises nor disavows Operation Car Wash. Instead, it presents a nuanced, sometimes contradictory set of reflections that invite critical engagement. If the operation failed to deliver systemic transformation, it is not because the law was too ambitious, but because the political and institutional environment was structurally resistant to reform. The attempt to modernise Brazil's accountability mechanisms collided with a political system that remains, in many respects, dependent on opacity, clientelism, and juridical ambiguity.

The testimonies contained here—diverse in their tone, rigorous in their detail—converge on one essential point: that combating corruption cannot be entrusted to isolated legal efforts. It requires a reconfiguration of incentives, the insulation of key institutions, a judiciary that is consistent and principled, and a political system that does not treat impunity as a condition for governability. Most of all, it demands sustained civic vigilance to prevent the erosion of democratic achievements through institutional complacency or strategic sabotage.

To those committed to integrity and the rule of law, this volume offers both a chronicle of what was possible and a reminder of how fragile that possibility remains. In this sense, *Brazil's Biggest Corruption Scandal* is not merely a retrospective. It is a warning—and a call to memory. As a documentary record of Brazil's largest and most consequential anti-corruption investigation, this book seeks not only to preserve institutional memory but also to inform future efforts—academic, legal, and civic—that aim to confront corruption with clarity, courage, and accountability.

References

1. Becker, G. S. (1968). Crime and punishment: An economic approach. *Journal of Political Economy, 76*, 169–217.
2. Cartier-Bresson, J. (1997). Corruption networks, transaction security and illegal social exchange. *Political Studies, 45*(3), 463–476.
3. Carvalhosa, M. (2022). *From cleptocracy to democracy in 2019: A government, state project*. Revista dos Courts.
4. Carvalhosa, M. (2021). *A new constitution for Brazil: From a country of privileges to a nation of opportunities.* LVM Publisher.
5. Carvalhosa, M. (1995). *The black book of corruption.* Peace and Earth.
6. Chemim, R. (2017). *Clean hands and Car Wash: Corruption looks in the mirror*. Citadel.
7. Cohen, J., Mrazek, M., & Hawkins, L. (2007). Corruption and pharmaceuticals: Strengthening good governance to improve access. In J. E. Campos & S. Pradhan (Eds.), *The many faces of corruption: Tracking vulnerabilities at the sector level* (pp. 29–62). World Bank. https://openknowledge.worldbank.org/handle/10986/6848
8. Costa, L. M. (2020). Rebuilding an empire: The Odebrecht challenge after the corruption scandal. *Journal of Business Ethics Education, 17*, 255–272.

L. M. Costa, *Brazil's Biggest Corruption Scandal*, Crime Prevention and Security Management, https://doi.org/10.1007/978-3-031-99078-6

9. Costa, L. M., Padua Lima, M. L., & Goldschmidt, P. C. (2020). Anticorruption policies in Brazil and the Operation Car Wash: Institutional and economic analysis. In F. Bechara & P. Goldschmidt (Eds.), *Lessons of Operation Car Wash: A legal, institutional and economic analysis* (pp. 22–51). Wilson Center. https://direitosp.fgv.br/sites/direitosp.fgv.br/files/arquivos/bi-09212020-car_wash_report_v2.pdf
10. Costa, L. M. (2019). An evil that belongs to us. *GV-Executive, 18*(3), 12–15. https://bibliotecadigital.fgv.br/ojs/index.php/gvexecutivo/article/view/79170
11. Costa, L. M. (2019). Compliance or non-compliance? *GV-Executive, 18*(1), 45. https://bibliotecadigital.fgv.br/ojs/index.php/gvexecutivo/article/view/78196
12. Costa, L. M. (2018). The dynamics of corruption in Brazil: From trivial bribes to a corruption scandal. In O. E. Hawthorne & S. Magu (Eds.), *Corruption scandals and their global impact* (pp. 189–203). Routledge.
13. De Castro Biason, R., & Livianu, R. (2019). *Corruption in the history of Brazil*. Mackenzie Publisher.
14. De Moraes Pitombo, A. S. A. (2021). Prisoner's dilemma: Pretrial detention and torture. In *In search of the lost just* (pp. 15–20). Singular.
15. Ferraz, C., Finan, F., & Moreira, D. S. B. (2012). Corrupting learning: Evidence from missing federal education funds in Brazil. *Journal of Public Economics, 96*(9–10), 712–726. https://doi.org/10.1016/j.jpubeco.2012.05.012
16. Kaufmann, D. (1997). Corruption: The facts. *Foreign Policy*, (107).
17. Lagunes, P. F., & Svejnar, J. (2020). *Corruption and the Car Wash scandal in Latin America*. Routledge.
18. Moreno, L. A. (2017, December 14). How tech can fight corruption in Latin America and the Caribbean. *World Economic Forum*. https://www.weforum.org/agenda/2017/12/how-technology-is-becoming-a-powerful-ally-in-the-fight-against-corruption-in-latin-america-and-the-caribbean
19. Mungiu-Pippidi, A. (2011). *Contextual choices in fighting corruption: Lessons learned* (Report No. 4). OECD. https://www.oecd.org/countries/vietnam/48912957.pdf
20. Nijboer, K., Senden, S., & Telgen, J. (2017). Cross-country learning in public procurement: An exploratory study. *Journal of Public Procurement, 17*(4), 449–482.
21. Nye, J. S. (1967). Corruption and political development: A cost-benefit analysis. *American Political Science Review, 61*(2), 417–427.

22. OECD. (2009). *Principles for integrity in public procurement.* https://www.oecd.org/gov/ethics/48994520.pdf
23. Passas, N. (2005). Lawful but awful: 'Legal corporate crimes.' *Journal of Socio-Economics, 34*(6), 771–786.
24. Persson, A., Rothstein, B., & Teorell, J. (2013). Why anticorruption reforms fail: Systemic corruption as a collective action problem. *Governance, 26*(3), 449–471.
25. Pinotti, M. C. (Ed.). (2019). *Corruption: Car wash and clean hands.* Portfolio-Penguin.
26. Power, T. J., & Taylor, M. M. (2011). *Corruption and democracy in Brazil: The struggle for accountability.* University of Notre Dame Press.
27. Rose-Ackerman, S. (1978). *Corruption: A study in political economy.* Academic Press.
28. Rose-Ackerman, S. (1999). *Corruption and government: Causes, consequences, and reform.* Cambridge University Press.
29. Rothstein, B. (2011). Anti-corruption: The indirect 'big bang' approach. *Review of International Political Economy, 18*(2), 228–250.
30. Silva, M. F. da. (1999). The political economy of corruption in Brazil. *RAE, 39*(3), 26–41. http://www.scielo.br/scielo.php?script=sci_arttext&pid=S0034-75901999000300004
31. World Bank Institute. (2008). *Fighting corruption through collective action: A guide for business.* https://www.globalcompact.de/wAssets/docs/Korruptionspraevention/Publikationen/fighting_corruption_through_collective_action.pdf

Index

L. M. Costa, *Brazil's Biggest Corruption Scandal*, Crime Prevention and Security Management, https://doi.org/10.1007/978-3-031-99078-6

FSC
www.fsc.org
MIX
Papier | Fördert gute Waldnutzung
FSC® C083411

Kolibri 360 GmbH
Ferdinand-Jühlke-Straße 7
99095 Erfurt, Deutschland
produktsicherheit@kolibri360.de